*Exploring*

# Washington's
## *Wild Areas*

## A GUIDE FOR
### HIKERS • BACKPACKERS • CLIMBERS
### CROSS-COUNTRY SKIERS • PADDLERS

*Exploring*

# Washington's
## *Wild Areas*

### SECOND EDITION
## Marge and Ted Mueller

THE MOUNTAINEERS BOOKS

Published by
The Mountaineers Books
1001 SW Klickitat Way, Suite 201
Seattle, WA 98134

First edition, 1994. Second edition, 2002

Published simultaneously in Great Britain by Cordee, 3a DeMontfort Street, Leicester, England, LE1 7HD

Manufactured in the United States of America

Project Editor: Laura Slavik
Copyeditor: Erin Moore
Cover and Book Design: Ani Rucki
Layout: Gray Mouse Graphics
Mapmaker: Gray Mouse Graphics
Photographer: All photographs by Kirkendall/Spring except as noted

Cover photograph: *Snowgrass Flats in Goat Rocks Wilderness, with Mount Adams in the distance*
Frontispiece: *Mount Hardy, in the Liberty Bell Roadless Area*

*Library of Congress Cataloging-in-Publication Data*
Mueller, Marge.
    Exploring Washington's wild areas : a guide for hikers, backpackers, climbers,
  x-c skiers & paddlers / Marge and Ted Mueller. —2nd ed.
      p. cm.
Includes bibliographical references and index.
   ISBN 0-89886-807-6  (pbk.)
    1. Outdoor recreation—Washington (State)—Guidebooks.  2.  Wilderness areas—Washington
(State)—Recreational use—Guidebooks.  3.  Washington (State)—Guidebooks.  I. Mueller, Ted.  II. Title
GV191.42.W22 M84 2002
796.5'09797—dc21
                                     2001008621

# TABLE OF CONTENTS

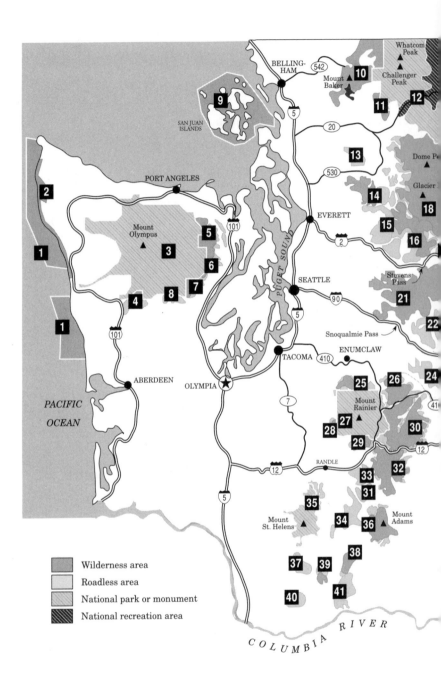

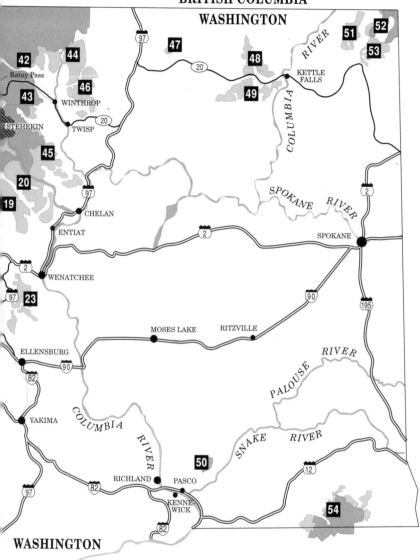

BRITISH COLUMBIA

WASHINGTON

**42** **44**

Rainy Pass

**46**

**43** WINTHROP

STEHEKIN TWISP

**45**

**20**

**19**

**97** CHELAN

ENTIAT

**23**

WENATCHEE

**97**

ELLENSBURG

YAKIMA

*COLUMBIA*

*RIVER*

**47** **48**

**49**

KETTLE
FALLS

**51** **52**

**53**

*COLUMBIA*

*SPOKANE* *RIVER*

SPOKANE

MOSES LAKE RITZVILLE

*PALOUSE* *RIVER*

**50**

RICHLAND PASCO

KENNE-
WICK

*SNAKE* *RIVER*

**54**

WASHINGTON

OREGON

Chapter Six. **Eastern Washington**

*Blue Lake lies just off the North Cascades Scenic Highway in the Liberty Bell Roadless Area. Cutthroat Peak rises above.*

# INTRODUCTION

"An area where the earth and community of life are untrammeled by man, where man himself is a visitor who does not remain"—it was thus that the United States Congress defined a wilderness area when, in 1964, it passed the initial Wilderness Act. The Wilderness Act further defined a wilderness as undeveloped federal land that has retained its primeval character and that meets the following criteria:

- Appears to have been affected only by the forces of nature, not man
- Has outstanding opportunities for solitude or primitive unconfined recreation
- Is at least 5,000 acres in size, or of a size that makes its preservation and use in an unimpaired condition feasible
- May contain ecological, geological, or other features of scientific, scenic, or historical value

Today, Washington state is fortunate to have more than 4.1 million acres (6,400 square miles) of national forests and parks protected as "designated wilderness areas." The state ranks behind only Alaska and California in the total size of areas so designated.

## WILD AREA MANAGEMENT

In the mid-1970s the Forest Service inventoried all national forest areas that had no roads or substantial development, and assessed the impact of various potential uses of these areas. The results of this study were published in 1979 as the Roadless Areas Review and Evaluation (RARE II). In 1984, after examining this inventory, Congress passed the Washington State Wilderness Act, which designated several large parcels of this roadless land as wildernesses. Those parcels not so designated were left without specific protection, their use to be established by the Forest Service planning processes.

Each national forest developed its own management plan that further partitioned the RARE II roadless areas into various categories, ranging from Timber Harvest units and Motorized Recreation sections (read "roads") to Wildlife Habitat Areas, Scenic Preservation Corridors, Primitive Areas, and Semiprimitive Areas. The latter category was further divided between Nonmotorized and Motorized, depending on whether or not motorcycles were permitted on trails.

In May 2000 the Forest Service completed a year-long study of a proposal for future management of the nation's existing roadless areas. The recommended action was to prohibit road construction and reconstruction within all inventoried roadless areas, unless required by existing rights or public health and safety. In addition, smaller uninventoried, unroaded areas could be managed as roadless at the local manager's discretion. Forest plans would be updated to reflect this policy change. Public meetings, attended by an estimated 16,000 citizens, were held in all 127 national forests, and more than 360,000 written comments were received on the proposal. Responses were overwhelmingly in favor of implementing the new roadless policy.

*The Yellow Aster Butte Trail, in the Mount Baker Wilderness, is dominated by views of Mount Baker.*

The new rules were published and due to become final in February 2001. In January a lawsuit to block implementation of the rules was filed by the state of Idaho and by logging, mining, and snowmobiling interests; and the new Bush administration delayed rule implementation pending the lawsuit's outcome. In May the new rules went into effect, although the legal challenge was still active, and the administration announced plans to further review and modify the proposal.

This book covers not only designated wilderness areas that are legally protected from exploitation, but also inventoried roadless areas (RAs) as of the date of publication (with the exception of four small isolated ones: Blue Slide, Jackson Creek, Bodie Mountain, and Clackamas Mountain).

Roadless areas have no formal protection other than the environmental impact statement review incorporated in the Forest Service planning process and the policy statement in the 2000 Roadless Area Conservation Plan. The authors are unabashed advocates of extending formal wilderness designation to such areas before these precious and irreplaceable resources are lost to logging, mining, or other commercial development. It is also our conviction that motorcycles and all-terrain vehicles (ATVs) are as inappropriate in semiprimitive areas as they are in a dedicated wilderness. Their raucous noise is incompatible with the sense of solitude treasured by wilderness visitors, and the damage they cause to trails and meadows is incompatible with the ethic of minimal impact use.

## Welcome to the Bureaucratic Maze

Both designated wildernesses and our broader category of wild areas, which include roadless areas, fall under the administration of a complex collection of state and federal agencies. At a cabinet level, responsibility is shared between the Departments of the Interior and Agriculture. Interior's Fish and Wildlife Agency manages the islands off the Washington coast and in the San Juan Islands, both national wildlife refuges and designated wildernesses. The Bureau of Land Management, also part of the Department of the Interior, administers the Juniper Dunes Wilderness. A third Interior agency, the National Park Service, manages Olympic, North Cascades, and Mount Rainier National Parks, as well as the Ross Lake and Lake Chelan National Recreation Areas (NRAs). Although large portions of the parks and NRAs are also designated wildernesses, sections with roads and commercial and tourist facilities developed prior to the Washington Wilderness Act are excluded from this status.

The remainder of federal lands are the responsibility of Agriculture's U.S. Forest Service (USFS). Portions of these forests have been formally protected as designated wilderness areas, and as a national recreation area and a national monument. However, even within the Forest Service administrative boundaries rarely coincide with the natural borders of the wild areas in this book. Wild areas are often split between two or more national forests, and each forest's management has independent control over planning, forest area classification, and budgets within their own purview. National forests are further subdivided into ranger districts; this is where the shoe leather hits the trail. These units are responsible for construction and maintenance of trails, logging unit sales, and personal contact with wilderness visitors. Rangers are the people you want to contact for the most current information on road and trail conditions. But when a continuous trail, totally within any given wilderness or wild area, crosses a ranger district boundary, it may suddenly acquire a different number, name, and maintenance status. This "your-turf, my-turf" game must be overcome to achieve coherent wilderness management.

Bordering these federal lands are extensive state and private holdings. The state and private lands are easy to identify: they are generally characterized by slope-balding clearcuts within a millimeter of the national forest boundary and self-promoting signs about how this naked hillside is really a tree farm that will once again flourish (only to be slashed to the ground in another 75 years). Portions of state lands, most of which were ceded by the federal government at the time of statehood, are constitutionally committed to maximizing cash return to support public schools (usually by timber sales). Other private inholdings on federal lands are mostly patented mining claims, vestiges of obscure and unrealistic mining laws created in 1872.

## Rules and Regulations

Increased numbers of wilderness visitors, and the need to preserve the natural environment that they come to see, requires constraints on wilderness use—some general, some specific to individual areas. General rules are:

- Entrance into a wilderness area is by permit only. Permits may be obtained at the nearest ranger station, or in many cases at self-monitored trailhead stations.
- Maximum party size is 12, which includes pack animals and humans.
- Maximum length of camping at any one site is limited, generally to 14 days.
- No mechanical means of transport are permitted in a designated wilderness: no ATVs (all-terrain vehicles), motorcycles, bicycles, or aircraft. In nondesignated roadless areas this rule varies by trail. Specific restrictions are included with each trail description.
- No motorized equipment, such as generators or chain saws, is permitted in a designated wilderness.
- Caching or storing equipment is limited to 48 hours.
- Use of unprocessed hay or grain livestock feed is prohibited.
- Grazing, hitching, tethering, or hobbling livestock within 200 feet of the shore of any lake, stream, or pond is prohibited.
- Shortcutting switchbacks is prohibited.
- Collecting cultural artifacts or disturbing archaeological or pictograph sites is prohibited.
- Digging plants requires a permit, and picking flowers of threatened or endangered species is prohibited.

In addition, specific local restrictions may apply:

- Entry quotas have been established for certain high-use areas.
- Most campgrounds and trailheads require a Northwest Forest Pass, either single day use or annual, for each vehicle using that facility. Passes may be purchased at USFS offices or many private vendors. Eighty percent of pass fees are retained locally for facility improvements and trail maintenance.
- Campfires might not be permitted; perhaps only camp stoves may be used.
- Cutting or trimming of trees, either live or dead, may be prohibited.
- Ecosystem restoration may preclude camping in certain areas, or preclude camping within a specified distance from lakes or streams.
- Pets (dogs, cats, or whatever) may not be permitted (and you should consider leaving pets at home in any case).
- Firearms may be prohibited, or if permitted may be subject to restrictions as to where they may be discharged.

Always check in advance with local Forest or Park Service rangers for current restrictions.

Aside from formal rules, there are other general guidelines for backcountry travel that all ethical visitors should follow in order to preserve the wilderness nature of the areas they visit. These include:

- Use existing campsites or unvegetated areas for camps rather than creating new sites and destroying more plants and grasses in the process.
- Minimize use of soaps (even biodegradable ones), wash cooking and eating utensils at least 100 feet from any stream or lake, and dump waste water on well-drained soil.
- Dig a cat hole, 4 to 6 inches deep, for human feces, and cover it with soil when finished. Locate the hole at least 100 feet from any water sources, and out of high-use camping areas.
- Pack out all refuse; don't burn or bury it. You packed it in full, it should be lighter going out.
- Store food in bags suspended from tree limbs at least 12 feet above the ground and 10 feet from the tree trunk to keep it away from animals.
- Follow the maxim "Take only pictures, leave only footprints."

*Hikers set up camp near Dishpan Gap along the Pacific Crest Trail in the Henry M. Jackson Wilderness. Glacier Peak rises above the fog-filled valley of the North Fork of the Sauk River.*

## USING THIS BOOK
### Topographic Maps

The topographic maps listed in the information blocks of this book are all USGS 7.5-minute-series maps, the most useful for wilderness navigation. These might not have the most current road and trail locations, so they may need to be supplemented by other maps, such as individual ranger district maps available from the Forest Service.

### Trail Descriptions

Unfortunately, space does not permit written descriptions of every trail within the areas covered in the book; however, all known, maintained trails, and most followable, unmaintained trails, are shown on the map accompanying the section.

Trail descriptions are deliberately brief; they are intended only to convey a sense of difficulty, both in length and elevation loss and gain, as well as some of the reasons to take the trail. For more extensive trail descriptions, refer to other guidebooks listed in Appendix B, Suggested Reading, or contact local ranger stations for guides to trails within their district.

**Coding Conventions.** Each trail description begins with the trail number and name, then the total trail mileage, followed by a difficulty rating.

| | |
|---|---|
| e | means easy. Easy trails offer a good, near-level grade and well-maintained tread that should offer no problems to inexperienced hikers. |
| m | means moderate. This rating covers a multitude of sins, but basically requires a fair degree of hiking and wilderness navigation ability. Moderate trails may include some miserable grades, rough treads, and a few obscure spots in the trail. |
| d | means difficult. Difficult trails may have terrible tread, fallen trees, and thick brush, and extensive wilderness navigation experience is required. Some trails in this grouping are abandoned or no longer maintained, but should be followable by very experienced hikers with polished navigation skills. |

The last letter(s) in the line, the letters in parentheses, define usage restrictions.

| | |
|---|---|
| (H) | means the trail is open only to hikers. |
| (S) | means the trail is open to saddle and pack stock. |
| (B) | means the trail is open to mountain bikes. |
| (M) | means the trail is open to motorized vehicles. |

The condition of trails and the forest roads accessing them varies over time. About 30 percent of the Forest Service budget comes from Congressional allocations, and in the past the remainder came primarily from timber sale proceeds. With growing restrictions on logging, this revenue source has greatly diminished, and funds for road and trail construction and maintenance have become hard to come by. Trail conditions have tended to degenerate, and remote, seldom-used, and difficult-to-maintain routes are often abandoned. This is unfortunate, for these trails are exactly the ones that can offer a degree of solitude not found on the more popular routes, as well as a way to disperse wilderness visitors and attract them away from more crowded areas. You can help address this problem by actively lobbying your Congressional representatives to adequately fund trail maintenance, and by participating in volunteer trail maintenance efforts by many of the outdoor groups in the state.

## Climbing

This book is not meant to be a climbing guide; however, in the descriptions we try to give a flavor of the climbing opportunities in a given region. Hundreds of peaks in the state offer every level of climbing challenge, but in general those mentioned in this book require technical climbing skills above mere scrambling, plus climbing equipment and experience in its use. As a shorthand means of giving a sense of a climb's difficulty, either of two commonly used classification schemes may be used.

The class system has five basic levels (C-1 to C-5), plus a decimal breakdown of C-5 into C-5.0 through C-5.14. In general, the higher the number, the more difficult the climb. C-1 and C-2 climbs are basically scrambles. A C-3 climb requires elementary climbing skills and involves moderate exposures, but a rope is generally unnecessary. A C-4 climb requires intermediate climbing skills, most often a rope is needed for safety, and sometimes pitons are required to secure belay points. C-5 climbs almost always require protection for safety on leads.

The grade system (G-I to G-VI) is more esoteric and subjective, and theoretically weighs factors such as length of climb, ascent time, route finding, weather problems, and so on. In general, a G-I technical segment can be completed in a few hours, a G-II takes half a day, and a G-III requires most of a day. A G-IV requires a long full day, and possibly a bivouac; usually its hardest pitch is rated C-5.7 or above. A G-V is probably a one-and-a-half-day technical challenge with a hardest pitch above C-5.8. A G-VI climb is a multiday affair with extremely difficult climbing, most likely requiring aid.

For a more complete list of summits and detailed descriptions of specific routes, refer to one of the climbing guides listed in Appendix B, Suggested Reading.

## Winter Sports

This category describes popular trips usually done on skis or snowshoes. These trips vary in length and difficulty from easy half-day tours up snowbound roads or trails to difficult cross-country routes that are only feasible when snow blankets rocks, brush, and other obstacles. Some of the more difficult routes are exposed to avalanches when conditions are right. (Or perhaps wrong?) Again, further details on the features, experience level required, and hazards are found in various guidebooks (see Appendix B, Suggested Reading). Typically, taking tours over snowbound roads outside of a designated wilderness may mean encountering snowmobiles.

The Washington State Parks and Recreation Commission has a Sno-Park program, where parking areas are plowed at the start of more than forty popular winter recreation tour sites. Several Sno-Parks have easy to intermediate, groomed, cross-country ski trails nearby, and some even have warming huts or sanitary facilities. A Sno-Park permit is required for use of these areas. A guide to these areas and their associated trails is available from Washington State Parks at the address listed in Appendix A.

## WILDERNESS SAFETY

The very concept of a wilderness experience implies a good deal of self-reliance in an environment not designed to protect visitors from natural hazards. As the title of an old Seattle Mountain Rescue film states, *Mountains Don't Care*. Although there certainly are trails, or portions of trails, that can be enjoyed by novice hikers, most of the recreational opportunities in this book demand backcountry experience, equipment, and map and compass navigation skills. The more remote and difficult routes may be physically punishing, with steep grades, boulder and tree root treads, and poorly marked or obscure sections. A great deal of determination, physical conditioning, experience, and wilderness navigation skills are required to safely sample such trails. Outdoor clubs in several Washington cities offer courses in hiking, camping, and climbing, as well as group hikes and climbs led by experienced members of the organization. This is an excellent way to develop the skills needed before tackling a wild-area trip on your own.

Make sure to pack the Ten Essentials on any trip you take: extra clothing, extra food, sunglasses, knife, firestarter, first-aid kit, matches in a waterproof container, flashlight, map, and compass.

### Weather

It is appropriate to begin this brief survey of "what's out there that can get you" with weather. Large portions of these wild areas are at elevations between 3,000 and 8,000 feet, and although summer temperatures are generally mild, sudden storms with wind, rain, or even snow are not unheard of. In open parkland or atop exposed ridge crests storms can quickly cause hypothermia in the unprepared—which will lead to death if not rapidly treated. On the eastern slopes of the Cascades, the confluence of moist air from the west and the hot, dry air from the Columbia Plateau often builds midafternoon thunderheads, and the high country is not a fun place to experience a lightning storm. Snow often persists on ridges and north-facing slopes until mid- to late July, and safely traversing steep, open, sidehill slopes requires an ice ax and knowledge of how to use it.

### Wildlife Hazards and Nuisances

Next in line are the critters out there in the woods. Although cougars, lynx, bobcats, coyotes, and, in some isolated instances, wolves inhabit Washington's wild areas, consider yourself very lucky if you ever see one. You are therefore very unlikely to be harmed by one.

Almost all areas have a resident population of black bear, but they are more likely to run when sighted than to cause a problem. The exception is in areas where mindless campers have left food or garbage lying around, training bears where to find easy pickings. Here, otherwise timid bears will delight in ripping into packs and food bags that are not properly hung out of reach. Most often, they have little appetite for leg-of-hiker tartare, and will depart to the tune of a banging kettle if they don't find a free lunch.

Wild areas in the northeast corner of the state are grizzly bear preserves; there are also reports of a few grizzlies in the North Cascades and one footprint was recently found in the South Cascades. However, the grizzly is an endangered species, which means that there are so few around that you'll likely hike a lifetime and never see one in these areas. Given the opportunity to avoid a hiker, old griz' will probably not cause a confrontation. Many hikers hang a bell on their packs to warn bears of their coming; however, an old joke says that the way you can tell black bear scat from grizzly scat is that the grizzly's has a bell in it.

Smaller on the scale of annoying mammals are raccoons, porcupines, squirrels, skunks, and mice, all of which delight in snaffling easy-to-reach food from campsites. The same precaution of hanging food bags out of reach or using bear-proof containers should also thwart these creatures.

Next come reptiles, or, more specifically, rattlesnakes. They are found in many areas on the hotter eastern side of the state, such as in lower portions of the Lake Chelan–Sawtooth, Wenaha–Tucannon, and Juniper Dunes Wildernesses. Given the opportunity, rattlers prefer to slither away and eat a mouse, and will strike out at a human only if surprised and without an avenue of retreat. Just watch out where you put your hands and feet. There are no poisonous snakes west of the Cascade crest.

In the insect world, the most troublesome critters are ticks, which are found in profusion east of the Cascades, and in a few spots on the west side, in spring and early summer. Potentially harmful effects of tick bites include Rocky Mountain spotted fever and Lyme disease. Early summer also brings out clouds of mosquitoes and deer flies throughout the Cascades; their bites are annoying and sometimes painful, but have no long-lasting impact.

The smallest threat, microscopic in size, is *Giardia*, a paramecium that is transmitted into water supplies from the feces of mammals. This organism causes nausea and severe diarrhea that requires medical treatment. Prevention, either by boiling water for at least 10 minutes or by filtering it through microfilters, is much easier than the cure.

Entire books have been written on recognizing and dealing with wilderness hazards, but no book can replace experience and prudent judgment for making trips safe and enjoyable. The recreational opportunities described in this book are in no way warranted to be hazard free; in fact, some are very difficult and even potentially dangerous for an inexperienced wilderness visitor. When you travel in the wild areas and over the routes described in this book, you are doing so at your own risk, and you must assume full responsibility for the safety and comfort of yourself and your party. In the wilderness, you must pay constant attention to potential problems from obscure treads, rockfalls, weather, avalanches, steep snow slopes, and the like, and be willing to turn back in the face of conditions for which you are not prepared.

## A NOTE ABOUT SAFETY

Safety is an important concern in all outdoor activities. No guidebook can alert you to every hazard or anticipate the limitations of every reader. Therefore, the descriptions of roads, trails, routes, and natural features in this book are not representations that a particular place or excursion will be safe for your party. When you follow any of the routes described in this book, you assume responsibility for your own safety. Under normal conditions, such excursions require the usual attention to traffic, road and trail conditions, weather, terrain, the capabilities of your party, and other factors. Because many of the lands in this book are subject to development and/or change of ownership, conditions may have changed since this book was written that make your use of some of these routes unwise. Always check for current conditions, obey posted private property signs, and avoid confrontations with property owners or managers. Keeping informed on current conditions and exercising common sense are the keys to a safe, enjoyable outing.

*The Mountaineers Books*

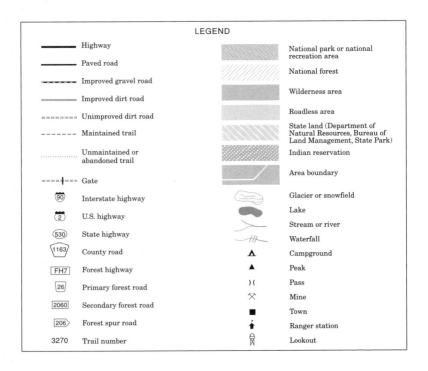

LEGEND

| | |
|---|---|
| ——— Highway | National park or national recreation area |
| ——— Paved road | National forest |
| ━━━━ Improved gravel road | Wilderness area |
| ═══ Improved dirt road | Roadless area |
| ======== Unimproved dirt road | State land (Department of Natural Resources, Bureau of Land Management, State Park) |
| −−−−−− Maintained trail | |
| ·············· Unmaintained or abandoned trail | Indian reservation |
| ====╪=== Gate | Area boundary |
| ⑩ Interstate highway | Glacier or snowfield |
| ② U.S. highway | Lake |
| ⑤③⓪ State highway | Stream or river |
| ⑪①⑥③ County road | —///— Waterfall |
| FH7 Forest highway | Ⓐ Campground |
| ②⑥ Primary forest road | ▲ Peak |
| ②⓪⑥⓪ Secondary forest road | )( Pass |
| ②⓪⑥〉 Forest spur road | ✕ Mine |
| 3270 Trail number | ■ Town |
| | ⚑ Ranger station |
| | ♑ Lookout |

Opposite: *Avalanche lilies edge the High Divide Trail in Olympic National Park.*

# chapter 1

# The Olympic Peninsula

# 1 Washington Islands Wilderness

**Location:** In Clallam, Jefferson, and Grays Harbor Counties, along the Pacific Coast of the Olympic Peninsula, from Cape Flattery on the north to Copalis Rock on the south
**Size:** About 486 acres of islands, rocks, and reefs, up to 3 miles offshore, stretching along 100 miles of coastline
**Status:** National Wildlife Refuge (1940), Designated Wilderness (1970)
**Terrain:** The wilderness consists of 870 reefs, rocks, and islands ranging from less than 1 acre to 36 acres in size. Most have little to no shore below vertical rock cliffs washed by wild surf.
**Elevation:** 0 to 223 feet
**Management:** U.S. Fish and Wildlife Service
**Topographic maps:** Allens Bay, Bodelteh Islands, Cape Flattery, Destruction Island, Hoh Head, La Push, Makah Bay, Moclips, Ozette, Quillayute Prairie, Shale Slough, Taholah, Toleak Point, Tunnel Island

The three Washington Islands Wilderness National Wildlife Refuges are a chain of offshore islands along the west side of the Olympic Peninsula that includes Flattery Rocks and the Quillayute Needles to the north, and Copalis Rock to the south. These islands are a stopover for thousands of migratory birds, and serve as both home and breeding ground for a dozen species of marine birds totaling more than 108,000 breeding pairs. Offshore waters host seals, sea lions, and whales.

## CLIMATE

The islands lie off the wet side of the Olympic Peninsula, exposed to weather patterns sweeping in from the Pacific. Annual precipitation ranges from 110 to 160 inches. Summers are cool and moist, with frequent stretches of persistent fog. Winter low-pressure systems bring storms with heavy rain, strong winds, and crashing seas. Temperatures are mild year-round, seldom dropping below 35 degrees or rising above 65 degrees.

## ECOSYSTEM

The tops of the larger islands have a thin layer of soil that permits growth of shrubs such as salal and salmonberry; a few have stands of Sitka spruce. This vegetation supports a small population of Townsend's voles, shrew moles, Trowbridge's shrews, salamanders, and garter snakes, a food source for raptors.

The lower rocks and reefs are haul-out sites for harbor seals and northern and California sea lions. Other mammals common in the waters surrounding the islands include Pacific right whales, gray whales, humpback whales, Pacific harbor porpoises, and fur seals. In 1970 sea otters were reintroduced after a nearly 100-year absence due to their near-extinction by fur hunters, and they appear to be thriving.

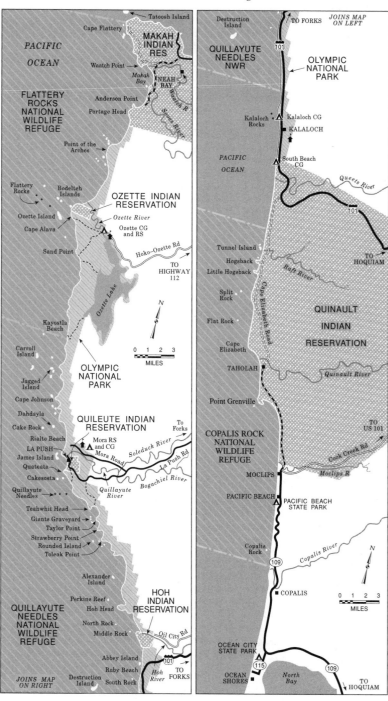

**Left map:**

PACIFIC OCEAN

Tatoosh Island
Cape Flattery
MAKAH INDIAN RES
Waatch Point
Makah Bay
NEAH BAY
Anderson Point
Portage Head
Waatch R
Sooes River

FLATTERY ROCKS NATIONAL WILDLIFE REFUGE

Point of the Arches

Flattery Rocks
Bodelteh Islands
Ozette Island
Cape Alava
Sand Point

OZETTE INDIAN RESERVATION
Ozette River
Ozette CG and RS
Hoko-Ozette Rd
TO HIGHWAY 112

Ozette Lake

Kayostla Beach

Carroll Island

Jagged Island
Cape Johnson
Dahdayla
Cake Rock
Rialto Beach
LA PUSH
James Island
Quateata
Cakesosta
Quillayute Needles

OLYMPIC NATIONAL PARK

QUILEUTE INDIAN RESERVATION
Mora RS and CG
Mora Road
Soleduck River
To Forks
La Push Rd
Bogachiel River
Quillayute River

N

0 1 2 3 MILES

Teahwhit Head
Giants Graveyard
Taylor Point
Strawberry Point
Rounded Island
Toleak Point

Alexander Island
Perkins Reef
Hoh Head
North Rock
Middle Rock

HOH INDIAN RESERVATION
Oil City Rd

QUILLAYUTE NEEDLES NATIONAL WILDLIFE REFUGE

Abbey Island
Ruby Beach
Destruction Island
South Rock
Hoh River
TO FORKS
101

JOINS MAP ON RIGHT

**Right map:**

JOINS MAP ON LEFT

Destruction Island
TO FORKS
101

QUILLAYUTE NEEDLES NWR

OLYMPIC NATIONAL PARK

Kalaloch Rocks
Kalaloch CG
KALALOCH

PACIFIC OCEAN

South Beach CG
Queets River
101

Tunnel Island
Hogsback
Little Hogsback
Raft River
TO HOQUIAM

Split Rock

Flat Rock

Cape Elizabeth

QUINAULT INDIAN RESERVATION

Cape Elizabeth Road

TAHOLAH
Quinault River

Point Grenville

TO US 101

COPALIS ROCK NATIONAL WILDLIFE REFUGE

Cook Creek Rd

MOCLIPS
Moclips R

PACIFIC BEACH
PACIFIC BEACH STATE PARK

Copalis Rock

Copalis River
109

N

0 1 2 3 MILES

COPALIS

OCEAN CITY STATE PARK

115
OCEAN SHORES
North Bay
109
TO HOQUIAM

Among the birds known to nest on the islands are bald eagles, peregrine falcons, auklets, cormorants, petrels, oystercatchers, murres, and gulls. These are joined by migrating flocks of passerines, scoters, shearwaters, and western grebes.

## GEOLOGY
The islands were formed by the collision between the North American and Juan de Fuca Plates some 50 million years ago. The western edge of this terrane consisted of sedimentary deposits overlaying the ocean floor. Repeated submerging and uplifting transformed these sediments into metamorphic rock, and its differential erosion created the reefs and islands that comprise the wilderness today.

## HISTORY
The sea and its resources were a vital part of the life of Northwest Indians, so these large offshore rocks were undoubtedly frequented by them. Shell middens found on Tsakawahyah Island indicate native visitation there. The top of this island, as well as caves on Ozette Island, served as native burial sites.

In 1907 President Theodore Roosevelt designated Flattery Rocks, Quillayute Needles, and Copalis Rock as migratory bird sanctuaries. Further protection was afforded in 1940 when these areas, with the exception of Destruction Island, were made national wildlife refuges. All were designated as a wilderness area in 1970.

## ACTIVITIES
Because of their wildlife sanctuary status, all the islands are closed to public entry and use. They can be viewed most closely from the coastal portion of Olympic National Park. Access points to this beach strip are at Ozette, Rialto Beach, Second and Third Beaches near La Push, Ruby Beach, Kalaloch, Taholah, Moclips, and Pacific Beach.

*Cormorants use rocks of the Washington Islands Wilderness as a resting site.*

# Olympic Coast

## Olympic National Park

**Location:** In Jefferson and Clallam Counties, along the Pacific Ocean shoreline of the Olympic Peninsula
**Size:** 42,900 acres
**Status:** National Park (1953), Designated Wilderness (1988)
**Terrain:** The Olympic Coast has sand, conglomerate, or rock beaches below steep rocky headlands, with hundreds of offshore rocks, reefs, and sea stacks. Headlands have wave-carved arches and caves, and are split by numerous creeks and rivers. Inland regions are low and densely forested, with a few lakes and several marshes.
**Elevation:** 0 to 650 feet
**Management:** National Park Service
**Topographic maps:** Allens Bay, Destruction Island, Dickey Lake, Hoh Head, La Push, Makah Bay, Ozette, Queets, Quillayute Prairie, Toleak Point, Umbrella Creek

This portion of Olympic National Park consists of a 57-mile strip of Pacific Ocean shoreline. The southern third of the ocean beach lies only a few hundred feet from a coastal section of US Highway 101, but the northern two-thirds are accessible only by hiking from one of four access points. Two sections, each more than 17 miles long, have no intermediate approaches.

Beaches range from long, wide expanses of sand to small coves framed by rocky headland cliffs, some impassable at sea level and others requiring low tide levels to round. Trails lead inland through dense, brushy forest to cross the most difficult of these heads. Offshore are more than 800 low rocks, submerging reefs, and spectacular sea stacks, all erosion-resistant vestiges of former heads and capes. Minus tides permit exploration of tide pools teeming with a fantastic variety of marine life.

The national park–managed ocean strip is interrupted briefly in three spots by small Indian reservations: the Hoh Reservation on the south side of the Hoh River, the Quileute Reservation south of La Push, and the Ozette Reservation on the north side of Cape Alava. Indians have lived in these areas for centuries; archaeological digs at a Cape Alava village site that was covered by a sudden mud slide more than 500 years ago, have recovered priceless artifacts that chronicle the culture and life of these early Native Americans. Many of these artifacts are displayed at the Makah Museum in Neah Bay.

Over the last 200 years, rugged offshore reefs have claimed numerous ships and sailors' lives. Remnants of a wave-battered shipwreck lie on the rocks north of Shi Shi Beach; elsewhere along the coast, rusting anchors and chains recall the destruction of other ships. Chilean and Norwegian Memorials, both located along the remote north wilderness beach, commemorate lives lost in nearby shipwrecks.

Near the north end of the beach strip, the park extends inland to enclose Ozette

Lake, the third-largest natural lake in the state. The lake, with numerous bays and coves, is 8.5 miles long and nearly 2 miles wide in most places. A boat launch by a small campground at the north end of the lake is its only means of access. Two trails lead from coves on the west side to the ocean beach; the rest of the lake is rimmed with impenetrable brush and forest.

## CLIMATE

The ocean beach strip is on the wet side of the Olympic Peninsula; precipitation here averages 120 inches per year, with three-fourths of this falling as heavy rains in fall and winter months. During this time, a continuous series of low-pressure cells roll in from the Pacific Ocean, accompanied by high winds, torrential downpours, and heavy seas. Although precipitation during the summer averages only 3 inches per month, this season is still cool, moist, and frequently foggy. Temperatures are mild year-round, seldom dropping below 35 degrees or rising above 65 degrees.

## ECOSYSTEM

The thick forest above the headland cliffs sports a band of shore pine immediately above the beach. Inland this is replaced by hemlock, red cedar, Pacific madrone, and Sitka spruce. A dense growth of kinnikinnick, salal, and oceanspray is underlaid by mosses, ferns, deerfoot vanillaleaf, wood sorrel, and fireweed. Because of its low elevation and the heavy rains, the forest floor has numerous bogs, marshes, and mud holes, making cross-country travel difficult.

Residents of the forest, and visitors to the beaches, include black-tailed deer, black bear, raccoon, skunk, and, on rare occasions, elk and porcupine. The ocean strip and its offshore rocks are both home and breeding ground for glaucous gulls, great blue herons, double-crested cormorants, black oystercatchers, crows, and ravens. Bald eagles also nest in the area, and may be spotted perched on snags above the beach. Seals often haul out on offshore rocks.

At low tide, the nearshore wave-cut benches are laced with tide pools that harbor colorful mussels, barnacles, limpets, periwinkles, rock oysters, purple shore crabs, hermit crabs, starfish, nudibranchs, chitons, anemones, and sea urchins.

## GEOLOGY

The headwall of the beach south of Ozette Lake is made up of sandstones and conglomerates formed from continental and marine sediments deposited 10 million to 25 million years ago. The area from Kayostla Beach north to Shi Shi Beach is composed of glacial deposits laid down by Pleistocene ice sheets and more recent alluvium. In places, the cliffs above the southern section of the ocean beach are intruded with breccia—fragments of broken sandstone compressed and cemented into solid rock in subterranean trenches. These outcrops are often permeated with crude oil that is compressed into spaces between the fragments.

The breaking surf focuses on projecting headlands, where it fractures blocks of rock by compressing air into small cracks, and undercuts the base of the sea cliffs,

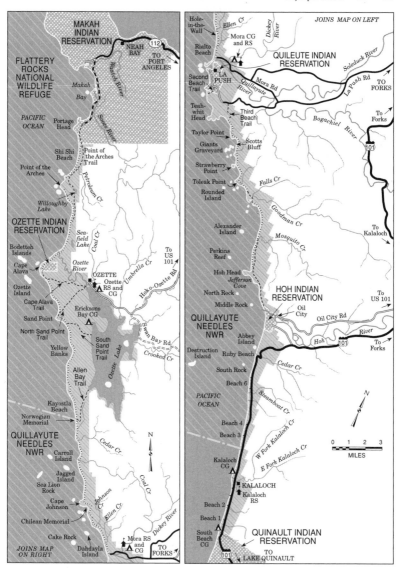

causing them to collapse. The resulting debris is eroded by the surf, carried off as sand and fine gravel, and deposited in the quieter water of coves. Over time, this erosion of seaward headlands results in the buildup of long stretches of sandy beach and smoothing of the coastline.

Offshore sea stacks are the less-fractured, more erosion-resistant remnants of former headland cliffs. Rocks and reefs at, or just below, the surface are portions of harder rock that form a broad, wave-cut bench near the shore.

*A rocky beach near Hole-in-the-Wall holds tide pools.*

## HISTORY

Archaeological digs at Cape Alava indicate that Indians lived along the Northwest ocean beaches as long as 2,000 years ago. The first white explorers arrived in the area between 1774 and 1778. The natives were hostile initially; a Russian expedition, shipwrecked near Rialto Beach in 1808, fought with both the Quileutes and Hoh before twenty-two of the sailors were killed or captured.

In the early 1800s the territory was jointly claimed by the United States and Great Britain; a boundary settlement in 1846 ceded the area to the U.S. Treaties concluded in 1855 assigned then-recognized tribes to reservations near their traditional hunting and fishing grounds on the peninsula.

Around 1890 the first white settlers moved to the southern portion of the beach strip at Kalaloch to open a fish cannery. The first non-native settler arrived at La Push in 1860. As early as the 1870s, schooners brought staples there, and the village served as a supply point for the nearby western peninsula. Rumors of a railroad or county road into the area led homesteaders to settle at Ozette Lake in the1890s. The road didn't arrive until 1935; meanwhile a tiny logging community grew at the site. The construction of the road prompted the building of a small resort at the north end of the lake at Ozette.

Recognizing its natural resource value, President Grover Cleveland established the Olympic Forest Reserve in 1897. The unique geography and ecology of the area was further recognized in 1909, when President Theodore Roosevelt created the 651,000-acre Mount Olympus National Monument. National park status was conferred on the area in June 1938; the ocean beaches were added to the park in 1953. The latest addition, in 1977, was the beach strip between Point of the Arches and Shi Shi Beach.

At the onset of World War II, the vulnerability of miles of coastline caused the Coast Guard to appropriate resorts at Kalaloch and Ozette as part of the Coastal Lookout System. This system ultimately included isolated four-man outposts every 5 to 10 miles along the coast. A few old cabins near creeks and headlands are vestiges of this wartime effort.

## HIKING

Hikers along the remote ocean beaches must contend with several hazards not common to hikes in other wilderness areas. Knowledge of tide levels and weather conditions is critical for a safe trip. Sheer cliffs drop directly to the surf at some of the headlands, forcing travelers to cross them via short inland trails through the dense coastal forest. The Park Service has installed "rope assists" (fixed ropes or wooden rungs strung on ropes) to help hikers up the steep soft cliffs adjoining the headlands. Other heads have steep sea cliffs and dense brush that make crossing them by trail impossible. As a result, hikers must schedule their travel to round such spots at low tide. Some creeks and rivers that can normally be waded become impassable with runoff from heavy rains or at extreme high tides. Severe storms combined with high tides can lash beaches with dangerous breaking surf that tosses huge driftwood logs around.

***Point of the Arches.*** *3.5 miles/e (H).* From the west end of Neah Bay find the road signed "OCEAN BEACHES" and follow it south. The road crosses the Waatch River, turns south along Makah Bay, then crosses the Sooes River. At 6.5 miles the passable road ends near some homes; the track that continues south across the reservation quickly degenerates to axle-deep mud. In 2 miles this path reaches the Olympic National Park boundary, above the north end of Shi Shi Beach. Slippery paths lead down to the beach at this point, and a short stroll north on the beach leads to small coves, tide pools, and sea stacks.

The trail continues south along the bluff for another mile before wandering down to the beach near Petroleum Creek. The way follows the beach to Point of the Arches, an exquisite collection of tiny coves, tide pools, and a line of sea stacks stretching nearly a mile offshore. Many of these stacks have caves and arches cut through them by the surf, giving the point its name. A few nearshore stacks can be explored at minus tides, but the tide-exposed bench has sharp rocks and slippery footing. The headlands immediately south of the point are inaccessible by beach.

***Cape Alava (Indian Village).*** *3.5 miles/e (H).* Beginning at the campground on the north end of Ozette Lake, the route crosses the footbridge over the Ozette River and follows the north fork west through hemlock forest to the sandy beach on the south side of Cape Alava, the westernmost point of the coterminous U.S. Much of the trail is on puncheon logs that bridge bogs. The cape lies within the Ozette Indian Reservation, which stretches about a mile along the beach.

*A family explores the fascinating Hole-in-the-Wall.*

The sandy beach can be hiked north through the reservation to the mouth of the Ozette River, which can be waded at low tide. A narrow strip of sand leads north from the river for nearly 4 miles to the southern edge of Point of the Arches.

The beach south from Cape Alava to Sand Point is a narrow, but easy, 3-mile walk except at very high tides. En route, at Wedding Rocks, is a series of Indian pictographs carved in the sandstone headland near the high-tide level.

**North Sand Point.** *2 miles/e (H).* At the start of the Cape Alava Trail, take the south fork, which heads through brushy forest to reach Sand Point. A good portion of this path is also on logs that cross bogs and marshes. A small rock spike marks the end of Sand Point, where a broad sandy beach sweeps south for 1.5 miles to cliffs north of Yellow Banks. A loop trip can be made by hiking north to Cape Alava.

**Rialto Beach to Cape Alava (the North Wilderness Beach).** *18.5 miles/m (H).* Because of the need to schedule rounding of several heads at low-tide levels, this is generally a 3-day hike, typically done by hikers dropped off at one end and picked up at the other. The south end leaves Mora Campground at the Rialto Beach Picnic Area. Hike the wide beach north for 0.5 mile, wade Ellen Creek, and in another mile reach Hole-in-the-Wall, a rock arch across the beach. A short distance north is the first headland that can be rounded only at low tide. Beyond, a sandy beach leads a mile north to the Chilean Memorial commemorating the 1920 shipwreck of the schooner *W. J. Pirrie*. A small offshore island with tide pools can be reached at minus tides.

North of the Chilean Memorial, the cliffs of Cape Johnson require a low tide to round, as does a small head another 0.5 mile to the north. The sandy beach continues for 1.3 miles to a head with a short, low trail across the inland side. A mile-long sandy stretch, with views offshore of Sea Lion Rock and Jagged and Carroll Islands, ends at a small, low-tide-only head, the last for several miles. In 2.4 miles the route reaches the Norwegian Memorial. The nearshore surf is peppered with low rocks from here to the next low-tide passage below a small head at the north end of Yellow Banks. The trip north to Sand Point and Cape Alava is described previously.

**Third Beach.** *1.5 miles/e (H).* The trailhead is on the south side of the road, 2.3 miles east of La Push. A forest hike ends in a steep switchback descent of the headland to the center of Third Beach, a mile-long strip of sand between Teahwhit Head and Taylor Point. At the south end of the beach a waterfall plunges from Taylor Point; nearshore tide pools are accessible at low tide.

**Third Beach to the Hoh River (the South Wilderness Beach).** *17 miles/m (H).* This long wilderness beach segment requires inland treks to cross heads impassable at sea level, and crosses three creeks that may not be fordable during heavy runoffs. Taylor Head blocks passage at the south end of Third Beach (trail described previously); a 1.5-mile wooded path leads inland across the head to a cove on its east side. Here a scramble over, or medium-tide-level passage around, a protruding cliff reaches a sandy respite before Scotts Bluff. The bluff is passable at low tide or can be bypassed by a short inland trail.

In 0.5 mile the offshore stacks of the Giants Graveyard mark the former location of a present-day sea cliff passable only at medium or lower tides. Once this obstacle is rounded, a sandy crescent-shaped beach leads to Strawberry Point, with nearshore sea stacks and tide pools. The broad beach continues south to Toleak Point, and more rocks and tide pools.

After another mile of beach, cliffs force the route inland past a waterfall at Falls Creek and to a waded crossing of Goodman Creek before the route once again returns to the beach. An easy hike of more than 2 miles leads to a ford of Mosquito Creek and a route choice. A minor head to the south can be skirted at minus tides, and the beach beyond can be followed for another mile before the cliffs of Hoh Head direct the route inland. Alternatively, at Mosquito Creek the Hoh Head Trail climbs to the brushy rim of the sea cliff and follows it south, with glimpses of the beach below. Both routes join for an inland trek over Hoh Head to Jefferson Cove.

At the south end of the cove, a steep cliff is the final low-tide-only obstacle before reaching the Hoh River trailhead at Oil City, a grandiose name for a site with neither oil nor residents.

**Southwest Beaches and US 101 Accesses.** Immediately south of the Hoh River, the park beach strip is interrupted by the Hoh Indian Reservation. US 101 swings west into the park about a mile south of the reservation and follows the rim of headlands for 11.5 miles to the south park boundary near the Queets River. En route several short paths lead through the forest to the wide, sandy beach strip. The few offshore stacks and rocks in this beach section occur near small eroded headlands, the only places where high tide might temporarily stall beach hikes. A few sea stacks are offshore from Ruby Beach, and Beach 4 has tide pools. Because of its accessibility, this strip is popular year-round, even in winter when the surf hurls huge driftwood about and whips up a froth of spindrift along the water's edge.

Paths to the beach are located at Ruby Beach (on the north end of this strip), Beach 6 (0.9 mile to the south), a small stream 0.9 mile south of Beach 6, Steamboat Creek (0.4 mile farther south), Beach 4 (in 2.4 more miles), Beach 3 (0.6 mile to the south), Kalaloch Beach (in another 2.5 miles), Beach 2 (1.3 miles south of Kalaloch), Beach 1 (0.9 mile to the south), and South Beach Campground (at the park's south boundary).

## 3    Olympic Peninsula Interior

### Olympic National Park; Rugged Ridge, Bald Mountain, and Madison Creek Roadless Areas

**Location:** In Clallam, Jefferson, Mason, and Grays Harbor Counties, in the heart of the Olympic Peninsula

**Size:** Park (interior), 878,973 acres; wilderness, 876,669 acres. Rugged Ridge, 4,564 acres; Mount Baldy, 3,895 acres; Madison Creek, 1,079 acres

**Status:** National Park (1938), Designated Wilderness (1988); Roadless areas are Roaded Natural and Semiprimitive Nonmotorized

**Terrain:** The region has a complex structure of rugged ridges, many supporting small glaciers or snowfields, divided by long, deep, glacier- and stream-carved drainages radiating from the high, remote interior.

**Elevation:** 80 to 7,965 feet

**Management:** National Park Service; Olympic National Forest, Pacific Ranger District

**Topographic maps:** Bob Creek, Bogachiel Peak, Bunch Lake, Chimney Peak, Colonel Bob, Elwha, Finley Creek, Hunger Mountain, Indian Pass, Kimta Peak, Kloochman Rock, Lake Crescent, Lake Sutherland, Lake Quinault East, Lake Quinault West, Maiden Peak, Matheny Ridge, McCartney Peak, Morse Creek, Mount Angeles, Mount Carrie, Mount Christie, Mount Deception, Mount Hoquiam, Mount Muller, Mount Olson, Mount Olympus, Mount Queets, Mount Skokomish, Mount Steel, Mount Tom, Mount Townsend, Mt. Washington, Owl Mountain, Port Angeles, Queets, Salmon River East, Salmon River West, Slide Peak, Spruce Mountain, Stequaleho Creek, The Brothers, Tyler Peak, Wellesley Peak, Winfield Creek, Wynoochee Lake

The inland portion of Olympic National Park is a huge wilderness, 50 miles wide east-to-west and 40 miles wide north-to-south. Here are a jumble of crumbling rocky summits between 6,500 and 7,700 feet high, flanked by sharp ridges, many topped by loose

*Hellebore graces the shore of Lunch Lake in the Seven Lakes Basin.*

rock towers. The faces of the higher peaks host more than sixty small, low-gradient glaciers. The heavy annual snowfall leaves steep snowfields, many that never totally melt. The park has more than 350 lakes, most quite small and tucked into alpine cirques; however, one, Lake Crescent, is more than 5,000 acres in size. Approximately 586 miles of trails, several 20 to 30 miles in length, explore the interior of the park. Many trace the long, radiating river courses that drain from the high country. None of the adjacent roadless areas have any formal trails.

## CLIMATE

The Olympic Range is a major barrier for storms from the Pacific Ocean; storm fronts drop tremendous amounts of precipitation on the range's western flanks, but the eastern slopes remain reasonably dry. The Hoh Rain Forest on the west receives an annual load of 133 inches of precipitation; the town of Sequim, on the northeast, sees only 16 inches. Most of this rain and snow falls between October and March, when few dry days are recorded. At lower elevations snow rarely remains on the ground for more than a few days, but a snowpack of 30 to 40 feet may accumulate on peaks and ridge tops. Year-round temperatures are relatively mild, ranging between the 20s to 40s in

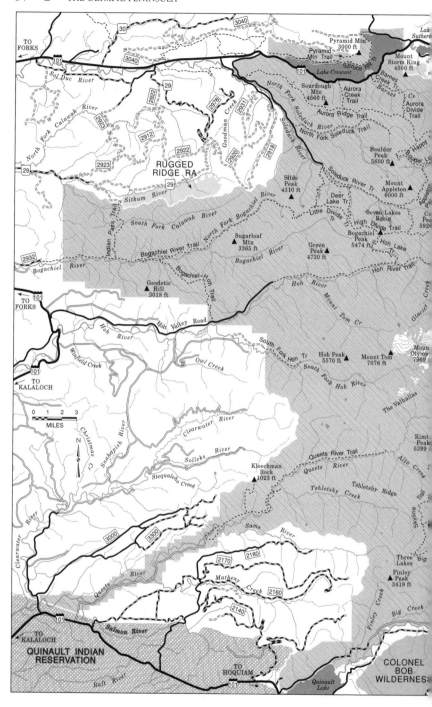

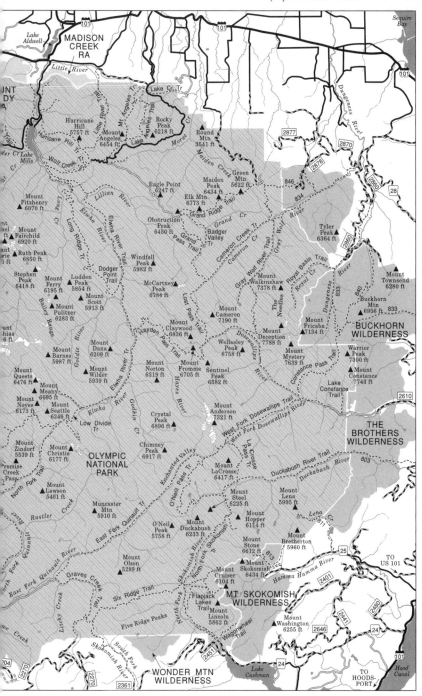

*Lunch Lake, in the Seven Lakes Basin, is a pretty alpine tarn.*

winter, and the mid-40s to 70s in summer. Weather is unpredictable, due to the proximity to ocean storm fronts; summer months frequently see persistent fog or low clouds below 3,000 feet that often disappear by early afternoon.

## ECOSYSTEM

The wide altitude variation in the park spans multiple forest zones. At the lowest elevations, forests are composed of Douglas-fir, western hemlock, Sitka spruce, and western red cedar, with bigleaf maple, red alder, and black cottonwood in drainage bottoms. The understory here contains salal, huckleberry, rhododendron, Oregon grape, devil's club, skunk cabbage, willows, salmonberry, and a variety of ferns and mosses. Farther up the slopes, trees change to Douglas-fir, western hemlock, silver fir, and western red cedar. Vine maple, alder, and devil's club grow profusely along streams and in avalanche tracks. Near timberline, the trees are subalpine fir, mountain hemlock, and Alaska cedar, and ground cover is dominated by willows, slide alder, huckleberry, heather, and colorful displays of wildflowers such as beargrass, paintbrush, lupine, and avalanche lilies. The highest ridges, in the alpine zone, have a sparse cover of phlox, sedges, anemones, spirea, mosses, and lichens.

Common mammals include shrews (several species), coast mole, snowshoe hare, mountain beaver, squirrels, chipmunks, vole, raccoon, weasel, mink, river otter, skunk, coyote, black bear, cougar, bobcat, elk, and black-tailed deer. Over 200 species of birds have been recorded in the Olympics, and a few dozen more species are transient visitors. Those most commonly seen are wrens, crows, woodpeckers, sparrows, kingfishers, owls, hawks, grouse, jays, finches, ravens, kinglets, juncos, and golden eagles.

## GEOLOGY

The rocks of the Olympic Peninsula were born in the waters off the western continental margin. Sediments and muds washed from the North American continent were layered and compressed offshore into sandstones and shales. Some 50 million years ago these deposits were intruded on their eastern edge by massive undersea lava flows that emerged as pillow basalts. These flows also penetrated the layers between the accumulated strata as sills. Collisions between the oceanic and continental plates caused shear fractures, and the layers overrode one another along the fault lines. Continued movement of the two plates toward each other tilted the strata sharply upward to a near-vertical plane. Further compression toward the northeast squeezed and distorted the strata into successive horseshoe-shaped bands wrapped around the north, east, and south sides of the Olympic Peninsula.

A general uplift raised the heart of the Olympics, and radial watercourses cut deeply through the base rock. Both continental and local glaciation during the last ice age, 12,000 years ago, further carved these drainages, leaving steep U-shaped valleys and glacial cirques in their wake. Since then, erosion has worn, sharpened, and narrowed ridges, cleaving the loosely bonded rock into rotten peaks and towers along ridge crests, and deepening the gorges of major rivers and streams. Local alpine glaciers, and the rivers and streams they feed with abrasive, scoured waste, continue this shaping and carving today.

## HISTORY

Native American tribes had several settlements on the shores of the Olympic Peninsula, some dating from more than 2,000 years ago. There is increasing archaeological evidence that they also ventured into the heart of the peninsula, now the Olympic National Park.

In 1774, crew members of the Santiago, under the command of Juan Perez, were the first Europeans to sight the Olympic Range. Mount Olympus was identified and named by Captain John Meares, a British explorer, in 1788; the name was applied to the entire range in the logs of the Vancouver Expedition in 1792.

The first homesteaders arrived on the lowland fringes of the Olympics in the 1850s. Although the U.S. Army built a trail from Fort Townsend to the Dungeness River in 1882, the interior of the range remained mysterious and unknown; some speculated that it contained a "Shangri-La" hidden valley. The first exploration into the range began in 1885 when Lieutenant Joseph O'Neil led an Army expedition through the northeast portion.

In 1889 the *Seattle Press* sponsored an expedition to cross the range and discover what lay hidden in its interior. A party of five headed into the Elwha Valley in December

1889. The group struggled upstream through deep snows in a tragicomic adventure. It took them until May 1890 to cross the range and reach the Quinault River, where they descended to the Pacific. The interior of the Olympics was no longer a mystery—and definitely not a Shangri-La!

O'Neil returned later in 1890 to lead a party into the range from the south. The expedition was intensive and thorough, mapping the Skokomish, Wynoochee, Quinault, Queets, Duckabush, and Dosewallips drainages. Although they claimed to have made the first ascent of Mount Olympus, evidence left by the party has never been found. When the Olympic Forest Reserve was created in 1897, a complete survey of the range was ordered. A USGS-contracted party led by Arthur Dodwell and Theodore Rixon completed this effort between 1898 and 1900, climbing many peaks in the range in the course of their activities. With the range and its peaks now plotted, a flurry of climbing activity took place in the early 1900s; by 1931 all major peaks had been climbed.

In 1909 President Theodore Roosevelt proclaimed 615,000 acres of the Olympic National Forest the Mount Olympus National Monument. The monument's size and

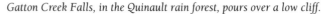

*Gatton Creek Falls, in the Quinault rain forest, pours over a low cliff.*

boundaries shifted markedly in subsequent years due to political pressures and commercial pursuit of its natural resources. Olympic National Park, 648,000 acres, was created in 1938 and since then has become almost 880,000 acres. Most of the interior was declared a designated wilderness in 1988.

## HIKING

Olympic National Park has instituted a program to loan bear-proof canisters for storing foods to backcountry hikers (with a voluntary donation accepted). Check with the park about this innovative way to address the problem of campsite predators.

### Dungeness–Gray Wolf River Trails

*Upper Gray Wolf Trail.* 12.9 miles/m (H,S). The Lower Gray Wolf Trail enters the park from the Buckhorn Wilderness (2,260 ft), 0.9 mile from the Upper Gray Wolf Trail (2,100 ft). The latter follows the bank of the Gray Wolf River upstream through fir and cedar forest and across avalanche tracks. It climbs steeply, switchbacking into meadows (5,200 ft), to reach Gray Wolf Pass (6,180 ft). Here are wide views of Mounts Deception, Mystery, Constance, and Olympus, The Brothers, Lost Peak, and The Needles. The path continues south, zigzagging abruptly down to the Dosewallips Trail (3,600 ft).

*Royal Basin Trail.* 7 miles/m (H,S). From Trail 832 (2,680 ft) on the Dungeness River, just east of the park boundary, the way heads west up Royal Basin Creek through Douglas-fir and hemlock forest. The path crosses multiple openings swept by avalanches originating on Gray Wolf Ridge. At Royal Falls the creek and trail bend south and the grade flattens; the trail crosses lower Royal Basin and climbs to Royal Lake (5,118 ft). The upper basin is rimmed on the west by the rock towers of The Needles, capped at its head by Mounts Deception and Mystery, and flanked on the east by spires along the Olympic National Park–Buckhorn Wilderness boundary.

### Dosewallips River Trails

*Lake Constance Trail.* 2 miles/m (H). From the Dosewallips River Road (1,460 ft), this route shoots up along Constance Creek, clawing over roots, ledges, and small cliffs to reach Lake Constance (4,664 ft). North from this beautiful, cliff-walled lake is 2-mile-long Avalanche Canyon, a snow-filled defile squeezed between cliffs and crags that rise abruptly 1,500 feet or more.

*Dosewallips Trail.* 15.4 miles/m (H,S). A long, easy-grade path from Dosewallips Campground (1,580 ft) follows the Dosewallips River northwest at the base of a deep, forested canyon. At Dose Forks, the West Fork Dosewallips Trail peels off, and shortly after, the Constance Pass Trail climbs to the north. The way follows the hook of the river west, then north, passing the south end of the Gray Wolf Trail. The forest opens at Dose Meadows, then the way contours around the head of the basin to Thousand Acre Meadow. Long, sweeping switchbacks climb to Hayden Pass (5,847 ft) to meet the trail of the same name. The pass is framed by Sentinel Peak and Mount Fromme, and has great views of Mount Anderson, Wellesley Peak, the Bailey Range, and Mount Olympus.

**West Fork Dosewallips Trail.** *9.1 miles/m (H,S).* From Dose Forks (1,930 ft) the route climbs west to a bridge over the 100-foot-deep gorge of the West Fork, then follows the river upstream through fir and hemlock forest. At 2,750 feet the trail crosses the river into open country at Honeymoon Meadows (3,520 ft). Above, at Anderson Pass (4,465 ft), it joins the Enchanted Valley Trail. Here a steep switchback chain leads to the moraine of the Anderson Glacier (5,100 ft), the largest in the east Olympics. Tiny, hardy wildflowers cling to niches in the rock; the glacier sweeps down from the two ragged summits of Mount Anderson.

**Constance Pass Trail.** *8.5 miles/m-d (H,S).* Switchbacks through Douglas-fir climb the steep spur above the Dosewallips Trail (2,181 ft) to Sunnybrook Meadows, where a long traverse east leads to Constance Pass (5,850 ft) and views of the ragged cliffs of the Inner Constance Peaks. The way drops north to Home Lake (5,308 ft), then descends into the Buckhorn Wilderness to Trail 833 at Boulder Camp (4,920 ft).

## Duckabush River Trails

**Duckabush Trail.** *22.2 miles/m-d (H,S).* Trail 803 enters the park from The Brothers Wilderness (1,320 ft), then rolls along the broad bottom of the Duckabush drainage as it continues upstream to pass the North Fork Skokomish Trail (2,620 ft). The valley narrows, the way becomes steeper, and switchbacks climb to Marmot Lake (4,390 ft). The route snakes uphill through parkland to O'Neil Pass (4,980 ft), where it meets the O'Neil Pass Trail.

## North Fork Skokomish River Trails

**North Fork Skokomish Trail.** *15.6 miles/m (H,S).* From Staircase Campground (840 ft), the route starts on an abandoned roadbed that heads up the North Fork Skokomish River. It passes the Flapjack Lakes Trail, then bends northeast as it thrusts upstream. The way leaves the timbered river bottom at Nine Stream (1,980 ft) to switchback up steep slopes and break into meadows at First Divide (4,688 ft). Here are views to Mount LaCrosse and White Mountain. Dropping down the north side of the pass, the way threads through meadows; Mount Steel frames the horizon to the west. Switchbacks descend steep wooded slopes north to the Duckabush Trail (2,710 ft).

**Flapjack Lakes Trail.** *5.6 miles/m (H,S).* Beginning at the end of an abandoned-road section of the North Fork Skokomish River Trail (1,480 ft), the route heads up the forested slope east of the river, crosses Madeline Creek, then rounds a ridge into the Donahue Creek drainage. It weaves up to Flapjack Lakes (3,847 to 3,850 ft) at the base of the towers of Sawtooth Ridge. The path continues northeast through meadows, past tarns flanked by the spires of The Fin, Castle Spires, The Needle, and the walls of Mount Cruiser. Flower meadows at Gladys Divide (5,350 ft) sweep gracefully up to the top of Mount Gladys.

## South Fork Skokomish Trails

**Upper South Fork Skokomish Trail.** *7 miles/m (H,S).* Trail 873 enters the park (2,600 ft) 4.4 miles from its trailhead on FR 2361. To this point, the grade is easy and well maintained, but at the park boundary it becomes rough and steep. After traversing a soggy basin (3,100 ft), the way switchbacks up to Sundown Pass (4,140 ft), then descends to the Graves Creek Trail (3,760 ft) just south of Sundown Lake.

## East Fork Quinault River Trails

*East Fork Quinault Trail. 18.9 miles/m (H,S).* From the end of the South Shore Quinault Road (620 ft) the route crosses Graves Creek, passes the Graves Creek Trail, then follows an abandoned roadbed up the ever-deepening Quinault River drainage. After crossing to the northwest side of the river, the road becomes a trail that traces the easy grade of the river upstream past numerous cascades from cliffs above. A suspension bridge over the river leads to the heart of Enchanted Valley and its two-story log chalet. Depending on the season, avalanches or myriad waterfall veils drop over the precipitous walls of Chimney Peak. Beyond Enchanted Valley, cliff walls constrict the route as it climbs past the O'Neil Pass Trail, then switchbacks steeply up to Anderson Pass (4,465 ft) to meet the West Fork Dosewallips Trail.

*Graves Creek Trail. 8.6 miles/m (H,S).* Near the start of the Enchanted Valley Trail (660 ft) this route climbs west through dense forest above Graves Creek to Success Creek. Here, creek and trail turn south and switchbacks climb the steep basin headwall. The way ascends east through meadows, passes the South Fork Skokomish Trail, and reaches Sundown Lake (3,811 ft).

*O'Neil Pass Trail. 7.4 miles/m (H,S).* From meadows west of Anderson Pass (3,250 ft) the route leaves the East Fork Quinault Trail and snakes southwest through forest and alpine meadows as it ascends past views of the cliffs of Chimney Peak above Enchanted Valley. It contours south through flower garden parks, rounds Overlook Peak, and climbs to O'Neil Pass (4,870 ft). The Quinault Valley stretches west to the Pacific, and close by is the massive summit of Mount Duckabush.

## North Fork Quinault River Trails

*Big Creek Trail. 7.1 miles/m (H,S).* From rain-forest bottomland on the North Shore Quinault Road, the route wanders west through fir and Alaska cedar to Big Creek. It heads abruptly uphill, breaks north along a steep-walled tributary drainage, then switchbacks up a wooded ridge to Three Lakes (3,180 to 3,230 ft) to meet the Skyline Trail.

*North Fork Quinault Trail. 16.4 miles/m (H,S).* Leaving the North Fork Ranger Station (500 ft), the way follows an abandoned road along the west bank of the North Fork Quinault River for 4 miles, then ascends into the narrowing valley. River and trail swing northwest, then hook sharply to the east. Steep walls near Geoduck Creek force the trail to the river. It crosses the river (hazardous at high water), climbs steeply through dense dark forest, and breaks into meadows as it meets the Skyline Trail. It reaches parkland at Low Divide (3,602 ft), where it joins the Low Divide Trail.

*Skyline Trail. 20.5 miles/m (H,S).* One of the most remote wilderness trails in the park leaves Big Creek Trail at Three Lakes (3,190 ft) to climb north past alpine tarns, meadows, and clumps of forest on the flank of Tshletshy Ridge. The way continues north above Three Prune Basin, then follows the divide between the Queets and Quinault basins north toward Kimta Peak. Ridge-top meadows afford views of Mount Olympus and the Bailey Range. After skirting the summit of Kimta Peak at 5,200 feet, the way bends sharply eastward, descends the north flank of Kimta Creek Basin, then switchbacks up to Promise Creek Pass (5,100 ft) and views of the heart of the Olympics—Mounts Zindorf, Christie, Seattle, Noyes, and Meany. Northeast, the path gropes through snowfields broken by rocks and heather as it descends to Hee Haw Pass (4,550 ft), then climbs past a spur to Lake Beauty (4,681 ft), and Beauty Pass (5,070 ft). The way weaves around basin headwalls of Promise and Seattle Creeks, switchbacks up to a traverse of the south rib of Mount Seattle, then snakes down to join the North Fork Quinault Trail (3,550 ft) west of Low Divide.

## Queets River Trails

**Queets Trail.** *15.4 miles/e-m (H,S).* At Queets Campground (280 ft), ford the Queets River, follow the flat river bottom through huge moss- and fern-covered trees, pass the Kloochman Rock Trail, and continue upstream to enter a magnificent forest of Sitka spruce, Douglas-fir, and red cedar. The path fades at Pelton Creek (850 ft).

## Hoh River Trails

**Hoh River Trail.** *18 miles/e-m (H,S).* This rain-forest route leaves the Hoh Campground (600 ft) and meanders west through a flat bottomland forest of spruce, cedar, bigleaf maple, and Douglas-fir, draped in ferns and mosses. The path continues upstream on an easy grade to the Olympus Guard Station (948 ft) and the Hoh Lake Trail. In another 2 miles the canyon narrows and the way ascends to a bridge across the vertical walls of a 150-foot-deep gorge cut by the Hoh River. The route zigzags uphill past Martin Creek Falls to Elk Lake (3,011 ft). It climbs through Alaska cedar, mountain hemlock, and silver fir; crosses several avalanche tracks; then arrives at Glacier Meadows (4,387 ft), high camp for climbs of Mount Olympus. The trail forks: the west branch leads to Indian Rock (4,700 ft), overlooking the snout of the Blue Glacier; the east branch continues up to a notch on the lateral moraine, then traces the glacier's edge to 5,000 feet.

**Hoh Lake Trail.** *6.5 miles/m (H,S).* About 0.5 mile beyond the Olympus Guard Station, the route leaves the Hoh River Trail (990 ft) and immediately starts long switchbacks up the steep north wall of the drainage. It climbs through the heart of a 1978 burn where the forest is in the process of regeneration. From the crest the way contours into the Hoh Creek basin, climbs round its head, and snakes up to Hoh Lake (4,520 ft). The route ascends the east rim above the lake to meet the High Divide and Bogachiel River Trails (5,170 ft) on the south side of Bogachiel Peak.

## Bogachiel River Trails

**Bogachiel River Trail.** *32.7 miles/e-m (H,S).* From the end of FR 2932 (300 ft) the way continues up a former bottomland roadbed for 1.6 miles to the park boundary. About 1 mile from the park boundary it enters old-growth spruce and hemlock forest. At the mouth of the North Fork of the Bogachiel (770 ft) the canyon narrows;

the route leaves the main river to follow its north fork. A steady ascent continues through thick forest to the river headwaters; it steepens as it climbs to a saddle (3,600 ft) in the basin headwall. East of Little Divide (4,130 ft), the route slides to the south side of the ridge, descends past Bogachiel Lake (3,540 ft), climbs over a saddle (4,120 ft), then weaves east down to Deer Lake (3,520 ft) and the Deer Lake Trail. South from the lake the way passes a half-dozen tarns en route to the top of the divide (4,750 ft) between the Bogachiel and Soleduck Rivers. A spur drops north down steep open slopes to the parkland of Seven Lakes Basin and its namesake collection of lakes. The narrow meadowed crest is followed east to a col just below the summit of Bogachiel Peak, where it ends at the junction with the High Divide and Hoh Lake Trails (5,170 ft).

## Soleduck River Trails

**Soleduck River Trail.** *8.4 miles/m (H,S).* From the end of the Soleduck River Road (1,950 ft) the route heads up the north bank of the river on an easy grade through Douglas-fir forest. At Soleduck Falls it passes the Deer Lake Trail, then wanders upstream to the Appleton Pass Trail. In less than a mile the way swings into the Bridge Creek drainage; switchbacks climb steeply to the meadows of Soleduck Park, where the path wraps around tiny Heart Lake (4,760 ft). It joins the High Divide Trail (5,050 ft) a short distance uphill at the crest.

**Deer Lake Trail.** *3.1 miles/m (H,S).* At the start (1,950 ft) of the Soleduck River Trail, an old wooden bridge crosses the river through the spray-filled air of Soleduck Falls. The way zigzags uphill, twisting along the convoluted, lushly vegetated slope above Canyon Creek to Deer Lake (3,520 ft). Here it meets the Bogachiel Trail.

**High Divide Trail.** *6.2 miles/m (H,S).* The Bogachiel and Hoh Lake Trails join at a col (5,170 ft) just below the top of Bogachiel Peak. On the ridge to the east a spur leads to the summit (5,474 ft), an old lookout site with unbeatable views of the northwest corner of the Olympic Peninsula. The path follows the divide east; one side looks into the meadows of Seven Lakes Basin, the other over precipitous timbered slopes dropping to the Hoh River. As the way progresses eastward it meets the Soleduck River Trail above Soleduck Park, then gradually descends to the rim above Cat Creek Basin. The path slides off the rising ridge, contours the steep, rocky south face of Cat Peak, then abruptly ends at the cliffs of the Catwalk (5,045 ft). Funding ran out before the trail could be extended through the Bailey Range, then plans were dropped to preserve the wilderness character of the range.

## Lake Crescent Trails

**Aurora Ridge Trail.** *15.5 miles/m (H,S).* After leaving the Soleduck River Road in clearcuts (1,400 ft), the way climbs east into virgin Douglas-fir forest as it heads up Aurora Ridge. At Sourdough Mountain (4,560 ft) the path breaks into meadows with views of Mounts Tom and Olympus. Here it descends to a saddle, then traverses east to just below the top of Aurora Peak (4,720 ft). Ridge-top forest and meadow alternate as the crest is traced east to the junction with the Aurora Divide Trail (4,750 ft), which it follows southeast to the Happy Lake Ridge Trail.

## Elwha River Trails

**Happy Lake Ridge Trail.** *10 miles/m (H,S).* The way leaves the Olympic Hot Springs Road (1,700 ft) and climbs northwest up forested slopes to the ridge top (4,550 ft). The narrow divide is followed west to a saddle (5,290 ft) with views north to the straits and south to Mounts Olympus, Anderson, and Carrie. A spur drops northwest to Happy Lake (4,870 ft); the main trail continues west along the crest to meet the Aurora Divide Trail. Ridge-top meadows are traversed southwest, then the way drops to the basin rim above Boulder Lake (4,332 ft), where it joins the Boulder Lake Trail.

**Boulder Lake Trail.** *2.8 miles/m (H,S).* About 2.5 miles above Boulder Creek Campground at Olympic Hot Springs (1,950 ft), the trail forks; left is the Appleton Pass Trail, straight ahead is the Boulder Lake Trail. The way climbs through Douglas-fir forest on the hillside north of Boulder Creek to the rim north of the lake, meets the Happy Lake Ridge Trail, then descends to Boulder Lake (4,332 ft).

**Appleton Pass Trail.** *7.8 miles/m (H,S).* From the junction (2,340 ft) above Boulder Creek Campground, the route bends south past a series of falls on the south fork of the creek, then climbs via several switchbacks through forest and flower-splashed alpine meadows to Appleton Pass (5,000 ft). South of the pass more switchbacks drop steeply to the Soleduck River Trail (3,100 ft).

**Wolf Creek Trail.** *8 miles/m (H,S).* From the end of the Elwha Road at Whiskey Bend (1,150 ft) the trail follows an abandoned road to the top of Hurricane Ridge. From deep forest in the lower portions, the way makes easy-grade switchbacks up to meadows near the end of the current Hurricane Ridge Road (5,050 ft).

**Elwha River Trail.** *25.6 miles/m (H,S).* A long, hooked thrust into the heart of the Olympics leaves Whiskey Bend (1,150 ft) above Lake Mills, and ascends slowly east away from the river through forest regenerating from a 1977 fire. The Long Ridge Trail heads off to explore country to the south. The Elwha River Trail stays high above the Grand Canyon of the Elwha, wandering through dense old-growth forest, before descending to the river near Prescott Creek (1,300 ft). A level grade traces the riverbank south past Elkhorn Ranger Station and the Dodger Point Trail to Hayes River Ranger Station (1,700 ft), near the junction with the Hayden Pass Trail.

The broad bottomland and adjoining terraces are followed south, then east to the Low Divide Trail, as the river hooks back toward the Bailey Range. The canyon narrows and the way climbs to Elwha Basin (2,700 ft), where it deteriorates to a boot track up the drainage via the Elwha snow finger to Dodwell–Rixon Pass (4,780 ft).

**Long Ridge Trail.** *13.3 miles/m (H,S).* From the Elwha River Trail (1,125 ft) the route descends to the Elwha River, crosses a suspension bridge, then begins a long sidehill ascent through Douglas-fir forest. The path swings back and forth across Long Ridge in a series of easy-grade switchbacks, then shifts this switchback pattern to the west side of the ridge. The trail finally stays atop or just below the crest as it enters meadows and subalpine forest with wide views east across the valley to the Bailey Range and beyond to Olympus. The path finishes its ascent through meadows to meet the Dodger Point Trail (5,290 ft). The trail was to be extended across the Bailey Range, but those plans were abandoned.

**Dodger Point Trail.** *5.8 miles/m (H,S).* At Semple Plateau the route leaves the Elwha River Trail (1,451 ft), fords the river, crosses terraces, then bends west above the Goldie River. Switchbacks surmount steep slopes as the way climbs a broad wooded ridge, then makes a long diagonal uphill to the northwest. With altitude, Douglas-fir and hemlock forest changes to subalpine growth, and flower meadows appear. The way reaches the crest (5,050 ft) northeast of Ludden Peak, where it meets the Long Ridge Trail and briefly shares tread with it en route to Dodger Point (5,760 ft). The old look-out cabin perched atop the point has unsurpassed views: Mount Olympus, the Bailey Range, the Elwha Valley, Mount Anderson, and, in the distance, Mount Rainier.

**Hayden Pass Trail.** *8.4 miles/m (H,S).* From the Elwha River Trail at the Hayes River Ranger Station (1,710 ft) the way climbs to a small wooded terrace, then snakes through cliffs beside a plummeting creek. It begins a gradual diagonal ascent southeast, emerging into meadows at a rib west of Mount Fromme. Rounding the rib, the track contours around alpine meadows to Hayden Pass (5,847 ft), tucked between Mount Fromme and Sentinel Peak. Here it meets the Dosewallips Trail.

**Low Divide Trail.** *3.1 miles/m (H,S).* At the southernmost point of the hook of the Elwha River, the route leaves the Elwha River Trail (2,190 ft), wanders through dense forest, then abruptly switchbacks up through headwall cliff bands to Lakes Mary and Margaret (3,590 and 3,630 ft). It continues uphill to Low Divide (3,602 ft), where it joins the North Fork Quinault Trail.

## Port Angeles Trails

**Mount Angeles Trail.** *10 miles/m (H,S).* The route heads southwest from Heart of the Hills (1,957 ft) and immediately begins climbing through second-growth forest on the north side of Mount Angeles. Increasingly steeper slopes force multiple switchbacks to reach the meadows of Heather Park (5,620 ft) in a lovely basin between the mountain's first and second summits. The way crosses the crest south of Second Summit, zigzags below the cliffs of Third Summit, then traverses to a notch in Klahhane Ridge (5,850 ft), where it meets the Lake Angeles Trail. Switchbacks drop south to a contour of the south face of Mount Angeles, then the way descends gradually over the meadow knolls and dips of Sunrise Ridge to the Hurricane Ridge Visitor Center (5,250 ft).

**Lake Angeles Trail.** *6.5 miles/m (H,S).* From Heart of the Hills (1,790 ft) the way heads into forest alongside Ennis Creek, climbs 1,000 feet, crosses the creek, and heads up the steep ridge on its east flank. At the cliff-walled cirque embracing Lake Angeles (4,240 ft), switchbacks gain the narrow rim above the lake, and the way twists up open rocky slopes with increasing views of Port Angeles, the Strait of Juan de Fuca, and Victoria. A path crosses the top of Klahhane Ridge (6,046 ft), then traverses west on a cliff-blasted grade to join the Mount Angeles Trail (5,850 ft).

**Grand Pass Trail.** *8 miles/m (H,S).* At the end of the Obstruction Point Road (6,120 ft), the trail fork to the south continues along the open tundra crest with expansive views into the heart of the Olympics. At a notch (6,400 ft) between two sharp knobs, the way swings east above a steep-walled basin, then drops via a switchback chain to a small meadow in a hillside bench. It descends to the Grand Creek valley and heads upstream to Moose Lake (5,056 ft). The way continues uphill through meadows past Gladys Lake (5,399 ft), then scales the rocky basin headwall to Grand Pass (6,420 ft). South of the pass it noses downhill, and nearly three dozen switchbacks later arrives at the Cameron Creek Trail.

**Grand Ridge Trail.** *7.6 miles/m (H,S).* The east fork from the end of Obstruction Point Road (6,120 ft) stays above timberline for several miles, providing outstanding views of the eastern Olympics. The track follows the south rim of the ridge and gradually descends along the south flank of Maiden Peak. It wanders down the crest to the east, dropping into forest as it passes Green Mountain, then continues down the narrow wooded ridge to the road (5,233 ft) below Deer Park.

## CLIMBING

Climbs of most of the major summits in Olympic National Park can be summarized as steep snowfields or modest-size glaciers, and C-2 to C-3 rotten rock. Since the climbs are, for the most part, multiday affairs due to the remoteness of the region, most parties are content just to bag the summit of a significant peak and not worry about variations that exist on the walls and faces of many peaks. There are hundreds of one- to two-lead rotten towers on ridgelines, but these are typically regarded as a nuisance en route to a summit rather than a climbing objective. For gendarme and face enthusiasts who enjoy loose rock, there are still many unclaimed firsts in the Olympics.

Probably the best rock climbing in the Olympics is found in Sawtooth Ridge; since this range is on the border between the park and the Mount Skokomish Wilderness, the climbs are described in the latter section. Other major peaks (5,758 to 6,250 ft) in the southeast corner of the park are Mount Stone, Mount Steel, Mount Duckabush, and O'Neil Peak. All are C-3 except the west summit of Duckabush, rated C-4 via either an exposed ridge from the middle summit or the south ridge.

A challenging group of peaks is located on the east edge of the park surrounding Avalanche Canyon just above Lake Constance. Here are Mount Constance (7,743 ft), a peak that dominates the skyline as seen from Seattle, with routes ranging from C-3 to C-5.7; Desperation Peak (7,150 ft) and Inner Constance (7,667 ft), mixed snow and rock routes between C-3 and C-4; The Thumb (6,600 ft), C-2 to C-4; and several towers on the ridge south of Inner Constance.

Immediately north of Constance is Warrior Peak (7,300 ft), a striking rock double summit. All routes are rated C-3. At the head of the West Fork Dosewallips is Mount Anderson (7,321 ft), the most prominent peak (with the largest glaciers) in the eastern Olympics. Exposed rotten rock routes, C-3, lead to both east and west summits.

Surrounding Deception Basin are Mount Mystery (7,639 ft), Little Mystery (6,941 ft), and Mount Deception (7,788 ft), the highest peak in the eastern Olympics. All are scaled via C-2 to C-4 routes. Rimming Royal Basin, west of the Buckhorn Wilderness, are another group of challenging, albeit rotten, rock climbs in The Needles (7,000 to 7,650 ft), with routes rated between C-3 and C-5.5. Among this group are Arrowhead, The Incisor, Sweat Spire, Gasp Pinnacle, and Devils Fang. On the east side of the basin, the Royal Shaft (6,000 ft) has a 120-foot, C-5.3 route.

In the Hurricane Ridge area, the most popular and easiest ascent is Mount Angeles (6,454 ft), which affords wide views north to Port Angeles, the Strait of Juan de Fuca, and Vancouver Island. Several routes from both north and south are at most C-3 in difficulty. Because of its proximity to the Obstruction Point Road, Steeple Rock (5,567 ft) sees intensive climbing activity, and a plethora of routes ranging from C-3 to C-5.8 have been placed up its various faces, gullies, and crack systems.

The crown jewel of the Olympics, Mount Olympus (7,969 ft), was purportedly climbed by the O'Neil Expedition in 1890, but the first authenticated ascent occurred in 1907. The classic Blue Glacier–Snow Dome route is frequently used by climbing parties, although other routes climb the C-5.3 west ridge, and over lesser summits from the east. Mount Tom (7,076 ft), a subsidiary peak to the west, is most easily climbed from Olympus routes to avoid other lowland jungle approaches. A horseshoe of short rock pinnacles (6,246 to 7,365 ft) around the Hoh and Humes Glaciers bears

*Climbers negotiate crevasses on the Blue Glacier of Mount Olympus.*

names from the pantheon of Greek gods and legends: Athena, Hermes, Aphrodite, Aries, and Icarus. All are relatively easy C-3 climbs, though exposed and rotten.

The Valhallas are an obscure group of rugged pinnacles encircling the Grei-Freki Glacier southeast of Mount Tom. Nordic gods rule here; among the pinnacles (5,400 to 6,038 ft) are Mimir, Thor, Woden, Baldur, Villi, and Freyja. All of these peaks are short, sometimes challenging C-2 to C-4 rock climbs.

Striking through the heart of the inner Olympics is the Bailey Range. The highest summit in the range, Mount Carrie (6,995 ft), is little more than a narrow, exposed ridge walk to the top. More challenging peaks in the range (6,283 to 6,950 ft) are Mount Fairchild, Mount Michael, Ruth Peak, and Mount Pulitzer, all involving exposed C-3 rotten rock.

In the vicinity of Low Divide are a number of easy walk-up summits and two that are more difficult: Mount Queets (6,476 ft), with four routes, and Mount Christie (6,177 ft), with mixed glacier and rock climbs. In the upper Quinault Valley are Chimney Peak (6,917 ft), with steep, exposed snow slopes; a nearby tower, The Chimney, a 100-foot, C-5.3 lead; and Bicentennial Peak (6,722 ft).

Farther south, on either side of the Quinault Valley, are Mount Olson (5,289 ft), a C-3 scramble via the west ridge, and Muncaster Mountain (5,910 ft), snow and rock rated C-3 to 4. Along the park's south border, seldom climbed because of their remoteness, are the Five Ridge Peaks (5,077 ft), a series of short pinnacles on the ridge between Five and Six Streams.

## WINTER SPORTS

The interior of the Olympics is remote and fraught with avalanche hazards, so most winter recreational activities are found on the perimeter. The road to Hurricane Ridge is plowed in winter, and a small ski and tubing area operates at the visitor center atop the ridge. This is also a starting point for several cross-country tours. Excellent day trips with outstanding views are those to the top of Hurricane Hill, a 6-mile round trip; up the southwest ridge of Mount Angeles to the base of the summit block, 3 miles (the mountain is also climbed in winter); and following the Obstruction Point Road, to the north side of Eagle Point, 3.5 miles. The latter trip can be extended to Obstruction Point, 6 miles, generally as an overnight trek.

From the Elwha Road, cross-country tours follow unplowed roads and summer trails to Boulder Lake, 6 miles; Appleton Pass, 7 miles; and Happy Lake Ridge, extended to a loop via Boulder Lake. All trips are generally 2-day affairs.

On the west side of the park, a long 2- to 3-day tour for advanced skiers starts from the end of the Soleduck River Road and follows the Soleduck and Deer Lake Trails to the Bogachiel Trail atop the divide. After great open-bowl skiing in the Seven Lakes Basin, the trip climbs over the intervening ridge to Soleduck Park, and returns to the starting point via the Soleduck River Trail.

At the southeast corner of the park a very popular tour heads out of Staircase and climbs to an overnight camp at Flapjack Lakes. From here there are excellent open meadow slopes to ski near Gladys Divide.

# 4 Quinault Lake Region

## Colonel Bob Wilderness; Moonlight Dome and South Quinault Roadless Areas

**Location:** In Grays Harbor County at the southwest corner of Olympic National Park, immediately east of Quinault Lake

**Size:** Wilderness, 11,961 acres; Moonlight Dome, 5,931 acres; South Quinault Ridge, 9,852 acres

**Status:** Designated Wilderness (1984); Roadless areas are mostly Semiprimitive Nonmotorized

**Terrain:** Heavily forested ridges rise steeply to alpine meadows and a few rocky peaks along ridge crests at the heart of the wilderness and roadless areas.

**Elevation:** 400 to 4,509 feet

**Management:** USFS, Olympic National Forest, Pacific Ranger District

**Topographic maps:** Bunch Lake, Colonel Bob, Finley Creek, Lake Quinault East

On the south side of the Quinault River alluvial plain, foothills rise abruptly, gaining more than 4,000 feet of elevation in a horizontal distance of just over a mile. Two parallel ridges that run northeast to southwest join at the heart of the Colonel Bob Wilderness, then continue to the southwest as a single contorted crest, Quinault Ridge, that tapers downward to the southwest. Several steep creek beds bound by lateral ridges drop from the upper reaches of this small wilderness and roadless area to either the Quinault River or the Humptulips River, which border the north and south sides of the wilderness. Dense, lush rain forest cloaks the steep hillsides, making cross-country travel virtually impossible except in ridge-top alpine meadows.

*Wood sorrel (oxalis) fills shadowy forest nooks in the Colonel Bob Wilderness.*

A fire lookout once graced the small rock summit of Colonel Bob, the second-highest point of the wilderness. This location commands views spreading from northwest to south across miles of clearcuts, once virgin rain forest. Beyond, to the west, fog banks often define Pacific Ocean beaches. Cliff-bound Fletcher Canyon drops away steeply to the northeast, directing views to the jagged backbone of Olympic National Park.

As a result of the precipitous terrain, the few trails that penetrate the wilderness are strenuous. Access to streams is limited, and lakes, aside from a few minuscule tarns at the head of Fletcher Creek, are nonexistent; thus, camping is available at only a few primitive sites near sparse water supplies.

Southeast of the wilderness, the small Moonlight Dome Roadless Area has steep, heavily forested ridges rising to two bald, rocky summits, Moonlight Dome and Stovepipe Mountain.

## CLIMATE

This rain-forest country is drenched by over 120 inches of precipitation annually. Clear weather occurs most frequently from mid-June to October, but rain can be expected

*A bridge crosses a moist gully near Ziegler Creek on the Colonel Bob Trail.*

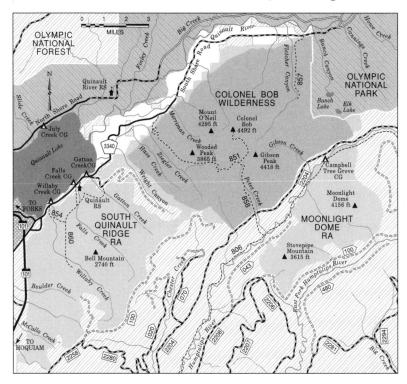

every month of the year. Winter temperatures are mild, seldom dipping below freezing at lower elevations, while summer weather rarely exceeds 70 degrees. Snow blankets elevations above 3,000 feet during winter months. Because the wilderness lies so near the Pacific, winds off the ocean bring heavy precipitation and weather patterns change abruptly with little notice. Visitors should be prepared for drizzle or downpour, even if the day starts clear and sunny.

## ECOSYSTEM

The ground cover in the lowest portions of the wilderness is a jumble of mosses, lichens, sword fern, and maidenhead fern, typical of rain forests. Creek beds are edged by dense borders of currant and salmonberry; vine maple and slide alder choke breaks in the adjoining forest. The low-level forest is a moss-encrusted profusion of western hemlock, Pacific silver fir, and western red cedar, with some Douglas-fir. Higher, silver fir and western hemlock predominant. Above 3,500 feet the forest thins to mountain hemlock and Alaska cedar, then gives way to grassy ridge-top meadows holding lush growths of huckleberry and salmonberry, as well as beargrass and brilliant displays of daisies, avalanche lilies, lupine, and other alpine flowers. Steep, open talus slopes that drop from the highest ridge crests and rock outcrops are painted with hardy lichen. Short spiky rock summits cap these ridges.

The dense forest is home to black-tailed deer, elk, and black bear, and occasionally mountain goat and cougar may be seen. Look overhead or to tree snags for bald and golden eagles. Spotted owls have been seen in both roadless areas.

## GEOLOGY

A crescent of uplifted, near-vertical strata of volcanic rock rims the north, east, and south sides of the Olympic Range. The Colonel Bob Wilderness lies at its southwest cusp, between two thrust faults. The steep narrow ridges were sculpted primarily by Pleistocene glaciers.

## HISTORY

The first settlers arrived in the Quinault Lake region in the late 1800s. About 1915, Mart and Purl Mulkey roughed a trail up Ziegler Creek and built a trapper's cabin near the headwaters of its north fork. Although no trace of this trail can be found, in 1922 the Forest Service followed a similar route when it laid out the trail to the newly constructed fire lookout atop Colonel Bob. The Civilian Conservation Corps (CCC) replaced the Mulkey cabin with a trail shelter about the same time. The lookout collapsed under heavy snows and was removed in 1967.

## HIKING

**Trail 851, Colonel Bob.** *7.3 miles/d (H; S up to the junction with Trail 858).* From the Quinault Lake South Shore Road (230 ft), the trail climbs steeply along the hillside northeast of Ziegler Creek to the Mulkey shelter at 4 miles. From here it switchbacks relentlessly to a 3,200-foot saddle on Quinault Ridge and traverses below cliffs to meet Trail 858. After crossing open, rocky slopes below Gibson Peak, it reaches Moonshine Flats at the head of Fletcher Creek. Switchbacks continue around the basin at the head of the creek and up the ridge to the final face of Colonel Bob, where steps carved in the rock lead to the summit (4,492 ft) and former lookout site.

**Trail 858, Petes Creek.** *2.4 miles/d (H,S).* The trailhead is located northeast of Humptulips on FR 2204 (1,195 ft). After a moderate 0.25 mile, the trail climbs a steep sidehill, crosses Petes Creek, and switchbacks up avalanche slopes below Gibson Peak to join Trail 851 (2,850 ft).

## CLIMBING

The eight or more rocky spikes that form the crown of the wilderness were once known collectively as McCallas Peak (3,865 to 4,492 ft). Four of these points are now named Wooded Peak, Mount O'Neil, Colonel Bob, and Gibson Peak. A trail leads to the top of Colonel Bob. The lookout formerly located there was not actually on the highest point in the wilderness; the true summit is on the ridge 1,200 feet to the east. All the other summits can be reached by cross-country routes no more strenuous than C-3. A spire on the ridge between Colonel Bob and Mount O'Neil, Mike's Spike (4,175 ft), requires one C-4 lead. Moonlight Dome (4,156 ft ) and Stovepipe Mountain (3,615 ft) are short C-3 rock scrambles reached via steep forest-clad ridges.

# 5 Dungeness River Region

## Buckhorn Wilderness; MacDonald, Quilcene, Mount Zion, and Green Mountain Roadless Areas

**Location:** In Jefferson and Clallam Counties, in two sections on the east side of Olympic National Park and north of the Dosewallips.

**Size:** Wilderness, 44,258 acres; MacDonald, 491 acres; Quilcene, 19,017 acres, Mount Zion, 5,384 acres; Green Mountain, 4,561 acres

**Status:** Designated Wilderness (1984); Roadless areas are Roaded Natural and Semiprimitive

**Terrain:** Creeks and rivers flowing from the eastern flank of the Olympic Range drain through glacier-carved canyons bounded by steep, forested ridges. Alpine meadows at timberline give way to narrow, jagged, rocky ridges that end in rugged summits. The Mount Zion and Green Mountain areas cover the top of a northwest/southeast crest on the eastern flank of the Olympic Mountains.

**Elevation:** 1,000 to 7,134 feet

**Management:** USFS, Olympic National Forest, Hood Canal Ranger District

**Topographic maps:** Mt. Deception, Mt. Jupiter, Mt. Townsend, Mount Zion, The Brothers, Tyler Peak

The Buckhorn Wilderness is in two sections: the northern portion covers the transition zone between the peaks on the northeast corner of Olympic National Park and the forested lowlands south of Sequim. The Gray Wolf River splits the north end of this section; its tributaries cut through heavily forested lateral ridges. From the south side of the river these steep ridges rise to a 6,000-foot-high rocky crest that arcs across the southern edge of this portion of the wilderness. High points along this ridge provide broad views north and northeast to the Strait of Juan de Fuca and Mount Baker, and west to the northern rim of Olympic peaks.

The southern section of the wilderness is larger and more rugged than the northern. From its headwaters, the Dungeness River threads along the west and north sides of the wilderness through a valley carved by Pleistocene glaciers. Steep forested hillsides on both sides of the river rise to rugged crests between 6,000 and 7,000 feet. Two large tributaries, Copper and Silver Creeks, flow north to the Dungeness, cutting deep canyons into adjoining ridges. Their names reflect early prospectors' ambitious hopes for the region. A 216-acre plot of patented mining property, the Tubal Cain Mine, still exists on Copper Creek within the wilderness. The eastern face of the wilderness is gouged by glacier-cut valleys, down which flow Tunnel Creek and the Big Quilcene and Dosewallips Rivers. The latter drainage forms the southern boundary of the wilderness.

More than 67 miles of trails penetrate the wilderness. Most reach the higher elevations along paths of least resistance—the valley floors. Other way-trails provide climbing, fishing, and exploring routes to more rugged sections of the wilderness. The region's dozen lakes are all quite small, and most are hidden in cirques high in the headwaters of creeks and rivers.

A fringe of roadless areas (the McDonald and Quilcene RAs) adjoin the east side of the Buckhorn Wilderness; these forests should have been included within the wilderness boundaries, but the region's insatiable appetite for harvestable timber overrode this choice. A lower range of hills a couple of miles east is topped by two long, narrow, stand-alone roadless areas, Mount Zion and Green Mountain, whose flanks have been sheared of timber.

## CLIMATE

Because this portion of the Olympic Peninsula lies in the rain shadow of the Olympic Range, it is much drier than the western slopes. Annual precipitation, which usually accompanies winds from the south and southwest, ranges between 40 and 60 inches. Temperatures are mild at lower elevations, rarely going below freezing or above 80 degrees. Heavy snowfall occurs at elevations above 3,000 feet, generally between November and March.

## ECOSYSTEM

Lower elevations host dense forests of western hemlock, Pacific silver fir, western red cedar, and Douglas-fir. Above 3,000 feet these trees give way to mountain hemlock, subalpine fir, and western white pine, while the highest elevations see open stands of stunted subalpine fir, whitebark pine, and dwarfed juniper. In the northern portion of the wilderness a large area of virgin forest was destroyed in the early 1900s by a major forest fire, the Maynard Burn.

The understory below 3,000 feet consists of a rich tangle of mosses, ferns, salmonberry, huckleberry, Oregon grape, devil's club, and a profusion of native rhododendrons. Higher, the vegetation thins to mountain ash and mountain spirea accompanied by bunchberry, western columbine, pearly everlasting, and the cream-white wands of beargrass. Alpine meadows are covered with grasses, heathers, and bright seasonal flowers such as avalanche lily, phlox, and penstemon, while rock outcroppings shelter the white blossoms of saxifrage.

Large mammals include black-tailed deer, occasional black bear, cougar, and bobcat in forested areas, and a few mountain goats at higher elevations. In addition to a wealth of smaller birds, raptors such as northern spotted owls, bald eagles, and goshawks may be seen. Hikers in alpine meadows may be greeted by the shrill whistle of Olympic marmots.

## GEOLOGY

The lower elevations at the north end of the Buckhorn Wilderness were part of the lateral moraine of the Vashon Ice Sheet that carved out Puget Sound and the Strait of Juan de Fuca some 14,000 years ago. The remainder of the wilderness consists mainly of older (40 million to 50 million years) upthrust submarine volcanic flows that form

*Native pink rhododendrons decorate the Tubal Cain Mine trail in the Buckhorn Wilderness.*

a crescent around the north, west, and south rims of the Olympic Peninsula. This pillow basalt has limestone lenses containing a form of manganese ore that is unique to the peninsula. During the past 10,000 years, montane glaciers carved the deep, steep-sided valleys that frame most of the drainages and sculpted the spires, towers, and narrow, ragged ridgelines.

## HISTORY

The Olympic National Forest, of which the Buckhorn Wilderness is now a part, was created in 1897 when President Grover Cleveland designated 1.5 million acres as the Olympic Forest Reserve. In 1902 visions of mineral wealth led prospectors to the Tubal Cain Mine, where the mining camp of Tull City (a cookhouse, two bunkhouses, and a blacksmith shop) sprang up. Manganese and copper ores were gouged from nearby hillsides, but fortune eluded the prospectors, and by 1920 active mining had ceased. Rotting fragments of cabins and campsites in the depths of the wilderness bear mute witness to later visits by prospectors, trappers, and hunters.

## HIKING
### North Section Trails

**Trail 834, Gray Wolf.** *7.7 miles/m (H,S).* From its start on FR 2870 (970 ft), the trail meanders through a mix of virgin forest and clearcuts for 2 miles before reaching the Buckhorn Wilderness boundary. Canyon walls close in as the route continues up the steep sides of the Gray Wolf River gorge to Camp Tony (1,600 ft) to meet Trail 838. The trail leaves the river in a long diagonal ascent to Slide Camp (2,150 ft). From here it descends 2 miles through dense forest to the Olympic National Park boundary, then continues into the heart of the park.

**Trail 838, Slab Camp.** *3.1 miles/d (H,S).* It's downhill all the way from the starting point (2,540 ft) on FR 2875 to the junction with Trail 834 at Camp Tony (1,600 ft). Trailhead views of Baldy quickly disappear as the path descends the forested hillside above Slab Creek in a series of gentle steps linked by short, steep segments.

## Dungeness River Trails

**Trail 833, Dungeness.** *8.1 miles/m (H,S).* From the FR 2860 trailhead (2,520 ft), a near-level grade follows the Dungeness River upstream for 3.2 miles to Camp Handy (3,100 ft). Here a diagonal ascent features intermittent views of the precipitous west face of Mount Constance. At Boulder Shelter (4,950 ft) the Constance Pass Trail continues south into the park. From Boulder Shelter the Dungeness Trail switchbacks up alpine slopes to Marmot Pass (6,000 ft), where it keeps the same number but becomes the Big Quilcene Trail.

**Trail 840, Tubal Cain.** *8.6 miles/m (H,S).* From the north bank of Silver Creek (3,300 ft), this trail rounds an intervening ridge and begins a gentle ascent along Copper Creek, reaching the ruins of the Tubal Cain Mine in 3.6 miles (4,350 ft). Little is left of the mining operations; nearby mine shafts are unsafe for exploration. After crossing the creek, the trail heads upstream, climbing diagonally up open slopes with views to the imposing north faces of Iron and Buckhorn Mountains. An unmarked spur 1.9 miles south of the Copper Creek crossing drops to tiny Buckhorn Lake. South from Buckhorn Pass (5,820 ft), an ascent along the west shoulder of Buckhorn Mountain, followed by a short drop to Marmot Pass (6,000 ft), leads to Trail 833.

## Eastside Trails

**Trail 839, Mount Townsend.** *6.7 miles/m (H,S).* From FR 2760 (2,850 ft) rhododendrons crowd the trail as it climbs along Townsend Creek. At the head of the creek, switchbacks lead up a wall to a small lake and Camp Windy (5,300 ft). A stiff climb through alpine meadows gains the ridge top. Rather than a definitive peak, Mount Townsend (6,280 ft) is a mile-long alpine meadow atop a narrow ridge. Wide, unobstructed views encompass Discovery Bay, the Strait of Juan de Fuca, the Cascades, Mount Constance, The Brothers, and a wall of Olympic National Park peaks. From the summit ridge, the trail descends north into forest to end near the midpoint of Trail 835; it can be hiked either east or west to access roads.

**Trail 833, Big Quilcene.** *5.3 miles/m (H,S).* From FR 2750 at Tenmile Shelter (2,500 ft) the trail climbs through old-growth cedar, fir, and hemlock, and masses of rhododendrons as it follows the north side of the Big Quilcene River. In 2.5 miles the trail leaves the river on a steep traverse across scree and avalanche slopes below Buckhorn and Iron Mountains. The way levels at Camp Mystery (5,400 ft), then continues to the head of the basin and switchbacks up a basalt cliff to Marmot Pass (6,000 ft).

***Trail 841, Tunnel Creek.*** *7.9 miles/d (H,S; pack stock not recommended).* From the north access at FR 2740 (2,600 ft) the track heads up the steep-walled, narrow valley of the South Fork of Tunnel Creek. The lower section is in old-growth hemlock and silver fir. In 2.7 miles the work begins; switchbacks lead up the valley wall to a small, wooded cirque that harbors tiny Harrison Lake (4,750 ft). A rocky path leaves the lake and climbs south to the Tunnel Creek–Dosewallips River divide (5,050 ft). En route, the vertical east walls of Mount Constance and Warrior Peak flash into view, seeming

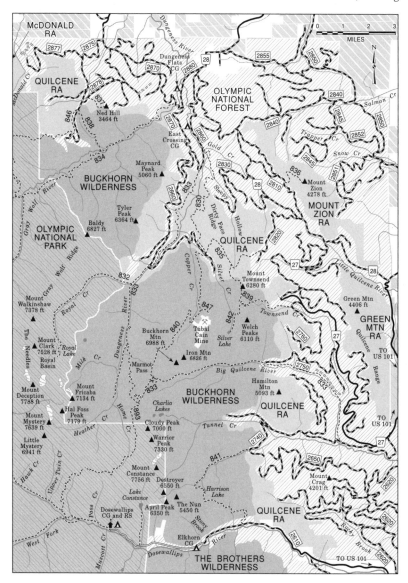

only an arm's length away. The descent to the Dosewallips begins in gentle alpine meadows, then follows endless switchbacks through old- and second-growth forest to reach FR 2610 (500 ft).

## Roadless Area Trails

**Trail 835, Little Quilcene.** *4.2 miles/m (H,S,B).* From FR 2820 (4,000 ft), in the headwaters of the Little Quilcene River, the route winds up to the notch of Little River Summit, then contours the head of Sleepy Hollow to intersect Trail 839 from Mount Townsend. The path then follows the crest of Dirty Face Ridge north for a mile before descending to the Silver Creek drainage and FR 2860 (3,350 ft). Rhododendrons and other wildflowers abound en route in spring.

**Trail 836, Mount Zion.** *1.8 miles/m (H,S,B,M).* Starting from FR 2810 (2,950 ft) the route climbs through second-growth fir and cedar to a camp and picnic site atop Mount Zion (4,278 ft) with expansive views of Mount Baker, the Cascades, and Puget Sound.

## CLIMBING

The northern section of the wilderness has no significant climbing challenges. Its highest summits, Baldy (6,827 ft) and Tyler Peak (6,364 ft) are alpine scrambles. In the southern portion of the wilderness there are numerous climbing opportunities in the small north–south subrange on the east side of the Dungeness River and on lateral ridges flowing east from that ridge. Most of the highest summits have routes no more difficult than C-3; their steeper faces are unappealing, loose, friable rock. The peripheral ridgelines are narrow, sheer, and serrated by 200- to 300-foot-high towers that offer several leads of C-4 to C-5 climbing.

At the northeast end of this subrange, Iron Mountain (6,826 ft) and Buckhorn Mountain (6,988 ft) are multi-summited rock arêtes with steep faces. Both can be climbed via talus gullies from the south. Iron Mountain and the northeast summit of Buckhorn are the most challenging. Mount Fricaba (7,134) and Hal Foss Peak (7,179) are alpine scrambles.

South of Marmot Pass are a series of sharp ridges running northeast from

*Stars streak the sky at high camp in the Buckhorn Wilderness; the lights of metropolitan Seattle glow in the distance.*

the Mount Constance–Warrior Peak massif. The second narrow rib to the south, Ridge of Gargoyles (6,400 ft), has a number of precipitous rock towers that range from C-3 to C-5.3 in difficulty.

Alphabet Ridge (7,000 ft), which extends from the park into the wilderness northwest of Cloudy Peak, is a chain of C-3 to C-4 rock spires that can be reached from Charlia Lakes. A similar ridge northwest of Warrior Peak, Warrior Arm (6,900 ft), has a number of towers in the C-4 to C-5 range, as well as a few easier spires on the northeast end of the arm.

The basin at the head of the South Fork of Tunnel Creek has at least four challenging rock spires around its periphery: Destroyer, Enigma, April Peak, and The Nun. All offer steep, exposed slab climbing.

## WINTER SPORTS

Most of the upland country of the wilderness is sealed off in winter by steep, snow-laden, avalanche-prone slopes. The gentler terrain to the northeast, in the vicinity of Mount Townsend, offers opportunities for ski mountaineering or snowshoeing. Snow-covered forest roads permit ski access to the lower slopes; advanced ski-tourers can follow lightly timbered slopes along the approximate route of the summer trail to the mountain's long summit ridge.

# 6  Duckabush River Region

### The Brothers Wilderness; Jupiter Ridge Roadless Area

**Location:** In Jefferson County, on the east side of Olympic National Park between the Dosewallips and Hamma Hamma Rivers
**Size:** Wilderness, 16,682 acres; Jupiter Ridge, 8,308 acres
**Status:** Designated Wilderness (1984); Roadless area is mostly Semiprimitive Nonmotorized
**Terrain:** A maze of steep forested ridges bordering the Duckabush River drainage rise to two major rocky summits surrounded by a tangle of narrow, rock-topped lateral ridges.
**Elevation:** 600 to 6,866 feet
**Management:** USFS, Olympic National Forest, Hood Canal Ranger District
**Topographic maps:** Mt. Jupiter, Mt. Washington, The Brothers

The Duckabush River drains east from Olympic National Park through a deep, glacier-cut valley that slices through the center of The Brothers Wilderness. The backcountry centers around its two major summits: Mount Jupiter, north of the Duckabush, and The Brothers, south of the river.

Only three trails lead into the wilderness; one is an access route for climbs of The

Brothers. The area's few lakes, with the exception of a sprinkling of small tarns north of The Brothers, are clustered around Mount Jupiter. None is accessible directly by trail; they are at best challenging cross-country scrambles from the Mount Jupiter Trail.

## CLIMATE

The wilderness and adjacent roadless area lie on the dry side of the Olympics in the rain shadow of the range. As a result, precipitation averages only 60 to 80 inches per year, and rain generally accompanies weather fronts moving in from the south or southwest. Temperatures are mild year-round, rarely getting above the 70s in the summer or below freezing in the winter at lower elevations. Snow is heavy in higher elevations during winter months, but most of it has cleared from the area by late July.

## ECOSYSTEM

Heavy forests of western hemlock, western red cedar, and Douglas-fir cover lower elevations, with a thick understory of bracken fern, salal, and Oregon grape. Rhododendron, salmonberry, huckleberry, vine maple, alder, and devil's club crowd the forest floor. At mid-altitudes the timber is mostly Pacific silver fir and mountain hemlock; ground cover includes clumps of rhododendron, mountain ash, beargrass, and spirea, while trilliums, fawn lilies, and other delicate flowers provide springtime accents. Higher, phlox and

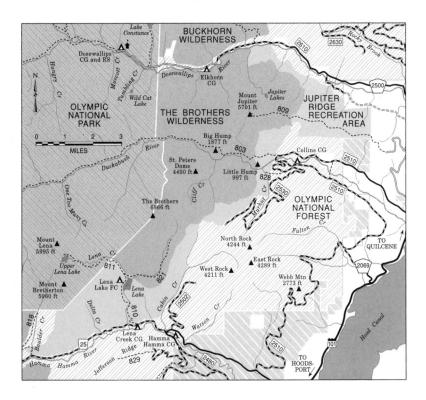

*The view from the summit of Mount Ellinor into the Mount Skokomish Wilderness: Mount Pershing in the foreground, Mount Stone in the far distance.*

buttercups snuggle into heathers and mosses amid subalpine fir. At ridge top, most vegetation gives way to rock.

Black-tailed deer are the most common mammal in this wilderness, but the area also hosts elk, black bear, and mountain goat. Occasionally marmots, pine marten, cougars, and golden and bald eagles are seen, as well as smaller birds and animals.

## GEOLOGY

The Brothers Wilderness lies in the crescent of upthrusted submarine pillow basalt that rims the north, west, and south sides of the Olympic Peninsula. Pleistocene montane glaciers carved the major features of the area, including the immense canyon of the Duckabush drainage. Two of its major features, Little Hump and Big Hump, are steps cut from the underlying rock by the glacier that carved the valley. Big Hump appears to have dammed the melting glacier, forming a lake above it until the river finally breached the barrier.

## HISTORY

Narrow-gauge railroads were used in the 1920s for logging the forest below Little Hump and the valley between Little Hump and Big Hump. Big Hump proved too formidable an obstacle for the trains, so the valley above was relatively untouched by ax and saw. A fire lookout once stood on the rocky summit pyramid of Mount Jupiter, and its sweeping views caused it to be used as an aircraft warning site during World War II. The lookout was removed in 1969.

## HIKING

**Trail 809, Jupiter Ridge.** *7.2 miles/d (H,S).* The trail leaves FR 2610-011 (2,000 ft), climbs steeply to the ridge top (3,200 ft), and becomes a long slog along the ridge. It switchbacks up a rise and shifts to the south side of the crest, with the north wall of The Brothers in view. More switchbacks regain the rough basalt of the ridge top, which is followed to the final zigzags up rock-hewn steps to the summit of Mount Jupiter. The climb becomes worthwhile, as nothing obstructs the sweeping scenery. Nearby, although a difficult climb away, is the summit of The Brothers; to the south, distant Mounts Rainier, Adams, and St. Helens punctuate the horizon; the Cascades, Puget Sound, and the Seattle skyline lie to the east; Mount Baker and the Coastal Range of British Columbia are north; and to the west is the jagged eastern face of the Olympics.

**Trail 803, Duckabush.** *6.7 miles/m (H,S).* From FR 2510-060 (370 ft), the trail climbs leisurely up the wide river basin and over Little Hump to the flat track leading to the base of Big Hump. Switchbacks negotiate the 800-foot rise to the top (1,800 ft), where the bald rock of St. Peters Dome comes into view across the river. Canyon walls now close in, and the trail drops close to the river for the remaining ascent to the park boundary.

**Trail 821, The Brothers.** *4.5 miles/d (H).* Take FR 25 to the Lena Lake trailhead (Trail 810, 780 ft). Hike the trail 3.5 miles to the lake and the start of The Brothers Trail (1,800 ft). The path follows the East Fork of Lena Creek through the Valley of the Silent Men, where climbers purportedly pass silently in the early morning hours when headed out to climb The Brothers. The maintained trail ends at a creek fork in 3 miles; beyond is a climbing route.

## CLIMBING

The double-summited peak of The Brothers (6,866 ft), a distinct landmark on the horizon west of Seattle, is one of the most popular climbs in the Olympics. The traditional routes follow Trail 821 to the alpine meadows below the peak's south face. From here a variety of steep C-3 to C-4 chutes and gullies rise to the exposed ridge leading to the south summit. The north summit can be reached by a ridge traverse from the south summit or via climbs up the east ridge of the peak.

# 7 Hamma Hamma River Region

## Mount Skokomish Wilderness; Jefferson Ridge Roadless Area

**Location:** In Mason County, at the southeast corner of Olympic National Park, immediately north of the upper end of Lake Cushman
**Size:** Wilderness, 13,105 acres; Jefferson Ridge, 9,369 acres
**Status:** Designated Wilderness (1984); Roadless area is Semiprimitive Non-motorized and Roaded Natural
**Terrain:** The headwater basin of the Hamma Hamma River is bounded by two long ridges with several massive summits that radiate narrow, exposed rock arêtes crowned with sharp spires.
**Elevation:** 2,000 to 6,434 feet
**Management:** USFS, Olympic National Forest, Hood Canal Ranger District
**Topographic maps:** Lightning Peak, Mt. Skokomish, Mt. Washington

The Mount Skokomish Wilderness is the southernmost of three wilderness areas created in 1984 to protect the remaining virgin forest on the east flank of Olympic National Park. The two parallel subranges of the wilderness, which run southwest to northeast, embrace the headwaters of the Hamma Hamma River. On the east, the chain of rock crests includes Mounts Ellinor, Washington, and Pershing, and Jefferson Peak. Narrow ridges that connect these summits are studded with smaller rock spires, and broader spur ridges lead off to the northeast. Access to the range is limited to a few trails leading up to timberline, where climbing routes continue onward to the summits. For hikers, the ends of formal trails deliver unimpeded views east to Hood Canal, Puget Sound, and the Cascades.

*At the edge of the Mount Skokomish Wilderness, a stream near Lake of the Angels holds a small cascade.*

The only route into the headwater basin of the Hamma Hamma, the Mildred Lakes Trail, was created by boot tread, not shovels, axes, and pulaskis, and as a result it is steep and difficult. Any other access to this area requires cross-country brush beating. Sawtooth Ridge, bounding the west side of this basin, is a mecca for climbers; its chain of sharp peaks, towers, and needles

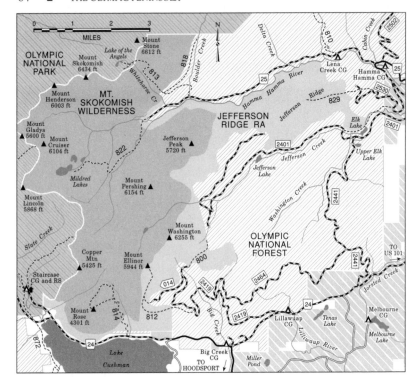

offers some of the best rock climbing on the Olympic Peninsula. After being broken by a fork of the Hamma Hamma River, a continuation of this ridge to the north culminates in Mount Skokomish, the namesake of the wilderness.

The Mount Skokomish Wilderness holds seven lakes, ranging from 1 to 38 acres in size, as well as a sprinkling of smaller ponds. Although technically in Olympic National Park, primary access to Lake of the Angels leads through the wilderness. Another beatific name has been applied to a nearby col: St. Peters Gate. Who knows—this may really be heaven on earth!

## CLIMATE

Because the wilderness lies in the rain shadow of the Olympic Range, precipitation is moderate, averaging 60 to 80 inches annually. Most of this accompanies weather systems from the south and southwest. Temperatures are mild, rarely exceeding 80 degrees in summer. Elevations above 3,000 feet receive snow between November and March, but by midsummer only the higher peaks retain snowfields.

## ECOSYSTEM

Lower slopes of the Mount Skokomish Wilderness are heavily forested with old-growth western hemlock, western red cedar, and Douglas-fir. Ground cover is predominantly

*The summit of Mount Ellinor offers views of the Olympic Mountains.*

ferns, salal, and kinnikinnick, with slide alder, willow, and vine maple choking stream-beds. At higher elevations the forest changes to hemlock, Alaska cedar, and Pacific silver fir, and then gives way to subalpine fir, western white pine, and dwarf juniper. Open hillsides sport thimbleberry and huckleberry, and in season, small meadows high on the ridges burst into color with Indian paintbrush, buttercups, bluebells, anemones, and asters. Ridge crests are barren rock, adorned only by lichen and tiny flowers that can survive in this harsh terrain, such as tolmie saxifrage and spreading stonecrop.

The forests are home for elk, black-tailed deer, bear, cougar, and Olympic mar-mot. Isolated groups of mountain goats might be seen glued to crags along the rocky ridgelines. Ravens frequently announce the approach of hikers, while bald and golden eagles circle overhead.

## GEOLOGY

The Mounts Pershing–Washington–Ellinor massif, the subrange that borders the east side of the wilderness, is uplifted pillow basalt, a portion of the crescent of such rock around the north, east, and south sides of the Olympic Peninsula. On the west side of the wilderness, the Sawtooth Range is composed of an erosion-exposed volcanic green-stone layer of the Soleduck Formation that makes up the core of the Olympic Moun-tains. Pleistocene glaciers gouged out the Hamma Hamma River drainage, and shaped and sharpened the surrounding ridges and peaks.

## HIKING
### Hamma Hamma Trails

**Trail 813, Putvin.** *3.7 miles/d (H).* This gentle path leads from FR 25 (1,530 ft) up Boulder Creek, then along an abandoned logging road to the Mount Skokomish Wilderness boundary in 1.5 miles. The route steepens to a diagonal climb through second-growth forest along Whitehorse Creek. At 3,600 feet the way levels a bit, and subalpine forest opens to glimpses of the rugged north face of Mount Pershing. The respite is short, as switchbacks scale a pair of rock walls to reach the Olympic Na-tional Park boundary and a beautiful flowered meadow that surrounds a few small ponds. A short descent reaches Lake of the Angels (4,880 ft), tucked in a glacial cirque below the walls of Mounts Stone and Skokomish. A scramble to a saddle on the ridge between these peaks is rewarded with views west to Mounts Duckabush and Steel and distant Mount Olympus; to the east are Hood Canal, Puget Sound, the Cascades, and Mount Rainier.

**Trail 822, Mildred Lakes.** *4.5 miles/d (H).* After a gentle start from FR 25 (1,800 ft), the trail quickly degenerates to a hard-to-trace boot-path that clambers over tree roots and around boulders, crosses a forested rib, and then descends to Huckleberry Creek. The route worsens as it crosses a ravine and heads straight uphill in a staircase of jumbled rock. At the ridge top the grade eases, then descends past a series of pools to the first of the Mildred Lakes (3,754 ft). Above, Sawtooth Ridge comes into view, stretching from Mount Lincoln on the south to Mount Cruiser on the north. Paths continue through open forest and meadows, past more ponds, to the remaining two Mildred Lakes. The westernmost is one of the largest subalpine lakes in the Olympics. Campfires are prohibited above 3,500 feet in Olympic National Forest.

## Lake Cushman Trails

**Trail 812, Mount Ellinor.** *2.5 miles/m (H).* Start at either of two trailheads, FR 2419 (2,666 ft) or FR 2419-014 (3,600 ft), then follow the route up through forest for a mile. Beyond this the unmaintained path climbs a very steep avalanche chute to a small subalpine basin, and from there continues as a moderate rock scramble west to the summit (5,944 ft).

**Trail 814, Mount Rose.** *4.8 miles/d (H).* Leaving FR 24 (750 ft) on an old roadbed, the route begins a relentless switchbacked climb north up wooded and once-cut slopes to finally reach a stream-head basin at 3,600 feet. From here a contour and ridgetop grade reach the summit of Mount Rose (4,301 ft). Lake Cushman is a zillion miles directly below. A return loop directly east drops steeply down to rejoin the uphill route.

## CLIMBING

The long, massive ridge between Jefferson Creek and the Hamma Hamma River holds several interesting climbs, although approaches are quite brushy and the volcanic rock that pervades the area is often rotten. At the north end of the crest a steep, narrow ridge leads south to Tran Spire (4,943 ft), a 250-foot-high tower conquered in a couple of C-5.3 leads. Lesser spires along the ridge are also tempting. Jefferson (Thorson) Peak (5,720 ft) is a small cluster of rock summits 0.5 mile to the south; C-3 routes end in gullies up its north and east sides.

Another mile southwest is tri-summited Mount Pershing (5,600, 5,871, and 6,154 ft); a number of unnamed spires sprout from the ridges leading to Pershing's summits. The Jefferson Creek and Lake Ellinor basins separate Pershing from the next summit to the southwest, Mount Washington (6,255 ft). This popular peak has a dozen routes on either snow or solid rock. Mount Ellinor (5,944 ft) has a trail and scramble route up the south side, and a more challenging approach from the north via Lake Ellinor.

The north end of the wilderness is anchored by the massive triple summit of Mount

Skokomish (6,434 ft), a relatively easy climb over rotten rock from Lake of the Angels.

The border between the west side of the Mount Skokomish Wilderness and Olympic National Park runs along the top of Sawtooth Ridge, renowned for its excellent rock climbing. This chain of pinnacles is composed of solid volcanic rock with few cracks for direct aid on vertical pitches. Most climbers approach the area from the west via the park's Flapjack Lakes Trail, rather than fight the heavy brush above Mildred Lakes. All of the pinnacles are near-vertical on their west faces, so most climbs attack less demanding eastside routes. The south end of the ridge is anchored by Mount Lincoln (5,868 ft), a relatively easy climb with steep, exposed rock. The lower North Peak of Mount Lincoln (5,690 ft) has a C-5.5 route up the south arête.

Along the ridge to the north are a series of gendarmes (5,600 to 5,700 ft), all with moderate single-lead routes. Two imposing towers, The Fin and The Horn (5,500 ft), have short exposed leads to the top on the south and east sides, and C-5.2 to C-5.5 routes up their near-vertical west faces. Castle Spires and The Needle (5,800 ft) have similar easy exposed routes on the southeast side and C-5 routes on the steeper north and west faces. The north end of the ridge, wholly within the Mount Skokomish Wilderness, is capped by Mount Cruiser (6,104 ft). The easiest route on the summit tower block is an exposed C-5, and other routes run up to 5.7. Several lower spires, all with short rock ascents, complete the north end of the ridgeline.

## 8 Skokomish River Region

### Wonder Mountain Wilderness; Upper Skokomish and Lightning Peak Roadless Areas

**Location:** In Mason County, on the southeast side of Olympic National Park, northeast of the South Fork of the Skokomish River
**Size:** Wilderness, 2,349 acres; Upper Skokomish, 6,182 acres; Lightning Peak, 7,174 acres
**Status:** Designated Wilderness (1984); Roadless areas are Primitive, Semiprimitive Nonmotorized, and Roaded Natural
**Terrain:** Rugged, heavily forested slopes rise to massive rock outcrops topped by steep pinnacles.
**Elevation:** 1,741 to 4,758 feet
**Management:** USFS, Olympic National Forest, Hood Canal Ranger District
**Topographic maps:** Lightning Peak, Mount Olson, Mount Tebo

Wonder Mountain Wilderness, a small triangle of land appended to the southeast side of Olympic National Park, is one of the smallest wilderness areas in the western United States; however, more extensive roadless areas on its southern perimeter still protect the wilderness. Wonder Mountain lies in the headwaters of east-flowing McKay Creek

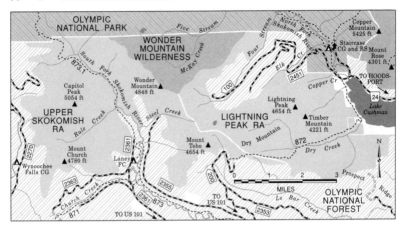

and Five Stream. The high ridge that wraps around the south end of the wilderness is capped near its southernmost point by the precipitous rock summit of Wonder Mountain (4,848 ft). Four small, unnamed lakes are hidden in cirques at the head of the two creeks that drain the wilderness. Two more lakes and a half-dozen tiny ponds lie to the north, across the national park border, at the head of forks of Five Stream. The ultimate in routefinding, primitive camping, and solitude is virtually guaranteed by the remoteness and extreme difficulty of access to the wilderness. Campfires are prohibited at the lakes and above 3,500 feet.

## CLIMATE

Annual precipitation ranges between 40 and 60 inches, as the wilderness is on the southern fringe of the Olympic Range rain shadow. A substantial portion of this occurs as snow. Temperatures are mild, rarely exceeding the 70s in summer.

## ECOSYSTEM

Lower elevations in the area are densely forested with western hemlock, Pacific silver fir, and Douglas-fir. Creek drainages are a tangle of slide alder, willow, and vine maple. Avalanche slopes off the north sides of the bordering ridge crests are covered in summer with thimbleberry, huckleberry, and vine maple. The wilderness is so seldom visited that there has been no attempt to catalog its native wildlife, although deer and elk are often seen, and spotted owls have been identified in the Upper Skokomish Roadless Area.

## GEOLOGY

The wilderness lies within the crescent of pre-Miocene uplifted volcanic rock that surrounds the north, east, and south sides of the heart of the Olympic Peninsula.

## HISTORY

In the late 1890s several prospectors staked claims in the area of the North Fork of the Skokomish River, east of the present wilderness, and made some unproductive attempts

*A climber surveys the Wonder Mountain Wilderness from a rocky point along its eastern boundary.*

at mining. It is thought that a few of these hardy souls searched for copper and manganese ore in the Wonder Mountain area, but no active mining took place.

## HIKING

The Wonder Mountain Wilderness has no hiking trails either in it or accessing it. All approaches are cross-country via steep, difficult, forested hillsides and ridges. The two forest roads that come closest to the wilderness lie on its southeast and southwest sides. Both roads are closed in fall and winter months to protect wildlife.

For the southeast approach, climb northwest from FR 2451-100 (2,360 to 2,900 ft) up forested sidehills to small saddles that breach the 4,200- to 4,000-foot-high ridge crest. The north side of the ridge is very steep; beyond here, cross-country routes depend on the destination.

The southwest approach from the end of FR 2355 (3,020 ft) follows the ridge east up steep wooded slopes to a flat (3,700 ft), then heads northeast toward the pinnacles on the end of the west ridge of Wonder Mountain. The ridge can be traversed west, then north, to lakes on the east side of the ridge. The ridges are all narrow, steep, and exposed.

## Roadless Area Trails

**Trail 872, Dry Creek.** *6.6 miles/m (H,S,B).* A side road from FR 24 at the north end of Lake Cushman (FR 2451) leads through summer homes to the trailhead (1,000 ft).

69

The path wanders south along the shoreline for about a mile, then turns west up Dry Creek, passing a short spur to an undeveloped state park. Following an abandoned logging road, the way continues west to the head of Dry Creek, then switchbacks up the steep basin wall, crosses a notch, and descends to meet FR 2353-200 (3,150 ft).

*Trail 873.1, Upper South Fork Skokomish.* *4.9 miles/m (H,S,B).* From the end of FR 2361 (1,300 ft) the trail wanders north through old-growth forest up the west side of the South Fork of the Skokomish River. It crosses and recrosses the river, then begins its climb to the park boundary, and beyond to Sundown Pass (4,103 ft) and a junction with the Wynoochee Lake Trail.

## CLIMBING

Climbing routes on Wonder Mountain (4,848 ft) all follow the southwest approach previously described in the Hiking section. The west ridge of the peak has several intermediate spires that must be either skirted or climbed before reaching the highest point on the east end of the summit ridge. The route is rated C-3.

# 9 San Juan Islands Wilderness

**Location:** In San Juan, Whatcom, Skagit, and Island Counties, in and around the periphery of the San Juan Island archipelago

**Size:** 355 acres

**Status:** Designated Wilderness (1976)

**Terrain:** The wilderness consists of 81 rocks, reefs, and islands ranging from 0.02 to 140 acres in size.

**Elevation:** 0 to 174 feet

**Management:** U.S. Fish and Wildlife Service

**Topographic maps:** Anacortes North, Blakely Island, Deception Pass, Eastsound, Eliza Island, False Bay, Friday Harbor, Lopez Pass, Lummi Island, Mt. Constitution, Richardson, Roche Harbor, Shaw Island, Stuart Island, Sucia Island, Waldron Island

The San Juan Islands Wilderness includes a major part of the San Juan Islands National Wildlife Refuge. The refuge was established to protect nesting seabirds and marine mammals, and includes 9 acres of reefs, 29 acres of rocks, 157 acres of grassy islands, and 259 acres of forested islands. A total of 84 individual properties are included in the refuge, 81 of which are now protected by wilderness designation.

## CLIMATE

The San Juan Islands are located in the rain shadow of the Olympic Range and Vancouver Island; as a result they enjoy a comparatively dry climate, with an average annual rainfall of only 25 inches, mostly occurring during winter months. Temperatures are also mild, averaging 60 degrees in summer and 39 degrees in winter.

*White Rock, in the San Juan Islands Wilderness, is a nesting site for several species of sea birds.* (Photo by Marge and Ted Mueller)

## ECOSYSTEM

The reefs in the wilderness are awash at high tide, and low rocks have no soil, so both lack vegetation. Nearly half of the acreage in the wilderness consists of low islands, where a thin layer of soil supports a growth of fescue mixed with some wheatgrass and bluegrass. The tops of the larger islands have a tree cover of Douglas-fir and Pacific madrone, with some occurrences of Rocky Mountain juniper, lodgepole pine, and Oregon white oak.

Glaucous-winged gulls are the dominant breeding species. Other nesting species include Brandt's cormorants, pelagic cormorants, pigeon guillemots, tufted puffins, black brants, black oystercatchers, and rhinoceros auklets. In addition to these residents, some 200 migratory species of birds visit the islands annually. Bald eagles nest in the trees of forested islands and are often seen perched in snags searching for prey, or feeding on fish along the shoreline. Harbor seals haul out on low rocks, and Dall's porpoises, harbor porpoises, pilot whales, minke whales, and pods of orca whales are common in surrounding waters.

## GEOLOGY

The geology of the San Juan Islands is more complex than their size might indicate. The granites and gneisses of the Turtleback Complex occur along the north rim of Orcas Island and make up the bulk of Blakely Island. These are the oldest rocks in the islands, dating from pre-Devonian times more than 400 million years ago. During the following 100 million years, most of this submerged base was overlaid with marine volcanic breccia and ash, and later with sedimentary deposits, which were metamorphosed into sandstones and shales.

Around 200 million years ago the entire region appears to have been lifted above sea level, after which portions subsided and were overlaid with more marine sediments.

1. Small Island
2. Rim and Rum Islands
3. Fortress Island
4. Skull Island
5. Crab Island
6. Boulder Island
7. Davidson Rock
8. Colville Island
9. Castle Island
10. Unnamed islands (3)
11. Unnamed rock
12. Swirl Island
13. Aleck Rocks
14. Unnamed islands (4)
15. Unnamed islands (3)
16. Hall Island
17. Unnamed island
18. Secar Rock
19. Unnamed rock
20. Unnamed islets (3)
21. Unnamed islets (13)
22. Mummy Rocks
23. Buck Island
24. Islets and rocks
25. Shark Reef
26. Harbor Rock
27. North Pacific Rock
28. Half Tide Rock
29. Unnamed rocks
30. Unnamed islands (7)
31. Low Island
32. Unnamed island
33. Barren Island
34. Battleship Island
35. Center Reef
36. Sentinel Island
37. Gull Reef
38. Ripple Island
39. Unnamed reef
40. Unnamed island
41. Gull Rock
42. Flattop Island

43. White Rocks
44. Mouatt Reef
45. Skipjack Island
46. Unnamed island
47. Bare Island
48. Clements Reef
49. Unnamed island
50. Matia Island
51. Puffin Island
52. Parker Reef
53. Little Sister Island
54. The Sisters
55. Eliza Rock ††
56. Viti Rocks ††
57. North Peapod Rocks
58. Peapod Rocks
59. South Peapod Rocks
60. Brown Rock
61. Unnamed rock
62. Shag Rock
63. Unnamed rocks (3)
64. Black Rock
65. Pointer Island
66. Lawson Rock
67. Dot Island ††
68. Bird Rocks (4)
69. Williamson Rocks (3)
70. Smith Island †/††
71. Minor Island †/††
72. Willow Island
73. Flower Island
74. Unnamed rock
75. Turn Island†
76. Turn Rock
77. Tift Rocks
78. Unnamed island
79. Unnamed island
80. Unnamed island
81. Low Island
82. Unnamed island
83. Nob Island
84. Bird Rock

†Non-wilderness status
††Not within area of map

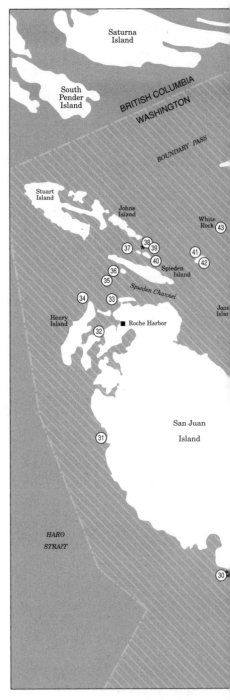

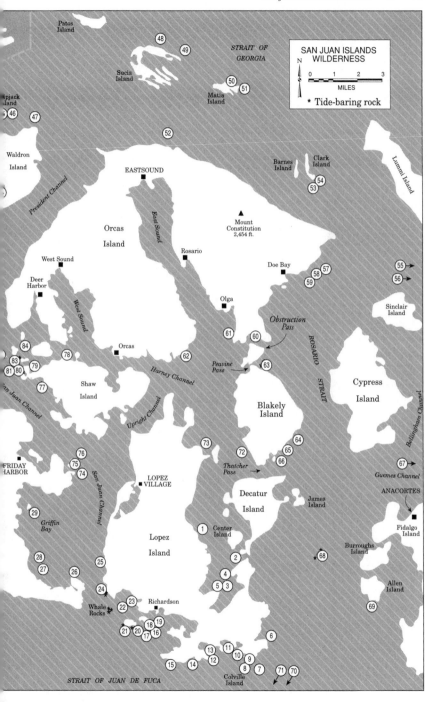

STRAIT OF GEORGIA

SAN JUAN ISLANDS
WILDERNESS

N

0          1          2          3
MILES

* Tide-baring rock

Patos
Island

Sucia
Island

Matia
Island

Barnes
Island

Clark
Island

Lummi Island

ppjack
land

Waldron

Island

EASTSOUND

President Channel

Orcas

Island

East Sound

Rosario

Mount
Constitution
2,454 ft.

Doe Bay

West Sound

Deer
Harbor

Olga

Sinclair
Island

West Sound

Obstruction
Pass

ROSARIO STRAIT

Orcas

Harney Channel

Peavine
Pass

Cypress

Island

Bellingham Channel

Shaw

Island

Upright Channel

Blakely
Island

an Juan Channel

Thatcher
Pass

FRIDAY
HARBOR

San Juan Channel

LOPEZ
VILLAGE

Decatur

Island

James
Island

Guemes Channel

ANACORTES

Griffin
Bay

Lopez

Island

Center
Island

Burroughs
Island

Fidalgo
Island

Whale
Rocks

Richardson

Allen
Island

STRAIT OF JUAN DE FUCA

Colville
Island

In the late Cretaceous period, low-angle thrusting in a northwest direction deformed the San Juan region, raising a northwest-bearing mountain range, and metamorphosed the sedimentary deposits into sandstones and siltstones. The northern islands, Sucia, Stuart, Spieden, and Waldron, were bent into open folds along the direction of the thrusting.

Pleistocene glaciers provided the final tailoring of the region, gouging deep channels through the range and smoothing and rounding its ridges. Later, the retreating ice left thick deposits of outwash sand and dropped large erratics. Weathering and wave action have combined to erode the softer siltstone and expose the harder layers of sandstone and conglomerate that form most of today's rocks and reefs.

## HISTORY

The value of the smaller islands in the San Juan archipelago as bird refuges was first recognized in 1914 when the Smith Island Reservation was created. In 1937 Jones and Matia Islands were added as migratory bird refuges. These three units were redesignated as national wildlife refuges in 1940. A fourth refuge, the San Juan Islands National Wildlife Refuge, was created in 1960. It was composed of the three Williamson Rocks and the four Bird Rocks, and Colville, Turn, and Bare Islands. Buck Island was added in 1967.

In 1975 three of these four rocky refuges were consolidated under the name of the San Juan Islands National Wildlife Refuge, and fifty-eight additional rocks, reefs, and islands were added. Jones Island was excluded, pending a potential trade to the State Parks and Recreation Commission in return for seventy-four state-owned rocks and islets in the San Juans. Sixteen more islands were added to the refuge in 1976, bringing it to eighty-four separate properties totaling 646 acres. In 1976, 355 acres of the San Juan National Wildlife Refuge were designated as the San Juan Islands Wilderness. Excluded from wilderness status were Smith, Minor, Jones, and Turn Islands, and the 5-acre state park property on Matia Island.

## ACTIVITIES

Matia Island has four small coves that offer anchorages. Rolfe Cove, on the northwest end of the island, has a dock, float, and mooring buoys associated with an adjoining state park. The rest of the island is part of the San Juan Islands Wilderness. A 1-mile loop trail leads from the campground past the remains of an old hermit's homestead to the island's south cove. Public use of this trail is subject to revocation if the wildlife in the refuge is disturbed.

All other rocks, reefs, and islands of the wilderness are closed to any public use, including landing, day use, and camping. Kayakers and small boaters can skirt the shoreline of these wilderness islands to observe birds and mammals, provided that wildlife is not bothered by their presence.

Opposite: *Mount Baker is reflected in a pool on the side of Park Butte in the Mount Baker National Recreation Area.*

*chapter 2*  **The North Cascades**

# 10 Mount Baker

## Mount Baker Wilderness and Mount Baker National Recreation Area; Adjacent Roadless Areas

**Location:** In Whatcom County, on the west side of North Cascades National Park, between Baker Lake and the Canadian border

**Size:** Wilderness, 117,900 acres; National Recreation Area, 8,600 acres; adjacent roadless areas, 74,664 acres

**Status:** Designated Wilderness, National Recreation Area (1984); Roadless areas Canyon Creek, Twin Lakes, and Loomis Mountain are Semiprimitive; Austin Pass is a Recreation Area; Twin Sisters Range is Primitive

**Terrain:** The dominant feature of the wilderness is the ice-clad summit of Mount Baker. Surrounding terrain is extremely rugged, with steep slopes terminating in ridge-top alpine meadows. Above these, jagged rock ribs lead to the summits of glaciated peaks. Creeks and rivers cut deep canyons into the lower forested slopes.

**Elevation:** 1,800 to 10,778 feet

**Management:** USFS, Mount Baker–Snoqualmie National Forest, Mount Baker Ranger District

**Topographic maps:** Bacon Peak, Baker Pass, Bearpaw Mountain, Cavanaugh Creek, Glacier, Groat Mountain, Mount Baker, Mount Sefrit, Mount Shuksan, Mt. Larrabee, Shuksan Arm, Twin Sisters Mountain, Welker Peak

Mount Baker, the fourth-highest summit in the state at 10,778 feet, is the northern-most of the chain of glaciated volcanoes that cap the Cascade Range in Washington. Although the mountain was first charted by explorers in 1790, dense forests, deep gorges cut by creeks and rivers flowing from its glaciers, and heavy snows lasting until midsummer thwarted exploration; it wasn't until 1868 that the first party reached its frozen summit. Fourteen glaciers cloak Mount Baker and its satellite peaks. With the addition of smaller glaciers found on other high summits in the area, the wilderness holds a total of more than 10,000 acres of permanent glacial ice.

The Mount Baker Wilderness, National Recreation Area, and adjacent roadless areas contain fifty-nine trails totaling more than 175 miles in length. Some are little more than climbing routes, others are brushy and poorly maintained, and a number are snowbound until mid-July. With the exception of the few routes that hug the bottom of densely forested drainages, the trails climb to alpine ridges with breathtaking vistas of glacier-shrouded Mount Baker, the much-photographed summit pyramid of Mount Shuksan, and a host of other peaks along the backbone of the North Cascades and in Canada's Cheam and Coast Ranges.

Most ridge tops have extensive, lightly forested heather meadows that burst into colorful displays of alpine flowers when the snow melts. A lush growth of huckleberries

*Artist Point affords outstanding views of Coleman Pinnacle and Mount Baker any time of year*

and blueberries ripens here in the fall. Although lowland forests once covered the region, logging has nibbled its way to the fringes of the wilderness and unprotected primitive and roadless areas.

## CLIMATE

Low-pressure systems from the Gulf of Alaska dominate the weather in the Mount Baker Wilderness. Heavy rain and snow are dumped on the region by successions of autumn and winter lows heavily laden with moisture gathered from the Pacific. Annual precipitation ranges from 80 inches in the lower areas on the western edge of the wilderness to 140 inches on the summit of Mount Baker and 150 inches at Baker Lake. Snow accumulates to an average depth of 18 feet in upper elevations. Even though most snow below 3,500 feet disappears by June, it persists above 5,000 feet until August. Glacial ice remains year-round above 6,000 feet; some permanent snowfields and pocket glaciers are found as low as 5,000 feet on north-facing slopes. When the Aleutian low retreats northward in summer, cool, dry air masses flow into the region.

## ECOSYSTEM

Vegetation in the wilderness is typical of that found on west Cascade slopes. Where not logged, valley floors are covered by a forest of Douglas-fir, cedar, and true fir with a thick understory of ferns and salmonberry. Devil's club and skunk cabbage thrive along creek beds, and open slopes are matted with vine maple and red alder. On higher slopes trees shift to Pacific silver fir and mountain hemlock, with Alaska yellow cedar in more open spots; the understory consists of salal, Oregon grape, and huckleberries. Between 4,000 and 5,500 feet, clumps of mountain hemlock and subalpine fir cluster in heather meadows covered by huckleberries, blueberries, and wildflowers. Higher yet, trees shrink to dwarf evergreens, then disappear entirely as sedges and tiny hardy flowers mat rock ribs that climb to the permanent ice fields.

In 1937, 1,407 acres were set aside as the North Fork of the Nooksack Research Natural Area (RNA) to preserve a baseline forest of Douglas-fir and western hemlock. A 2,460-acre addition has been proposed to track regeneration of a 75-year-old burn through Douglas-fir and other subalpine ecological communities. A second RNA of 1,920 acres has been proposed at Chowder Ridge, where alpine plants, flowers, and dwarfed subalpine fir (krummholz) are represented.

The forest is home to black-tailed deer, black bear, fishers, marten, blue grouse, and pileated woodpeckers. Mountain goats and hoary marmots are found at higher elevations. The basin on the south side of the wilderness between Dock Butte and Washington Monument, designated as an elk refuge, is one of the few places in the North Cascades where elk are found in any number.

## GEOLOGY

The geology of the Mount Baker Wilderness is surprisingly complex for the size of the area. The North Cascades consist of a microcontinent that collided with, and became attached to, the North American continent about 50 million years ago. The dominate rock of this "new" addition is the Chilliwack Group, a thick sheet of dark sandstone, shales, and marine lava flows laid down between 200 million to 300 million years ago. The

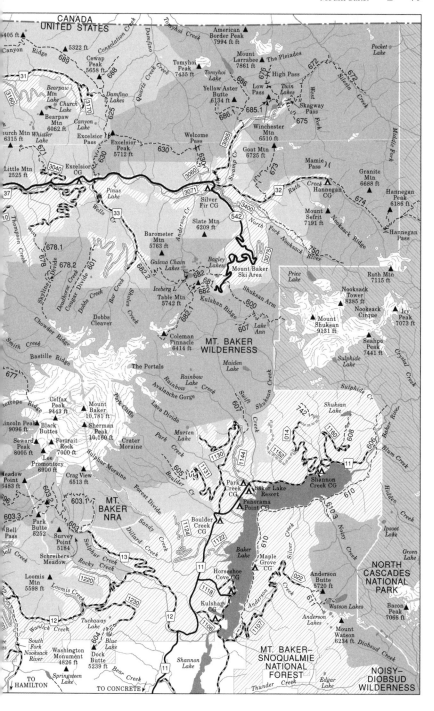

heart of this formation, from the Canadian border to Baker Lake, was overlaid 120 million to 150 million years ago by rock of the Nooksack Group, consisting of fossil-rich marine sediments, primarily of volcanic origin. This formation was intensely folded and sheared along the Church Mountain Thrust at its north and east edge.

A long fault line runs along the eastern border of the Mount Baker Wilderness, from the Skagit River to the Chilliwack River in Canada. East of the fault, the rock is primarily of the Shuksan Suite, a huge thrust sheet of green schist and phyllite meta-morphosed from marine volcanic flows. The upward thrust of this sheet, interposed with fragments of older crystalline core rock, is exposed in the peaks at the northeast corner of the wilderness.

Mount Baker volcanics overlay the center of the Nooksack Group in an east–west direction. West of the present summit, the Black Buttes mark the location of an older, eroded vent of the volcano. Mount Baker is relatively young; its flows were laid down over the past 10 million years, and there is less glacial erosion on the peak than on the other volcanoes farther south in the Washington Cascades. The mountain has been active as recently as 1975, emitting steam and a little ash from the summit crater.

Glacial flows in Pleistocene times carved the underlying rock, creating most of the cirques and valleys that are presently recognizable. Even today, this erosion con-tinues on a lesser scale where the massive glaciers of Mount Baker and smaller alpine glaciers on surrounding peaks carve and shape the surrounding rock.

The Sisters, at the southwest corner of the wilderness, is a massive intrusion of dunite, an ancient rock, probably of Precambrian origin, thought by some to be an exposed portion of the Earth's mantle. The intrusion appears to have been emplaced 50 million to 60 million years ago. The surface of the rock is olivine, imbedded with grains of chromite, which weathers to a distinctive reddish-brown color. The rough-textured tops of these peaks apparently escaped significant glacial erosion.

## HISTORY

Although there is evidence that Indians used a faint trail over Hannegan Pass to hunt mountain goats in the high Cascades, the first recorded explorations into the Mount Baker Wilderness occurred in connection with the boundary survey between 1857 and 1862. Tomyhoi Peak, Mount Larrabee, and either Goat Mountain or Winchester Moun-tain were possibly climbed by members of that survey party.

Prospectors poked into the South Fork of the Nooksack River in 1860 with scant success, but discoveries in the upper Skagit River and Ruby Creek in 1879 brought gold fever to the Nooksack as well. By 1885, the presence of gold in the South Fork was discounted; however, in 1896 promising prospects were found at the head of the North Fork of the Nooksack and its Swamp Creek and Ruth Creek tributaries. The Silver Tip Mine on Goat Mountain triggered a flurry of activity along Ruth Creek, and gold-laden veins of quartz were found at Twin Lakes and south of Skagway Pass. Word of riches quickly got out, and by 1902 nearly 500 miners inhabited five tent cities upriver from Nooksack Falls. Full-scale mining operations, complete with onsite stamp-ing mills, began at the Lone Jack, above Twin Lakes, and the Great Excelsior, on Wells

Creek. Mining was difficult; most sites were buried in snow for eight months of the year, and transportation of materials, supplies, and ore relied on humans and pack strings.

Additional lode mining occurred at the Boundary Red Mine on the north side of The Pleiades, the Gargett Mine on Mount Larrabee at Yellow Aster Meadows, and east of Glacier. Placer mining flourished on the North Fork of the Nooksack and many of its tributaries. As the mines played out in the early 1900s, logging became the chief economic driver in the region.

It wasn't until 1868 that a group led by Edmund Thomas Coleman made the first ascent of Mount Baker, via the glacier now named for him. Another sixteen years passed before the second ascent, when a pair of climbers approached the mountain from the south via the Easton Glacier. Some contend that this party actually reached the top of Sherman Peak, the lower, south summit of the mountain, rather than the true summit. Between 1911 and 1913, the Bellingham Chamber of Commerce introduced the annual Mount Baker Marathon. The race required contestants to get from Bellingham to the summit and back by auto, rail, bicycle, and foot, climbing to the summit via either the Coleman Glacier or Easton Glacier, and descending via the other. Poor weather, emotional stress, and the hazards of solo glacier travel caused cancellation of the marathon after its third year.

In the late 1920s, the Civilian Conservation Corps pushed a road up to Baker Lake and built the Komo Kulshan Guard Station. A fire lookout was constructed atop Park Butte in 1936, and many of today's trails were built to service the lookout and fire patrols in the area. The desire to exploit Mount Baker's scenic and recreational potential led to construction of a road to Heather Meadows, on the east side of the mountain, in 1924. By 1927, a resort there, complete with a lodge, hotel, and cabins, offered recreation that included skiing, hiking, and horseback riding. Most of the resort burned to the ground in 1931; the portions that were restored matured into today's Mount Baker Ski Area.

Federal management of the area was established in 1897 when President Cleveland created the Washington Forest Preserve, which included the region surrounding Mount Baker. From 1910 to 1917, Charles Finley Easton was one of the chief lobbyists promoting Mount Baker as a national park. In 1926, the Mount Baker Recreation Area, encompassing the entire mountain, was established; however, logging, mining, and water development were still permitted if they did not impair recreational values. Renewed proposals for park status for Mount Baker were introduced in the late 1930s and early 1940s, but it wasn't until 1984 that the bulk of the mountain and its surrounding virgin forests were designated as wilderness.

## HIKING
### Heather Meadows Recreation Area Trails

**Trail 600, Lake Ann.** *4.8 miles/m (H).* From Austin Pass (4,700 ft), the trail drops to the north fork of Swift Creek and follows it through mixed heather, forest, and scree for 1.5 miles to a saddle overlooking Lake Ann (4,700 ft). The lake is perched in a small meadow at the edge of precipitous cliffs surrounding the head of Shuksan Creek.

*Mount Shuksan's Lower Curtis Glacier leads to a popular climbing route up Fisher Chimneys.*

Across the basin, Fisher Chimneys and the lower 1,400-foot-high west wall of Mount Shuksan sweep up from the Lower Curtis Glacier.

**Trail 681, Table Mountain.** *2.6 miles/m-d (H).* From the end of Highway 542 (4,700 ft), the northernmost trail climbs a steep basalt cliff to reach the near-flat top of Table Mountain (5,742 ft) and spectacular views of Mounts Baker and Shuksan. The path wanders along the south and west rims of the mountain, descends a steep snowfield (ice ax recommended), then weaves down cliffs on its west side to join Trail 682 (4,980 ft).

**Trail 682, Chain Lakes.** *5.5 miles/e (H).* From the end of Highway 542 (4,700 ft), the southernmost path runs along the south wall of Table Mountain to a saddle in a little over a mile. Here the trail drops north along the west side of Table Mountain, passes an unmarked junction with Trail 681, and arrives at tiny Mazama Lake, the first of the Galena Chain Lakes. Next in the chain is Iceberg Lake (4,793 ft); a short spur leads from here to Hayes and Arbuthnet Lakes. The route climbs east to Herman Saddle (5,300 ft), then drops into the upper Bagley Creek Basin. A gradual descent past the flowered meadows surrounding Bagley Lakes reaches the lower Mount Baker Ski Area parking lot (4,200 ft).

**Trail 682.1, Ptarmigan Ridge.** *5 miles/m (H).* At the saddle west of Table Mountain (5,200 ft), a branch of Trail 682 continues west toward Mount Baker, skirting one side, then the other, of Ptarmigan Ridge. The trail continues to Camp Kiser, a small bench (6,180 ft) amid clumps of mountain hemlock on the west side of Coleman Pinnacle.

## Upper North Fork of the Nooksack River and Ruth Creek Trails

**Trail 750, Nooksack Cirque.** *6.5 miles/m (H).* From FR 32 (2,480 ft), a short, barrier-free path leads to a bridge viewpoint of Ruth Creek plunging through a narrow 100-foot-deep gorge. The track wanders through logged-over land along the north side of the Nooksack River, then fades into the braided channels of the Nooksack as it enters the deepest and darkest portion of the drainage. Obscure paths continue upriver to 2,800 feet to seldom-seen views of the glaciers and rock walls at the head of the Nooksack Cirque.

**Trail 674, Hannegan Pass.** *5 miles/e (H; S from August 15 to November 1).* From the end of FR 32 at Hannegan Campground (3,110 ft), a gentle climb up the forested hillside north of Ruth Creek reaches the heather meadows of Hannegan Pass (5,066 ft). The trail then enters North Cascades National Park as the Chilliwack Trail. En route are glimpses south to Ruth Mountain, Mount Sefrit, and Nooksack Ridge. From the pass, Trail 674.1 heads north up the ridge in lazy switchbacks, through heather and wildflowers, to the summit of Hannegan Peak (6,186 ft). Look east to see the peaks of the Picket Range, including Redoubt, Whatcom, Challenger, and Triumph. To the south, admire the ragged north face of Mount Shuksan; southwest is the stunning ice crown of Mount Baker.

## Swamp Creek Trails

**Trail 686, Tomyhoi Lake.** *4 miles/m (H).* The way leaves FR 3065 (3,700 ft) at the base of an avalanche-swept face, climbs around a forested ridge, and continues up a minor drainage to Gold Run Pass (5,430 ft). Yellow Aster Butte looms high to the west, and Mounts Shuksan and Baker dominate the skyline to the south. After a steep descent from the pass, hazardous until it melts out, the trail follows a creek northward to Tomyhoi Lake (3,722 ft). A cliff rises from the lake to a glacier falling from the summit of Tomyhoi Peak (7,435 ft).

**Trail 686.1, Yellow Aster.** *2 miles/m (H).* The original Keep Kool Trail to this beautiful ridge deteriorated to the point it was abandoned in the late 1990s and this new approach from the Tomyhoi Trail was built. The way leaves Trail 686 at Gold Run Pass (5,410 ft) and traverses west to Yellow Aster Butte (5,500 ft) and its chain of beautiful tarns that dimple lush, flower-tinted meadows. Old prospects and rusted mining gear testify to the origin of the trail. Late summer brings a feast of blueberries in the alpine meadows atop the butte.

**Trail 685.1, Winchester Mountain.** *2.1 miles/m (H).* From Twin Lakes (5,170 ft), this route climbs north through subalpine fir and small flower meadows, then traverses avalanche slopes. After rounding the ridge south of Winchester Mountain, the path switchbacks up through dwarf subalpine fir to the summit and an historic fire lookout (6,510 ft) maintained by a local climbing club. A sweeping 360-degree view encompasses Tomyhoi Peak, Mount Larrabee, American Border Peak, The Pleiades, the glaciated spires of the Chilliwack Range, the sawtoothed Picket Range, Mount Shuksan, and the glistening mass of Mount Baker. An ice ax is mandatory in steep snow chutes until late summer.

*Snow blankets Mount Baker's Austin Pass and distant Mount Shuksan.*

**Trail 676, High Pass.** *3 miles/m (H).* From 0.4 mile up Trail 685.1 (5,400 ft), a miners' route climbs north along the head of the Winchester Creek basin, then switchbacks up to Low Pass (5,650 ft). After ascending an open hillside to High Pass (5,900 ft), the trail climbs north up a ridge and a steep rock face to the shoulder of Mount Larrabee (6,730 ft). A spur northwest from High Pass leads to the abandoned Gargett Mine. The Forest Service has proposed extending this trail from High Pass to Trail 686, just north of Gold Run Pass.

## North of the North Fork of the Nooksack River Trails

**Trail 671, Church Mountain.** *4.2 miles/m (H).* Church Mountain is easily recognized from Highway 542 by its vertical green walls, which rise nearly a mile to a gable roof of rock and a slab-sided rock steeple. A fire lookout once stood atop the east peak, but weather collapsed the building and it was removed in 1966. From the trailhead on FR 3040 (2,313 ft), the route takes endless switchbacks up the forested hillside to reach heather meadows at the head of Deerhorn Creek basin. A long traverse and a steep ascent of a rock rib gains the summit ridge east of the lookout site. Here are imposing views a mile straight down to the Nooksack Valley, plus the panoramic sweep of The Sisters, Mount Baker, and Mount Shuksan, with peaks along the American border to the north.

**Trail 630, High Divide.** *13 miles/m (H; S from August 14 to November 1).* From the trailhead on Highway 542 (1,040 ft), incessant switchbacks climb a timbered mountain flank to Excelsior Pass (5,375 ft). This trail winds eastward through alpine meadows to Welcome Pass (5,400 ft), rarely dropping more than a few hundred feet below the ridge top. From Welcome Pass the route zigzags down a steep, forested ridge to

FR 3060 (2,450 ft). Wildflowers adorn the route from late July to September, and the crevassed glaciers of Mount Baker are continuous visual companions.

## Canyon Creek Trails

**Trail 689, Canyon Ridge.** *9.1 miles/d (H,B,M; S from August 15 to November 1).* From its west end at FR 3140 (4,470 ft) this trail wanders east along a 4,800- to 5,400-foot-high ridge crest, less than a mile south of the Canadian border. Once a part of the Whatcom Trail, which stretched from Bellingham to the Cariboo gold fields of British Columbia, this route is being restored as a segment of the new Pacific Northwest Trail system. The path is gentle, sometimes in timber, sometimes in heather meadows. The west end is being rebuilt, but may be difficult to follow, and it is often obscured by snow until late summer. As the ridge swings south from the border, the trail begins a gentle descent through mountain ash forest to the junction with Trail 625 at its eastern end.

**Trail 625, Damfino Lake–Excelsior Pass.** *2.5 miles/m (H).* Starting from FR 31 (4,277 ft), a gentle grade leads past Trail 689 to a meadow surrounding tiny Damfino Lake (4,470 ft). Beyond the lake the path switchbacks up a steep hillside, then crosses a notch to more alpine meadows. A gentle traverse rises another mile to Excelsior Pass to meet Trail 630. Here is the familiar panorama of Mounts Baker and Shuksan, the Border Peaks, and the crests of the North Cascades.

## South of the North Fork of the Nooksack River Trails

**Trail 601, Cougar Divide.** *3 miles/m (H).* At the end of FR 33 (4,680 ft) the route heads up a gentle forested rib that soon breaks out into eye-popping views of Mount Baker and the surrounding valleys. The ridge crest narrows as the trail climbs to a saddle at 5,800 feet, and a climbing route continues upward to Chowder Ridge.

**Trail 678, Skyline Divide.** *5.5 miles/m (H; S from August 15 to November 1).* From the trailhead at FR 37 (4,350 ft), switchbacks and a diagonal climb through a silver fir forest lead to the crest of Skyline Divide, between Thompson and Deadhorse Creeks. Atop the divide a short path leads north along the crest to a promontory (5,884 ft) with a clear view of the peaks lining the horizon and Church Mountain rising abruptly north across the valley. Trees dissolve to alpine meadows as the path ascends the slowly rising ridge. With altitude the meadows fade to a mat of sedges; the trail continues south along the crest, then disappears into snowbanks at a cliff on the west end of Chowder Ridge (6,400 ft). The upper portion of the divide is snow-covered until August. Once above timberline, the horizon-spanning scenery includes the Canadian Coast Range, the Border Peaks, Mount Shuksan, and a wall of ice breaking from the summit of Mount Baker. Below are the deep canyons of north-flowing tributaries of the Nooksack.

**Trail 677, Heliotrope Ridge.** *2.7 miles/e (H).* From the trailhead parking lot on FR 39 (2,880 ft), the route crosses Grouse Creek, zigzags uphill, then takes a climbing traverse through the forest to Kulshan Creek. An ascent east of the creek reaches the former site of Kulshan Cabin (4,700 ft), just below timberline. Here a path climbs a meadow-covered rib south to snowfields below Heliotrope Ridge (6,200 ft). These meadows are blanketed by wildflowers in late summer.

## Middle Fork of the Nooksack River Trails

**Trail 697, Elbow Lake.** 6.2 miles/m (H; S from August 15 to November 1). The route leaves FR 38 before its end, crosses a bridge over the Nooksack just below the trailhead (2,140 ft), and swings west to the mouth of Green Creek. It ascends the forested sidehill above the creek, then bends east up slopes above Hildebrand Creek. Canyon walls close in at tiny Hildebrand Lake. The way continues to Elbow Lake (3,380 ft) and nearby Lake Doreen; 200- to 400-foot-high walls embrace both lakes. From Doreen the path threads through a breach in the wall, traverses south, and drops down a timber-covered ridge to a spur trail that meets Trail 603.3 (3,300 ft). The route crosses Doreen Creek twice before reaching FR 12 at Pioneer Camp.

**Trail 696, Ridley Creek.** 3 miles/m (H; S between August 15 and November 1). From the end of FR 38 (2,610 ft) the way climbs a timber-covered rib to a bridge over the Middle Fork of the Nooksack. After a traverse of forested slopes, switchbacks climb the steep north side of the Ridley Creek drainage. The route then traverses southeast along the upper edge of the flower meadows of Mazama Park to join Trail 603.3 (4,500 ft).

## South Fork of the Nooksack River Trails

**Trail 604, Blue Lake.** 0.7 mile/e (H,M). From the end of FR 1230 (3,930 ft), an easy path climbs to the alpine meadows surrounding the north and east sides of Blue Lake (3,984 ft). From its common start with Trail 604, Trail 604.1 climbs a forested rib north of Blue Lake, then breaks into an alpine meadow bench above the cliffs west of the lake. A narrow ridge leads south, where switchbacks climb to the summit of Dock Butte (5,239 ft). The fire lookout once here was removed in 1964, but the views of Mount Baker and south as far as Mount Rainier remain.

**Trail 603, Park Butte.** 3.5 miles/m (H; S between August 15 and November 1; open to snowmobiles to the wilderness boundary). From the trailhead at the end of FR 13 (3,364 ft), the route passes through Schreibers Meadow, then begins a gradual climb of the wooded hillside. The ridge is surmounted in a series of switchbacks, and the forest is left behind at the lower end of Morovitz Meadows (4,600 ft). A diagonal ascent above the heather-covered basin south of Cathedral Crag leads to a saddle on South Fork Divide. A short hike up the ridge to the west reaches the fire lookout atop Park Butte (5,252 ft). The tower, constructed in 1936, is maintained by the Skagit Alpine Club. Views sweep up the Easton Glacier to the icy cap of Mount Baker; west is the ragged string of summits along the top of Twin Sisters Mountain; north are the steep crags of the Black Buttes.

**Trail 603.1, Scott Paul.** 6.5 miles/m (H). This trail leaves Trail 603 (3,364 ft) just beyond its starting point, then makes a few lazy switchbacks up a forested ridge to the north between two forks of Sulphur Creek. At the head of the basin above the east fork, trees fade to heather meadows. The path climbs to 4,800 feet; a boot-track continues atop the snowfields and rocks of the moraine to Crag View, where the Squak

Glacier focuses views upward to Sherman Peak, the south summit of Mount Baker. The trail traverses west above timberline along the 4,800-foot contour line to the head-waters of Rocky Creek on Metcalf Moraine. Here it drops to meet Trail 603 below Morovitz Meadows (4,600 ft).

**Trail 603.2, Railroad Grade.** *2 miles/m (H)*. From Trail 603 at the north end of Morovitz Meadows (4,670 ft), this way ascends the lateral moraine on the west side of the Easton Glacier. Above 5,000 feet a climbers' track continues along snow and jumbled rock to the edge of the glacier, 1,000 feet higher. This is the start of a climbing route to the summit.

**Trail 603.3, Mazama Park.** *6 miles/m (H; S between August 15 and November 1)*. At a saddle on the south side of Cathedral Crag (4,750 ft), the fork to the north is the upper end of Trail 603.3. It switchbacks downhill to a junction with Trail 696 (4,500 ft) near the southeast edge of the beautiful alpine meadow of Mazama Park. Trail 603.3 heads west over Bell Pass (3,964 ft) and ends on Trail 697 near Doreen Creek (3,300 ft).

## Baker Lake Trails

**Trail 608, Shuksan Lake.** *2 miles/d (H)*. Starting from FR 1160 in a clearcut (2,980 ft), the trail enters old-growth forest and without respite zigzags up a seemingly vertical ridge to a saddle (4,720 ft) above two tarns. Dropping past these, the route swings west along a cliff rim above the south side of Shuksan Lake, then descends to a small meadow at the west end of the lake (3,694 ft).

**Trail 606, Baker River.** *1.6 miles/e (H)*. A short, near-level jaunt up the west bank of Baker River from FR 11 (800 ft) ends at Sulphide Creek, just inside the national park boundary. Here are rewarding views up the wide, glacier-carved basin, extending into the heart of the North Cascades to Easy Ridge and Whatcom Peak.

## CLIMBING

The crown of the wilderness, Mount Baker (10,778 ft), was first climbed via the Coleman Glacier. This popular route on the northwest side ascends the glacier to the saddle between the summit and Black Buttes, then scales the steep ice of the Roman Wall to the flat summit plateau. Southside routes ascend the Boulder and Easton Glaciers. The latter is the easiest on the mountain, but even it has seen fatalities in a midsummer avalanche on the upper Deming Glacier. From the northeast, climbs start at the end of Trail 682.1 at Camp Kiser, head up the Sholes Glacier to either the Rainbow Glacier or Mazama Glacier, then finish via the steep Park Glacier headwall. On the north, extremely challenging ice routes claw up the Coleman Glacier headwall, the upper Roosevelt Glacier, and the north ridge of the mountain. All glaciers become heavily crevassed and difficult to cross by early fall.

The ridge west from the summit leads to the Black Buttes, a maze of sawtooth basalt spikes above the west end of the Deming Glacier that are remnants of an earlier cone of Mount Baker. Vertical walls line both the east and west sides of a crescent-shaped arête. The four named summits are Colfax (9,443 ft), Lincoln (9,096 ft), and Seward (8,005 ft) Peaks, and Lee Promontory (6,900 ft). Lincoln is the most difficult climb of the group, requiring exposed rock and glacier work. There are several other unnamed pinnacles along the crest between these peaks.

The Twin Sisters Range, southwest of Mount Baker, is named for the two distinctive pyramidal peaks, North Twin (6,570 ft) and South Twin (6,932 ft), which mark the north end of the range. The 6-mile-long crest to the southeast is topped by a number of towers ranging between 5,900 and 6,500 feet; small glaciers lie in pockets along the northeast side of the range. The rock throughout the range is rough-textured and solid, offering excellent short climbs in the C-4 to C-5 range. In keeping with the Sisters motif, many of the lesser peaks bear feminine names, such as Barbara, Nancy, Little Sister, and Cinderella.

The trails north from Swamp Creek access a group of peaks along the Canadian border. From Trail 686.1 at Yellow Aster Meadows, a boot-path heads up the ridge for an exposed C-3 scramble up Tomyhoi Peak (7,435 ft). From the south, the sharp summit pyramid of American Border Peak (7,994 ft) appears to be an imposing climb, although the long cross-country approach from the Gargett Mine is perhaps as difficult as the climb itself. A variety of rock features on the ridge southeast of the summit make the C-3 to C-5 route especially interesting. From the upper end of Trail 676 above the Gargett Mine, a scramble up talus, loose dirt, and rock reaches the top of Mount Larrabee (7,861 ft). The buttress east from the summit of Larrabee is capped by four ragged spires, The Pleiades (7,280 to 7,360 ft). Steep snow or ice gullies from either north or south reach a col between the east and west pairs of peaks, where C-3 scrambles over solid rock gain the summits.

Rugged Nooksack Ridge, between Ruth Creek and the North Fork of the Nooksack River, is anchored on the north end by Mount Sefrit (7,191 ft) and on the south by Ruth Mountain (7,115 ft). Ruth is a simple scramble south from Hannegan Pass via the glacier on its north ridge, and the final summit pyramid of Sefrit has several C-4 to C-5 leads on solid rock. The crest between Sefrit and Ruth is laced with several lower pinnacles.

## WINTER SPORTS

Mount Baker Ski Area, a major commercial facility at the east end of Highway 542, is surrounded by its namesake wilderness. The open alpine slopes are among the most popular cross-country ski touring areas in the state, with due caution paid to avalanche hazards. One of the Cascades' best cross-country trips heads south from the ski area, crosses the snowbound Bagley Lakes, and climbs to Herman Saddle. The return trip offers excellent runs down deep untracked snow. Another tour heads south from the ski lodge to Austin Pass and Artist Point for outstanding views of Mounts Shuksan and Baker in their cloaks of winter snow. The more daring can follow the general route of the summer trail along Ptarmigan Ridge to Camp Kiser; avalanche hazards occur on the south side of Table Mountain, but rewards include miles of untracked open basins.

Access roads to the wilderness become ideal ski tours when snows seal them to vehicular traffic. In the North Fork of the Nooksack drainage, such tours include FR 32 and 3400 into the upper reaches of the Nooksack River and Ruth Creek, FR 3075 at the head of White Salmon Creek, FR 3071 up Anderson Creek above Silver Fir Campground,

FR 33 up Wells Creek, and FR 3065 toward Twin Lakes. Farther west, FR 39 up Glacier Creek offers outstanding views of the northwest side of Mount Baker and access for skiing the open bowls below Heliotrope Ridge.

On the south side of Mount Baker, the difference between a recreation area and a wilderness area is readily apparent in the winter. Snowmobiles are permitted on roads and some of the trails of the recreation area, and the snow-covered forest roads between Baker Lake and Schreibers Meadow are heavily used.

From Schreibers Meadow, the summer trail to Park Butte has excellent snow for advanced cross-country skiers well into late spring. Ski mountaineers often use the Railroad Creek route for glacier skiing on the lower Easton Glacier or even conduct spring climbs from this side of the mountain. The snow-covered loop connecting FR 1144 up Morovitz Creek to FR 1130 up Park Creek has scenic side trips to Rainbow Falls and the opportunity for a welcome warming dip in Baker Hot Springs (nude bathing prohibited).

# Baker Lake Region

## Noisy–Diobsud Wilderness; Oakes Peak and Noisy–Diobsud Roadless Areas

**Location:** In Whatcom and Skagit Counties, on the west side of North Cascades National Park between Highway 20 and Baker Lake

**Size:** Wilderness: 14,300 acres; Noisy–Diobsud, 50,385 acres; Oakes Peak, 1,604 acres

**Status:** Designated Wilderness (1984); Roadless areas are Primitive and Semiprimitive Nonmotorized

**Terrain:** Rugged, extremely steep, forested slopes are split by numerous creek drainages. Ridges are topped by alpine meadows; those on the northeast border of the wilderness are capped by rocky summits.

**Elevation:** 900 to 6,234 feet

**Management:** USFS, Mount Baker–Snoqualmie National Forest, Mount Baker Ranger District. A few sections outside the designated wilderness are managed by the Washington State Department of Natural Resources (DNR) or are in private hands.

**Topographic maps:** Bacon Peak, Damnation Peak, Lake Shannon, Marblemount, Sauk Mountain, Welker Peak

Ridges on the northeast and southwest sides of Noisy Creek (flowing to the north) and Diobsud Creek (flowing to the south) define the official boundaries of the Noisy–Diobsud Wilderness. The national forest land wrapping around three sides of the wilderness, about two-and-a-half times the size of the designated wilderness itself, is currently

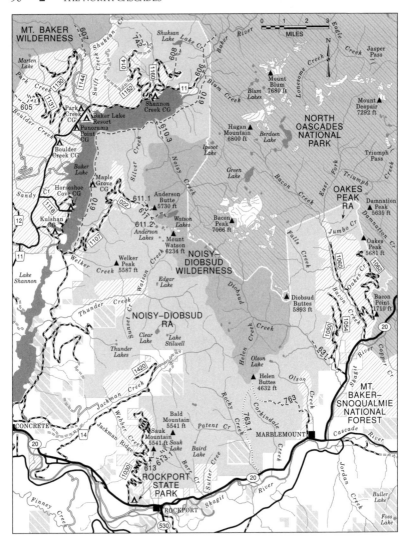

managed by the Forest Service in a primitive or semiprimitive status, which gives it de facto, although not legal, protection similar to the wilderness. Eleven-mile-long Baker Lake lies along the northwest edge of this extended wilderness at the foot of a steep hillside covered with old-growth forest. The southwest side of this region, including the lower portions of the Anderson, Welker, Thunder, and Jackman Creek drainages, has been heavily logged; fortunately, a 0.5- to 5-mile-wide buffer of old-growth forest still exists along the perimeter of the designated wilderness. Extremely steep rock walls rise from the Skagit River on the south and southeast sides of the extended wilderness.

Only 12 miles of maintained trails exist in the wilderness and adjacent roadless areas; another dozen or so miles of abandoned routes are so obscure and difficult that their use demands polished navigation skills. The wilderness itself holds only a dozen lakes, most above 4,000 feet; the roadless area outside the wilderness has more than double that number of lakes, most not reached by trails.

Hikers enjoy relatively easy trails to two abandoned fire lookout sites at Anderson Butte and Sauk Mountain. Both offer unparalleled views of hundreds of miles of forested ridges cut by lakes and deep river valleys. Above loom the jagged crest of the Cascades and the huge masses of the ice-clad volcanoes on the forefront of that range. Climbers are the most frequent visitors to the ragged, rocky boundary between the wilderness and North Cascades National Park.

## CLIMATE

Alternating high- and low-pressure cells from the North Pacific dominate the weather pattern on the west side of the North Cascades. Summers are generally mild and dry, but a continuous series of low-pressure fronts from the south, southwest, and west bring rain and snow in the autumn and winter. Annual precipitation here is about 150 inches, much of it delivered as snow that reaches depths of 18 feet or more. The snow is generally gone below 3,500 feet by early June.

## ECOSYSTEM

Vegetation in the Noisy–Diobsud Wilderness is typical of that found on the west side of the Cascades. Low-level forests are old-growth Douglas-fir, cedar, true fir, and western hemlock, with an understory of mosses, ferns, salal, Oregon grape, elderberry, and salmonberry, joined by vine maple and devil's club along creek beds. Buttercups, foam flower, and youth-on-age add color to the forest floor. With increasing altitude the timber shifts to mountain hemlock, and ultimately gives way to alpine meadows along ridge tops.

The dense forest canopy is habitat for black-tailed deer, elk, black bear, and northern spotted owls. Mountain goats are common in the Diobsud Buttes area, and peregrine falcons are occasionally seen.

## GEOLOGY

Most of the wilderness consists of Paleozoic sedimentary rocks, formed more than 250 million years ago as ocean sediments accumulated off a microcontinent impinging northeastward on the coastline of North America. At a thrust fault along the northeast side of the wilderness, pre-Jurassic metamorphosed rock overrode this plate, forming the crest of today's Diobsud Buttes. A similar-aged metamorphic intrusion rises in the southeast end of the extended wilderness in the vicinity of Sauk Mountain.

## HISTORY

Little is known of the early history of the Noisy–Diobsud Wilderness, although there are sketchy records of visits by pioneer trappers. Most prospectors bypassed the area in their rush to more lucrative claims along the upper Skagit and Cascade Rivers.

Marblemount, the tiny community at the southeast corner of the wilderness, began the 1880s as the last point for miners to purchase supplies and slake their thirst for whiskey.

The first surveys of the region took place in the early 1900s, and records indicate exploration of the Baker River area in the 1920s. The present shoreline of Baker Lake was created in 1924 by the construction of Baker Dam, erected to supply power to the Bellingham area. Fire lookouts were built on Anderson Butte in 1920 and on Sauk

*Valerian blossoms and hellebore decorate the hillside above Watson Lakes.*

Mountain in 1928. For a time, cattle were driven to alpine meadows for summer grazing; the path up to Helen Buttes is still known as the Cow Heaven Trail. In recent years, logging, primarily on state and private land, has clearcut hundreds of acres along the southwest side of the extended wilderness.

## HIKING

**Trail 610, East Bank.** *13 miles/e (H,S).* The trailhead (980 ft) is on the west side of the FR 1107. A gentle descent along a steep forested hillside crosses Anderson Creek, then drops to the east shore of Baker Lake, which it follows north to Maple Grove Campground (724 ft), accessible only by foot or boat. North from the campground, a recently constructed trail follows the east bank of Baker Lake for 2 miles, then climbs over a forested knob at the elbow where the lake turns east. At the mouth of Noisy Creek is a junction with a short spur, Trail 610.3, that heads up into the creek. The main trail continues northeast, maintaining altitude, to Hidden Creek, then descends to the east bank of the Baker River. Just beyond Blum Creek the way crosses a bridge over the Baker River and meets Trail 606.

**Trail 611, Watson Lakes.** *2.3 miles/e (H).* From FR 1107-022 (4,200 ft) a few switchbacks reach the ridge top, and the path heads southeast along the gentle crest; in a little over a mile it climbs to the saddle above Watson Lakes. Switchbacks lead down to the upper lake (4,418 ft); the path follows its north shore, then descends to the lower lake (4,407 ft). Glassy surfaces of the two deep blue lakes mirror Anderson Butte and the snowfields leading to the summit of Mount Watson.

**Trail 611.1, Anderson Butte.** *1.5 miles/m (H).* About 0.8 mile from the start of Trail 611, a fork leads east up switchbacks to the ridge top, a former fire lookout site. Choice of the site is obvious, as views extend north over hundreds of acres of forest, crowned by the icy summits of Mounts Baker and Shuksan. The actual top of the butte (5,730 ft) is 0.25 mile to the east via an easy ridge-top scramble.

**Trail 611.2, Anderson Lakes.** *0.4 mile/m (H).* At the point Trail 611 starts its climb to the Watson Lakes saddle, a spur continues downhill to the largest of the Anderson Lakes (4,475 ft). Two small ponds lie uphill in open basins south and east of this lake. The other three lakes of the group (5,000 to 5,300 ft) lie in a rocky basin above a band of cliffs to the east. These lakes usually remain frozen until mid-June.

**Trail 613, Sauk Mountain.** *2.1 miles/e (H).* From Highway 20 at the west side of Rockport State Park, turn north onto FR 1030. A series of hairpin turns leads 7 miles uphill to the ridge top, where a spur to the south ends at the present trailhead (4,500 ft). Be thankful—once the trail to this point was a tedious 5-mile grind from the highway up the steep ridge to the southeast. The remaining 2 miles of trail are not a snap; however, the path takes twenty-nine switchbacks up a steep alpine meadow to reach the ridge leading north to the summit (5,541 ft). Here a spur (613.1) heads south down the ridge, then contours northeast, crosses a finger ridge, and descends in a few lazy switchbacks to a cirque that holds Sauk Lake (4,104 ft).

The main trail continues on to the summit. The original fire lookout was built here in 1928; its 1957 replacement was removed in 1985. To the north is a sweeping view of the entire Noisy–Diobsud Wilderness and beyond to the jagged peaks of North Cascades National Park. Below, the blue ribbons of the Skagit and Sauk Rivers thread through valley floors.

**Trail 763, Cow Heaven.** *6.4 miles/m (H).* The trail starts at the end of an unmarked road beyond the barn of the Marblemount Ranger Station (500 ft). Once herds of cattle were driven up this route for a summer feast on alpine meadows; now only hikers and hunters struggle up the steep, tedious path. An initial gentle grade through cool virgin forest soon leads to switchbacks up forested rock outcrops to a broad flat (2,200 ft). After a short respite, switchbacks continue up the steep sidehill to an indistinct ridge that breaks into alpine meadows (4,200 ft). The way becomes obscure; one fork traverses the slopes east of Corkindale Creek, and another continues up the crest to the top of Helen Buttes, while a third obscure, unmaintained path (763.1) descends the south face of the ridge along Rocky Creek. The higher up the mountain you go, the better are the views to the snowcapped peaks of North Cascades National Park and the upper gorge of the Skagit River.

## CLIMBING

While Sauk Mountain (5,541 ft) has an easy trail to the top, cliffs on three sides of the summit offer short, challenging rock climbs. In winter these faces are also used by ice climbers.

On the southeast side of the wilderness, dense vegetation covers a tangled succession of cliffs rising nearly 5,000 feet from Diobsud Creek to the near-vertical southeast rock face of Diobsud Buttes (5,893 ft). A series of short, ragged summits lines the top of the buttes, and small glaciers hang from their northern edge. Most of these high points are scrambles, but a few have one or two leads of C-4 climbing.

The twin summits of Mount Watson (6,234 ft), nearly 1,000 feet higher than nearby Anderson Butte, offer even better views of the miles of forested valleys and ridges culminating in the glaciated summits of Mounts Baker and Shuksan and the sheer west face of Bacon Peak. Good C-3 to C-4 routes lead over rock or a rock-and-snow combination to the summit.

## WINTER SPORTS

The combination of snow and steep avalanche-prone terrain seals off much of the Noisy–Diobsud Wilderness and adjoining roadless areas to winter recreation. However, the Sauk Mountain Road, from snowline to a cliff band at about 3,900 feet, offers a relatively safe intermediate midwinter tour, with good views of the Skagit and Sauk Valleys from the upper portions of the road. Avalanche slopes make travel higher up the mountain inadvisable.

At the north end of the wilderness, the relatively gentle, lightly timbered ridge leading to Anderson Butte and Anderson Lakes (Trail 611) is an excellent advanced basic trip, with good downhill runs in the basin below the lakes. Snow levels will determine how much of FR 1107 must be skied to reach the ridge trail route.

# 12 North Cascades Region

## North Cascades National Park Complex (Stephen Mather Wilderness); Glacier Peak H, Alma–Copper, and Hidden Lake Roadless Areas

**Location:** In Whatcom, Skagit, and Chelan Counties, between the Canadian border and Lake Chelan

**Size:** Total park: 505,000 acres; wilderness: 504,614 acres. Total Ross Lake National Recreational Area: 117,600 acres; wilderness: 74,000 acres. Total Lake Chelan National Recreational Area: 62,000 acres; wilderness: 56,000 acres. Glacier Peak H, 7,939 acres; Alma–Copper, 8,193 acres; Hidden Lake, 6,652 acres

**Status:** National Park, Ross Lake NRA, Lake Chelan NRA, and Designated Wilderness (1988); Roadless areas are Semiprimitive Nonmotorized

**Terrain:** Rugged, rocky, glaciated peaks rise locally as much as 7,000 feet above deep, forested, glacier-gouged, and stream-cut valleys. Ross, Diablo, and Gorge Lakes were created by Seattle City Light dams.

**Elevation:** 400 to 9,210 feet

**Management:** National Park Service, Mount Baker–Snoqualmie National Forest, Mount Baker Ranger District

**Topographic maps:** Bacon Peak, Big Devil Peak, Cascade Pass, Copper Mountain, Crater Mountain, Damnation Peak, Diablo Dam, Eldorado Peak, Forbidden Peak, Gilbert, Goode Mtn., Hozomeen Mtn., Jack Mtn., Marblemount, McAlester Mtn., McGregor Mtn., Mount Blum, Mount Sefrit, Mount Shuksan, Mount Triumph, Mt. Arriva, Mt. Challenger, Mt. Logan, Mt. Lyall, Mt. Prophet, Mt. Redoubt, Mt. Spickard, Pinnacle Mountain, Pumpkin Mtn., Ross Dam, Shuksan Arm, Skagit Peak, Sonny Boy Lakes, Stehekin, Sun Mountain

The "National Park Complex" or Stephen Mather Wilderness consists of three components: the park itself, and the Lake Chelan and Ross Lake National Recreation Areas. The latter area divides the park into two separate pieces, one to its north and one to its south. Each of these sections is a vast wilderness in its own right, with outstanding peaks, spire-laden ridges, and an extensive collection of alpine glaciers.

The North Cascades National Park encompasses some of the wildest, most rugged, and untracked terrain in the Cascade

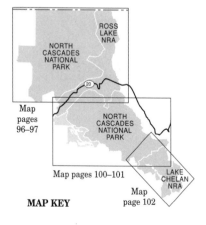

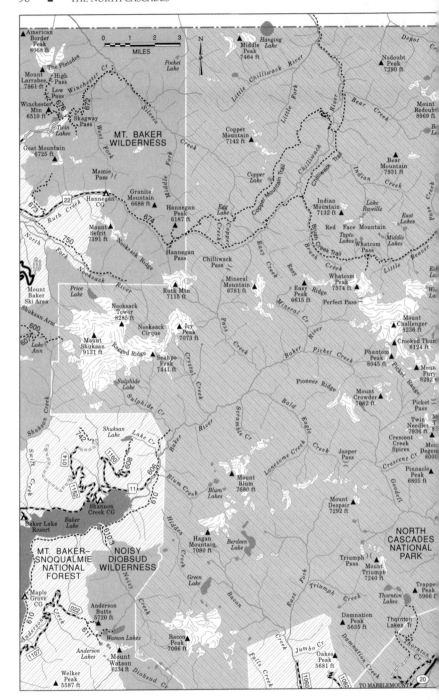

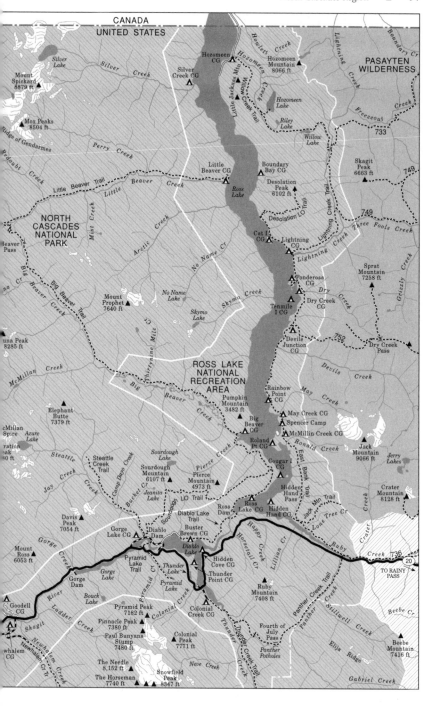

*Paddlers on Ross Lake view a waterfall tumbling from Devils Creek.*

Range. Although there are nominally 390 miles of maintained trails in the park, this figure is somewhat misleading, as most individual trails are quite long, and vast stretches of the park are accessible only by cross-country travel, much of which requires mountaineering skills. Multiday mini-expeditions are required to reach many of these remote areas. The most popular day-use area is Cascade Pass, due to its relative ease of access as well as its spectacular alpine scenery. Unfortunately, hordes of visitors are severely stressing this fragile environment, despite valiant efforts by the Park Service to preserve it.

The Ross Lake National Recreation Area consists of a narrow corridor along the North Cascades Scenic Highway, which bisects North Cascades National Park, and a similar corridor along the east side of the park enclosing Ross Lake. The highway and the usage of the Skagit River drainage for hydroelectric power are the reasons for excluding the NRA from the national park. Recreation in this area is heavily boat-oriented; there are nineteen different campsites along the shores of Ross and Diablo Lakes, many accessible only by boat. The outstanding alpine scenery of the adjacent park and Pasayten Wilderness, with their many glaciers and jagged peaks, can be admired from a number of spots along the area's lakes and trails.

The broad, deep, glacier-carved valley of the Stehekin River, in the Lake Chelan NRA, is one of the most remote such valleys in the state. It can be reached only by ferry from Chelan, 51 miles to the south, by private boat, floatplane, private aircraft, or by hiking or riding horseback over connecting trails to the east and west. The valley floor is framed by steep cliffs rising more than 7,000 feet to rugged peaks. Streams cascade down these slopes, often ending in beautiful waterfalls near the valley floor. One of these, 312-foot Rainbow Falls, can be seen from a campground and picnic area 2 miles northwest of Stehekin. During summer months, the park runs a shuttle van service (fee charged) up the Stehekin Valley Road, with stops at trailheads and campgrounds en route.

## CLIMATE

The climate varies dramatically by location: the west side of the park complex receives much heavier precipitation than the east slopes. West of the north–south backbone ridges, the annual precipitation is near 110 inches, most falling between November and May in the form of snow; annual snowfall exceeds 500 inches. Although the Ross Lake RNA is technically on the wetter western side of the Cascade crest, it is in the rain shadow of the Skagit and Picket Ranges, and therefore receives significantly less precipitation than one would expect for a westside region. The mean annual precipitation at Ross Lake ranges between 66 to 75 inches.

Westside temperatures tend to be mild; mean January temperatures on the lower slopes range between 15 and 25 degrees, with temperatures dropping below those at higher altitudes. Average summer highs are in the mid-70s in the valleys, and in the 60s to low 70s at upper elevations.

Because Lake Chelan is on the drier east side of the Cascades, annual precipitation there averages only 33 inches. Most of this falls between October and April as snow that accumulates to depths of 5 to 7 feet. The higher trails are generally clear by July. Rain in the east is a rarity between May and September. Temperatures here reach the high 80s to 90s in summer, and lows in winter average between zero and 20 degrees.

## ECOSYSTEM

Forest communities within the park vary both by location, east or west of the backbone ranges, and altitude. Forests in westside valleys consist of western hemlock, red alder, Douglas-fir, and western red cedar, and in damper spots willows, vine maple, big-leaf maple, birch, dogwood, black cottonwood, and chokecherry. In the understory are salal, Oregon grape, huckleberry, Oregon boxwood, twinflower, and bracken fern, and in drier spots kinnikinnick, dogbane, and spirea.

With increasing altitude the forest mix is dominated more by Pacific silver fir; some Alaska cedar joins the community, as do Sitka alder and mountain hemlock. In the highest zone on the west, mountain hemlock and subalpine fir prevail; there are local occurrences of alpine larch, whitebark pine, juniper, and several species of willow. Alpine meadows above treeline have a ground cover of grasses and heathers, and summer wildflowers such as glacier lily, cinquefoil, phlox, lupine, saxifrage, and penstemon.

At the highest levels east of the crest, mountain hemlock and subalpine fir make up large portions of the forest; Sitka alder, whitebark pine, juniper, and willow are still present, but a new addition to the forest is Engelmann spruce. With decreasing elevation, Douglas-fir, western hemlock, Alaska cedar, western larch, and western white pine reappear.

Lower-level forests east of the divide shift to Pacific silver fir, grand fir, Douglas-fir, western hemlock, western red cedar, ponderosa pine, lodgepole pine, whitebark pine, willows, Sitka alder, vine maple, and dogwood. The Big Beaver Valley in the Ross Lake NRA holds one of the largest stands of old-growth western red cedar in the coterminous United States. The forest floor at lower levels is made up of Oregon grape, spirea, Oregon boxwood, willow, western prince's pine, twinflower, bracken fern, serviceberry, starflower, orange honeysuckle, and oceanspray; these are joined by kinnikinnick and dogbane in drier locations.

On the slopes east of the Stehekin the woodlands shift to Pacific silver fir, whitebark fir, and western larch; higher still the forest becomes subalpine fir, Engelmann spruce,

and subalpine fir. At upper elevations the forest tapers to subalpine larch, and under-
foot, heather and rock.

Among the larger mammals found in the park's interior are elk, mule deer, white-
tailed deer, moose, mountain goat, black bear, mountain lion, lynx, and red fox. Smaller
inhabitants include porcupine, mink, raccoon, striped skunk, wolverine, ermine, river
otter, beaver, marten, snowshoe hare, and long-tailed weasel. The smallest creatures
found here are moles, pika, hoary marmot, chipmunks, squirrels, voles, deermouse,
and bog lemming.

The most often seen of the 150 bird species in the area are blue and ruffed grouse,
American flicker, red-breasted nuthatch, black-capped chickadee, Steller's jays, and ptarmigan. Species on state or federal threatened and endangered lists that have been sighted

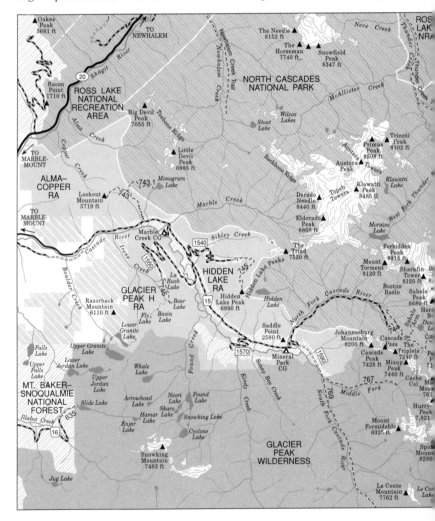

in the park are fishers, gray wolf, grizzly bear, peregrine falcon, bald eagle, northern goshawk, pileated woodpecker, northern spotted owl, sandhill crane, American white pelican, Swainson's hawk, trumpeter swan, ferruginous hawk, and common loon.

## GEOLOGY

The southeast–northwest orientation of the major geological structures in the North Cascades tends to confirm tectonic theories that the region was once a microcontinent located in the mid-Pacific that collided with the North American continent some 50 million to 90 million years ago. This terrane is thought to have made initial contact in southern California, then slid northwest before becoming firmly docked to North America between the Pacific Northwest and Alaska. The collision triggered the uplift of

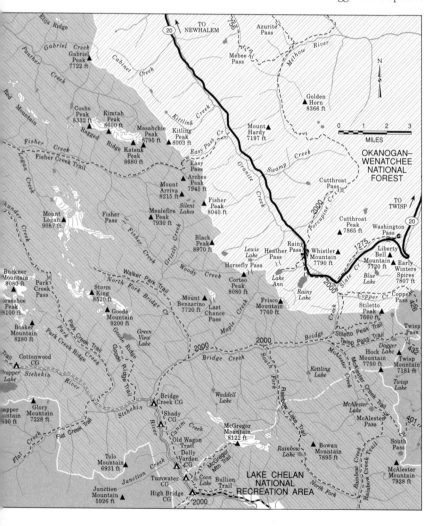

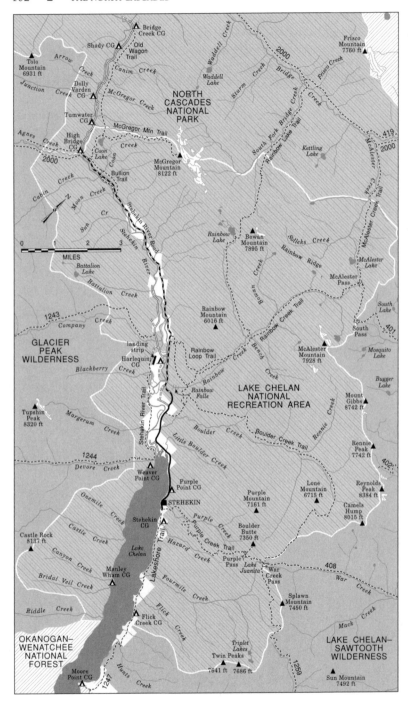

the Cascade crest, and folding and fracturing, oriented in the direction of the movement of the plates, created the sheer north faces characteristic of peaks in this region.

The backbone of the area is composed of older metamorphic gneisses formed between 500 million and 700 million years ago, the crystalline core of the microcontinent. A long thrust fault runs north–south along the west side of Mount Shuksan. On its west side are slates and schists ranging between 300 million and 600 million years in age. The rock on the east side of the complex consists of metamorphosed schists, gneisses, and a good deal of migmatite, more than 180 million years old, formed off the east coast of the North Cascades long before it joined the west coast of North America.

This base was intruded about 100 million years ago by granodiorite and quartz diorite in the area northeast of Bridge Creek and along the line of ridges between the upper Stehekin River and the town of Newhalem. The Picket Range and the Mount Redoubt area are made up of relatively young granite and granodiorite intrusions that occurred 10 million to 40 million years ago, after the docking of North Cascades terrane.

*A hiker surveys Easy Ridge in North Cascades National Park. In the background is Mount Ruth (center) and the rocky summit of Mount Shuksan.*

A major north–south fault line runs along the east bank of Ross Lake. The region between this fault and the Hozomeen fault line to the east that marks the west boundary of the Methow graben, is composed of uplifted greenstone, a metamorphosed basalt. Jack Mountain, on the southwest edge of the Ross Lake RNA, is believed to have been thrust to the east along a horizontal fault line as it overrode younger sedimentary rocks.

An ice age that began 2 million to 3 million years ago created thick glaciers that carved deep valleys in the underlying rock. About 15,000 years ago the Puget lobe of the Cordilleran ice sheet reached east up the Skagit Valley to the vicinity of Newhalem. Another lobe of that glacial ice rode down the Skagit headwaters from Canada, flowing over divides untouched in previous periods of glaciation. However, the portion of the Skagit Valley between Newhalem and Ross Lake was not in the route of the glacial flow; the deep, V-shaped river course here was cut solely by erosion.

As the glaciers that formed the Stehekin Valley and Lake Chelan retreated, a lobe of the continental ice sheet advanced across the Columbia River Plateau to deposit a moraine that blocked the lower end of the valley now filled by Lake Chelan, causing the level of the lake to rise by hundreds of feet. The 51.5-mile-long, 1,548-foot-deep lake has seen many adjustments in its water level over the ages, some caused by earthquakes, others by people. Today it is the largest lake in the coterminous United States that is so deeply carved through the mountains that frame it. Damming the Chelan River at its outlet in 1928 stabilized the lake at its current level.

Most of the present, surface features of the park are a result of glacial erosion by both continental ice sheets and alpine glaciers. The major drainages have steep walls and the wide, U-shaped floors characteristic of glacier-formed valleys. The lower ends of many creeks and rivers have carved narrow, steep-walled gorges through alluvial deposits near their mouths. Alpine glaciers, the ancestors of those remaining today, are responsible for cutting the dozens of cliff-walled cirques and chiseling the sharp ragged peaks that line the major ridges throughout the region.

## HISTORY

There is some evidence of prehistoric use of the North Cascades by natives who quarried chert for tools and weapons, fished for salmon, and visited the high country to hunt mountain goat. Artifacts found near Hozomeen Mountain indicate a long period of Indian habitation, and two tribes lived in or regularly visited the area: the Lower Thompson tribe above the Skagit Gorge, and the Skagits below it. Fading lines of petroglyphs on lakeside cliffs opposite Stehekin retain an indecipherable record of early inhabitants in the Lake Chelan area. The few passes through the rugged mountains were critical trade routes between tribes in the Puget Sound and those in the Columbia River Basin. One of the most popular routes, still followed by today's trails, crossed the Cascade crest at Twisp Pass, descended along Bridge Creek to the Stehekin River, then headed upstream over Cascade Pass and dropped to the Skagit River via the Cascade River.

The earliest non-natives in this part of the Cascades were trappers and fur traders who first entered the area in the late 1700s via Cascade Pass, using the old Indian trade route. A Swiss topographer surveyed the boundary between Great Britain (Canada) and the United States between 1857 and 1859, and mapped some of the upper Skagit drainage.

The first whites to explore the head of Lake Chelan were surveyors who, in the 1870s, were seeking possible rail routes over the Cascades. In 1882 an Army group under Lieutenant H. H. Pierce claimed to have discovered the head of the lake and the river flowing into it; the officer graciously named the river for himself, but it is now called the Stehekin.

In 1877 prospectors headed up the Skagit but found only traces of placer below the mouth of its gorge. They later struggled upstream to the vicinity of Ruby Creek, where they found increasingly better placers, enough to trigger a minor gold rush. Prospectors poured into the area at the end of the 1870s, but access was a constant inhibitor to mining production, since the Skagit Gorge could only be traversed via precarious cliff-wall ledges and, at Devils Elbow, a shaky suspension bridge and a system of ladders. The Fraser River and Caribou gold strikes soon lured most prospectors north, although limited mining was carried on in the area until the 1950s.

Between 1885 and 1889, highly promising galena ledges were discovered in Boston Basin, near Cascade Pass. These were traced into the Doubtful Lake and Horseshoe basins. All three basins were rapidly plastered with claims over the next three to four years. The ore, rich in silver and lead, with traces of gold, piled up near tunnel mouths for lack of a means to get it to market.

In 1889 the first steamer on Lake Chelan was launched, and settlers moved to the head of the lake during 1889 and 1890. By 1891, a trail ran 6.5 miles up the south side of the river, then crossed it and followed its north side into the upper valley. The initial road up the valley was platted in 1891, and the current route was built in 1897. In ensuing years prospectors worked downstream from Cascade Pass to Bridge Creek, Flat Creek, Agnes Creek, Coon Lake, Company Creek, Rainbow Creek, and Boulder Creek. The influx of 700 to 800 miners in 1892 eventually dissipated as the value of the ore played out. Limited mining activity continued in Horseshoe Basin until 1948. A rich silver strike was discovered at the head of Thunder Creek in 1892, but again transportation difficulties thwarted exploitation of the find, and operations there folded by 1913. Today the economic mainstays of the tiny community of Stehekin are recreation and tourism.

Opening access to the upper Skagit and creating a link between the Skagit and Methow Valleys concerned both regions as early as 1893. Whatcom County partisans lobbied for a route over Hannegan and Whatcom Passes, while Skagit County citizens preferred one up the Skagit River and over Cascade Pass. When the former route was ruled not feasible, proponents of the latter split into the Cascade Pass crowd and another faction who wished to extend the crude road that had been cut from Winthrop to the Harts Pass mines.

Cascade Pass was selected, money was appropriated in 1895, and construction in 1896 pushed a rough road on the west to within three miles of the pass, where the road end remains today. A dirt road was cut up the east side of the pass from Stehekin to Bridge Creek in 1899, and was later extended to the Black Warrior Mine in Horse-shoe Basin. Despite heavy lobbying to complete the road across the pass, nothing was achieved by 1929, when the stock market crash eliminated funding. The scenic and wilderness value of the area was recognized before momentum for construction could be regenerated, and in 1934 it became part of the newly created North Cascades Primitive Area.

The die was cast in 1940 when Forest Service managers, probably out of a desire to retrieve logs cut during the Ross Dam construction, convinced the Highway Department to back a route over Rainy and Washington Passes. Road construction from Newhalem to Thunder Creek was started in 1958, and from the Methow toward Washington Pass in 1962. The long-awaited North Cascades Scenic Highway opened in 1972.

Skagit Power was the first to attempt damming the Skagit in 1909; the effort failed due to problems getting construction materials into the gorge. In 1918 Seattle City Light began construction of a diversion dam at Gorge Creek to supply power to the city and to other dam projects upriver. The railroad was extended up the Skagit to Newhalem in 1921 to support construction, and the first dam was finished in 1924. The design and construction of a second dam at Diablo began immediately. After delays caused by the financial market crash in 1929, the 389-foot Diablo Dam was finished in 1936. A year later the need for additional power triggered design work on the Ross Dam. This 540-foot-high structure was completed in 1949. The last dam built replaced the original diversion dam at Newhalem with the present 300-foot-high Gorge Dam in 1960. Although City Light applied for permits for three additional dams in the drainage, rising environmental consciousness in the 1980s stymied any further hydroelectric projects.

Vestiges of the region's history still remain within the park, and have been designated or proposed as National Historic Register sites. These include old log cabins and backcountry shelters, the Black Warrior Mine, monuments marking the international boundary, and the three remaining lookouts of the six originally constructed in the region.

## HIKING
### Nooksack River Trails

*Copper Mountain Trail.* 15 miles/m (H). At a junction (4,240 ft) northeast of Hannegan Pass, this path heads up the steep, forested face on the north side of the drainage. After a few switchbacks it crosses the upper forks of Hells Gorge, where it breaks into alpine meadows and traces the ridge top (5,500 ft) east. The open crest offers endless views of Ruth Mountain, Mount Shuksan, and the vast expanse of the wilderness heart of the park. At 3 miles a spur drops to tiny Egg Lake (5,180 ft); the main route continues along the scenic ridge top to the lookout atop Copper Mountain (7,142 ft). Here a sweeping panorama embraces the Border Peaks, Slesse, Nodoubt, Redoubt, Bear, and Mox Peaks, and the whole jagged crest of the north Pickets. Switchbacks descend northeast from the open crest past the tight, cliff-bound cirque containing Copper Lake (5,263 ft). The way enters broken subalpine forest,

*Mount Challenger, swathed in the Challenger Glacier, lies deep in the North Cascades National Park.*

then continues down through long switchbacks in old-growth forest to rejoin the Chilliwack Trail north of Indian Creek (2,320 ft).

**Chilliwack Trail.** *17 miles/m (H,S).* This is an old miners' route to the Caribou gold fields in Canada. From Hannegan Pass (5,046 ft) a few switchbacks through sub-alpine forest lead to meadows at the head of the Chilliwack River, where the Copper Mountain Trail takes off. The rapid, wooded descent to Copper Creek Camp (3,100 ft) is followed by a gentler grade that works its way down near the river. In another mile a cable car provides safe passage across the Chilliwack for hikers. The route bends around a ridge nose and past a junction with the Brush Creek Trail, then continues down the widening valley bottom, most of the way in brush and dense timber. Beyond Indian Creek it meets the north end of the Copper Mountain Trail. The Chilliwack is followed downstream to the Canadian border (2,050 ft), and on to Chilliwack Lake.

**Brush Creek Trail.** *5.1 miles/m (H,S).* This route leaves the Chilliwack Trail near the mouth of Brush Creek (2,640 ft) and traces the north side of the creek upstream, always deep in woods and along a brushy stream bottom. A gradual climb gives way to a steady uphill grind to Whatcom Pass (5,206 ft) and the Little Beaver Trail. Spectacular views from the pass are but a hint of what is available from short boot-paths south to the shoulder of Whatcom Peak or north to the meadowed arm above Tapto Lakes (5,670 to 5,750 ft). To the south lie the massive summit of Whatcom Peak and the immense white swath of the Challenger Glacier sweeping up to rugged, rocky summit pinnacles.

## Westside Ross Lake Trails

**Big Beaver Trail.** *15 miles/m (H,S).* Reach Ross Dam either by boat uplake from Diablo or via the Happy Falls Trail from Highway 20. Cross the dam (1,617 ft) and pick up the trail on its north side as it contours the sidehill 200 feet above the lake. After passing Ross Lake Resort, a gentle grade ascends across open sidehills with views of the lake, Ruby Arm, and Jack Mountain. The path swings north; contours northwest through Douglas-fir, hemlock, silver fir, and cedar; then drops in a few lazy switchbacks to a footbridge across Big Beaver Creek (1,618 ft). This point can also be reached by water taxi from the resort to Big Beaver Camp.

The way follows the north side of the creek up the broad, glacier-carved valley, passing lush green creek-bottom marshes, ponds, small lakes, and huge western red cedars. At 6.2 miles (1,900 ft) the trail enters the park and climbs rapidly along plunging Big Beaver Creek. Upstream the grade eases as it ascends to Beaver Pass (3,620 ft). The way is mostly in heavy forest with occasional avalanche-track vistas west to the vast glacial cirques and towers of the Pickets. After crossing the pass, switchbacks wind down into the Little Beaver Valley to meet the Little Beaver Trail (2,440 ft).

**Little Beaver Trail.** *16.9 miles/m (H,S).* The trailhead, on the trackless west shore of Ross Lake, must be reached via a boat to Little Beaver Campground (1,650 ft). The path climbs switchbacks above the narrow channel at the mouth of Little Beaver Creek, then heads west above the creek. At 2.5 miles it enters the park and wanders up the bottom of a wide, glacier-cut valley between high, forested walls to meet the Big Beaver

*Big Beaver Valley holds a spectacular stand of old-growth western red cedar.*

Trail (2,440 ft). A gradual ascent continues up an ever-narrowing valley, with cliffs en-croaching on either side. At 2,950 feet kiss the easy grade good-bye and fight through fifty-six switchbacks hacked up wooded cliffs to Whatcom Pass (5,206 ft). Here are outstanding views of the northern Pickets and the immense expanse of the Challenger Glacier.

## Skagit River Trails

*Thornton Lakes Trail.* 4.8 miles/m (H). From the end of the Thornton Creek Road (2,500 ft), 11 miles east of Marblemount, the tread swings into the Thornton Creek drainage on an abandoned logging road, passing through clearcuts. After crossing the creek and reversing direction, the old road gives way to a true trail, which turns uphill with a vengeance. The route switchbacks up through old-growth forest, then pauses briefly in a small flat at the park boundary before switchbacks resume to gain the ridge crest (5,050 ft). A ridge-top scramble north to Trappers Peak (5,966 ft) is rewarded by an outstanding view of the ragged Picket Range. The path drops a short distance west to lower Thornton Lake (4,486 ft), nestled below the cliff wall of Trappers Peak. Scramble routes work up to Middle (4,700 ft) and Upper (5,040 ft) Thornton Lakes. These two lakes are not free of ice until mid- to late summer.

**Newhalem Creek Trail.** *4 miles/e (H,S).* An old logging road leaves the campground (520 ft) on the south side of Highway 20 at Newhalem, and heads south up Newhalem Creek and becomes a trail. In 2.8 miles it enters the park and passes through a series of large clearcuts to a trail-end campsite (2,300 ft). The slashes in the forest offer views of jagged Teebone Ridge.

**Sourdough Mountain Trail.** *5.5 miles/m (H,S).* The route starts at the northwest side of Diablo (900 ft), and shoots straight up the wooded hillside, resorting to switchbacks only when the slope gets *really* steep. The nose of the ridge is gained at 3,800 feet, where the route enters the park and continues a long gradual ascent north to Sourdough Creek. It climbs east and, with a few more switchbacks, reaches the rocky meadow atop Sourdough Mountain. The lookout, originally built in 1916 and rebuilt in 1933, sits atop the high point (5,985 ft) at the east end of the mountain. The panorama includes nearby Colonial, Snowfield, Pyramid, and Pinnacle Peaks, and in the distance Boston and Buckner, the Picket Range, Canada's Chilliwack Range, Skagit Peak, and Jack and Crater Mountains. Below are Diablo and Ross Lakes.

**Pyramid Lake Trail.** *2.25 miles/e (H).* The track leaves the south side of Highway 20 (1,100 ft) east of the spur road to Diablo, and climbs a forested rib on the east side of Pyramid Creek. A gradual ascent through old-growth Douglas-fir and hemlock and up a last few switchbacks ends at the pocket meadow holding tiny Pyramid Lake (2,630 ft). The clearing gives a glimpse of the impressive 1,000-foot-high summit block of Pyramid Peak.

**Diablo Lake Trail.** *3.8 miles/m (H).* About 1.5 miles east of the spur to Diablo, turn north on the road down to Diablo Dam, cross the top of the dam, and in little over a mile reach a onetime resort, the home of the North Cascades Environmental Center (1,227 ft). A path leaves east and wanders upstream along the banks of Deer Creek to the base of cliffs above Buster Brown Flat. It picks its way up and across a narrow bench between cliff bands and contours a rocky bluff (1,820 ft) with great views down to Diablo Lake and Thunder Arm and up to the Colonial Glacier and its surrounding peaks. The route rounds a steep ridge nose, traverses lightly forested cliffs, then descends to the suspension bridge (1,220 ft) across the Skagit below Ross Dam. From the east side of the river, the powerhouse road is followed uphill to the Happy Falls Trail, which leads back to Highway 20.

**Thunder Creek Trail.** *18.9 miles/m (H,S).* From the south end of Colonial Creek Campground (1,220 ft) a path heads along the bank of Thunder Arm to a bridge across Thunder Creek. The way continues through dense old-growth Douglas-fir, hemlock, and cedar into the heart of the Thunder Creek Valley. A few meadows resulting from old forest fires offer dramatic views up to the Neve Glacier and Snowfield and to the Colonial Creek peaks. At 6 miles (1,940 ft) the trail enters the park south of McAllister Creek. It crosses Fisher Creek and follows it steeply uphill to avoid a large valley-bottom swamp in the Thunder Creek basin. At 3,130 feet the Fisher Creek Trail breaks

*Hikers pause along the banks of Thunder Creek.*

away, and this route descends steep slopes to the valley floor (1,950 ft) near the south end of the swamp.

Creek and trail climb a narrowing drainage to Skagit Queen Creek (3,040 ft), then the route switchbacks up a steep shelf to an alpine valley as it traces the creek bed upstream through narrowing canyon walls. The way weaves up the basin headwall above the source of Thunder Creek to the rock cleft of Park Creek Pass (6,080 ft), where it meets the Park Creek Trail from the Stehekin.

**Fisher Creek Trail.** *10.5 miles/m (H).* After leaving the Thunder Creek Trail (3,130 ft), this route follows the densely forested bottom of Fisher Creek east below Ragged Ridge to a basin meadow (5,200 ft) north of Mount Arriva. The trail turns abruptly up the steep north slopes and grinds in switchbacks to Easy Pass (6,500 ft).

## Eastside Ross Lake Trails

**East Bank Trail.** *20 miles/m (H).* From the Panther Creek Bridge (1,800 ft) on Highway 20, the trail drops north to cross Ruby Creek, then heads west above the shore of Ruby Arm. In 3 miles the route passes the Jack Mountain Trail, then swings north through Hidden Hand Pass (2,540 ft). It wanders slowly downhill to the north to close with the east bank of Ross Lake near Roland Point. The trail remains near the shore of this inland fjord for the remainder of its 20-mile length. The Dry Creek Pass Trail heads east into the Pasayten Wilderness about a mile north of Devils Creek, and the Lightning Creek Trail heads inland on the north side of its namesake. The East Bank Trail ends at the lakeshore 2 miles farther, at the start of the Desolation Lookout Trail (1,750 ft).

**Jack Mountain Trail.** *3 miles/m (H).* From the 3-mile point of the East Bank Trail (1,930 ft), this route heads in the only direction it seems to know—up! Fifty-four switchbacks later, the way breaks into beautiful meadows for a more gradual lateral ascent east to its end at a ridge-top saddle (6,000 ft). Gentle, open slopes lead north to a pair of knobs with breathtaking views of Jack and Crater Mountains, the Picket Range, and Pyramid, Pinnacle, Colonial, and Snowfield Peaks.

**Desolation Peak Lookout Trail.** *4.5 miles/m (H).* At the north end of the East Bank Trail (1,720 ft) the route heads sharply upward, switchbacking all the way, through young forest regenerated after a 1926 burn. Occasional open spots give glimpses down to Ross Lake. The way breaks out into meadows at 4,500 feet, but unrelenting switchbacks continue up to the ridge crest and north along the crest to a bald knob (5,895 ft). Fields of flowers escort the track to the lookout atop Desolation Peak (6,102 ft). North, the sheer 2,000-foot walls of Hozomeen Mountain loom close at hand. South, the icy expanse of the Nohokomeen Glacier sweeps up to the massive summit of Jack Mountain. In the distance are the Pasayten highlands, Eldorado, Snowfield, Colonial, the Picket Range, and Mount Baker, and below is the blue ribbon of Ross Lake.

**Lightning Creek Trail.** *10 miles/m (H,S).* This link between the East Side Trail and the Canadian border leaves that trail at Lightning Creek (1,700 ft). It switchbacks out of the narrow creek bottom to the sidehill above the creek, follows the drainage east and north, then descends gradually to meet the creek at Deer Lick Cabin (1,920 ft). Just beyond, Trail 749 heads east into the Pasayten Wilderness. The route continues north, along the east bank of Lightning Creek to the dense, foreboding cedar grove of Nightmare Camp. A gradual ascent traces Lightning Creek as it swings west to its western source, Willow Lake (2,853 ft).

**Willow Creek (Jackass Pass) Trail.** *5 miles/e (H,S).* The last link between the East Bank Trail and Canada heads west from Willow Lake (2,853 ft), descending a shallow, forested valley. It passes a short spur to Hozomeen Lake (2,923 ft), then wanders down to the Hozomeen Campground, on Ross Lake just south of the Canadian border. This trailhead can be reached via the road south into the Skagit Valley Recreation Area from Trans-Canada Highway 1, near Hope, British Columbia.

## Stehekin River Trails

**Walker Park (North Fork of Bridge Creek) Trail.** *9.5 miles/m-d (H,S).* This old miners route leaves the PCT at its 2.7-mile point, and heads north along the North Fork of Bridge Creek in a deep, densely wooded, U-shaped valley. Avalanche tracks offer brief, brushy peeks to the high cliffs that frame the drainage. The original route led north past prospects in Grizzly and Fisher Creeks to Fisher Pass. The present trail fords Grizzly Creek (3,150 ft) and continues along the North Fork, breaking into valley-bottom meadows with breathtaking views of waterfalls cascading from the hanging glaciers at the base of the faces of Goode and Storm King Mountains. The way fades into meadows (4,200 ft) in the great cirque on the south side of Mount Logan.

**Twisp Pass (Fireweed) Trail.** *5 miles/m (H,S).* From the PCT at the mouth of McAlester Creek (3,640 ft), this old Indian path climbs gradually but relentlessly along the East Fork of McAlester Creek to Dagger Lake (5,508 ft). The way then climbs to the head of the drainage and Twisp Pass (6,064 ft), where it becomes Trail 432 as it leaves the park.

**Stiletto Peak Trail.** *3.5 miles/d (H).* From Trail 2000, 0.6 mile north of the Twisp Pass Trail, switchbacks climb a steep wooded slope with no respite for 2,100 vertical feet. The way then contours ridge-top meadows, crosses a small notch to a tiny creek-head cirque, then climbs once more through parkland to the site of a fire lookout (7,223 ft) removed in 1953. The 360-degree views remain; these include Goode Mountain's face and broad glacier, Mount Benzarino, Frisco Mountain, Early Winter Spires, and Silver Star.

**Goode Ridge Trail.** *5 miles/m (H).* This route leaves the Stehekin Road (2,200 ft) and climbs steadily up the broad, forested rib complex of Goode Ridge. Near the head of Theis Creek the way breaks into the open as it continues inexorably up the narrowing ridge. It follows the crest to end on a small plateau (6,600 ft) atop the cliffs above Green View Lake. Here are outstanding views of the Bridge Creek, Park Creek, and Stehekin River drainages, as well as the surrounding summits.

**Park Creek Trail.** *8 miles/m (H,S).* Starting on the Stehekin River Road (2,310 ft) 18.5 miles from Stehekin, the route switchbacks up above the Park Creek gorge, bends into the drainage, skirts 800-foot-high cliffs at the southeast end of Park Creek Ridge, and enters the broadening valley bottom to the northwest. The way breaks into meadows as the valley opens to a wide cirque surrounded by waterfall-laced walls rising 4,000 feet to Booker and Buckner Mountains, the Buckner Glacier, Storm King, and Goode Mountain. The track leaves the valley floor in a chain of switchbacks up a steep face to a pocket valley, where flowered meadows, heathers, and snowfields lead to the narrow, rockbound notch of Park Creek Pass (6,080 ft).

## Cascade River Trails

**Cascade Pass Trail.** *6.5 miles/m (H).* This historic trail, a route across 5,423-foot-high Cascade Pass that was used by Indians and early explorers, has been so loved to death in recent years that the Park Service has turned it into a near city-park path to protect the fragile ecology. On the west the trail leaves the end of the Cascade River Road (3,650 ft). Easy-grade switchbacks crawl through forest to break into parkland, fingertips away from Cascade Peak, The Triplets, and the rumble of ice peeling off the north face of Johannesburg. The route descends east of the pass to Pelton Basin campsites, the Horseshoe Basin Trail, and a constantly changing horizon of jagged peaks on either side. At its east terminus the path joins the Stehekin River Road at Cottonwood Camp (2,750 ft).

**Horseshoe Basin Trail.** *1.5 miles/m (H).* In pre-wilderness days this road was used to transport ore and mining supplies between Stehekin and the Black Warrior Mine. Today the path leaves the Cascade Pass Trail between Doubtful and Basin Creeks (3,640 ft), then bends north into the latter's basin. A few switchbacks at the end of the gradual climb end at the mine (5,000 ft), wrapped in lower cirque cliffs draped by dozens of ribbon waterfalls. The mine ruins are interesting to explore (with care). Don't remove artifacts! The more hardy may choose to search for old miners' tracks through the cliffs east of the mine to gain the wider upper cirque, which blazes with a rainbow of wildflower colors soon after the snows melt. Mining claims once filled this basin up to the base of aptly named Ripsaw Ridge, as prospectors chased galena ledges exposed by glaciers.

**Trail 745, Hidden Lake.** *4.5 miles/e-m (H).* From the clearcut end of FR 1540 (4,000 ft), the path climbs first through forest, then breaks into meadows and wildflowers as it switchbacks up to the head of the East Fork of Sibley Creek. A long diagonal ascent followed by a lazy pair of zigzags reaches a saddle (6,590 ft) above Hidden Lake. The main trail continues a short distance to the lookout cabin atop Hidden Lake Peaks (6,890 ft), maintained by volunteers. A rough way-trail drops from the saddle down talus slopes to the tight cirque holding Hidden Lake (5,733 ft).

**Trail 743, Lookout Mountain.** *4.7 miles/m (H).* East of Lookout Creek the track leaves the Cascade River Road (1,250 ft) for a knee-numbing switchback assault on the wooded ridge to the north. The grade tapers to just steep 2,200 feet higher as it continues its climb to the junction with Trail 743.1 (4,150 ft). More twisty trail gains a meadowed side-slope with views into the Cascade River drainage. After zigzags conquer a steep cliff, the way winds around the east and south sides of a knob to a volunteer-maintained fire lookout (5,699 ft) with grand views of the Skagit River valley and the peaks of Cascade Pass.

**Trail 743.1, Monogram Lake.** *2.2 miles/m (H).* Leaving Trail 743 (4,150 ft), this spur climbs steep timbered slopes and breaks into meadows as it swings around an open nose (5,400 ft), then descends to the shore of Monogram Lake (4,873 ft). North slopes sweep up to the Monogram Glacier and the peaks at the south end of Teebone Ridge.

## Lower Stehekin Trails

In summer a Park Service shuttle van will carry you up the Stehekin Valley Road for a fee. Private businesses also have taxi services available.

**Lakeshore Trail.** *4 miles/e (H,S).* From the Golden West Visitor Center in Stehekin, the path heads south along the northeast shore of Lake Chelan. The grade is easy, with a few ups and downs that never rise more than 500 feet above the shore. The trail runs through stands of ponderosa pine and Douglas-fir with an understory decorated by a botanical dictionary of flowers, running from balsamroot to yellow bells. There are two campgrounds along the route, one a short distance from the trailhead and one near the NRA boundary beyond Flick Creek. At the NRA boundary, the route enters the Lake Chelan–Sawtooth Wilderness as Trail 1247, then continues another 13.2 miles to Prince Creek.

**Purple Creek Trail.** *8 miles/m (H,S).* Also starting at Stehekin's Golden West Visitor Center, this route strikes uphill through Douglas-fir, ponderosa pine, and whitebark pine, twisting through twenty-seven tight switchbacks before crossing Purple Creek. Another thirty switchbacks in mountain hemlock and subalpine fir, then in larch-rimmed meadows, reach tiny Lake Juanita (6,665 ft). A 0.5-mile spur leads west to the top of Boulder Butte (7,350 ft), the site of a fire lookout in the 1930s and '40s. Views span Lake Chelan, the Stehekin Valley, and a horizon of jagged peaks. Just above the lake, the Summit Trail heads southeast to the NRA border and Trail 1259. A few hundred feet farther is War Creek Pass (6,770 ft) where Trail 408 heads east into the Lake Chelan–Sawtooth Wilderness, and the Boulder Creek Trail drops north to the valley below.

**Rainbow Loop Trail.** *3.2 miles/e (H,S).* The south trailhead (1,170 ft) is 2.7 miles up-valley from Stehekin Landing. It climbs to a forested bench, and, after passing the start of the Boulder Creek Trail, reaches an open bluff (2,200 ft) with views down to the valley and Lake Chelan. The path contours the bench, then crosses Rainbow Creek to the lower end of the Rainbow Creek Trail. A gradual descent rejoins the Stehekin Valley Road (1,230 ft) 5 miles from Stehekin Landing.

**Boulder Creek Trail.** *11.5 miles/m (H,S).* Starting 0.8 mile from the south end of the Rainbow Loop Trail (2,100 ft), this route begins a steady grind up Boulder Creek, first through Douglas-fir, ponderosa, and whitebark pine, then through meadows. A traverse reaches the creek at 3,700 feet; the way traces the bank as the creek swings south into the head of the drainage. Here switchbacks gain the shoulder (6,530 ft) of Lone Mountain, where the forest opens to views of flowered meadows flowing from the summits of Reynolds and Rennie Peaks. The wooded rib is followed southeast to a ridgeline hump (7,484 ft), the NRA border. The boundary is followed south across a few undulations to War Creek Pass (6,770 ft), to meet the Purple Creek Trail and Trail 408.

**Rainbow Creek Trail.** *10 miles/m (H,S).* This route leaves the Rainbow Loop Trail 1.5 miles from its south trailhead. Switchbacks climb above the west side of Rainbow Creek, then a traverse merges with the rising creek. Crossing to the east bank, the ascent continues through meadows to Bench Creek, the beginning of the Rainbow Lake Trail. A climb through dense old-growth forest recrosses the creek, and switchbacks gain McAlester Pass (6,017 ft). At the pass, meadows spotted with a few pines afford views of the steep north side of McAlester Mountain and the summits of the crest running north to Twisp Pass. The McAlester Creek Trail continues northwest, and the South Creek Pass Trail strikes southeast for 1.4 miles to South Pass (6,300 ft), where it continues into the Lake Chelan–Sawtooth Wilderness as Trail 401.

**Rainbow Lake Trail.** *6.1 miles/m (H,S).* From the Rainbow Creek Trail at Bench Creek (3,750 ft) this path switchbacks down to cross Rainbow Creek, then back up the opposite side as it heads west along the north fork of the creek. The track continues a gradual ascent through meadow breaks in the spruce forest to the head of the drainage. A brief climb of a rocky basin headwall reaches Rainbow Lake (5,630 ft), which sits in a forested bowl with meadows at either end. From Rainbow Lake the route climbs to the west shoulder (6,230 ft) of Bowan Mountain, then switchbacks down steep rocky meadows to the South Fork of Bridge Creek. The trail follows the creek downstream to the PCT at Bridge Creek (3,250 ft).

**McAlester Creek Trail.** *5.5 miles/m (H,S).* From McAlester Pass (6,017 ft) gentle switchbacks drop to McAlester Lake (5,507 ft), where lake-edge meadows poke out of open forest cover. From the lake, the track drops down steep, wooded side-slopes to follow the bank of McAlester Creek to the Twisp Pass (Fireweed) Trail (3,820 ft).

**Stehekin River Trail.** *4 miles/e (H,S).* This valley-bottom path follows the original wagon trail used before the present road was built. From the road spur along the southwest side of the Stehekin landing strip (1,200 ft), the near-level path weaves through open woods along the southwest side of the river. The way passes tiny flowered clearings and beaver ponds to reach Weaver Point Campground (1,100 ft), the original starting point of the Stehekin Valley wagon road. Just above the campground, Trail 1244 heads up Devore Creek into the Glacier Peak Wilderness.

**Coon Lake Trail.** *1.2 miles/m (H,S).* Heading north from the High Bridge Guard Station (1,600 ft), a couple of lazy switchbacks gain the bench (2,210 ft) holding shallow Coon Lake, an excellent spot for watching waterfowl. A pretty waterfall cascades from a narrow cleft in the cliffs on the northeast side of the lake. The McGregor Mountain Trail leaves the north end of the lake.

**McGregor Mountain Trail.** *6.8 miles/d (H,S).* Steep is an understatement! This route leaves the north end of Coon Lake (1,980 ft) and heads up the precipitous slope along the west side of Coon Creek. One hundred forty-four tedious switchbacks later, it reaches a small, larch-rimmed basin holding Heaton Camp (7,000 ft). Beyond the camp, a tough scramble follows paint splotches marking a path over talus and ledges to the summit (8,122 ft). Breathtaking scenery abounds: the valley floor is a vertical mile and a half below; to the south are Bonanza, Agnes, Dome, Spire, and a host of other jagged summits; at the head of the Stehekin Valley are the Cascade Pass peaks; farther north are the Park Creek Pass summits; and due north is Mount Benzarino, with Ragged Ridge in the distance.

### Trail 2000, Pacific Crest National Scenic Trail. *13.2 miles/m (H,S).*

This trail, commonly known as the PCT, continues its journey north from the Stehekin River Road at Bridge Creek (2,170 ft), 16 miles upstream from Stehekin. It follows the broad, forested rim above the 200-foot-deep Bridge Creek gorge, with occasional glimpses northwest to Ragged and Memaloose Ridges, then drops to meet the Walker Park Trail (2,580 ft) at the mouth of the North Fork. The route continues upstream above the steep north bank of Bridge Creek, then enters a widening valley floor as it drops to the creek bank. Avalanche swaths provide breaks in the forest cover as the way heads east past the Rainbow Lake Trail to the Twisp Pass Trail. The path continues along the west bank of the creek to Highway 20 at Rainy Pass (4,900 ft).

## CLIMBING

North Cascades National Park combines glaciers, technical rock, and local altitude differentials exceeding 5,000 feet for some of the best alpine climbing in the coterminous

United States. Limited trails and rugged cross-country terrain mean that, with the exception of Mount Shuksan and some of the Cascade Pass peaks, most climbs are multiday efforts, with much of this time spent getting to and from climbing bases near objective peaks.

In the southeast corner of the park, a line of glaciated rock summits (7,760 to 8,970 ft) stretches northwest from Frisco Mountain. Some are nontechnical ascents; others are rock climbs of varying difficulty. The more difficult climbs, C-4 to C-5.5, are the narrow, rounded thumb of Fisher Peak (8,040 ft), the 1,000-foot north face of Meulefire Peak (7,930 ft), and the wide, unstable 1,400-foot north face of Arches Peak (7,945 ft). At the northwest end of this group is Ragged Ridge, a chain of ridge-top spikes between 7,230 feet and 8,795 feet. The highest of these, Mesahchie Peak (8,795 ft), is the only real challenge, between C-3 and C-5.

In the triangle between Fisher, Park, and Thunder Creeks are three huge glaciated massifs: Mount Logan (9,087 ft), Storm King (8,520 ft), and Goode Mountain (9,200 ft). Logan has challenging ice and rock routes, some in the high C-5 range. Storm King has four summits of nearly the same altitude, with rock routes rated C-4. Goode, with a dramatic glacier on the northeast face, has a half-dozen different approaches between C-3 and C-5.5.

Major summits along the crest north and east of Cascade Pass include Booker (8,280 ft), with a C-5.8 face; Buckner (9,080 ft), scramble and C-3 to C-4 ridge routes; Ripsaw Ridge (8,000 ft), dozens of closely spaced spires rated C-3 to C-5; Boston Peak (8,894 ft), C-3 to C-4; and Sahale Peak (8,680 ft), a relatively easy ascent.

The Boston Basin peaks offer several striking challenges for rock climbers. Sharkfin Tower (8,120 ft) and Sharks Tooth are narrow ridge-crest blades with all routes rated above C-5. Forbidden Peak (8,815 ft) is a stark tower rising above the huge Boston Glacier, with several exposed ridge and face routes between C-4 and C-5.10. Nearby Mount Torment (8,120 ft) has rock ledges and towers mostly in the C-3 to C-4 range.

Framed between McAllister, Thunder, and Marble Creeks are a host of rugged glacier-bound crags capped by the distinctive ice slope leading to the top of Eldorado Peak (8,868 ft). This glacier route is easier than several others rated as high as C-5.7. Southwest of Eldorado is The Triad (7,520 ft), with an exposed, steep C-5.6 wall. To the north are a host of spectacular needles (8,102 to 8,508 ft) between Eldorado and Klawatti Peak (8,485 ft). There are weeks of climbing challenges here, on solid C-3 to C-5.5 granite. Backbone Ridge (7,160 to 7,675 ft), to the northwest, has a string of short one- to four-pitch climbs up spires whimsically named The Coccyx, The Sacrum, Lumbar Point, and Thoracic Point.

Along the western rim of this segment of the park is Teebone Ridge, rising sharply above surrounding valleys. The ridge, between 6,840 and 7,055 feet, includes Little Devil, Baksit, and Big Devil Peaks; Fallen Angel; and a group of short gendarmes known as the Six Hellions. Although approaches are tedious, the rock summits are mostly short, enjoyable C-3 climbs.

Clustered south of Highway 20 in the vicinity of Diablo and Gorge Lakes are a group of pinnacles (7,182 to 8,347 ft) framing two good-sized glaciers. Here are Pyramid,

Pinnacle, Colonial, and Snowfield Peaks; Paul Bunyan's Stump; The Needle; and The Horseman. All rise more than a vertical mile above nearby valleys. Climbs are mixed ice and rock, with some routes up 40- to 45-degree ice and narrow, knife-edge arêtes rated C-4 to C-5.6.

Northwest from Diablo is the renowned Picket Range, a jumble of sharp rock summits rising above hanging glaciers that peel off 1,000-foot-high walls into deep valleys below. The southern component of this range, between 6,800 and 8,000 feet, contains McMillan Spire, twin summits that rise more than 2,000 feet from the glacier at their base. Inspiration Peak has a long, slabby, exposed C-5.9 face. Mount Degenhart and Pinnacle Peak (The Chopping Block) have classic, mixed ice and rock alpine routes. Mount Terror has C-3 to C-5.5 routes up various ridges and faces.

The northwest continuation of the Picket Range presents more jagged peaks. Mount Fury (8,292 ft) has no route easier than C-4, and several more difficult. Phantom Peak (8,045 ft) and Crooked Thumb (8,124 ft) are spectacular rock needles with sheer east faces. The capstone of the north Pickets is Mount Challenger (8,236 ft), with an imposing 2-square-mile glacier on its northeast flank. Steep, crevassed ice leads to rock summit blocks rated in the C-5 range. Anchoring the north end of the range is Whatcom Peak (7,574 ft), a massive ice and rock summit.

Another small subrange is framed by Goodell Creek, the East Fork of Bacon Creek, and Bald Eagle and Lonesome Creeks. The two significant peaks in this group are Mount Triumph (7,240 ft) and Mount Despair (7,292 ft). Triumph is a rock thumb with near-vertical to overhanging faces on three sides. Dual-summited Despair has a slabby 4,500-foot east face and a hanging glacier.

The group of summits along the park's west boundary south of Baker River are seldom climbed, due to long, tedious, cross-country approaches. Among these is Bacon Peak (7,066 ft), a massive, heavily glaciated summit with a broad, exposed 2,000-foot west face. Hagan Mountain (7,080 ft) is a string of short rock pyramids flanking an alpine glacier. The summits are interesting one- to two-lead pitches between C-3 and C-5.5. Mount Blum (7,680 ft) is a bulky peak with both nontechnical routes and exposed C-3 to C-5.9 ridge climbs.

The classic alpine beauty featured on more postcards, calendars, and book covers than any other peak in the North Cascades is Mount Shuksan (9,131 ft). Shuksan's distinctive pyramidal peak is draped with a jumble of hanging glaciers and flanked with knife-edge arêtes that offer some of the best mixed alpine climbing in the park. A dozen or more routes have been put up Shuksan itself; these run from a romp up the Sulphide Glacier and the traditional Fisher Chimneys combination of rock and ice, to the broken 55-degree ice cascade of the Price Glacier and the C-5.7 Northwest Rib. East of the summit, enclosing the huge Nooksack Cirque, are the impressive Nooksack Tower and Jagged Ridge. The Nooksack Tower combines near-vertical ice couloirs and a headwall face with 7 of 16 pitches classed over C-5.7.

In the remote north-central portion of the park is another subrange with rugged glaciated summits, long ridgelines of gendarmes, and striking near-vertical north faces. Bear Mountain (7,931 ft) has a wide 2,500-foot-high north wall, the upper third of

*Mount Shuksan offers fine climbing as well as classic beauty.*

which overhangs. Routes on this face run to 17 leads rated between C-5.3 and C-5.9. Mox Peaks (also known as Twin Spires; 8,407 and 8,504 ft), at the north end of Ridge of Gendarmes, are a pair of exposed rock fangs with no easy routes. The signature summit of this group is Mount Redoubt (8,969 ft); although it has a 1,700-foot rock wall to the northeast, easier routes reach the top from other sides and ridges. The third major summit in the area is Mount Spickard (8,879 ft), one of the few peaks in the area that has a steep glacier route to within 200 feet of the top.

The narrow confines of the Ross Lake RNA enclose few peaks of climbing interest. Hozomeen Mountain, marking the northeast border, is an impressive exception. This massive multi-summited peak rises abruptly more than 5,000 feet above the valley floor on the east side of Ross Lake. The sharply pointed summit pyramids have precipitous 2,000-foot rock faces and numerous individual crags on flanking ridges. The North Peak (8,066 ft) is the highest point on the massif; it has been climbed by several long C-4 to C-5 routes. The South Peak (8,003 ft) is the most difficult, with upper pitches ranked C-5.4 to C-5.6. The lesser Southwest Peak (7,471 ft) has a relatively easy route from the southwest and two from the south and west rated C-4 to C-5.

There are no truly difficult climbs in the Lake Chelan NRA, but a number of the summits have impressive faces. At the southwest corner of the NRA is Castle Rock (8,137 ft), named for the imposing west flank that rises 7,000 feet above the lake. Cross-country routes from Devore Creek gain the south ridge for an easy approach.

McGregor Mountain (8,122 ft), is a huge east–west trending massif that rises in a continuous succession of cliffs above the north side of the Stehekin Valley. The McGregor Mountain Trail (see Hiking, above) climbs the west corner of the peak, where a scramble continues to the top. Several other lower satellite summits are scattered along the arête to the east.

The crest along the boundary between the NRA and the Lake Chelan–Sawtooth Wilderness has the highest peak in the area, and probably its best climbing. Reynolds Peak (8,384 ft) has an awesome 2,500-foot north face and two distinct summit pyramids. Approaches from War Creek Pass or Trail 402 lead to C-3 to C-4 leads on the final summit block. The crest continues north, then west to Rennie Peak, Mount Gibbs, and McAlester Mountain. All follow the vertical north-face theme of the other peaks, but are easy scrambles from the southeast.

## WINTER SPORTS

Although most of the backcountry in the park is sealed by heavy snows and avalanches during winter, Mount Shuksan's Sulphide Glacier is an excellent late-spring trek once roads in the Baker Lake area melt out and make the approach viable. The lower portion of the trip roughly follows Trail 742 up the steep, timbered slopes of Shannon Creek to the lower edge of the Sulphide Glacier, then continues up the broad, easy-grade slope to the summit pyramid. Weather, crevasses, and lower-altitude avalanche slopes all add spice to the trip.

## WATER SPORTS

The Skagit River between Newhalem and Copper Creek is popular for rafting and kayaking. In addition to high mountain scenery, wildlife such as deer, raccoon, fox, coyote, beaver, and otter may be spotted along the river. Fall brings spawning salmon runs, and bald eagles winter along the river. The put-in point is Goodell Campground, and take-out spots are at Bacon Creek and Copper Creek. The water level fluctuates daily, depending on the power demands on the dams, but the river is always runable by paddlers with Class 3 experience.

The lower Stehekin offers diverse paddling opportunities. For the first 0.5 mile below the High Bridge Guard Station the river runs through a narrow channel with very challenging white-water rapids. Below that point, the river is rated Class 2 or lower, with major hazards being downed trees and logs, and the propensity of the river to shift its channel periodically. Put-ins are found at Bullion Camp and Harlequin Campground, and the take-out is at Weaver Point Campground at the mouth of the river.

Opposite: *Prusik Peak and adjoining Mount Temple Ridge are the capstones of the Upper Enchantment area.*

*chapter 3*   # The Central Cascades

# 13 Mount Higgins Region

## Higgins Mountain and Pressentin Roadless Areas

**Location:** In Skagit County, between Highway 530 and Highway 20, 4 to 20 miles west of Darrington
**Size:** Higgins Mountain, 13,177 acres; Pressentin, 15,057 acres
**Status:** Semiprimitive Nonmotorized
**Terrain:** Extremely steep timbered ridges culminate in sharp rocky summits.
**Elevation:** 500 to 5,274 feet
**Management:** USFS, Mount Baker–Snoqualmie National Forest, Darrington Ranger District
**Topographic maps:** Day Lake, Fortson, Gee Point, Mt. Higgins

West of Darrington, the valley floor drained by the North Fork of the Stillaguamish River is rimmed on the north and south by steep, forested hillsides that sweep nearly a mile to the sky. To the south lies the Boulder River Wilderness, and to the north are two small, rugged, roadless areas surrounded by an onslaught of logging roads and clearcuts. Only precipitous terrain and the presence of old-growth spotted owl habitat have saved these areas from a similar fate. A high, Y-shaped ridge, bounded by near-vertical walls, runs east and west through the center of the Higgins Mountain area, and steep-sided drainages pinwheel around Gee Point in the Pressentin area. Six small lakes are tucked into shelves below the ridge top.

Each area contains a trail leading to the sites of former fire lookouts. The two major summits of the Mount Higgins massif can be gained only by cross-country climbing routes. The highest point in the vicinity, Round Mountain (5,274 ft), was once scheduled for a lookout; a trail was put in to the top, but the structure was never built. Portions of the abandoned trail may still be found, and volunteers have proposed to reopen it.

The summits offer spectacular views down to the valley floor and across to the nearby ragged summits of Whitehorse and Three Fingers on its south side. The backbone of the Cascades, capped by ice-clad Glacier Peak, frames the eastern horizon. To the west, the Olympic Range rises above the waters of Puget Sound.

## CLIMATE

Annual precipitation in the area ranges between 80 and 100 inches, mostly falling as snow during fall and winter. The steep walls of the backbone ridge are laced with avalanche tracks from the heavy snowfall. Higher slopes become accessible by July, when most of the snow has melted. Temperatures are relatively mild year-round, with an average high in the mid-80s and an average low in the 20s.

## ECOSYSTEM

Although the lower slopes have some Douglas-fir, true fir, and western red cedar, the bulk of the dense forest consists of western hemlock at lower elevations, and mountain hemlock higher up. A few small, alpine meadows are found near the heads of creek drainages. Clearcuts and avalanche slopes along the access routes have a dense brush cover of vine maple, slide alder, and dwarf willow.

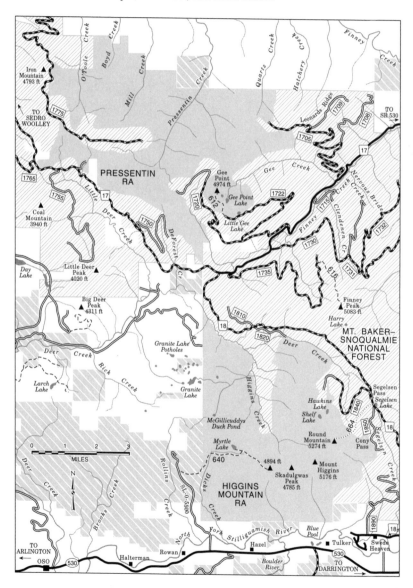

*Mount Higgins offers high views of the valley of the North Fork of the Stillaguamish River; Whitehorse Mountain is on the right.*

The forest is home to black-tailed deer, black bear, blue grouse, marten, and pileated woodpeckers. Old-growth forest remaining along the northwest edge of the area hosts spotted owls.

## GEOLOGY

The Mount Higgins massif is composed of metamorphosed sandstone and shale sharply folded into steep, southwest-dipping strata.

## HIKING

**Trail 640, Mount Higgins.** *4.5 miles/m (H,B,M).* Although the trailhead is on the east side of the SL-0-5500 road at 1,460 feet, a boot-path departs from the end of a switchback in another 1.5 miles (2,500 ft), shortcutting the lower first mile of the formal trail and meeting it near the national forest boundary. Both trailheads are on DNR land. The route climbs up the west side of the Dicks Creek drainage, eases at 3,400 feet, and passes a spur that drops west to Myrtle Lake (3,515 ft). After wending through a meadow at the head of Dicks Creek, the trail resumes its ascent through forest broken by boulder fields. The path ends at the top of the westernmost of the three summits of the massif (4,849 ft), the site of a former fire lookout built in 1926. The building collapsed from heavy snow in 1965.

**Trail 612, Gee Point.** *1.2 miles/m (H; S,B,M between 8/1 and 11/1).* This short hike starts from the end of FR 1722 (4,400 ft), where a brief climb to the north through timber reaches the ridge overlooking Gee Point Lake. The route follows the gradually ascending ridge top to Gee Point (4,974 ft) and broad views north to the Skagit River valley.

## CLIMBING

Skadulgwas Peak (4,785 ft) is the middle of three peaks along the Mount Higgins massif. The 1,000-foot north face of the summit block is nearly vertical, and its south face is a steep rock slab; however, there is a scramble route via the southwest ridge.

Mount Higgins (5,176 ft) is the easternmost, and highest, of the three summit peaks. Its east ridge is reached via a cross-country route that leaves FR 1850 near Deer Creek Pass, or from the end of FR 1890, north of Swede Heaven. The ridge can be followed west to a 200-foot, C-3 rock pitch just below the summit.

## 14  Boulder River Region

### Boulder River Wilderness; Boulder River Roadless Area

**Location:** In Snohomish County, 15 miles east of Granite Falls, between the North and South Forks of the Stillaguamish River and the Sauk River
**Size:** Wilderness, 49,000 acres; Boulder River, 32,307 acres *
**Status:** Designated Wilderness (1984); Roadless area is Semiprimitive Nonmotorized
**Terrain:** Brushy wooded slopes rise steeply from 1,000 feet to ridge tops in the range of 4,000 to 5,000 feet. The north–south backbone ridges have several rock peaks and pinnacles.
**Elevation:** 1,000 to 6,850 feet
**Management:** USFS, Mount Baker–Snoqualmie National Forest, Darrington Ranger District
**Topographic maps:** Bedal, Helena Ridge, Mallardy Ridge, Meadow Mountain, Mount Higgins, Silverton, White Chuck, Whitehorse Mountain

The Boulder River Wilderness and adjacent roadless area are located at the heart of a small subrange framed on the north and south by forks of the Stillaguamish River, and on the east by the Sauk River. A narrow, north–south axis ridge, serrated with sharp rock summits, runs through each area. Numerous steep, heavily wooded lateral ridges run east and west from these backbones. Cross-country travel below timberline is extremely difficult due to the steep terrain and thick brush, slide alder, and devil's club. However, exquisite alpine meadows are found on some ridge tops at timberline.

Several small glaciers fill cirques on Whitehorse Mountain and Three Fingers, and a number of small permanent snowfields are found in other pockets throughout the area. The wilderness has twenty-two charted lakes and ponds, and the roadless area has another two dozen. Trails lead to only a half-dozen of these lakes—the remainder require cross-country brush-beating to reach. One trail at the southeast end of the roadless area leads to a rocky summit with outstanding views south to the nearby range of peaks that run from Big Four to the Monte Cristo group.

## CLIMATE

Average annual precipitation for the area, ranging between 80 and 100 inches per year, starts in the form of rain in early October, changing to snow at higher elevations before the month is out. Southwesterly storm patterns during winter months bring heavy rain and snow, especially on the south and west sides of the area. By the end of November the snow level is generally down to 2,000 feet, where it remains until May. Most snow is gone below 4,000 feet by early July. Temperatures are relatively mild, seldom below zero in winter or above 80 in summer.

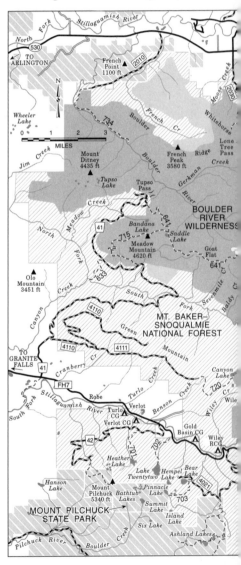

## ECOSYSTEM

Dominant trees at lower altitudes are western hemlock, Douglas-fir, and western red cedar. Creek drainages hold a dense understory of slide alder, dwarf willow, vine maple, ferns, and devil's club. One of the few lowland old-growth forest areas in this part of Washington State can be found in the lower reaches of the Boulder River, where ancient stands of Douglas-fir, true fir, western red cedar, and western hemlock grow in abundance.

The 640-acre Long Creek Research Natural Area (RNA), located in the southwest corner of the wilderness area, was established in 1947 to preserve a baseline forest of western hemlock and climax red alder, some nearly 2 feet in diameter and 100 feet tall. The Perry Creek drainage has been proposed as a 2,066-acre RNA. It contains various rare species of ferns, along with untouched stands of Alaska cedar, mountain hemlock, subalpine fir, and a heather and huckleberry community.

The forest at midaltitudes consists mainly of mountain hemlock, Pacific silver fir, Alaska cedar, and subalpine fir. Alpine parks can be found between 4,000 and 5,000 feet. Typical of these are the top of Meadow Mountain and Goat Flat on the west side of the wilderness axis ridge, where the forest dwindles to patches of subalpine fir and mountain hemlock, and meadows support heather, huckleberry, blueberry, dwarf lupine, phlox, salmonberry, anemone, fleabane, valerian, paintbrush, penstemon, bistort, and avalanche lilies. Rocky peaks have a sparse cover of heather and sedge, interspersed with a few hardy flowers.

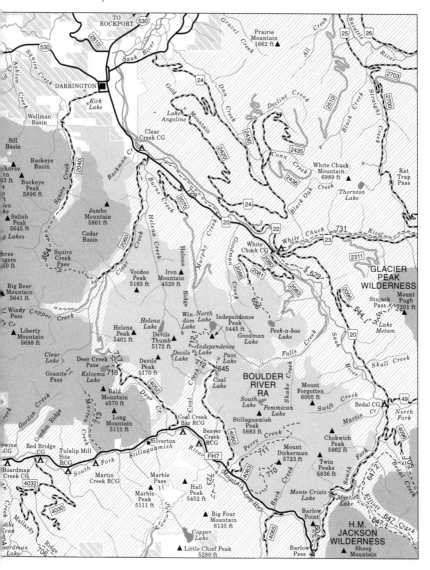

*A beautiful little waterfall dropping into the Boulder River can be seen from the trail.*

Forest inhabitants include black-tailed deer, black bear, spotted owl, marten, and pileated woodpeckers. Isolated groups of mountain goats are found in the higher elevations.

## GEOLOGY

This portion of the North Cascades lying west of the Straight Creek fault was created about 50 million to 90 million years ago when a microcontinent carried by tectonic plates became attached to the western edge of the North American plate. Over time, the edges of this terrane had been overlaid with sedimentary layers and basalt flows that were later metamorphosed into Darrington phyllite. The binding of the terrane to the continent was accompanied by uplift, folding, and faulting of the ancient rock base.

Volcanic activity that occurred between 10 million and 40 million years ago overlaid the southeast corner of the area near Barlow Pass where volcanic flows interbedded with sedimentary rock. This vulcanism was followed by another major uplift of the area, and intrusions of granodiorite between the high north–south axis ridges. Between 2 million and 12,000 years ago the alpine glaciers that formed on the higher peaks flowed down to merge with thick ice sheets covering the lowlands, in the process carving out most of the presently recognizable geographic features.

Peaks of the backbone ridges consist mainly of older, metamorphosed shale and sandstone exposed by erosion of younger volcanic rocks. Granite walls on the east side of Salish Peak and along Squire Creek are examples of the Squire Creek granodiorite intrusion. Mineralization in the form of veins, gold-containing placers, and disseminated sulfides occurred along the contact zones between the intrusion and the older metamorphic rock. Mount Forgotten is composed of loose volcanic breccia; the area northwest from it is predominantly pre-Jurassic metamorphic rock.

## HISTORY

As late as 1890 the entire Boulder River Wilderness area was uncharted, and the headwater sources of the Stillaguamish River were unknown. In 1889, the discovery of lead, silver, and gold ore just east of here in the Monte Cristo basin brought miners and speculators into the area; however, all initial approaches to that area were from the south, from the vicinity of Index. Surveys of routes by which heavy machinery could be brought in and ore could be taken out led to the construction, in 1891, of a wagon road from the north following the Sauk River. In 1892, another road was built along the South Fork of the Stillaguamish. By the fall of 1893 the rails of the Everett and Monte Cristo Line were added to the latter route.

The Monte Cristo finds led to other prospecting and mining in the mountains between Silverton and Monte Cristo, and the mining camp at Silverton served as a base for prospectors staking claims in the vicinity of Long Mountain, on the southern rim of the present wilderness area. Prospecting out of Darrington, on the northeast side of the area, led to several active claims on Whitehorse Mountain, Jumbo Mountain, and in Buckeye Basin, which all lie within the present wilderness area. By 1900 the mines had begun to play out.

Rough mining trails laced the area; prospectors showed total disdain for precipitous ridges if there was a vein of gold or silver to be found. Their only concern on the equivalent of a C-5 climbing route was whether they could make it with a cast-iron cookstove lashed to their packs. During the 1920s and '30s, the Forest Service expanded the rough miners' trail network with routes to reach and supply the fire lookout perched atop Three Fingers and patrol cabins spotted about the area.

Logging followed mining as the next economic boom for the region, and major timber sales in ensuing years have pushed logging roads into the periphery of the roadless area, along Clear Creek, Coal Creek, Beaver Creek, and several of the tributaries flowing north into the Sauk River, obliterating most of the older trail systems. Only the heart of this designated and de facto wilderness remains roadless and covered by old-growth forest.

## HIKING
### Wilderness Trails

**Trail 734, Boulder River.** *4.3 miles/e (H)*. The trailhead is located at the end of FR 2010. Old-growth forest and waterfalls from side streams are prime attractions as the trail meanders up and down above the north side of the canyon carved by the Boulder

River. Due to its low elevation, this trail is hikeable year-round, but it offers no views of wilderness peaks.

**Trail 654, Squire Creek.** *4 miles/m (H).* The trail runs between the end of FR 2040, on the north, and Squire Creek Pass. The route climbs along Squire Creek, offering spectacular views of the precipitous east side of the peaks on the backbone ridge of the wilderness.

**Trail 641, Three Fingers.** *6.2 miles/m (H).* The path starts from near the end of FR 41 at Tupso Pass. A short spur 2 miles east of the pass leads to Saddle Lake; the main trail continues to Goat Flat, 4.5 miles from the trailhead. Goat Flat is a pleasant alpine meadow thick with early-season flowers and late-season berries. A crude path continues climbing westward to reach Camp Saddle and Tin Can Gap, two cols that lead to the Queest-Alb Glacier at the west base of Three Fingers. From here, a climbers' track over glacier and rock reaches the South Peak summit block, where ladders lead up the final sheer face to a lookout cabin atop a minuscule rock platform blasted from the top of the mountain.

**Trail 653, Niederprum.** *2 miles/d (H).* This trail from FR 2030 is a classic miners' track that doesn't dillydally in switchbacks—it climbs from 1,000 feet to 4,000 feet up the north side of Whitehorse Ridge by the shortest (and steepest) route possible. It ends in a brush-covered meadow where miner Mat Niederprum once worked his claims. A track that continues over Lone Tree Pass is the most popular route for climbing Whitehorse Mountain.

## Roadless Area Trails

**Trail 712, Independence Lake.** *0.7 mile/e (H).* The trail starts at a clearcut at the end of FR 4060 (3,580 ft), then traverses a steep sidehill through old-growth forest to reach Independence Lake (3,720 ft). Meadows at either end of the lake flank a rock wall that rises above its east shoreline.

**Trail 712.1, North Lake.** *2.5 miles/m (H).* This path starts at the northeast end of Independence Lake, where switchbacks twist up the steep hillside to a pair of saddles on the ridgeline (5,000 ft). The first of these offers views of Mount Baker and the peaks of the Boulder River Wilderness, the second overlooks Glacier Peak. More switchbacks lead east from the saddle down to the cirque filled by North Lake (4,158 ft).

**Trail 711, Perry Creek.** *3.6 miles/e-m (H).* The trailhead is located at Perry Creek on FR 4063 (2,100 ft). The track follows the sidehill above Perry Creek, alternating between forest and open talus slopes. Falls are visible in streams cascading off the south side of Stillaguamish Peak; at 1.9 miles the trail crosses just above a waterfall on Perry Creek itself (3,300 ft). The ascent continues to a hillside covered by old-growth forest. Ridge-top meadows (5,000 ft) offer exhilarating views of the Cascade peaks from Mount Baker to Mount Rainier; to the south Big Four looms just a touch away. A climbers' scramble route to the summit of Mount Forgotten (6,005 ft) follows the narrowing ridge to the north.

**Trail 710, Dickerman Mountain.** *4.3 miles/m (H).* From the Mountain Loop Highway (Forest Hwy 7; 1,875 ft), never-ending switchbacks work up the sheer south flank of Mount Dickerman through a dense forest regrown from a major fire in the early 1900s. At 4,400 feet the climb moderates at meadows containing a tiny lake. However, the pause is brief and the way continues up the steep west ridge to the summit (5,723 ft). The vertical north face of the peak overlooks Perry Creek and the rock spires surrounding its headwaters: Stillaguamish, Chokwich, and Twin Peaks, and Mount Forgotten. To the east are Sloan and Glacier Peaks, and to the south the chain of Monte Cristo–area summits serrate the skyline.

**Trail 656, Peek-a-boo Lake.** *2.5 miles/m (H).* From FR 2086 (3,160 ft), the trail enters old-growth forest as it climbs the broad drainage at the head of Dutch Creek. At 3,800 feet, switchbacks up a forested face gain a ridge-top meadow (4,300 ft) with views northeast to White Chuck and beyond to Dome Peak and Mount Shuksan. The path then descends to beautiful Peek-a-boo Lake (3,902 ft), tucked in a forested hillside pocket.

## CLIMBING

Within the wilderness, with the exception of Jumbo Mountain, climbing activity is concentrated on the peaks along the major north–south axis ridge. Most of these have near-vertical faces ranging from 600 to 2,000 feet on one or more sides, but many have other relatively easy routes. Several of these peaks are climbed in the winter, when snow covers the brush and makes cross-country travel easier.

Whitehorse Mountain (6,563 ft) rises dramatically above the town of Darrington, offering a combination of glacier or rock climbing routes, most of the latter below C-5.

*North Cascades peaks spread to the northeast from Mount Dickerman; Mount Forgotten is on the left, and Mount Pugh in the distance.*

The most popular route leaves the end of Trail 653. South from Whitehorse Mountain are Buckeye Peak (5,896 ft), Mount Bullen (5,974 ft), and Salish Peak (5,645 ft), as well as intermediate short towers along intervening ridges. Although approach routes involve brush-beating up valley floors and steep sidehills, routes of C-4 or lower can be found on all of these peaks. The southeast face of Salish Peak is 600 feet of excellent granite with routes varying from C-5.6 to C-5.8.

The visual showpiece of the area is Three Fingers. The South Peak (6,850 ft), which tops the Boulder River Wilderness, has a restored lookout cabin perched on its top. It is reached via Trail 641 and a climbers' path across steep snow and rock to a vertical face, where a ladder spans the final 40 feet to the lookout. The Middle Peak (6,600 ft) is an easy rock climb from the col between it and the North Peak. The North Peak (6,720 ft) has several interesting routes combining glacial ice with C-4 to C-5 rock climbs.

South of Three Fingers are Big Bear Mountain (5,641 ft) and Liberty Mountain (5,688 ft). Both require brush-beating approaches but have easy rock routes to the final summits. Liberty also has a more challenging C-5.6 route on its north ridge. At the southeast lobe of the axis ridge is Long Mountain (5,111 ft), where a series of individual rock summits are linked by a mile-long exposed ridge.

Jumbo Mountain (5,801 ft) lies between the Squire Creek and Clear Creek drainages, east of the main line of peaks. Once above timberline, its three summits are easy rock scrambles.

There are two areas of climbing interest on the west and southeast sides of the roadless area. On the far west side are Voodoo Peak (5,193 ft), a short C-4 ascent; Helena Peak (5,401 ft), a walkup with a C-3 face; and the more challenging Devils Peak (5,170 ft), C-4. Several short rock towers along the ridge to the south offer one- to two-lead challenges. Nearby Devils Thumb (5,172 ft), an exposed outcrop of dunite, has a C-4 approach from Devils Lake. Independence Peak (5,445 ft), a small rock outcrop, is accessible by C-3 scrambles from Trail 712.1.

The higher southeast portion of the area includes several peaks above 5,500 feet. Northernmost are Stillaguamish Peak, a scramble, and Mount Forgotten, an exposed C-3 ridge scramble; both are reached from Trail 711.

The triple summits of Twin Peaks (5,836 ft) are normally approached from the Perry Creek basin, where notches lead to the sheer exposed C-4 slabs protecting the summits. A spire-studded ridge leads northeast to Chokwich Peak (5,662 ft), a flat-topped summit with several short towers on ridges to the north, west, and south.

## WINTER SPORTS

The Mountain Loop Highway is not plowed beyond the vicinity of Silverton during the winter, but ski tours from here can follow summertime logging roads for excellent winter scenery and reasonable downhill runs. One of the more popular tours follows snow-covered FR 4060 from its start 2.5 miles beyond Silverton up the Coal Creek basin to Coal Lake. More experienced skiers can continue on to either Pass Lake or Independence Lake. The wide Coal Creek drainage frames wondrous winterscapes of Big Four Mountain, Hall and Sperry Peaks, and Mount Pilchuck.

# Ragged Ridge Region

## Glacier Peak K Roadless Area

**Location:** In Snohomish County, along the south side of the Mountain Loop Highway between Silverton and Monte Cristo and between Spada Lake and the North Fork of the Skykomish River
**Size:** 45,509 acres
**Status:** Semiprimitive Nonmotorized; unprotected DNR and private land
**Terrain:** Rugged, extremely steep, forested hillsides rise to a chain of jagged rock crags that line the narrow tops of steep forested ridges.
**Elevation:** 720 to 6,610 feet
**Management:** USFS, Mount Baker–Snoqualmie National Forest, Skykomish and Darrington Ranger Districts. Some land adjacent to the roadless area is managed by the Washington State Department of Natural Resources (DNR) or are private patented mining claims.
**Topographic maps:** Baring, Bedal, Gold Bar, Index, Mallardy Ridge, Monte Cristo, Mount Stickney, Silverton, Wallace Lake

The 15-mile-long crest on the south side of the South Fork of the Stillaguamish River, between Mallardy Ridge and Silvertip Peak, bristles with some of the most beautiful alpine summits on the western flank of the Cascades. Although the area has remained roadless, mainly due to its rugged topography, it has still seen heavy use by humans.

Ragged Ridge, west of the North Fork of the Skykomish River, is one of the most remote and impenetrable areas still remaining on the west flank of the Cascades. The edges of the area have been chewed by logging, especially in the state DNR properties. Two short trails penetrate the periphery of the area, but the seldom-visited interior has no constructed accesses, and (thankfully) has yet to feel a chain saw.

Discovery of gold, silver, and copper lodes here in the 1890s led hordes of prospectors into the rugged peaks. The few trails that exist today were put

*Sheep Gap Mountain rises above Gothic Basin.*

in by miners intent on getting from place A to place B via the shortest distance possible. As a result, these trails are strenuous and challenging, more often used as climbing routes rather than for casual hiking. Several other paths are abandoned and overgrown; those interested in bushwhacking their way into the area's history can locate their traces using old maps.

A dozen distinct peaks, all topping 6,000 feet, and many more smaller spires and towers line the crest of the region. Hikers are lured here by the scenic beauty; climbers are challenged by the solid rock pyramids with vertical faces framed by knife-edge ridges. The convoluted crests for which Ragged Ridge is named have steep, densely forested walls cut by creek drainages. Narrow ridge tops are liberally sprinkled with rock horns and spike-like gendarmes. Two large lakes, Big Greider and Boulder, lie on the northwest side of the area, and a third, Isabel, is on the southwest. A sprinkling of smaller lakes is found west of Mount Stickney and along its southern border.

## CLIMATE

Summer weather is generally dry and mild, with temperatures rarely exceeding the 80s. Rains start in October and turn to snow at higher elevations by month's end. Precipitation—60 to 100 inches annually—continues to fall as snow throughout winter, when snow levels drop to around 2,000 feet. Temperatures remain mild through winter, seldom dropping below zero. Snow is gone below 4,000 feet by July, but upper elevations are not snow-free until August.

## ECOSYSTEM

The lower portions of the backbone ridges are heavily forested, primarily with western hemlock, some Douglas-fir, and western red cedar. Avalanche tracks that lace the precipitous hillsides are covered with slide alder and vine maple, joined by dwarf willow and devil's club along creekbeds. Silver fir, mountain hemlock, and red cedar also share the hillsides. Red mountain heather, western cassiope, blue-leaved huckleberry, luetkea, and elephant's head pedicularis are found in subalpine meadows near creeks and lakes. A few small alpine meadows, with seasonal wildflower displays, are found atop the ridges. The ragged rock summits support little vegetation other than patches of heathers and sedges. Unique local climatic conditions at the Big Four Ice Caves foster the growth of subalpine wildflowers rarely seen at this low elevation.

Forests are inhabited by elk, black-tailed deer, and black bear. Both deer and elk descend to lower elevations adjoining the North Fork of the Skykomish for winter range, and bald eagles use the river as a winter feeding ground. Spotted owls are found in the vicinity of Snowslide Lake and the South Fork of Salmon Creek.

## GEOLOGY

The geology of the area reflects dramatic deformations of the base metamorphic rock. The phyllite and slate of Big Four dates to pre-Jurassic times. The peaks southwest of Big Four are mostly younger, metamorphosed sandstones, shales, and conglomerates formed from Cretaceous and Paleocene continental deposits from about 70 million years ago. The folded strata here dip steeply to the east and northeast. Vesper Peak and the area south of Big Four are made up of a Tertiary intrusion of quartz diorite. Near Red Mountain, strata of metamorphosed sedimentary and volcanic rock are cut by a dike of serpentine. The western edge of the region consists mostly of older, Mesozoic sedimentary deposits. The heart of Ragged Ridge is an intrusion of 35-million-year-old granitic rock, a part of the Index batholith. Sheer rock faces, narrow ridgelines, and high cirques were carved by local alpine glaciers 15,000 to 20,000 years ago.

## HISTORY

In the mid-1800s the dense virgin forests of the Pacific Northwest presented a serious obstacle to new settlers in the region; thus, rivers were relied on for transportation and commerce. The first trading centers along the Skykomish River were located at Snohomish City and Gunn's Place (present-day Index). In 1859 a syndicate was organized to push roads into the area, and Ed Cady was hired to explore the upper Skykomish to look for a possible route across the Cascades to the Columbia River basin. Cady and his partner discovered that local Indians traded with tribes east of the Cascades using a route that went up the North Fork of the Skykomish River, through a pass (now named Cady Pass), and down the Wenatchee River. In 1860 Cady began blazing a path along this route that is still followed by forest roads and trails. This trail is now in the Henry M. Jackson Wilderness.

The new trail brought prospectors into the region, and a small way station called Scott's Camp was built at the confluence of Silver Creek and the Skykomish. This later became the mining camp of Galena, a site still marked on today's maps although it has long since disappeared. By 1874 prospectors had filed claims on Silver Creek upstream from Scott's Camp, and by 1880 another mining camp, Mineral City, was thriving at the junction of the north and south forks of Silver Creek.

In 1890 prospectors discovered the mineral wealth of Glacier Basin, across the ridge to the north, and miners poured into the Monte Cristo area between 1891 and the 1920s, beating out hardscrabble trails to impossible spots in their search for riches. The Everett and Monte Cristo Railway was completed in 1893 to support mining operations here. Portions of the railroad grade are still recognizable today along the bank of the South Fork of the Stillaguamish River.

In 1897 a 2-mile-long aerial tram was run from Silverton (1,500 ft) south over 4,200-foot Marble Pass to reach the "45" copper mine at the head of Williamson Creek. The very week the tram was completed, heavy snows and floods wiped out the railbed, and mining operations were suspended. The railway was not restored until the spring of 1900, and the "45" tram was returned to operation in July of 1901. The operation was never profitable, and the mortgage on the mine was foreclosed in 1903.

*Lake Isabel is one of three large lakes found in the Ragged Ridge region.*

Despite the decline in mining activity at Monte Cristo itself, in 1911 the Del Campo Metals Company opened prospects on Weden Creek, and by 1913 it had announced that they were ready to produce. However, by 1918 these two mines in Gothic Basin were also abandoned.

As mining played out, the scenic value of the area was recognized, and in 1921 Everett investors built an elaborate resort with a lodge, cabins, golf course, and tennis courts, and created a lake at the base of Big Four Mountain. The 1929 depression cut deeply into the inn's clientele, and a devastating blow was dealt in 1933 when the railroad discontinued operation. Automobiles with wheels modified to run on the railroad track continued to serve the inn until 1937, when the CCC converted the old railbed to the present Mountain Loop Highway. The inn burned to the ground in 1949. A picnic area now stands near its foundation.

## HIKING
### South Fork of the Stillaguamish River Trails
*Trail 723, Ice Caves.* 1 mile/e (H). A near-flat path leaves the Big Four Picnic Area parking lot (1,715 ft) on a boardwalk over beaver-pond marshes, enters the woods,

and then crosses a footbridge over the South Fork of the Stillaguamish. After a short forest hike, the trail breaks out to up-close views of the mile-high face of Big Four Mountain and the avalanche-born snowfield that harbors the ice caves. The caves form when meltwater from the face of the mountain creates pockets under the ice, which are then enlarged by warm drafts of summer air. The caves are subject to sudden collapse, so are dangerous to enter or climb upon. Avalanches that create the snowfield obviously also make close approaches dangerous in winter.

**Trail 707, Sunrise Mine.** *3 miles/m (H).* The trail starts from FR 4065 in a clearcut (2,380 ft), then enters forest as it heads to a log crossing of the South Fork of the Stillaguamish River. It continues up a branch of the river, breaking out to a steepening avalanche slope. The final mile, marked by cairns, heads straight uphill to Headlee Pass (4,600 ft). The rock in the final chute below the pass is very steep and loose. The pass, a knife-edge slot in a spire-dotted ridge between Sperry and Morning Star Peaks, is the start point of climbing routes for these peaks.

**Trail 724, Weden Creek.** *1.8 miles/d (H).* From Barlow Pass (2,361 ft), hike the old Monte Cristo Road 1.7 miles to the trailhead on the southwest side of the road. The Sauk River is sometimes difficult to cross here; an alternative path on the opposite bank, cut by volunteers, runs from the Twin Bridge Campground, 1 mile from Barlow Pass, to the normal trail at Weden Creek.

The trail was originally put in to reach the two Del Campo mine sites at the head of the creek. A steep diagonal up a forested hillside crosses several gullies en route that require ice axes for safety when filled with snow. From the lower mine site (3,700 ft), switchbacks gain the top of a cliff above Weden Lake, the site of the upper mine. Here the way enters the Foggy Lake basin, framed on both sides by 1,000-foot faces rising to the craggy summits of Del Campo and Gothic Peaks and Castle Rocks. The snow-covered basin melts to meadows in late summer, but the lake often remains frozen year-round.

## Ragged Ridge Trails

**Greider Lakes Trail.** *2.5 miles/d (H).* From the trailhead picnic area on FR 61 (1,580 ft), a path leads into the forest, then starts endless switchbacks up a jarring root-and-boulder tread. In just under 2 miles a scramble traverse of a steep cliff leads to Little Greider Lake (2,910 ft). A path around the northwest shore continues 0.5 mile to Big Greider Lake (2,932 ft). Both lakes are rimmed by a 1,000-foot-high band of cliffs. Just before the second lake, a spur switchbacks 0.7 mile up the steep, brushy hillside to the base of a rock wall and great views up Williamson Creek to Big Four, Vesper, and Little Chief Peaks.

**Boulder Lake Trail.** *4 miles/d (H).* The trail leaves the south side of FR 61 (1,650 ft) on an abandoned logging road that deteriorates to a rough traverse of a large rock slide above the east bank of Boulder Creek. In 0.5 mile the path enters forest and zigzags up, then traverses as it climbs the hillside to the head of the drainage. After a final marshy contour, the northwest end of Boulder Lake (3,706 ft) is reached. Cliffs 600 feet high border the cirque that holds the lake.

## CLIMBING

The ridge between Mallardy Ridge and Silvertip Peak is a climber's mecca, with challenges for all skill levels. Big Four (6,135 ft) is a massive mountain with an imposing near-vertical north face. Two bands of cliffs, one between 2,000 and 4,000 feet and a second between 4,800 feet and the summit, are its major challenges. Several routes have been put up the mountain; most range from C-3 to C-4, with one variant rated C-5.8.

North of Headlee Pass are two sharp rock towers, Vesper (6,214 ft) and Sperry (6,125 ft) Peaks. Vesper's north face is a near-vertical 900-foot slab, with routes ranging from C-5.6 to C-5.9. The summit pyramid of Sperry has three sheer faces separated by steep, narrow arêtes. Routes are C-2 to C-5.8.

On the south side of Headlee Pass is Morning Star Peak (6,020 ft). The final summit pyramid has no routes below C-3 to C-4. There are several minor spikes on the spur ridges from both Sperry and Morning Star. One of these, Vega Tower (5,480 ft), is a striking spire offering both C-3 and C-5.8 climbs.

North of Foggy Lake is Del Campo Peak (6,610 ft), a solid rock summit pyramid, difficult from all sides. On the rim above the lake is Gothic Peak (6,213 ft), solid sandstone with precipitous east and west faces. Along the ridge north from Gothic are Castle Rocks (5,800 ft), a series of difficult crags.

South of the Foggy Lake basin is the multisummited massif of Sheep Gap Mountain (5,683 to 5,819 ft). The lower north peak is an easy scramble, but near-vertical walls of the bell-shaped main peak are rated C-3, as is Rams Horn (5,400 ft), a tower south of the main peak.

Although individual summits in the Ragged Ridge area are not high in comparison to other Cascade peaks, many rise nearly 4,000 vertical feet above the adjoining drainages, presenting a climbing challenge belied by their altitude. Since most of the area is intrusive granite, the rock offers solid, stable climbing. Ridges throughout the area are topped with a multitude of short gendarmes worthy of a lead or two of serious rock climbing.

Mount Stickney (5,367 ft) is the highest peak on the west edge of the Ragged Ridge area. Cross-country approaches from the northwest reach narrow ridge-crest scrambles from its east or west ribs. The convoluted crest dividing the North Fork of the Sultan River and the Salmon Creek and Elk Creek drainages has several attractive rock horns and pyramids ranging from C-3 to C-5.5 in difficulty; all approaches require considerable bushwhacking. The ridge encircling Greider Lakes is capped by Greider (4,838 ft) and Static (4,897 ft) Peaks. The latter has excellent climbing routes up solid granite, with short leads to C-5.8.

The highest point in the Ragged Ridge area is Red Mountain (5,550 ft). The summit block is protected on all sides by near-vertical faces, breached only by steep brush-choked gullies; a C-4 route climbs from the Sultan River basin.

The northeast end of the area is anchored by Crested Buttes (5,338 ft), a ragged subridge south of Sheep Gap. A series of crags atop the ridge can be approached from either the east via Silver Creek or from the west via the Sultan River. Thick, brushy approaches lead to C-3 to C-4 rock spires.

# 16 North Fork Skykomish River Region

### Henry M. Jackson Wilderness; Glacier Peak A, B, and L, Heather Lake, and Eagle Rock Roadless Areas

**Location:** In King, Snohomish, and Chelan Counties, straddling the Cascade crest between Stevens Pass, the South Fork of the Skykomish River, and the North Fork of the Sauk River

**Size:** Wilderness, 103,591 acres; Glacier Peak A, 443 acres; Glacier Peak B, 18,646 acres; Glacier Peak L, 14,227 acres; Heather Lake, 11,067 acres; Eagle Rock, 35,035 acres

**Status:** Designated Wilderness (1984); Roadless areas are Semiprimitive Nonmotorized

**Terrain:** The wilderness features steep slopes and finger ridges separated by glacier-cut valleys. Ridge-top alpine meadows lie to the south and east, and sharp, serrated ridges with distinctive peaks to the northwest. Eagle Rock has three major ridges tending northwest to southeast that rise abruptly 3,000 to 4,000 feet above intervening drainages. Ridge crests are capped by rock gendarmes and craggy peaks with near-vertical faces.

**Elevation:** 660 to 7,835 feet

**Management:** USFS, Mount Baker–Snoqualmie National Forest, Darrington and Skykomish Ranger Districts; Okanogan–Wenatchee National Forest, Lake Wenatchee Ranger District; Washington State Department of Natural Resources (DNR); private patented mining claims

**Topographic maps:** Baring, Bedal, Bench Mark Mountain, Blanca Lake, Captain Point, Evergreen Mountain, Grotto, Index, Labyrinth Mountain, Monte Cristo, Poe Mountain, Scenic, Skykomish, Sloan Peak, Stevens Pass

The Henry M. Jackson Wilderness honors Washington's longtime senator, who was a major force in creating many of the state's present wilderness areas. The area straddles more than 30 miles of the Cascade crest from Stevens Pass to Kodak Peak, traversed by a portion of the Pacific Crest National Scenic Trail (PCT). Ridges separated by deep, glacier-carved valleys radiate east and west from the crest; many are routes for other trails leading from the perimeter of the wilderness to the PCT.

The northwest corner of the wilderness encompasses several glaciated basins rimmed by narrow, ragged ridges capped by spires, towers, and toothlike summits ranging between 6,000 and 7,800 feet. Their imposing, 4,000- to 5,500-foot local relief makes them a mecca for mountain climbers, hikers, and photographers who relish Alps-like scenery. Since this area saw major mining activity in the late 1800s, history buffs can have a field day exploring the ruins of mines and mining camps, envisioning what the area must have looked like in its heyday.

*Wildflowers fill a meadow in the Henry M. Jackson Wilderness.*

More than sixty alpine and subalpine lakes are spattered about the area, ranging from pond-sized to the substantial 179 acres of Blanca Lake. Although the Glacier Peak L and B, Heather Lake, and Eagle Rock Roadless Areas on the periphery of the designated wilderness were not included under its protection, they are included here in the hope they may be joined to the wilderness before they succumb to timber harvest or development.

East from Gold Bar on US Highway 2, the stupendous 3,000-foot vertical north face of Mount Baring suddenly looms dead ahead. On the opposite side of the valley the massive, jagged thumbs of Gunn and Merchant Peaks protrude above forested hillsides. These peaks mark the southwest corner of the Eagle Rock Roadless Area. This

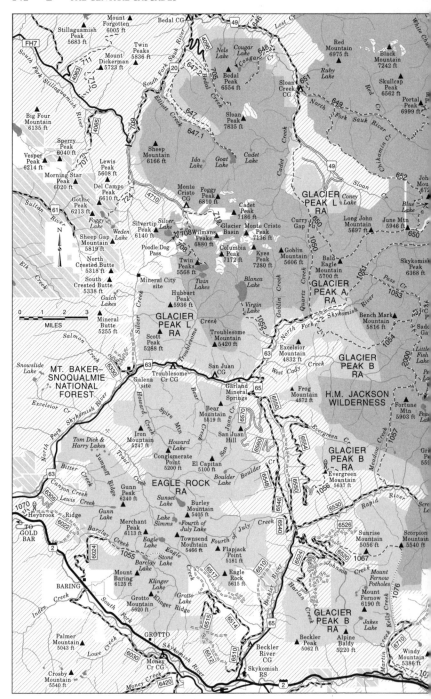

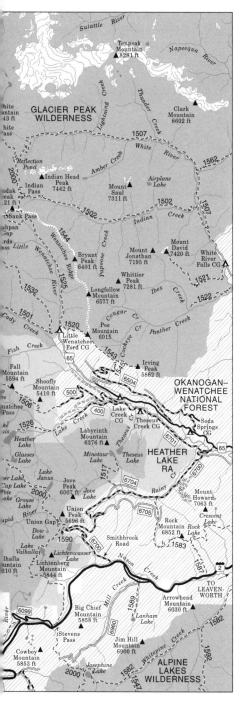

de facto wilderness fills a triangular wedge framed by the North and South Forks of the Skykomish River and the Beckler River. Although logging has gnawed at the south and east sides of this area, and mining has made deep intrusions into its western edge, the heart of the region remains virgin forest at elevations below 4,000 feet, with precipitous ridges and peaks rising steeply above.

Access to the interior of Eagle Rock is restricted to faint boot-paths; only two short trails are maintained. Nonetheless, many of the dozen and a half alpine lakes that dot the heart of the area are reached by determined fishermen. Climbers also visit Eagle Rock, drawn by the beauty and challenge of its jagged peaks.

## CLIMATE

Annual precipitation ranges from 60 to 80 inches, mostly falling in the form of snow at medium and high elevations. Periods of heavy precipitation start in November, often causing runoffs in rivers and streams late in the year. Snow accumulates as deep as 20 feet on higher terrain, and often remains there until late July. Elevations below 3,500 feet are generally snow-free by early June, when snowmelt again causes peak flows of rivers and streams.

Temperatures are relatively mild year-round. Summer highs average in the 80s, and winter lows average in the 20s, with a few extended below-zero periods.

## ECOSYSTEM

On the west side of the Cascade crest, most valleys and ridges up to about 4,500 feet are covered with western

*Glacier Peak can be seen in the distance from Poe Ridge, on the border of the Henry M. Jackson Wilderness.*

hemlock, Alaska cedar, Douglas-fir, true fir, Pacific silver fir, and spruce. Drainages contain a tangled web of slide alder, vine maple, dwarf willow, ferns, and devil's club, and avalanche slopes have a thick cover of slide alder and vine maple. Subalpine meadows, most commonly found along and at the head of creek drainages, contain red mountain heather, huckleberry, western cassiope, and luetkea. At higher elevations the timber changes to subalpine fir and mountain hemlock. Basin heads and ridge tops frequently have open parklands carpeted with heathers and mosses and fringed by blueberry and huckleberry bushes. When snows melt these meadows are a canvas of colorful wildflowers such as avalanche lilies, dwarf lupine, penstemon, phlox, bistort, valerian, and Indian paintbrush.

Black-tailed deer are the most common species in the area, but the forest also harbors black bear, bobcat, cougar, marten, and lynx. Bald and golden eagles, osprey, spotted owls, blue grouse, ruffed grouse, and several species of songbirds are found in the area. At rocky upper elevations, mountain goats and hoary marmots may also be seen.

## GEOLOGY

The geology of the Henry M. Jackson Wilderness is complicated by the Straight Creek fault, which cuts through it from north to south. According to plate tectonic theories, this fault line marks a slippage between sections of the northwest-moving North Cascades microcontinent.

The base rock east of the fault is older continental crust, mostly metamorphosed sedimentary deposits that accumulated on the eastern coastal plain of the North Cascades terrane over 180 million years ago. The base rock west of the fault is thick volcanic ocean crust overlaid with metamorphosed mudstones and sandstones, all heavily folded 25 million to 35 million years ago. Most of the peaks of the Monte Cristo group represent eroded remnants of this base.

The area east of the Straight Creek fault and north of Stevens Pass was intruded by a large mass of granitic rock between 60 million and 100 million years ago. Later granitic intrusions, about 25 million years old, occurred east of the fault in the vicinity of Sloan and Foggy Peaks, and to the west in the vicinity of Hubbart Peak.

The core of the Eagle Rock area is a portion of the Grotto batholith, a 25-million-year-old granodiorite intrusion, flanked on the east by metamorphosed pre-Miocene volcanics and Permian sedimentaries, and on the west by Paleozoic sedimentary rock. Quartz veins containing a variety of sulfides are found along the borders of the intrusion. Trout Creek, the major drainage north of the Gunn Peak massif, has been a significant producer of copper ores. Prospectors working along the Mount Baring ridge have discovered quartz veins containing tourmaline, blue shorl, albite, and epidote.

The sharp, jagged, spire-laden arêtes and incisor summit blocks in the north end of the wilderness all result from the carving of local alpine glaciers that reached their maximum about 15,000 years ago. These same glaciers are responsible for shaping the steep-sided drainages that pervade the region.

## HISTORY

Trappers and then prospectors made the first non-Indian explorations in the area. To facilitate their travel, Ed Cady blazed a trail across the Cascades in 1860, following a route used by coastal Indians to trade with tribes east of the mountains. Cady's trail across the pass now named for him never materialized into the wagon road and railroad envisioned by his Everett business patrons. Today it remains accessible only to boots and hooves.

In 1897, rich copper ores were found in lower Trout Creek, and other claims were staked higher up the creek on the north side of Gunn Peak. The lower of these, the Sunset Mine, operated continuously from the time of its discovery until 1932, with the peak of its production occurring between 1918 and 1920. Prospectors worked north from the Skykomish River up Silver Creek, lacing the area with claims and dreaming of rich gold, silver, and copper strikes. In 1889, Joseph Pearsall, prospecting north of Hubbart Peak, reached a saddle now known as Wilmans Pass, where he saw the peaks surrounding Glacier Basin. Spotting rust streaks on the basin walls and the red-gold glint of galena, he worked his way into the basin to collect ore samples. Assays showed both gold and silver; Pearsall got a grubstake and headed back to the basin to stake claims. By fall a dozen claims marked rich-looking prospects in Glacier Basin and Seventysix Gulch. In 1890 more claims were filed, and the campsite in the valley was named Monte

Cristo, after the wealthy count of that name in the novel by Alexander Dumas.

The year 1893 saw the town of Monte Cristo platted, the construction of a concentrator, and the arrival of the first train via a new route up the Stillaguamish River. Aerial tramways were built from the mines to the concentrator in 1894. In 1896 a wagon road reached mines at Goat Lake in the drainage north from Glacier Basin. Tunnels were bored 250 feet beneath the floor of Glacier Basin, and a hole was started through lower Wilmans Peak between Glacier Basin and Seventysix Gulch.

More than 22,500 tons of ore concentrate had been shipped out of Monte Cristo by 1897, but for the next two years floods and washouts closed the railroad line to the town, shutting down mining. The railroad was restored in 1900, and mining resumed at a steady pace the following year. Although more than $7 million in gold was taken from Monte Cristo, the mines were never profitable, and 1904 mine closures and bankruptcies foretold the end. The mines closed in 1907; in 1915 heavy snows crushed most of the town's buildings, leaving it a ghost town save for visits by tourists to the remaining hotel. The last mines shut down in 1920; the final vestige of mining, the remaining tramway cable, fell in 1973.

The southern perimeter of the wilderness was opened by the construction of the Great Northern Railroad line across Stevens Pass in 1893. The original path over the summit required a series of switchbacks on either side; spurs at the ends of the switchbacks held trains while switches were thrown to permit them to reverse direction for the next section of track. This laborious method of crossing the pass was eliminated in 1900, when a 2.6-mile-long tunnel was completed through the mountain just north of the pass. Despite construction of massive snowsheds above the section of track west of the tunnel, a 1910 avalanche killed 96 people aboard two trains that had been trapped by prior slides. The track was relocated to a new 7.8-mile-long tunnel south of the pass in 1929.

## HIKING
### North Fork of the Sauk River Trails

*Trail 648, Sloan Peak.* 4.5 miles/d (H). From FR 49 (1,900 ft), the trail follows an old road across beaver ponds to the North Fork of the Sauk River; it must be forded in the vicinity. The miner origins of the route become apparent as it climbs relentlessly up a forested rib, then delicately tiptoes across Cougar Creek between two waterfalls. A respite in the ascent, followed by two more crossings of Cougar Creek and a chain of short switchbacks, surmounts the final 1,000 feet. Here the path breaks out to meadows (4,800 ft) with awesome views of nearby Sloan Peak and more distant ones of Red Mountain and Glacier Peak. Travel beyond here requires mountaineering skills.

*Trail 650, Bald Eagle (Curry Gap).* 10 miles/m (H,S). A footbridge crossing Sloan Creek (2,400 ft) leads to a 2.5-mile hike up abandoned FR 4920 to the trailhead (2,950 ft). The trail enters the forest and ascends to Curry Gap (3,950 ft), where meadows open to views of glaciers falling from the east side of the Monte Cristo peaks. The trail continues southeast, switchbacks to the ridge top (5,000 ft), then follows the crest to the north side of Bald Eagle Mountain.

*The distinctive shape of Sloan Peak, in the Henry M. Jackson Wilderness, can be spotted from viewpoints within a hundred miles.*

The route follows a ridge northeast to Long John Mountain, then continues east atop the crest to June Mountain. A side-trip scramble to the top of June Mountain (5,946 ft) opens expansive views of Sloan, Glacier, and the Monte Cristo Peaks. The trail meets Trail 652 from the north at a small saddle east of June, then swings across the ridge to traverse south-slope meadows. It gains the ridge top, then hooks south to join the PCT at Dishpan Gap (5,600 ft).

## South Fork of the Sauk River Trails

***Trail 647, Elliott Creek.*** *5.2 miles/e (H).* From the gate at the end of FR 4080 (1,850 ft), walk the abandoned road, now trail, for a mile to its junction with Trail 647.2. Head southeast on the old roadbed through forest and clearcuts for 2.5 miles to the junction with Trail 647.1 at the wilderness boundary, and the beginning of the true foot trail to Goat Lake. In 0.5 mile a side path leaves the trail and crosses Elliott Creek to the site of a former hotel and mining camp. Switchbacks surmount a steep hillside below the lake outlet; enjoy glimpses here of McIntosh Falls. The trail rounds the east side of Goat Lake (3,161 ft) and is overwhelmed by brush near its south end. Views here rise up the basin to cliffs below the glaciers hanging from the sides of Cadet and Foggy Peaks.

**Trail 647.1, Elliott Creek Loop.** *2 miles/m (H).* This trail variation follows an 1896 wagon route to mining claims in the Goat Lake basin, and it is one of the nicest valley walks in the region. From the shared trailhead with Trail 647 at the end of FR 4080 (1,850 ft), the path follows the north bank of Elliott Creek through creek-side old growth for two miles, then swings uphill to rejoin Trail 647 (2,720 ft).

**Trail 708, Poodle Dog Pass.** *2 miles/m (H).* Once a brutal path that stumbled over roots and boulders as it clawed up to Poodle Dog Pass, this trail has recently been relocated to steep, but more accommodating environs. From the Monte Cristo townsite (2,756 ft), the route switchbacks up the steep rib west of Seventysix Gulch to 4,200 feet, then traverses below the face of Wilmans Peaks to Poodle Dog Pass (4,350 ft). From the pass, a short spur continues west to the cirque surrounding Silver Lake (4,260 ft).

**Trail 708.1, Twin Lakes.** *2.7 miles/m (H).* From Poodle Dog Pass (4,350 ft), a rugged path climbs east to Wilmans Pass (4,850 ft), the original route used by the prospector who discovered the Monte Cristo basin. Here the way follows a steep, narrow rib with views down the wall of Seventysix Gulch to the pinnacles of Wilmans Peaks, and up to the summit of Columbia Peak. Beyond a col between the Twin Peaks summits (5,350 ft), the trail scrambles along a shelf above a 600-foot-high cliff, then descends to the east bank of the northern, and larger, of the Twin Lakes (4,710 ft).

**Trail 719, Glacier Basin.** *2.1 miles/m-d (H).* From the south side of the bridge over Glacier Creek near Monte Cristo (2,850 ft), the trail follows a gentle railroad grade for nearly a mile, to a no-nonsense climb that heads straight up badly eroded dirt and rock where trailside tree roots provide vital hand holds. As it rounds Mystery Hill, the path breaks into meadows at the heart of Glacier Basin (4,700 ft). On all sides, vertical, glacier-pocked walls sweep up to rugged peaks: Wilmans, Monte Cristo, Cadet, and The Cadets. Ruins and rusting debris are all that remain of the mine shafts, ore bins, and aerial tramways that once filled this beautiful place.

### North Fork of the Skykomish River Trails

**Trail 1052, Blanca Lake.** *3.5 miles/d (H).* There is no hesitation in the uphill grind from FR 63 (1,900 ft) through thirty-seven switchbacks to reach a tiny meadow enclosing the perfectly circular shoreline of Virgin Lake (4,220 ft). From here, a 0.5-mile path swings down a forested sidehill to the south shore of Blanca Lake (3,972 ft). Rock cliffs rise above the east shore of the lake, whose water is stained a pale turquoise green by glacial till. At the north end of the lake is a broad talus fan, plowed by the Columbia Glacier before it retreated farther up the basin. Rimming the glacier are walls and pocket glaciers below the summits of Kyes, Monte Cristo, and Columbia Peaks.

**Trail 1054, West Cady Ridge.** *8 miles/m (H,S).* After numerous switchbacks climb through old-growth forest from FR 63 and the Skykomish River (2,470 ft), the route breaks into meadows atop West Cady Ridge (4,800 ft). The heather parkland follows a ridge-top arc to Bench Mark Mountain. A short spur to the top of the mountain (5,816 ft) offers vistas to the Monte Cristo peaks, as well as Sloan, Baker, Glacier, and Rainier. The route continues a short distance east, dropping to meet the PCT just north of Saddle Gap (4,700 ft).

**Trail 1051, North Fork of the Skykomish River.** *8 miles/m (H,S)*. At the end of FR 63 (3,000 ft) this path heads up the valley floor of the North Fork of the Skykomish River. It continues up the narrowing drainage to the river headwaters and an open alpine park (4,500 ft). Switchbacks attack the steepening hillside, and the route gains the ridge top at Dishpan Gap (5,600 ft) to merge with Trail 650 and the PCT.

## Beckler River Trails

**Trail 1067, Johnson Ridge.** *4.3 miles/m (H; B,M)*. This trail originally started at the Beckler River, but logging roads and clearcuts annihilated its lower portion. It now begins near the upper end of abandoned FR 6526 (3,800 ft) in an area burned by a 1967 forest fire. The sometimes obscure path follows the crest east; as it passes over Sunrise Mountain (5,056 ft) trees give way to views of Mount Fernow and Glacier Peak. The ridge-top trail descends to a saddle, then climbs again to Scorpion Mountain (5,540 ft). A spur drops from the mountaintop to tiny Joan Lake (5,040 ft), cupped in a bench on Scorpion's east slope. An old unmaintained route, Trail 1076, continues south from here down Kelly Creek to FR 6710.

**Trail 1057, Meadow Creek.** *8 miles/m (H,S)*. The route leaves the Rapid River and FR 6530 just east of Meadow Creek (2,000 ft) and switchbacks up the slope above the creek through the remains of a 1967 forest fire. A gradual ascent reaches the head of the creek, then heads uphill to reach alpine meadows surrounding Fortune Ponds (4,700 ft). A short scramble to the top of Fortune Mountain (5,903 ft) opens views of the backbone of the Cascades. South from the ponds the way follows the old PCT tread to meet its new route above Pear Lake (4,809 ft).

## US 2 Trails

**Trail 1055, Barclay Lake.** *2.2 miles/e-d (H)*. The trail leaves the north side of FR 6024 (2,200 ft) and slogs through mudholes along the riverbank as it wanders up to the inlet of Barclay Lake (2,422 ft). A footpath from the lake inlet heads northeast up the hillside and across talus slopes to a low saddle and Stone Lake (3,875 ft). From here it continues northwest through Paradise Meadows to Eagle Lake (3,888 ft), which lies just below the east face of Merchant Peak.

**Trail 1074, Iron Goat.** *4 miles/e (H)*. Once the railroad route across Stevens Pass, the portion of track between the old Cascade tunnel and Scenic was abandoned when the trains were rerouted to a new tunnel on the south side of the pass. Four miles of this railbed has since been converted to a trail. There are two segments, both starting at a switchback on the east side of Martin Creek (2,600 ft). The lower piece of trail traces the old track from the switchback down to Twin Tunnels, 1.2 miles. The upper part of the route ends at the west end of the Windy Point tunnel (2,840 ft). Plans are being developed to extend this section to the old railroad tunnel at Stevens Pass.

## Little Wenatchee River Trails

**Trail 1506, Top Lake.** *5 miles/m (H,S).* From the end of FR 6701-500 (3,700 ft), the trail traverses a forested hillside below Shoofly Mountain until it reaches cliffs rising above the north fork of Lake Creek. Switchbacks gain the ridge above the cliffs, where the route follows the crest northwest to Fall Mountain, skirts its south side, then descends to Top Lake (4,580 ft). The trail continues west through the meadows to join the PCT north of Wenatchee Pass.

**Trail 1501, Cady Pass.** *5 miles/m (H,S).* Three trails leave the Little Wenatchee Ford Campground (2,960 ft); this is the shortest of the three to reach the PCT. For most of its length the route follows the valley bottom beside Cady Creek, and it can be quite muddy in places. When the main drainage of the creek swings north, the trail climbs west and joins the PCT at Cady Pass (4,500 ft).

**Trail 1532, Cady Ridge.** *6 miles/d (H).* This fork leaves Trail 1501 (3,000 ft) 0.2 mile beyond the Little Wenatchee Ford Campground and begins a grueling 1-mile climb north to the top of Cady Ridge (5,000 ft). Once the crest is gained, the path follows it northwest through open forest and ridge-top meadows to join the PCT south of Wards Pass (5,700 ft).

**Trail 1525, Little Wenatchee River.** *7.5 miles/m (H,S).* From the Little Wenatchee Ford Campground (2,960 ft), the trail heads north up the brushy valley floor of the Little Wenatchee River. In 5 miles the route leaves the Little Wenatchee and climbs an eroded path up a steep hillside to Meander Meadow (4,900 ft). Here heathers, sprinkled with colorful wildflowers, line the path as it continues the gentle ascent to the PCT at Sauk Pass (5,500 ft).

## Trail 2000, Pacific Crest National Scenic Trail

**PCT: Stevens Pass to Union Gap.** *7 miles/m (H,S).* The trail crosses US 2 just east of Stevens Pass (4,030 ft) and initially follows an old railroad grade across slopes with low brush cover and open views of the Nason Creek drainage and Nason Ridge. It traverses west into the headwaters of Nason Creek, where it ascends through marshes and meadows to a rock knob (5,010 ft) above the west shore of Lake Valhalla. The route drops into a meadow at the northwest end of the lake (4,900 ft), then climbs, staying well below the east side of the crest until it reaches Union Gap (4,700 ft), and meets Trail 1590.

**PCT: Union Gap to Wenatchee Pass.** *10.5 miles/m (H,S).* From Union Gap, the track drops down the west side of the crest to meadow-wrapped Lake Janus (4,146 ft). After climbing west from the lake, it regains the crest (5,200 ft) with the path weaving from one side to the other. Passing high above Glasses Lake, a few switchbacks gain the top of Grizzly Peak (5,597 ft), with views down to Heather Lake and northeast to Glacier Peak. Beyond a balding knob north of Grizzly Peak the route follows the forested crest as it descends to Wenatchee Pass (4,210 ft).

**PCT: *Wenatchee Pass to Cady Pass.*** *6.2 miles/m (H,S).* A short climb from Wenatchee Pass reaches meadows west of Top Lake, and Trail 1506. A slow ascent gains a saddle above the east end of Pear Lake (4,809 ft). The trail was rerouted in 1987 to continue along the ridge and bypass Pear Lake, Frozen Finger Pass, and Fortune Ponds. Trail 1057 from Meadow Creek now incorporates the old route from Fortune Ponds past Pear Lake to the PCT. The route swings west of the ridge for a long traverse to Saddle Gap (5,050 ft) and, just north of it, Trail 1054. A series of switchbacks descends to Pass Creek, to meet Trail 1053. The route then reaches Cady Pass (4,300 ft) where it is joined by Trail 1501.

**PCT: *Cady Pass to Wenatchee Ridge.*** *8.3 miles/m (H,S).* After dodging east of the crest at Cady Pass, the track regains the top at 5,400 feet, then maintains that altitude across talus slopes and alpine meadows on the south side of Skykomish Peak. Tiny, cliff-rimmed Lake Sally Ann (5,479 ft) is passed, and Trail 1532 merges from the east. The path continues through flower-laced heathers and crosses Wards Pass (5,700 ft) to reach Dishpan Gap (5,600 ft); here it is joined by Trails 1051 and 650. More alpine meadows are crossed to Sauk Pass (5,500 ft), where Trail 1525 ascends from Meander Meadow. A short traverse below the east side of Kodak Peak (named for a camera lost there by a USGS topographic survey party) leads to Wenatchee Ridge, the south boundary of the Glacier Peak Wilderness.

## CLIMBING

The northernmost peak in the Henry M. Jackson Wilderness is tri-summited Bedal Peak (6,554 ft). Routes vary from a scramble up timbered slopes on the north to several C-5.7 leads up solid rock on the southeast face. South of Bedal is the signature mountain in this part of the Cascades, Sloan Peak (7,835 ft). It is the highest point in the wilderness, and its distinctive "Matterhorn" summit is easily identified from any viewpoint within a hundred miles. Climbs combine alpine meadow treks, glacier travel, and steep solid rock. The easiest route, a C-3, follows a shelf traversing the south side to the upper southwest face. The southwest face and the north ridge are a tougher C-4 to C-5. The vertical east, southeast, and west faces require several leads from C-5.7 to C-5.8.

The horseshoe ring of peaks around Monte Cristo and Glacier Basin have climbs enough to fill a season. At the northwest corner is Addison Ridge, a long jagged massif divided into three distinct summits and a multitude of ridge-top crags (6,640 to 6,799 ft). The highest are Gemini North, Gemini South, and Pirate Peak. Farther east along this arête are Eyre Tower and the rock pyramid of Foggy Peak (6,810 ft), whose various routes range from C-4 to C-5.

On the north side of Glacier Basin are Cadet Peak (7,186 ft) and The Cadets (6,800 ft), a row of easy-scramble crags. Capping the head of the basin is Monte Cristo Peak (7,136 ft). Combination snow and rock routes up its ridges and faces are in the C-3 to C-4 range, although one rates C-5.5. The south side of the basin is framed by multi-towered Wilmans Peak and several companion spires. West Wilmans (6,840 ft) and East Wilmans (6,880 ft) Peaks have two small glaciers hanging from their east flanks,

*The Pride Glacier lies below peaks of the Monte Cristo region. Summits seen here are, left to right, Kyes Peak, Columbia Peak (in the distance), Monte Cristo, Wilmans Peaks (either side of the U-notch), and The Cadets (far right).*

and vertical rock faces on both north and south sides. Most ascents are ranked C-3 to C-4. Farther west along the ridge are East Wilmans Spire, C-5.4, South Wilmans Spire, C-3, and North Wilmans Spire, C-4 to C-5.2. Lower down on the ridge is an impressive stone monolith, the Count of Monte Cristo, with several routes ranging from C-5.4 to C-5.10.

A companion basin south of Glacier Basin surrounds the broad Columbia Glacier. On its east side is Kyes Peak (7,280 ft), with pocket glaciers wrapped around a jagged crest. Monte Cristo Peak is also at the head of this basin. On the west rim, a series of C-5 towers leads to the summit of Columbia Peak (7,172 ft). An easy C-3 route up the west spur gains its summit, although C-4 to C-5 routes exist on other ridges and faces.

More remote and less known summits lie on the outer flanks of the Monte Cristo group. These include Goblin Mountain (5,606 ft), east of Kyes Peak, and a long rugged ridge south of Poodle Dog Pass capped by Hubbart Peak (5,936 ft) and Scott Peak (5,288 ft). Both of the latter peaks have impressive vertical east faces.

The terrain south and east in the Henry M. Jackson Wilderness, while rugged and remote, has few appealing climbs. A possible exception is Mount Fernow (6,190 ft) a subalpine mass just north of Highway 2, south of Johnson Creek and west of Kelly Creek. A few crags of C-3 difficulty stand atop its steep, forested ridges. Lichtenberg Mountain (5,844 ft), rising above Lake Valhalla, north of Stevens Pass, has a west face and northwest ridge of solid rock with C-5.7 routes.

In the Eagle Rock Roadless Area, the imposing 3,100-foot-high vertical north face of Mount Baring (6,125 ft) has long been regarded as one of the most difficult climbs in the western Cascades. Some of the northwest's top climbers struggled with this C-5.8 to C-5.10 challenge before it was finally conquered in 1960. Since then it has been climbed several times, including once in the winter. Its equally challenging north prow, Dolomite Tower, is a C-5.9 climb, first done in 1986.

Baring and the striking thumbs of Gunn and Merchant Peaks are bookends on either side of Barclay Creek. Gunn (6,240 ft) is approached from Barclay Creek, where gullies and slabs lead to a notch on its southeast ridge. A basin traverse leads to the C-3 ascent of the final summit block. The northwest face of this block can be climbed in three C-4 to C-5 rock leads. Merchant Peak (6,113 ft) is topped by relatively easy C-3 ridge routes from the saddle between its east and west summits.

On the Bear Creek–Howard Creek divide, Spire Mountain (6,213 ft) is a sharp, narrow rib topped by three distinct summits and several other rock gendarmes. C-3 to C-4 routes up chimneys on the east face access the tops of the spires. Bear Mountain (5,519 ft) is a triple-towered, rough rock peak at the northeast corner of the Eagle Rock area. Ascents start from FR 6574, an unmaintained spur off of FR 6570 at the north end of the Beckler River Road. Ribs connecting the individual summits are sharp knife-edges; traverses on them are rated C-3 to C-5.

## WINTER SPORTS

Most of the Henry M. Jackson Wilderness is locked in deep snow all winter, and its high-angled, remote slopes present too great an avalanche hazard for winter travel. The exceptions are areas immediately north of Stevens Pass, which are accessible to cross-country skiing and snowshoeing from the ski area. Skyline Ridge, on the north side of the pass, is a strenuous 1,000-foot climb from the highway past the radio relay shed to the snow-covered flat of Skyline Lake. A continuation of the tour uphill to the ridge top offers views of Mount Stuart and Glacier Peak. Downhill runs are good via the ascent route or in the powder snow in the timbered basin northwest of the ridge (with due caution for lower avalanche slopes above Nason Creek). Under stable snow conditions the open slopes on the east side of the summit ridge offer excellent advanced skiing, though ridge-top cornices often make them difficult or dangerous to reach.

The open bowl of Smithbrook Basin can be reached from snow-covered Smithbrook Road (FR 6700), 4.7 miles east of Stevens Pass. Halfway up the basin, avalanche slopes on both sides bear a cautious watch, as do those farther into the basin on the north side of Lichtenberg Mountain. Expert skiers can pick up the general route of the PCT near the head of the basin and follow it south across a saddle to steep slopes leading to Lake Valhalla. The tour should only be taken under stable snow conditions.

# 17　Nason Ridge Roadless Area

**Location:** In Chelan County, between US 2 and the Little Wenatchee River
**Size:** 19,567 acres
**Status:** Special Interest Area for scenery and recreation
**Terrain:** A long, steep, east–west ridge with a broad, rounded top capped by spurs leads to rock summits. Lower slopes are covered with open mixed-conifer forest, but the ridge top is barren rock and talus.
**Elevation:** 2,200 to 7,063 feet
**Management:** USFS, Okanogan–Wenatchee National Forest, Lake Wenatchee Ranger District; plus a few private sections owned by Longview Fiber
**Topographic maps:** Labyrinth Mountain, Lake Wenatchee, Mount Howard, Plain

Throughout its 16-mile, east–west length, Nason Ridge rises abruptly for 4,000 feet above adjoining drainages. Its top is broader and less jagged than other Cascade massifs of similar altitude, but the barren crest above 6,000 feet is marked with steep cliffs falling away to broad talus slopes. Small lakes and tarns hide in basins and cirques below. Several peaks mark the top of the ridge, but none presents any climbing challenge. Although the total acreage enclosing the ridge is relatively small, the wide vistas of the Cascade crest from the open upper slopes make the ridge area feel larger than it actually is.

Many sidehills, especially those above Nason Creek and US 2, are regularly swept clean of trees by avalanches. The low-lying replacement growth of vine maple, mountain ash, and slide alder turns these slopes into palettes splashed with brilliant golds and scarlets in late fall.

## CLIMATE

Nason Ridge receives 55 to 65 inches of precipitation annually, more than half in the form of snow between the months of October and April. Snow accumulates to an average of 6 to 7 feet during winter months, but most of the area is snow-free by mid-July. Summer temperatures are warm, with highs averaging in the upper 80s, and winter is chilly with lows averaging in the teens.

## ECOSYSTEM

Lower elevations are covered by grand fir and Douglas-fir. The mid-elevation forest is western hemlock, western red cedar, and Pacific fir, with an understory of vine maple, salal, salmonberry, Oregon grape, sticky currant, elderberry, and devil's club. The upper-elevation forest is mostly subalpine fir, lodgepole pine, whitebark pine, and Engelmann spruce. Alpine meadows have a profusion of wildflowers. Steep avalanche-swept sidehills are covered with willow, mountain maple, mountain ash, Sitka alder, huckleberries, and grasses. The highest elevations are barren, save for sedges and heathers.

Nason Ridge is known for its concentration of mountain goats, which are often seen around Alpine Lookout early or late in the day. For study purposes, the herd in the lookout vicinity is protected from hunting.

## GEOLOGY

The central portion of Nason Ridge, from Rock Mountain to Round Mountain, is primarily folded metamorphic biotite schist and gneiss of the continental crust that makes up the Cascade core. It is probably 100 million to 200 million years old. The far west end of the ridge is a portion of the Mount Stuart batholith, a younger granitic intrusion that occurred 50 million to 60 million years ago. The Leavenworth fault, marking the west edge of the Chiwaukum graben, runs north–south along the east side of the ridge. The graben is thought to have subsided as the area was overlaid with sedimentary deposits. Cobbles and boulders mark the fault boundary. Although adjoining drainages were gouged by alpine glaciers, the upper portion of the ridge appears to have escaped glaciation; its rock outcrops are rugged and angular, not smoothed by glacial polishing.

## HISTORY

The earliest use of the Nason Ridge area was for grazing sheep. In the early 1900s herds were driven up to ridge-top meadows for summer forage. Fire lookouts were constructed

*Mom and Junior relax on Nason Ridge.*

between 1933 and 1936 atop Rock Mountain and Alpine Lookout. The former was abandoned in 1973; the latter, replaced in 1975, is one of the few forest lookouts actively manned for fire detection.

## HIKING
### Lake Wenatchee Trails

*Trail 1583, Nason Ridge.* *16.7 miles/m (H,S,B; M from its east end to the Alpine Lookout spur trail).* From the Kahler Glen trailhead (1,980 ft) south of Lake Wenatchee State Park, the track follows and crosses old logging roads as it heads up the east end of Nason Ridge for 3 miles to 5,270 feet, where it meets Trail 1529. It traverses the south slope of Round Mountain, then follows the crest west. In 2.5 miles, a spur leads uphill to a ridge high-point and Alpine Lookout (6,235 ft). Motorized vehicles are prohibited beyond the start of this spur. Views north are down to Lake Wenatchee, the White River drainage, Dirtyface Mountain, and the peaks of Chiwawa Ridge. To the south, US 2 follows Nason Creek far below, and across the valley are the Chiwaukum Mountains and the north end of the Alpine Lakes Wilderness.

From Alpine Lookout, the path continues west on the south slope of the ridge, first through meadows, then in open alpine forest. In 3.2 miles it switchbacks down to Merritt Lake (5,003 ft). From the lake, it descends to a basin where the upper end of Trail 1588 is met (4,840 ft). A traverse west along south slopes reaches the meadows of Royal Basin (4,900 ft); horse travel is not recommended west of here. Switchbacks

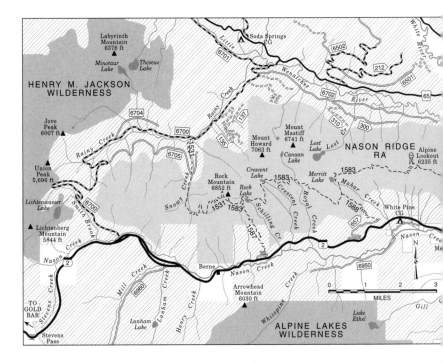

up talus gain a forested bench that continues west to Crescent Lake (5,450 ft). A climb from the lake basin rounds a narrow rib, then traverses rock and talus slopes to the open bowl above Rock Lake (5,870 ft). Skirting cliffs above the lake, the path rounds a bare rib to pass Trail 1587 (6,110 ft) and end on Trail 1531.

## US 2 Trails

**Trail 1529, Round Mountain.** *1.6 miles/m (H,B,M).* This is the shortest of the trails that reach the east end of Nason Ridge and its spectacular viewpoints at Round Mountain and Alpine Lookout. From FR 6910 (3,960 ft), the route uses a dozen easy-grade switchbacks up the hillside to gain the ridge top just east of Round Mountain. Here it joins Trail 1583 (5,270 ft) as the latter continues west along Nason Ridge.

**Trail 1588, Merritt Lake.** *3 miles/m (H,S,B).* From the end of FR 657 (3,040 ft), twenty-three switchbacks through old-growth forest gain a basin above the west side of Mahar Creek, where Trail 1583 is met (4,840 ft). That trail can be followed 0.5 mile uphill to Merritt Lake (5,003 ft), a tarn with a small meadow near its outlet and rock cliffs framing the opposite shore.

**Trail 1587, Rock Mountain.** *4 miles/m (H,S,B).* From the end of a powerline service road east of Berne on US 2 (3,010 ft), this grueling trail heads up the avalanche-stripped hillside where, sixty-two switchbacks later and 2,000 feet higher, it gains the top of a rib projecting southeast from Nason Ridge. There is little respite, however, as the path continues up steep, heather-covered slopes. At the south rim of the basin

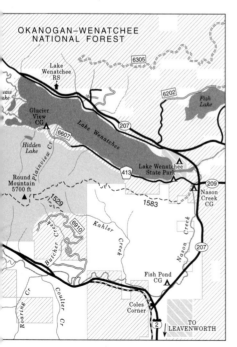

enclosing Rock Lake, the trail meets the west end of Trail 1583 (6,110 ft). The Rock Mountain Trail climbs a rock rib to the crest of Nason Ridge and Trail 1531 (6,600 ft). The way goes straight up the narrow crest to the Rock Mountain summit (6,852 ft), a former lookout site atop cliffs that drop 1,000 feet east to Rock Lake. A ridge leads 1.5 miles to the north, to the top of Mount Howard, the highest point on Nason Ridge. Beyond, Sloan and Glacier Peaks loom above a host of lesser summits. To the south, the tip of Mount Rainier rises above the summit of Mount Daniel.

**Trail 1531, Snowy Creek.** *4 miles/ m (H,S,B).* Where FR 6705 crosses Snowy Creek, find the trailhead on the south side of the road (3,580 ft). The track climbs gently south through cool, streamside forest, then takes switchbacks east up to a large flat meadow. The pleasant hike is

*Looking southwest from Rock Mountain, a portion of the serrated edge of Nason Ridge can be seen.*

over, and thirty-two switchbacks, first in open timber, then up rock and heather, gain the top of Nason Ridge (6,600 ft). Here, Trail 1587 is passed as Trail 1531 begins its final thrust to the Rock Mountain summit.

## WINTER SPORTS

Nason Ridge is too steep and avalanche-prone for much winter recreation; however, the summer route up the logging roads of Butcher Creek and Trail 1529 to the top of Round Mountain offers a safe, though strenuous, 5-mile winter trip to the top of the mountain. Here are shimmering views of snowclad peaks and lakes, and an excellent downhill run through open timber.

# 18 Glacier Peak

### Glacier Peak Wilderness; Glacier Peak I, J, and M, Twin Lakes, Canyon Creek, Prairie Mountain, White Chuck, and Chelan (North of Holden) Roadless Areas

**Location:** In Skagit, Snohomish, and Chelan Counties, astride the Cascade crest between Cascade Pass and the Wenatchee River

**Size:** Wilderness, 576,900 acres; Glacier Peak G, 8,737 acres; Glacier Peak I, 12,755 acres; Glacier Peak J, 25,971 acres; Glacier Peak M, 1,055 acres; Prairie Mountain, 3,822 acres; White Chuck, 5,723 acres; Twin Lakes, 22,048 acres; Canyon Creek, 9,158 acres; Chelan (Holden–Lucerne), 9,270 acres

**Status:** Designated Wilderness (1964, 1984); Roadless areas are Semiprimitive Nonmotorized and Motorized

**Terrain:** Deep, glacier-cut valleys with steep sidehills are heavily forested up to 5,000 to 6,000 feet. Above, meadows and parklands along lower ridge crests give way to heavily glaciated, ragged rock summits ranging between 7,000 and 9,000 feet. Centerpiece of the wilderness is the ice-draped volcanic cone of Glacier Peak.

**Elevation:** 1,600 to 10,541 feet

**Management:** USFS, Mount Baker–Snoqualmie National Forest, Mount Baker and Darrington Ranger Districts; Okanogan–Wenatchee National Forest, Chelan, Entiat, and Lake Wenatchee Ranger Districts; some private patented mining claims

**Topographic maps:** Agnes Mountain, Bench Mark Mtn., Cascade Pass, Clark Mountain, Dome Peak, Downey Mtn., Gamma Peak, Glacier Peak East, Glacier Peak West, Goode Mtn., Holden, Huckleberry Mtn., Illabot Peaks, Lime Mountain, Lucerne, McGregor Mtn., Mount David, Mt. Lyall, Pinnacle Mountain, Prairie Mtn., Pugh Mountain, Pyramid Mountain, Saska Peak, Schaefer Lake, Sloan Peak, Snowking Mtn., Sonny Boy Lakes, Stehekin, Suiattle Pass, Trinity, White Chuck Mtn.

A glorious hodgepodge of peaks and glaciers along the Cascade crest surrounds Glacier Peak, the most remote of the range's high volcanoes. Creeks drop from snow- and ice fields to rush through deep, glacier-scoured drainages. Walls swoop up from the brush-choked valley bottoms past avalanche scars on forested slopes to vertical rock faces and knife-edge summits. Wilderness ridges are pocked with cirques and basins holding 210 lakes, many so remote that only half of them have been named.

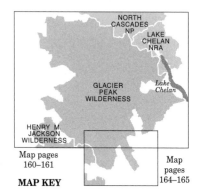

Map pages 160–161

**MAP KEY**

Map pages 164–165

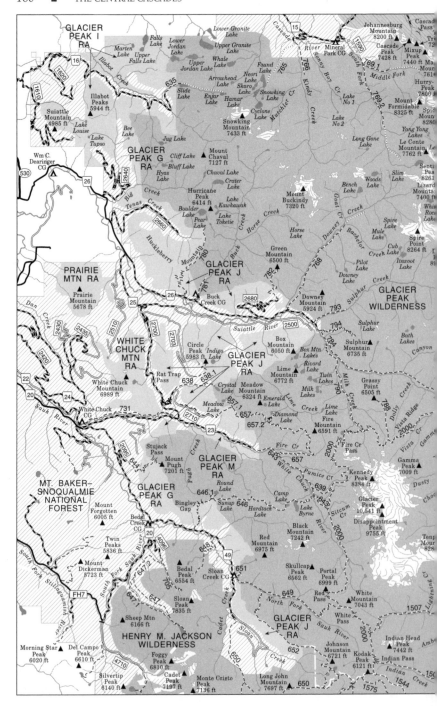

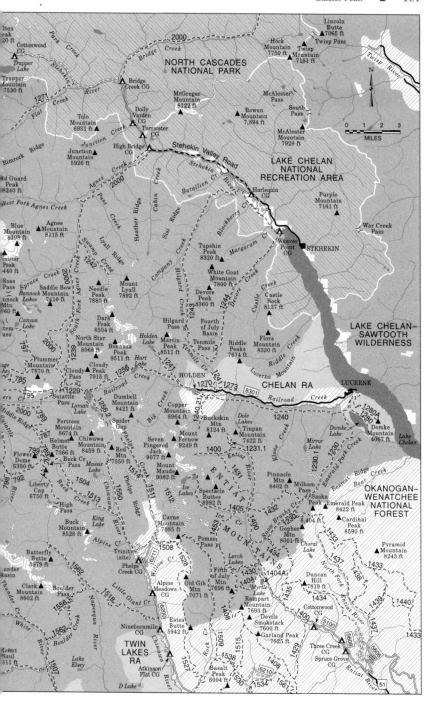

One hundred cataloged trails spread through the region, offering 450 miles of hiking. These range from easy well-maintained paths to rugged old sheep drives, poorly marked and never cared for. Once above timberline, experienced cross-country hikers have many more miles of alpine country at their disposal. Such treks include the classic Ptarmigan Traverse, a 15-mile-long climbers' route, mostly on rock and glaciers, from Cascade Pass south to Dome Peak. The exit south from Dome requires another 10 to 20 miles of cross-country and trail travel to reach the nearest road.

Glacier Peak, 10,541 feet, is the highest summit in its namesake wilderness. The remainder of the significant peaks in the region range between 7,000 and 9,500 feet; most have either alpine glacier or hanging glaciers plastered to their sides. The wilderness has more active glaciers than any other region in the Lower 48 states. The relatively low elevation of the wilderness peaks belies their climbing challenge and scenic beauty; most rise about 5,000 vertical feet above adjacent valley floors, and many sheer faces are more than 2,000 feet high.

## CLIMATE

Because the Glacier Peak Wilderness spans the Cascades, its climate varies by location —east or west of the crest. The high range blocks storm systems that sweep in from the Pacific; as the damp, warm ocean air bumps into the mountains, it rises, cools, and deposits its moisture content on the western slopes. Once across the crest precipitation levels drop significantly as the cool, dry air continues east across the state. On the west side of the wilderness the average annual precipitation is 110 inches, much falling as snow between October and April, accumulating up to 45 feet deep. On the east side of the Cascades the annual precipitation averages only 35 inches, and snow depths range from 10 to 12 feet. Temperatures follow much the same pattern. West of the crest the ocean air patterns keep summer highs down to the balmy 80s, and winter lows in

*A shoulder of Red Mountain is a fine spot for a high campsite.*

the teens to lower 20s. East of the crest summers are warmer, with highs in the 90s, and winter lows range slightly above zero.

## ECOSYSTEM

Valley bottoms are covered by a dense forest of hemlock, spruce, cedar, fir, cotton-wood, alder, and willow, with an understory of woody plants such as huckleberry. Side-wall forests consist of true fir, spruce, and hemlock, and some larch in upland meadows. Eastern slopes also have substantial pine, mostly lodgepole. Steep slopes are regularly cut by avalanche tracks where alder and low alpine plants are the primary survivors. Clusters of subalpine fir and mountain hemlock frame alpine meadows carpeted with sedges, heathers, and a variety of wildflowers.

Wildlife includes both mule and black-tailed deer, a few elk, black bear, marten, fisher, and lynx. Among smaller animals are Douglas squirrels, chipmunks, and golden-mantled ground squirrels. Higher rocks and cliffs are home to mountain goats, hoary marmots, pika, and ptarmigan. Rarely seen, though possibly present, are grizzly bear, gray wolf, and wolverine.

Birds of the area include grouse, goshawks, red-tailed hawks, gray jays, red-shafted flickers, Clark's nutcrackers, great horned owls, and the more rare spotted owls and peregrine falcons.

## GEOLOGY

The core rocks in the area are schists and gneisses, metamorphosed from sediments and lava flows beneath the ocean on the coast of the North Cascades microcontinent, before it reached North America. The core rock was lifted above the sea, and granitic plutons, such as the one forming the Dumbell Mountain peaks, intruded through the newly raised crust in places as long as 220 million years ago. As this microcontinent drove northeast and impinged on the west coast of North America about 50 million years ago, these metamorphic rocks were squeezed and folded to form the base structure of the northwest-trending Cascade Range. When the rocks cooled and hardened, the residual northward motion of the newly accreted North Cascades caused shear stresses resulting in several parallel fault lines, generally running in a northwest–southeast direction.

Erosion wore away the surface of the new mountain range, carrying the sediments down to valley floors to form sandstones and conglomerates. Uplifting of the region continued, accompanied by lava flows from volcanoes along the Cascade crest, until about 25 million years ago, when most volcanic action ceased. Fissures caused by fault-ing were intruded with still more granite from deep within the Earth's crust. The largest of these intrusions, in the heart of the wilderness, is the Cloudy Pass batholith, which formed about 22 million years ago.

The cone of Glacier Peak began to build atop the western edge of the Cloudy Pass batholith about 700,000 years ago in a series of passive dacite flows. Lime Ridge, to the west, first blocked the westward flow of lava, so most spread to the east into the

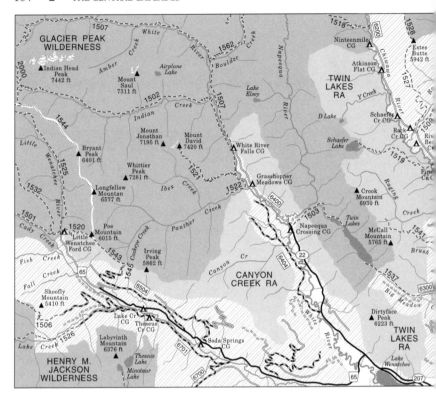

Suiattle River valley. As the volcano cone grew higher, flows surmounted Lime Ridge and poured into the White Chuck River drainage as well. Most volcanic flows that built the primary cone of the peak ceased after 12,000 to 15,000 years; however, two more recent eruptions formed smaller subcones on the flanks of Glacier Peak. Extruded dacite formed Disappointment Peak on a rib to the south. A second cone on the east flank of the mountain, beneath the Chocolate Glacier, collapsed and oozed down in the form of mud flows and debris fans to push the Suiattle River into the bedrock to the east. In what we hope was a final burst of activity about 12,000 years ago, the mountain exploded violently in nine or more closely spaced eruptions, sending pumice mud slides into the White Chuck and Suiattle Valleys, and distributing a carpet of ash and pumice up to 12 feet thick over the mountains downwind to the east. This ash has been traced as far east as Saskatchewan.

About a million years ago sculpting of the region was begun by glaciers, which waxed and waned until the last advance of the continental ice sheets about 12,000 years ago. The glaciers cut the deep U-shaped valleys characteristic of the region, carved the sharp peaks and ridges, and scooped out the bowls now filled by mountain lakes. Since then the glaciers have been in retreat, but their past work can be observed in the long moraines extending well beyond today's glacial snouts, and in the high rock ribs

from the summit of Glacier Peak that mark the original surface level of the volcanic cone prior to glacial grinding.

## HISTORY

The earliest users of the Glacier Peak Wilderness were nearby Indian tribes, who foraged its forests and meadows for plants and game. Indian trails used for trade between the coastal tribes and those of central Washington crossed Cloudy, White, and Indian Passes. The first Euro-Americans in the area were traders and trappers; their travel through the area followed existing Indian trails. In the 1870s railroads sent survey crews into the region in search of Cascade crossings suitable for rail lines.

The Northwest gold rush of the 1880s and '90s brought in prospectors, with the first claims filed in the Chiwawa River valley, Phelps Creek drainage, and along Railroad Creek. Prospectors found not only gold, but ores of copper, silver, lead, zinc, and molybdenum. By 1896, red stains had led to prospects at Red Mountain and other spots on Phelps Ridge; the Royal Development Company bought out claims and built a large mill at Trinity. Mines extracted low-grade copper ore in the 1930s, but production ceased to be profitable, and the operation closed.

A railroad survey in 1887 reported copper ore outcrops along Railroad Creek, and J. H. Holden staked claims there in 1896. Holden could never raise capital for a full-scale operation, but Howe Sound Company later bought the property, and by 1938 began production. In 1939 a 2,000-ton mill was built at Holden, and the population of the mining community grew to 450. Over the next 19 years, the Holden mine produced more copper than any other in the state; 106,000 tons of concentrate were shipped to the Tacoma smelter, and 600,000 ounces of gold were recovered. The total value of the minerals extracted exceeded $66 million. A precipitous drop in copper prices in 1957 made Holden's low-grade ore no longer profitable. Mining ceased, and the property was eventually sold to the Lutheran church for a retreat village.

Settlers first arrived in the Wenatchee Valley in the 1870s, and by the 1900s sheepherders had blazed trails into the Glacier Peak Wilderness and were regularly moving herds from valley bottoms to alpine meadows for summer pasture. Many of the more rugged (and, unfortunately, poorly maintained or abandoned) trails in the high country are old sheep drives. Fire-prevention strategies in the 1920s prompted the Forest Service to build more trails to support fire lookouts on peaks throughout the region and to provide access for fire patrols and fire suppression crews. Lookouts were located atop Green, Huckleberry, Red, Johnson, Domke, and Poe Mountains, Sulphur Point, Miners Ridge, Flower Dome, Glacier Creek Ridge, and Mount David.

The Glacier Peak Wilderness Area was created in 1964; it encompassed portions of what is now the south end of North Cascades National Park, but did not extend as

*Mining took place at Big Copper Mine, near Holden, from the 1930s through the 1950s. The mine is now closed.*

far south or west as the current wilderness boundaries. In 1984 the boundaries were expanded, adding 112,600 acres to the wilderness.

## HIKING
### Suiattle River Trails

**Trail 780, Huckleberry Mountain.** *7 miles/m (H,S).* From FR 26 (990 ft), long switchbacks sweep up a hillside to the ridge top (5,180 ft). The trail follows the crest northwest, where subalpine meadows give views of Glacier Peak and the north face of White Chuck Mountain. A ridge-top ramble to a bald knob (5,856 ft) opens views of the snow-draped span of Mount Chaval, Snowking Mountain, Mutchler Peak, Mount Buckindy, and beyond the ragged backbone of the Cascade crest. At the end of the ridge, 0.6 mile north, is the site of an abandoned lookout (6,267 ft).

**Trail 782, Green Mountain.** *4 miles/m (H,S).* The route leaves FR 2680 (3,350 ft) to diagonal up a forested hillside then climb more steeply northward to break into meadows. A few switchbacks and another traverse lead to a small pond in an open cirque. The route now climbs an alpine flower–bedecked slope, then follows the ridge top to the summit of Green Mountain (6,500 ft), a onetime lookout site. Reasons for its choice are obvious, to the southeast is Glacier Peak, to the northeast the peaks of the Ptarmigan Traverse, and stretching east-to-west the deep Suiattle drainage.

**Trail 768, Downey Creek.** *6.8 miles/m (H,S).* From FR 26 (1,450 ft), the track slogs steadily up through forest, streams, and mud holes above the east side of Downey Creek, occasionally dropping near the creek itself. In 6 miles, at Bachelor Creek (2,440 ft), the trail passes a long abandoned trail up that creek, then follows Downey as it bends east from Goat Creek and dwindles away a mile upstream.

**Trail 784, Suiattle River.** *10.8 miles/e (H,S).* The major westside gateway to the Glacier Peak Wilderness leaves the end of FR 26 (1,592 ft), then wends east up the deep Suiattle drainage to its junction with the PCT (2,800 ft). At 9.4 miles, Trail 785 swings northeast up Miners Ridge.

**Trail 785, Miners Ridge.** *9.9 miles/e (H,S).* At 9.4 miles on Trail 784 (2,760 ft), switchbacks head north up the forested hillside. Above the west end of Trail 795, switchbacks continue up to flowered meadows atop Miners Ridge. A spur heads west 0.1 mile to a lookout site; the cabin here is used in summer as a wilderness ranger station. The main trail continues east through ridge-top parkland to Image Lake (6,056 ft), one of the most photogenic spots in the wilderness. The lake, set amid flower garden meadows, reflects the icy summit of Glacier Peak. A path circles the grassy basin east of the lake, and other spurs lead away from the lake to separate camp areas for backpackers and horses. Scrambles east along the heather crest to Plummer Mountain (7,870 ft) open vistas of the Dome Peak area. From Image Lake the trail traverses east, then switchbacks down to meet Trail 795 at the Glacier Peak Mine property (5,630 ft).

**Trail 795, Miners Cabin.** *2.1 miles/e (H).* This track avoids the final ascent to the top of Miners Ridge; instead, it traverses the south side of the ridge at the 5,400-foot level as it heads toward Suiattle Pass. It is rejoined by Trail 785 at some miners' shacks (5,630 ft), then ends as it meets the PCT (5,470 ft) 0.7 mile west of Suiattle Pass.

## White Chuck River Trails

**Trail 657, Meadow Mountain.** *17.6 miles/m (H,S).* After a 5-mile hike up gated FR 2710, the trail leaves the north side of the road (3,570 ft), makes a gentle traverse, then switchbacks up to open meadows (4,900 ft) on the south slopes of the crest. At a saddle in 0.5 mile is a spur that descends to Meadow Lake (4,763 ft). The path continues east through forest and meadows that become wildflower gardens in early summer and berry patches in fall. At a sharp saddle (5,800 ft) south of the Meadow Mountain summit, switchbacks drop to a traverse above Owl Creek. The route continues east around creek-head basins to a tiny bench (5,400 ft) below the cliffs of Fire Mountain. It zigzags down to Fire Creek (3,720 ft), crosses it, heads west along a bluff, then switchbacks down a nose to join Trail 643 (2,570 ft).

**Trail 643, White Chuck.** *6.9 miles/e (H,S).* At the end of FR 23 (2,240 ft), this path heads east into the old-growth forest of the White Chuck Valley. The junction with Trail 657 is passed at 1.4 miles, as the route continues into the steep-walled river drainage. At 4.2 miles, Trail 643.1 leads to Kennedy Hot Springs and the east end of Trail 646. Trail 643 switchbacks up a nose to the east to join the PCT at Sitcum Creek (3,900 ft).

## North Fork of the Sauk River Trails

**Trail 646, Lost Creek Ridge.** *11.1 miles/m (H,S).* The route shows no mercy as it switchbacks from FR 49 (1,849 ft) up the slopes to Bingley Gap (4,390 ft), then zig-zags up the ridge to a saddle (5,520 ft) where a spur to Round Lake (5,070 ft) drops off. Here are unobstructed views of Bedal and Sloan Peaks. The track becomes vague as it traverses the parkland on the south slopes below the crest; it becomes recogniz-able again near Hardtack Lake (5,430 ft). The path crosses to open north-facing slopes, climbs briefly, then descends to the cirque containing Camp Lake (5,681 ft). A climb up the rib north of the lake leads to a meadow bench, then switchbacks down to the north shore of Lake Byrne (5,544 ft). The trail swings back and forth through the for-est as it drops with knee-jarring vengeance to Kennedy Hot Springs (3,300 ft).

**Trail 649, North Fork of the Sauk.** *8.4 miles/m (H,S).* From Sloan Creek Camp-ground on FR 49 (2,072 ft), a gentle track heads east along the North Fork of the Sauk River. Huge cedars decorate the river bottom as the way passes the beginning of Trail 652 at 2 miles. At Mackinaw Shelter (2,970 ft) the gentle grade is history as switchbacks press up forest and avalanche slopes to timberline (5,260 ft). A long traverse through a subalpine park meets the PCT, 0.5 mile west of White Pass (6,000 ft).

**Trail 652, Pilot Ridge.** *11 miles/d (H,S).* This route leaves Trail 649 at the 2-mile point (2,400 ft). After a foot-log crossing of the Sauk, the path zigzags up the steep wooded slope to gain the top of Johnson Ridge (5,175 ft). The way follows the crest southeast for 7 miles as it undulates between 5,000 and 5,700 feet, alternating between forest and meadows with unsurpassed views of Glacier Peak, the Monte Cristo–area summits, and Mount Rainier. The path rounds the head of the Sloan Creek basin, passes a spur to Johnson Mountain, then twists around a rib and drops to Little Blue Lake (5,194 ft). After contouring a basin above another fork of Sloan Creek, the trail climbs to join Trail 650 east of June Mountain (5,700 ft).

## White River Trails

**Trail 1521, Mount David.** *7 miles/m (H).* From the end of FR 6400 (2,300 ft), follow Trail 1522 downstream along the west bank of the White River for 1 mile to the start of Trail 1521. The route leads southwest up a steep forested slope, where switchbacks gain the ridge crest (5,200 ft). After a brief respite, the climb resumes, and, with ups and downs, reaches timberline. It continues, weaving through ridge-crest cliffs, to the summit pinnacle, where a lookout once stood. Concrete steps set in holes blasted from the rock cliff lead to the top (7,420 ft). Wide views here stretch to Sloan Peak, Clark Mountain, Mount Daniel, Mount Rainier, Lake Wenatchee, and, way below, the White River and Indian Creek.

**Trail 1502, Indian Creek.** *11 miles/m (H,S).* Cross the bridge at the end of FR 6400 (2,300 ft) to the west side of the White River, and wander the valley floor up-stream for 2 miles. After crossing Indian Creek the route switchbacks above the lower creek gorge, then returns to the level creek bottom upstream. After a gradual grind upstream, the grade steepens near the upper end of the Indian Creek drainage, and the forest thins and breaks into intermittent meadows. A few final zigzags reach Indian Pass (4,990 ft) and the PCT.

**Trail 1507, White River.** *15 miles/m (H).* At the end of FR 6400 (2,300 ft), the route on the east side of the White River wends through old-growth forest as it follows the river upstream. At mile 4, Trail 1562 branches east at Boulder Creek; the White River Trail then makes two rather tenuous crossings of the river and heads uphill southwest to Lower White Pass and the PCT (5,400 ft).

**Trail 1562, Boulder Creek.** *14.5 miles/d (H).* At Boulder Creek (2,530 ft) this route leaves Trail 1507 and switchbacks east up forest slopes. The way crosses the creek in an upper basin and continues a moderate ascent along its east bank. It threads through cliffs of the basin headwall to reach the meadows of Boulder Pass (6,200 ft) for a peek into the upper Napeequa Valley. The downhill grade northeast from the pass is moderated by a long chain of switchbacks. Crossing the Napeequa River (4,290 ft) is a final challenge; it can be nearly impossible during high-water periods. On the opposite side of the river the way meets Trail 1518 from Little Giant Pass, and continues up the wide green swath of Napeequa Valley. An imposing rim of glaciers and peaks rise above. A number of cross-country routes probe the enclosing walls.

## Chiwawa River Trails

**Trail 1518, Little Giant.** *8.5 miles/d (H).* A mile north of Nineteenmile Campground on FR 6200, the trail drops east from the road (2,606 ft) to the Chiwawa River, where a barricade indicates the obvious—the bridge is out. Cross the river on a nearby logjam, or in low water wade, and follow old roads through an abandoned campground to the trailhead. The original sheep drive that went straight uphill has been enhanced by switchbacks, but the tread is very eroded. A pine forest is traversed to the south fork of Little Giant Creek, where the steep ascent resumes, first in forest, then brush, and then atop a rocky rib to finally reach Little Giant Pass (6,408 ft). A rough tread leads down to the valley floor to meet Trail 1562.

**Trail 1511, Phelps Creek.** *9.5 miles/m (H,S).* From the gate on FR 6211 (3,500 ft), the track heads up an old mining road, past the start of Trail 1508, to the road end near Chipmunk Creek. The path continues along the creek bottom, alternating between meadow and forest to reach Spider Meadows (4,700 ft), framed by 2,000-foot-high cliffs topped by Dumbell Mountain. At 5,300 feet the trail splits; one path continues a short distance to the headwaters of Phelps Creek, the other heads west toward a seemingly impenetrable wall. A miners' path picks its way up the cliff to a gully that contains the Spider Glacier. A scramble up the rib east of the glacier leads to Spider Gap (7,100 ft), with good views of Mount Maude and Seven Fingered Jack en route. On the north side of the gap, a snow and rock descent (ice ax recommended) along the side of the Lyman Glacier reaches the end of Trail 1256.2 from Lyman Lake.

**Trail 1508, Carne Mountain.** *3.5 miles/m (H,S).* Moderate-grade switchbacks climb through forest from Trail 1511 (3,500 ft) to the open slopes of a small basin (4,800 ft) on the southwest side of Carne Mountain. The larch-rimmed meadows of the basin are stippled with wildflower colors in early summer. At the head of the basin (6,420 ft) the way meets Trail 1509 joining from the northeast. A short amble south to a small saddle gives views of the vertical north face of Old Gib, and a ridge scramble north reaches the top of Carne Mountain (7,085 ft).

**Trail 1550, Chiwawa River.** *4.9 miles/e (H,S).* An old mining road to the Red Mountain prospects near the head of the Chiwawa River starts on private mine property at the end of FR 6200 at the site of Trinity (2,772 ft). At 1.5 miles pass the beginning of Trail 1513 and climb away from the river along the west flank of Phelps Ridge. The river is rejoined as it swings north. In another mile the trail forks (4,760 ft). Trail 1550.1 continues up the basin to a meadow at the forks of the Chiwawa River; views sweep up to Fortress and Chiwawa Mountains. Trail 1550 switchbacks through avalanche-scored timber to prospects on the west slope of Red Mountain (6,440 ft).

**Trail 1513, Buck Creek.** *8 miles/m (H,S).* From the 1.5-mile point of Trail 1550 (3,200 ft), the route crosses the Chiwawa River, then follows Buck Creek northwest. After rising over a pair of glacier-cut benches, the way breaks into a meadow with views to hanging glaciers on the face of Buck Mountain. A long switchback takes the path out of the creek bottom to a traverse of slopes high above the creek. The trail rejoins the creek at its source in a basin at 5,600 feet. Continue west to Buck Creek Pass (5,810 ft) and tremendous views of Glacier Peak. Trails 1513, 789, and 792 meet at the pass.

**Trail 789, Buck Creek Pass.** *5 miles/m (H,S).* The route northwest from Buck Creek Pass (5,810 ft) wends through meadows as it descends to Small Creek, then ascends to cross Middle Ridge (6,245 ft). An easy wooded grade leads to the PCT (4,640 ft) near Miners Creek.

## Entiat River Trails

**Trail 1400, Entiat River.** *14.7 miles/e (H,S).* From Cottonwood Campground at the end of FR 5100 (3,144 ft), a wide track heads northwest through river-bottom timber along the Entiat River. Leaving this route to the west are Trail 1404, at 3.5 miles; Trail 1430, at 5 miles; and Trail 1405, at 8.3 miles. Headed east at 6.5 miles is Trail 1230. As the Entiat River hooks west, the dense forest occasionally breaks into meadows. The valley widens, and the trail finally ends (5,482 ft) in a cliff-bound meadow below glaciers hanging from the summit blocks of Mount Fernow, Seven Fingered Jack, and Mount Maude.

**Trail 1404, Cow Creek Meadows.** *3.2 miles/e (H).* From Trail 1400 (3,749 ft), the path passes the north end of Myrtle Lake, climbs northwest through a notch, then contours a forested rib to reach Cow Creek, where a short spur leads to Cow Creek Meadows (5,180 ft). The trail continues uphill in a chain of switchbacks through rocky meadows and larch on the east side of Fifth of July Mountain to intersect Trail 1408 from the Entiat Mountains (6,637 ft).

**Trail 1430, Larch Lakes.** *5.4 miles/m (H,S).* After leaving Trail 1400 (3,784 ft) and crossing the Entiat River, the path climbs through timber beside Larch Lakes Creek. Trees give way to the brushy slopes of an old burn, and tedious switchbacks weave uphill to the small bench holding lower Larch Lake (5,670 ft). A short ascent leads to the meadow encircling the upper lake (5,750 ft), and the north end of Trail 1408. The route now crosses a saddle (6,450 ft) on the northwest rim of the basin and begins a long traverse to Pomas Pass (6,420 ft), where it meets Trail 1453.

**Trail 1405, Ice Creek.** *4.1 miles/e (H,S).* After leaving Trail 1400 (4,363 ft) and crossing the Entiat River on a log, the route swings west into the Ice Creek drainage, where it meets the north end of Trail 1453. The path continues up Ice Creek Valley, in forest at first, then in alternating trees and meadows. At the head of the creek the trail ends in a pretty basin (5,210 ft) surrounded by the rock walls of the Entiat Mountains.

From these meadows, a rugged, 2-mile boot-tread heads east to the base of cliffs, then scrambles up alongside a fork of Ice Creek to a rock and pumice bench that holds lower Ice Lake (6,822 ft). Follow the bench southwest to the creek cascading from the upper lake. The route scrambles up along the creek to upper Ice Lake (7,188 ft), tucked below the 1,600-foot-high face of Mount Maude.

**Trail 1453, Pomas Creek.** *3.1 miles/m (H,S).* As Trail 1405 enters the Ice Creek drainage, this path drops off south (4,398 ft), then climbs a hogback on the west side of Pomas Creek. A traverse beneath cliffs and a few switchbacks lead to Pomas Pass (6,420 ft), where the route meets Trail 1430.

## Lucerne Trails

**Trail 1230, Emerald Park.** *12 miles/m (H,S).* At the 2.2-mile point on Trail 1280 (2,182 ft), between the community of Lucerne and Domke Lake, this route strikes southwest along the flat west of the lake. A long traverse of a forested hillside leads to Emerald Park Creek; here the trail steepens as it climbs above the northwest side of the drainage. The way levels as it enters the meadows of Emerald Park (5,200 ft). Farther up the drainage the meadows expand, with views opening to jagged Bearcat Ridge to the south. The path climbs to steep-walled Milham Pass (6,663 ft) and views east to Lake Chelan and the Sawtooth Range. From the pass, descend steep, larch-covered slopes, and in 1.3 miles pass Trail 1433 leading south. The path continues its descent to reach avalanche-cut meadows with views of the north faces of Gopher Mountain and Saska Peak. After passing the north end of Trail 1434, the route drops through timber and brushy creek bottom to reach Trail 1400.

**Trail 1256, Railroad Creek.** *10.5 miles/m (H,S).* An easy grade leaves the end of FR 8301 at Holden (3,310 ft) and heads west up the Railroad Creek drainage. The track through the dark green jungle continues upstream, to a hillside ascent past waterfalls at the outlet to Hart Lake (3,982 ft). Switchbacks up a side-slope bypass cliffs below Crown Point and offer views of the cascades. The route ascends past another waterfall to its source, Lyman Lake (5,598 ft), a picture-postcard spot below the Lyman Glacier and Chiwawa Mountain. To the west, subalpine forest gives way to meadows as the route climbs to Cloudy Pass (6,438 ft). From Cloudy Pass the route switchbacks down into the basin at the head of Agnes Creek to meet the PCT.

**Trail 1256.2, Lyman Lake.** *3 miles/m (H).* A relatively new trail from the north end (5,580 ft) of Lyman Lake heads along a rib east of the lake, then crosses an old moraine into a meadow that holds four upper lakes at the snout of the Lyman Glacier.

*Image Lake holds a postcard-perfect reflection of Glacier Peak.*

From the lower edge of the glacier, gullies, rock, or snow (depending on the season) lead up to Spider Gap (7,060 ft).

## Stehekin River Trails

**Trail 1244, Devore Creek.** *16 miles/m (H,S).* From Weaver Point Campground (1,150 ft) at the north end of Lake Chelan, the route switchbacks up the hillside to bypass a short gorge near the mouth of Devore Creek. It then follows the creek bottom south through steep, narrow walls, occasionally passing through avalanche-cut meadows.

At the head of the creek in Fourth of July Basin, switchbacks climb the headwall to Tenmile Pass (6,442 ft), then more drop south through larch and pine into the Tenmile Creek drainage. At 5,200 feet a side-slope traverse to the northwest joins the upper reaches of the creek. The route continues upstream to meadows below basin-rimming cliffs. Zigzags up a rocky gully on the east side of the cliff reach Hilgard Pass (6,638 ft), the south end of Trail 1243.

*Trail 1243, Company Creek.* 11 miles/m (H,S). The route leaves the Stehekin Valley (1,250 ft) and climbs a rib above cliffs on the north side of Company Creek. It traverses high above the creek at the base of cliffs; a flat grade continues south until Company Creek rises to meet it. The trail proceeds up the creek bottom, and at 5 miles makes a difficult crossing to the east side of the stream. At the confluence of Company and Hilgard Creeks the route swings up the Hilgard drainage, following it south to basin-end cliffs. Switchbacks work up the headwall to Hilgard Pass (6,638 ft), where the south end of Trail 1244 is met. The pass can be dangerous until snow melts.

*Trail 1271, Flat Creek.* 3.5 miles/e (H,S). From the Stehekin Valley Road (2,285 ft), 14.5 miles from Stehekin, this route heads southwest up the Flat Creek drainage. An easy grade through forest and meadows ends in a bowl (2,800 ft) below the impressive cliffs of Rimrock Ridge. The glacier-wrapped summit of Le Conte Mountain rises to the west above the end of the valley.

## Trail 2000, Pacific Crest National Scenic Trail

The PCT enters the Glacier Peak Wilderness from the Henry M. Jackson Wilderness near Indian Pass. It follows the Cascade backbone north, and next contacts civilization at the High Bridge Guard Station on the Stehekin River, at the mouth of Agnes Creek.

*PCT: Indian Pass to Sitcum Creek.* 12.4 miles/m (H,S). The ridge at Indian Pass (4,980 ft) can be reached from the south via the PCT from the Henry M. Jackson Wilderness or from the east on Trail 1502 from Indian Creek. The route climbs gently through meadows to Lower White Pass (5,400 ft), where it meets the upper end of Trail 1507. The ascent continues on open northeast slopes to White Pass (5,904 ft), with Glacier Peak in view the entire way. At White Pass the trail crosses the ridge, traverses below White Mountain, and meets the east end of Trail 649. The way climbs gradually to Red Pass (6,550 ft), a narrow defile south of Portal Peak, where the Monte Cristo group of peaks lines the western horizon. The way swings east after crossing the pass; meadows give way to cliffs and talus slopes on the south side of White Chuck Cinder Cone, a remnant of a small volcano. The trail drops to Glacier Creek Meadows in a broad basin at the head of the White Chuck River, then descends through subalpine forest. After crossing the White Chuck, a long river bottom descent reaches Sitcum Creek (3,900 ft) and Trail 643 from the west.

*PCT: Sitcum Creek to Vista Ridge.* 18.6 miles/m (H,S). The route heads north, traverses the valley wall to Kennedy Creek, crosses the creek, and climbs the opposite wall to Kennedy Ridge (4,250 ft). The parkland crest is followed up to timberline, close to the snouts of the Scimitar and Kennedy Glaciers. A long ascent weaves northwest, crossing meltwater creeks, to reach Fire Creek Pass (6,350 ft), the most technically troubling pass on the PCT. Switchbacks east of the pass drop first to cliff-bound Mica Lake (5,443 ft), then to Milk Creek (3,800 ft). Thirty-six switchbacks up the opposite side of the drainage regain lost altitude and reach the meadows of Milk Creek Ridge (5,600 ft). A gentle grade through the basin at the head of the East Fork of Milk Creek leads to Vista Ridge (5,900 ft) and a sweeping view up the Vista Glacier to the summit of Glacier Peak. Here are the first glimpses northwest to the glaciers in the Dome Peak area.

**PCT: *Vista Ridge to Suiattle Pass.*** *12.3 miles/m (H,S).* After a chain of switchbacks drops through cliffs to Vista Creek, the route follows the wooded creek bottom downstream to Skyline Bridge over the Suiattle River (2,780 ft), where it crosses Trail 784. The route zigzags up the nose of Middle Ridge, traverses east above Miners Creek, crosses it, and climbs to Suiattle Pass (5,984 ft), passing Trails 789 and 785 en route. The pass overlooks the deep Agnes Creek drainage and the jagged knife-edge ridge on its east border.

**PCT: *Suiattle Pass to the Stehekin River.*** *17 miles/m (H,S).* The route drops into the headwaters of the South Fork of Agnes Creek, where it meets Trail 1256 (5,600 ft). As the path swings around a basin southeast of Bannock Mountain, glimpses open east to the bulk of Bonanza Peak (9,511 ft). The way descends to rejoin Agnes Creek at Glacier Creek (3,600 ft) and begins the long trek down the valley floor. Meadows in this section of the trail offer views upstream to the rock finger summit of Agnes Mountain, and downstream to the south face of McGregor Mountain. Civilization of sorts is reached at the High Bridge Guard Station on the Stehekin (1,600 ft).

## CLIMBING

Climbing guides catalog routes up 140 peaks and spires in the wilderness, far too many to list individually here. Many of these have impressive faces exceeding 1,000 feet in height, but also have easy ridge scrambles to their summits. Following is a summary of the most impressive or technically challenging climbs.

In the northwest corner of the wilderness, the highest and most glaciated peak is four-summited Snowking Mountain (7,433 ft). Routes exist from all sides, but none are technically difficult. Southwest of Snowking is Mount Chaval (7,127 ft), with three craggy summits. Easiest routes are from the west; more challenging are the northwest flank, C-3 to C-4, and the north ridge, 1,500 feet of solid granite with moves up to C-5.7. The third peak of interest in this area is Mount Buckindy (7,320 ft), the highest of a group of fractured, loose breccia spires that rise above the Kindy Glacier. Routes from the north and east combine snow and rock pitches. A half-dozen lesser spires in the group have short vertical faces of low C-5 difficulty.

The remoteness of Glacier Peak (10,541 ft), the highest summit in the wilderness, adds to the difficulty of its ascent. Routes have been put up all of its major glaciers: the Sitkum, Scimitar, Kennedy, Ptarmigan, Vista, Ermine, Dusty, Chocolate, Gerdine, North Guardian, and Cool. The upper reaches of most of these are very steep and heavily crevassed. The only rock route to the summit follows the southern rib via Disappointment Peak, then up the cleaver beyond to the summit. Southeast of Glacier is Tenpeak Mountain (8,281 ft), a long summit block above the Honeycomb Glacier with several rock routes in the C-5 range.

Popular, easily accessible peaks (7,240 to 8,200 ft) lie along the boundary between the wilderness and North Cascades National Park at Cascade Pass. Most impressive of these is Johannesburg Mountain, with its wide, vertical, 2,200-foot-high north face; several routes rate up to C-5.8. Next along this ridge is Cascade Peak, with C-3 to C-5.8 ascents on all sides. East of Cascade are The Triplets, three rock spikes with several hundred feet of C-3 to C-5.3 leads. The ridge turns southeast to Mixup Peak, a long knife-edge crest rising from a steep, downsloping rock apron. Routes vary from C-4 to C-5.

The classic 15-mile-long, cross-country Ptarmigan Traverse south from Cascade Pass reaches some of the best climbs in the wilderness. The traverse crosses Cache Col south of the pass to its first summit, Magic Mountain (7,610 ft). Its summit tower has an impressive vertical west face; however, most climbs involve only C-3 to C-4 chimney or ridge routes. A traverse south leads to a col between Mount Formidable (8,325 ft) and Spider Mountain (8,286 ft). Formidable is a massive peak above the Middle Cascade Glacier with a summit chopped into several towers. Steep routes on both snow and rock have a few exposed leads. Spider is renowned for its loose rock, which endangers otherwise simple C-4 ascents.

A long traverse south leads to Le Conte Mountain (7,762 ft), an elongated summit. The highest point is an easy ridge climb, but the 100- to 200-foot spires at the south end of the summit block are more challenging. The Le Conte Glacier is traversed south past Sentinel Peak (8,261 ft) and its companion, Old Guard (8,240 ft); both are easy snow and rock scrambles. After contouring the upper South Cascade Glacier the route crosses a saddle and drops to White Rock Lakes (6,194 ft). Sharp, knife-blade spires along an arête southwest of the lakes culminate in Spire Point (8,264 ft), at the apex of the Dana and Spire Glaciers. This crag has several difficult rock routes ranging from C-4 to C-5.7.

East of Spire, on a rib between the Dome Glacier to the west and the massive Chickamin Glacier to the east, is the highest summit in the area, Dome Peak (8,920 ft). Travel over crevassed glaciers leads to the final assault on the narrow summit flake. There are also several interesting towers on ridges radiating from Dome, and two more peaks rise above the Chickamin Glacier. East of Dome is Sinister Peak (8,440 ft), a bulky rock summit with a steep snowfield on its shoulder. Ice and rock routes are rated C-4. Northeast of Sinister is Blue Mountain (8,198 ft), sometimes known as Gunsight Peak for the pair of rabbit-ear flakes that form its top. It is a striking peak with a solid, vertical, 700-foot granite face. There are no easy routes, and those on the face range as high as C-5.10.

Agnes Mountain (8,115 ft) is a rugged, isolated peak 1.5 miles east of Blue. Its distinctive "Matterhorn" shape protrudes high above surrounding crags. The slabs and blocks of the summit pyramid hold several C-5 to C-5.6 routes. The South Fork of Agnes Creek is framed by two impressive ridges. To the west is Bannock Mountain (7,760 ft), with a massive northwest face rising 1,700 feet above a glacier base. On the east side of the creek is a long, jagged ridge with Needle Peak (7,880 ft) at its north end. The pointed summit is an exposed C-3 climb. The ridge continues south past Dark Peak (8,504 ft) to culminate in the huge mass of Bonanza Peak (9,511 ft), the highest nonvolcanic summit in the Cascades. The top of the mountain is a complex, multi-horned rib that long thwarted climbing attempts. Glacier approaches lead to several rock pitches of C-5 and harder on any summit routes.

At the northeast end of the wilderness three impressive peaks rise above the west side of Devore Creek. The northernmost, Tupshin Peak (8,320 ft), has a broad 1,300-foot north face and a series of pinnacles along its summit ridge. Ticklish, exposed C-4 to C-5.4 rock work is required to reach the top. Southwest of Tupshin is White Goat Mountain (7,800 ft), a narrow granite blade with sheer 1,000-foot sides. Even the normally easier arête approaches are rated C-5.3 to C-5.5. The southernmost of this trio is Devore Peak (8,360 ft), with a vertical 900-foot north face. Ridge routes have a few brief C-4 leads.

Fortress Mountain (8,674 ft) is the highest summit in the Chiwawa Mountains, but a relatively easy scramble from the southwest flank or east ridge. The Entiat Mountains terminate in three peaks of climbing interest. Mount Maude (9,082 ft) is a bulky summit rising above the Entiat Glacier. A difficult icefall route ascends from the glacier; all other routes, none higher than C-5, are on rock. North of Maude is Seven Fingered Jack (9,077 ft); as its name implies, its crest comprises seven pointed crags. All may be climbed via moderately difficult gullies. Mount Fernow (9,249 ft), the third peak, is the highest point in the Entiat Mountains. Its three main ridges are all easy climbs.

## WINTER SPORTS

Few visitors venture into the interior of the Glacier Peak Wilderness in winter, as the proliferation of avalanche tracks on side-slopes makes such expeditions inadvisable; nonetheless, winter ascents have been made on some peaks. Several classic ski and snowshoe tours on the west side of the wilderness can be recommended. One of these is Green Mountain, best done early or late in the season to reduce avalanche danger. The route follows Trail 782 from the Suiattle River. There is some avalanche danger in the meadows near timberline, before reaching the ridge top. The reward is a panorama of peaks, including Sloan, Glacier, Dome, Shuksan, Baker, and nearby Buckindy.

A safer tour, with equally spectacular views of Glacier Peak, is Meadow Mountain via Trail 657. It is a 5-mile road slog to reach the trailhead, and the lower portion of the trail is a narrow path through dense timber with only light snow cover. But once into timberline meadows, the deep snow on the broad ridge crest offers endless skiing opportunities.

An expert-level trek follows Trail 643 up the White Chuck River to Kennedy Hot Springs. The feasibility of this trip depends on snow depths; too much and it is impossible to drive the 11 miles up FR 23 to the trailhead, too little and the low-altitude trail will have only sparse snow cover. In the "just right" case, the reward for the long valley-bottom trip is a dip in the warm springs before heading back.

# 19 Entiat Mountains

## Myrtle Lake (West), Rock Creek, and Entiat (West) Roadless Areas

**Location:** In Chelan County, on the southeast border of the Glacier Peak Wilderness Area, between the Chiwawa and Entiat Rivers

**Size:** Entiat Mountains, including Entiat (west of the Entiat River), 60,565 acres; Rock Creek, 32,924 acres; Myrtle Lake (west of the Entiat River), 2,730 acres

**Status:** About 30 percent is Semiprimitive Nonmotorized; most of the remainder is open to motorized recreation

**Terrain:** A high-altitude plateau, with steep side-slopes, leads to interconnecting alpine ridge tops that rise to rugged summits at the northeast end of the range.

**Elevation:** 2,500 to 7,610 feet

**Management:** USFS, Wenatchee National Forest, Lake Wenatchee and Entiat Ranger Districts

**Topographic maps:** Brief, Chikamin Creek, Plain, Pyramid Mountain, Saska Peak, Schaefer Lake, Silver Falls, Sugarloaf Peak, Trinity, Tyee Mountain

The Entiat Mountains are a southern extension of the Glacier Peak Wilderness Area, and their exclusion from it is somewhat illogical. Perhaps it was because their geography was less rugged, more a transition from the ice-clad peaks of the wilderness to the alpine and mid-range forest of central Washington. Or perhaps it was because of their extensive trail use by motorcycles—more's the pity.

The mountain range rises abruptly from the base level of about 2,500 feet in the two wide, glacial-cut valleys that frame either side. The center of the range varies between 5,000 and 7,000 feet. The Mad River has carved a deep longitudinal drainage through the heart of the area. Its tributaries, as well as those of the Chiwawa and Entiat Rivers on either side, further divide the range into an interconnecting series of ridges and valleys.

The forests are typical of the Cascades' east slopes, giving way to broad meadows along and near the heads of creeks, and alpine meadows on ridge tops. The entire range has only a half-dozen lakes larger

*The Mad River area offers fine mountain biking as well as hiking.*

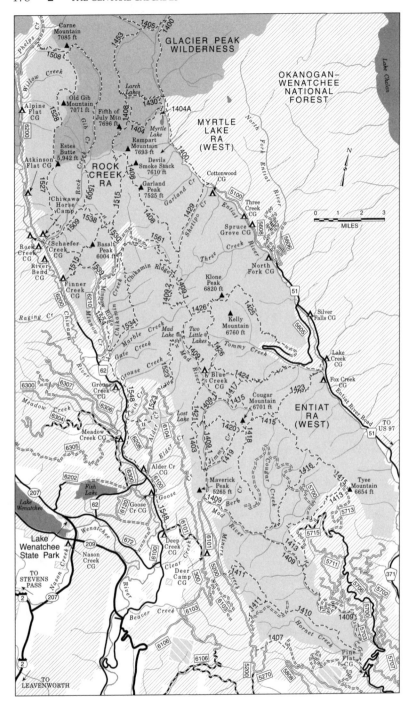

than pond-size, and most of these are shallow and heavily silted. In a few centuries they will probably be swallowed by encroaching meadows.

Some 185 miles of trail lace the Entiat Mountains Roadless Area; however, the roadless designation does not preclude motorized use. About 145 trail miles are open to motorcycles, and a half-dozen trails have been widened and graded (nearly paved) specifically for motorized use. Some of the remaining miles default to foot travel only by virtue of being abandoned and unmaintained. The snarl of engines certainly does not contribute to a wilderness experience, and the ash and pumice soil of the mountains is easily eroded by boots, let alone speeding, spinning wheels. It may be too late to protect this wonderful area with a wilderness designation, but we should at least lobby for no further degradation.

## CLIMATE

The west side of the Entiat Mountains receives more precipitation (45 to 90 inches annually) than the east side (35 to 50 inches annually). On both sides, from 60 to 70 percent falls between November and April in the form of snow. Valley snow depths reach an average of 5 feet, and at higher elevations snow stacks up to about 7 feet. Most is gone from all elevations by mid-July. Summer temperature highs average in the 80s and 90s; winter lows average between 10 and 20 degrees.

## ECOSYSTEM

Forests on the west side of the Entiat Mountains are composed of Douglas-fir, Pacific silver fir, grand fir, western hemlock, western white pine, and western red cedar, while timber on the drier eastern side is primarily Douglas-fir, alpine fir, and lodgepole pine. Large portions of the southeast end of the mountains have been burned by a succession of forest fires, and a dense lodgepole pine forest has regenerated since then.

The forest understory contains huckleberry, vine maple, mertensia, and prickly currant; in meadow breaks cheatgrass brome, starry Solomon-plume, heartleaf arnica, twinflower, arctic lupine, pyrola, prince's pine, wood violet, and anemone prevail. Alpine meadows at or near ridge tops are covered with arctic lupine, Sitka valerian, showy sedge, American false hellebore, and feathery miterwort. Side-slope avalanche paths support a growth of Sitka alder, mountain ash, elderberry, and trailing blackberry.

The forest is a summer range for mule deer, a small herd of elk, black bear, marten, and grouse. Spotted owls have been identified in the southern end of the mountains, and peregrine falcons have been sighted on the east side of the range.

## GEOLOGY

The underlying rocks in the Entiat Mountains, primarily evident in a wedge-shaped area between Miners Ridge and the lower Mad River, are old pre-Jurassic metamorphics. A major fault line marking the eastern edge of the Chiwaukum graben runs along the west crest of the mountains in the vicinity of Miners and McDonald Ridges. Chiwaukum graben rock is a pale sandstone, younger (30 million to 40 million years old) and less tightly folded than the older metamorphics on either side. Most of the folding occurred before the graben filled with sedimentary rock of volcanic origin. The remainder of the mountains between the fault line and the Entiat River are part of the Chelan batholith, a complex, massive, granitic intrusion between 60 million and 70 million years old.

Continental glaciers, which reached their maximum southern progress about 12,000 years ago, carved the valleys on either side of the Entiat Mountains through which the Entiat and Chiwawa Rivers flow. Although the soils covering the mountains include glacial alluvium, they are predominantly volcanic ash and pumice, ranging from 6 inches to 60 feet in depth, deposited by Glacier Peak eruptions 12,000 years ago. This light volcanic mix erodes easily when vegetation is removed.

## HISTORY

Local Indian tribes were known to visit the Entiat Mountains for hunting and food gathering. There is also some evidence of early-day trappers in the Rock Creek and Blue Creek areas. By the early 1900s, sheepherders were driving their flocks to ridge-top alpine meadows for summer grazing. At the heart of the mountains, on the Mad River, is Blue Creek Campground, accessible only by trail. This was once the site of the Mad River Dude Ranch, a popular 1920s vacation spot.

When fire protection became a key mission of the Forest Service in the 1920s and '30s, fire lookout sites were placed atop many of the area's high points, including Basalt Peak, Tyee Mountain, Klone Peak, Cougar Mountain, and a knob south of Estes Butte. All of these lookouts were removed or destroyed by the 1960s, but many of the region's trails, built to access and support the lookouts, are their legacy.

## HIKING
### Chiwawa River Trails

**Trail 1523, Alder Ridge.** 11 miles/m (H; S,B,M after July 15). The lower portion of this trail leaves FR 62, crosses logging roads, and wanders up through clearcuts from the Chiwawa River near Twin Creek (2,350 ft) to FR 6104 (3,900 ft), where the roadless area begins. Here the path continues up the ridge, covered with grand old Douglas-fir and ponderosa pine. At 5,800 feet the trail gains the crest of the Entiat Mountains, then continues north, alternating between woods and meadows, to reach its high point (6,229 ft). Rock outcrops en route offer views of Glacier Peak. The trail descends to meet Trail 1409.1 at the south fringe of Mad Meadow (5,810 ft).

**Trail 1515, Basalt Ridge.** 7.7 miles/m (H,S,B). From Finner Creek Campground on FR 62 (2,475 ft), the trail switchbacks up steep, wooded side-slopes to a bench at the head of Minnow Creek. It resumes the climb to the summit of Basalt Peak (6,004 ft), then drops north to a rock nubbin with views of the Rock Creek drainage and the crowns of the Entiat Mountains: Garland Peak, Devils Smoke Stack, and Rampart Mountain. Switchbacks gain the crest of the ridge heading north and follow its undulations to a junction with Trail 1408 (7,348 ft) near Devils Smoke Stack.

**Trail 1509, Rock Creek.** 11.5 miles/m (H,S; B to the Glacier Peak Wilderness). Near Rock Creek Campground on FR 62 (2,500 ft), the path leads up timbered slopes above the southeast side of Rock Creek. The route continues north along the creek in alternating forest and meadow, then enters the Glacier Peak Wilderness (3,650 ft). A creekside cliff forces the path high above the bank; beyond, it returns to the thickly wooded creek bottom. The forest thins to meadows as the trail climbs to the head of the drainage and switchbacks up the basin headwall. The route swings around to a saddle (5,980 ft) south of Carne Mountain, crosses it, and meets Trail 1508.

**Trail 1527, Estes Butte.** *2.5 miles/m (H,S,B,M).* Just north of Rock Creek Campground, spur FR 6200-460 heads a short distance up the north side of Rock Creek to the trailhead (2,600 ft). Switchbacks work up the steep forested hillside, where breaks in the trees offer views down the Chiwawa River valley. The climb eases at 4,600 feet as the ridge continues north to an abandoned lookout site (5,397 ft) with views of Glacier Peak, the Entiat Mountains, and the Chiwawa River valley. The path continues north along the ridge, dipping in saddles and rising over hummocks to reach the summit of Estes Butte (5,942 ft).

## Miners Ridge Trails

**Trail 1411, Miners Ridge.** *4.5 miles/e (H,S,B,M).* FR 5200, which rides the major fault line on the east side of the Chiwaukum graben, joins both ends of this trail. The north trailhead (4,950 ft), crosses Miners Creek, then climbs gently to the broad ridge top (5,500 ft). The track heads southeast through broad meadows, laced with lupine and Indian paintbrush, that provide wide views of Glacier Peak, Mount Stuart, and Lake Wenatchee. Just beyond a knob on the south end of the ridge (5,600 ft) is the west end of Trail 1410. From here the path swings downhill above the Hornet Creek Basin to rejoin FR 5200 (5,350 ft).

**Trail 1410, Hornet Ridge.** *6 miles/d (H,S,B,M).* A route between Miners Ridge and the Mad River leaves Trail 1411 just below the high point on the south end of the ridge. An easy grade follows Hornet Ridge southeast above the steep north slope of the Hornet Creek drainage. After a saddle, a rise, and another saddle, the route traverses south slopes below the ridge top to a narrow rib between Hornet Creek and a drainage to its north. A no-nonsense drop downhill followed by a few switchbacks leads to Trail 1409 in the Mad River canyon (1,970 ft), 1.5 miles north of Pine Flat Campground.

## Mad River Trails

**Trail 1409, Lower Mad River.** *14.9 miles/e (H,S,B,M).* From Pine Flat Campground on FR 57 (1,620 ft), the route follows the twists of the river as it heads northwest into the canyon. Old-growth cedar and Douglas-fir frame the trail, and vestiges of a 1970s fire that devastated the area can be seen on the side-slopes above the river. The first of many side trails, Trail 1410, leaves the west side of the river at 1.5 miles, just beyond Hornet Creek. In another mile the path leaves the riverbank and zigzags up to side-slopes, where it contours for a mile before returning to the river.

At 9.8 miles the route crosses the river to avoid cliffs along the east bank. It recrosses to the east bank at 10.6 miles, just below Cougar Creek. Here Trail 1416 heads uphill to the northeast. For the next mile the canyon widens, then closes in again at

13 miles near Berg Creek. Another mile leads to Maverick Saddle (4,300 ft), the end point of the lower river trail, and the start of the upper one.

**Trail 1409.1, Upper Mad River.** *12.2 miles/e (H; S,B,M after July 15).* From FR 6101 at Maverick Saddle (4,300 ft), the route follows the west side of the river for a mile, crosses the river, and meets the lower end of eastbound Trail 1419. The path breaks into clearings, and at 3 miles passes the lower end of Trail 1421 to the west. Meadows continue for the next mile; the river is crossed and recrossed before meeting Trail 1415 heading east up Whistling Pig Creek. At 5 miles the south end of expansive Blue Creek Meadow is reached; its campground is another 0.5 mile farther on the bank of Blue Creek (5,430 ft).

This campground is at the heart of the upper Mad River trail system, and a favorite base camp for numerous one-day loop trips using various interconnecting paths. Trail 1426 leaves east from the campground, and Trail 1421 heads to the west. To the north the river flows through a wide basin with a string of broad meadows. Near the south end of Mad Meadow, Trail 1523 drops in from the west, and a short spur leads southwest to Mad Lake, the river's source. At 7.5 miles, in the heart of Marble Meadow, Trail 1426 takes off to the east. The track now switchbacks up the rim of Three Creek Basin, and ends at the ridge top at 12.2 miles, where it joins Trails 1408 and 1429. Motorcycles are prohibited on trails north of here.

**Trail 1418, Cougar Ridge.** *4.5 miles/m (H,S,B,M).* Near the end of FR 5700 (5,200 ft) this route sets out along the top of a broad north-flowing ridge. The route follows this undulating crest for more than 5 miles, finally breaking into meadows and rock outcrops with views of Glacier Peak. It meets Trail 1419 (6,210 ft) just below the final rise to the summit of Cougar Mountain. The path continues along basalt slopes on the south and east sides of Cougar Mountain. It ends in another 0.2 mile on Trail 1415 (6,140 ft) as that trail crosses the mountain's north slope. A short spur climbs to the summit of Cougar Mountain (6,701 ft), a former lookout site well chosen for its unbroken views of the Cascades from Mount Rainier to Glacier Peak, as well as peaks around Mount Stuart.

**Trail 1415, Tyee Ridge.** *8.7 miles/m (H,S,B,M).* This scenic trail atop Tyee Ridge starts from FR 5713 at the last switchback (6,400 ft) below the Tyee Mountain lookout site. The first portion of the trail wanders the ridge through the silvering snags remaining after a large 1970s forest fire. For the next mile the route stays on south slopes just below the crest, with the Mount Stuart peaks in sight, until it reaches an open saddle (6,700 ft) on the south shoulder of Signal Peak. A slow descent along a roller-coaster ridge reaches a pocket meadow where Boiling Springs bubbles up to fill a tarn. Beyond is the head of Trail 1423 from the Entiat River valley, and in another mile the trail reaches an intersection with Trail 1418 on the northeast rib of Cougar Mountain. A descent along the north side of the mountain leads through Cougar Meadow (5,870 ft), then down Whistling Pig Creek, to the bank of the Mad River and Trail 1409.1.

**Trail 1421, Lost Lake.** *3.9 miles/e (H,S,B,M).* From the Upper Mad River (4,800 ft), 3.2 miles south of Blue Creek Campground, a recently reconstructed trail makes a

*Glacier Peak as seen from the Klone Peak Trail, with Whittier Peak, highest of the American Poet Peaks, on the left.*

series of lazy switchbacks up the forested west slope to a 5,650-foot-high flat, then descends to tiny Lost Lake (5,550 ft). The route climbs slowly north to a 5,930-foot high point, then makes a beeline descent to Blue Creek Meadow (5,400 ft).

**Trail 1426, Blue Creek.** *4.8 miles/e (H,S,B,M).* From the Blue Creek Campground (5,430 ft), this route heads up the west bank of Blue Creek, passes the west end of Trail 1424, then near the head of the drainage swings steeply uphill to Lake Ann (5,830 ft), the first of the Two Little Lakes. A few hundred feet downhill is the second lake, Lake Louise (5,750 ft). The path ascends gradually north along Tommy Creek, then swings west at Klone Meadow (6,200 ft), where it meets Trail 1425. From here a gradual descent to Marble Meadow (5,930 ft) rejoins Trail 1409.1.

**Trail 1408, Garland Peak.** *11.1 miles/m (H,S).* From its junction with Trails 1409.1 and 1429 at the headwaters of Three Creek (6,270 ft), the route follows the rocky crest of the Entiat Mountains north, sometimes atop the ridge, other times on the west slopes, shying away from the vertical faces on its north and east sides. Views are continuous and spectacular; close at hand are the ragged summits of the Entiat Mountains, south are Rainier and the Stuart subrange, east is the Cascade crest, and north are the ice-cloaked crags of the Glacier Peak Wilderness. At its high point (7,350 ft), midway between Garland Peak and Devils Smoke Stack, the route meets Trail 1515.

From a pass on the shoulder between Devils Smoke Stack and Rampart Mountain (7,160 ft), the trail drops to timberline to round the west side of Rampart, then enters the Glacier Peak Wilderness (5,860 ft) and switchbacks up the south shoulder of Fifth of July Mountain to Cow Creek Pass (6,920 ft). Scramble routes to the mountaintop reach eye-popping views of Rainier, Glacier, Maude, Spectacle Buttes, and the ragged north end of the Chelan Mountains. The way traverses north, drops below a band of cliffs, then passes the upper end of Trail 1404 as it heads to a rocky spur above Larch Lakes (6,350 ft). It drops into the cirque (5,740 ft) enclosing the upper two lakes, where it meets Trail 1430.

## Entiat River Trails

**Trail 1423, South Tommy.** *5.7 miles/m (H,S,B,M).* Two trails head west from FR 51 at Lake Creek Campground (2,215 ft); this one stays close to the west bank of the Entiat River for a short distance, then begins a torturous ascent of steep slopes in a series of switchbacks. A respite at a small bench (3,500 ft) is followed by more zigzags to the top of a spur (5,300 ft). This rib tilts abruptly upward for the final climb to a 6,485-foot-high knob on the northwest end of Tyee Ridge. The path tops the crest, then drops down the south side to join Trail 1415 (6,020 ft) west of Boiling Spring.

**Trail 1424, Middle Tommy.** *8.8 miles/m (H,S,B,M).* The second trail from Lake Creek Campground (2,215 ft) swings up the north bank of Tommy Creek, touches a logging spur in 0.7 mile, then crosses the creek and switchbacks to a mid-ridge bench at 5,150 feet. It drops around the head of a creek basin, then resumes switchbacks up a steep rib to a saddle. The way continues west through the flower fields of East Blue Creek Meadow, then ascends to end on Trail 1426 (5,500 ft).

**Trail 1425, North Tommy.** *9 miles/e (H,S,B,M).* FR 5605 does the first 2,000 feet of climbing up the steep north side of Tommy Creek. From the road's end (4,500 ft), the trail climbs west, switchbacking first broadly, then tightly, to m1

aintain an easy grade for motorbikes. At a helipad knob (5,863 ft) the route swings northwest atop the ridge, undulating over hummocks to reach Three Creek Ridge. From here a short ridge romp leads to the old lookout site atop Klone Peak (6,820 ft) and great views of the summits of the Glacier Peak Wilderness, the Pyramid Mountain portion of the Chelan Mountains, and the Mount Stuart–area peaks. The route then circles the south side of Klone to end on Trail 1426.

**Trail 1429, Shetipo.** *4.7 miles/m (H,S,B,M).* From the Entiat River's Cottonwood Campground (3,082 ft) at the end of FR 51, this route heads southwest, crosses Shetipo Creek, switchbacks up above the west bank, and stays high enough to avoid steep walls above the creek. The way crosses the creek in about 3 miles, then works up a series of side-slopes and benches to the pass at the head of Three Creek, where it meets Trails 1409.1 and 1408 (6,270 ft).

## CLIMBING

There are no serious climbs in the Entiat Mountains, although several of the high points have precipitous north or east faces, ranging from 100 to 1,500 feet or more in height. The longest and most prominent faces are on Signal and Garland Peaks, Devils Smoke Stack, and Rampart Mountain. Their faces feature routes up gullies and broken rock ranging from C-3 to C-5 in difficulty.

## WINTER SPORTS

Although the interior of the Entiat Mountains is too steep and avalanche-prone to be attractive for winter sports, snows turn peripheral access roads into potential cross-country ski and snowshoe tours. They are also attractive to the wintertime cousin of the motorcycle, the snowmobile.

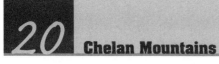

# 20 Chelan Mountains

## Chelan (West), Entiat (East), Myrtle Lake (East), and Stormy Mountain Roadless Areas

**Location:** In Chelan County, south of Glacier Peak Wilderness, between the Entiat River and Lake Chelan

**Size:** Chelan (west of Lake Chelan), 38,015 acres; Entiat (east of the Entiat River), 10,690 acres; Myrtle Lake (east of the Entiat River), 8,190 acres; Stormy Mountain, 32,500 acres

**Status:** About 60 percent is Primitive and Semiprimitive Nonmotorized; the remainder is open to motorized use.

**Terrain:** A high plateau and backbone ridge are joined by numerous lateral drainages. Mountains rise steeply from deep, glacier-carved valleys on either side. Ragged rocky peaks are located along the northern third of the range.

**Elevation:** 1,098 to 8,590 feet

**Management:** USFS, Wenatchee National Forest, Entiat and Chelan Ranger Districts

**Topographic maps:** Big Goat Mtn., Brief, Lucerne, Pyramid Mountain, Saska Peak, Silver Falls, South Navarre Peak, Stormy Mtn.

The Chelan Mountains lie between two wide, deep, glacier-carved valleys, one containing the Entiat River, the second filled by the crystal blue waters of Lake Chelan. The side-slopes of both valleys rise abruptly to the 6,000- to 7,000-foot backbone of the range. Glaciers and creeks have carved these abrupt hillsides into a series of lateral ridges that run perpendicular to the crest of the mountains. The North Fork of the Entiat River thrusts deeply into the northwest corner of the region.

A dense pine forest climbs from the creek bottoms up the slopes to timberline meadows on ridge tops. The forest cover on the sidehills is streaked by avalanche tracks. The northern portion of the area, bordering on the Glacier Peak Wilderness, contains the region's highest and most rugged peaks, some with near-vertical faces on their north and east sides. A few tiny pocket glaciers hide in cirques below these rock bastions.

*A curious bee explores a thistle blossom.*

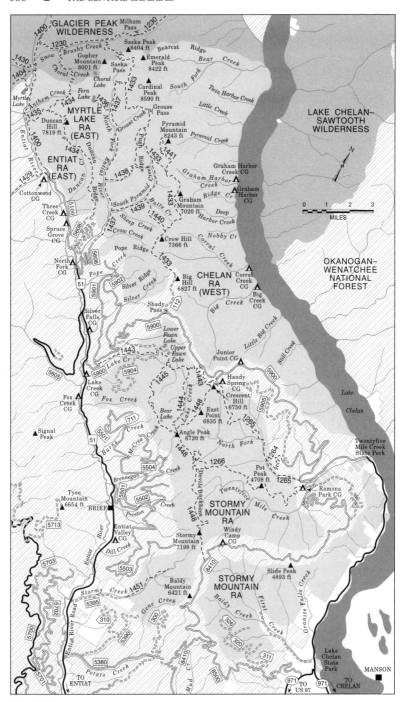

Ridge-top trails run the length of the backbone crest, fed on the west side by multiple trails that run up drainages and lateral ridges. These permit a host of loop trips that use only portions of the long crest route. The east side of the range has no maintained trails between the crest and the lake.

The mountains are not truly roadless; they are cut laterally at their midpoint by a heavily used forest road between Twentyfivemile Creek State Park on Lake Chelan and the Entiat Valley. The south and southwest borders of the roadless area have been heavily logged, and the threat of continued infringement on the present virgin forest is ever present. Some of the ridge tops had wide fire breaks cleared to contain the massive 1970 Entiat forest fire; several decades will be required before these tracks regain their natural appearance. Unfortunately, roadless also does not mean motorless; a large portion of the trail mileage in the mountains is open to the destruction of tread and solitude by motorcycles.

## CLIMATE

Because the Chelan Mountains form a high north–south divide, weather conditions vary somewhat between the west and east sides of the range. The wetter west side receives 40 to 70 inches of precipitation annually, while the drier east side gets 25 to 60 inchs. Sixty to 70 percent falls in the form of snow between November and May, and snow depths can vary between 6 and 15 feet, depending mostly on elevation. Temperatures in summer are warm, with highs averaging in the high 80- to 90-degree range. Lows in winter average in the teens and low 20s.

## ECOSYSTEM

Forests in the Chelan Mountains are Engelmann spruce, Pacific silver fir, subalpine fir, lodgepole pine, and alpine larch. Small Douglas-firs are also found in lower elevations on the west. Lodgepole pine is especially dense in old burn areas, where it is the dominant regenerative species. The forest understory includes pinegrass, oceanspray, dwarf huckleberry, and false azalea. Sheep fescue, cinquefoil, penstemon, and lupine are found in alpine meadows.

The area is used as a summer range by mule deer and a few elk. Black bear, cougar, marten, grouse, and a variety of smaller non-game birds and mammals also inhabit the forest. A few mountain goats are found in the rugged rock cliffs at the north edge of the range.

## GEOLOGY

The rock on the west side of the Chelan Mountains is a portion of the Chelan Batholith, a granitic intrusion that occurred in the late Mesozoic era. The eastern flank of the mountains is a complex of pre-Jurassic metamorphic rock and migmatite, a heterogeneous mix of igneous and metamorphic rocks swirled together along the eastern boundary of the batholith. Surface soils are either granitic residuum or a combination of pumice and volcanic ash, from 6 inches to 30 feet deep, expelled during the eruption of Glacier Peak about 12,000 years ago.

The deep valleys on both sides of the mountains were carved by the last continental ice sheet. The terminus of the lobe of continental ice on the east side of the mountains stopped prior to carving through bedrock near present-day Chelan, and when the ice retreated the valley filled with the waters of Lake Chelan. The glacial lobe from the Okanogan Valley was slower to retreat and temporarily blocked the head of Lake Chelan, raising its level far above today's height, causing the waters to carve a temporary escape coulee west from Twentyfivemile Creek.

## HISTORY

Long before Euro-American intrusion, the Lake Chelan area was home to the ancestors of the Chelan Indians, who lived on the margins of the lake. At least one site with pictographs has been reported along the lakeshore bordering the Chelan Mountains. The first whites in the area were trappers in the Domke Lake area who ran extensive traplines into the north end of the range. These pioneers were followed in the early 1900s by sheepherders who ran flocks up to alpine meadows for summer grazing. In the 1920s fire lookouts were constructed at several high points in the region. Among these were Duncan Hill, Big Hill, Pyramid Mountain, and Stormy Mountain. Only debris fragments and incomparable views remain today at these lookout sites.

## HIKING
### Entiat River Trails

**Trail 1434, Duncan Hill.** *10.4 miles/m (H,S; B,M to the Glacier Peak Wilderness).* From the trailhead on FR 5608 (5,146 ft) at the southeast end of Duncan Ridge, this seldom-used track follows the pine-covered crest over minor knobs to reach meadows at the head of Duncan Creek. In another 0.5 mile the way gains the rocky ridge south of Duncan Hill, where views extend from distant Mount Rainier to the nearby rocky crown of the Entiat Mountains. At 7,400 feet the path traverses the west side of Duncan Hill past a spur to the old lookout site at the summit (7,819 ft). The route wiggles downhill, climbs diagonally through forest, then meadows at the head of Anthem Creek, and rises to the Glacier Peak Wilderness boundary at a pass between Anthem and Choral Creeks (6,900 ft). The way drops to a small bench, then zigzags down the steep, forested slope along Choral Creek to Trail 1230 (4,915 ft).

**Trail 1437, North Fork of the Entiat River.** *8.1 miles/m (H,S,B).* This is the quickest route into the high rock summits at the north end of the Chelan Mountains. From the end of FR 5606 (4,150 ft), the trail meanders through thick forest along the east bank of the river, crosses South Pyramid Creek, and meets the lower end of Trail 1439. In another mile the trail passes the lower end of Trail 1438 as it works its way up the North Fork. Avalanche tracks provide view breaks in the woods as the way climbs along the valley floor to meet Trail 1436 to Fern Lake. In another mile the route leaves the river (5,760 ft) and ascends the east side-slope to merge with Trail 1433 (6,605 ft).

**Trail 1436, Fern Lake.** *1.5 miles/d (H).* This primitive track leaves Trail 1437 (5,201 ft) 6.1 miles from its start. The path climbs west after a logjam scamper or a frigid wade crosses the North Fork of the Entiat. The tread becomes more rugged as it breaks into steep rock for the final ascent to Fern Lake (6,894 ft). The lake reflects the glacier-polished cliffs that rim it, and in fall the color accents of surrounding golden larch.

**Trail 1439, South Pyramid Creek.** *4 miles/e (H,S,B).* This is the quickest route to the expansive views from Pyramid Mountain. From the 1.3-mile point of Trail 1437 (4,110 ft), just north of South Pyramid Creek, the route climbs through dense lodgepole pine, crosses the creek three times, then meets Trail 1433 (5,849 ft) at the south base of Pyramid Mountain.

## FR 5900 Trails

**Trail 1433, Pyramid Mountain.** *16.8 miles/m (H,S,B).* This long, ridge-top route extends from the heart of the Chelan Mountains north into the Glacier Peak Wilderness. From the end of FR 5900-112, north of Big Hill (6,550 ft), the route follows an old firebreak along the ridge, then slides west of the crest at the confluence of Silver and Pope Ridges (6,930 ft).

The path traverses the flank of Crow Hill, descends to a wooded saddle (6,442 ft), then rounds the head of Butte Creek. A climb up the open south flank of Graham Mountain leads to a traverse of the fir-dotted slope on the west side of the mountain, then across meadows to Trail 1441 (6,250 ft), the spur to the summit of Pyramid Mountain.

At South Pyramid Creek the track joins the upper end of Trail 1439 (5,849 ft), then follows the creek northwest to its headwaters. Climbing resumes, and after crossing Grouse Pass (7,190 ft) the way descends around Grouse Creek basin to the bald ridge on its north side. More downhill travel passes the intersection with Trail 1437 (6,605 ft), then a wooded traverse reaches a platform at the head of the North Fork of the Entiat, with wide views down that drainage. The way contours a rock shelf to switchbacks up the steep sidehill to Saska Pass, the wilderness boundary (7,450 ft). From the pass, the trail descends through larch-rimmed meadows to pine-covered slopes and ends on Trail 1230.1 (5,831 ft).

**Trail 1441, Pyramid Point Viewpoint.** *2.9 miles/m (H,S,B).* From Trail 1443 on the south slope of Pyramid Mountain (6,250 ft), the old lookout path climbs diagonally up the west side of Pyramid Mountain, then zigzags up to the summit (8,243 ft). Peer down the sheer northeast face to Lake Chelan, or turn around and admire Glacier Peak and its entourage of ice-trimmed summits.

**Trail 1443, Lake Creek.** *7.6 miles/e (H,S,B,M).* The lower sections of the original trail have been decimated by logging, and a recent logging road cuts the path midway up Lake Creek basin, but the trail still offers some forested solitude in its remaining sections. From a logging spur off FR 5900 (3,900 ft), the path ascends above the north bank of Lake Creek, mostly through lodgepole pine. It crosses FR 5904 (4,570 ft) at the base of the bowl containing Fawn Lakes and ascends the south slope of the basin. Switchbacks clamber up the wooded side-slope to the ridge top. The way proceeds east to Crescent Hill, to join Trail 1448 (6,720 ft).

**Trail 1448, Devils Backbone.** *13 miles/e (H,S,B,M).* This motorbike racetrack follows the top of the south end of the Chelan Mountains. From the north trailhead on

FR 5900-118 at Crescent Hill (6,750 ft), shared with Trails 1265 and 1443, the route follows the ridge south to Angle Peak (6,720 ft). The long trek southeast runs along the backbone ridge through alpine timber and meadows. In a mile switchbacks drop below the cliffs of Point 6709, then regain the ridge east of the cliffs. Trail 1266 (6,680 ft) from Pot Peak is passed as the path continues south, following a roller-coaster ridge-top dip to a zigzag climb to the summit of Stormy Mountain (7,198 ft). Here the vista spans green orchard oases in the parched Wenatchee hills, the volcanoes of the South Cascades, the frosted cone of Glacier Peak, and the chain of North Cascade summits. The track then drops down the west slopes of the crest to end at FR 8410 (6,100 ft).

## FR 8410 Trails

**Trail 1265, North Fork of Twentyfivemile Creek.** *10 miles/d (H,S,B,M)*. From FR 5900 on the east side of Darby Draw (2,390 ft), the path takes an easy grade west along the north bank of Twentyfivemile Creek. The route continues through riverbank fir and pine forest for three miles, then swings abruptly uphill, first in switchbacks, then just a relentless climb. The woods give way to meadows near the ridge top (5,850 ft), and the open crest climbs arrow-straight to the northeast, with continuous views of Lake Chelan. A hook at the end of the ridge ends at Crescent Hill, where it meets Trail 1448 (6,720 ft).

**Trail 1266, Pot Peak.** *9.5 miles/m (H,S,B,M)*. From Ramona Park Campground on FR 8410 (1,920 ft), switchbacks climb the forested ridge to the southwest to a breather in a flat, mid-ridge meadow. The slope again steepens; a traverse, a swing around the shoulder of the ridge, and yet another climbing traverse gain the ridge (4,300 ft) east of Pot Peak. The way circles the peak, then begins a steady ascent of a west-bound ridge. Meadows open at 6,800 feet, with views across Twentyfivemile Creek basin. Trail 1448 is met at 6,680 feet.

## CLIMBING

Although several of the Chelan Mountains high points have sheer north faces, most have trails or easy scramble routes from other sides. Only the summits along and immediately south of the Glacier Peak Wilderness are of climbing interest. These boundary peaks (7,900 to 8,428 ft) from west to east are: Choral Peak, Gopher Mountain, and Saska, Emerald, and Bearcat Peaks. Most have scramble routes from the south and steep C-3 rock ascents on the north and east faces.

Southeast of Bearcat Ridge are two companion arêtes, Devils Divide and Cloudcomb Ridge. The west end of Devils Divide is anchored by tri-topped Cardinal Peak (8,590 ft). The narrow crest on the south ridge is blocked by four near-vertical gendarmes requiring C-4 to C-5 climbing. East from Cardinal Peak, the divide is a series of craggy gendarmes with impressive rock routes up their south faces, and non-trivial ridge routes.

Cloudcomb Ridge, extending northeast from Squaretop Mountain, has four distinct summits and several intervening gendarmes along the ridge top. Gully systems on the flanks provide summit routes up steep, friable C-3 rock.

*The Lake Creek trail climbs slopes of the Chelan Mountains through stands of lodgepole pine.*

## WINTER SPORTS

Forest roads on the fringes of the Chelan Mountains are heavily used for wintertime snowmobiling, but most backcountry trails have dangerous avalanche slopes along their routes, so winter use is limited. A possible exception is Trail 1433 between Big Hill and Pyramid Mountain. The Entiat River Road (FS 51) is generally open as far as Brief, and from there skis or snowshoes can be used to reach FR 5900 and climb to Shady Pass. From the pass, follow the crest trail north to the vicinity of Pyramid Mountain. The south slopes of the summit are avalanche-prone, so the trip in can be retraced from that point, or a loop trip can be made by dropping to Trail 1439 in South Pyramid Creek, then continuing to the Entiat River Road.

# 21 Alpine Lakes Wilderness

**Location:** In King, Snohomish, Kittitas, and Chelan Counties, between US 2 and Interstate 90

**Size:** 393,360 acres

**Status:** Designated Wilderness (1976)

**Terrain:** Densely forested valleys rise to rugged rocky ridges and peaks with small glaciers and permanent snowfields. More than 700 lakes and tarns fill glacial cirques.

**Elevation:** 1,000 to 9,415 feet

**Management:** USFS, Mount Baker–Snoqualmie National Forest, Snoqualmie and Skykomish Ranger Districts; and Wenatchee National Forest, Cle Elum, Lake Wenatchee, and Leavenworth Ranger Districts

**Topographic maps:** Bandera, Big Jim Mountain, Big Snow Mtn., Blewett, Cashmere Mountain, Chikamin Peak, Chiwaukum Mountains, Davis Peak, Devils Slide, Enchantment Lakes, Grotto, Index, Jack Ridge, Lake Phillipa, Leavenworth, Mount Daniel, Mount Howard, Mount Phelps, Mount Si, Mount Stuart, Polallie Ridge, Scenic, Skykomish, Snoqualmie Lake, Snoqualmie Pass, Stevens Pass, The Cradle

The Alpine Lakes Wilderness exemplifies many of the problems faced in trying to preserve our wilderness heritage. Its jagged and irregular boundaries bespeak its history, namely that the prospectors, railroads, and loggers got here first, before recreationists and environmentalists, and staked claim to large segments of this wild and beautiful country. Long road fingers, built to support mining and logging activities, thrust up drainages into the wilderness. Patented mining claims stake out small privately owned chunks of property in the heart of the wilderness. Around the perimeter, a checkerboard pattern of private and national forest land marks the alternate sections of land given to railroads under the 1862 Union Pacific Act. This property was subsequently sold to timber companies for large profits. By the time the irreplaceable beauty and natural treasures of the region were recognized and its preservation was lobbied for, these intrusions had already gnawed deeply into its periphery.

The Alpine Lakes Wilderness was created in 1976 to preserve the heart of this beautiful area. The act creating it charged the Forest Service to manage its perimeter under a common resource plan and to acquire as rapidly as feasible the private properties within the proposed wilderness boundaries. Although preserva-

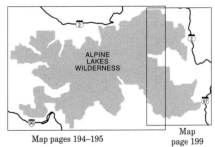

Map pages 194–195

Map page 199

**MAP KEY**

tion of the land was legally assured, preservation of its wilderness nature wasn't. The 450 miles of trails, 700 lakes, and countless peaks and pinnacles are but an hour's drive from population centers of more than 4 million people, a large number of whom surge into the wilderness during summer and fall, especially on weekends, for 1- to 2-day hiking, camping, and climbing trips. The result in some places is a degree of solitude and wilderness experience similar to that found in New York's Central Park. Alpine lakes are elbow-to-elbow campsites, fragile vegetation is boot-trampled out of existence, and the natural resources the wilderness was created to protect are threatened by use-it-to-death recreation.

The Forest Service has struggled with alternatives that attempt to address overuse of this popular wilderness. Proposals would enforce strict limits on the number of people permitted to enter the wilderness at any given time, set entrance fees, severely restrict camping sites, and so on. To some these seem like draconian measures, impinging on taxpayers' God-given rights to go where and when they choose on public property—but maybe it is time for us to recognize that by overusing the wilderness we are destroying the very essence of a wilderness experience.

## CLIMATE

The variation in altitude from valley floors to the Cascade crest, as well as the barrier formed by the crest itself, creates a wide variance in local weather conditions. The western lowlands see precipitation of around 55 inches annually, while the crest averages 180 inches. At lower altitudes on eastern slopes, precipitation drops to 10 inches a

*A waterfall can be seen on Sawyer Creek, off the Deception Creek Trail.*

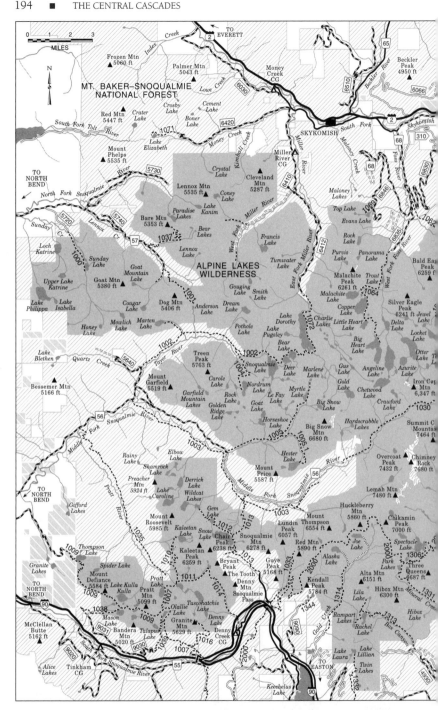

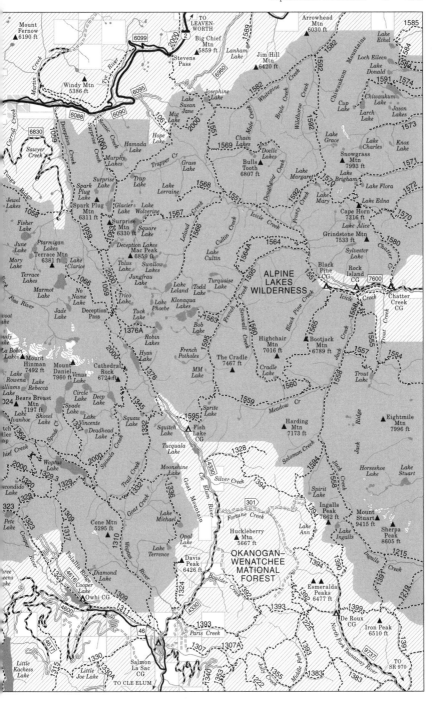

year. Higher elevations are not snow-free until mid-July and often see first snowfalls by mid-October. Because of the steep gradient, summer thunderstorms often occur over the crest. Warm summer weather in the Puget Sound region frequently results in temperature inversions that blanket the lowlands along the sound with fog and low clouds, while the mountains enjoy warm, sunny conditions.

On the west side of the Cascades summer temperatures are typically in the mid-70s, with occasional days in the 90s. Near the crest, days rarely exceed the mid-60s, and frosty nights are common. On the east side of the range temperatures in the 90s are the norm, and many days exceed 100. Sudden weather changes can create winterlike conditions anytime during the year. Fall and winter storms exact their toll on the forest, when steep barometric gradients can generate winds as high as 75 miles per hour.

## ECOSYSTEM

The wide, east–west span of the wilderness, as well as its elevation extremes, encompass multiple ecological zones. Forests in lower regions on the west are mostly Douglas-fir, western hemlock, western red cedar, and red alder. Avalanche courses are coated with vine maple, and the understory includes salal, salmonberry, Oregon grape, and devil's club. With altitude the cedar and alder give way to Pacific silver fir, noble fir, and mountain hemlock, and open slopes see more Sitka alder and Douglas maple. Kinnikinnick and twinflower are introduced into the ground cover. Meadows have a profusion of blackberry, elderberry, and currant. Above 4,000 feet the dominant forest species are mountain hemlock and silver fir, with smatterings of subalpine fir. Near 6,000 feet the forest is mostly subalpine fir and dwarf juniper, and many meadows host a plethora of wildflowers, including avalanche lily, bluebells, phlox, and Indian paintbrush. Above timberline, heather, lupine, and snow lily fill spots between clumps of subalpine fir, larch, and mountain hemlock.

East of the crest occasional stands of Engelmann spruce, alpine larch, and white-bark pine mix with subalpine fir, mountain hemlock, white fir, and silver fir. Lower on slopes the trees shift to Douglas-fir, hemlock, grand fir, and white fir, with the forest floor covered by pinegrass, sedge, huckleberry, elderberry, and vine maple. At the lowest elevations the forest is Douglas-fir, ponderosa pine, western hemlock, and lodgepole pine. The understory is mostly grasses and sedges decorated by rock lily, mariposa lily, hawkweed, and balsamroot.

The wilderness harbors typical wildlife species including black-tailed deer, elk, black bear, beaver, weasel, mink, bobcat, and cougar. Higher elevations are home to mountain goats, and there are reported sightings of such endangered species as gray wolf, bald eagle, grizzly bear, and spotted owl. The area also hosts some 13 species of amphibians, 12 reptile species, and 177 species of birds.

## GEOLOGY

The geological history of the region can be traced back about 350 million years to deposition of sedimentary and volcanic rock, probably off the shores of the North Cascades microcontinent while it was still in the mid-Pacific. Major granite batholiths intruded the crustal rocks about 80 million to 90 million years ago; today they are represented in the granite peaks of the Stuart Range and the Snoqualmie Pass area. On the south perimeter of this range is a band of serpentine rock representing older oceanic crust metamorphosed in the trench off the east coast of the microcontinent before the Stuart Range intrusions. South of this band are rocks of the Swauk Formation, sandstones that were probably deposited on the eastern edge of the North Cascades terrane during Eocene times. This formation has been folded and faulted as a result of the continental collision.

Most of the surface features recognizable today are a result of glaciation, both continental and local. Many of the hundreds of lakes for which the region is named lie in glacier-carved cirques, and exposed slabs of the granite substrate are smoothed and marked with striations from glacial erosion. The deep, U-shaped valleys owe their characteristic form to glacial gouging, and many exhibit steps and hanging valleys formed by the retreat of glaciers with global warming.

*Mount Stuart dominates the Alpine Lakes Wilderness.*

## HISTORY

Many central Washington Indian tribes attribute the Alpine Lakes region with the source of all human life in the Cascades. Most early native visits to the high mountains were limited to hunting and gathering trips, and "vision quests," where tribal members went alone to peaks to establish contact with their guardian spirits. Trails that developed over mountain passes became essential for exchange of goods between plains- and saltwater-based Indian tribes. The first whites in the region, in the early 1800s, were trappers and fur traders. They were soon followed by missionaries and the pioneer settlers in the 1850s. Stress between the natives and immigrants culminated in the brief "Indian Wars" in 1855.

By 1853 surveys were seeking railroad routes across the Cascades. The search for routes was accelerated by the 1858 gold strikes in the Fraser River valley. Portland interests could transport goods east of the Cascades via the Columbia River, but Puget Sound merchants needed railroads to transfer goods across the range. Coal discoveries in the Roslyn area offered the cheap fuel required by railroads to run trains across the range, and the grants of alternate sections of land to railroads provided economic incentives to develop these routes. The Northern Pacific laid tracks across Stampede Pass in 1888, the Great Northern drove a tunnel through Stevens Pass in 1893, and the Chicago, Milwaukee, St. Paul, and Pacific went through Snoqualmie Pass in 1909. Most of the checkerboard sections of grant land were sold to timber companies, and this weird pattern of land holdings persists and thwarts logical management of major ecosystems today.

The Fraser River gold strikes triggered prospector searches for mineral wealth in the Alpine Lakes region, and more than 1,900 lode and placer claims and 137 patented claims were filed in the area. The minerals were mostly copper ores, with smatterings of gold and silver deposits. A presumably rich copper claim is still held in the heart of the wilderness near La Bohn Gap; it is a pain in the side for efforts to acquire all private land holdings within the wilderness.

Many eastside trails originated in the early 1900s as sheep drives. In 1905 the Forest Service was assigned management responsibility for the federal lands in the region, and during the 1930s the CCC built many of today's trails (and now-abandoned lookouts) to support the fire suppression mission of the Forest Service.

In the early 1900s, recreationists, mostly mountain climbers, recognized the unique character of the area, and by 1920 outdoor groups were strongly lobbying for its inclusion in the national park system. Formal protection was not provided until 1976, when the current wilderness area was created.

## HIKING
### Middle Fork Snoqualmie River Trails

***Trail 1002, Snoqualmie Lake.*** *10 miles/e-m (H; S,B on the Taylor River Road from the gate to the trailhead).* From a gate on FR 5640 (1,225 ft), walk the abandoned roadbed up the Taylor River for 6 miles to the old trailhead (1,865 ft). At a Y, Trail 1004 heads south to Nordrum Lake, and Trail 1002 climbs east through old growth to

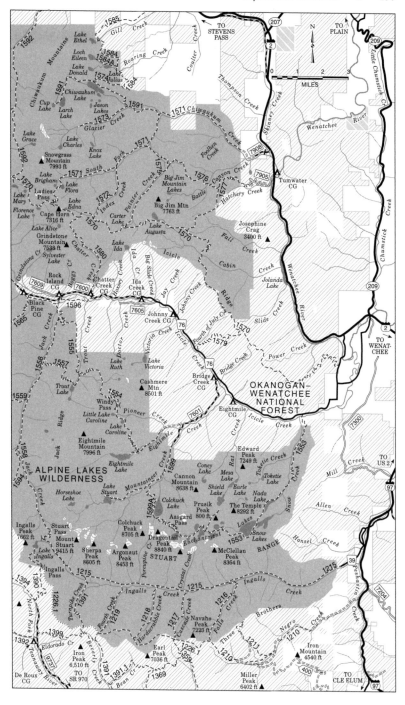

Snoqualmie Lake (3,147 ft). After skirting the north shore, switchbacks reach Deer (3,583 ft) and Bear (3,610 ft) Lakes. Trail 1072 continues east from Bear Lake to Lake Dorothy.

**Trail 1005, Dingford Creek.** *6.7 miles/m (H,S).* Leaving FR 56 (1,450 ft) the trail switchbacks up the steep forested slope to the wilderness boundary where the grade eases. Never straying far from Dingford Creek, the way climbs gradually through old-growth forest to a junction (2,840 ft) with Trail 1005.1 to Hester Lake. The route continues its gradual creek-side ascent, and after one long switchback reaches Myrtle Lake (3,780 ft). Looming above are the impressive cliffs and pocket glaciers of Big Snow Mountain. A one-time trail, now just a boot path, climbs a steep rib to Upper Myrtle Lake and views north into the Miller Creek drainage.

**Trail 1030, Dutch Miller Gap.** *7.4 miles/m (H).* From the end of FR 56 (2,990 ft), the route continues northeast up the Middle Fork of the Snoqualmie River on a gentle grade with minor ups and downs. After closing to the river near a steep cascade, the way enters meadows in the broadening upper valley, with views south to Overcoat Peak and Summit Chief, Middle Chief, and Little Big Chief Mountains. Passing Trail 1024 to Williams Lake, the way bends southeast to Dutch Miller Gap (4,980 ft) and an awesome view of Bears Breast Mountain. The route continues east as Trail 1362.

## South Fork Snoqualmie River Trails

**Trail 1039, Talapus Lake.** *3.1 miles/m (H).* At the end of FR 9030 (2,640 ft) the route leaves clearcuts for forest and twists uphill through two sets of switchbacks to Talapus Lake (3,230 ft). More zigzags climb the rib to the east to Olallie Lake (3,780 ft). Campfires are not permitted at either lake.

**Trail 1007, Pratt Lake.** *6 miles/m (H).* From FR 9034 (1,910 ft), the way swings east, then west past Trail 1016 as it climbs diagonally through second-growth forest. It bends north into the Talapus Creek drainage, passes a spur trail to Olallie Lake, then makes a horseshoe bend above the lake. The route meets Trail 1009 at a saddle (4,150 ft) with views of Mount Rainier, then twists downhill to Pratt (3,385 ft) and Lower Tuscohatchie (3,430 ft) Lakes.

**Trail 1016, Granite Mountain.** *3.1 miles/m (H).* From the 1-mile point on Trail 1007 (2,600 ft), the route wiggles up the steep wooded sidehill, breaks out of trees, and heads east diagonally across avalanche slopes (dangerous until early summer). Switchbacks reach the ridge top and broad views south to Rainier. The way ascends slopes just north of the crest, then reaches the summit lookout (5,629 ft). Fantastic panoramic views here encompass Rainier, Stuart, Glacier, Baker, and the backbone of the Cascades.

**Trail 1009, Mount Defiance.** *7.8 miles/m (H).* At the saddle above Olallie Lake (4,150 ft) this route leaves Trail 1007 and gradually ascends wildflower meadows west to Rainbow Lake (4,290 ft). It continues west, then rounds cliffs above Lake Kulla Kulla. The way climbs around the base of Mount Defiance, then circles the wide, open hillside above the Spider Creek basin before zigzagging down to cross a rib above Thompson

Lake. More switchbacks drop to the lake (3,670 ft). Another mile of poorly maintained tread crosses a saddle to reach the end of the Granite Creek Road.

**Trail 1011, Melakwa Lake.** *3 miles/m (H).* From Lower Tuscohatchie Lake (3,430 ft), the route crosses forested sidehills above the Pratt River before switchbacking up to Melakwa Lake (4,510 ft), where it meets Trail 1014. Above the lake are the sheer faces of Chair and Kaleetan Peaks.

**Trail 1014, Denny Creek.** *4.3 miles/m (H).* Just beyond Denny Creek Campground, a spur from FR 1021 heads west to the trailhead (2,240 ft). The way crosses Denny Creek, ducks under westbound freeway lanes, then heads upstream to recross the creek below Keekwulee Falls. The route passes Snowshoe Falls, then snakes up Denny Creek to Hemlock Pass (4,600 ft). It descends to join Trail 1011 at the outlet stream from Melakwa Lake (campfires prohibited).

## Snoqualmie Pass Trails

**Trail 1013, Snow Lake.** *8.5 miles/m (H,S).* One of the most heavily used trails in the wilderness heads north from the Alpental Ski Area parking lot (3,140 ft), then traverses through forest and talus slopes above the South Fork of the Snoqualmie River. At the head of the basin a short path leads west to a viewpoint above Source Lake overlooking Chair, Bryant, and Hemlock Peaks, and The Tooth. Trail 1013 switchbacks up steep slopes to a broad heather and huckleberry saddle (4,400 ft) between Chair Peak and Snoqualmie Mountain; more zigzags descend to Snow Lake (4,016 ft), where campfires are prohibited. After skirting the east shore the path descends around the steep east headwall of Rock Creek. Switchbacks drop down the forested hillside to Trail 1003 (1,620 ft) and follow it west to cross the Middle Fork of the Snoqualmie near Dingford Creek.

**Trail 1033, Commonwealth Basin.** *2.5 miles/m (H).* At the 2.5-mile point (3,800 ft) of the PCT, Trail 2000, north of Snoqualmie Pass, the route drops into Commonwealth Basin, meets the steep ridge leading toward Red Mountain, then begins a sharp switchback chain up its nose to a tiny tarn (4,870 feet). From here it heads up open rocky slopes to Red Pass (5,350 ft), between Red Mountain and Lundin Peak. Views from the saddle span nearby peaks, the South and Middle Forks of the Snoqualmie River, Mount Thompson, Chikamin Peak, Lemah Mountain, and Chimney Rock.

**Trail 1314, Gold Creek.** *4.5 miles/m-d (H).* From a spur of FR 4832-142 (2,600 ft), follow the roadbed for nearly a mile before a rough tread heads upstream along the narrow, rising valley floor. Marshy meadows and beaver dams slow progress up the valley as the way struggles upstream. It passes a primitive path uphill, then climbs over rockslides and through vine maple and slide alder to Alaska Lake (4,230 ft). The trail's continuation up Gold Creek degrades rapidly to a bushwhack route up roots and boulders to Joe Lake (4,624 ft). Cross-country routes climb to the PCT.

**Trail 1313, Rachel Lake.** *4.8 miles/m (H).* The route leaves FR 4930 at Box Canyon Creek (2,770 ft) and follows the narrow wooded canyon floor upstream to a headwall where all pretense of a civilized tread ends. Switchbacks worm up cliffs, with the rough ascent mitigated somewhat by views of beautiful waterfalls. The way passes

Rachel Lake (4,760 ft), then snakes up bare rock slopes to a T-junction atop Rampart Ridge. The path north leads past a spur to Lila Lake (5,195 ft), then up the knife-edge crest to the summit of Alta Mountain (6,151 ft) and outstanding views of the peaks of Chikamin Ridge. To the south the path follows the crest to the plateau bowl holding the seven Rampart Lakes (5,100 ft). Views south from here span Snoqualmie Pass, Adams, and Rainier.

**Trail 1331, Mineral Creek.** 5.4 miles/m (H). From FR 4600 north of Little Kachess Lake (2,365 ft), the route follows an abandoned mining road up Mineral Creek to the wilderness boundary, then continues upstream to a steep headwall climb to meadows surrounding Park Lakes (4,710 ft). Beyond, the path ascends a short distance to join the PCT (4,940 ft).

## Cooper River Trails

**Trail 1309, Polallie Ridge.** 8.8 miles/m (H,S). This route leaves the Salmon La Sac Campground (2,410 ft) and heads directly up the steep wooded nose of Polallie Ridge. At 4,600 feet the way traverses the northeast side of the ridge, crosses a notch, and descends to Diamond Lake (4,940 ft). The trail continues north, alternately crossing saddles and dropping into basin-top benches, then regains the crest and follows it to its high point (5,547 ft). It continues along the crest to an old lookout site, en route enjoying outstanding views of Cascade backbone peaks: Mount Daniel, Bears Breast, the Summit Chief group, Lemah Mountain, and more. Dropping north, the way follows a wooded spur down to end on Trail 1329 (4,240 ft).

**Trail 1323, Pete Lake.** 7.5 miles/m (H,S). From Owhi Campground on Cooper Lake (2,788 ft), the route works through the bottomland old growth of the Cooper River, passing a spur from the end of FR 4616-113 (2,820 ft). The way meets Trail 1329 at Pete Lake (2,980 ft), then turns west along Lemah Creek to a fork. The northwest branch heads up to the PCT at Lemah Meadows (3,220 ft). The southwest branch either fords or crosses foot-logs over Lemah Creek, then ascends to join the PCT (3,440 ft) 1.4 miles south of the first fork.

**Trail 1306, Spectacle Lake.** 1.4 miles/m (H,S). A brief route weaves up rocks and ledges from the PCT to the finger of Spectacle Point on Spectacle Lake (4,250 ft). The convoluted shoreline of this enchanting lake has vistas sweeping up cliff faces to the rugged crests of Four Brothers, Chikamin Peak, and Lemah Mountain. Trail 1339, an alternate access from the PCT to the lake, claws straight up tree roots and rocks, passing a pretty waterfall en route.

## Waptus River Trails

**Trail 1310, Waptus River.** 11.2 miles/m (H,S). From Salmon La Sac Campground (2,410 ft) this route crosses over low, lumpy forestland to the Waptus River, then follows the southwest side of the drainage upstream. The way ascends a step to the outlet of Waptus Lake (2,963 ft), where a hikers' spur leads west to Trail 1329. The main route crosses the river, and meets Trail 1310.1, a connector to the PCT. After passing the stock

*Alpine meadows in the Rampart Lakes area hold weathered rock and heather; Mount Hibox is in the distance.*

access to Trail 1329, the path wanders along the north shore of the lake. The trail ends as it meets the PCT (3,040 ft) 0.5 mile upstream from the head of the lake.

**Trail 1329, Waptus Pass.** *6 miles/m (H,S).* At the southeast corner of Waptus Lake, a horse route leaves Trail 1310 (3,000 ft) and crosses a ford of the Waptus River. Hiker and horse routes merge at the southwest corner of the lake, then begin a strenuous climb of more than fifty switchbacks up the Quick Creek gorge. The way flattens in broad meadows near Waptus Pass, where it meets Trail 1309. At the pass itself (4,570 ft) Trail 1329.3 heads off to the north. The brutal climb from Waptus Lake is now reversed; more than two dozen switchbacks drop abruptly west to meet Trail 1323 (2,990 ft) at Pete Lake.

**Trail 1362, Dutch Miller Gap.** *4.7 miles/m (H,S).* From the PCT (3,030 ft) near its Waptus River crossing, this route snakes back and forth up a forested slope, then climbs along a narrow bench to Lake Ivanhoe (4,652 ft). Above is a vertical wall rising 2,000 feet to the top of Bears Breast. The path then switchbacks up the cirque headwall to Dutch Miller Gap (4,980 ft), where it meets Trail 1030.

## Cle Elum River Trails

**Trail 1595, Paddy Go Easy Pass.** *3 miles/m (H,S).* About 0.7 mile beyond the Fish Lake Campground, the route leaves FR 4330 (3,370 ft) and begins a gradual wooded ascent that soon shoots sharply up through dense forest, rarely using a switchback for a breather. At Paddy Go Easy Pass (6,100 ft) the way crosses the crest of the Wenatchee Mountains and enjoys views of The Cradle's cliffs. The route drops east from the pass and continues down French Creek.

**Trail 1345, Cathedral Rock.** *4.5 miles/m (H,S).* A few sweeping switchbacks climb the wooded valley wall from Tucquala Campground (3,350 ft), at the end of FR 4330, to Squaw Lake (4,841 ft). Above the lake the way climbs to a gentle bench that it follows northwest to a junction with the PCT (5,510 ft) near the fang of Cathedral Rock.

**Trail 1376, Deception Pass.** *5 miles/m (H,S).* From the end of FR 4330, a walk along the valley floor meanders through forest to Hyas Lake (3,448 ft). After wandering along the marshy east shore, the way encounters a smaller lobe of the lake, then begins a steep, switchbacked ascent of the basin headwall to Deception Pass (4,470 ft). Here it meets Trail 1059 and the PCT.

## Ingalls Creek Trails

**Trail 1215, Ingalls Creek.** *13.8 miles/m (H,S).* At the end of the Valley High turnoff from US 97 (1,940 ft) one of the longest valley trails in the central Cascades heads west up the narrow bottom of Ingalls Creek. The easy grade runs through forest with tantalizing avalanche-track glimpses of the stunning peaks of the Stuart Range. Steep sidehill routes rise up successive drainages on the south side of the trail: 1216 up Falls Creek, 1217 up Cascade Creek, 1218 up Hardscrabble Creek, 1219 up Fourth Creek, and 1391 up Turnpike Creek. At the head of Ingalls Creek the route climbs to just below Stuart Pass (6,270 ft), where it meets Trail 1558.

**Trail 1216, Falls Creek.** *4 miles/m (H,S).* At the 5.2-mile point of Trail 1215 (3,420 ft), this steep, narrow path wiggles up the Falls Creek drainage to a ridge-top saddle (6,040 ft) where it meets Trail 1210 from Negro Creek.

**Trail 1217, Cascade Creek.** *2.7 miles/m (H,S).* Just east of Cascade Creek (3,880 ft) a thin, rough track switchbacks up the creek drainage to a notch (6,040 ft), where it meets Trails 1359 and 1226.

**Trail 1219, Fourth Creek.** *3.6 miles/m (H,S).* A gentle grade up the wooded bottom of Fourth Creek (4,300 ft) climbs gradually to crest-top meadows and a junction with Trail 1391 (5,530 ft). Here are magnificent views of the Cashmere Crags.

## South Side of Icicle Creek Trails

**Trail 1553, Snow Lake.** *16.6 miles/m-d (H).* After leaving FR 76 (1,380 ft) the route zigzags up into the Snow Creek drainage, then follows the creek south, keeping well above the brushy bottom. At Nada Lake (4,910 ft) the way crosses the creek, then follows the northwest shore. A few zigzags climb to the dam between Lower and Upper Snow Lakes (5,415 feet and 5,420 ft); after skirting the south shore of the upper lake the trail becomes just plain mean.

Switchbacks work up through forest to open meadows, then polished granite slabs, as the way climbs into the fabled Enchantment Lakes. The first encounter is with Lake Viviane (6,795 ft); above is hook-shaped Leprechaun Lake (6,875 ft). Granite spires become more profuse and lake names more esoteric: Sprite; Perfection (Rune) (7,130 ft); Inspiration (Talisman) (7,190 ft); Isolation (Brynhild) (7,700 ft); and Tranquil (Lake Freya) (7,795 ft). Scattered to the sides are the Troll Sink and Gnome Tarn. The rough, primitive track continues uphill westward to Aasgard Pass (7,850 ft).

**Trail 1599, Stuart Lake.** *5.5 miles/m (H; S, closed to stock from May 1 to the first weekend after Labor Day).* From FR 7601 (3,430 ft), the route heads up the wooded bank of Mountaineer Creek on an easy grade, then switchbacks up a valley step past Trail 1599A. A marshy path wends upstream to Lake Stuart (5,064 ft) and awesome views up to the imposing north wall of Mount Stuart.

**Trail 1599A, Colchuck Lake.** *1.6 miles/m (H).* A strenuous route from Trail 1599 (4,890 ft) zigzags up through open forest and granite nubbins to Colchuck Lake (5,570 ft) below steep cliffs leading to Aasgard Pass. A climbers' path, marked by cairns, twists up the steep snow and boulder couloir to the pass (7,650 ft) and the Enchantment Basin.

**Trail 1552, Eightmile Lake.** *3.3 miles/m (H,S).* The 1.5-mile road/trail from FR 7601 (3,280 ft) travels through balding clearcuts to the wilderness boundary. There the way twists upstream past Little Eightmile Lake (4,404 ft) and a junction with Trail 1554, then continues to Eightmile Lake (4,641 ft).

**Trail 1554, Eightmile–Trout Creek.** *8 miles/m (H,S).* The route climbs from Little Eightmile Lake (4,404 ft) through a series of wooded switchbacks that break into flower meadows before reaching the final step to Lake Caroline (6,190 ft). Here are impressive views southwest to the Enchantments and Mount Stuart. The trail wanders up past Little Caroline Lake (6,300 ft), then climbs through subalpine meadows to Windy Pass (7,230 ft) and even broader views of the Stuart Range and Cashmere Mountain.

From the pass, the route traverses north through meadows into forest, then switchbacks down to join Trail 1555 (4,600 ft) at Trout Creek.

**Trail 1558, Jack Creek.** *10.5 miles/m (H,S).* From FR 7600-615 (2,800 ft), the route crosses Jack Creek and switchbacks up to pass Trail 1555 to Trout Creek. The side-slope path continues into the Jack Creek drainage to meet the rising creek. Upstream are muddy creekside sections as the way passes Trail 1557 and ascends to a Y (3,760 ft). The west fork, Trail 1559, heads up Meadow Creek, while Trail 1558 continues south up the bottom of Jack Creek. The way plows through forest and dense brush as it follows the creek uphill, crosses avalanche chutes, then reaches flower meadows and rocky slopes leading to Stuart Pass (6,400 ft). At the pass, rugged ridges rise east to the cliffs of Mount Stuart and west to the summit of Ingalls Peak. The way then drops over the pass to join Trail 1215 (6,240 ft).

**Trail 1557, Jack Ridge.** *4 miles/m (H,S).* From the junction with Trails 1555 and 1554 (4,600 ft), the way continues to Trout Lake (4,790 ft), then swings uphill to the west. Switchbacks climb steeply to the ridge crest (5,700 ft). After a brief sojourn in ridge-top meadows, knee-jarring switchbacks drop down the wooded slopes west to the 3-mile point of Trail 1558 (3,640 ft).

**Trail 1559, Meadow Creek.** *6 miles/m (H,S).* From the junction with Trail 1558 (3,640 ft), the route branches west and passes Trail 1560 as it heads up the flat, wooded bottom of the Meadow Creek drainage. The easy grade is mostly in forest, but periodically breaks into meadows with views north to the walls of The Cradle. An imperceptible pass is crossed (5,350 ft) and the way drifts down to join Trail 1595 near the head of the French Creek drainage (4,900 ft).

**Trail 1560, Snowall–Cradle Lake.** *12.6 miles/m (H,S).* One mile from the east end of Trail 1559 (3,980 ft), this route snakes steeply uphill. After topping wooded cliff bands it heads diagonally to Cradle Lake (6,180 ft). The way climbs through meadows above the lake to a col (6,400 ft) with impressive views of the precipitous south face of The Cradle, then drops abruptly through cliffs, and switchbacks down to soggy meadows at the head of Snowall Creek. An easy creek-bottom grade continues north, then in sweeping switchbacks breaks down the canyon wall to French Creek and Trail 1595 (3,350 ft).

**Trail 1551, Icicle Creek.** *11.5 miles/e-m (H,S).* At the end of FR 7600 (2,840 ft) the route heads through old-growth forest along the valley floor of Icicle Creek. The way passes a succession of side trails: 1595 up French Creek, 1592 into Frosty Creek, 1567 into Leland Creek, 1568 up Lorraine Ridge, 1569 to Chain Lakes, and 1582 down Whitepine Creek. For most of its length the way slowly creeps up the creek bottom, but near the confluence of Trapper, Basin, and Icicle Creeks it is forced abruptly uphill to the headwaters of the creek at Josephine Lake (4,681 ft). After circumnavigating the ridge above the lake, the route ends on the PCT (4,950 ft).

**Trail 1595, French Creek.** *9.3 miles/m (H,S).* This creek-bottom route through dense old-growth forest sees few scenic breaks along its entire length. Beginning 1.25 miles up Trail 1551 (2,900 ft), the way turns along French Creek and traces its sometimes muddy banks upstream past Trails 1564A and 1560 as it makes a long sweep west, then south, to meet Trail 1559 near the French Creek headwaters. An uphill burst via numerous switchbacks leads to Paddy Go Easy Pass (6,100 ft), from where it drops to Tecquala Lake.

**Trail 1568, Lorraine Ridge.** *4 miles/m (H,S).* At 6 miles up Trail 1551 (3,220 ft) this path fords Icicle Creek between Icicle and French Creeks (3,220 ft), passes Trail 1566, and tilts up the nose of a wooded ridge. As the slope becomes increasingly steeper, a straight-on attack relents to switchbacks. Near the crest the forest cover breaks to rock outcrops with views across and down the Icicle Creek Valley. The way contours just below the top of Lake Lorraine Point, an old lookout site, then follows the ridge-top bench to a break in cliff bands, where it heads down to Lake Lorraine (5,056 ft).

**Trail 1566, Leland Creek.** *5.3 miles/d (H,S, but not recommended for stock).* From Trail 1568, the route fords Leland Creek. It makes a gradual ascent up the wide valley bottom to Prospect Creek. Leland Creek bends south and narrows, and the route continues up the muddy valley floor. Steep canyon walls close in as the trail climbs steeply upstream to Lake Leland (4,461 ft).

## North Side of Icicle Creek Trails

**Trail 1570, Icicle Ridge.** *26 miles/m (H,S).* This long, scenic, ridge-top route starts east of the wilderness from FR 76 (1,180 ft), 1.5 miles south of Leavenworth. The inevitable series of more than three dozen switchbacks reaches the east end of Icicle Ridge; then the way continues its relentless ascent straight up the wooded ridge to the first meadow breaks at about 6,200 feet. Just after passing Trail 1579 at 8.7 miles it hits a high point (6,900 ft), and 0.5 mile farther enters the wilderness. Fires ravaged this area in 2001. However, trails are expected to be restored by 2002. The tread fades in and out on a roller-coaster route along the meadowed crest with continuous great views into deep flanking valleys and south to Cashmere Mountain and the Stuart Range.

From a saddle, the path zigzags down a steep wooded canyon wall, crosses Cabin Creek (4,990 ft), then reverses the pattern as it scales the north drainage slopes and regains a crest (6,400 ft) that parallels Icicle Ridge. This ridge is followed west to a meadow meeting with Trail 1577. The track drops west from the ridge into the upper valley of Cabin Creek, then twists up to its headwaters at Lake Augusta (6,854 ft). From there it heads west over a rocky saddle (7,300 ft), then drops to Carter Lake (6,150 ft). Once again it climbs to a notch (6,650 ft), then switchbacks down to Index Creek (4,890 ft).

The way swings back and forth out of the basin to reach a slabby shoulder of Icicle Ridge and pass Trail 1580. The path, obscure in places along the rock and meadow crest, climbs to Lake Edna (6,750 ft), then ascends glacier-smoothed slabs around the nose of Cape Horn to Ladies Pass (6,790 ft), where it meets Trail 1571. The route contours a cliffy basin to a 6,900-foot notch where the twisting path heads northwest, up and down through the meadows and rocks above Lakes Mary and Margaret, to end at Frosty Pass (5,960 ft). There it joins Trail 1592.

**Trail 1577, Hatchery Creek.** *6.5 miles/m (H,S).* From a spur off FR 7905 (2,800 ft), switchbacks charge up the broad wooded ridge, pause briefly at a bench junction with Trail 1576, then climb to a broad crest at 6,050 feet. A long contour through meadow and flower fields around the Fall Creek headwaters reaches Trail 1570 (6,700 ft).

**Trail 1575, Painter Creek.** *4.7 miles/m (H,S).* At 1.4 miles up the South Fork of Chiwaukum Creek this path leaves Trail 1571 and heads southeast along Painter Creek. After a brief steep section, at the junction with Trail 1576 (5,100 ft) both creek and trail bend to the southwest. The valley floor opens, and the long steep wall of Big Jim Mountain looms above to the east. At the head of the creek the trail climbs to meet Trail 1570 at Carter Lake (6,150 ft).

**Trail 1576, Badlands.** *5 miles/m (H,S).* A link between Trail 1575 (5,100 ft) and Trail 1577 (5,340 ft) crosses the broad grassy top of the Badlands (6,200 ft). The start and finish of the trail are steep, but the central highland portion is a moderate grade.

**Trail 1571, Chiwaukum Creek.** *12.2 miles/m (H,S).* Starting at a gate on FR 7908 (2,020 ft), hike the road 1.5 miles to the start of the trail. The way wends through old growth up the deep, narrow bottomland beside Chiwaukum Creek to a Y; Trail 1591 continues upstream, and Trail 1571 follows the south fork of the creek. As the path heads upstream past Trails 1575 and 1572, the valley widens and forest cover opens at Timothy Meadow. The gradual ascent through forest and across avalanche meadows reaches a cliff-rimmed cul-de-sac. Switchbacks snake up the south end of the headwall past meadow-draped Lakes Flora (5,700 ft) and Brigham (5,830 ft), then the path zigzags up rocky slopes to Ladies Pass (6,790 feet) to meet Trail 1570.

**Trail 1591, North Fork Chiwaukum.** *6.2 miles/m (H; S as far as junction with Trail 1573).* From Trail 1571 (3,320 ft), this route continues up the main fork of Chiwaukum Creek, where walls force switchbacks up to the base of cliffs. A traverse over talus and boulders reaches Chiwaukum Lake (5,210 ft). The way follows the shore, enters meadowed Ewing Basin above the lake, then fishhooks around the head of the basin as it climbs to Larch Lake (6,078 ft).

**Trail 1580, Chatter Creek.** *5 miles/m (H; S, but not recommended).* Starting off FR 7600 (2,760 ft), 0.2 mile above Chatter Creek Campground, the route slithers up the brushy, rocky canyon wall beside Chatter Creek to a flat pocket at 5,000 feet. Steep walls, including the vertical east face of Grindstone Mountain, surround the basin. The track picks its way up through talus and boulders to a notch (6,660 ft) in Icicle Ridge, then contours above cliffs to a junction with Trail 1570 (6,140 ft).

**Trail 1592, Frosty–Wildhorse.** *12.4 miles/m (H,S).* From Trail 1551 (3,050 ft), just past the upper crossing bridge, the way traverses uphill into Frosty Creek. Avalanche paths and meadows open near 5,000 feet as the way climbs to Lake Margaret (5,430 ft), then on beyond to Frosty Pass (5,760 ft) to meet Trail 1570. Views disappear as the route passes Trail 1578 to Lake Grace and leaves timberline for a long diagonal descent across timbered slopes above Wildhorse Creek. Switchbacks drop down to the valley floor where the path joins Trail 1582 at Whitepine Creek (4,300 ft).

**Trail 1569, Chain Lakes.** *4 miles/m (H,S).* As Trail 1551 begins its valley-head climb, this route (3,770 ft) climbs up east slopes in seventeen tight switchbacks, then begins a long diagonal ascent to Chain Lakes (5,628, 5,679, and 5,690 ft). The cliff face of Bulls Tooth rises above the lakes to the east, and an unnamed spike on the north side of the lakes towers 1,000 vertical feet above. A rugged path climbs northeast up talus slopes to a rocky col (6,200 ft), then drops abruptly to Doelle Lakes (5,775 and 5,635 ft).

## US 2 Trails

**Trail 1582, Whitepine Creek.** *8.1 miles/m (H,S).* From the end of FR 6950 (2,800 ft), the track follows the brushy bottom of the Whitepine Creek drainage southwest. The easy-grade route lies mostly in old-growth forest, with occasional avalanche tracks affording glimpses of flanking ridges. The path passes Trail 1592 as it continues upstream through some muddy spots to the creek's headwaters. After crossing a low wooded saddle (4,650 ft) it descends to meet Trail 1551 (4,390 ft) below Josephine Lake.

**Trail 1060, Surprise Creek.** *4.7 miles/m (H).* From FR 6090 (2,250 ft) near Scenic, the route follows the wooded bank of Surprise Creek upstream, then zigzags steeply up the basin wall to Surprise Lake (4,508 ft) where it joins the PCT. Cliffs rise above to Thunder and Surprise Mountains.

*An angler tests his fishing skills in Big Heart Lake.*

**Trail 1063, Surprise Mountain.** *1.5 miles/d (H,S).* An old lookout trail leaves the PCT at the largest of the Deception Lakes (5,053 ft). It follows the old route of the Crest Trail to Surprise Pass (6,400 ft), and climbs southwest to the ridge, then north to the lookout site atop Surprise Mountain (6,330 ft). Panoramic views of the Cascades from Glacier to Stuart provide a counterpoint to the sheer north face, which drops 1,500 feet to Glacier Lake.

**Trail 1059, Deception Creek.** *10.3 miles/m (H; S south of Trail 1059.1).* This densely forested creek-bottom route leaves FR 6088 (2,000 ft) and wanders upstream above the banks of Deception Creek. At 5 miles a junction with Trail 1058 drops 0.5 mile to FR 6830 in Fisher Creek. The way climbs high above the creek to a brief link, Trail 1059A, that snakes uphill to join the PCT just south of the Deception Lakes. The main trail drops back down to Deception Creek and follows it to Deception Pass (4,480 ft) to meet Trails 1066, 1376, and the PCT.

## Foss River Trails

**Trail 1058, Tonga Ridge.** *6 miles/m (H,S).* At the west end of Tonga Ridge the route leaves FR 6830-310 (4,320 ft), traveling in second growth, then in meadows along the crest. The way slips to the south side of the ridge below Mount Sawyer. At a broad, wooded saddle (4,760 ft) a spur climbs south over a bench, then descends to Fisher Lake (4,763 ft). The main trail continues east, drops to FR 6830 at Fisher Creek (3,650 ft), and joins Trail 1059.

**Trail 1062, Necklace Valley.** *7.5 miles/e-d (H).* An enchanting and very popular trail leaves FR 68 (1,650 ft) to follow the old bed of a narrow-gauge railroad through forest up the East Fork Foss River. The way crosses the river and strikes abruptly up a narrow drainage as it presses relentlessly on to tiny, cliff-rimmed Jade Lake (5,442 ft). Heather and glacier-smoothed rock accompany the path up Necklace Valley past Emerald (4,700 ft) and Opal (4,790 ft) Lakes. Numerous angler tracks seek out other small lakes in the valley.

**Trail 1064, West Fork Foss River.** *6.8 miles/e-m (H).* At the end of FR 6835 (1,640 ft), the route heads up the rapidly narrowing valley of the West Fork Foss River as it climbs to Trout Lake (2,030 ft). Above the lake switchbacks grind up open slopes beside a tributary stream to Copper Lake (3,961 ft). En route a spur climbs 0.2 mile to Malachite Lake (4,089 ft). From Copper Lake the way weaves up to Little Heart (4,204 ft) and Big Heart (4,545 ft) Lakes. Boot-paths explore another half-dozen alpine lakes in the vicinity.

## Miller River Trails

**Trail 1072, Lake Dorothy.** *4.5 miles/e-m (H).* From the end of FR 6412 (2,240 ft), a heavily used track climbs through forest to Lake Dorothy (3,058 ft), then winds along its east shore and across its soggy inlet marsh. Switchbacks grind west up a steep wall to the basin holding Bear (3,610 ft) and Deer (3,583 ft) Lakes, and meet Trail 1002.

## Trail 2000, Pacific Crest National Scenic Trail

**PCT: Snoqualmie Pass to Park Lakes.** *12.5 miles/m (H,S).* From the Snoqualmie Pass parking lot (3,000 ft), the route heads into Commonwealth Basin, passing Trail 1033. A pair of sweeping switchbacks reach the ridge top (5,400 ft) north of Kendall Peak, where the trail crosses the crest and picks its way gingerly along the Kendall Katwalk, a narrow path blasted from the side of a rock cliff. The route descends a bit to heather meadows, then contours high above Alaska Lake. It twists around the base of Alaska Mountain, swings along the ridge above Joe Lake, then contours flower meadows below Huckleberry Mountain. The trail traverses along the base of the 600-foot-high cliffs of Chikamin Peak and Four Brothers, crosses a col (5,600 ft), and descends to Trail 1331 (4,950 ft) above Park Lakes.

**PCT: Park Lakes to Waptus Lake.** *19.7 miles/m (H,S).* A few switchbacks reach the top of Chikamin Ridge (5,350 ft) northwest of Three Queens, then the path wiggles down past Trails 1306 and 1339. A long traverse passes Trail 1323 en route to Lemah Meadow (3,200 ft), to meet Trail 1323.2. Compensating for the grueling switchbacks that climb out of the meadow are striking views of Lemah Mountain and Chimney Rock. After gaining the top of the ridge (5,600 ft) south from Summit Chief Mountain, the way contours basin walls above Escondido Lake, then begins its descent into the Waptus River drainage. After a few switchbacks Trail 1329.3 is met; next, a traverse across an old burn with a view of the impressive face of Bears Breast leads to two more series of zigzags descending to the Waptus River (3,030 ft) and Trail 1362. The way bends southeast and traverses the side-slope above Waptus Lake, passing Trail 1310.

**PCT: *Waptus Lake to Deception Pass.*** *14.7 miles/m (H,S).* The route heads away from Waptus Lake up Spinola Creek, passes Trail 1310.1, and climbs once again to meadow country and Deep Lake (4,382 ft). Trail 1345 is met near the base of the sharp vertical thumb of Cathedral Rock. The way dips into the Cle Elum River basin to 3,700 feet before climbing again to reach Deception Pass (4,470 ft) and to meet Trails 1066, 1376, and 1059.

**PCT: *Deception Pass to Trap Pass.*** *8.3 miles/m (H,S).* A long, gradual ascent reaches Deception Lakes (5,053 ft), joining Trail 1059.2 just below the lakes and Trail 1063 at the lakes themselves. The way continues a gradual ascent along the west flank of Surprise Mountain, crosses its north shoulder (5,550 ft), then switchbacks down to Glacier Lake (4,806 ft). To save a miserable drop and climb, the trail has been rerouted horizontally across the slope east of Slippery Slab Tower to the final half-dozen switchbacks to Trap Pass (5,800 ft).

**PCT: *Trap Pass to Stevens Pass.*** *12.3 miles/m (H,S).* The way slips east of the pass, contours through a cliff band, then follows a forest and meadow sidehill northeast before descending to Hope Lake and Trail 1061 (4,400 ft). The route wraps around tiny Mig Lake (4,661 ft) and weaves up to a saddle (5,200 ft) above Swimming Deer Lake. Contouring above cliffs, the way reaches the ridge (4,950 ft) above Josephine Lake, where it meets Trail 1551. A few zigzags descend to Lake Susan Jane (4,595 ft), then a short ridge-top run leads to FR 6960. Final switchbacks climb an easy rib to the head of the ski lifts, then descend the groomed ski area slopes to Stevens Pass (4,056 ft).

## CLIMBING

Although there are hundreds of individual peaks and towers in the Alpine Lakes, the tops of many are simple scrambles, possibly overlooking terrifying faces dropping away from easily attained summits. Others, however, are true climbing challenges. The solid, stable granite walls of the Stuart batholith offer some of the best and most challenging rock climbing in the Cascades. By virtue of their ease of access, many difficult alternative routes have been placed up otherwise easy peaks; here attaining the top is not so much the achievement as is how you get there.

On the west flank of the wilderness is isolated, difficult, and dangerous Mount Garfield (5,519 ft). Its height belies its challenge since it rises nearly 4,000 feet from its low-lying base in a complex structure of spires, gullies, and faces. Route finding is almost as challenging as climbing, and most routes score in the mid- to high C-5 range.

The most popular climbs are those in the vicinity of Snoqualmie Pass (5,168 to 6,554 ft), all easy 1-day assaults from the highway. The more interesting, with C-4 to C-5 plus routes, are The Tooth, Chair Peak, the north ridge of Kaleetan Peak, the west face of Guye Peak, and Lundin Peak. A bit more north is Mount Thompson (6,554 ft), a particularly striking peak with sheer faces; most routes are no more difficult than C-4.

Farther north along the crest are the isolated spire of Chikamin Peak (7,000 ft) and the tri-topped summit of Three Queens (6,687 ft). Lemah Mountain (7,480 ft) has five sharp summit pinnacles ranging between C-3 and C-5.5. Nearby companions north along the crest are Chimney Rock (7,680 ft), with multiple routes rated C-5 and C-5.8; the castlelike top of Overcoat Peak (7,432 ft), and the Summit Chief group (7,120 to 7,464 ft): Summit Chief, Middle Chief, and Little Big Chief, all rated between C-3 and C-4. One of the most imposing peaks in the Waptus Lake area is Bears Breast Mountain (7,197 ft), a huge tower with vertical faces, multiple spires and crags, and no routes below C-5.4. North from Waptus Lake is massive multisummited Mount Daniel (7,960 ft) and companion Mount Hinman (7,492 ft). Both have large glaciers on their north flanks, but easy summit routes. The distinctive rock thumb of Cathedral Rock (6,724 ft) is skirted by the PCT; it offers various C-3 and C-5.7 routes.

The crown jewels of climbing in the central Cascades are the Cashmere Crags in the Enchantment Lakes region. Dozens of solid, distinctive granite spires, ranging from one to two leads to 1,500-foot faces, spike ridgelines throughout the area. Provocative names such as Crocodile Fang, Razorback Spire, Prusik Peak, Bloody Tower, Cruel Thumb, and Cynical Pinnacle proclaim their challenge. Almost all of the climbs are in the high C-5 range, with some rated as high as C-5.11. They are grouped geographically into the Rat Creek group at the northwest corner of the plateau; Mount Temple Ridge on the northeast side; Three Musketeers Ridge to the far northeast; McClellan Ridge on the southeast; The Knitting Needles, low on the southeast flank; Nightmare Needles on the south slopes; Flagpole Needles, near Little Annapurna; and the Dragontail Plateau group. The northwest face of Dragontail Peak is one of the most challenging walls in the Cascades, with a dozen routes rated from C-5.6 to C-5.11.

The highest peak in this portion of the wilderness is massive Mount Stuart (9,415 ft). Its fractured buttresses and enormous 2,000-foot-high faces are distinctive from 50 miles away. There are a dozen or more routes on the mountain, the simplest rated C-3, the most difficult C-5.10. Surrounding this impressive peak are comparably challenging companions: Ingalls (7,662 ft), Sherpa (8,605 ft), and Argonaut (8,453 ft) Peaks.

## WINTER SPORTS

Winter visitors can follow the summer trail up Gold Creek and the gentle valley floor for 2 miles from a Sno-Park before the slopes above become steep avalanche hazards. East from the pass the Mount Margaret Trail is a popular winter tour, especially when the maze of logging roads are snow-covered, and more direct up and downhill routes become available.

On the east side of the wilderness the valley-floor route to Cooper and Pete Lakes makes an easy tour, given proper discretion during avalanche conditions. Trips can also be made up the Ingalls Pass Trail. For a long northside trip, leave Stevens Pass and follow the Pacific Crest Trail south to Lakes Susan Jane and Josephine; extend the trip either by a descent down Whitepine Creek or continue on to the Surprise Creek valley and Glacier Lake.

# 22 Teanaway River Region

## Teanaway and Thorp Mountain Roadless Areas

**Location:** In Kittitas County, between the Alpine Lakes Wilderness on the north and Interstate 90 on the south, and between Kachess Lake on the west and US 97 on the east

**Size:** Teanaway, 66,293 acres (2,400 acres owned by timber companies); Thorp Mountain, 15,667 acres (8,000 acres owned by timber companies)

**Status:** 30 percent is Semiprimitive Nonmotorized, the remainder is Semiprimitive Motorized

**Terrain:** High, north–south ridges run between Lakes Kachess and Cle Elum, and between the three forks of the Teanaway River. The peaks and alpine meadows of the Alpine Lakes Wilderness form the northern boundary of the region.

**Elevation:** 2,400 ft to 7,000 ft

**Management:** USFS, Okanogan–Wenatchee National Forest, Cle Elum and Leavenworth Ranger Districts; private timber companies

**Topographic maps:** Blewett, Cle Elum Lake, Davis Peak, Easton, Enchantment Lakes, Kachess Lake, Liberty, Mt. Stuart, Polallie Ridge, Red Top Mtn, Teanaway Butte

The Thorp area has a high backbone ridge running north/south between Kachess and Cle Elum Lakes. Almost three-quarters of the area is heavily forested, but ridge crests are sparsely timbered, covered mostly with grasses broken by rock outcrops. Until recently the entire area was plagued by a checkerboard ownership, with alternate sections owned by timber companies. In 2000 a major land swap was negotiated and the Forest Service acquired over half of the private sections in the area, insuring a more consistent management of contiguous ecosystems.

The area is popular with recreationists; there are 32 miles of trails, some more than 10 miles in length. Unfortunately more than 80 percent of these are open to motorized use. One of the area's major attractions is the Thorp Mountain fire lookout, one of the few lookouts active in northwest forests.

The Teanaway area is bordered on the north by a steep, bald crest along the south edge of the Alpine Lakes Wilderness. The three south-draining forks of the Teanaway River frame high, broad, sparsely timbered ridges. These ridges and the intervening drainages have long north–south trail systems extending their full length, as well as several lateral connecting trails. There are 147 miles of trails within the area, about half of which are open to motorized use. The Teanaway area was also decimated, although less than Thorp, by the checkerboard ownership of alternate sections by timber companies. The 2000 land swap cut private ownership in this area by two-thirds, to less than 2,500 acres.

## CLIMATE

Average annual precipitation for the region is 40 to 80 inches, with about half of that falling as snow. Snow depths vary by location and elevation, but range from 4 to 15 feet. Winter temperatures seldom get below the teens, and summers are a pleasant 70 to 90 degrees.

## ECOSYSTEM

Thorp is more heavily forested than the Teanaway drainage, with the predominant species being Douglas-fir, Pacific silver fir, noble fir, and western hemlock. In the Teanaway most of the vegetation is found on north slopes and stream bottoms where brush such as bitter cherry and willow abound. Ridge tops are covered with grasses broken by patches of subalpine fir and lodgepole pine. Wildflowers thrive in meadow areas; among those seen are trillium, spring beauty, lupine, scarlet gilia, and glacier lilies.

Spotted owls have been sighted at various locations within the region, and deer and elk are the most notable large mammals found here. All of the usual smaller forest critters such as mice, pocket gophers, chipmunks, and squirrels are omnipresent. One of the less pleasant species, ticks, are a frequent annoyance in spring.

## GEOLOGY

The Thorp area, between Kachess and Cle Elum Lakes, is predominantly Eocene volcanic rock interspersed with sandstones and shales deposited earlier off the east coast of the North Cascades microcontinent prior to its docking with North America. Most of the Teanaway area is underlain with the Swauk Formation, thick layers of sandstone laid down about 50 million years ago off the east coast of the North Cascades

*Balsam root makes a bold splash of gold along Thorp Mountain trails.*

microcontinent. Folding and uplifting of these layers accompanied the collision of this terrane with North America.

Sometime after this event portions of this area were intruded and overlain by volcanic eruptions from dikes between Cle Elum and Blewett Pass. The northern boundary to the Teanaway area is formed of serpentine, a metamorphic rock on the southern periphery of the Mount Stuart batholith which intruded this area about 88 million years ago.

## HISTORY

Although little specific is known of prehistoric use of the Thorp/Teanaway area, Kachess is an Indian name meaning "many fish," so native fishing in the lake was very likely. Indians also conducted hunting and berry picking expeditions in the vicinity of Salmon La Sac and Koppen Mountain; these activities continued well into the 1920s.

The earliest whites in the area were trappers who arrived in the early 1800s. The first formal exploration in the region took place in 1853 when Captain George McClellan conducted a scouting expedition looking for Cascade passes suitable for wagon roads and railroads. McClellan got as far as Yakima Pass, but totally missed Snoqualmie Pass. On his return trip he camped at both Kachess and Cle Elum Lakes.

In 1873 gold was discovered in Swauk Creek on the east side of the area, and in following years the Cle Elum Mining District was alive with prospectors. Starting in 1881, ninety-two claims were staked on Red Mountain and along the upper Cle Elum River in the Howson, Camp, Fortune, Silver, and Scatter Creek drainages. A mining camp was located at Galena City near Camp Creek. Prospectors found gold, silver, copper, lead, iron, nickel, and cinnabar. At present three abandoned mill sites, 187 mining claims, several cabin sites, and a number of today's trails are all that remain from the extensive mining activity.

The broad, grassy ridge tops were heavily used for sheep grazing between the late 1800s and the 1920s, and remnants of herder camps can still be identified. A few such allotments exist to this day. With the expanding fire suppression mission of the Forest Service, fire lookouts were erected in the 1930s atop Red, Jolly, and Thorp Mountains, Teanaway Butte, and Three Brothers; and trail systems were created to support them. The only lookout remaining is on Thorp Mountain.

## HIKING
### Thorp Mountain Trails

**Trail 1308, *Domerie Peak*.** *9 miles/d (H,S,B; M not recommended).* This long ridge-top trail starts near the south end of Cle Elum Lake at FR 4303-201 (3,350 ft). It begins steep and soon gets steeper as switchbacks struggle up an open face to the crest and great views of the lake and Domerie Creek. The way skirts the top of Domerie Peak (4,771 ft) with the summit just a scramble away. The narrow ridge is followed north to a traverse around the top of Mount Baldy, then a ridge-top meander northwest to meet Domerie Divide Trail 1308.2. The wooded crest broadens as the path continues north to Thomas Mountain (5,269 ft). The trail switchbacks steeply down to a saddle, climbs a timbered knob, then descends to another saddle. Here it begins a gradual ascent up a narrow crest to meadows and a junction with Trail 1308.1 just below the South Peak (5,580 ft) of French Cabin Mountain. The route takes a knife-edge ridge top north through wildflower gardens, skirts the upper flank of North Peak (5,498 ft), then descends the rib to the northeast to FR 4308-115 (3,840 ft).

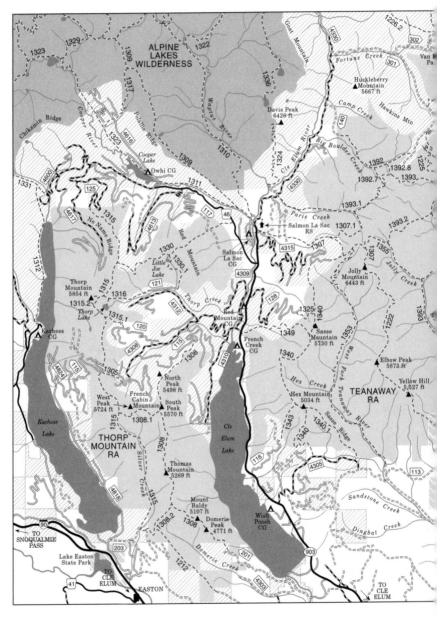

**Trail 1315, Kachess Ridge.** *14.7 miles/m (H,S,B)*. Another long north–south route leaves a spur from FR 4818-203 (2,360 ft) and switchbacks up a wooded slope to avoid the deep canyon of lower Silver Creek. Above this obstacle the way rejoins the now-broad creek bottom framed by steep forested slopes on either side. The route continues its gradual upstream climb, then bends west with the steepening creek around

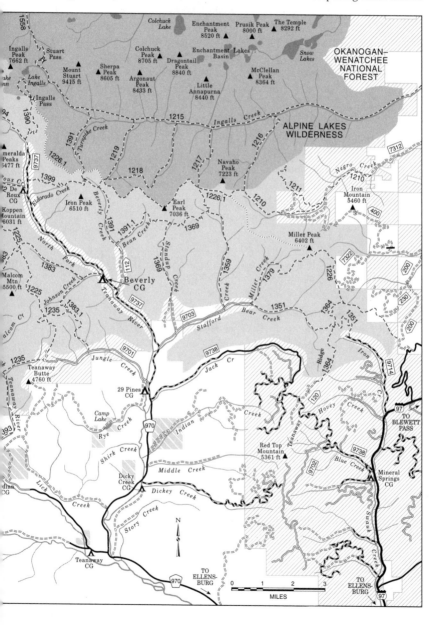

French Cabin Mountain. The way climbs from forest to open meadows below West Peak, where it meets Trail 1308.1 (4,660 ft). It then climbs to a basin-head saddle at the head of Silver Creek.

A traverse of the rocky, open slopes above French Cabin Basin leads to Trail 1305 (4,850 ft), and a switchback chain up the steep rounded, nose end of Kachess Ridge. The crest narrows and the obscure path traverses a steep side-slope to avoid an intermediate peak, then regains the thin, bare ridge top with sweeping views. At a Y in the crest, Trail 1315.1 drops eastward into Knox Creek, while this route heads northwest on the crest of the basin holding Thorp Lake. The main trail traverses the east face of Thorp Mountain, but spur Trail 1315.2 loops steeply to the top of the peak (5,854 ft) and stupendous views from the only active fire lookout in the area.

The route passes the top of Trail 1316, then leaves the north end of Kachess Ridge. The way meets the west end of Trail 1330, then follows the top of No Name Ridge as it hooks to the northwest. At the end of the ridge the trail ends on FR 4617-125 (4,920 ft).

**Trail 1330, Red Mountain.** *6.7 miles/m-d (H; S not recommended).* From FR 46 (2,600 ft), the route heads west into the forest and soon starts a switchback chain up the flank of Red Mountain. After passing through prospects by Elven Thorp (namesake of the roadless area) the way climbs to the crest just north of the summit of Red Mountain (5,722 ft). There was once a fire lookout on a slightly lower summit a half-mile to the south. A rather obscure route continues westward, and drops to the shore of Little Joe Lake (4,700 ft) where it passes Trail 1330.1 to FR 4312-121. It then climbs open slopes to the west to meet Trail 1315 (5,300 ft).

## West Fork Teanaway Trails

**Trail 1340, Sasse Mountain.** *9 miles/d (H,S,B,M).* From the end of FR 4305-118 (3,600 ft), this old sheep drive climbs north up the timbered ridge to meet Trail 1340.1, then crosses the open slopes of Hex Mountain (5,034 ft), flower-clad in spring. The way wanders northwest along the ridge above Hex Creek, rounds the creek-head basin, then follows the near-level grassy crest of Sasse Ridge north past Trail 1349 to Sasse Mountain (5,730 ft). The route continues north atop Sasse Ridge, then traces the upper end of FR 4315 before merging with Trail 1307 (5,600 ft).

**Trail 1307, Jolly Mountain.** *6.2 miles/d (H,S,B).* Starting at Salmon La Sac (2,400 ft), this trail heads east through old clearcuts in a series of long switchbacks that climb toward the head of Salmon La Sac Creek. After passing spur 1307.1 to Paris Creek, the route twists up the basin headwall to a junction with Trail 1340 (5,600 ft), then follows the crest northeast past the upper end of Trail 1353. Trail and ridge bend to the south around a tributary of the West Fork of the Teanaway River where the way breaks into ridge-top meadows and broad vistas. After passing the end of Trail 1355, the path zigzags south to the summit of Jolly Mountain (6,443 ft), a onetime lookout site, and continues as Trail 1222.

**Trail 1353, West Fork Teanaway.** *9.6 miles/d (H,S,B,M).* From the end of FR 4305-113 (2,700 feet), the route follows the tight, narrow creek bottom of the West Fork of the Teanaway River upstream, crossing and recrossing the river below Hex Creek. After once more crossing the river, the route stays 100 to 200 feet higher on the west canyon wall for the next few miles, then drops to three successive river crossings within a mile. As the drainage bends northwest, the trail remains above its north bank, then at a split in headwater streams many long switchbacks climb to the crest of Sasse Ridge to meet Trail 1307 (5,700 ft).

**Trail 1222, Yellow Hill.** *9.8 miles/d (H,S,B,M)*. The south end of this route leaves FR 4305-113 (3,250 ft) to weave up the wooded ridge top west of a tributary of the Middle Fork of the Teanaway River. The long uphill slog finally breaks out into small meadows near the summit of Yellow Hill (5,527 ft). The way traces the ridgeline northwest in a narrow rocky climb to Elbow Peak (5,673 ft). Rounding the peak the path stays atop the thin, exposed ridge, with broad views in all directions, as it weaves northward for the next two miles. A bend northwest past bare unnamed summits leads to Jolly Mountain and Trail 1307 (6,443 ft).

**Trail 1392, Boulder–De Roux.** *7.9 miles/d (H,S,B,M)*. This route departs FR 4330-140 (3,650 ft) along an old miners' route on the north slope above Big Boulder Creek. In just over a mile, two short spurs to the south connect to Trail 1393 in the headwaters of the Middle Fork of the Teanaway River. This trail continues upstream along Big Boulder Creek to reach the upper end of FR 4330-301 (5,450 ft) where a short road walk north leads to Gallagher Head Lake (5,420 ft). The route now swings southward, descending into the De Roux Creek drainage in long sweeping switchbacks. After passing Trail 1225, the trail begins a steep, twisted descent alongside the creek, crosses it, and breaks out of the narrow drainage at the De Roux Campground (3,770 ft).

## Middle Fork Teanaway Trails

**Trail 1393, Middle Fork Teanaway.** *12 miles/m (H,S,B,M)*. As FR 4305-113 crosses the Middle Fork of the Teanaway River (2,650 ft), this old wagon road heads up the east bank and makes the first of many river crossings. Three more crossings in the next two miles lead to Way Creek and a junction with Trail 1235 (3,000 ft). In five more crossings Jolly Creek and Trail 1355 are reached. Another crossing returns the route to the east side of the river and a junction with Trail 1383 near Medra Creek (3,900 ft). A mile upstream the route returns to the west side of the river where spur Trail 1393.2 makes a rugged, switchbacked climb over a saddle to the west to connect to Trail 1395 up Jolly Creek. One last crossing takes the trail along the north slopes of the headwater basin where long switchbacks climb to a narrow saddle (6,850 ft) above the head of Big Boulder Creek, and beyond junctions with two spurs from Trail 1392. The route swings westward to another wide swale (5,500 ft), where it becomes Trail 1393.1.

**Trail 1225, Koppen Mountain.** *10 miles/d (H,S)*. This poorly defined, old sheep drive leaves Trail 1235 atop the ridge between Johnson and Malcom Creeks (4,820 ft). It continues northward along the open rib, with wide views of the Wenatchee Mountains, then crosses east–west Trail 1383 (5,400 ft). The way gradually climbs northward along the narrow open crest to the summit of Koppen Mountain (6,031 ft). The path now begins a gradual descent of the north ridge of the mountain, crosses Trail 1392.1, and bends down steep wooded slopes to end on Trail 1392 at De Roux Creek (5,280 ft).

**Trail 1235, Way Creek.** *4.9 miles/d (H,S,B,M).* The two segments of this trail leave the end of FR 9701 at an unnamed saddle (5,620 ft) at the head of Jungle Creek. The section to the west down Way Creek starts steep, but offers an easy access to the Middle Fork of the Teanaway that eliminates the seven river crossings downstream of its junction with Trail 1393 (2,990 ft). The segment of trail north from the road end climbs a wooded rib, traverses around the head of Way Creek, then crosses the ridge top at a junction with Trail 1225. The way then traverses to the east to a saddle junction with Trail 1383.1 (4,500 ft).

*Trails on Teanaway Ridge are ideal for mountain biking.*

## North Fork Teanaway Trails

**Trail 1394, Esmeralda Basin.** *5.1 miles/m (H,S,B).* In the headwaters of the North Fork of the Teanaway River, the trail leaves the end of FR 9737 (4,243 ft), and follows the east bank of the river to the north where Trail 1390 splits off to Ingalls Pass. This route climbs steadily up the drainage, passing through springtime flower fields, then switchbacks up to Fortune Pass (6,000 ft) and knockout views of surrounding peaks. A segment of old, poorly maintained County Line Trail 1226.2 wanders to the north, headed for Lake Ann, Van Epps Pass, and Scatter Creek. Unending switchbacks drop from Fortune Pass to FR 4330-301 (5,040 ft).

**Trail 1390, Ingalls Way.** *4.4 miles/m (H).* A quarter mile from the end of FR 9737 this route leaves Trail 1394 (4,500 ft) for a switchbacked ascent of the steep open slope to the east with great views of Esmeralda Peaks. At 5,400 feet the Longs Pass Trail 1229 breaks away; this route takes a climbing traverse to the north, followed by a switchback ascent to Ingalls Pass (6,500 ft). After crossing the pass, the way contours around the Headlight Creek basin, then crosses a low rib to the south shore of Lake Ingalls (6,463 ft) and dramatic views of Mount Stuart. A boulder and slab scramble around the lake's west shore reaches the junction of Trails 1215 and 1558 at Stuart Pass.

**Trail 1391, Beverly–Turnpike.** *3.8 miles/m (H,S).* The trail leaves the end of FR 9731-112 (3,640 ft), heading up Beverly Creek to a junction with Trail 1391.1 up Bean Creek to Standup Creek Trail 1369. From this meeting point, the way continues up the flower-covered east bank of Beverly Creek, zigzags higher up the slope, and passes the west end of Trail 1226.1, another segment of the County Line Trail. The route crosses the creek and climbs to a junction with Trail 1399. From here, a short, steep climb to a saddle (5,820 ft) continues as Trail 1391 down Turnpike Creek.

**Trail 1383, Johnson–Medra.** *6 miles/d (H,S,B,M).* This link between the North and Middle Forks of the Teanaway River leaves FR 9737 (3,150 ft) to head up Johnson Creek. In half a mile Trail 1383.1 continues up the creek to cross the headwater ridge and drop to FR 9701 in Jungle Creek. This route, however, breaks away along a brushy tributary stream to the northwest. At the drainage headwall, switchbacks climb to a ridge crest intersection with Trail 1225 (5,400 ft). The trail then twists downhill to Medra Creek, and follows its north bank west to the Middle Fork (3,900 ft).

## Eastern Teanaway Roadless Area Trails

**Trail 1369, Standup.** *5.9 miles/d (H,S).* From the end of FR 9703-112 (3,100 ft), the path starts up the west bank of Standup Creek, but crosses the creek three times in the next 2 miles. The creek swings west into a small gorge, which the trail avoids with switchbacks up a steep nearby face. More switchbacks follow, and at 5,800 feet Trail 1391.1 from Bean Creek is met in a small meadow. Yet more switchbacks climb through the woods to a saddle (6,200 ft) on the southwest shoulder of Earl Peak. The route then descends into basin meadows at the head of Stafford Creek to meet Trail 1359 (5,040 ft).

**Trail 1359, Stafford Creek.** *6 miles/m (H,S).* Closely following Stafford Creek uphill through forest from FR 9703 (3,040 ft), the route joins the head of Trail 1369 in headwater meadows (5,040 ft). A continuing climb reaches a ridge-top saddle (6,050 ft) with glorious views of Mount Stuart and the peaks of the Enchantments. Here the trail changes to 1217 as it heads down Cascade Creek to Ingalls Creek.

## Climbing

Most of the summits along the Wenatchee Mountains crest are walk-ups or scrambles, all with great views. More challenging is triple-summited Ingalls Peak (7,662 ft). The North Peak is the most difficult with several C-4 routes, and other C-5 and above variations. The South Peak is mainly a strenuous hike, and the East Peak has C-4 to C-5 routes. In the North Fork of the Teanaway the Esmeralda Peaks (6,477 ft) present an imposing appearance from the north, but all summits have easy routes from the south or east. Hawkins Mountain (7,160 ft), at the head of the South Fork of Fortune Creek, has an impressive 1,500-foot-high north face, but its two main summits are simple scree scrambles from the south or east.

## WINTER SPORTS

Although most trails are not accessible in winter, many of the forest roads on the perimeter of the roadless areas offer excellent opportunities for snowshoers, cross-country skiers, and snowmobilers. Some of the most popular areas are the roads on the west side of US 97 in Iron, Blue, and Scotty Creeks.

## 23 Naneum Region

### Devils Gulch, Lion Rock, and Naneum Roadless Areas

**Location:** In Chelan and Kittitas Counties, south of US 2 and east of US 97
**Size:** Devils Gulch, 25,186 acres; Lion Rock, 4,834 acres; Naneum, 6,911 acres
**Status:** 8 percent is Semiprimitive Nonmotorized; the remainder is Semiprimitive Motorized
**Terrain:** The Devils Gulch area culminates in steep-sided Mission Ridge, whose flanks are cut by lateral creek drainages separated by twisted spur ridges. To its south, the Naneum area encompasses the head of the Naneum Basin. The Lion Rock area is to the southwest, dominated by Table Mountain.
**Elevation:** 1,600 to 6,500 ft
**Management:** USFS, Okanogan–Wenatchee National Forest, Leavenworth and Cle Elum Ranger Districts; Washington State Department of Natural Resources (DNR)
**Topographic maps:** Mission Peak, Monitor, Naneum Canyon, Reecer Canyon, Swauk Pass, Swauk Prairie, Tiptop

Forest roads carve this region into three separate roadless areas. To the north, the largest is Devils Gulch. It is comprised of a long, sparsely vegetated crest, Mission Ridge, that is punctuated with large fractured blocks of sandstone. On both sides of this crest deep couloirs, many dry most of the year, have carved a complex pattern of lateral ridges. South of Mission Ridge and east of the Table Mountain bench, a broad basin with a gentler topography wraps around the headwaters of Naneum and Pearson Creeks. The west rim of Table Mountain falls away abruptly in the basalt cliffs and talus slopes that are the main features of the Lion Rock Area.

The three "roadless" areas see heavy recreational use from motorcycle traffic. Devils Gulch has 36.7 miles of trails, Naneum 13.8 miles, and Lion Rock 6.2 miles. All are open to motorized recreation.

## CLIMATE

The entire area is in a relatively dry zone in the rain shadow of the Cascades. Annual precipitation ranges 15 to 25 inches, most in the form of winter snows. Snow depths vary with elevation, but range from 3 to 5 feet. Winter temperatures hover in the lower teens, but summers are hot and dry, with the mercury often reaching into the 90s.

## ECOSYSTEM

Forest cover varies within the area, but is heavier in the southern reaches. Lower-slope timber is mostly Douglas-fir, ponderosa pine, grand fir, and western larch, which changes to lodgepole pine, subalpine pine, and Englemann spruce at higher elevations. Southwest slopes are more sparsely forested, with broken stands of ponderosa pine surrounded by pinegrass, bitterbush, and other vegetation. Willow, oceanspray, service-berry, and false hellebore may be found in creek drainages.

The mammal population is typical of the region: mule deer, elk, black bear, marten,

*Mule deer (black-tailed) frequent open meadows of the Naneum Roadless Area.*

bobcat, coyote, and cougar. Grouse are often seen, as are hawks, golden eagles, owls, and jays; there have been reports of peregrine falcons and isolated sightings of spotted owls. Canyons support a sizeable population of rattlesnakes. Sections on the south perimeter of Naneum belong to the Colockum State Wildlife Area.

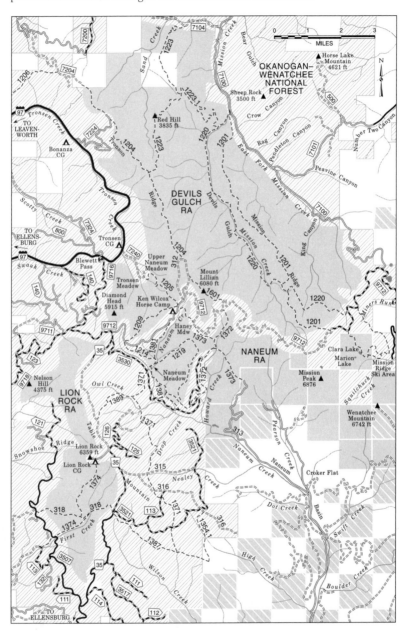

## GEOLOGY

Table Mountain, at the heart of the area, is made up of Miocene Grande Ronde basalt flows; it is on the western fringe of the area covered by the Columbia River basalts. The Lion Rock area, on the west flank of the mountain, has extensive talus slopes eroded from this basalt lying atop Eocene continental sedimentary rock. The northern part of the region in the Devils Gulch Roadless Area is predominantly Tertiary and Cretaceous continental sedimentary rock.

## HISTORY

The area's history is not marked by striking events. The region was a travelway for natives who took advantage of its natural resources to gather food, berries, roots, and household materials, and held an annual trading conclave southeast of Table Mountain. Early white exploration included trappers and miners; although the region is adjacent the former Swauk mining district, no significant mineral extraction occurred here. In the early 1900s much of the open high country was used for sheep and cattle grazing, and substantial grazing allotments continue to this day.

*A large rail fence marks the precipitous edge of Table Mountain in the Lion Rock Roadless Area.*

## HIKING
### Devils Gulch Roadless Area

**Trail 1223, Red Hill.** *8 miles/m (H,S,B; M June 15 to Oct 1).* This ridge-top trail heads south from FR 7104 at Sand Creek (1,670 ft) to immediately switchback up a wooded nose and cross a logged-off section of private land. Returning to virgin public forest, the way passes spur Trail 1223.1 (3,300 ft) that connects to the Devils Gulch Trail 1220. The way follows the crest southeast to the top of Red Hill (3,835 ft), then heads south along the ridge top with some open scenic views. Switchbacks ascend a steep knob to Tronson Ridge where Trail 1204 is met (4,870 ft).

**Trail 1220, Devils Gulch.** *10.5 miles/d (H,S,B,M).* The route, sharing a trailhead with Trail 1201, leaves FR 7100 (1,550 ft) to follow Mission Creek into Devils Gulch. For the first 2.5 miles the trail hugs the west bank of the creek, then it crosses to the east bank and climbs 100 feet above the stream. Another crossing is made as the drainage narrows, and the way stays above the creek at the base of cliffs. At 6.5 miles (3,450 ft) is one last stream crossing, then a switchback chain climbs the steep canyon wall to the top of Mission Ridge, where the route crosses Trail 1201 (4,420 ft). A long traverse of the wooded side-slope leads to FR 9712 (4,580 ft).

**Trail 1201, Mission Ridge.** *7.7 miles/m (H,S,B,M).* From a shared trailhead on FR 7100 (1,550 ft) with Trail 1220, the route climbs ceaselessly up the steep, wooded north end of Mission Ridge. The grade tempers somewhat at 3,400 feet, and ridge-top meadows offer wide views over adjoining drainages. The upward grind continues along a narrowing crest with several open, bare, rocky stretches. After topping out at 4,800 feet, the path descends to a crossing of Trail 1201 (4,420 ft), takes a couple of roller-coaster ups and downs, then climbs again to meadows and FR 9712 (5,700 ft).

### Naneum Roadless Area

**Trail 1381, Naneum Creek.** *4.7 miles/m (H,S,M).* Heading south from Ken Wilcox Horse Camp (5,600 ft) the route follows Naneum Creek down through tree-fringed pocket meadows to the broader opening of Naneum Meadow where it meets the east end of Trail 1219. A few switchbacks briefly gain the top of a bluff before the way passes Trail 1372 and begins a gradual descent along a cliff face to FR 3530 (4,750 ft).

### Lion Rock Roadless Area

**Trail 1374, First Creek.** *3.3 miles/d (H,S,M).* Starting from Lion Rock Campground (6,410 ft) the route descends gradually southward through tree-framed meadows, where it is sometimes difficult to follow. At 2 miles it meets 4wd road 318 (5,200 ft), an old stock driveway. A few hundred feet to the east the trail leaves the road at First Creek and follows its wooded north bank steeply downhill to the southwest to end on FR 3507 (3,550 ft).

## WINTER SPORTS

Many of the area's roads and trails are heavily used in winter by snowmobilers and cross-country skiers.

# 24 Little Naches River

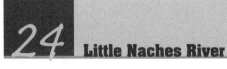

## Manastash, Quartz, and Taneum Roadless Areas

**Location:** In Kittitas and Yakima Counties just east of the Pacific crest between Highway 410 and Interstate 90

**Size:** Manastash, 8,798 acres (6,996 acres privately held); Quartz, 8,756 acres; Taneum, 25,122 acres (11,735 acres privately held)

**Status:** 25 percent is Semiprimitive Nonmotorized, the remainder is Semiprimitive Motorized

**Terrain:** A broad, convoluted backbone ridge runs northwest to southeast across the high plateau making up the roadless areas. Multiple drainages with intervening ridges divide the flanks of the main ridge.

**Elevation:** 3,000 to 6,300 ft

**Management:** USFS, Okanogan–Wenatchee National Forest, Cle Elum and Naches Ranger Districts; private timber company holdings

**Topographic maps:** Blowout Mountain, Cle Elum, Cliffdell, Easton, Frost Mountain, Manastash Lake, Mount Clifty, Quartz Mountain, Raven Roost, Ronald

The Taneum and Manastash Roadless Areas are underlain by a checkerboard pattern of ownership between the Forest Service and Plum Creek Timber. The latter acquired its holdings from railroads, which were originally granted alternating sections of land to entice them to build transcontinental lines through the area. In 2000, a major land swap was brokered between the Forest Service and the timber company to eliminate some of the checkerboard holdings and develop a more contiguous environment under public management. Roughly ten sections of land in this area reverted to public ownership. Environmentalists are attempting to raise funds to acquire even more of the presently unroaded timber company land before it succumbs to harvest.

The roadless areas are heavily used for recreation; Taneum has 124 miles of trails, and Quartz and Manastash each have 18 miles. Unfortunately all of the trail mileage is heavily used by motorcyclists, and

*Rabbits found along the Little Naches River provide a food source for coyotes, as well as hawks, and owls, and other raptors.*

some trails are open to 4WD traffic, which significantly impacts the wild area experience for other users.

## CLIMATE

Since the area lies east of the Pacific crest, weather is drier and temperatures are more extreme than those immediately to the west. Precipitation ranges from 45 to 70 inches annually, with more than half of that accumulating as winter snows. Snow depths average 6 to 7 feet. Winter temperatures range in the teens to lower 20s, and summer highs often hit the high 80s to 90s.

## ECOSYSTEM

Most of the lower portions of this region is heavily wooded; western slopes have a cover of fir and hemlock, while eastern slope forests are primarily Douglas-fir with lesser occurrences of western white pine and western larch. Higher up the trees change to subalpine fir, lodgepole pine, and Englemann spruce, while most of the broad ridge tops are sparsely timbered and covered with bunchgrass and springtime wildflowers.

Wildlife includes elk, deer, black bear, and a few cougar and mountain goats. Smaller mammals found here include coyotes, weasels, and badgers. Grouse are quite common, and a few nests of peregrine falcons and golden eagles have been sighted.

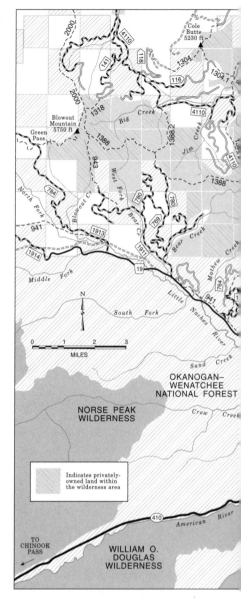

## GEOLOGY

Geologically, the entire region included in the three roadless areas is laced with extensive northwest- to southeast-tending faults indicating extensive folding of the surface rock. The top of backbone Manastash Ridge displays the oldest stock, pre-Jurassic metamorphic schist and amphibolite exposed by erosion of the Eocene volcanic rock which makes up most of the higher portions of the slopes on either side of the backbone. Lower slopes and creek

bottoms consist primarily of Eocene continental sediments, although extensive Quaternary landslide sediments are found at the southeast end of the region. The chain of ridges along the northern boundary of the area is also older Jurassic orthogneiss. Blowout Mountain, at the northwest end of the region, presents a small intrusion of Miocene quartz diorite.

*Lookout Mountain in the Taneum Roadless Area provides views of snowy Cascade Mountain peaks and miles of forest between.*

## HISTORY

Prehistoric inhabitants used the area as a major travel artery between the plains natives and those of the coast, and several sites of archaeological interest have been found in the area. Sheep grazing allotments in the early 1900s led to flocks being moved to ridge-top meadows in summer, and several of today's trails follow the routes of these annual migrations. Fire lookouts were constructed atop many of the area summits in the 1930s, and additional trail systems were developed to support them and the Forest Service fire suppression mission. All of the lookouts were removed in the 1950s.

## HIKING
### Taneum West Trails

**Trail 1388, Manastash Ridge.** *16.7 miles/m (H,S,M).* The longest and most scenic trail in the area begins near the summit of Quartz Mountain at the end of FR 3100

(6,200 ft). A short ridge crest jog reaches the head of Peaches Ridge, and the top of Trail 1363. A half-mile to the west the way intersects Trail 948 from the Little Naches River (5,580 ft), then continues northwest on the sometimes wooded, sometimes open ridge top with great views to the west across the Norse Peak Wilderness to the Cascade crest. The twisting ridge is followed northwest to a saddle junction with Trail 1326 (5,380 ft), where the route crosses a col on the east shoulder of Mount Clifty and traverses below its south-face cliffs. The way crosses Trail 947 (5.650 ft) on the southwest rib of the mountain, then bends northward to intersect Trails 1321.2 and 1333 at the top of Blazed Ridge. The path weaves along the forested crest to the west, passes two more feeder spurs, then traverses a broad open slope to join the PCT at Blowout Mountain (5,260 ft).

**Trail 1321, North Ridge.** *9.5 miles/m (H,S,B,M).* From the end of FR 4517 spur Trail 1321.3 heads west and shortly joins Trail 1321; the route then swings into a steep, switchbacked grind up wooded North Ridge. It meets Trail 1334 at the edge of an old burn where meadows bristle with huckleberries. At a saddle on the west flank of the ridge (5,440 ft) the trail splits. Trail 1321.2 drops in tight switchbacks to the Greek Creek headwaters (4,500 ft), then makes an equally grueling zigzag climb to the top of Blazed Ridge and Trail 1388 (5,420 ft). The main trail continues uphill, then splits again. Trail 1321.1 continues up the steep, narrowing, rocky ridge to the summit of Mount Clifty (6,245 ft), while 1321 rounds the head of Little Creek basin and ends west of Windy Pass on South Cle Elum Ridge Trail 1326 (5,410 ft).

**Trail 947, Mount Clifty.** *5.6 miles/m (H,S,B,M).* This westside approach to Mount Clifty leaves FR 19 at Four Way Meadow (3,330 ft) to pick its way through logged-off patches to the ridge between Mathew and Pileup Creeks. Wading through more old clearcuts, the trail reaches virgin timber at a saddle at 4,420 ft, then follows a steep narrow crest up to Trail 1388 (5,660 ft). The way switchbacks up an open southwest rib to the summit of Mount Clifty (6,245 ft) where it meets Trail 1321.1 from the north.

## Taneum East Trails

**Trail 1367, South Fork Taneum.** *5.3 miles/m (H,S,B,M).* A reasonably scenic, albeit rough, river bottom trail leaves FR 3322 (3,780 ft) and heads west up the broad drainage of the South Fork of the Taneum River. After passing Trail 1366, the narrowing river canyon forces the trail to close with the river. The route continues into the widening headwater basin, then gradually climbs wooded slopes to a junction with Trail 1363 (5,000 ft) at the foot of Peaches Ridge. The way then descends to meet Trail 1377 and the north fork of the river (4,210 ft).

**Trail 1363, Taneum Ridge.** *12.1 miles/m (H,S,M).* Starting well east of the roadless areas on FR 3300 (2,860 ft), the route follows the top of Taneum Ridge through heavily cut sections of timber before gaining unlogged stands at 4,800 feet. The way follows the gradually climbing crest, with open patches offering views of the valleys harboring the forks of the Taneum River. The way crosses Trail 1367 (5,000 ft) at the base of Peaches Ridge, then climbs to the ridge top in a series of long switchbacks. The route ends as it joins Trail 1388 (6,240 ft) a half-mile north of Quartz Mountain.

## Quartz Trails

**Trail 948, Quartz Mountain.** *7.5 miles/m (H,S,B,M)*. The westside approach to Quartz Mountain leaves FR 1903 (2,700 ft) and begins an arduous climb through old logged patches, crossing several logging spurs en route. A chain of switchbacks up a steep wooded wall gains the ridge top and virgin forest. The crest is followed north, sometimes in timber, sometimes in meadows with expansive views west into the Norse Peak Wilderness. Ridge and trail make a sharp turn to the northeast, twisting ever upward, to reach a bench at 5,200 feet. The route then skirts the head of a steep-walled cirque and joins Trail 1388 (5,580 ft) a mile northwest of the Quartz Mountain summit.

## Manastash Trails

**Trail 1207, Hereford Meadow.** *3.8 miles/e (H,S,B,M)*. From its junction with Trail 1385 (5,040 ft) off FR 31, the route closely follows the bank of the South Fork of Manastash Creek as it gradually climbs to the northwest. A pleasant alternation between meadow and forest accompanies the trip upstream. The path ends on FR 3100 at Hereford Meadow (5,790 ft) just short of a pond at the creek headwaters.

**Trail 1350, Manastash Lake.** *4.4 miles/m (H,S,M)*. From the saddle on 4WD road 694 (5,550 ft), the trail winds down a wooded slope to Manastash Lake (5,063 ft). Rounding the west shore of the lake the way weaves across a forest bench, then switchbacks down a steep hillside where Lost Lake (5,040 ft) is squeezed into a narrow defile. Crossing the outlet stream the route splits; Trail 1350.1 climbs westward from the narrow valley. The main trail heads to the east, climbs through second-growth, then crosses several logging roads as it descends to FR 3100 (4,200 ft).

Opposite: *Mount St. Helens from the southeast. The Shoestring Glacier descends from the prominent notch.*

*chapter 4*     **The Southern Cascades**

## 25 White River Region

### Clearwater Wilderness; Sun Top and Tolmie Roadless Areas

**Location:** In Pierce County, on the northwest corner of Mount Rainier National Park, 15 miles southeast of Enumclaw

**Size:** Wilderness, 14,300 acres; Sun Top, 2,386 acres; Clearwater, 8,803 acres; Tolmie Creek, 274 acres

**Status:** Designated Wilderness (1984); Roadless areas are Semiprimitive Motorized and Semiprimitive Nonmotorized

**Terrain:** A jumble of high, narrow ridges are cut by headwater branches of the Clearwater River, Huckleberry Creek, Tolmie Creek, and South Prairie Creek.

**Elevation:** 2,000 to 6,089 feet

**Management:** USFS, Mount Baker–Snoqualmie National Forest, Snoqualmie Ranger District

**Topographic maps:** Bearhead Mtn., Clear West Peak, Golden Lakes, Mowich Lake, Sunrise, Sun Top, Old Baldy Mtn.

This small vestige of unlogged federal land sits on the northwest edge of Mount Rainier National Park. Over half of the land was designated as Clearwater Wilderness in 1984. The three roadless areas, patches of forest on the edge of the wilderness, as well as a

*Beargrass blossoms mingle with other wildflowers in the Clearwater Wilderness.*

narrow strip between Sun Top and the park, remain unroaded and untouched. By stark contrast, surrounding private land and national forest land has been heavily logged. Fortunately, this island of westside Cascade old-growth forest, with its dozen small lakes and exceptional viewpoints, is thus far preserved from a similar fate, and provides a buffer to Mount Rainier National Park.

## CLIMATE

The weather picture in the area is mild and wet. Total annual precipitation ranges between 59 and 80 inches, depending on elevation, with 90 percent falling between October and May, much of it in the form of snow. The average annual snowfall is between 6 and 25 feet, and snow often persists in higher elevations until late July. Winter temperatures are relatively warm, with midwinter lows averaging in the low 20s; summers are comfortable, with highs averaging in the lower 70s.

## ECOSYSTEM

The forest is typical of the west side of the Cascades: the major tree species are Douglas-fir, western hemlock, and western red cedar. The moist understory is made up of swordfern, deerfern, ladyfern, Oregon oxalis, deerfoot vanillaleaf, wild ginger, white inside-out flower, and a variety of liverworts and mosses. The animals found here are the usual black-tailed deer, black bear, cougar, bobcat, small mammals, and marmots, along with a few elk. You are likely to see raptors such as golden eagles, goshawks, and sharp-shinned hawks soaring over peaks, and bluebirds, flycatchers, jays, and nutcrackers flitting about the forest understory.

## GEOLOGY

The Ohanapecosh Formation, the base upon which all of the Mount Rainier vicinity is built, consists of sedimentary deposits laid down about 40 million years ago. Folding and faulting created a syncline that ran northwest through the park and continued through the heart of the Clearwater Wilderness. About 25 million years ago the base

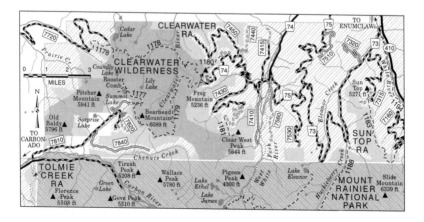

layers were overlaid by the rhyodacitic ash flows of the Stevens Formation, which covered the southeast side of the wilderness. The heart of the area is a large pluton, the Carbon River Stock, which intruded into the older formations some 10 million to 15 million years ago. This pluton is composed mainly of granodiorite, quartz diorite, and quartz monzonite. Clear West Peak, at the southeast corner of the wilderness, is a huge plug of flow-banded vitrophyre and welded tuff, which may have been extruded contemporaneously with the pluton intrusion. The current surface features of the area were carved by a number of small local glaciers that flowed northward from the area's east–west backbone ridge between 15,000 and 20,000 years ago.

## HISTORY

Although the Puyallup Indians undoubtedly hunted animals and gathered berries in the area, there is no evidence of any extended habitation by them. In the 1930s lookouts were built on three of the high spots, Bearhead Mountain, Clear West Peak, and Sun Top. The buildings at two of the sites were removed in the 1960s; however, the lookout on Sun Top remained, and was reconstructed in 1990, making it a favorite scenic destination. It is still staffed, partially by volunteers. A steep narrow road, open only in the summer, reaches the lookout.

## HIKING
### Carbon River Trails

*Trail 1177, Summit Lake.* 2.5 miles/e (H,S). From a road-end clearcut on FR 7810 (4,400 ft), the route heads into the old-growth forest of the wilderness and switchbacks up to Twin Lake (4,810 ft). Here it meets the west end of Trail 1179, then weaves up a small rib before starting a long, gradual ascent to Summit Lake (5,439 ft). In meadows on the northwest shore, enjoy a striking view of Mount Rainier's Willis Wall mirrored on the surface of the lake. The meadows have suffered badly from inconsiderate use, so please treat them gently. A footpath leads to the top of a 5,740-foot-high knob on the west side of the lake, with an even better mountain view.

### Clearwater River Trails

*Trail 1178, Clearwater.* 8.1 miles/d (H; S, but not recommended). From the east, the route leaves Trail 1179 just beyond its trailhead at the end of FR 74 (4,140 ft), and descends northwest around the head of a basin densely covered with old-growth forest. Switchbacks drop sharply to a long, gradual descent to the Clearwater River (2,110 ft). The route heads west, crosses Lily Creek, then climbs determinedly above its west fork to a small lake in Celery Meadows. After a short ascent to a flat, the path continues west to the wilderness boundary and crosses into private land. A few switchbacks lead south through clearcuts to FR 7720 (4,320 ft).

*Trail 1179, Carbon.* 9.4 miles/d (H; S, but not recommended). Leaving the end of FR 74 at Martin Gap (4,140 ft), the trail twists down around basins and ridges to the Clearwater River (3,140 ft), then crosses it. After switchbacking up above the brushy river bottom, the way follows the drainage south to its head, where more switchbacks surmount the steep wall leading to Hurricane Gap (4,960 ft). The track heads west in a gentle ascent around the steep south and southwest sides of the long massif of Bearhead Mountain, en route passing over an open knob with outstanding views of Mount Rainier. Trail 1179.1 to the old lookout site atop Bearhead Mountain is passed at 8.1 miles, and the path ends as it meets Trail 1177 at Twin Lake (4,810 ft).

**Trail 1181, Clear West Peak.** *0.8 mile/m (H,S).* This short path leaves the end of FR 7430 (4,720 ft) and follows the top of a narrow rib uphill to the site of a former lookout (5,644 ft). The open summit offers great views up the tongue of the Winthrop Glacier to the summit of Mount Rainier and down the deep valley of the White River drainage.

**Trail 1183, Sun Top.** *8.3 miles/m (H,S,B,M).* Although this trail officially starts on FR 7160-210 (2,583 ft) at the Ranger Creek airstrip, it crosses FR 7160 and its spurs three more times higher uphill, which can shorten the hike if open gates permit. From the upper road crossing (4,300 ft), the route contours the wooded head of Buck Creek, then gains the top of the ridge to the north (5,300 ft). The long, old-growth-clad crest descends gradually to cross FR 7315-510 (4,760 ft) before switchbacking up to the lookout site (5,271 ft).

# 26 Norse Peak Region

## Norse Peak Wilderness; adjacent and Silver Creek Roadless Areas

**Location:** In Pierce and Yakima Counties, on the north and east sides of Highway 410 northeast of Chinook and Naches Passes
**Size:** Wilderness, 50,923 acres; Norse Peak Adjacent, 11,380 acres; Silver Creek, 1,055 acres
**Status:** Designated Wilderness (1984); Roadless areas are Semiprimitive Motorized and Semiprimitive Nonmotorized
**Terrain:** Steep, rocky ridges at higher elevations enclose narrow valleys, while open parkland basins hold mountain lakes.
**Elevation:** 3,200 to 6,858 feet
**Management:** USFS, Mount Baker–Snoqualmie National Forest, Snoqualmie Ranger District; and Okanogan–Wenatchee National Forest, Naches Ranger District
**Topographic maps:** Chinook Pass, Goose Prairie, Mount Clifty, Noble Knob, Norse Peak, Raven Roost, Sun Top, White River Park

The Norse Peak Wilderness straddles the Cascade crest on the east side of Mount Rainier National Park. The historic Naches Pass Trail, which was cut across the Cascades in 1853 by pioneer immigrants to the Puget Sound, lies just north of the wilderness boundary; the leg of Highway 410 east of Chinook Pass marks its southern limits.

The southwest corner of the area is flecked with abandoned prospects, mine shafts, and cabin remnants, memorials to the search for elusive mineral wealth that embraced the area in the late 1800s to early 1900s. Deep narrow drainages cut into the heart of the wilderness—the Greenwater River west of the crest, and Union and Crow Creeks and the South Fork of the Little Naches River on the east. Nearly two dozen lakelets and tarns, only half with names, dapple flats and pockets at mid- and upper altitudes.

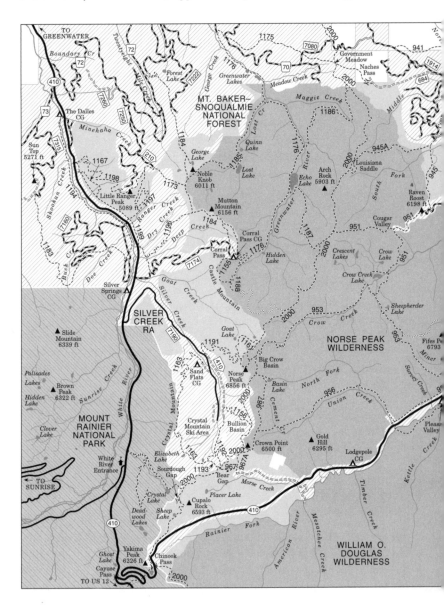

## CLIMATE

Climate varies somewhat, depending on location and elevation. In general, the annual precipitation runs about 100 inches, 80 to 90 percent of which falls as snow, accumulating to depths of up to 10 feet. Most snow is generally gone from higher elevations by late July. Winter low temperatures average between 10 and 20 degrees, and summer highs are in the mid-70s.

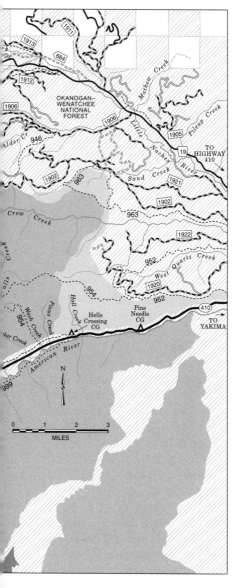

## ECOSYSTEM

At lower altitudes west of the crest, the forest is Douglas-fir, true fir, western hemlock, and western red cedar. The understory includes ferns, white inside-out flower, Oregon oxalis, vanillaleaf, wild ginger, liverworts, and various mosses. At higher elevations, mountain hemlock and subalpine fir become more prevalent, and the forest frequently breaks into meadows with a covering of huckleberry, luetkea, helebore, Indian paintbrush, woolly everlasting, cinquefoil, lupine, and sedges. On the eastern rim of the wilderness, some larch and Engelmann spruce appear, as well as larger stands of lodgepole pine and white pine.

Wildlife found here includes mule deer, black-tailed deer, elk, black bear, cougar, fisher, wolverine, mountain goat, and several species of grouse. Bald and golden eagles have been seen in the Greenwater River drainage.

## GEOLOGY

The bulk of the area is composed of the Fifes Peak Formation, a composite of lava flows, mud flows, and volcanic clastic rock, from 50 to 500 feet thick. Rhyolite flows are exposed in the Fifes Peak–Fifes Ridge area at the head of Falls Creek, and on Castle Mountain, along the western rim of the wilderness. This formation is thought to be about 25 million years old, and lies on top of the earlier Stevens Ridge Formation, a slightly thicker layer of ash flows and volcanic clastic rock. About 10 million to 15 million years ago these lava flows were intruded by granitic plutons along the southwest side of the wilderness; the mineralized contact zone along the perimeter of the plutons has been heavily prospected for both placer and lode gold.

## HISTORY

Names such as Bullion Basin, Gold Hill, Placer Lake, and Pickhandle Gap all attest to the early-day gold fever that drew prospectors to the southwest corner of the wilderness in the 1880s. Although the Summit Mining District recorded nearly fifty active claims in the headwaters of Morse and Silver Creeks, and extensive hydraulic mining on Morse Creek recovered some nuggets, the gold extracted never covered the costs of recovery. A large fire swept the northwest section of the wilderness around 1900, creating alpine meadows that were later leased by the government for cattle and sheep grazing. After the Washington Forest Reserves were created, the Forest Service built fire lookouts atop Noble Knob, Norse Peak, and Raven Roost, and cut trails into the region to support the lookouts and fire patrols. The 1950s and '60s saw the creation of Washington's largest ski resort, Crystal Mountain, in the Silver Creek basin along the west boundary of the wilderness; this in turn has increased interest in winter use of the adjoining wilderness backcountry.

## HIKING
### Greenwater River Trails

**Trail 1176, Greenwater.** *11.9 miles/e-m (H,S).* From the junction with the historic Naches Trail near the beginning of FR 7033 (2,480 ft), the route follows the banks of the Greenwater River southeast through dense Cascade forest past Greenwater (Meeker) Lakes (2,860 and 2,906 ft) and Trail 1185. The way continues upstream between encroaching forested walls, passes Trail 1186, then climbs to the wooded pocket enclosing Echo Lake (3,819 ft) and a junction with Trail 1187. The path continues upstream to a spur to Hidden Lake (4,190 ft), Trail 1176.1. A pair of switchbacks climb to a steep side-slope traverse to FR 7174 at Corral Pass (5,550 ft).

**Trail 1185, Lost Lake.** *5.1 miles/m (H,S).* At the 3.2-mile point on Trail 1176 (3,070 ft), this path heads south into the Lost Creek drainage. A brief ascent out of the basin floor bypasses Quinn Lake (3,890 ft); the way then continues to Lost Lake (3,985 ft). Here the route heads west and a strenuous climb tops the divide between Lost and George Creeks (5,240 ft). A traverse of the steep, open, rocky face of Noble Knob meets Trail 1184 (5,700 ft) on the rib south of that high spot.

### Corral Pass Trails

**Trail 1155, Rainier View.** *2.2 miles/m (H,S).* From the FR 7174 trailhead (5,550 ft), the route starts southwest, then winds south as it slowly climbs to the elongated summit ridge of Castle Mountain (6,100 ft). Once atop the crest, hikers are rewarded by a horizon-filling view of the White River side of Mount Rainier. In a short distance the way drops west atop a minor rib to join Castle Mountain Trail 1188 (5,900 ft).

That trail is badly deteriorated, and its restoration is a multi-year project.

**Trail 1184, Noble Knob.** *7.9 miles/m (H,S).* The trail leaves FR 7174 at Corral Pass (5,651 ft) to head north along the west side of the crest, often on open slopes with knock-out views of Mount Rainier. After traversing below Mutton Mountain and passing the heads of Trails 1196, 1173, 1185, and a spur to the top of Noble Knob, the path crosses a steep, open sidehill on the west flank of the knob, and regains the crest at a junction with a spur trail to George Lake. Shortly thereafter the route enters a maze of logging roads and ends on FR 7222 (3,500 ft).

## Dalles Ridge Trails

**Trail 1197, Ranger Creek.** *5.8 miles/m (H,S,B).* From Trail 1199 at Ranger Creek (2,700 ft), this route switchbacks up the north slope above the creek, and in a long sweep tops a ridge finger. More zigzags up the steep north wall of the creek lead to a crest north from Little Ranger Peak, a junction with Trail 1198, and a scout-built shelter. Another easy mile uphill leads to Trail 1173 (5,450 ft).

**Trail 1198, Palisades.** *6.6 miles/m (H,B).* From Trail 1199 (2,520 ft) at Dalles Creek, the route heads into a narrow, rocky cleft in multiple tight switchbacks. After surmounting the cliff band, the way weaves eastward through old growth to Snoquera Creek, then skirts the cliff edge to reach clearcuts near Little Ranger Peak. The flat ridge to the north is followed to a junction with Trail 1197 at the scout shelter (4,960 ft).

## Silver Creek Trails

**Trail 1191, Norse Peak.** *5.2 miles/m (H,S).* The trail leaves FR 7190-410 (3,990 ft) north of the Crystal Mountain Ski Area and switchbacks up a steep sidehill. The tread has been reconstructed at an easy grade to combat erosion problems caused by its steeper predecessor. At 4 miles a spur leads to the top of Norse Peak (6,856 ft), once the site of a fire lookout. Panoramic views include the Puget Sound basin, Snoqualmie Pass summits, the rolling hills east to the Columbia Plateau, Mount Adams, and the icy bulk of close-at-hand Mount Rainier. The way tops the ridge (6,040 ft), and drops east into Big Crow Basin to join the PCT (6,280 ft).

**Trail 1156, Bullion Basin.** *2.2 miles/m (H,S).* Climbing to the east from FR 7190-410 (4,720 ft) the route gradually makes its way through subalpine trees to and above Bullion Basin where it joins the PCT (6,160 ft).

## American River Trails

**Trail 956, Union Creek.** *7.1 miles/m (H,S).* The trail leaves a roadside pull-off (3,410 ft) from Highway 410 east of Chinook Pass, and crosses Union Creek below an impressive waterfall. The way tightly switchbacks up the wooded rib along the east side of the falls, then follows Union Creek upstream, staying a few hundred feet above the dense creek-bottom brush. At the North Fork of the creek, the trail crosses a foot-log over another foaming waterfall, then continues east, dropping to creek level at 4 miles. A gradual ascent into the widening basin leaves the creek and swings up the headwall to meet Trail 987 (5,920 ft).

*The steep walls of Fifes Peaks are favored by rock climbers.*

**Trail 987, Lake Basin.** *2.5 miles/m (H,S).* After leaving the PCT southeast of Crown Point (6,200 ft) the trail traverses the lightly timbered slope on the east side of the Cascade crest, passes the upper end of Trail 956, and wanders through the meadows of Cement Basin. It crosses a saddle into Lake Basin, where a spur descends to Basin Lake, then climbs to rejoin the PCT (6,400 ft) east of Norse Peak.

**Trail 953, Crow Lake.** *12.7 miles/m (H,S).* The trail leaves Highway 410 (3,390 ft) east of Chinook Pass, heads northwest along Miner Creek, and grinds uphill in a succession of thirty switchbacks. It tops the divide between Miner and Survey Creeks, then traces it uphill, staying near the edge of its sheer southwest face. At 5,800 feet the way swings west around the head of Survey Creek, then bends north to broad meadows and a tiny tarn at Grassy Saddle (5,600 ft). From the saddle, a leisurely wooded descent passes spurs to Sheepherder and Marsh Lakes, then meets Trail 951 (4,580 ft), 0.5 mile west of Crow Creek Lake. The way now wanders west along the broad bottomland to the headwaters of Crow Creek, then switchbacks up a steep headwall to join the PCT in Big Crow Basin (6,230 ft).

**Trail 954, Fifes Ridge.** *8.8 miles/m (H,S).* From Highway 410 (3,360 ft) east of Chinook Pass, the route makes a steady ascent up Wash Creek to near its headwaters. Switchbacks claw up the wooded basin headwall to a saddle on Fifes Ridge (5,190 ft) just east of Fifes Peaks. Trail 954 heads east along the crest and shortly tops a bare knob with views west to the vertical battlements and sharp pinnacles of Fifes Peaks. The route traces the convolutions of the descending ridge east to end on Trail 952 (5,100 ft), off FR 1920.

## Raven Roost Trails

**Trail 951, Cougar Valley.** *5.2 miles/m (H,S).* The old road west of Raven Roost has been converted to trail. In a mile it splits; the section heading south winds down Cougar Valley to the meadows beside Crow Creek Lake (4,550 ft), then continues up Crow Creek another 0.5 mile to end on Trail 953 (4,580 ft). The segment heading west wanders through meadow and forest near the top of the east–west ridge to meet the PCT (5,830 ft) near the head of the South Fork of the Little Naches River.

**Trail 945A, Louisiana Saddle.** *3.2 miles/m (H).* After leaving Trail 945 (4,200 ft) this route soon enters the wilderness and traces the ridge top west in a gradual ascent, interrupted once by a short face requiring switchbacks to surmount. The path then wends through wildflower meadows to meet the PCT at Louisiana Saddle (5,210 ft).

## Trail 2000, Pacific Crest National Scenic Trail. *26.6 miles/m (H,S).*

From Highway 410 at Chinook Pass (5,432 ft), the route runs northeast on the sidehill above the highway for a little more than a mile. It then rounds a hogback and turns north, climbing to Sheep Lake (5,750 ft). A weaving path up a steep, rocky side-slope crosses Sourdough Gap (6,410 ft). After a short descent north of the gap, the path traverses the treeless head of Morse Creek Basin to Bear Gap (5,882 ft), the junction with Trails 1192 and 1193 from the west, and 967 from the east. As the route swings north around Pickhandle Point, views open down the Silver Creek Basin. The way recrosses the crest at Pickhandle Gap (5,980 ft), then passes Trail 987 on the southeast side of Crown Point, where a switchback returns the path west of the crest for the next segment of the trek.

Trail 1156 is joined at the head of Bullion Basin, and a long, gradual ascent recrosses the crest at Scout Pass (6,550 ft). A traverse above the rocky slopes of Lake Basin meets Trail 987, then traces a flat wooded track around the head of Big Crow Basin, passing Trails 1191 and 953. A gradual wooded descent meets Trail 1188 at Martinson Gap (5,780 ft), then the way weaves back and forth across the crest, passing Trail 951. The path now follows the ridge top to Louisiana Saddle (5,210 ft), where it meets Trail 945A. The wooded west side of the crest is followed to Rods Gap (4,850 ft), where the track descends to Government Meadow (4,730 ft) on the west side of Naches Pass.

## CLIMBING

The main climbing interests in the wilderness are the multiple andesite summits of Fifes Peaks, most with high vertical walls, and a collection of crags and spires that line the ridge between them (6,375 to 6,917 ft). Although the peaks have challenging faces, the rock is very loose and friable. The defined summits are the Far East Peak, with nearby Teddy Bear Pinnacle and Mainmast; the East Peak, the largest and most imposing of the summits, with adjoining Cannonhole Pinnacle; the West Peak, sheer on three sides, but easy from the east; and the Northwest Peak, the highest and easiest of the summits, with a detached tower close by.

On the ridge east of Sourdough Gap is Cupalo Rock (6,593 ft), part of the granitic intrusion at the southwest corner of the area. The east face has a number of two- to three-lead, solid rock climbs in the C-5 to C-5.7 range.

## WINTER SPORTS

One of western Washington's major ski resorts, Crystal Mountain, lies adjacent the southwest corner of the wilderness, and several strenuous backcountry ski/snowshoe treks fan out from there into the Norse Peak Wilderness and adjoining roadless areas. One of the more popular of these tours is to Bullion Basin, east of Crystal Mountain. Extensions of this tour head north along the crest to the summit of Norse Peak, and on to Lake and Big Crow Basins east of the peak, or south to Crown Point. Expert-level tours cross Bear Gap and head east down Morse Creek, or follow the Pacific Crest Trail southwest from the gap to make a loop trip around Threeway Peak.

A less demanding trip follows the snowbound road toward Corral Pass, then at timberline swings south up the ridge to the top of Castle Mountain. A second route continues on to the pass, then heads north, following the route of Trail 1184 to the top of Mutton Mountain.

## 27 Mount Rainier National Park

**Location:** In Pierce and Lewis Counties, surrounding Mount Rainier
**Size:** Park, 235,613 acres; wilderness, 228,480 acres
**Status:** National Park (1899), Designated Wilderness (1988)
**Terrain:** This high, heavily glaciated, dormant volcano is surrounded by alpine parks framed between rugged, precipitous canyons.
**Elevation:** 1,950 to 14,411 feet
**Management:** National Park Service
**Topographic maps:** Chinook Pass, Cougar Lake, Golden Lakes, Mount Wow, Mt. Rainier East, Mt. Rainier West, Mowich Lake, Ohanapecosh Hot Springs, Sawtooth Ridge, Sunrise, Tatoosh Lakes, Wahpenayo Peak, White Pass, White River Park

Just as the summit of Mount Rainier marks the highest point in the state of Washington (and the fifth-highest spot in the Lower 48 states), the park abounds with other superlatives. It contains 382 lakes and ponds, 470 rivers and streams, and 9 major watersheds. Its 27 named glaciers cover a surface area of about 37 square miles, the largest glacial system on a single peak in the coterminous United States. The forests and alpine meadows around the mountain are habitat for 787 plant species, 54 mammal species, 130 bird species, and 17 species of reptiles and amphibians.

*Edith Creek Basin, near Paradise on Mount Rainier, features tumbling cascades and spectacular views.*

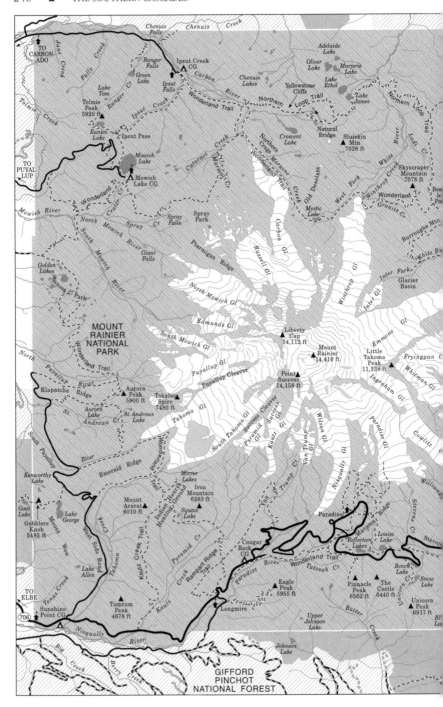

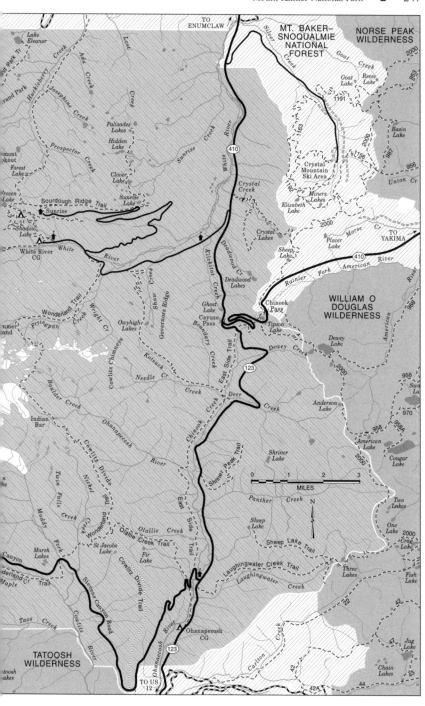

The park is also a recreationist's paradise. There are more than 300 miles of maintained trails within its borders; one, the Wonderland Trail that encircles the mountain, is 93 miles long. Five standard campgrounds in the park contain nearly 600 campsites, and the 41 backcountry camps can accommodate more than 1,000 wilderness hikers and climbers. Each year from 6,000 to 8,000 people attempt to climb the mountain, some in private parties, others using the Rainier Mountaineering Service. Fewer than half succeed in reaching the summit.

## CLIMATE

Both temperature and precipitation vary markedly with altitude and location. At lower elevations, midsummer temperatures range between 48 and 80 degrees; at Paradise (5,400 ft), the range is between 44 and 64 degrees; and at the summit, summer temperatures have been recorded between minus 10 and 32 degrees. Average midwinter temperatures at Longmire are in the upper 20s to low 40s; at Paradise, lower 20s to lower 30s. At the summit, temperature records are sketchy, but a low of minus 80 has been recorded. Valleys below 5,000 feet are frequently draped in local clouds or fog when the high country is clear and sunny. Winds increase with elevation; on the summit they are almost nonstop at about 30 mph, and are known to reach as high as 100 mph.

Rain or snow starts falling in October, and there are only intermittent sun breaks until mid- to late April. Total annual precipitation at lower elevations is about 80 inches; at Paradise, 100 inches. There are no reliable figures for the summit; however, because cold, high-altitude air has less moisture-carrying capacity, it is safe to assume that precipitation levels there are somewhat less than on the slopes below. A substantial portion of this moisture falls as snow that accumulates to depths of 2 to 4 feet at lower elevations, grading up to 20 feet or more at the altitude of Paradise. July, August, and September are generally dry and pleasant, with only two to four rainy days a month.

The mountain is said to "generate its own weather," which to a certain extent is true. The 14,411-foot peak is both high and massive enough to significantly disrupt area wind flows (witness the lenticular cloud cap that often forms above the summit).

## ECOSYSTEM

The 12,000-foot altitude differential within the park spans multiple forest zones. The portions of the park below 4,000 feet are covered with a dense old-growth forest consisting of Douglas-fir, western hemlock, and western red cedar. Grand fir, cottonwood, and maple are found in drainage bottoms, and avalanche-stripped slopes are blanketed with red alder and vine maple. Understory elements include devil's club, huckleberry, oxalis, skunk cabbage, twinflower, trillium, and many other flowers. Ferns and more than a hundred species of mosses and fungi flourish in the shady, damp environment.

Between 4,000 feet and 6,500 feet, the forest constituents change to mountain hemlock, Alaska cedar, whitebark pine, and subalpine fir, spaced more openly with increasing altitude. This woodland cover is broken by meadows stippled with a spectrum of wildflower color: lupine, Indian paintbrush, western anemone, penstemon, mountain bistort, aster, pedicularis, cinquefoil, and Sitka valerian, to name but a few.

Above timberline are broad subalpine meadows with only a few short, gnarled tufts of mountain hemlock and subalpine fir. Between late June and early September these meadows are a sea of multihued wildflowers. More than seventy-six species have been identified, among them beargrass, heather, avalanche lily, goldenrod, monkey-flower, shooting star, fireweed, larkspur, buttercup, Jacob's ladder, and columbine. The harsh alpine zone at the lower fringes of the glaciers features mosses, lichens, sedges, moss campion, and phlox, hardy plants uniquely adapted to this environment.

Among the fifty-four mammal species found in the park, the most often seen are elk, black-tailed deer, black bear, mountain goat, raccoon, pine marten, beaver, porcupine, skunk, cougar, bobcat, hoary marmot, pika, snowshoe hare, golden-mantled ground squirrel, and yellow pine chipmunk. Of the 130 species of birds that live or nest in the park, or pass through in migratory travel, the more common residents are blue grouse, jays, Clark's nutcracker, flickers, Vaux's swift, thrushes, kestrels, rough-legged and red-tailed hawks, Steller's jay, red-breasted nuthatch, red-winged blackbird, mountain chickadee, hummingbirds, and yellow-bellied sapsucker.

## GEOLOGY

The geological story of Mount Rainier begins some 40 million years ago when the base Puget Group of siltstones and arkoses, probably deposited in a shallow inland sea, was gradually overlaid by layers of lava flows, mudflows, ash flows, and rhyolites of the Ohanapecosh Formation. The interleaving of tuff breccias with laminated siltstones and thin-graded sandstone indicates that most of these eruptions occurred underwater. As eruptive material accumulated, parts of the basin may have risen above water level. The only identified centers for this volcanic activity are the Mount Wow and the Cowlitz Chimney–Sarvent Glacier areas. The Ohanapecosh Formation built to a thickness of about 10,000 feet over a period of 8 million to 10 million years. After its deposition the formation was subjected to folding along a north–northeast axis.

The next phase of volcanic activity started some 25 million to 30 million years ago when the ash flows and volcanic clastic rocks of the Stevens Formation overlaid the Ohanapecosh Formation and its erosion debris to a depth of 450 to 3,000 feet. This volcanic activity occurred mostly in the southern part of the park, although smaller outcrops have been identified in the north and northwest sections.

About 5 million years later a third phase of volcanism began. The lava flows, mudflows, and clastic rocks of the Fifes Peak Formation were layered over the Stevens Ridge Formation to a depth of 1,000 to 3,000 feet. These lava streams appear to have radiated from vents just east of the present park boundary. Continued deformation along the old fold axes deepened and distorted the Ohanapecosh Formation, and this syncline was partially filled by flows of the Stevens and Fifes Peak Formations.

The last geological element to impact the area prior to the volcanism that built the present peak occurred 8 million to 15 million years ago. The huge Tatoosh Pluton intruded the overlying formations, slicing through them and warping and distorting their structure. As the top of the pluton forced through the other formations, a spider's web of sills and dikes radiated from its dome, especially along the base of the Stevens Ridge Formation. In places the pluton magma broke through the surface in volcanic explosions; the eroded plugs of these vents make up Sourdough Mountain and the Palisades.

About 3 million years after the Tatoosh Pluton intruded, a general uplift of the whole Cascade Range began; the three older formations were raised to an altitude of about 4,000 feet, and were heavily eroded by rivers and streams that cut deep canyons through their layers. The birth of the current volcano began about 1 million years ago with a rapid outpouring of lava flows, the oldest occurring in the north and west sections of the park. This lava filled the deep canyons first, inverting the ancestral drainages of the White, Carbon, Mowich, and Puyallup Rivers, which were forced to find new courses along the sides of these new masses of lava. Today those canyon-filling flows comprise the alpine plateaus of Grand Park, Sunset Park, and Burroughs Mountain.

Continuing eruptions built up successive layers of lava flows interspersed with breccias from pyroclastic flows. Strata on lower slopes included mudflows triggered by steam explosions when hot lavas mixed with snow or meltwater. Smaller lava flows that reached the base of the new stream-cut canyons banked against the older lava to form a series of terraces. The cone of the volcano continued to build over succeeding centuries to reach an estimated height of about 15,500 feet.

Two satellite volcanoes appeared on the mountain's north flank during the Pleistocene glaciation period, erupting olivine andesite that flowed into the valleys below, flooding the headwaters of the Carbon and North Mowich Rivers. Divided remnants of these two cones form Observation and Echo Rocks. The blunt summit of Rainier then lost nearly 1,000 feet of its height, either because the core of the volcano subsided due to diversion of magma to the two satellite volcanoes, or because the core, softened by meltwater, found breaches in the rim and flowed down the volcano's sides in massive mudflows. Approximately 5,800 years ago, something triggered the massive Osceola mudflow; nearly half a cubic mile of debris swept down the White River valley to the site of present-day Auburn. The three current summits—Liberty Cap, Point Success, and Columbia Crest—lie on the lip of the older summit cone.

Rainier's last known volcanic activity, minor pumice eruptions, occurred 500 to 600 years ago and briefly between 1820 and 1854. More recent historical changes have taken the form of floods and mudflows. Major floods from the Nisqually Glacier occurred in 1926, 1932, 1934, and 1955; a large slurry flood surged down the Kautz River in 1947; in 1963 a massive debris avalanche peeled off the north side of Little Tahoma and raced down the Emmons Glacier to the White River Campground; twenty debris flows have moved down Tahoma Creek since 1967; and more recent South Tahoma debris flows have washed out portions of the West Side Road.

## HISTORY

Indians living on the perimeter of the park hunted, fished, and gathered berries within its boundaries for centuries. Their legends are rich with stories of Takhoma, as they called the imposing volcano centerpiece, and some of its satellite peaks. Although portions of the park were at one time claimed by the Muckleshoot, Nisqually, Yakama, Puyallup, and Taidnapum tribes, there is no solid evidence of any permanent native residence within the current boundaries.

The first European explorers to see Mount Rainier were members of the 1792 Vancouver expedition; its leader, Captain George Vancouver, named the peak for a friend, Rear Admiral Peter Rainier of the British Navy. The next recorded sighting of the mountain was by the Lewis and Clark Corps of Discovery in 1806. In 1833, William Tolmie, the physician at the Hudson's Bay Company's Fort Nisqually, made the first attempt to approach the peak. With five Indian guides he made his way up the Puyallup and Mowich Rivers to Mowich Lake, on the mountain's northwest flank. He pressed higher and climbed an intermediate peak, possibly Hessong Rock, for close views of the rugged north face of the mountain.

In the 1850s settlers began trickling into the Puget Sound area. One of them, James Longmire, made the second thrust into the park area as he followed the Nisqually River upstream, searching for an alternative to troublesome Naches Pass across the Cascades. Longmire blazed a trail into the southwest corner of the park in 1861, and for the next 20 years he guided approach marches of many of the first climbing parties. In 1870 he discovered a mineral spring in a meadow in the Nisqually River valley, filed a claim there, and later constructed a rough tourist resort at Longmire Hot Springs.

An old Indian guide recounted having taken a party of two unnamed white men, purportedly Indian Treaty boundary surveyors, to the summit in 1855 by way of the Emmons and Winthrop Glaciers. Although his description of the crater's features seems to verify this story, the men remain unknown. Lieutenant A. V. Kautz made the first reported summit attempt in 1857 via Wapowety Cleaver; the party turned back near Point Success, a few hundred feet short of the summit in elevation, and a half-mile away in distance. The first recorded successful ascent of the peak was made in August 1870 by General Hazard Stevens and Philemon Beecher Van Trump. They approached from south of the present park, crossed the Tatoosh Range, descended to Mazama Ridge, and climbed from there to the present site of Camp Muir, where they used the Gibraltar Rock route to reach the summit.

The surge of prospecting in the late 1800s also hit Mount Rainier; by the turn of the century more than 300 mining claims had been filed in the park. Copper was the only mineral of significance found, and most mining rapidly folded. Three mines became producers: the Eagle Peak Copper Mining Company's mine in the Tatoosh Range, the North Mowich Glacier Mine at the base of Eagle Cliff, and the Mount Rainier Mining Company's mine at Starbo, in Glacier Basin. All mining ceased in 1948.

The mountain rapidly became a major tourist attraction, featuring Longmire's resort in the Nisqually Basin, where an inn opened in 1906; a tent lodging business at Paradise, which operated between 1898 and 1915; and the Ohanapecosh Hot Springs Resort, which was in full swing by the late 1920s. In 1893 the striking beauty of the mountain and its outstanding natural features led to intensive lobbying by several national scientific and outdoor organizations for its preservation. Congress established the national park in March 1899, the fifth such area in the United States to be so designated.

Further protection for its unique backcountry was assured in 1988 when all undeveloped portions of the park became a designated wilderness.

## HIKING
## Westside Trails

Because of repeated washouts, the West Side Road is closed at Dry Creek, 3.1 miles up the road. This means that additional road hiking is required to reach westside trails.

**Gobblers Knob Trail.** *2.5 miles/m* (H). From the West Side Road at Round Pass (3,900 ft), an easy grade ascends 1 mile to Lake George (4,292 ft). Most visitors stop here to camp or fish, but the trail continues more steeply up the forested slope west to the lookout atop Gobblers Knob (5,485 ft), where views of the Tahoma Glacier and Sunset Amphitheater reward the extra effort.

**Kautz Creek Trail.** *5.7 miles/m* (H). The trail leaves the Nisqually–Longmire Road (2,410 ft) near the Kautz Creek bridge, passing initially along the top of the 1947 mudflow amid regenerating forest. The near-level grade ends in a mile after crossing the creek, and more than two dozen switchbacks weave up the steep, densely forested, northwest wall of the drainage to a forest-and-meadow bench. One more steep open stretch of trail, followed by gentle parkland, leads to the Wonderland Trail at Indian Henrys Hunting Ground (5,450 ft). The Mirror Lakes Trail continues up another 0.7 mile to flower fields at its namesakes.

**South Puyallup Trail.** *1.6 miles/m* (H). The trail heads east from the West Side Road (3,500 ft) through the deep forest on the sidehill above the South Puyallup River. Just before reaching the Wonderland Trail (4,070 ft) it passes one of the most distinctive and photogenic examples of columnar basalt in the park.

**St. Andrews Trail.** *2.2 miles/m* (H). This route departs the West Side Road (3,770 ft) for the steep wooded hillside north of St. Andrews Creek. Switchbacks reach the top of Klapatche Ridge (4,600 ft), then the way follows the crest east to Aurora Lake (5,500 ft) and the Wonderland Trail. The lake, at the edge of Klapatche Park, reflects the icy west side of Rainier.

**North Puyallup Trail.** *2.75 miles/e* (H,S). The last 3 miles of the old West Side Road (4,000 ft) have been converted to a trail that runs along the steep wooded hillside, 600 to 800 feet above the North Puyallup River. It follows the drainage upstream to meet the Wonderland Trail at river's edge (3,700 ft).

## Mowich Trails

**Spray Park Trail.** *8.7 miles/m* (H). The path to the outstanding flower fields of Spray Park leaves the south end of Mowich Lake (4,929 ft) and descends through subalpine forest along the west flank of Fay Peak to the rim of Eagle Cliff (4,640 ft). Switchbacks climb up along the edge of the cliff to a short viewpoint spur (4,900 ft) near the base of the 400-foot-high ribbon of Spray Falls. More than twenty tight switchbacks now scale the wall along Grant Creek to reach the lower fringes of Spray Park. This flower-covered meadow is but a sample of those to come. The way ascends eastward

*Spray Park is renowned for spectacular fields of avalanche lilies.*

into expansive fragrant meadows that blend upwards into snowfields below Observation and Echo Rocks. Above, narrow, fragmented Ptarmigan Ridge sweeps up beside the Mowich Face for 6,000 feet to Liberty Cap. The way, marked by cairns, crosses a permanent snowfield (6,360 ft), then descends the ridge framing the west side of Seattle Park. At timberline the route zigzags down the steep wooded bank of Marmot Creek to Cataract Creek (4,000 ft). A gradual descent of this drainage meets the Wonderland Trail at the Carbon River (3,190 ft).

 ***Tolmie Peak Trail.*** *2.8 miles/m (H).* This path leaves the Wonderland Trail at Ipsut Pass (5,140 ft), north of Mowich Lake, eases up past Eunice Lake (5,354 ft), then in a pair of long switchbacks gains the top of Tolmie Peak (5,920 ft). The lookout here has around-the-compass views of Mount Baker, the Olympic Range, Mount St. Helens, the northwest face of Rainier, and the Cascades.

## Carbon River Trails

 ***Northern Loop Trail.*** *10.6 miles/m (H).* A long swing through the lightly visited north segment of the park leaves the Wonderland Trail (2,860 ft) as a switchback chain up a steep, forested wall to a flat at the base of Yellowstone Cliffs (5,200 ft). A climb through steep meadows past pretty little lakes reaches Windy Gap (6,020 ft), overlooking the ragged top of nearby Sluiskin Mountain. A short side trail heads north along the meadowed east flank of Independence Ridge, then drops to Natural Bridge, a 100-foot-long, 100-foot-high andesite arch carved by stream erosion.

The way drops east from the gap, first in meadows, then forest, as it descends to Lake James (4,430 ft). It then zigzags down precipitous wooded slopes near Van Horn Creek to cross the West Fork of the White River (3,160 ft). The trail immediately regains all of its recently lost altitude. The wooded uphill haul climbs to an open promontory (5,696 ft) with wide views of Grand Park, Mount Fremont, Skyscraper Mountain, the West Fork drainage, Redstone Peak, and Lake James. The Grand Park Trail to Lake Eleanor is passed as the path skirts the southwest edge of Grand Park. It descends to the head of Cold Basin (5,380 ft), then heads up the upper Lodi Creek basin, squeezed between Mount Fremont and Skyscraper Mountain. A steeper grade reaches Berkeley Park and rejoins the Wonderland Trail (6,400 ft).

**Grand Park Trail.** *3.3 miles/m (H).* Splitting from the Northern Loop Trail (5,650 ft) at Grand Park, the route skirts the northwest fringe of this broad, meadowed plateau, then gradually descends through woods to secluded Lake Eleanor (4,985 ft).

## Sunrise Trails

**Palisades Lakes Trail.** *3.5 miles/e (H).* From the Sunrise Road at Sunrise Point (6,120 ft), the path drops past a short spur to Sunrise Lake (5,725 ft), then wanders by Clover Lake (5,732 ft). It crosses a low notch, meanders near Tom, Dick, and Harry Lakes (5,500 to 5670 ft), and passes a boot-path to Hidden Lake (5,915 ft). After crossing a meadowed bench, it ends at Upper Palisades Lake (5,805 ft), perched below the rock cliff of the Palisades.

**Fremont Lookout Trail.** *1.3 miles/e (H).* From the west end of the Sourdough Ridge Trail (6,500 ft), continue west to Frozen Lake (6,850 ft). This trail leaves the lake and ascends parkland to Fremont Lookout (7,140 ft), where in clear weather hikers can scan the Cascades, Olympics, Rainier, and downtown Seattle.

**Burroughs Mountain Trail.** *4 miles/m (H).* From Sunrise Campground (6,350 ft), the way passes the spur to the Emmons Overlook before heading up steep snow slopes to First Burroughs Mountain (7,170 ft). The route continues west across the delicate tundra crest to Second Burroughs Mountain (7,402 ft). An easy downslope to a broad saddle leads to twenty-eight tightly linked switchbacks that drop abruptly to the Glacier Basin Trail (5,530 ft). An alternative route from First Burroughs Mountain heads northeast down a steep snow bank to the Wonderland Trail, just west of Frozen Lake.

## White River Trails

**Glacier Basin Trail.** *3.5 miles/e (H).* An easy grade from White River Campground (4,310 ft) follows an old wagon road past the Emmons Moraine Trail to mining ruins at Starbo in Glacier Basin. Near the head of the basin is the lower end of the Burroughs Mountain Trail (5,530 ft).

## Eastside Trails

**Crystal Lakes Trail.** *3 miles/m (H).* Leaving Highway 410 opposite the Highway Department maintenance sheds (3,530 ft), the route heads up the heavily forested hillside in a series of tight switchbacks. The twisting trail continues uphill, crosses avalanche slopes, passes Lower Crystal Lake (5,460 ft), and breaks into alpine meadows as it arrives at Upper Crystal Lake (5,828 ft). Elk and mountain goat are often seen in the vicinity.

**East Side Trail.** *16.5 miles/e-m (H,S).* A long hike with shortcut options leaves Highway 410 (5,340 ft) southwest of Chinook Pass, weaves down to cross Highway 123 at 4,560 feet, then dives into deep forest at the head of Chinook Creek. The first 2 miles drop steeply along the sidehill above the creek to the intersection with the Owyhigh Lakes Trail (2,850 ft) near the mouths of Kotsuck and Deer Creeks. From here a gentle grade follows the wooded bank of Chinook Creek to its confluence with the Ohanapecosh River. The way continues south on the low slopes above the river, crosses the east end of the Stevens Canyon Road (2,200 ft), passes the Olallie Creek trailhead, and ends at the Ohanapecosh Campground (1,850 ft).

**Olallie Creek Trail.** *1.3 miles/m (H,S).* From the east end of the Stevens Canyon Road (2,320 ft), the route slips into dense old-growth forest as it heads north up the sidehill to the Olallie Creek drainage. Here it bends west, continuing its wooded ascent to the creek's headwaters. Switchbacks climb the basin headwall to a junction with the Wonderland Trail at the ridge top (4,760 ft).

**Laughingwater Creek Trail.** *7 miles/m (H,S).* From Highway 123 (2,150 ft) south of the park's Stevens Canyon entrance, the track climbs up a wooded sidehill and over a ridge-top knob to a bench and a small marshy lake beside Laughingwater Creek. The way follows the creek upstream to where the lilting waters break into a crescendo at a waterfall, then climbs upslope away from the creek to Three Lakes (4,650, 4,650, and 4,678 ft), straddling the park boundary. The route continues east, weaving back and forth across the border of the park, to a junction with the PCT (5,700 ft).

## Paradise Valley Trails

**Lakes Trail.** *2.3 miles/e (H).* The easy-grade path passes through the alpine meadows of Mazama Ridge, from the Skyline Trail (6,010 ft) near Sluiskin Falls to Reflection Lakes (5,600 ft).

**Pinnacle Peak Trail.** *1.5 miles/e (H).* From the Stevens Canyon Road (4,870 ft) at Reflection Lakes, the easy grade steepens as it twists uphill through open woods, meadows, snowfields, and talus to the saddle (5,940 ft) at the west base of Pinnacle Peak. Here is an awesome view of the south side of Rainier; turn around to a complementary scene to the south that includes Mount Adams and the Goat Rocks.

## Longmire Trails

**Eagle Peak Trail.** *3.5 miles/m (H).* The route heads south from Longmire (2,800 ft) wrapped in dense old-growth forest. It soon bends east and climbs steep wooded slopes using easy-grade switchbacks. Trees give way to a steep meadow, splashed with wildflower color, as the path nears a saddle (5,740 ft) on the south ridge of Eagle Peak. The reward is great views of the sweep of the Nisqually Glacier from Paradise to the summit of "The Mountain."

**Rampart Ridge Trail.** *3 miles/m (H,S).* Starting from the Trail of the Shadows

Nature Loop at Longmire (2,800 ft), the way snakes up a steep forest slope at the southwest end of The Ramparts. After topping the ridge, the route continues up the crest to an open viewpoint (4,100 ft) with a wide view up the Nisqually River valley. The track continues along the ridge to a junction with the Wonderland Trail (3,870 ft), which can be used as a return leg to Longmire.

**Van Trump Park Trail.** *6.4 miles/m* (H). From the Wonderland Trail atop Rampart Ridge (3,830 ft), this path ascends the gentle wooded crest northeast to a short, steep, switchbacked slope that breaks to the alpine meadow bench of Van Trump Park (5,400 ft). A spur climbs to Mildred Point (5,935 ft) and great views of the steep-walled snout of the Kautz Glacier. From the parkland, the track contours to cross Van Trump Creek, then begins a zigzag descent past the spray-crowned ribbon of 250-foot-high Comet Falls. More falls are passed as the way drops down the narrow canyon cut by Van Trump Creek, then crosses a bridge above Christine Falls to return to the Longmire–Paradise Road (3,610 ft).

## The Wonderland Trail

This 93-mile-long loop encircles the mountain, alternately climbing to high alpine meadows dotted with lakes and carpeted with wildflowers, then dropping swiftly into deep river canyons carved into the mountain's lava slopes. Scenery is varied and breathtaking throughout its length, as every profile of Rainier's upper slopes is presented. Access trails from the perimeter provide opportunities for loop hikes, as well as resupply points for around-the-mountain hikers. Only a few segments of the trail are open to pack stock.

**WT: Longmire to Rampart Ridge.** *2 miles/m* (H,S). From Longmire (2,800 ft), the route zigzags up steep wooded slopes to top Rampart Ridge, where it meets the Van Trump Park (3,850 ft) and Rampart Ridge (3,870 ft) Trails.

**WT: Rampart Ridge to Indian Henrys Hunting Ground.** *5.1 miles/m* (H). After crossing Rampart Ridge, the way descends gradually to cross Kautz Creek (3,500 ft), then wanders through regenerating forest atop the thick deposits of the 1947 Kautz mudflow. Switchbacks that climb the steep wall out of the drainage near Fishers Hornpipe Creek are followed by a diagonal wooded ascent to the deep cleft of Devils Dream Creek. The path swings through marsh meadows past Squaw Lake (5,070 ft) before entering the flowered park of Indian Henrys Hunting Ground. Here the Kautz Creek (5,250 ft) and Mirror Lakes (5,230 ft) Trails are passed.

**WT: Indian Henrys Hunting Ground to North Puyallup River.** *13.3 miles/m* (H). A steep, switchbacked drop leads to a suspension bridge crossing Tahoma Creek (4,250 ft). A bouldery grade east atop a lateral moraine is followed by a zigzag climb to the base of cliffs at the east end of Emerald Ridge. Open slopes overlook the west wall of Glacier Island—watch for mountain goats. After crossing a narrow saddle (5,620 ft) with views of the Tahoma Glacier, Puyallup Cleaver, and Tokaloo Spire, the way slinks down the rim of a 200-foot-high cliff before dropping to the South Puyallup River (4,070 ft) and its parallel access trail.

It's uphill once more as switchbacks work up the drainage wall to St. Andrews

Park and St. Andrews Lake (5,886 ft). The way then descends to Aurora Lake (5,500 ft), embraced by the flower fields of Klapatche Park. Here the head of the St. Andrews Trail is met. The way drops abruptly northeast below Aurora Peak, then wiggles precipitously down to the old end of the West Side Road (now trail) at the North Puyallup River (3,700 ft).

**WT: North Puyallup River to Mowich Lake.** *14.9 miles/m (H,S).* A gradual ascent through cool, pleasant forest passes an old burn, then climbs more steeply into the meadowland of Sunset Park (5,250 ft). A twisty, contouring path arrives at Golden Lakes, a group of lakes and tarns scattered along the rim of Sunset Park between 4,230 and 5,000 feet. The path traces a ridge-top arc west to a saddle (4,677 ft) just inside the park boundary, then heads down again through two dozen wooded switchbacks to the South Mowich River (2,710 ft). The path through bottomland woods crosses both forks of the Mowich River; an uphill grind, mitigated by switchbacks, finally reaches Mowich Lake (4,929 ft), just beyond the junction with the Spray Park Trail.

**WT: Mowich Lake to Carbon River.** *5.5 miles/m (H,S).* A gentle grade north from Mowich Lake reaches Ipsut Pass and the start of the Tolmie Peak Trail. The way snakes down the steep basin headwall northeast of the pass to follow Ipsut Creek down through

*The Wonderland Trail crosses the chasm of Tahoma Creek on a suspension bridge.*

huge old-growth cedar to the Carbon River and Ipsut Creek Campground (2,340 ft).

**WT: *Carbon River to Sunrise.*** *13.3 miles/m (H).* An easy grade from the camp-ground traces the bank of the Carbon River through broad bottomland to two river-crossing alternatives. The first, at the junction with the Northern Loop Trail (2,860 ft), is a sometimes washed-out log bridge. Farther upstream at the base of Echo Cliffs (3,230 ft), just beyond the Spray Park Trail, a bouncy, swaying suspension bridge has a better survival record, but adds thrills for the nervous. A parallel path on the oppo-site side of the river links the two crossing points. A short distance beyond the upper bridge the trail reaches a viewpoint at the snout of the Carbon Glacier below North-ern Crags (3,600 ft), then ascends along the moraine for another 2 miles. A steep climb through woods crosses the saddle at the south end of Old Desolate, then descends through tree clumps and meadows to Mystic Lake (5,700 ft).

East of Mystic Lake the path wanders down the bank of the West Fork of the White River, rounds the snout of the Winthrop Glacier (4,720 ft), and threads below Garda Falls. Switchbacks climb along Granite Creek to Skyscraper Pass (6,730 ft), where the view west encompasses the Winthrop Glacier, Old Desolate, Vernal Park, and Sluiskin Mountain. The route heads across meadows and pumice slopes around the head of Berkeley Park, passes the east end of the Northern Loop Trail, then reaches a major intersection at Frozen Lake (6,850 ft). Here the Burroughs Mountain Trail goes southwest, the Fremont Lookout Trail heads north, and the Wonderland Trail splits, with one leg descending to the Sunrise Campground (6,350 ft) and a second to the Sunrise Ranger Station (6,430 ft).

**WT: *Sunrise to White River.*** *4.2 miles/m (H).* One of the less popular segments of the Wonderland Trail is the brief civilization-to-civilization link that zigzags down from Sunrise to the White River Campground (4,300 ft).

**WT: *White River to Indian Bar.*** *9.8 miles/m (H).* The trail resumes east of White River Campground at the junction of the White River and Sunrise Roads (3,950 ft), then follows the wooded south edge of the road to Fryingpan Creek, where there is an alternative access from the road. The next woodland stretch traces the creek upstream for 3 miles before breaking into meadows where Rainier and Little Tahoma appear. The way wiggles uphill to Summer Land (5,950 ft), a popular alpine park below the Fryingpan Glacier and Little Tahoma. The track southeast crosses snowfields that per-sist until August, passes frigid tarns, then climbs to Panhandle Gap (6,750 ft). Here are great views of the Sarvent Glaciers and the Cowlitz Chimneys, jagged remnants of an old volcanic plug, and Mounts Adams and Hood; above are glaciers sliding from the rock pyramid of Little Tahoma.

Beyond the gap is the highest and most remote stretch of the trail; it crosses smooth, glacier-polished rock, steep snowfields, and windswept benches reaching 6,700 feet before heading down a skinny ridge top to Indian Bar (5,100 ft). Near the shelter here is unpronounceable Wauhaukaupauken Falls.

**WT: *Indian Bar to Cowlitz Divide.*** *4.2 miles/m (H).* Rocks, slabs, and meadows accompany the ascent southeast to a bald viewpoint (5,930 ft) at the north end of Cowlitz Divide, featuring Rainier, the Tatoosh peaks, Mount Adams, Mount St. Helens,

Shriner Peak, the Cascade crest, and the Cowlitz Chimneys. The way rolls along the minor ups and downs atop the narrow divide, gradually descending through trees to the junction with the Olallie Creek Trail (4,760 ft).

**WT: *Cowlitz Divide to Reflection Lakes*.** *10.2 miles/m (H,S).* From the top of the divide, sixteen switchbacks drop to Nickel Creek (3,310 ft). After crossing the creek, the trail continues down to the Stevens Canyon Road at Box Canyon (3,140 ft). From the south side of the road, the route swings down around a forested nose, then begins a gradual ascent of Stevens Canyon, en route passing several waterfalls. (The most striking are Sylvia and Martha Falls.) The Stevens Canyon Road is crossed at 4,150 feet, and met again at 4,600 feet, where the trail parallels the road to Louise Lake (4,597 ft) and Reflection Lakes (4,854 to 4,865 ft).

**WT: *Reflection Lakes to Longmire*.** *5.6 miles/m (H,S).* The route leaves the lakes after crossing the Stevens Canyon Road, swings back and forth down past the Narada Falls Trail, then continues a descent of the narrow Paradise River canyon. After crossing the river and passing Carter Falls, the way runs beside remnants of a decaying wooden pipeline that funneled water to a powerhouse that once delivered electricity to mines high on Eagle Peak, and also later to the park at Longmire. Passing the powerhouse ruins (3,250 ft), the way crosses the Nisqually River and continues parallel to its bank to Longmire (2,800 ft).

## CLIMBING

The obvious climbing attraction within the park is "The Mountain" (14,411 ft), which attracts thousands of summit aspirants every year; however, only 40 percent of the parties, both guided and private, reach the summit. Weather and the rapid transition in altitude eliminate a major portion of the climbers; unfortunately, Rainier has also claimed many climbers' lives. Routes have been put up every side of the peak, and most have one or more variations, either to attack new challenges or to accommodate seasonal changes in crevasse patterns, sloughing off of ledges, and so on. The easiest routes are on the south and east sides of the mountain, while those on the west and north sides range from difficult to terrifying.

The easy to moderate routes, all less than G-III, are Gibraltar Ledge, Ingraham Glacier–Disappointment Cleaver, Nisqually Ice Cliff, Nisqually Ice Fall, Fuhrer Finger, Wilson Glacier Headwall, Kautz Glacier, Kautz Glacier Headwall, Kautz Cleaver, Success Cleaver, Tahoma Glacier, Russell Cliff, and Emmons–Winthrop Glaciers.

The more difficult or dangerous routes, all G-III to G-V, include South Tahoma Headwall, Tahoma Cleaver, Sunset Amphitheater–Tahoma Glacier, Sunset Amphitheater Headwall, Edmunds Headwall, Central Mowich Face, North Mowich Headwall, North Mowich Face Icefall, Ptarmigan Ridge, Liberty Wall, Liberty Ridge, Willis Wall, and Curtis Ridge.

The second-highest peak in the park (and the third-highest in the state) is Little Tahoma (11,138 ft), a subsidiary partner of Rainier. The rocky summit pyramid is normally climbed via combination rock-and-glacier routes out of Summer Land that range from C-3 to C-4 in difficulty. The loose north and northeast faces are rated at C-4 to

*Camp Muir, at the 10,000-foot level of Mount Rainier, is a popular ski destination, as well as a way-stop for summit-bound climbers.*

C-5, and the west ridge has been climbed in winter when ice glues the C-5.7 rock leads together.

South of Paradise is an arc of striking rock peaks (the Tatoosh Range), most of whose 5,900- to 6,900-foot summits are just a few leads of solid rock above cross-country hikes from easy access trails. Among the most interesting of these are Unicorn Peak, C-3 to C-4; The Castle, C-3; Pinnacle Peak, C-3 to C-4; and Eagle Peak, C-4. The rest of the summits are scrambles or easy walk-ups.

Although there are a number of interesting, distinctive summits on the west and northwest sides of the mountain, few offer any serious climbing challenge. One exception is Tokaloo Spire (7,480 ft) on the Puyallup Cleaver, a 70- to 150-foot-high dike with two vertical faces. A C-4 crack-and-chimney route reaches the top from its east rib.

Sluiskin Mountain, between Windy Gap and Vernal Park, is a scraggly crest with some challenging climbing on the major summit, The Chief (7,026 ft), C-3. The secondary high spot, The Squaw (6,960 ft), and The Papooses, a series of pinnacles to the ridge on the west, are easy scrambles.

The eroded volcanic plugs that make up the pinnacles of the Cowlitz Chimneys and Governors Ridge, on the east side of the park, are more strenuous rock climbs. In the Cowlitz Chimneys, the Main Chimney (7,605 ft) has a contorted, hard-to-follow C-3 route to its top; the North Chimney (7,105 ft), one of the most inaccessible spots in the park, has pitches ranging from C-5 to C-5.8 in difficulty. Governors Peak (6,600 ft) is a steep pyramidal C-3 to C-4 summit, and nearby Governors Needle (6,500 ft) is a slender, friable C-5 pinnacle.

## WINTER SPORTS

The road from the Nisqually entrance to Paradise is the only one presently open in the winter. Sledding, snowshoeing, tubing, and cross-country skiing are the winter activities at Paradise. Depending on year-to-year budgets, the sledding and tubing areas may or may not be groomed. Three marked but ungroomed trails run from Paradise to Nisqually Vista, Paradise to Narada Falls, and Narada Falls to Reflection Lakes.

Cross-country skiing and ski mountaineering reach other untracked areas. Among the more popular one-day trips are the broad open snowfield ridge between Paradise and Camp Muir, Paradise to Reflection Lakes via Mazama Ridge, Narada Falls to Reflection Lakes, and Reflection Lakes to the Castle Peak saddle in the Tatoosh Range. On the north side of the mountain is the road trek to Mowich Lake, and on the east side is the advanced tour into Crystal Lake Basin.

Longer ski/snowshoe trips involving multiday snow camps and mountaineering skills head into Seattle Park and the Russell Glacier, Steamboat Prow, the Carbon Glacier, Van Trump Park, the Nisqually Glacier, the Wilson Glacier, and the traverse from Paradise to White River via the Ingraham and Emmons Glaciers.

In recent years there has been increased interest in winter climbs, both of Rainier and Little Tahoma. The easier routes often become simpler as crevasses are filled by snow. Some of the most difficult, hazardous in summer because of loose muddy pumice and constant rockfall, have faces that are thankfully glued together by ice; alas, avalanches become a new hazard.

 **Glacier View Region**

### Glacier View Wilderness; Deer Creek Roadless Area

**Location:** In Pierce County, on the southwest corner of Mount Rainier National Park
**Size:** Wilderness, 3,080 acres; Deer Creek, 890 acres
**Status:** Designated Wilderness (1984); Roadless area is Semiprimitive Nonmotorized
**Terrain:** A high U-shaped ridge with two long north–south fingers encloses meadows and alpine lakes in the headwaters of a fork of the South Puyallup River.
**Elevation:** 3,320 to 5,507 feet
**Management:** USFS, Gifford Pinchot National Forest, Cowlitz Valley Ranger District
**Topographic maps:** Mount Wow

Nine lakes, some small or intermittent, lie in cirques or on benches in a pleasant little basin shielded from outside noise and distraction by long ridges on either side. A thin strip of roadless area on the northwest side of the wilderness separates it from the logged hillsides farther west. A trail paralleling the western boundary of the wilderness offers access to the area's highest points, with breathtaking views east of Mount Rainier and the thin rock dikes separating the long frozen tongues of the Tahoma, Puyallup, and South Mowich Glaciers; above them is the frigid bowl of the Sunset Amphitheater. To the west the view is another story—denuded slopes along winding, caterpillar-like logging roads, most on privately owned tree farms, that have nibbled up to within inches of the wilderness and roadless area boundaries.

## CLIMATE

The precipitation in the area averages around 85 to 90 inches annually, with a large portion of that falling as snow. More than 30 feet of snow falls during the winter months, but most is gone by mid-July. Winter temperatures are generally in the low 20s, and summer highs average between 65 and 70 degrees.

## ECOSYSTEM

The area is forested with Pacific silver fir, western hemlock, noble fir, Douglas-fir, western red cedar, white pine, and true fir. Typically found in the understory are oakfern, ladyfern, white trillium, queencup beadlily, deerfoot vanillaleaf, twinflower, purple twisted stalk, white inside-out flower, bunchberry dogwood, starry Solomon-plume, dwarf blackberry, a variety of huckleberries, three-leaved coolwort, devil's club, and a wide assortment of mosses. The basin is an important summer range for elk and mountain goats.

*The summit of Glacier View, appropriately, provides views of Mount Rainier's glaciers.*

## GEOLOGY

The rock exposed in the wilderness is that of the Ohanapecosh Formation, which is the original base on which the entire Mount Rainier area is built. It consists of multiple layers of volcanic breccias, sandstone, and siltstone more than 9,000 feet thick that resulted from volcanic epiclastic and pyroclastic flows. Best evidence indicates that this succession of thick volcanic mudflows, with intervening sedimentary sheeting, occurred underwater in a relatively placid lake or bay about 36 million years ago. The strata of the Ohanapecosh Formation in the Glacier View Wilderness tilt upward to the west at a 25- to 30-degree angle along a north–south strike. The small cirques notched in the basin walls were carved by local glaciation some 12,000 to 15,000 years ago.

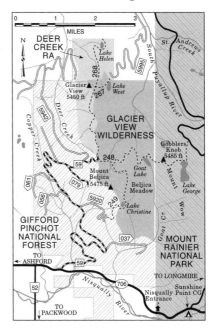

## HISTORY

In support of the Forest Service fire-suppression mission in the 1920s and '30s, a fire lookout was built atop Glacier View; it was removed in the 1960s. A temporary lookout (a telephone and a toolshed) was placed atop Mount Beljica. Maps in the early 1960s show the typical one-section checkerboard pattern of private and federal land reaching all the way to the national park boundary. In subsequent years the Forest Service consolidated a dozen contiguous sections of forest under federal ownership, and the virgin portion of that land was designated as the Glacier View Wilderness in 1984.

## HIKING

**Trail 249, Lake Christine.** *1.8 miles/e (H,S).* From the end of FR 5920 (4,420 ft), the route rises out of a clearcut to traverse the steep slopes of a forested knob, then climbs abruptly along an outlet stream to Lake Christine (4,802 ft). After circling the east side of the lake, the trail ascends north through virgin timber to a rib (5,080 ft) east of Mount Beljica, where a faint, unmaintained boot-path leads west to its summit (5,475 ft). The way now descends to Beljica Meadow, and meets Trail 248 (4,580 ft).

**Trail 248, Puyallup.** *2.5 miles/m (H,S).* From the junction with Trail 267, this route traverses south to Beljica Meadow, rounds the north side of a finger ridge, then descends gradually to Goat Lake (4,343 ft). A long diagonal ascent up slopes to the east reaches the park boundary (4,700 ft), where the trail continues on to Gobblers Knob, Lake George, and Round Pass.

**Trail 267, Glacier View.** *3 miles/m (H,S).* At a low saddle (4,550 ft) a shortcut drops 100 feet down to FR 59. The route heads north, sometimes atop the boundary ridge, sometimes skirting the west side of ridge-top knobs. At a notch south of Glacier View, a short unmaintained spur climbs to the summit (5,450 ft) and meditation-worthy views of Mount Rainier. From the notch, the way drops northeast, passes the end of Trail 268, and continues down through the woods to the tiny pocket holding Lake West (4,582 ft).

**Trail 268, Peak Two.** *1.3 miles/m (H,S).* After leaving Trail 267 (5,040 ft) on the east slopes of Glacier View, the way crosses the northern wilderness boundary and continues a long gradual descent to Lake Helen (4,612 ft), just a few hundred yards south of the clearcuts that mark the national forest and roadless area boundary.

# 29 Tatoosh Region

## Tatoosh Wilderness; Dixon Mountain and Backbone Roadless Areas

**Location:** In Lewis County, along the southern boundary of Mount Rainier National Park

**Size:** Wilderness, 15,800 acres; Dixon Mountain, 6,070 acres; Backbone, 1,210 acres

**Status:** Designated Wilderness (1984); Roadless areas are Semiprimitive Nonmotorized

**Terrain:** The wilderness is framed by two long, steep, rugged ridges, with forested lower slopes leading up to subalpine and alpine parklands. Roadless areas are two long ridges flanking the wilderness.

**Elevation:** 1,230 to 6,310 feet

**Management:** USFS, Gifford Pinchot National Forest, Cowlitz Valley Ranger District

**Topographic maps:** Tatoosh Lakes, Ohanapecosh Hot Springs, Wahpenayo Peak

The steep flanks, formidable ridges, and high-altitude meadows of this southern end of Mount Rainier's Tatoosh Range were saved by wilderness designation in 1984. The only accesses to the area are a pair of trails with a few short spurs to lakes and the high point of the wilderness. The steep, rough terrain does not abet easy cross-country travel, and the trails are tedious and demanding in their climb to the more pleasant ridge-top treks. Once in the high-country parkland, the flower fields, berry patches, and views of the major Cascade volcanic summits reward the effort to get there. Of the half-dozen lakes in the backcountry, only three are more than tiny tarns, and these have so delicate an ecology surrounding them that camping is not permitted there. Dixon Mountain, on the west side of the wilderness, is a forested, steep-sided ridge with no developed recreation facilities. Backbone, on the east flank of the wilderness, is a steep ridge with substantial

*The Tatoosh Range, seen here from Edith Creek Basin, edges the south side of Mount Rainier National Park.*

old-growth forest. A trail runs its length from Backbone Lake to the Mount Rainier National Park boundary.

## CLIMATE

Precipitation and temperatures vary between the lower elevations of flanking drainages and the ridge crest that dominates the wilderness. The following information applies to the higher heart of the region, since this is the area of most interest to recreationists. Precipitation is heavy, averaging about 100 inches annually, a large part falling as snow. A total of about 40 feet of snow is dropped on the area each winter, some of which persists on the ground until late July. Midwinter lows average in the mid- to high teens, and summer highs are a comfortable 70 degrees.

## ECOSYSTEM

The lower-level forest is made up of Pacific silver fir, western hemlock, noble fir, western red cedar, and Douglas-fir. The understory includes oakfern, ladyfern, deerfoot vanillaleaf, white trillium, twinflower, queen-cup beadlily, bunchberry dogwood, various huckleberry species, dwarf blackberry, devil's club, and mosses. Higher elevations see the addition of mountain hemlock, pyrola, and beargrass. Parklands have a ground cover that includes blue-leaved huckleberry, dwarf blackberry, luetkea, woolly everlasting, Indian paintbrush, and, in varying locations, pedicularis, lupine, sedge, cinquefoil,

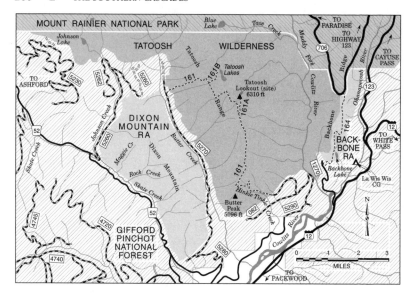

and alpine aster. A 560-acre RNA has been established in the Butter Creek drainage, in conjunction with an adjoining one in the national park, for the study of watersheds, stream biology, and subalpine plant communities.

Black bear, cougar, bobcat, black-tailed deer, elk, and mountain goat are found at upper elevations in summer and early fall, and the bottom of the Muddy Fork of the Cowlitz River drainage serves as a winter range for these animals. In addition, hikers are likely to see marmots, pikas, white-tailed ptarmigans, snowshoe hares, golden eagles, and Swainson's hawks.

## GEOLOGY

The geology of the Tatoosh area is among the more complex in the Mount Rainier vicinity. At the far west side of the area, exposed rock is a part of the Ohanapecosh Formation, composed of volcanic breccia, sandstone, and siltstone resulting from underwater volcanic epiclastic and pyroclastic flows some 36 million yeas ago. The formation was folded on a northwest to southeast line, and a major syncline follows the Butter Creek drainage, on the west side of Tatoosh Ridge. A vertical fault along the east side of the ridge marks a sharp delineation between the exposed Ohanapecosh Formation on the west, and the Stevens Ridge Formation, which overlaid it, on the east. Tatoosh Ridge itself is multilayered, and the lowest layer is the Ohanapecosh Formation. The next layer of basaltic andesite flows was overlaid by the Stevens Ridge Formation, consisting of rhyodactic ash flows deposited about 30 million years ago. This is topped by the Fifes Peak Formation, a heterogeneous composite of lava flows, mudflows, and volcanic clastic rock about 25 million years old. The Stevens Ridge Formation that pervades the east side of the wilderness has been intruded by numerous east–west trending basalt dikes and sills from roughly the same period.

## HISTORY

The Taidnapam Indians, who had summer fishing camps near the confluence of the Muddy and Clear Forks of the Cowlitz, would head to Tatoosh Ridge in the fall to hunt, gather materials for making baskets, and harvest and dry huckleberries. According to legend, Coyote visualized a mountain named "neq'u't," where there would be a thick growth of berries for the tribe to pick and dry; this mountain was Tatoosh Ridge. The major trail through the area was put in by the Forest Service to reach and support the Tatoosh fire lookout, which stood atop the ridge between the 1920s and 1960s.

## HIKING

**Trail 161, Tatoosh.** *9 miles/d (H,S).* Starting from the northwest at FR 5270 (2,920 ft), switchbacks climb an abrupt 1,000 feet through thick forest. A sidehill ascent continues east to just below a notch on Tatoosh Ridge (5,530 ft), where Trail 161B heads northeast to Tatoosh Lakes (4,288 ft) (camping is prohibited at the lakes). The route contours the west side of the ridge, twisting around the heads of basins, most of the time in subalpine meadows ablaze with the colors of wildflowers in early summer. The tread may be indistinct; hold a level grade to reach a ridge-top saddle (5,760 ft) and the start of Trail 161A to the former site of the Tatoosh lookout (6,310 ft). The lookout site has spectacular views; Mount Adams looms to the southeast, the Paradise side of Mount Rainier is close at hand to the north, and to the south is the gaping maw of Mount St. Helens.

*Mount Rainier rises above ridges of the Tatoosh Wilderness.*

The way swings to the east side of the crest as it continues south and, with the ridge, starts a gradual descent toward Butter Peak, at its southern end. The trail bends east 0.4 mile from that peak and heads downhill in steep switchbacks. It crosses Hinkle Tinkle Creek and, swinging back and forth, finally reaches FR 5290 (2,355 ft).

**Trail 164, Backbone Lake.** *3.3 miles/m (H,S).* Starting in a clearcut at the end of FR 1270 (1,880 ft), the trail climbs into woods before passing a fork to Backbone Lake. From here, the path abruptly climbs the steep nose of Backbone Ridge, then wanders the ridge crest to reach the Mount Rainier Park boundary and join Highway 706 at 3,360 feet. Mountain goats are frequently seen along the ridge.

## 30 Bumping Lake Region

### William O. Douglas Wilderness; adjacent, Cortright, Carlton Ridge, and Laughingwater Roadless Areas

**Location:** In Lewis and Yakima Counties, mostly east of the Cascade crest, between the American and Tieton Rivers

**Size:** Wilderness, 167,195 acres; William O. Douglas Adjacent, 22,938 acres; Cortright, 3,380 acres; Carlton Ridge, 2,260 acres; Laughingwater, 1,050 acres

**Status:** Designated Wilderness (1984); Roadless areas are Semiprimitive Nonmotorized, Motorized, and Roaded Natural

**Terrain:** Two broad, high ridge complexes, deeply cut by lateral streams, rise abruptly on either side of the Bumping River drainage to a crest of subalpine meadows and rocky summits. The two ridges meet on the Cascade crest at the Bumping River headwaters in a wide, flat plateau, lightly timbered and with numerous meadows, lakes, and ponds.

**Elevation:** 3,200 to 7,766 feet

**Management:** USFS, Gifford Pinchot National Forest, Cowlitz Valley Ranger District, and Okanogan–Wenatchee National Forest, Naches Ranger District

**Topographic maps:** Bumping Lake, Chinook Pass, Cougar Lake, Goose Prairie, Meeks Table, Norse Peak, Old Scab Mtn., Rimrock Lake, Spiral Butte, Timberwolf Mtn., White Pass

The William O. Douglas Wilderness is named for the conservation-minded Supreme Court justice who had a cabin here at Goose Prairie. He hiked extensively throughout the area for years, and wrote about it in the book *Of Men and Mountains*. The wilderness contains a magnificent spectrum of geological, biological, botanical, scenic, and recreational treasures. Its geography includes deep drainages at the headwaters of four major rivers, high rugged ridges topped by subalpine meadows and rocky crags, dense old-growth forests, juvenile volcano cinder cones, and a broad, lightly forested parkland plateau with 59 named lakes of various sizes and more than 250 unnamed lakes, ponds,

*Cougar Lake, in the William O. Douglas Wilderness, is reached via Trail 477.*

and puddles. The eastern portions of the wilderness drop to open ridges and stands of ponderosa pine.

The area's sixty-six trails, totaling more than 250 miles, offer similar variety. The Pacific Crest National Scenic Trail runs north–south along its western backbone, crossing the meadow-and-lake parkland with a web of interlinked paths leading from one scenic spot to another. The route along the top of American Ridge is the longest continuous trail in the Naches Ranger District, twisting, climbing, and diving along the contorted crest for nearly 27 miles. On the eastern side of the wilderness is Nelson Ridge, a narrow, bald, alpine rib reached by grueling, straight-up switchback chains that only a miner could build.

## CLIMATE

Since the wilderness stretches east from the Cascade crest for more than 17 miles, there is a significant difference in the precipitation falling on its east side versus its west side. On the west it totals nearly 120 inches, while the east, in the rain shadow of the

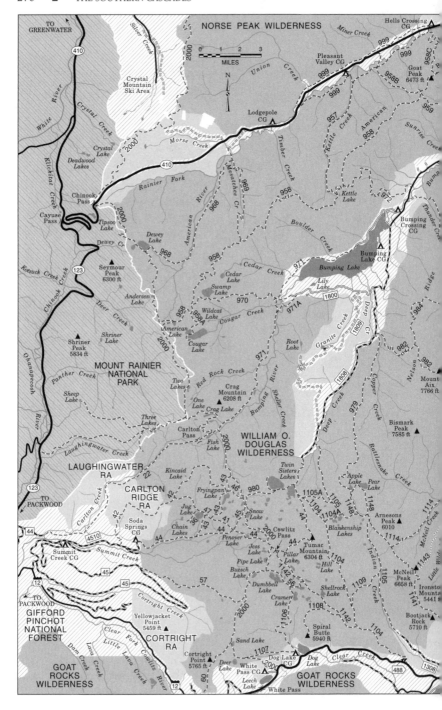

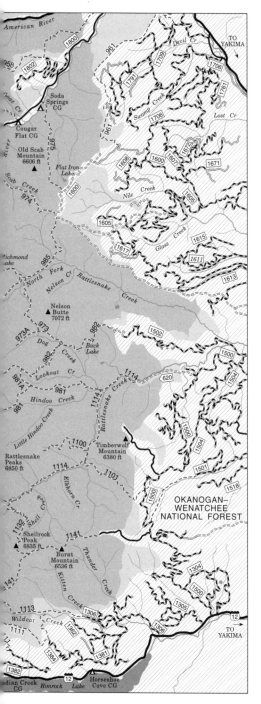

Cascades, precipitation measures only 24 inches. The bulk of the moisture falls during winter months as snow, with accumulations of 10 to 15 feet at upper elevations. Winter minimums throughout the area are in the 15-degree range; summer highs on the west side are in the low 70s, while the east side enjoys significantly more sunny days, with highs averaging in the upper 70s to lower 80s. The lower east side of the wilderness is generally snow-free by early June, but snow patches linger on the west, and at higher elevations, until mid-July; first flakes fall in October.

## ECOSYSTEM

By virtue of its location astride the Cascade crest, the wilderness has a diverse group of plant communities representing both the wet west side of the Cascades and the drier east slopes. On the west, the dense old-growth forest at lower elevations typically consists of Douglas-fir, western hemlock, and western red cedar. With a gain in altitude the forest composition shifts to western hemlock, Pacific silver fir, noble fir, western white pine, and Engelmann spruce. At the upper elevations along the crest, and across the parklands of the Tumac Plateau, Alaska cedar, mountain hemlock, and subalpine fir predominate. Many of these species are also found on the east side of the wilderness, but they are joined by whitebark pine at upper elevations and ponderosa pine lower down. A sixty-four-acre RNA at Meeks Table, on the eastern rim of the area, has a representative ecology of the ponderosa pine–pinegrass community in combination with Douglas-fir. A second RNA of 2,205 acres with a mixed old-growth and shrub forest and a Pacific silver fir forest has been proposed in the Cedar Creek drainage.

The eastern portion of the wilderness has substantial herds of elk and mule deer that winter in the meadows of the Bumping River drainage. Other species found in the area include cougar, fisher, wolverine, Cascade red fox, mountain goat, and blue and ruffed grouse.

## GEOLOGY

For a region of its size, the geology of the area is relatively complex. The base structure, exposed in only a few sites along the south edge, is old pre-Miocene sandstone and pillow basalt formed on the east coast of the North Cascades subcontinent prior to its becoming attached to the North American continent. The northern half of the region has been overlaid with Eocene andesite and rhyolite, while the southern portion of the wilderness, immediately north of White Pass, is covered by a thick layer of High Cascade volcanic flows between 10 million and 30 million years old.

Several granodiorite plutons, or perhaps several exposures of the same pluton, intruded through the lava flows about 10 million years ago. One lobe of this pale gray granite runs up the Bumping River drainage and hooks back along Miners Ridge; an arm also slices through American Ridge near Sunrise Creek. A second outcrop is found at the northwest corner of American Ridge, a third is in the vicinity of Carlton Pass, and a fourth lies adjacent to US 12 at Cortright Creek. Mineralization along the pluton borders, typical of such intrusions, has led to extensive prospecting in some of these areas.

Continental ice sheets later covered the area, smoothing the high plateau along the Cascade crest and carving the deep drainages in the center of the wilderness and on its north and south flanks. More recent volcanic activity, probably contemporary with the last glaciation some 10,000 to 15,000 years ago, is represented by the cinder cones of Spiral Butte and Tumac Mountain.

## HISTORY

For centuries the Yakama Indians hunted, fished, and gathered berries in the wilderness region, and trod paths across Cowlitz Pass to trade with Puget Sound tribes. The first white surveyors followed these trails over the pass in 1861, and a railroad survey party cut a path from Summit Creek over Cowlitz Pass to Bumping River in 1867. An 1881 map shows a trail from the Nisqually River to the upper Cowlitz, across Cowlitz Pass, then down Indian Creek to the Tieton River and on to Yakima, a route apparently used for cattle drives.

Bumping Lake and Bumping River were discovered in the 1850s; they were also known by their Indian names of Tanum Lake and Tanum River well into the 1880s. The Northern Pacific Railroad attempted, unsuccessfully, to dam the river in 1894, a feat that was finally accomplished by the Bureau of Reclamation in 1910. The Bumping Lake area was the site of prospecting in the late 1880s as miners, operating out of

*A pack string crosses a meadow on a trail ride through the William O. Douglas Wilderness. Tumac Mountain is in the distance.*

the Copper City camp at the head of the lake, burrowed into quartz sulfide veins in search of gold and copper ores.

By 1897 the present wilderness area was incorporated in the Pacific Forest Reserve, and the early 1900s saw herds of sheep annually grazing in the high meadows. The availability of CCC crews, and the increased emphasis on fire suppression in the 1930s, led to an extensive trail system in the area and construction of fire lookouts at Goat Peak, Little Bald Mountain, Miners Ridge, Mount Aix, Tumac Mountain, Timberwolf Mountain, and Clover Springs.

## HIKING
### Southeast of Bumping River Trails

*Trail 975, Soda Springs.* 5.2 miles/m (H,S). From Soda Springs Campground (3,020 ft) on FR 1800 (note there are two Soda Springs Campgrounds in the area), a footbridge crosses the Bumping River and heads south. After a straightforward climb to a wooded saddle (3,670 ft) the trail heads up a broad ridge toward Old Scab Mountain. The way becomes steeper as it attacks a finger northeast of the summit, then grudgingly eases at a marsh and meadow flat (5,600 ft) below the peak's east face, where it bends to the southeast to meet FR 1600 (5,900 ft).

**Trail 974, Nile Ridge.** *6.1 miles/d (H,S).* After 2 miles of level track along the Bumping River northeast from Bumping Crossing Campground (3,370 ft), this route bends uphill along Scab Creek and in another mile begins a progressively steeper climb. It then switchbacks with a vengeance up the drainage headwall, tops out at 5,900 feet, then follows the crest east to the junction of FR 1600 and Trail 985 (6,351 ft).

**Trail 985, Windy Ridge.** *3.2 miles/m (H,S).* Not capriciously named, this route leaves FR 1600 at Clover Spring (6,351 ft). It angles down an exposed, breezy south ridge, then descends a steep forested nose, turns southwest, and continues down to meet Trail 973 on the North Fork of Rattlesnake Creek (4,400 ft).

**Trail 973, Richmond Mine (Thunder Creek).** *10.2 miles/m-d (H,S).* A miners' track, redirected out of a soggy creekbed by the Forest Service, departs a road spur (3,370 ft) northeast of Bumping Crossing Campground. It winds up a rib north of Thunder Creek, crosses the creek twice, attacks a seemingly vertical face head-on to gain a saddle (6,200 ft), then descends to Richmond Lake (5,990 ft). From the lake, the way drops east, passing the north end of Trail 984, to meet Trail 985 (4,400 ft) above the North Fork of Rattlesnake Creek, then switchbacks south up the drainage wall to a narrow col (6,405 ft) west of Nelson Butte. The trail drops downhill one more time into the Dog Creek drainage, where it continues downstream to end on Trail 982 (4,430 ft).

**Trail 982, Mount Aix.** *13.8 miles/m-d (H,S).* An uphill grind from FR 1808 (3,670 ft) climbs through thirty-six switchbacks before relaxing to a steep sidehill diagonal climb to the top of Nelson Ridge (7,100 ft) and a junction with Trail 984. Here views of Rainier, Adams, and the Goat Rocks reward the tongue-dragging climb. A scramble east up a narrow rock-and-heather ridge reaches the top of Mount Aix (7,766 ft). The trail traverses the steep, rocky south slopes of the peak, follows a narrow, barren crest east, then drops to the headwaters of Lookout Creek. The way snakes across subalpine meadows, dives to Dog Creek to meet Trail 973 (4,420 ft), then climbs past Buck Lake (4,740 ft) to end at FR 1502-695 (4,780 ft).

**Trail 979, Pear Butte.** *8.2 miles/m (H,S).* From FR 1808 (3,670 ft), the route climbs into the wooded slopes of the Copper Creek drainage to twenty puckered switchbacks that gain a ridge nose (5,200 ft) leading south to Pear Butte. Once atop the ridge the way flows through alternating forest and meadows to the north flank of Pear Butte. It then drops southwest to a broad saddle (5,220 ft), where it eases downhill to meadows around Apple Lake (5,060 ft), then meets Trail 1148.

**Trail 1114, Rattlesnake.** *13 miles/m-d (H,S).* Like to wade streams? This is the trail for you (but not during high-water times). The trail starts on logging spur FR 1500-620. After leaving Trail 981 at the confluence of Dog and Rattlesnake Creeks (3,235 ft), the path crosses Rattlesnake Creek twelve times as it follows it upstream. The route meets several side trails en route. At 4,180 feet the way turns southwest up McNeil Creek, then switchbacks up the drainage headwall to join Trail 1141 (5,270 ft).

**Trail 1141, Ironstone Mountain.** *10.6 miles/m-d (H,S).* From the end of FR 1500-199 at Cash Prairie (6,335 ft), the route follows the ridge top west past the head of

Trail 1140 to the bald top of Burnt Mountain (6,536 ft) and great views of the Goat Rocks and Mount Adams. The way undulates up and down along the ridge, contours a steep side-slope, then bends around the south side of Ironstone Mountain. At Russell Ridge (5,990 ft) it follows the crest north to a junction with Trail 1143 and a steep, rough switchback chain across McNeil Peak (6,658 ft), where there are good views down the Indian Creek drainage to Rimrock Lake. A rugged track slides off the northwest side of the peak to meet Trail 1114 at the divide between the McNeil Creek and Indian Creek drainages. From here, the way crosses a shallow saddle, then descends through forest to end on Trail 1105 at Indian Creek Meadow (4,930 ft).

## Northwest of Bumping River Trails

**Trail 958, American Ridge.** *26.8 miles/m-d (H,S).* The northeast end of the trail leaves FR 1800, 0.7 mile from Highway 410 (2,800 ft). After a brief climb, a gentle grade heads southwest across a wooded bench to the sharp end of American Ridge. Switchbacks climb the forested face, and after a brief ridge romp (4,300 ft) more switchbacks drop to a wooded shelf that is followed southwest to Fifes Creek. A gradual ascent above the creek headwaters regains the ridge (5,050 ft) above Goat Creek basin. In another mile the fun is over; forty-three tight switchbacks grind up to the top of Goat Peak (6,473 ft), a former lookout site. The upper end of Trail 958C is passed about halfway to the summit. Here are dramatic views across the American Creek valley to the spikes of Fifes Peaks, farther west to Rainier, and south to Adams.

More switchbacks drop west to a diagonal descent to the saddle junction with Trails 959 and 958B (5,690 ft). The way now twists, turns, and rolls up and down through alternating forest and meadows atop the ridge. After passing Trail 972 (6,020 ft) from Goose Prairie, the route zigzags down the east face of the ridge to little Kettle Lake (5,670 ft). A gentle ascent around the upper Kettle Creek basin then crosses a saddle (6,340 ft) to a traverse below cliffs at the head of Timber Creek. Switchbacks regain the crest of American Ridge (6,880 ft); the way crosses the ridge, then contours the head of Big Basin (6,350 ft). It regains the ridge top and tracks its ups and downs southwest past Trail 969 to an overlook of the cirque holding Cedar Lake. After more bends and jogs on the forested slopes above Swamp Lake, the way descends to a broad woods-and-meadow flat where it meets Trail 970. Trail 958 climbs west to meadow-wrapped American Lake (5,260 ft) and its end on the PCT (5,360 ft).

**Trail 958C, Goat Peak.** *2.8 miles/m (H).* From Hells Crossing Campground on Highway 410 (3,320 ft), the route makes a relentless climb south up a steep hogback ridge, sometimes in forest, sometimes in meadow. It joins Trail 958 (5,900 ft) for that trail's final thrust to the summit of Goat Peak (6,473 ft).

**Trail 959, Goat Creek.** *3.7 miles/m (H,S).* The way leaves FR 1050 (3,100 ft) near Cougar Flat Campground and heads up the steep forested hillside with determination. The grade tempers somewhat at 4,500 feet, but in another mile the trail resorts to switchbacks to surmount a final face and reach Trail 958 at the ridge top (5,690 ft) west of Goat Peak.

**Trail 972, Goose Prairie.** *5.1 miles/m (H,S).* Immediately northeast of Bumping

Lake Campground, Trail 972 leaves FR 1800 (3,340 ft) for a steady ascent to the west, augmented by a few switchbacks. It weaves up forested hillsides to join Trail 958 (6,020 ft) north of Kettle Lake.

**Trail 957, Kettle Creek.** *6.2 miles/m (H,S)*. A gradual valley-bottom trail departs Trail 999 (3,460 ft) to follow the bank of Kettle Creek upstream to its headwaters. Here it switchbacks up the steep drainage headwall and joins Trail 958 on the shore of Kettle Lake (5,670 ft).

**Trail 969, Mesatchee.** *5.3 miles/m (H,S)*. At the end of FR 1700-685 (3,640 ft) the route crosses Morse Creek and the American River, then begins a rapid zigzag ascent to gain the steep wooded slopes above the east bank of Mesatchee Creek. A steady climb leads to a creek crossing (4,900 ft), then a long switchback works up the side-slope to meet Trail 958 at the head of the basin (5,850 ft).

**Trail 968, Dewey Lake.** *6.5 miles/m (H,S)*. Just beyond the point where Trail 969 crosses the American River (3,630 ft), this route heads south along the east bank of the river and follows it upstream for 4 miles. The way crosses the main river course to track a tributary up steep forested slopes to Dewey Lake (5,112 ft), where it joins the PCT at the lake's south shore.

**Trail 971, Bumping Lake.** *10.1 miles/e (H,S)*. From the end of FR 1800-394 (3,460 ft), on the northwest side of Bumping Lake, the track follows the lakeshore west to its input stream, then heads upstream through an ever-broadening valley, browsing grounds for elk and deer. The way crosses Red Rock Creek, passes an unnamed lake, then follows the bank of the Bumping River to meet the PCT (4,090 ft) just east of Fish Lake.

**Trail 970, Swamp Lake.** *4.6 miles/m (H,S)*. At the end of FR 1800 (3,550 ft) the trail cuts quickly to a tenuous crossing of Bumping River, crosses Trail 971, then climbs steadily up forested slopes to Swamp Lake (4,795 ft). The way weaves through flowers and blueberry fields to end on Trail 958 (5,040 ft).

## Cascade Crest Trails

**Trail 1105, Indian Creek.** *8 miles/m (H,S)*. At the end of FR 1308 (3,380 ft) this path heads up the lower Indian Creek gorge to meet Trail 1109 a few footsteps away from a gorgeous 150-foot-high waterfall. The way continues upstream to Indian Meadows, where it meets Trail 1141, then both ends of loop Trail 1148 to Pear and Apple Lakes, before bending west to Blankenship Lakes (5,270 ft). The trail continues north through Blankenship Meadows and Mosquito Valley before descending to FR 1808 (4,050 ft) at Deep Creek.

**Trail 1104, Sand Ridge.** *8.5 miles/m (H,S)*. At the end of Spur 488 on the north side of US 12 (3,400 ft), the route ascends Sand Ridge, then heads northwest to meet Trail 1142 on the east side of Spiral Butte. The gentle grade continues north through the forest and meadows of the Tumac Plateau, passes the McAllister Trail 1109 connector to Trail 1105, and rounds the east side of Tumac Mountain. The way then passes eastbound Sandy Trail 1104A and Round Lake 1105A, both short connectors to Trail 1105.

The path then meets the north end of Trail 44, and ends on Trail 980 on the shore of the smaller of the Twin Sisters Lakes (5,190 ft).

**Trail 980, Twin Sisters.** *4.2 miles/m (H,S).* The trail leaves the end of FR 1808 (4,270 ft) (a stock trailhead is 0.5 mile to the east) to head up wooded slopes above Deep Creek. In 1.5 miles the way meets Trail 1104 on the north shore of the smaller of the Twin Sisters Lakes (5,190 ft). After crossing a wooded neck to the larger lake (5,152 ft) the route descends through pond-and-pothole meadows to the PCT (4,950 ft).

**Trail 1142, Shellrock Lake.** *4.4 miles/m (H,S).* Taking off northwest from Trail 1104 (4,600 ft), the route follows the east base of Spiral Butte past Trail 1108, then enters the lake country of the Tumac Plateau. It skirts Shellrock Lake (4,926 ft), then passes Trail 1106, which leads to more of the area's lakes. After passing spur trails 1142B to Long John Lake and 1142A to Dumbbell Lake, the route ends on Trail 44 (5,190 ft), just east of the PCT (5,145 ft).

**Trail 1106, Cramer Lake.** *5.4 miles/m (H,S).* From the Dog Lake Campground on US 12 (4,240 ft), this popular route starts up the marshy North Fork of Clear Creek drainage, then makes a diagonal climb up a steep forested slope west of Spiral Butte. An easier grade leads north to Cramer Lake (5,025 ft). Above the lake the way bends east and weaves past Otter Lake (5,030 ft) and a smattering of other ponds, to end on Trail 1142 (5,075 ft).

**Trail 44, Cowlitz.** *5.2 miles/m (H,S).* The route, part of the prehistoric native Yakima–Cowlitz Trail, leaves Soda Springs Campground (3,220 ft) at the edge of the Carlton Ridge Roadless Area; (the stock trailhead 44A is on FR 4510) to follow Summit Creek upstream to its headwaters. The way heads east past connector Trails 43, 41, and 45 between various lakes to reach Penoyer Lake (5,005 ft), then wanders up through meadow hummocks and ponds to the PCT (5,180 ft), whose tread it shares for a short distance. After passing the end of Trail 1142 the route ascends the west side of Tumac Mountain (6,304 ft). At the top are sweeping views of the entire plateau with its myriad meadows and tiny lakes, as well as a tiny pond below in the heart of the crater. The way drops through subalpine forests and meadows to join Trail 1104 near Twin Sisters Lakes.

**Trail 42, Kincaid.** *8.8 miles/m (H,S).* This old sheepherders' route leaves from near the end of FR 4510 (3,900 ft), drops to a fork of Carlton Creek, then begins a steep, forested, switchback climb to the

*Orange Columbia lilies brighten the trailside along the Cascade Crest.*

top of Carlton Ridge at Log Spring (4,932 ft). The way follows a once-burned-off ridge to the east, with outstanding views of Mount Rainier. After crossing the Cascade crest (5,200 ft) and entering the wilderness, the route passes Trail 47 and continues on to Kincaid Lake (5,300 ft). The trail then circles along the ridge top to Fryingpan Mountain (5,700 ft) and makes a rapid descent to Trail 43 (4,800 ft) north of Fryingpan Lake.

**Trail 22, Carlton Creek.** *9 miles/d (H; S, but not recommended).* From the end of FR 44 (2,250 ft), the route follows an abandoned section of this road for 4 miles to the former trailhead. The trail, surveyed in 1905 for a possible railroad route across the Cascades, traces the twists of Carlton Creek upstream to Carlton Pass (4,140 ft), then wanders down to Fish Lake (4,112 ft) to meet the PCT.

### Trail 2000, Pacific Crest National Scenic Trail. *27.6 miles/m (H,S).*

From US 12 at White Pass (4,470 ft), the PCT passes the east shore of Leech Lake, then climbs steeply to the wilderness boundary. It passes a marshy meadow near Deer Lake (5,206 ft), then heads north to meet Trail 60 at shallow Sand Lake (5,295 ft). The way wanders up to a saddle (5,480 ft) junction with Trail 57, with glimpses through open timber stands to Spiral Butte and the Goat Rocks.

The route winds down to Buesch Lake (5,100 ft), then twists north past Trail 56 and the shore of Pipe Lake (5,210 ft) and temporarily comingles with Trail 44. It now heads northwest and winds through meadows, ponds, and puddles south of Snow Lake (4,935 ft); 0.6 mile north it meets Trail 980 and several spur trails from lakes to the west. The way starts a long, uninterrupted descent to Trail 971 on the bank of the Bumping River. About 0.3 mile upstream is Fish Lake (4,112 ft), and a junction with Trail 22.

Switchbacks climb a precipitous south-facing slope to a contour path above Buck Lake, then bend around a rib to Crag Lake (5,010 ft). A flower-meadow basin is traced west to a pair of lazy switchbacks that gain the Cascade crest (5,740 ft) with views of Rainier, Adams, and St. Helens. The path meets Mount Rainier National Park's Laughingwater Trail just west of the crest, then swings to eastside slopes above the Red Rock Creek drainage. The way now recrosses the crest (5,700 ft) to wildflower meadows and a knockout picture of Mount Rainier. The trail contours westside slopes across lateral ribs to a col (5,340 ft); the way crosses east to Trail 958, then climbs to another saddle (5,580 ft). A descent of wooded westside slopes leads past Anderson Lake (5,350 ft), and yet another crest crossing. Sideslopes are descended gradually to Dewey Lake (5,112 ft) and Trail 968. The route then climbs northwest to meet Highway 410 at Chinook Pass (5,432 ft).

### WINTER SPORTS

Although the rugged ridge country framing the Bumping River drainage is either inaccessible or dangerous for winter travel, excellent ski and snowshoe trips are available along the north and south borders of the wilderness and into the heart of the westside plateau. Sno-Parks at Hells Crossing and Pleasant Valley Campgrounds on Highway 410 east of Chinook Pass offer two access points to Trail 999, an easy, near-flat, 13-mile-long loop on both sides of the highway. Although the trail is not groomed, there is enough traffic to make it easy to follow.

Across the highway from the White Pass Ski Area, a groomed track around Leech Lake links up with the south end of the PCT. The trail can be followed west to Deer Lake, a short easy tour. With careful navigation, the trail can be followed north past Sand and Buesch Lakes to Cowlitz Pass. A base camp here permits tours of the meadow- and lake-pocked plateau. An extended tour can continue east to the summit of Tumac Mountain and Blankenship Meadows. Aside from possible bad weather and the ease of getting lost in the look-alike maze of meadows, this trip is relatively danger-free. Tours farther north along the crest are unwise, because slopes quickly become steep and avalanche-prone.

# 31 Cispus River Region

## Blue Lake and Wobbly Roadless Areas

**Location:** In Lewis and Skamania Counties, between the Cispus River and its North Fork

**Size:** Blue Lake, 11,040 acres; Wobbly, 6,400 acres

**Status:** The core areas are Semiprimitive Motorized; the remainder of the periphery is managed for Timber Harvest.

**Terrain:** High northwest-to-southeast tending ridges frame deep creek drainages. Lateral streams divide lower slopes into ridges perpendicular to the main crests.

**Elevation:** 1,600 to 5,738 feet

**Management:** USFS, Gifford Pinchot National Forest, Cowlitz Valley Ranger District

**Topographic maps:** Blue Lake, East Canyon Ridge, Hamilton Buttes, Tower Rock

The dichotomy in the names of Blue Lake's creeks, Doe Creek and Buck Creek, Cat Creek and Mouse Creek, Slickrock Creek and Smoothrock Creek, is perhaps reflected in people's view of the area: exploitation versus preservation. Fifteen years ago the Blue Lake Roadless Area was nearly double its present size and had a splendid buffer of old-growth forest along slopes leading up to the top of its backbone ridge. Today the lower flanks of the area have been heavily logged. With the recent shift in the management direction of the Forest Service, this "harvest" concept has changed. Unfortunately, many old trails and abandoned logging roads have been reconstructed to ATV standards, assuring little solitude for the wilderness-seeking visitor. Elk Peak, Wobbly's high point, offers superlative views of the North Fork of the Cispus River, the peaks of the Goat Rocks Wilderness, and ice-capped Mount Adams. Several old burns in the area have regrown with berry bushes, and fall berry-picking is one of the area's prime attractions.

*The Blue Lake Butte Trail leads through fields of beargrass.*

## CLIMATE

Blue Lake and Wobbly are on the wet side of the Cascades, so they enjoy about 90 to 100 inches of precipitation annually. Most falls as snow between November and April, and the trails are generally not snow-free until early July. Midwinter lows average around 15 degrees, and summer highs range in the mid-70s.

## ECOSYSTEM

The forest spared from chain saws is typical of the west side of the Cascades. Principal tree species are Pacific silver fir, western hemlock, and subalpine fir, with nominal occurrences of red alder, and mountain hemlock. Among other wildlife, mule deer, elk, and black bear are found in the area.

## GEOLOGY

The base rock of the area is composed of layers of volcanic andesite flows, flow debris, and volcanic sandstones that form a thick cover over the continental crust. Most of the rock is of Oligocene or Miocene age, about 30 to 36 million years old. Some older Eocene andesite and rhyolite are also found in the vicinity. Blue Lake itself was formed when a young volcano vent on the ridge to the west erupted beneath glacial ice sometime between 60,000 to 300,000 years ago, blocking the glacially carved canyon to form the lake.

## HIKING

**Trail 271, Blue Lake Ridge.** *11.7 miles/d (H,S,B,M)*. From FR 23 (1,916 ft), the route climbs diagonally up the steep southwest slope of Blue Lake Ridge. After a breath-catching pause at a bench above Blue Lake Creek, the way climbs to yet another bench and splits. The motorized expressway, Jump-Off Trail 271A, continues uphill to join

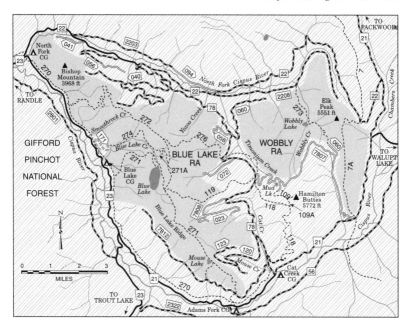

Trail 272 (4,960 ft). The segment of trail that passes the camp area at the outlet from Blue Lake (4,058 ft) and continues uphill to meet Trail 272 southeast of the lake is restricted to hikers. From the Trail 272 junction, the path wanders south along the northeast side of the ridge, passes the upper end of Trail 119, climbs to a high of 5,040 feet, then descends a forested drainage to Mouse Lake (4,475 ft). A newly constructed section, rerouted to avoid logging, rounds the lake and drops southwest to FR 7812. It descends the road for about a mile before rejoining the original trail route down to FR 21 (2,790 ft).

**Trail 274, Blue Lake Hiker.** *2.5 miles/d (H).* A rugged new route that avoids motorized congestion in the area leaves the end of FR 2300-171 to climb along the north bank of Blue Lake Creek. Crossing steep exposed sidehills and climbing rock stairways, the way passes below a striking 250-foot-high wall of columnar basalt before it meets Trails 271 and 271A at Blue Lake (4,058 ft).

**Trail 272, Bishop Ridge.** *8.7 miles/d (H,S,B,M).* After leaving FR 23 (1,540 ft) the way climbs a steep bank, then turns up the south slopes of Bishop Mountain. The track weaves back and forth to avoid steeper spots before finally switchbacking to the ridge top south of the mountain's summit. Open timber and a few small meadows offer broad views of the Cispus River valley. The way follows the 5,000-foot-high crest southeast past the junction with Trail 271A, to end on Trail 271 southeast of Blue Lake (4,520 ft).

**Trail 119, Blue Lake Butte.** *3.5 miles/m (H,S,B,M).* This old sheepherders' route from FR 78 (4,166 ft) heads up a lateral ridge running east from the area's backbone.

A grade wanders up through alternating forest and meadow to its junction with Trail 271, at the head of the Blue Lake basin (4,610 ft).

**Trail 273, Wobbly Creek.** *2.9 miles/e (H,S,B,M).* This route, through a semi-open old burn, leaves FR 2208 (2,845 ft) and climbs gradually for 1.4 miles to Wobbly Lake (3,333 ft). The lake was created when a landslide off the face of Elk Peak blocked the creek drainage. The track then deteriorates as it continues the ascent to FR 7807-060 (4,000 ft). The latter road is very rough, and may be passable only by 4wd vehicles.

**Trail 7A, Klickitat Loop.** *4 miles/d (H,S).* This short segment of trail, lying within the Wobbly Roadless Area, is part of a 27-mile loop trail. Since the roadless area is restricted to nonmotorized recreation, the path is a pleasant respite from the motor mania in the rest of Blue Lake/Wobbly. The trail leaves FR 22 (4,400 ft) on the east slope of Elk Peak. It switchbacks into the headwaters of Elk Creek, then crests the south ridge of the peak a short scramble from the summit. Here it follows the ridge southward, sometimes in timber, and sometimes on open ridgeline with great views. A gradual descent along the ridge ends at FR 21 (3,190 ft).

# 32   Goat Rocks Region

## Goat Rocks Wilderness; adjacent, White Pass, Coal Creek, Bluff, Packwood Lake, Angry Mountain, Chambers, and Walupt Roadless Areas

**Location:** In Lewis and Yakima Counties, astride the Cascade crest south of US 12
**Size:** Wilderness, 105,633 acres; adjacent, 7,357 acres; White Pass, 1,160 acres; Coal Creek Bluff, 1,170 acres; Packwood Lake, 1,130 acres; Angry Mountain, 450 acres; Chambers, 2,120 acres; Walupt, 700 acres
**Status:** Designated Wilderness (1964, 1984); Roadless areas are Semiprimitive Nonmotorized and Unroaded Natural
**Terrain:** The region holds a series of moderately high summits, with north slope glaciation, that run north–south along the Cascade crest. Deep lateral drainages are separated by steep ridges that rise to timberline meadows and parklands.
**Elevation:** 2,200 to 8,201 feet
**Management:** USFS, Gifford Pinchot National Forest, Cowlitz Valley Ranger District, and Okanogan–Wenatchee National Forest, Naches Ranger District
**Topographic maps:** Hamilton Buttes, Jennies Butte, Ohanapecosh Hot Springs, Old Snowy Mtn., Packwood Lake, Pinegrass Ridge, Spiral Butte, Walupt Lake, White Pass

The Goat Rocks represent what today's Cascade volcanic giants, Rainier, Adams, and St. Helens, will look like (barring further eruptions) 2 to 5 million years from now. The present-day Goat Rocks are remains of a volcano cone (or cones) that once stood

*The headwaters of the South Fork of the Tieton River rise out of this meadowy basin in the Goat Rocks Wilderness.*

more than 12,000 feet high. Glacial and stream erosion since Pliocene times has reduced this ancient giant to a string of moderate summits linked by ridges capped with short pinnacles of more resistant basalt.

Much of the area's 120 miles of trails travel high ridges near or above timberline, passing through beautiful alpine meadows that flame with wildflower color as soon as the snow melts. There are two large lakes on the western edge of the wilderness, and the high-altitude parklands are sprinkled with dozens of smaller ponds and lakes (and accompanying mosquitoes).

## CLIMATE

Climatic conditions vary dramatically with altitude in the Goat Rocks; warm summer days at lower elevations are a sharp contrast to the possibility of sudden near-blizzard conditions at higher elevations, even in midsummer. Higher trails may be impassable due to snow until early August, and September can see the first flurries of winter storms. In general, the area receives between 90 and 110 inches of precipitation annually, over 90 percent of which falls as snow between October and May. Total snowfall averages more than 25 feet, with accumulated depths of 10 feet or more. Temperatures are mild; winter minimums average in the lower teens, and summer maximums rarely rise above the balmy lower 70s.

## ECOSYSTEM

Because of its altitude differential, the Goat Rocks Wilderness spans three separate vegetation zones. Dense low-level forests, primarily found in the area's deep stream drainages, are composed of Pacific silver fir, Alaska yellow cedar, western white pine, and noble fir, with associated plants such as boxwood, princess pine, mountain blueberry,

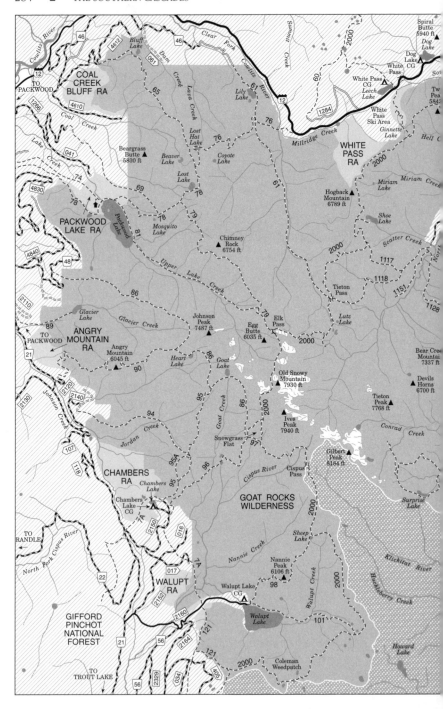

pipsissewa, and bunchberry dogwood. Higher slopes have forests of mountain hemlock, subalpine fir, and whitebark pine. Here broad meadows are covered by golden fleabane, sandwort, sheep fescue, penstemon, cinquefoil, and sedges. When the snow melts, the meadows are painted with wildflower color; look for prairie lupine, goldenrod, saxifrage, aster, arnica, paintbrush, phlox, marigold, and avalanche lily. Surrounding the highest peaks are areas of barren rocky soil, talus slopes, lingering snowfields, and small glaciers. Even here, Lyall lupine, mountain hare sedge, white heather, and other small hardy plants find ways to survive in the short growing season.

Among the animals of the wilderness are blacktailed deer, elk, black bear, coyote, pine marten, and cougar. In alpine country hikers can find pikas, and hear the shrill whistle-welcomes of hoary marmots. Mountain goats are frequently seen near Nannie Basin, in the Upper Lake Creek valley, and around the area's highest summits. Several species of grouse are found, and among the sensitive species in the wilderness are the three-toed woodpecker and great horned owl.

## GEOLOGY

During the Pliocene epoch, volcanic vents erupted at Hogback Mountain, Old Snowy, Ives, and Lakeview Mountain, spewing flows of basalt, andesite, and rhyolite into adjoining river drainages formed from folds of crustal bedrock. Over time erosion from streams and glaciers cut away the older soft rock, exposing sharp ridges composed of these volcanic flows. Further erosion ground volcanic summits down to the present form of the Goat Rocks. On the southwest edge of the region, the younger Mount Adams laid new lava over the ancient basalt. Deposits of glacial till and volcanic detritus were recently overlaid with a thick ash cover from the 1980 eruption of Mount St. Helens; the process of blending this latest of many such volcanic deposits into surface soil can be traced in the alpine meadows of the wilderness.

## HISTORY

Both the Klickitat and the Cowlitz Indians visited the area for hunting game and gathering herbs and roots. Elk Pass

*Conrad Creek threads through a beautiful meadow below Gilbert Peak.*

was one of the routes regularly used for trading between Columbia Plateau and Puget Sound tribes. In 1931, 44,500 acres at the heart of the area were dedicated as the Goat Rocks Primitive Area. This was expanded to 72,440 acres in 1935, and in 1940 to 82,680 acres, when it was designated as the Goat Rocks Wild Area. Official wilderness protection was bestowed on the area in 1964, and in 1984 the most recent addition increased its size to 105,633 acres. In the 1930s CCC crews built several trails here to support new fire lookouts atop Lakeview Mountain, Goat Ridge, Hawkeye Point, Nannie Peak, Lost Lake, Round Mountain, and Bear Creek Mountain. None of these lookouts survive today.

## HIKING
### FR 21 Trails

**Trail 98, Nannie Ridge.** *4.5 miles/m (H,S).* From Walupt Lake (3,950 ft), this route heads north via grinding switchbacks and a rough tread to reach the ridge-top (5,880 ft) south of Nannie Peak. An unmarked path leads to the top of the peak (6,106 ft), a former fire lookout site with great views of Adams, St. Helens, and the heart of the Goat Rocks. The trail drops east of the ridge to skirt cliffs on the peak's east face. The ridge is regained northeast of the peak, and the path contours around an intervening knob to the flower meadows surrounding Sheep Lake (5,710 ft) to join the PCT.

**Trail 96, Snowgrass.** *5.3 miles/m (H,S).* There are two trailheads, 0.5 mile apart, one on FR 2150-405 (4,660 ft) designated for hikers, and one at Berry Patch on

FR 2150-040 (4,680 ft) for horses; both join a short distance uphill. The way ascends gently through dense forest to a swampy, mosquito-laden crossing of Goat Creek. A climb up the wooded wall to the east leads to a trail reroute that swings west, away from Snowgrass Flat. The famous flower fields of the flat, buried in 1980 by ash from the St. Helens eruption, are being carefully nurtured to assist their comeback. The way climbs through open meadows, passes Bypass Trail 97, and then joins Trail 86 near Alpine Camp (5,930 ft). A 0.5-mile talus and heather scramble uphill meets the PCT (6,440 ft).

**Trail 95, Goat Ridge.** *4.6 miles/m-d (H,S).* Leaving the Berry Patch trailhead (4,680 ft), the route climbs northward along an open ridge top, soon passing the lower end of a side loop, Trail 95A, to a former lookout site atop the ridge. In little over a mile it meets the other end of the loop, and then the head of Trail 94. The way then continues its ridge crest ascent to end at its junction with Trail 86 (6,580 ft).

**Trail 90, Angry Mountain.** *8.4 miles/d (H,S).* Not for the lazy, this trail leaves FR 2120 (2,700 ft), leans back, and heads for the sky. Eighteen sweaty switchbacks later, the way tops the west end of Angry Mountain (6,045 ft). An easy grade wanders 2 miles east along the crest to a reality check, twenty-three more switchbacks that grind uphill to the crest east of the mountaintop (5,800 ft). Finally, a pleasant respite, as an open, flower-decked alpine crest leads eastward up a ridge of imposing Johnson Peak to end on Trail 86 (6,150 ft).

## FR 48 Trails

**Trail 86, Lily Basin.** *12 miles/m-d (H,S).* A long, long ridgeline route, with endless breathtaking scenery, leaves FR 48 (4,220 ft) on a long gentle grade to the top of the divide (5,200 ft) between Upper Lake and Glacier Creeks. Here is the first glimpse down to the broad, blue-glass surface of Packwood Lake and, on the horizon above, the glacier-clad summit of Mount Rainier. The route follows the ridge east, first on one side, then the other, then contours around the head of Glacier Creek, skirting the base of cliffs rising to Johnson Peak. The upper end of Trail 90 is passed (6,150 ft) on the ridge west of the peak, and the horizon view now shifts to Mount Adams. The way contours the steep barren slope on the south side of the peak around the cirque above Heart Lake. It continues through alpine parkland at the head of the Middle Fork of Johnson Creek to Goat Ridge (6,600 ft) where it meets Trail 95. A traverse of talus slopes to the east reaches Goat Lake (6,430 ft), often ice-clad until late summer. A long gradual descent of alpine meadows meets Trail 96 (5,950 ft) above Snowgrass Flat.

## FR 1260 Trails

**Trail 78, Packwood Lake.** *9.6 miles/m (H,S).* The section of trail outside the wilderness is blessed with a parallel route to Packwood Lake for motorcycles (Trail 74), leaving a degree of solitude for the foot trail as it ascends through old-growth forest from FR 1260 (2,700 ft) to the lake (2,857 ft). A mass of humanity is rejoined briefly at the Packwood Lake Campground and Resort, where there is also a guard station. The trail heads along the north shore, then leaves the lake and climbs through dense forest to Mosquito Lake (4,853 ft). An uphill grade past the north end of Trail 79 reaches the flower-trimmed shores of Lost Lake (5,165 ft). A stiff climb from here breaks onto an open ridge to meet Trails 65 and 76 (6,250 ft), just below the former site of the Lost Lake lookout.

**Trail 79, Coyote.** *6.8 miles/d (H,S).* About 0.5 mile before Trail 78 reaches Lost Lake (5,150 ft), this route splits off for a long gradual ascent on the west side of the ridge above Upper Lake Creek, with frequent glimpses down the deep valley to Packwood Lake. After skirting the base of Chimney Rock, the track makes an easy descent along the top of a southeast-tending ridge to Packwood Saddle (5,530 ft). Switchbacks negotiate the ridge to the southeast to reach the PCT at Elk Pass (6,700 ft).

## FR 46 Trails

**Trail 65, Bluff Lake.** *6.6 miles/d (H,S).* A long, grinding climb begins (2,840 ft) on FR 4612, and continues relentlessly through old-growth forest to Bluff Lake (3,841 ft). A steep grade clambers uphill to the 5,000-foot level of Coal Creek Mountain, then the way makes a long, diagonal ascent just below the crest of the deep, dark Coal Creek valley. Timber opens to alpine meadows with views north to Rainier as the track climbs to meet Trails 76 and 78 (6,250 ft) just below the summit that once bore Lost Lake lookout.

**Trail 61, Clear Fork.** *9.6 miles/m-d (H,S).* A long, forested ascent leaves the end of FR 46 (3,150 ft), passes Lily Lake (3,660 ft), crosses Trail 76, and wanders gradually up through dense timber above the Clear Fork of the Cowlitz River. At 6.5 miles the way fords the river to begin an uphill thrust to Tieton Pass (4,780 ft), where it meets the PCT and Trail 1118.

## US 12 Trails (west of White Pass)

**Trail 76, Clear–Lost.** *6.6 miles/d (H,S).* Heading west from US 12 (3,750 ft), the trail descends to cross the Clear Fork of the Cowlitz River, then works gradually uphill to cross Trail 61. The way heads up a very steep forested hillside, climbing through ragged palisades to Lost Hat Lake (5,590 ft). A diagonal climb up talus slopes reaches the site of the Lost Lake lookout (6,376 ft), and, just below, meets Trails 65 and 78.

## FR 12 Trails (from US 12 east of White Pass)

**Trail 1144, Round Mountain.** *5.5 miles/d (H; S, but not recommended).* Starting at the end of FR 1200-830 at Indian Spring (4,310 ft), a wooded uphill slog on a rough, rutted tread climbs past a spur to the top of Round Mountain (5,970 ft), a former lookout site with commanding views of the Tieton River basin. The way continues to the bare, sharp point of Twin Peaks (5,843 ft), with views across the valley to Spiral Butte, down to White Pass, and up the Tieton River drainage into the heart of the wilderness. The route follows the ridge west to meet the PCT (5,400 ft) near Ginnette Lake.

**Trail 1118, North Fork Tieton.** *4.9 miles/e (H,S).* The trail leaves the end of FR 1207 (3,330 ft) at an easy grade up wooded slopes on the west side of the North Fork of the Tieton River. It continues a gradual ascent to Tieton Pass (4,780 ft), where it ends at a junction with the PCT and Trail 61.

**Trail 1128, Tieton Meadows.** *4.7 miles/m (H,S).* After leaving the end of FR 1207 (3,330 ft), the trail spends a brief period on the gentle valley floor along the east side of the North Fork of the Tieton, then lets it rip as seventeen switchbacks twist up a wooded hogback to the east. A long, diagonal climb winds around three stream headwater basins to meet Trail 1130 (6,230 ft).

**Trail 1130, Bear Creek Mountain.** *7.4 miles/m (H,S).* From the end of FR 1204 at Section Three Lake (6,030 ft), the route heads southwest to a saddle, then slowly ascends through alpine meadows as it winds around the head of Bear Creek Basin. From the midpoint of the trail (6,250 ft), a spur switchbacks up the rocky face of Bear Creek Mountain to the old lookout site (7,337 ft) and knockout views of Dev-

*The Pacific Crest Trail passes Shoe Lake south of White Pass.*

ils Horn, Tieton, Old Snowy, Ives, and Gilbert. The way then drops to a forested bench and contours west for more than 2 miles to the west rim of the South Fork of the Tieton drainage. Switchbacks drop down the steep hogback to Conrad Meadows and a gate barring further vehicle traffic up FR 1000 (4,030 ft).

**Trail 1120, South Fork Tieton Loop.** *10.1 miles/m (H,S).* From the gate on FR 1000 at Conrad Meadows (4,030 ft), the way follows the South Fork of the Tieton upstream, and at 4 miles splits into a loop high above the headwall of the basin. A clockwise course zigzags up a steep, wooded wall to Surprise Lake (5,255 ft), where a bench (5,700 ft) between cliff bands is followed north to the upper headwater trickle of the South Fork. An unmarked path climbs north up a raw rock slope to another alpine bench below Gilbert Peak; this can be wandered north as far as Conrad Creek. The loop trail continues around the north side of the basin rim, then switchbacks abruptly down to the trail split point.

## Trail 2000, Pacific Crest National Scenic Trail. *31.1 miles/m-d (H,S).*

**PCT: White Pass to Elk Pass.** *13.2 miles/m (H,S).* From US 12 opposite White Pass Campground (4,390 ft), the trail makes long, lazy switchbacks south to Ginnette Lake (5,420 ft). Passing the upper end of Trail 1144 above the lake, the way heads southwest up the easy ridge, then follows the open rib southwest to Hogback Ridge. A traverse of the shale slopes of the Miriam Lake basin reaches a saddle above the Shoe

Lake basin. Camping is prohibited in the basin to preserve the fragile habitat.

The way descends into the upper Scatter Creek basin, meets Trail 1117, then climbs and crosses to the west side of the crest and winds down to Tieton Pass (4,790 ft), where it joins Trails 61 and 1118. The route recrosses the crest at Lutz Lake (5,100 ft), then climbs back over the crest and traverses meadows and talus slopes to Elk Pass (6,500 ft), where it meets Trail 79 from the west.

**PCT: Elk Pass to Snowgrass Flat.** *3.8 miles/d (H,S)*. The trail segment between Elk Pass and Snowgrass Flat is the highest portion of the PCT in the state (7,100 ft), and the most dangerous section to cross. The track tiptoes along the top of a steep, narrow ridge, not wide enough for horses and hikers to pass each other safely, and exposed to the rake of sudden dangerous storms at any time of the year. At the south end of this catwalk the route traverses between the upper end of the Packwood Glacier and the slopes below the top of Old Snowy, then gradually descends to the parkland above Snowgrass Flat, where it meets Trails 96 (6,440 ft) and 97 (6,290 ft).

**PCT: Snowgrass Flat to South Wilderness Boundary.** *14.1 miles/m (H,S)*. The route contours eastward above the headwaters of the Cispus River to Cispus Pass (6,450 ft). After a brief sojourn east of the crest, the way returns to the west side and works down into the Nannie Creek drainage to meet Trail 98 at Sheep Lake. The track descends into the forested hillside above Walupt Creek, passes Trail 101, and swings west on easy slopes above the flower fields of the Coleman Weedpatch. After a slow ascent along alpine ridges, the trail leaves the wilderness.

## CLIMBING

Although the highest peaks of the Goat Rocks range around 8,000 feet and support a band of glaciers along their north sides, all are relatively easy ascents over mixed rock and snow routes. The northernmost, Old Snowy Mountain, is a large gentle summit only a scramble away from the PCT. Ives Peak has easy routes from either east or west. Although the summit ridge of Gilbert Peak (8,184 ft), the highest point in the Goat Rocks, is an easy scramble, there are interesting rock climbs on the south and glaciers on the north. A number of basalt horns (7,750 to 7,960 ft) on the ridge west of Gilbert offer a few pitches of C-4 climbing. Among these are Big Horn, Little Horn, and Black Thumb.

## WINTER SPORTS

The ridges south of the White Pass Ski Area are popular with cross-country skiers and snowshoers, partly because much elevation can be gained by using the area's main chairlift. From the top of the lift, tours head west through bizarre sculptures of snow-plastered trees to the open ridge of Hogback Mountain and great views of the Goat Rocks. With due caution for avalanche conditions, some parties push on to snow camps at Shoe Lake, or even as far as Tieton Pass. The summer route to Round Mountain is another vigorous tour out of the White Pass area. Those willing to put up with a long snow-covered road approach can also enjoy a pleasant trip into Packwood Lake, peaceful without its motorized summer crowds.

# 33   Pompey Peak Roadless Area

**Location:** In Lewis County, wrapping around the Smith Creek drainage south of Packwood, between the Cowlitz River and the North Fork of the Cispus River
**Size:** 23,530 acres
**Status:** Semiprimitive Nonmotorized and Mountain Goat Habitat
**Terrain:** This high divide with steep, rugged north-tending ridges is cut by deep creek canyons.
**Elevation:** 1,030 to 5,900 feet
**Management:** USFS, Gifford Pinchot National Forest, Cowlitz Valley Ranger District
**Topographic maps:** Blue Lake, Packwood, Packwood Lake, Purcell Mountain, Tower Rock

On the south side of US 12 between Randle and Packwood, densely wooded hillsides climb abruptly from the Cowlitz River valley to a cockscomb rim of rock-faced cliffs. Dark, V-shaped valleys drive deep into this mountain mass, and for a brief moment one can imagine what the surrounding country must have looked like before it was logged. Only the horseshoe-shaped ridges surrounding the Smith Creek drainage are currently managed by the Forest Service as semiprimitive areas, and all of their periphery, as well as the thrust of Smith Creek into their heart, has been heavily harvested. The historic old cross-Cascades Indian trade route along the south rim of the area is only a stone's throw from clearcuts in places, but fading, unmaintained tracks atop two north-tending crests still offer real solitude, route-finding challenges, and unsurpassed scenery.

## CLIMATE

Due to nearly 4,000 feet of vertical elevation difference, the area's climate differs significantly with altitude. In general, precipitation levels are high, averaging around 100 inches per year, with the bulk of this falling as snow between November and April. The snowpack at lower elevations ranges between 2 and 4 feet, while upper elevations see snow depths of 10 feet or more. Most trails are clear of snow by mid-July. Temperatures are relatively mild, with winter lows averaging between 10 and 20 degrees, and midsummer highs in the mid-70s.

## ECOSYSTEM

The altitude differential in the Pompey area spans three separate forest zones. The lower valley floors are covered with western hemlock, Douglas-fir, and Pacific silver fir; red alder, western red cedar, and bigleaf maple are also found in damper locations. The understory in cool, moist areas includes swordfern, Oregon oxalis, oakfern, and devil's club; white foamflower, vanillaleaf, Oregon grape, salal, and oceanspray are found in drier spots. With elevation the forest mix shifts to mountain hemlock, Alaska yellow cedar, subalpine fir, and (in old burns) lodgepole pine. Queencup beadlily, huckleberry, Cascade azalea, and beargrass occur in the ground cover. On the highest ridge tops, clusters of small subalpine fir fringe parklands covered by sedges, beargrass, mountain blueberry, partridgefoot, and heathers, as well as floral displays of asters, shooting star, lupine, Indian paintbrush, and cinquefoil.

Among forest inhabitants are black-tailed deer, elk, black bear, bobcat, pine marten, cougar, raccoon, mink, snowshoe hare, marmot, and a variety of squirrels, chipmunks, and mice. Frequently seen birds are gray jays, Clark's nutcracker, blue and spruce grouse, and white-tailed ptarmigan. The valley floors are winter range for deer and elk, and mountain goats have both summer and winter ranges in the area.

## GEOLOGY

The base rock in the area, common throughout the region, is mostly thick volcanic flows of andesite and rhyolite laid down over a period between 15 million and 35 million years ago. The surface features, the hills and valleys, were shaped by glacial and stream erosion over the last 15,000 years.

## HISTORY

The area has been visited by local Indian tribes for perhaps as long as 6,000 years. The Taidnapam Indians headed into the higher elevations in summer and fall to hunt game and gather berries, medicinal plants, roots, and bark. A major Indian trade route between the Puget Sound tribes and tribes east of the Cascades ran through the area; Trails 7 and 128 follow portions of this route. In the late 1920s to early 1930s, the Forest Service built fire lookouts at area high spots, including South Point, Dry Creek Point, Pompey Peak, and Cispus Butte. None of them remain today. The most obvious activity throughout the region over the past 50 years has been logging, and miles of roads linking clearcut scars snake up the slopes of every drainage.

## HIKING

**Trail 7, Klickitat.** *17.1 miles/m (H,S,B).* This trail follows an old ridge-top Indian trade route across the Cascades. Much of the original west end of the trail has been obliterated by logging; the route now starts at the end of FR 5508-024 (4,320 ft), atop the divide between the North Fork of the Cispus River and Kilborn Creek. The crest is followed east for over a mile, where a gradual ascent across the south side of Twin Sisters reaches the east end of Trail 128 (5,260 ft). The way bends southeast, crossing alpine parklands below Castle Butte, to reach a spur trail (127) to the top of Cispus Point (5,686 ft). Here are great views of Rainier, Adams, St. Helens, and Hood, and an endless succession of clearcuts hacked from the valley walls of the North Fork of the Cispus River. A diagonal descent southeast skirts rock walls to logging on either side of Jackpot Lake (4,551 ft). This spot can also be reached via FR 20 up Smith Creek.

To the east the original trail has been rerouted out of the Smith Creek drainage to

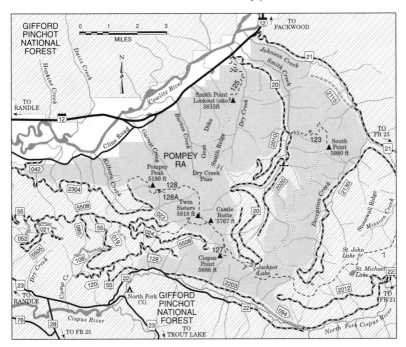

avoid logging; it rejoins the old route at the divide between Smith and Deception Creeks. After skirting clearcuts at the head of Deception Creek, the way makes a diagonal climb up the hillside between Cold Springs Butte and St. Michael Lake, then descends to St. John Lake (5,110 ft). A sidehill traverse and a climb across ridge-top meadows leads around the north side of Mission Mountain (5,698 ft). The route now starts a long, gradual descent of the forested rib arcing to the south to reach its present east end at FR 22 (4,400 ft).

**Trail 128, Pompey Peak.** *5 miles/d (H,S,B).* From the end of FR 2304 (3,520 ft), a short, gentle grade northwest swings up through the old-growth forest on the west shoulder of Pompey Peak, then skirts its steep south side to the gentler east ridge. A spur leads up the shoulder of Pompey Peak to the summit (5,180 ft), an old lookout site. All other faces of the peak drop away sharply. An impressive view spans the broad Cowlitz River valley, the vertical east face of Goat Dike, the Twin Sisters, and on the horizon the ice-clad summits of Rainier and Adams, and the blast-opened face of St. Helens. The way continues along the narrow ridge around the head of Kilborn Creek to break into alpine meadows. The route then traverses beneath the rocky cliffs of Twin Sisters to a saddle between them and Castle Butte, where it meets Trail 7 (5,260 ft).

**Trail 125, Dry Creek.** *3.5 miles/m (H,S,B,M).* From the Cowlitz River valley the forested slopes rise with neck-craning abruptness beside the deep dark gash of Dry Creek. From FR 20 (1,060 ft), endless long switchbacks work up an imposing hillside to its

*Cispus Point provides high views of meadows and valleys of the Pompey Peak Roadless Area.*

northernmost point (3,815 ft), once a fire lookout site. Here are great views north across the broad Cowlitz River valley to Mount Rainier. A continuation of the trail along the ridge to the south is no longer maintained and takes expert routefinding skills to follow.

**Trail 123, South Point Lookout.** *3.3 miles/d (H,S,B).* The route leaves FR 20 (2,740 ft), deep in the Smith Creek drainage, and begins a grueling climb up the forested west side of South Point Ridge, mitigated by ceaseless switchbacks. Two long diagonal sweeps lead to final zigzags to the top of South Point (5,980 ft), a former fire lookout, now a microwave relay station site. The lookout's views remain, including Rainier and Adams, the Goat Rocks, and the rocky face of Smith Ridge across the valley. An abandoned continuation of this trail along the ridge south to join Trail 7 can only be followed with superior cross-country navigation skills.

# 34 Dark Divide

## Dark Divide and Spencer Ridge Roadless Areas

**Location:** In Lewis and Skamania Counties, between the Cispus and Lewis Rivers on the north and south, and Mounts Adams and St. Helens on the east and west

**Size:** Dark Divide, 55,000 acres; Spencer Ridge, 5,700 acres

**Status:** Unroaded Recreation; Semiprimitive, part Nonmotorized, part Motorized. Includes the Shark Rock Special Scenic Area and the Table Mountain Special Wildlife Area

**Terrain:** In the Dark Divide, two narrow north–south ridgelines rise abruptly more than 4,000 feet above the adjoining valley floors to form the northern lobes of an area with twelve peaks over 5,000 feet scattered along the craggy crests. In the broad southern portion of Dark Divide, ridges frame the headwaters of several creeks that have cut deeply into bedrock as they flow south to the Lewis River. Spencer Ridge is a thumb of roadless area extending southwest from Dark Divide, with ridges framing both sides of the Clear Creek drainage.

**Elevation:** 1,550 to 5,880 feet

**Management:** USFS, Gifford Pinchot National Forest, Cowlitz Valley Ranger District, and Mount St. Helens National Volcanic Monument

**Topographic maps:** Blue Lake, East Canyon Ridge, French Butte, McCoy Peak, Quartz Creek Butte, Spencer Butte, Steamboat Mtn., Tower Rock

As logging gnawed at the periphery of Dark Divide and old trails were consumed, the Forest Service tried its best to redirect these paths to avoid, or at least accommodate this disruption. The voracious appetite for old-growth timber has been stemmed by new Roadless Area Conservation Rules, and several roads in these areas have been decommissioned and restored to roadless conditions. The two northern lobes of the region which frame the McCoy Creek drainage rise with neck-popping abruptness to narrow, twisting crests. For the most part these are topped by alpine meadows and rugged rocky outcrops. Ridge-top trails offer splendid views throughout their length, down to creeks and rivers more than 4,000 feet below, and across to the giant ice-clad Cascade volcanoes on the horizon. Although once crowded by logging activity, the lower southern portion of Dark Divide still retains prime examples of

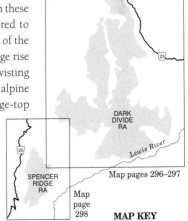

Cispus River

23

DARK DIVIDE RA

Lewis River

25

SPENCER RIDGE RA

Map page 298

Map pages 296–297

**MAP KEY**

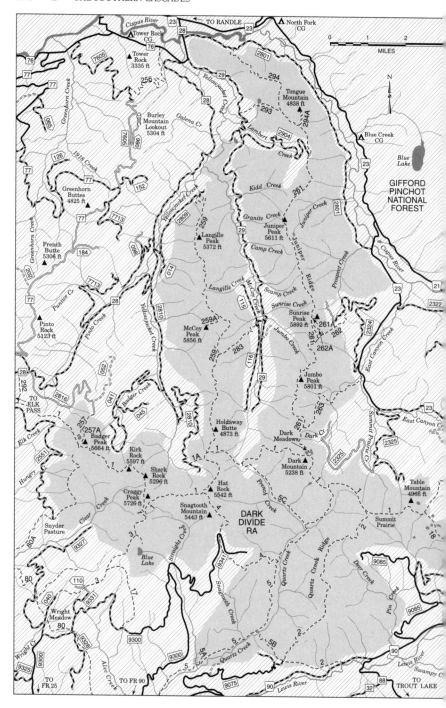

old-growth forest that can wrap one in a blanket of wilderness solitude. The major creeks that drain the area have cut deep, narrow gorges along much of their courses, and play a rushing-water symphony as they drop steeply down cascades and roll over waterfalls.

## CLIMATE

Average annual precipitation runs about 90 inches, varying with location and altitude. Less than 5 percent of this falls in peak summer months; much of it makes up the 23 feet of snow that drops on the area each year. Except for shaded gullies and north slope pockets, snow is gone at most elevations by July, and the first flakes don't generally fall until November. Temperatures are relatively mild—midwinter lows average 24 degrees, and summer highs run in the low 70s.

## ECOSYSTEM

The forest in Dark Divide and Spencer Ridge is predominantly Pacific silver fir and western hemlock, with lesser occurrences of subalpine fir, mountain hemlock, and red alder. In the ground cover are huckleberry, prince's pine, bunchberry dogwood, rhododendron, queencup beadlily, twinflower, salal, rustyleaf, and dwarf blackberry. The lower southern portion of the area is noted for occurrences of fringed pinesap, on the state Sensitive Plant Species list. Old fires are generally credited as the source of the meadows, pastures, and prairies that cover the remainder of the area. These clearings are covered with beargrass and huckleberries, complemented by a variety of wildflowers that bloom in early summer.

Small meadows and ponds at lower elevations are important elk calving habitats. The forest also contains black-tailed deer, black bear, marten, and northern spotted owl. The subalpine communities support northwestern salamander, western toad, northern pigmy owl, northern goshawk, evening grosbeak, Clark's nutcracker, and mountain chickadee.

## GEOLOGY

The bedrock underlying the area is multilayered andesite and rhyolite, from volcanic flows about 24 million years ago. The long finger ridges extending north–south are composed of stacks of lava flows, flow debris, and volcanic sandstones that accumulated between 18 and 25 million years ago. In the middle to north portions of the roadless area are a number of small Miocene dunite intrusions with mineralization along their edges. These have led to placer gold mining along McCoy and Camp Creeks. Low-grade copper ores have also been found in the area. The most recent volcanic activity occurred about 650,000 years ago when lava flows from vents in the Badger Peak area partially filled valleys to the north in the Yellowjacket Creek drainage. Continental, then local, glaciers, carved and shaped ridges, sharp arêtes, and cirques enclosing lakes and tarns are found throughout the area. Ridge-top soils are shallow and insecure, while those in the valley bottoms are deep and stable. The 1980 eruption of Mount St. Helens overlaid portions of the region with a layer of fine pumice that will take decades to merge with native soils.

## HISTORY

Dark Divide contains sites with stone fragments and peeled cedars that would indicate the region was used by natives for hunting and gathering before recorded history. Trail 1, the Boundary Trail, marked the border between the Rainier Forest Reserve, established in 1897, and the Columbia National Forest, which was created from it in 1908. The latter was redesignated the Gifford Pinchot National Forest in 1949. During the 1930s, fire lookouts were built atop McCoy Peak, Tongue Mountain, Sunrise Peak, Summit Prairie, Badger Peak, Spencer Butte, and Smith Creek Ridge; many of the area's trails were put in to support the lookouts and associated fire patrol activities. All of these lookouts were removed, vandalized, or burned by the late 1960s; only the views remain. Many of the trails have been consumed by the region's omnivorous logging, although some were preserved and rerouted by the Forest Service once chain saws had gorged themselves.

## HIKING
### Southside Trails

**Trail 1, Boundary.** *32.4 miles/m (H,S,B,M).* This historic old trail runs east to west across the region. The path has been cut by logging roads and nibbled on the fringes

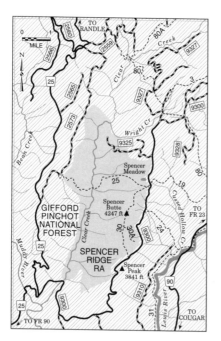

by clearcuts, but it still retains a vestige of its former stature. On the east side of Dark Divide the route begins on FR 2334 (4,320 ft) and proceeds southwest along the base of Table Mountain. The way winds up to Summit Prairie, where it meets Trail 2 (5,070 ft) north of a former lookout site. A gradual descent northwest reaches a pair of shallow lakes at Dark Meadows (4,360 ft) and finally joins Trail 261.

A jagged contour west crosses logged areas at the head of McCoy Creek, joins the south end of Trail 259, passes spur Trail 1A to FR 2810 (3,980 ft), then swings around the basin at the headwaters of Yellowjacket Creek. After slinking below the sheer north face of Hat Rock, the route switchbacks down to Yellowjacket Pass (4,350 ft). The way follows the narrow ridge west toward Craggy Peak, contours its southeast side to meet Trail 3, then turns north along the west base of the peak.

The route snakes up the steep, bare east face of Shark Rock, then traces a narrow ridge west to Kirk Rock. A ridge-top path continues northwest, traverses below Badger Peak, then swings down to a fringe of meadows at Badger Lake (4,940 ft). From here, the way follows undulations of the ridge west, between logging incursions from both sides, to Elk Pass (4,080 ft) on FR 25.

**Trail 257, Badger Ridge.** *1 mile/m (H,S,B,M).* The shortest approach to Badger Lake and Badger Peak leaves the end of FR 2816 (4,880 ft) atop Badger Ridge. In early summer the meadowed crest is carpeted with wildflowers, and fall brings a feast of huckleberries. All seasons offer great views of the truncated cone of Mount St. Helens and Pinto Rock, a rugged old volcano core. The path crosses a notch (5,300 ft), passes spur Trail 257A to the top of Badger Peak (5,664 ft), and circles down a basin wall to meadows west of Badger Lake.

The Badger Peak spur leads across a 300-foot gully from the summit that can be dangerous before snowmelt. This rocky point of the peak had its top blasted off for a onetime lookout cabin. The view here is stupendous; close by is the ragged Shark Rock Scenic Area, and Cascade volcanoes—Hood, St. Helens, Adams, and Rainier—glisten on the horizon.

**Trail 2, Summit Prairie.** *9 miles/m (H,S,B,M).* Starting on FR 90 (2,310 ft), the relocated lower end of this route begins as deceptively easy with a diagonal ascent up wooded slopes to the end of FR 9075 (3,220 ft). Here the fun is over, as switchbacks twist uphill to a broad, forested ridge top (4,520 ft). The way heads north along the top of steep-walled Quartz Creek Ridge, the divide between Quartz and Deer Creeks. Most of the time is spent atop the narrow crest, but occasionally the track drops to talus slopes on its east side. The route wiggles east atop the ridge, then north to the former lookout site (5,238 ft) above Summit Prairie, before it descends north to Trail 1 (5,235 ft).

**Trail 5, Quartz Creek.** *10.6 miles/m (H,S,B).* This is the premier trail on the south side of Dark Divide. It leaves FR 90 near the mouth of Quartz Creek (1,770 ft) on an old mining road, then winds along the steep-walled creek bank to cross Platinum Creek. The way climbs out of the narrowing gorge past mining relics, crosses a clearcut, then drops to a newly constructed bridge across Straight Creek that overlooks the lip of a waterfall. A few switchbacks regain a shelf above the deep, narrow course of Quartz Creek. After skirting another clearcut, the way enters magnificent old-growth forest as it continues upstream along the rim of the creekbed wall.

The route crosses Straight Creek (2,270 ft), where an unmarked path works uphill for a peek at a beautiful, wide, 50-foot-high falls. The way gradually climbs away from the stream, meets the east end of Trail 4, then drops again to cross Quartz Creek at a wider spot in the drainage. The route recrosses the creek just above French Creek, where Trail 5C heads up that drainage. The path switchbacks up out of the upper Quartz Creek gorge, then climbs to join Trail 1 (4,280 ft) on the divide above Dark Creek.

**Trail 3, Craggy Peak.** *4.4 miles/m (H,S,B,M).* A well-maintained trail from

FR 9327-040 (3,840 ft) ascends through clearcuts, the last of which can also be reached by FR 9331-110 (4,280 ft). The route then swings around the head of Alec Creek with glimpses down into the cirque containing Blue Lake. A short spur trail leads down into the cirque, and a boot-path continues on to the lake itself. Ridge-top meadows are followed to join the southern sweep of Trail 1 (5,200 ft) south of Craggy Peak.

## Northwest Lobe Trails

**Trail 259, Langille Ridge.** *10.4 miles/d (H,S,B,M).* This trail, which runs the length of the northwest lobe of Dark Divide, leaves FR 2809 (2,630 ft) in switchbacks up a densely forested slope. The path passes the west base of Langille Peak, then gains the open, meadowed crest at 5,200 feet. Beargrass, wildflowers, and huckleberries (depending on season) accompany the route south along the high narrow ridge, which is broken by weird rock outcrops. The way contours above Bear Creek, then climbs its headwall. It follows the east side, then the top of the ridge south to join Trail 1 (4,525 ft) south of Holdaway Butte.

## Northeast Lobe Trails

**Trail 294, Tongue Mountain.** *5.4 miles/m (H,S,B,M).* There are two ways to reach the top of Tongue Mountain. The long, tedious route leaves FR 2801 (1,380 ft) to puff and pant through endless switchbacks up a broad ridge (2,800 ft), then continues southeast to Trail 294A (4,020 ft) to the top. A second path leaves FR 2904 at 3,580 feet and ascends north along a broad, wooded ridge for 1 mile to Trail 294A (4,020 ft).

*The volcanic cone of Mount St. Helens can be seen from Badger Mountain.*

The open slopes below the summit trail provide a sweeping panorama of Burley Mountain, Tower Rock, Mount Rainier, and Mount St. Helens.

Trail 294A slithers up a difficult, fractured, washed-out path through crumbling rock to the onetime lookout site atop Tongue Mountain (4,838 ft). The weathered trail, not for the faint hearted, rewards its conquerors with outstanding views of Adams and Rainier and breathtaking glimpses down precipitous wooded slopes to the Cispus River, 3,000 feet below.

**Trail 261, Juniper Ridge.** *11.6 miles/d (H,S,B,M).* From FR 2904 (3,640 ft), along the headwaters of Lambert Creek, the way switchbacks up to the ridge top and follows the crest south to the base of Juniper Peak (5,611 ft). This old sheep drive picks its way along narrow huckleberry meadows atop Juniper Ridge, then slips up cliffs to the crest south of Sunrise Peak. A 0.3-mile spur (Trail 261A) leads to the top of the peak, an old lookout site with impressive views of Hood, Adams, St. Helens, and Rainier. The way then descends an open berry-field hillside to the broad saddle of Old Cow Camp (4,707 ft). Next the trail strikes up along the rock cliffs northwest of Jumbo Peak, skirts the west side of this summit, then drops south along the ridge past Trail 263 to meet Trail 1 at Dark Meadows (4,400 ft).

**Trail 263, Dark Meadows.** *3.2 miles/m (H,S,B,M).* From FR 23 (2,500 ft), the way heads southwest through second-growth forest, then heads for the sky up the wooded cliffs of the lower Dark Creek drainage. After crossing the creek it climbs through old-growth timber to meet Trail 261 at meadows near the head of Dark Creek (4,480 ft).

## Spencer Ridge

**Trail 30, Spencer Butte.** *3 miles/m (H,S,B,M).* The south end of the trail across Spencer Butte leaves FR 9300 (3,450 ft) and begins a gradual, climbing traverse through forest changing from white pine to noble and subalpine fir. As the path levels near the top of the butte, look for a spur, Trail 30A to Breezy Point. Since the lookout atop Spencer Butte could not see into the Lewis River drainage, an emergency lookout site was prepared atop a cliff face at Breezy Point 0.5 mile to the southeast, where remnants of a frame to support a fire finder can still be seen. The broad clearing atop the butte itself has a few traces of the old lookout and knockout views of Mounts Adams and St. Helens. The trail returns to forest as it descends the north ridge of the butte to Spencer Meadow (3,420 ft)—watch for elk here.

## CLIMBING

Although there are no major peaks of climbing interest in the area, several solid and interesting rock outcrops (5,000 to 5,725 ft) offer near-vertical 200- to 400-foot solid rock faces for challenging short climbs. Those along Trail 1 include Kirk Rock (5,597 ft), Shark Rock (5,296 ft), Craggy Peak (5,726 ft; which can be approached by a scramble trail up its south ridge from Trail 1), Hat Rock (5,542 ft), and Table Mountain (4,966 ft). Similar rock faces are found on peaks along Trails 261 and 294. Among these are Tongue Mountain (4,838 ft), Jumbo Peak (5,801 ft), and three nearby unnamed summits (5,445 to 5,610 ft).

# 35　Mount St. Helens

## Mount St. Helens National Volcanic Monument; Tumwater and Strawberry Roadless Areas

**Location:** In Cowlitz, Lewis, and Skamania Counties, surrounding Mount St. Helens
**Size:** Monument, 110,330 acres; Tumwater, 9,370 acres; Strawberry, 5,070 acres
**Status:** National Volcanic Monument (1982); Roadless areas are Semiprimitive Motorized and Nonmotorized
**Terrain:** The shattered crater of Mount St. Helens is surrounded by steep, rugged ridges denuded by the 1980 eruption, and numerous unique geological features reflecting the effect of this and past eruptions. The roadless areas are ridges on the northeast periphery of the St. Helens scorched timber zone.
**Elevation:** 800 to 8,365 feet
**Management:** USFS, Gifford Pinchot National Forest, Mount St. Helens National Volcanic Monument, and Cowlitz Valley Ranger District
**Topographic maps:** Cougar, Cowlitz Falls, Elk Rock, Goat Mountain, Hoffstadt Mtn., Mount St. Helens, Mt. Mitchell, Smith Creek Butte, Spirit Lake East, Spirit Lake West, Vanson Peak

Mount St. Helens gained worldwide fame on May 18, 1980, when an earthquake triggered a massive landslide, releasing the forces within the mountain in a catastrophic eruption that blew away the north side of the peak, leveled more than 230 square miles of forest with a hot lateral blast, and filled rivers as far as the Columbia with a surge of hot mudflows.

In 1982 Congress created the 110,000-acre Mount St. Helens National Volcanic Monument to preserve this unique environment for research into ongoing volcanism, the natural process of recovery from the eruptive destruction, and visitor education and recreation. The roadless areas on the northeast periphery of the monument are forested ridges only moderately affected by the eruption.

## CLIMATE

Climate in the monument varies with altitude; precipitation ranges from 65 inches in the valleys to more than 140 inches on the upper portions of the mountain. Snow, much of which falls between October and March, accounts for most of this precipitation. Lower-level snowpacks are between 2 and 4 feet; mid-altitudes accumulate 7 to 14 feet. July and August are the driest months; only 5 percent of the total annual rainfall occurs during those two months. Midsummer temperatures run between 45 and 72 degrees, and winter averages are between 24 and 33 degrees. Extreme temperatures, most occurring with continental, easterly winds, can drive winter minimums to minus 15 degrees and raise summer highs above 90.

*The north side of Mount St. Helens reveals the blasted-out side, with a new cinder cone growing inside the crater.*

## ECOSYSTEM

The May 1980 eruption drastically altered the biosphere within the monument. The debris avalanche, pyroclastic flows, and mudflows covered an area of 24 square miles on the north side of the summit, in the headwaters of the North Fork of the Toutle, with a layer of debris between 150 and 640 feet thick. Mudflows also wiped out the forest around the South Fork of the Toutle River, and in the Swift Creek, Pine Creek, and Muddy River drainages. The lateral blast and pyroclastic flows leveled the forest as far as 23 miles north of the crater, and scorched trees on the perimeter of this area, including portions of the Tumwater and Strawberry Roadless Areas.

 With a few exceptions, all wildlife in the blast zone was killed, including the entire mountain goat and ptarmigan populations, and an estimated 5,000 deer, 1,500 elk, and 200 black bear. The only mammal survivors on the north side of mountain were those underground at the time of the eruption: gophers, deer mice, Pacific jumping mice, and moles. Where still covered by snow, young trees and plants were unharmed, as were amphibians and fish in secluded snow-covered lakes.

Since the eruption, recolonization has started, first with fireweed, thistles, bracken fern, huckleberry, and willow. Over time a typical conifer forest will once again develop in the area. Toads, frogs, and salamanders have returned to the region, as have elk, black-tailed deer, beaver, and coyote. Birds now seen are ravens, flickers, juncos, bluebirds, sandpipers, killdeer, and several species of ducks.

Some areas were untouched by the eruption; the deep Green River Valley on the northern border of the monument has a dense forest of old-growth Douglas-fir, and the area on the west side of the mountain near Blue Lake has one of the largest known stands of old-growth noble fir. The southwest corner of the monument was touched only by ashfall, and there a healthy forest is dominated by Douglas-fir, Pacific silver fir, western hemlock, and lodgepole pine. The understory contains red huckleberry, rustyleaf, kinnikinnick, creambush, salal, oceanspray, beargrass, oval-leaf huckleberry, western fescue, swordfern, and penstemon.

Among the mammals in the undisturbed area are elk, black-tailed deer, black bear, cougar, snowshoe hare, porcupine, coyote, bobcat, river otter, beaver, weasel, muskrat, raccoon, skunk, and marten. Birds seen here are grouse, ptarmigan, several

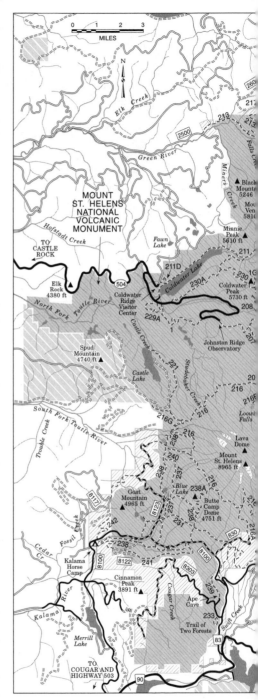

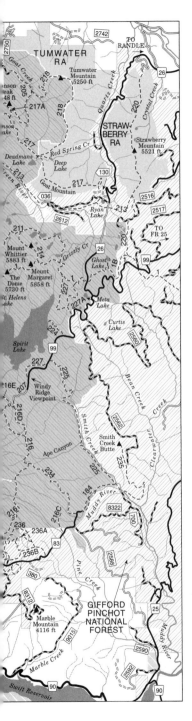

species of woodpeckers, sparrows, finches, swallows, vireos, thrushes, wrens, blackbirds, nutcrackers, crows, ravens, spotted owls, screech owls, great horned owls, red-tailed hawks, sharp-shinned hawks, goshawks, osprey, and bald eagles.

## GEOLOGY

Ancestral Mount St. Helens probably formed about 40,000 years ago, when eruptions of andesite and dacite formed a relatively small cone at the present site of the peak. This primordial mountain was later modified, about 19,000 years ago, by mudflows, lava flows, and pyroclastic eruptions. Some of these flows are evident in the Kalama, Lewis, and North Fork of the Toutle River drainages. About 10,000 years ago, further eruptions were accompanied by pyroclastic flows and ash deposits that can be traced as far east as central Washington.

Some 3,500 years ago, a series of explosive eruptions, accompanied by surges of pyroclastic flows and mudflows into the North Fork of the Toutle River, created a dam that formed the original Spirit Lake. Five hundred to 700 years later, smaller eruptions resulted in pyroclastic flows on all sides of the mountain, and a number of small dacite domes formed.

About 2,000 years ago, ejected materials shifted from dacite to andesite and basalt, and the more recent cones began to form. The Dogs Head dome emerged from the northeast side of the mountain; basalt flows on the south side of the mountain created the lava tube caves and dammed the Kalama River to create Merrill Lake.

Around 1,000 years ago, a lateral blast on the north side of the mountain dumped lava boulders and thick ash deposits north and east of the peak, and two new domes formed, Sugar Bowl on the northeast side of the mountain, and East Dome on the east side.

The once-familiar symmetrical cone was built 300 to 500 years ago in a series of andesite and pyroclastic flows on the west, north, and south sides of the mountain. The most recent eruptions (prior to

1980) were in the Goat Rocks, where a dome formed and lava flowed down both the northeast and south sides of the mountain.

May 1980 marked the cataclysmic event that created the current Mount St. Helens. Two summit fumeroles formed and merged, and the north side of the mountain took on an ominous bulge. A magnitude 5.1 earthquake triggered the total collapse of the north flank, and 0.65 cubic mile of debris surged from the north face at speeds greater than 200 miles per hour, blocked the mouth of Spirit Lake, and drove over intervening ridges at the headwaters of the North Fork of the Toutle. The collapse of the north side of the mountain released pressure on the underlying magma tubes. A huge lateral blast cloud of hot gases and pulverized mountain fragments raced north at speeds to 250 miles per hour and temperatures up to 680 degrees, leveling and destroying everything in its path. A column of powdered ash rose more than 15 miles high, floated east with prevailing winds, and blanketed eastern Washington, Idaho, Montana, and southern British Columbia. Rapid melting of snow and ice, as well as water squeezed from the debris avalanche, caused mud to race down Smith and Pine Creeks, the Muddy River, and the North and South Forks of the Toutle River, in hot flows as much as 12 feet above normal river levels. Hot pyroclastic flows followed, depositing lava blocks and pumice on top of debris and mudflows.

The lava dome inside of the crater has since had several eruptive cycles and grown to its present size of 2,700 feet wide and 876 feet high. In view of the history of St. Helens, the present quiescent state of the mountain is certain to give way to similar violent episodes at some time in the next few centuries.

## HISTORY

Indians lived in the vicinity of Mount St. Helens since prehistoric times; at the time the first Euro-Americans arrived, the Klickitats and Cowlitz, along with a half-dozen other minor tribes, inhabited the area.

The mountain was initially seen by Europeans when it was named by Captain George Vancouver during his northwest coastal surveys between 1792 and 1794. The first overland explorers to note the mountain were the Lewis and Clark Corps of Discovery, who visited the area in 1805–06. White settlers were introduced to the violent nature of St. Helens during an eruptive cycle between 1842 and 1853. There were eyewitness reports of steam plumes rising from the summit, lava flowing from a crater on the south side of the mountain, a new smoking crater on its northwest flank, and sporadic heavy ashfall. By 1860 the mountain had entered a temporary dormant period.

Homesteaders, loggers, and miners soon probed the mountain's flanks; the community of Toutle was established in 1876, and a trading post was opened near Spirit Lake in 1876. A logging railroad was extended into the North Fork of the Toutle in 1895, and two years later major logging also began in the South Fork. Miners arrived in 1891, and shortly thereafter claims were staked near Spirit Lake and in the Green River Valley. In 1901, the county completed a wagon road into Spirit Lake to support mining efforts, but mineral wealth proved illusory, and most mines folded by 1911.

*Slopes on Mount Margaret, once covered by ash, now hold dense fields of lupine and other wildflowers, with a few shattered tree stumps. Mount Adams is in the distance.*

St. Helens was included in the Rainier forest reserve in the 1890s, and became a part of the Columbia National Forest in 1908. A ranger station was established at Spirit Lake in 1913, and a fire lookout was built on the summit of the mountain between 1918 and 1921. Although the lookout was abandoned in 1929, lumber fragments from the building were still visible on the site in the late 1970s. Most of the area's trails not destroyed in the 1980 eruption were built by the CCC in the 1930s.

## ACTIVITIES
Day-use passes with a per person charge are required to visit the Silver Lake and Coldwater Ridge Visitor Center, Johnston Ridge Observatory, and Ape Cave.

## HIKING
### Highway 504 Trails
**Trail 211, Lakes.** *12 miles/m (H).* The route leaves the boat launch area at the southwest end of Coldwater Lake (2,490 ft), or from an alternate path (Trail 211D) at the Coldwater Ridge Visitor Center, and follows the northwest shore past fishing spurs.

Above is a blast-bared, 1,400-foot-high wall. After wandering along the flat valley bottom above the lake, the way climbs into the narrowing drainage of Coldwater Creek, where it meets Trail 230 (2,880 ft). A new trail extension continues upstream into the tightening canyon, then switchbacks north up a lateral drainage to Snow Lake (4,700 ft). It climbs the basin headwall above the lake and follows the ridge crest east to a junction with Trail 214. Continuing eastward, the path descends a ridge finger to Shovel Lake (4,700 ft), then traverses the steep sidehill above Panhandle Lake before crossing a low saddle and dropping to Obscurity Lake (4,350 ft). The route then contours to the south around the head of the Grizzly Creek drainage, crosses below Grizzly Lake, and climbs a spur ridge to join Trail 1 at Bear Pass (4,940 ft).

**Trail 230, Coldwater.** *4.5 miles/m (H).* A strenuous grind leaves Trail 211 (2,880 ft) and weaves uphill, following onetime roads past destroyed logging equipment. It snakes through ridge-top notches to join Trail 1 (5,050 ft) above St. Helens Lake.

## Northern Monument, Tumwater, and Strawberry Trails

**Trail 213, Green River.** *7.5 miles/m (H,S,B).* In sharp contrast to the devastation in most areas north of St. Helens, the Green River Valley was protected from the eruption (and, equally astonishing, from encroaching chain saws). From FR 2612-036 (2,640 ft), negotiate 0.5 mile of blast-leveled timber, then enter huge old-growth Douglas-fir as the way traces the deep, steep-walled river course downstream. The path, originally blazed to access mining claims, passes the Minnie Lee Mine, then at 5 miles meets the lower end of Trail 213A. In slightly more than a mile the way reaches the monument boundary and ends on a private logging road (1,879 ft). An eastward extension of the trail parallels FR 2612, passes through the Green River Horse Camp, rounds Ryan Lake, and a mile or so farther joins Trail 220.

**Trail 213A, Vanson Ridge.** *3.3 miles/m (H,S,B).* This link between Trails 213 (2,330 ft) and 217 (4,110 ft) heads east through deep forest, wiggles uphill to the base of wooded cliffs, then sweeps northwest in a bold diagonal climb of the face. On reaching the bench above (3,400 ft), it winds uphill in a more leisurely fashion to join Trail 217 west of Vanson Peak.

**Trail 217, Goat Mountain.** *8.6 miles/m (H,S,B).* After leaving FR 2600-130 (3,320 ft), a rugged switchback chain gains the ridge top (5,000 ft), where the way breaks out of timber to rock and pumice studded with patches of wildflowers and huckleberry bushes. The next 2 miles of open crest have horizon views of Rainier and St. Helens complemented by vistas below of both blowdown and lush old-growth forest. The route drops off the ridge top to a saddle junction with Trail 218 (4,400 ft), where one short spur drops east to Deep Lake (3,986 ft), and a second (Trail 217D) descends southwest to the shore of Deadmans Lake (4,352 ft). Surrounding woods survived the 1980 blast, but the bottom of this clear, shallow lake is coated with a heavy cover of pumice from the eruption.

Trail 217 continues northwest, regains the crest, follows it a way, then descends to a saddle to meet Trail 205 and the southeast end of Trail 217A (4,700 ft), a loop trail to the old lookout site atop Vanson Peak (4,948 ft). The route drops into a wooded basin to join Trail 213A and a brief path (Trail 217B) to Vanson Lake (4,190 ft), tucked in a forested bowl on the southwest side of Vanson Peak. A short distance farther is the other end of Trail 217A, and beyond that the monument boundary, well defined by private logging clearcuts. The trail ends on Weyerhaueser Road 2600, which may or may not be open to public access.

**Trail 218, Tumwater.** *9 miles/m-d (H,S,B).* The route leaves Trail 217 (4,400 ft) near Deadmans Lake to follow a wildflower-decked ridge crest, first east, then north along the monument boundary. The grade is gentle, with easy ups and downs over ridge-top knobs. At 5 miles a spur scrambles up a narrow ridge to the rocky summit of Tumwater Mountain (5,250 ft) and great panoramic views. The way drops west into a pocket meadow where elk are often seen. It then swings north around a finger rib, diagonals down its cliffy west face, then switchbacks down to reach Goat Creek. A short distance downstream it joins Trail 205 (2,560 ft).

**Trail 205, Goat Creek.** *6 miles/m (H,S,B).* From the end of FR 2750 (2,400 ft), the route traverses the steep, forested hillside to Leona Falls. Here it ducks into a 300-foot-long hollow behind the 100-foot-high falls. Another mile upstream the way meets Trail 218, then bends up the west fork of Goat Creek and climbs steeply to a pocket meadow near its source. It weaves westward up a ridge through another meadow, and across the south face of Vanson Peak to the saddle, where it joins Trail 217 (4,700 ft).

**Trail 220, Strawberry Mountain.** *10.7 miles/m (H,S,B).* From Trail 1 (4,400 ft) east of Ghost Lake, this old miners' trail climbs northward along the ridge top, passes a spur to a onetime lookout site, then descends to cross FR 2516 (4,834 ft). From here, it gradually ascends northward along the crest at the fringe of the St. Helens blast zone to pass below the summit of Strawberry Mountain (5,521 ft). The way then skirts along the west side of the ridge and begins a long, gradual, forested descent to end on FR 2600-045 (2,700 ft).

## Eastside Trails

**Trail 1, Boundary.** *20.2 miles/m (H,B).* The western segment of this 70-mile-long east–west trail is picked up on FR 99 (4,100 ft) west of Bear Meadow. It climbs west, passes the south end of Trail 220, continues through dense forest, then contours a creek-head basin. Bending around a ridge, the way enters the monument and descends to Clearwater Creek (3,700 ft), where clumps of surviving trees are intermixed with blast-downed forest. Trail 1B wends upstream through blast-flattened trees and clumps of smaller conifers to Ghost Lake (3,785 ft), where downed trees along the shoreline support its name. Trail 1 ascends west to a saddle, then drops through flattened forest to cross FR 26 (3,680 ft). The route weaves up westward, passes the north end of Trail 227A, then continues through blowdown to Norway Pass (4,500 ft) to meet Trail 227 and a spectacular view of the crater and lava dome glaring down on Spirit Lake.

After swinging north to Bear Pass (5,600 ft) and a junction with Trail 211, the way snakes along the bare, convoluted ridge west to Mount Margaret (5,858 ft), where a short spur gains the summit for great views of St. Helens and Spirit Lake. The bald crest is followed west of Margaret and around the west side of the St. Helens Lake basin to Trail 1G, a steep switchback path to the former lookout site atop Coldwater Peak (5,730 ft). Here are impressive views of the crater, the lava dome, St. Helens Lake, Johnson Ridge, and the Coldwater Creek basin.

After passing Trail 230 the way ducks under a natural arch framing Adams in one direction and St. Helens in the other. The short spur of Harrys Ridge Trail 208 leaves to the south for bird's-eye views of the crater and Spirit Lake. A contour of the headwaters of Coldwater Creek then passes Trail 207. The way heads west to the Johnston Ridge Observatory, en route crossing the fractured, barren landscape of the debris avalanche that overrode the ridge. From the first road switchback west of the observatory, the path descends west to the debris and lahar plain south of Coldwater Lake (2,580 ft).

**Trail 227, Independence Pass.** *3.5 miles/m (H).* From Independence Pass on FR 99 (4,030 ft), the way climbs past a junction with Trail 227A, an interesting loop trail option that skirts the head of the Bean Creek drainage and links Trail 227 to Trail 1 between Norway Pass and the Norway Pass trailhead. Trail 227 then climbs to a grand viewpoint of St. Helens and Spirit Lake. It continues uphill through blowdown, then bends west to the barren slopes 1,000 feet above the lake, where it heads north toward Norway Pass. En route it passes basalt monoliths, once hidden by forest, now exposed rock-climbing challenges. The route ends on Trail 1 at Norway Pass (4,500 ft).

**Trail 224, Harmony.** *1 mile/m (H).* This is the only access to the shoreline of Spirit Lake. It drops from FR 99 (4,100 ft) to the lake (3,406 ft), passing through blowdown and bleached, blast-sanded stumps. Note the scoured high-water mark formed as waves surged up the shoreline following the eruption, and the mat of dead trees still floating on the lake's surface.

**Trail 207, Truman.** *6.5 miles/m (H).* From the Windy Ridge Viewpoint parking lot (4,040 ft), the route begins on a gated 4WD road used by researchers to access the Pumice Plain below the crater. From the road end (4,550 ft), the way, marked by wooden posts, passes the Willow Spring Trail 207A shortcut to Trail 216, and heads north across a desolate, multilayered product of the 1980 eruption. Buried deepest are portions of the massive debris avalanche that obliterated part of old Spirit Lake and created a huge dam at the outlet of new Spirit Lake. Overlaying this debris are pyroclastic flows and mudflows whose heat sterilized the Pumice Plain. The route wanders across this bleak area, then climbs a portion of the debris avalanche that overrode Johnston Ridge to end on Trail 1 (4,010 ft).

## Southeast Trails

**Trail 225, Smith Creek.** *9 miles/m (H,B).* Starting on FR 99 (4,320 ft) 1.5 miles north of the Windy Ridge Viewpoint, the route follows a twisting, bald, pumice-covered ridge down to the headwater canyon of Smith Creek. It continues atop the broad mudflow that surged down the creek, leveling everything in its path. Near the halfway point the creek, 3 to 4 feet deep, must be forded. The trail leaves the blast area near the creek dropping from Ape Canyon, then continues, marked by wooden posts, atop the broad mudflow along the stream course. The way ends on FR 8322 (1,680 ft) near the confluence of Smith Creek and the Muddy River, as it meets Trail 184.

**Trail 234, Ape Canyon.** *5.5 miles/m (H,B).* From the end of FR 83 (2,860 ft), the route climbs northwest through old-growth forest as it snakes along a ridge on the northeast side of the Muddy River lahar. It occasionally breaks from the trees for glimpses of this broad mudflow plain. At 4,150 feet the trail reaches the deep, narrow defile of Ape Canyon, sliced through 3,600 years of lava flows by the grainy, rasping water. A short distance farther it ends on Trail 216.

**Trail 184, Lava Canyon.** *3 miles/e-d (H).* From a geological point of view this is one of the most interesting trails in the monument. The 1980 mudflows scoured all vegetation from the walls of this narrow canyon, exposing lava flows depicting nearly 2,000 years of the mountain's eruptive history. From the end of FR 83 (2,860 ft), a barrier-free boardwalk leads to the top of a beautiful waterfall. The trail loop beyond becomes more challenging, and includes a shaky-kneed suspension bridge over the top of a high waterfall. The route below the bridge gets a bit dicey, with a steep un-protected sidehill, wet slippery areas, and ladders on short cliff faces. A short side jaunt climbs a ladder to a razor-thin pinnacle overlooking falls and river. The trip is worth it, as it passes more falls and huge columns of basalt that were hard enough to resist the savage carving of the mudflow. The trail ends as it meets Trail 225 and crosses a bridge over the Muddy River to meet FR 8322 (1,680 ft) at its confluence with Smith Creek.

## Southwest Trails

**Trail 238, Toutle.** *13.6 miles/m (H,S,B).* The lower end of this route leaves FR 8100 at Kalama Horse Camp (2,030 ft) and follows the north bank of the Kalama River in a gradual ascent east to FR 8100-600 (2,670 ft). After passing McBride Lake (2,677 ft) the route climbs to a wooded side slope traverse to Redrock Pass (3,100 ft), where it crosses FR 8100. The way ascends north across an open lava flow into trees to reach the lower end of Trail 238A. The path gradually ascends along the base of Butte Camp Dome, then swings west across a mudflow to reach FR 8123 (3,213 ft).

The trail continues due north along wooded slopes above Blue Lake (3,346 ft), then enters one of the largest stands of old-growth noble fir in the Cascades. It descends into Sheep Canyon to cross a creek, mudflow, and Trail 240 in the drainage bottom. The track climbs out of the canyon, bends around a minor rib, and drops steeply to the barren drainage of the South Fork of the Toutle to end on Trail 216 (3,300 ft).

**Trail 238A, Butte Camp.** *2.7 miles/m (H,B).* The second most popular climbing route on St. Helens leaves Trail 238 (3,300 ft) and heads north up a steep, wooded slope. The path twists up around the east base of the Butte Camp Dome to a pocket wildflower meadow at Lower Butte Camp, then zigzags up a steep lava wall, and ends on Trail 216 (4,720 ft) with a sweeping view of the rock and snow slopes leading up to the crater's rim. Climbing permits are required to travel higher.

**Trail 240, Sheep Canyon.** *2.2 miles/m (H,B).* From the end of FR 8123 (3,420 ft), the route passes through an overgrown clearcut, then follows Sheep Creek uphill to views of the ribbon of a 75-foot-high waterfall below its junction with Trail 238. Crossing the latter, the way continues ceaselessly uphill along the edge of a drainage

*Hikers rest on the lip of Mount St. Helen's crater. Mount Adams is in the distance.*

scraped bare by mudflows accompanying the 1980 eruption. The path ends at its junction with Trail 216 (4,780 ft)

**Trail 221, Castle Lake.** *3.2 miles/m (H).* A maze of private logging roads leads to other trail accesses, but the only route to Castle Lake through the monument leaves Trail 216G and heads north along the line between a barren ridge and the mudflow that filled the North Fork of the Toutle. The route follows this demarcation line northeast to the mouth of Castle Lake (2,510 ft), formed when the debris avalanche dammed the South Fork of Castle Creek.

## Round-the-Mountain Trail

**Trail 216, Loowit.** *27 miles/m-d (H; B on the south side of the mountain between Windy Pass and South Fork Toutle).* This rugged trail, bearing the Indian name for Mount St. Helens, wraps around the mountain between the 4,000- and 4,700-foot levels. Starting from the northeast corner of the crater, at the end of access Trail 216E (3,960 ft), the route contours the rugged jumble of the pyroclastic flow and debris avalanche to a spur trail up to hot-water Loowit Falls tumbling from the yawning mouth of the blown-away crater. Farther west the trail becomes very difficult, often washed out, as it weaves through rough moonscape gullies below the open gap in the crater wall, passing Trail 207A. When it reaches the precipitous rim of the South Fork of the Toutle, Trail 216G breaks off to the west, and the main route snakes down to the river bottom to meet Trail 238 (3,300 ft).

The route ascends tight switchbacks east up Crescent Ridge along the fringe of the blast zone, then crosses a mudflow to meet the upper end of Trail 240 (4,600 ft). It then snakes southeast at timberline to Butte Camp Dome, where it passes Trail 238A (4,750 ft). A timberline traverse, difficult because of numerous stream-cut gullies, continues across old lava flows. Trail 216A (4,700 ft) is met after crossing the Swift Creek lava flow. The way now follows the treeline downhill, scrambling in and out of stream-washed gullies with poor tread. At the wall above June Lake, Trail 216B is joined (3,400 ft).

Lost altitude is regained in a very difficult ascent across the Worm Flows and the deep, unstable gashes cut by the headwater forks of Pine Creek and the Muddy River. After negotiating the upper edge of the Muddy River mudflow, the route joins Trail 234 (4,180 ft) near the Ape Canyon overlook. Scenery here is outstanding; Adams and Hood are on the horizon, and above is the breach in the crater wall at the head of the Shoestring Glacier. Below is the broad Muddy River lahar and the narrow cleft carved through old basalt by Ape Canyon Creek.

The grade becomes easier; after fording Ape Canyon Creek the track is nearly flat as it crosses the Plains of Abraham (4,400 ft), swept and leveled by eruption mud-flows. After passing Trail 216D at the north end of the Plains, the path turns west and climbs abruptly to Windy Pass (4,850 ft). A gradual downhill grade completes the circuit at the junction with Trail 216E.

**Trail 216A, Ptarmigan.** *2.1 miles/d (H).* Part of the most-used climbing route on the south side of the mountain, this trail leaves FR 8100-830 (3,720 ft) in noble fir forest and climbs, gradually at first, then more steeply, to break out on the Swift Creek lava flow as it meets Trail 216 (4,700 ft).

**Trail 216B, June Lake.** *1.4 miles/m (H).* A popular trail, both in summer and winter, leaves the end of FR 8300-250 (2,700 ft) and gradually ascends through second-growth forest to the walled pocket holding tiny June Lake (3,150 ft). A beautiful waterfall cascades over cliff walls into the northeast end of the lake. A mean pair of switchbacks climb to join Trail 216 (3,400 ft) on a bench above the lake.

**Trail 216D, Abraham.** *2 miles/m (H,B).* This route heads south from Trail 207 at the end of the gated road section of that trail (4,100 ft). It follows a narrow, eroded pumice ridge south to 4,600 feet, then traverses the headwater basin of Smith Creek to meet Trail 216 at the north end of the Plains of Abraham (4,430 ft).

## CAVING

There are at least sixty known caves, all lava tubes, located in the long basalt flow on the south side of Mount St. Helens. Many of these caves have unique, delicate geological features, as well as a varied collection of vegetation, mammals, insects, and invertebrates, many of which are rare and vulnerable species. Casual cave visitors can severely damage this precarious environment by carelessness, ignorance, or vandalism, and the caves' geological features are not likely to be reproduced short of another major basalt flow like the one that created these. Even then, if ever, centuries would pass before the diversity of biota would be replicated. By their very nature caves force even the most careful explorers to trace the same routes, and each visit further disturbs surface features. For this reason, only one of these caves, Ape Cave, is open to monument visitors. The locations of other caves, and paths to their entrances, are not publicized; experienced cavers should contact local speleological groups for more information regarding them.

Ape Cave is the third longest known lava cave on the North American continent: 12,810 feet. It was first discovered in 1947, and mapped in detail in 1978. During

*The famed Ape Cave of the Mount St. Helens area is an ancient lava tube.*

summer months the Forest Service operates "Ape Headquarters" on FR 8303, near the main entrance. The cave has had no artificial development except metal staircases at the main and upper entrances. When visiting the cave, visitors must bring their own lanterns, or rent some at the information center. The cave extends 4,000 feet downslope from the main entrance and 8,000 feet upslope. The upper end of the cave has a stairway exiting a skylight entrance; Trail 239 leads from there back to the information center. Portions of the upper cave are rough going due to breakdowns in the basalt, and there are dropoffs up to 8 feet that must be climbed. The downslope portion of the cave has a sand floor, and is the easiest section for most visitors.

## CLIMBING

The south side of Mount St. Helens was reopened to climbing in 1987; however, permits are required between May 15 and October 31 to climb above 4,800 feet on the mountain. A fee is charged for the permit, and reservation applications are accepted at the monument headquarters. A limited number of unreserved permits are available daily at Jacks Restaurant and Store on Highway 503, 28 miles east of Woodland. The permit system restricts climbing parties to 100 people per day to help preserve the fragile alpine vegetation. There are no quotas or permit charges between November 1 and March 31.

The mountain is no longer a technical climb, just a long, dusty, 6-hour uphill slog once the snow has melted off. The view from the rim down to the crater and the lava dome is impressive, and worth the effort, but use extreme caution near the lip, as it is still unstable. There are three commonly used approaches for climbing the mountain: the Butte Camp route, via Trails 238 and 238A; the Monitor Ridge route, via Trail 216A; and the Worm Flows route, via either Trail 244 or 216B. The latter is primarily used in the winter.

## WINTER SPORTS

The popular winter recreation area at Spirit Lake disappeared in the 1980 eruption, but it has been replaced by new recreation areas on the south side of the mountain. Two Sno-Parks are located here: Cougar, at the junction of FR 81 and FR 83, and Marble Mountain, at the junction of FR 83 and FR 8312. The latter has a log cabin warming hut, and both have several groomed snowmobile routes. Since the area is popular with both snowmobilers and cross-country skiers, the Forest Service provides separate trails strictly for skiers. Shared trails are marked by orange diamonds, skier-only trails by blue diamonds.

Although a number of winter trails simply follow summer roads, others have been constructed primarily for winter use. The Wapiti Ski Loops, near Marble Mountain, are five trails of varied length, all flat and relatively easy. More difficult are the Sasquatch Ski Loops, three loop trails totaling 6.7 miles, that climb higher on the mountain. The June Lake and Swift trails climb to timberline following summer Trails 244 and 216B. All of the Cougar routes trace snowbound roads, some as long as a 15-mile round trip. There are several excellent views of snow-mantled St. Helens en route.

# 36 Mount Adams

### Mount Adams Wilderness; South Midway, West Adams, and Gotchen Creek Roadless Areas

**Location:** In Yakima and Skamania Counties, surrounding Mount Adams
**Size:** Wilderness, 42,280 acres; South Midway, 2,300 acres; Horseshoe, 7,600 acres; West Adams, 2,300 acres; Gotchen Creek, 7,500 acres
**Status:** Designated Wilderness (1964, 1984); Horseshoe is Semiprimitive Motorized and Roaded Natural; South Midway and West Adams are Semiprimitive Nonmotorized; Gotchen Creek is Unroaded Recreation
**Terrain:** Rising above forested slopes and subalpine meadows is the massive volcanic peak of Mount Adams, with steep rock faces and several large glaciers radiating from the summit.
**Elevation:** 3,300 to 12,276 feet
**Management:** USFS, Gifford Pinchot National Forest, Mount Adams Ranger District; Yakama Indian Nation
**Topographic maps:** Glaciate Butte, Green Mountain, Jungle Butte, King Mountain, Mount Adams East, Mount Adams West, Steamboat Mountain, Trout Lake

The second-highest and the most massive of the Cascade volcanoes in the state, Mount Adams, is the focal point and namesake of the wilderness. Forested slopes climb gradually to a timberline level of about 6,600 feet, above which ten major glaciers cloak the

*Campsites at Glacier Meadows, in the Mount Adams Wilderness, have views of distant Mount Rainier.*

mountain to its 12,276-foot summit. The low gradient of the mountain's south side contrasts with the steep icefalls and arêtes on the west side, and the sheer cliffs, precipitous hanging ice, and deep rugged valleys on the east. Most of the wilderness's 64 miles of trails lie at or below timberline. Three link to encircle three-fourths of the base of the mountain; the rest serve primarily as feeder routes to these three. The east side of the mountain, which lies in the Yakama Indian Nation, has no path along its base, and the few short trails in Tract D of the reservation are open only on a permit basis.

Presently there are four semiprimitive roadless areas on the periphery of the wilderness, all deserving equal protection. South Midway is a wedge of meadow and forest at the north edge of the wilderness; Horseshoe is a forested area with several lakes, marshes, and meadows on the northwest corner of the wilderness; West Adams is a thin strip of woodland along the west boundary; Gotchen Creek, on the south side of the mountain west of the Tract D boundary, is a timbered section that includes the geologically and botanically important A. G. Aiken Lava Bed, one of the most recent and accessible lava extrusions on the mountain.

## CLIMATE

Average annual precipitation in the area ranges from 90 to 100 inches, almost all of which falls between September and May, mainly in the form of snow. The annual snowfall ranges between 10 and 25 feet, dependent on elevation. Midwinter lows average between 10 and 20 degrees, and summer highs are a mild 70 to 80 degrees.

## ECOSYSTEM

Mount Adams's diversity of trees, shrubs, and flowers represents both the wet west side and the dry east side of the Cascades; its wide elevation range also spans several ecological zones. On lower slopes the forest is made up of Pacific silver fir, western hemlock, noble fir, Douglas-fir, western red cedar, and western white pine, with less frequent occurrences of grand fir, Engelmann spruce, and lodgepole pine. The understory is composed of huckleberry, salal, prince's pine, rhododendron, queencup beadlily, dwarf blackberry, and twinflower. Higher up the slopes, whitebark pine, mountain hemlock, and subalpine fir are more common, with a groundcover of huckleberry and beargrass. Wet meadows and bogs in subalpine regions host a variety of unique species such as water sedge, bog willow, tall cotton grass, pale laurel, horsetail, elephant's head pedicularis, western tofieldia, and Oregon saxifrage. Among the flowers found in alpine meadows are avalanche lily, white marsh marigold, monkeyflower, Indian paintbrush, gentian, phlox, lupine, mountain red heather, cinquefoil, and penstemon. The harsh environment of lava flows supports rugged plant communities, mostly mosses and lichens.

Common animal species are black-tailed deer, elk, and coyote. Less frequently seen are black bear, pine marten, and mountain goat. At higher elevations, pika and hoary marmot abound. Among the avian population are blue, ruffed, and spruce grouse, white-tailed ptarmigan, mountain chickadee, Clark's nutcracker, prairie falcon, red-tailed hawk, gray jay, golden-crowned kinglet, and gray-crowned rosy finch.

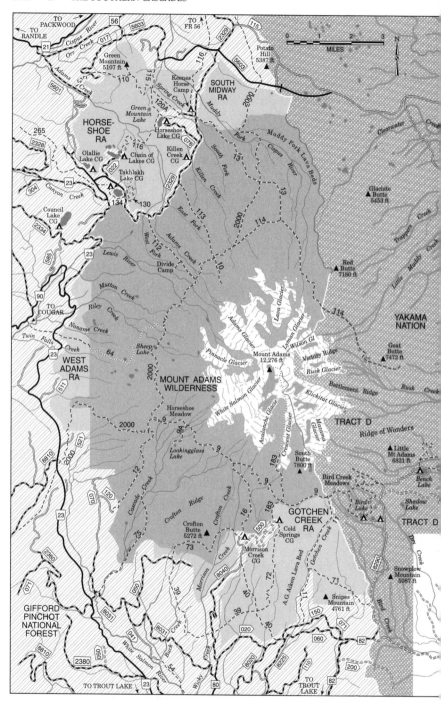

## GEOLOGY

The broad summit of Mount Adams was built from the eruptions from several cones over a wide span of time, rather than through a series of peak-building eruptions forming a single cone, as is common in other Cascade volcanoes. Its lower slopes are pocked with eroded cones and lava flows from numerous other minor eruptive vents. Underlying most of the Mount Adams area is 10-million- to 15-million-year-old Yakima basalt. The earliest eruptions in the immediate vicinity occurred in Pleistocene times, about 450,000 years ago, when andesite flows created most of the mass of the present mountain. More recent additions to the south side of the mountain are a result of eruptions between 12,000 and 25,000 years ago. These occurred during the last advance of the continental ice sheets, which shaped and polished the ragged lava surface of the mountain. The most recent eruptions happened somewhere between 2,000 and 6,000 years ago. A vent near Red Butte extruded the blocky andesite that forms the 10.4-square-mile Muddy Fork flow, one of the largest lava fields in the Cascades. A similar eruption in the vicinity of South Butte also created the A. G. Aiken Lava Bed on the south side of the mountain.

The mountain continues to be sculpted by its active glaciers. Four of these, the White Salmon, Adams, Lyman, and Klickitat Glaciers, originate from the summit; the Mazama, Avalanche, Pinnacle, Lava, Wilson, and Rusk Glaciers all lie on lower slopes below steep rock headwalls. With the exception of the Rusk and Klickitat Glaciers, which have cut deep canyons on the east face of the peak, these lower glaciers are in broad, shallow cirques and fan out to low gradients near their snouts.

The combination of hydrogen sulfide and glacial meltwater, forming sulfuric acid, has weakened rock faces, causing huge avalanches to break off rocky headwalls. About 5,000 years ago one such avalanche peeled from the west side of the summit above the White Salmon Glacier to form the sheer face of The Pinnacle. More recent avalanches broke off the same area in 1921 and 1983. Other such avalanches have been noted near Devils Garden, Avalanche Valley, and Battlement Ridge, and in 1998 a major avalanche occurred near the terminus of the Mazama Glacier.

## HISTORY

There is evidence of Indian visitation to Mount Adams as long as 9,000 years ago. According to Yakama and Klickitat tribal legends, Pah-to (Mount Adams), one of five wives of the Sun, became jealous of other wives, Wahkshum and Plash-Plash (the Goat Rocks), because each day they were touched by the Sun before Pah-to. She fought with the other two wives and broke their heads off, leaving them the less significant summits of today.

The egotistical Pah-to then went south of the Columbia River and from there brought back all of the forest plants and animals to flourish on her slopes. Klah-Klahnee (Oregon's Three Sisters) convinced Wy-east (Mount Hood) to fight Pah-to;

*Heather meadows, bubbling brooks, and close-up views of Mount Adams are found at Adams Glacier Basin.*

in the ensuing battle Pah-to's head was knocked off and scattered to the north (today's Muddy Fork Lava Beds); all of the animals and plants returned south, and the slopes of Pah-to became barren. Since the Great Maker knew that people waiting to be born near Pah-to would need plants and animals to survive, he gave her a new head, the Great White Eagle from the Land Above, who caused her slopes to once again be fruitful and populated with game. The mountain is considered sacred by local Indian tribes.

The 1792 Vancouver expedition to Puget Sound failed to notice the mountain, perhaps because of its more easterly location. The first explorers to note seeing it were the Lewis and Clark expedition in 1805, although observations at the time often confused it with Mount St. Helens. An 1839 proposal to call the Cascades the Presidents Range and name its summits after past presidents, recommended renaming Hood and St. Helens as Adams and Jefferson. Amid confusion in surveys, the name Mount Adams was given to the present peak (and, fortunately, the rest of the renaming scheme fell from favor).

The first verifiable ascent of the mountain took place in 1854, and the second (the first by women) occurred in 1867. In 1897 Mount Adams was included in the newly created Mount Rainier Forest Reserve, and its slopes were opened to grazing leases. As many as 100,000 sheep grazed on the mountain in the early 1900s; this use gradually tapered off until the last permit expired in the 1970s. Between 1918 and 1921 the Forest Service constructed a fire lookout atop the summit, but frequent poor visibility and the arduous supply route caused it to be abandoned as an active lookout in 1924.

A mining claim was filed on the broad summit in 1929, and sulphur mining began in 1932. A wagon road and pack trail route to support the mining operations saw as many as 168 pack trains a year during the height of operations. Today's South Spur climbing route follows this old path. Sporadic mining occurred here until 1959.

In 1908 the Columbia National Forest, which included Mount Adams, was cut from the Mount Rainier Forest Reserve; the forest was renamed for Gifford Pinchot in 1949. Mount Adams was initially designated as a wild area in 1942; when the 1964 Wilderness Act was signed, 36,356 acres around the mountain became one of its first units. When an old survey error defining the border with the Yakama Indian Reservation was corrected in 1972, 1,000 acres of the wilderness were returned to the tribe, who manage it as a primitive area. The Washington Wilderness Act of 1984 added 6,914 acres along the north and west borders to the wilderness, bringing it to its present size.

## HIKING

The east side of Mount Adams, including Tract D along the southeast side of the wilderness, lies in the Yakama Indian Nation. Permits are required to use trails and campgrounds and to fish within Tract D; the rest of the reservation is closed to the public. Fees are charged for such use; the amount varies with the duration of the stay. During summer months permits may be obtained from the Tract D ranger stationed at Bird Lake.

### Southside Trails

**Trail 9, Around the Mountain.** 8.3 miles/m (H,S). Somewhat misnamed, this trail does not go "around the mountain," but only skirts its south flank. Starting on the west from the Pacific Crest National Scenic Trail (PCT) at Horseshoe Meadow (5,900 ft), the route meanders southeast through subalpine forest and intermittent wildflower-splashed meadows just below timberline. The path rolls up and down, passes Trail 9A to Lookingglass Lake and Trail 16 at the head of Crofton Creek (6,160 ft), and crosses Trail 183 at the head of Hole in the Ground Creek (6,280 ft). After crossing the upper edge of the A. G. Aiken Lava Bed (6,250 ft), the way meets Trail 11 at the Tract D boundary, then continues to Bird Creek Meadow (6,100 ft).

**Trail 11, Snipes Mountain.** 5.7 miles/m (H,S; B to the junction with Trail 71). From its start on FR 8225-150 (3,800 ft), the trail climbs through open pine forest along the east side of the A. G. Aiken Lava Bed. At 4,800 feet the path meets the west end of Trail 71, then veers away from the lava beds to follow Gotchen Creek northeast to the Tract D boundary, where it meets Trail 9 (6,290 ft) at the wilderness boundary.

**Trail 71, Pine Way.** 2.7 miles/m (H,S,B). This old cattle drive leaves FR 8290 at the Tract D boundary (4,270 ft) to climb northwest along a rocky path through second-growth timber before reaching Trail 11 at the edge of the A. G. Aiken Lava Bed (4,800 ft). Bikes are not permitted on Trail 11 above this junction.

**Trail 183, South Climb.** *3.4 miles/m (H,S)*. Once part of the old trail used by pack strings serving the sulfur mines at the summit of Mount Adams, this trail today is the most popular and heavily used route for summit climbs. Starting at Cold Springs Campground (5,600 ft), the route heads uphill, crosses Trail 9 (6,380 ft), then climbs the rib west of the Crescent Glacier to 8,200 feet. Here the maintained trail ends, and a footpath continues up to the Lunch Counter (9,000 ft). Above this point the climbing route follows névé slopes to the false summit (11,500 ft), and then on to the true summit (12,276 ft).

**Trail 12, Stagman Ridge.** *4.1 miles/d (H,S)*. From a clearcut at the end of FR 8031-120 (4,400 ft), the way enters the wilderness and old-growth forest as it proceeds up the crest of Stagman Ridge. To the southeast cliffs drop abruptly nearly 1,000 feet to Cascade Creek. In 1.5 miles the path swings west from the drainage wall to broader slopes with open timber broken by small meadows. The trail jogs west, then climbs a short distance to join the PCT (5,800 ft) west of Horseshoe Meadow.

## Northside Trails

**Trail 112, Divide Camp.** *2.8 miles/m (H,S)*. This route starts on FR 2329 (4,720 ft) southeast of Takhlakh Lake, then climbs gradually southeast up forested slopes interspersed with small meadows. At 5,678 feet a spur leads southwest to Divide Camp on the West Fork of Adams Creek. The main trail ascends another 0.8 mile to meadows to meet the PCT (6,020 ft).

**Trail 113, Killen Creek.** *3.1 miles/m (H,S)*. From FR 2329 (4,584 ft) south of Killen Creek Campground, this old sheep route ascends south–southeast through timber and small meadows. It breaks into a meadow with a wildflower carpet as it meets the PCT (6,084 ft).

**Trail 13, Muddy Meadows.** *4 miles/m (H,S)*. From the end of FR 2329-087 (4,410 ft), the route slogs through Muddy Meadows, with glimpses of the north side of Adams soon wiped out by dense old-growth forest. The way now heads seriously uphill over rough, rocky footing through open timber to cross the PCT (5,231 ft). An easy grade heads east, then swings south as it ascends a wooded wash to end on Trail 114 (5,860 ft).

**Trail 114, Highline.** *7 miles (5.3 miles to the Yakama Nation boundary)/d (H,S)*. From the PCT at the head of Killen Creek (5,900 ft), this route heads east on a roller-coaster course across forested slopes on the north side of Mount Adams. After passing the upper end of Trail 13, it ascends to a pleasant little meadow at Foggy Flat (6,000 ft). The way swings south and gets down to serious climbing as it scrambles up through the jumble of the terminal moraines of the Lava and Lyman Glaciers. The icefalls of these two glaciers tower above, and below are the huge Muddy Fork Lava Beds. The indistinct tread, marked by large rock cairns, continues up to top a barren, wind-swept ridge (7,750 ft) just below the Devils Garden (the Yakama Nation boundary, permits are required for travel beyond). Switchbacks drop down rock slopes, then the track skirts the lower end of the Wilson Glacier to reenter subalpine forest at a saddle (7,020 ft) between Mount Adams and Goat Butte. The path weaves through open timber and meadows as it descends into Avalanche Valley and a pleasant campsite (6,600 ft) at a tarn above Rusk Creek.

**Trail 116, High Lakes.** *7.7 miles/e-m (H,S,B; M west of Horseshoe Lake).* From Chain of Lakes Campground at the end of FR 2329-022 (4,400 ft), this path soon switchbacks down to cross an old lava flow and Adams Creek. The route then weaves uphill through open forest to Horseshoe Lake (4,140 ft). It rounds the north side of the lake, passes Trail 115, and meets Trail 120 from Keenes Horse Camp. From here, the near-level path heads north through wildflower meadows and sparse timber, crosses FR 5603, and ends at FR 2329-117 (4,320 ft).

**Trail 110, Green Mountain.** *5.9 miles/m (H,S,B,M).* Starting from Trail 115 (4,000 ft) north of Green Mountain Lake, the path switchbacks up to the ridge crest southeast from Green Mountain and continues uphill to the summit (5,107 ft) and great views of Adams, Rainier, and St. Helens. The route then drops down slopes to the west, crosses FR 5603-017 (4,450 ft), and zigzags down a steep face to FR 5601 (2,800 ft).

## Trail 2000, Pacific Crest National Scenic Trail. *20.8 miles/m (H,S).*

After crossing FR 23 (3,854 ft) east of Swampy Meadows, the PCT climbs north to the wilderness boundary. It then swings east for a gradual ascent through dense old-growth Douglas-fir to the headwaters of the White Salmon River. A recent relocation of the trail weaves uphill to meet the upper end of Trail 12 (5,800 ft). From there, the way passes Trail 9, contours north to Sheep Lake (5,768 ft), and a short distance farther meets vestiges of Trail 64. After a brief journey across a lava-bed moonscape at the head of Mutton Creek, the way bends northeast, crosses meadows and forks of the Lewis River, then meets the upper end of Trail 112 (6,020 ft). Crossing rocky slopes at Adams Creek, the way wends through open forest and meadows to meet Trails 113 and 10 (6,110 ft). The trek continues northeast past the west end of Trail 114 (5,910 ft) near a splattering of small ponds and marshes. The way now descends gradually north through thick forest to cross Trail 13 (5,231 ft), then weaves around the south and west sides of the Muddy Fork Lava Beds before descending to FR 5603 (4,750 ft) north of the wilderness boundary.

## CLIMBING

Mount Adams (12,276 ft), the second-highest peak in the state, is the only summit in the Mount Adams Wilderness. At least twenty-five routes have been put up this popular mountain, ranging in difficulty from nontechnical scrambles to very challenging ice and rock climbs. The 6,000-foot elevation gain from timberline to the summit, and the possibility of sudden storms, whiteouts, and below-zero wind-chill temperatures, require good physical conditioning, proper equipment, and navigation skills for a safe ascent, even on the easiest routes.

The easiest routes—Mazama Glacier, South Spur, Southwest Chute, and Avalanche–White Salmon Glacier—are on the long, mild-gradient south slope. Routes on the west and north sides of the mountain, up the Pinnacle, Adams, Lava, and Lyman Glaciers and intervening cleavers, are more difficult, and all are rated at G-II. They often involve heavily crevassed glacier segments, up to 1,000 feet of 40- to 50-degree ice, or narrow exposed ridges. The most challenging routes, ranging from G-II to G-III, are found on the remote east side of the mountain, where vertical headwalls tower above the steep, narrow cleavers dividing the long narrow icefalls of the Wilson, Rusk, and Klickitat Glaciers.

## WINTER SPORTS

Sno-Parks are maintained south of the wilderness (north of Trout Lake) at Pine Side and Smith Butte. Sixteen miles of groomed, signed ski trails follow snowbound logging roads from these two locations. The South Spur climbing route is a popular spring skiing or snowshoeing trek, but it may involve several miles of approach march, depending on how high the roads have melted out. The climb is crevasse-free, but it can be avalanche-prone and very hazardous in stormy weather or whiteout conditions. The summer route must be followed meticulously, and placing wands to mark a descent route is advisable.

## 37 Siouxon Creek Roadless Area

**Location:** In Clark and Skamania Counties, south of Yale Lake and the Swift Reservoir
**Size:** 26,800 acres
**Status:** Mostly Semiprimitive Nonmotorized and Semiprimitive Motorized; small portions are Roaded Natural and Roaded Modified
**Terrain:** A broad creek basin, includes low-elevation watercourses and high, forested bordering ridges.
**Elevation:** 600 to 4,169 feet
**Management:** USFS, Gifford Pinchot National Forest, Mount St. Helens National Volcanic Monument; Washington State Department of Natural Resources (DNR); some private logging company lands
**Topographic maps:** Bare Mountain, Cougar, Mount Mitchell, Siouxon Peak

The Siouxon Creek basin is a bastion of uncut forest land amid an otherwise heavily logged-off region. The multiple forks of the creek flow from high, bounding ridges down deep, quiet canyons covered with a canopy of second-growth trees, not replacements for logged generations but the rebuilding, of a forest destroyed by fires more than ninety years ago. The creek and its tributaries are famous for the numerous flashing waterfalls, plunge pools, and rippling cascades that mesmerize visitors along trails through the area. The Siouxon Creek trail has become a favorite of mountain bikers, who can enjoy its low elevation challenge nearly year-round.

*A frothing cascade drops into a pool on Siouxon Creek.*

## CLIMATE

The local climate varies with elevation, but in general the area receives between 90 and 100 inches of precipitation annually, 95 percent of which falls between September and May as snow. Annual snowfall varies between 8 and 20 feet depending on altitude. Temperatures are quite mild; winter lows average in the mid-20s, and summer maximums range in the upper 70s. Lower-elevation trails are generally usable from the end of May to the end of November; those on the ridge tops are open from July through October.

## ECOSYSTEM

Although the Siouxon Creek basin is mostly forested, its near-uniform tree cover is less than 100 years old. The Yacolt burn of 1902 denuded much of the old-growth forest, and the current forest is mostly second-growth Douglas-fir. Other significant timber species include western hemlock, western red cedar, and bigleaf maple. The understory brush is made up of vine maple, Pacific rhododendron, western yew, Oregon grape, salal, red huckleberry, and trailing blackberry. Vegetation here includes evergreen violet, twinflower, swordfern, sweetscented bedstraw, and cutleaf goldthread; berries and mushrooms are abundant.

The creek bottom is a winter range for elk and black-tailed deer, and black bear are also found in the vicinity. Much of the area surrounding Horseshoe Ridge has been identified as spotted owl habitat. The snags that remain standing from the Yacolt burn also provide homes for cavity-dwelling mammals and birds.

## GEOLOGY

The entire area is underlain by thick, multilayered volcanic flows of andesite breccia of the Ohanapecosh Formation. These range from 25 million to 50 million years in age. The surface soil is an eroded volcanic mix that tends to be unstable along Siouxon Creek. The highest summits in the basin have rock outcrops atop broad talus slopes.

## HISTORY

The higher ridgelines of Siouxon are rumored to contain prehistoric artifacts, indicating they were probably used by native tribes for berry and herb gathering for several thousand years. The large September 1902 forest fire that swept the region completely destroyed the forest cover, with the exception of isolated pockets of trees along the creek bottoms. When the Forest Service intensified its fire-prevention efforts in the 1930s, most of the present trails were put into the area, several by CCC crews. Hickmans

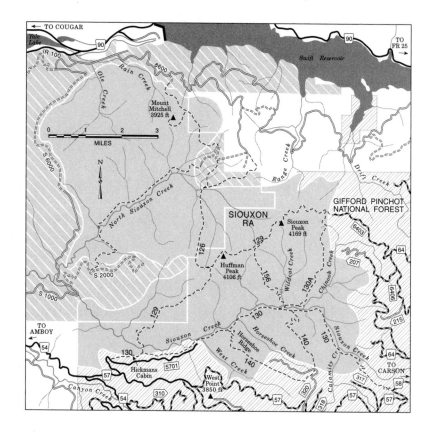

Cabin, alongside Trail 130, was built in the same period for use as a fire-crew base camp; it is one of the few standing artifacts of that era. Fire lookout sites were manned at times atop Horseshoe Ridge, Huffman Peak, and Mount Mitchell.

## HIKING

**Trail 130, Siouxon.** *12 miles/m (H,S,B).* The lower end of the trail can be accessed from two points on FR 5701. From the westernmost of the two (1,820 ft), the way gradually descends the forested slopes on the south side of Siouxon Creek, passes Hickmans Cabin and the lower end of Trail 129, then meets FR 5701 again at the road's end (1,360 ft), the second access point. The route crosses West Creek and passes near the first of several delightful cascades and waterfalls that enrich the trip upstream. In less than a mile the west end of Trail 140 is passed. Shortly, the way crosses Horseshoe Creek at yet another waterfall, then bends away from the creek to bypass a narrow, steep-walled section of the streambed. In another mile the route returns to water's edge to meet the east end of Trail 140 and the lower end of Trail 156. After passing the start of Trail 130A, the way crosses beneath a foaming falls on Chinook Creek (1,540 ft), then swings southwest up the ever-steepening walls of the Siouxon Creek canyon. It's all uphill from here, first in a long diagonal sweep up the east slope above the creek, then in rugged switchbacks to a bluff above the west drainage rim. More switchbacks surmount the final rib and reach FR 58 (3,500 ft).

**Trail 129, Huffman Peak.** *8.4 miles/m (H,S,B).* Just east of Hickmans Cabin, the route leaves Trail 130 (1,340 ft), zigzags down to a challenging wade of Siouxon Creek (1,190 ft), then starts a haul up the steep, forested sidehill to reach a saddle on the ridge top (2,000 ft). The cliff-rimmed crest is followed northeast for 2 miles to a talus slope below a rocky knob, then swings around the north side of Huffman Peak. The summit (4,106 ft) can be reached by a rock-and-meadow scramble. The track stays atop a narrow, wooded crest to the northeast, passes the upper end of Trail 156, and continues on to the summit of Siouxon Peak (4,169 ft), with great views of Rainier, St. Helens, and Hood, as well as Swift Reservoir and Mount Mitchell, to the north. North of the summit the track follows an abandoned logging road eastward for 1.5 miles to meet FR 6403 (2,868 ft).

**Trail 140, Horseshoe Ridge.** *6.9 miles/d (H,B).* At its west end the route leaves Trail 130 (1,290 ft) 1 mile from the end of FR 5701. Switchbacks work up through dense forest to the northwest end of Horseshoe Ridge (2,600 ft). The way continues east atop the narrow, steep-walled ridge, enjoying breaks of tiny meadows clad in beargrass and huckleberries. After reaching the ridge high point (3,495 ft) the path merges with FR 5700-320 for 0.1 mile at the toe of the horseshoe, then starts down its north web. After a long diagonal descent, a few switchbacks complete the drop back to Trail 130 (1,400 ft).

**Trail 130A, Chinook.** *3.8 miles/m (H,S,B).* The way leaves Trail 130 near the confluence of Chinook and Siouxon Creeks (1,600 ft) to climb steeply up the side of the Chinook Creek drainage, passing beautiful cascades en route. After following an abandoned logging road, it ends on FR 6403 (2,868 ft).

***Mount Mitchell Trail.*** *2.5 miles/d (H).* This route to an old lookout site hasn't been maintained, and may be in poor condition. The way starts from the 8600 road (2,100 ft) about 2 miles east of IR 100 at the east side of Yale Lake. The route climbs a very steep wooded ridge, then contours the head of a drainage to a saddle (2,950 ft) with outstanding displays of native rhododendrons in late spring. From the saddle the trail traverses cliffs to the south ridge of Mount Mitchell, then ascends this alpine rib to the summit lookout site (3,925 ft).

## WINTER SPORTS

The lower portions of Trail 130 can be reached in early winter or late spring for short periods of cross-country skiing. The snowy solitude of the valley floor makes a good 1-day tour with no avalanche danger.

# 38 Indian Heaven

## Indian Heaven Wilderness; Red Lake Roadless Area

**Location:** In Skamania County, between the White Salmon and Wind Rivers
**Size:** Wilderness, 20,960 acres; Red Lake, 2,700 acres
**Status:** Designated Wilderness Area (1984); Red Lake is Roaded Natural
**Terrain:** The region is a 4,500-foot-high bench with forest, open meadows, a wealth of ponds and small lakes, and several alpine ridges and volcanic cinder cones.
**Elevation:** 3,020 to 5,927 feet
**Management:** USFS Gifford Pinchot National Forest, Mount Adams Ranger District
**Topographic maps:** Gifford Peak, Lone Butte, Sleeping Beauty

Indian Heaven Wilderness, which in early summer could justly be known as Mosquito Haven Wilderness, covers a mid-altitude plateau spattered with over 150 small lakes, marshes, and ponds amid meadows and open forest. The meadows lie at the base of many wooded warts and knobs, as well as the area's highest summits, all bearing the easily identified shape of old volcanic cones. Summer visitors up to the challenge posed by biting bug hordes will find a sea of color as the meadow wildflowers burst into bloom. A more pleasant time to visit, however, is fall; the pests have mostly died off, and the palette of early frosts mixes the brilliant scarlets and golds displayed on huckleberry bushes and other deciduous plants. A feast of ripe purple huckleberries is an added attraction.

## CLIMATE

Indian Heaven receives moderately heavy precipitation, on the order of 90 to 100 inches annually. Most falls between November and April as snow, with 4 to 6 feet accumulating by midwinter. The snow is mostly gone by mid-July. Temperatures in the winter are relatively mild, with minimums ranging in the low 20s. Summer highs average a pleasant 74 to 78 degrees.

## ECOSYSTEM

The forested segments of the wilderness contain Pacific silver fir, noble fir, and subalpine fir, with less frequent occurrences of Douglas-fir, mountain hemlock, white pine, and lodgepole pine. The extensive meadow communities on the plateau support a wide variety of plants including water sedge, cotton grass, bog willow, western aster, marsh horsetail, camas, willow weed, shooting star, elephant's head pedicularis, marsh violet, northern starflower, and several species of sphagnum mosses.

The area is a summer and fall habitat for black-tailed deer and elk; black bear love to feast on its huckleberries. Most lakes over three acres in size have some rainbow and eastern brook trout, and several are stocked regularly.

## GEOLOGY

The entire Indian Heaven Plateau is made up of recent volcanic rock, dating from Pleistocene times. Virtually every knob and high spot along the crest was once a volcanic cone that released basalt and andesite flows and scattered bursts of volcanic fragments on the surrounding landscape. These eruptions were mainly one-shot affairs, building a cone of only a few hundred feet. Two larger cones are East Crater, with 600-foot-high walls and a soggy meadow in its depressed center, and Lemei Rock, whose broad, fractured crater now contains Lake Wapiki.

## HISTORY

Native tribes regularly visited the Indian Heaven area for more than 9,000 years. The area's rich huckleberry fields resulted from periodic fires that cleared off the encroaching forest. These fires were either intentionally set by Indians, accidentally triggered by berry-drying fires, or caused by lightning. During the early 1900s, Indian Heaven saw large groups from the Yakama, Klickitat, Cascade, Wasco, Wishram, and Umatilla tribes meet here annually to pick and dry huckleberries, fish the lakes, hunt and dry meat, tan hides, make baskets, and engage in trading and socializing. The Indian Race Track, in the southern part of the wilderness, was the site of one such gathering. The track, 10 feet wide and about 2,000 feet long, was used by the Indians to race horses; fast, strong horses were prized possessions.

## HIKING
### Westside Trails

**Trail 171, Race Track.** *3.1 miles/m (H,S)*. At Falls Creek Horse Camp on FR 65 (3,490 ft), the way heads southeast through second-growth forest, crosses the creek, and climbs a rocky tread to reach flatland forest (4,200 ft). In another mile, a shallow pond at the edge of the receding meadow marks the Indian Race Track. Trees are rapidly reclaiming most of the 2,000-foot-long path over which Indians held riding competitions for half a century. The route continues south from the meadow as it climbs toward the Red Mountain lookout (4,968 ft) at the end of FR 6048.

**Trail 111, Thomas Lake.** *3.3 miles/d (H,S).* Starting from a clearcut on FR 65 (4,450 ft), the way heads uphill through thick timber to a passage between Dee, Heather,

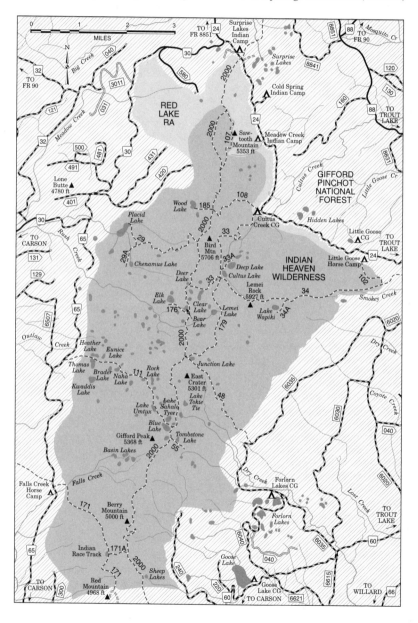

and Thomas Lakes (4,300 ft). It continues uphill east past Brader Lake (4,470 ft), several smaller ponds, and Naha Lake (4,740 ft), to the west shore of Rock Lake (4,780 ft). Here the way wends southeast past more small lakes and ponds to the narrow path between Lake Sahale Tyee (4,670 ft) and Blue Lake, where it joins the PCT (4,640 ft).

**Trail 29, Placid Lake.** *3.5 miles/m (H,S).* Leaving FR 3000-420 (4,120 ft), the path descends gradually through old-growth forest to Placid Lake (4,042 ft). It skirts the north end of the lake, passes Trail 29A to Chenamus Lake, then weaves up the steepening wooded slopes to the east. Subalpine meadows, adorned with wildflowers, are entered on the west flank of Bird Mountain, where the way joins the PCT (4,980 ft).

## Eastside Trails

**Trail 108, Cultus Creek.** *1.5 miles/d (H,S).* Originating at Cultus Creek Campground (3,988 ft) on FR 24, the route switchbacks up through steep, lightly timbered slopes, then into huckleberry meadows and talus to a saddle (5,237 ft) on the north end of Bird Mountain. Here enjoy views of Adams and Rainier before crossing west of the crest to meet the PCT (5,150 ft).

**Trail 33, Indian Heaven.** *3.3 miles/m (H,S).* From Cultus Creek Campground (3,988 ft), the way heads southwest through dense forest as it works up the steep east flank of Bird Mountain. It swings south past cliffs on the upper portion of the mountain, then passes a short spur to Deep Lake (5,087 ft). At Cultus Lake (5,070 ft) the way meets Trail 34 at a saddle (5,100 ft) between Bird Mountain and Lemei Rock. The path descends 0.3 mile south, turns west along a shore-side meadow at Clear Lake (4,950 ft), and ends on the PCT at Deer Lake (4,770 ft).

**Trail 34, Lemei.** *5.3 miles/d (H,S).* The way leaves FR 24 (3,650 ft) on an abandoned roadbed on the north side of Smoky Creek. It then starts a long, gradual ascent due west through thick second-growth forest, passing Trail 102 to Little Goose Horse Camp. The path plods uphill through older and less dense timber, then passes a spur to Lake Wapiki (5,250 ft), tucked in a pocket that was once part of the crater cone of Lemei Rock. Trail 34 breaks into meadows and steepens as it climbs to a saddle (5,600 ft) on the north shoulder of Lemei Rock, a scenic spot with views of Lake Wapiki and the cliff face of the rock. The way descends west to Cultus Lake, where it joins Trail 33 (5,100 ft).

**Trail 48, East Crater.** *2.5 miles/m (H,S).* From FR 6035 (4,080 ft), the route starts in forest and wiggles uphill to meadows spattered with a dozen or more small lakes and ponds. A gradual ascent around the east base of East Crater leads to Junction Lake (4,730 ft), where the way meets the PCT.

## Trail 2000, Pacific Crest National Scenic Trail. *16.4 miles/m (H,S).*

The trail leaves FR 60 at Crest Horse Camp (3,490 ft) to ascend through forest to the southern wilderness boundary. The path wanders down a broad bench between two wooded volcano cones, past Trail 171A to the Indian Race Track. Switchbacks climb to the long, flat top of Berry Mountain (5,000 ft) and views of Hood, St. Helens, and Adams. More switchbacks drop off the north end of the mountain to a contour of the

*Rock Lake is reached via Trail 111, on the west side of the Indian Heaven Wilderness.*

southeast side of Gifford Peak. The path passes Trail 55 to Tombstone Lake, then arrives at Blue Lake (4,630 ft), meeting Trail 111. A rerouted segment of trail continues north, winds around the base of East Crater, and arrives at Junction Lake (4,730 ft), where it meets Trails 48 and 179.

The new trail, uphill from the boggy old pond-and-puddle route, continues north to Bear Lake (4,750 ft), passing spur Trail 176 to Elk Lake. A short distance farther is Deer Lake (4,770 ft) and an intersection with Trail 33. The way picks up the 5,000-foot contour line along the southwest side of Bird Mountain, passes the upper end of Trail 29, then ascends to a saddle (5,237 ft) on the north side of the mountain, where it is joined by Trail 108 and spur Trail 185 to Wood Lake. After skirting a small knob, the route traces the crest north to Sawtooth Mountain.

The PCT stays on the west side of the mountain; those wishing to climb along its summit can take Trail 107, a rugged 2-mile parallel route along a narrow ridge. Cautious scrambles over loose rock to its top (5,353 ft) give acrophobic views down the sheer east face. Just north of the mountain, the trail leaves the wilderness and descends gently to the berry fields straddling FR 24 (4,238 ft) just south of Surprise Lakes Indian Camp.

## WINTER SPORTS

With some of the adjoining forest roads now being plowed in winter, the gentle terrain of the wilderness, relatively avalanche-free, is becoming more popular as a ski-touring destination. Check with the Mount Adams Ranger Station to learn which roads are clear when planning such a trip.

**Wind River Region**

## Trapper Creek Wilderness; Bourbon Roadless Area

**Location:** In Skamania County, between the Wind River and Siouxon Creek
**Size:** Wilderness, 6,050 acres; Bourbon, 4,540 acres
**Status:** Designated Wilderness (1984); Roadless area is 30 percent Semiprimitive Nonmotorized, 70 percent Roaded Natural
**Terrain:** Steep, heavily forested ridges make a horseshoe wrap around the deep Trapper Creek drainage.
**Elevation:** 1,200 to 4,268 feet
**Management:** USFS, Gifford Pinchot National Forest, Mount Adams Ranger District
**Topographic maps:** Bare Mountain, Termination Point

This major creek drainage, and its delightful variety of ecological zones, have been preserved from omnipresent chain saws by a 1984 grant of wilderness status. An equal amount of virgin territory that borders the northeast side of the region begs for the same protection. Trapper Creek runs nearly the length of the wilderness; it and its clear, sparkling tributaries dive steeply downhill, cutting deep canyons and rolling tumultuously over waterfalls before settling down to a valley-floor meander to the Wind River. A single lake is captured in a cliff-walled cirque at the southwest corner of the wilderness. The high enclosing ridges offer spring wildflower displays, fall huckleberry feasts, and horizon-stretching scenic views.

## CLIMATE

Although the wilderness receives annual precipitation of 90 to 100 inches, fortunately for recreationists only 5 percent of this falls between June and August. The amount dropping as snow varies with altitude, ranging from 8 feet at lower levels to 20 feet at upper elevations. Low temperatures in midwinter are around 24 degrees, and mid-summer highs average a mild 74. Most trails are accessible to hikers from May to December, although in the highest areas snow clings through June, and flurries can be expected in October.

## ECOSYSTEM

Lower-level forest cover is made up of Pacific silver fir, western hemlock, noble fir, western red cedar, Douglas-fir, and western white pine. The understory includes salal, rhododendron, rustyleaf, prince's pine, queencup beadlily, twinflower, bunchberry dogwood, huckleberries, and dwarf blackberry. Meadows on the higher subalpine ridges here have a carpet of beargrass and huckleberries, along with a wide assortment of wildflowers that appear as soon as the snow melts.

Among the woods' residents are black-tailed deer, elk, black bear, cougar, bobcat, and pine marten. Pikas and whistling marmots inhabit higher-elevation rock outcrops. Grouse, northern spotted owl, barred owl, goshawk, pileated woodpecker, gray jay, and Clark's nutcracker all make their homes here.

At a northern corner of the wilderness is the Sister Rocks Research Natural Area. The RNA is preserved for the study of subalpine forests and soils, as well as the ecology of the Pacific silver fir, a handsome tree that occurs in the area in a variety of vegetation communities.

## GEOLOGY

The base rock of the Trapper Creek area is a thick series of basalt and andesite flows dating between 25,000 and 50,000 years ago. The region has numerous basalt outcrops that fracture and drop to talus slopes.

## HISTORY

In 1910 a Portland brewing company built a hotel and resort at Government Mineral Springs, a half-mile upstream from the mouth of Trapper Creek. Guests were brought 15 miles by horse-drawn wagon from Carson to this vacation spot. The resort was elegant

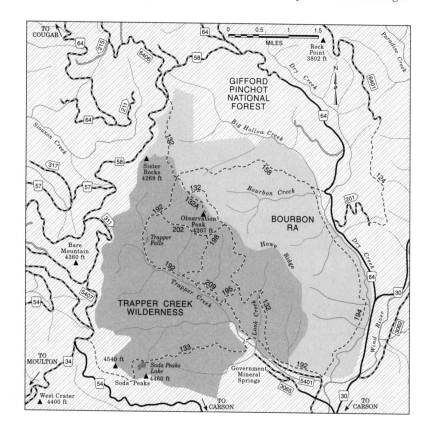

for its day, with flower gardens, mineral baths with purported curative powers for all sorts of ailments, a dance pavilion, and a riding stable. A campground, very popular with families, was built east of the hotel. The resort flourished in the Prohibition era, when it was said to have been a haven for liquor and gambling. The hotel burned to the ground in 1935; but vestiges of the campground, enhanced by the work of CCC crews in the 1930s, remain as a picnic area today. The Trapper Creek Wilderness has the resort to thank in part for its existence. Early forest plans required non-logged buffer zones beside roads and near places such as the resort. Because the property, plus its buffer space, effectively sealed off any easy access to the Trapper Creek basin, the forest there escaped cutting.

Although the path to the top of Observation Peak predates Forest Service activity in the area, most of the area's trails were built in the 1930s to support fire-suppression activities. Fire lookout sites were once staffed atop Observation Peak and Sister Rocks.

## HIKING

**Trail 133, Soda Peaks Lake.** *5.5 miles/d (H).* From the 1.5-mile point on Trail 192 (1,450 ft), the way drops 100 feet southwest to a bridge over Trapper Creek, then heads west up a steep, forested hogback. It weaves and bobs up the crest at the edge of the steep north face to reach a tiny saddle (3,250 ft). The ridge top widens for 0.5 mile, then in a final uphill thrust arrives at the cirque holding Soda Peaks Lake (3,760 ft). From the lake, the way ascends the north and west sides of the cirque to a gap between Soda Peaks (4,250 ft). Here it drops northwest down a narrow, wooded finger ridge to meet FR 54 near its junction with FR 5407 (3,670 ft).

**Trail 192, Trapper Creek.** *6 miles/e-d (H; S to the junction with Trail 132).* This long route traces Trapper Creek from its mouth to its headwaters. From a common trailhead with Trail 194 on FR 5401 (1,150 ft), the gentle, wooded grade parallels the road to Government Mineral Springs. Here Trail 132 takes off to the northeast, and in another 0.5 mile Trail 133 leaves to the southwest. The way now steepens as it ascends diagonally up the slope on the east side of Trapper Creek. It soon passes two short, primitive spur trails; Trail 195 up the steep slope to the east, connecting to Trail 32, and Trail 209 which parallels the main trail, then reconnects with it in less than a mile to offer a loop possibility. Trail 192 then climbs into second-growth forest and maintains its distance above the creek as it snakes up the drainage. The route crosses Trapper Creek, then abruptly climbs the 700-foot basin headwall to a spectacular view of 100-foot-high Trapper Falls. A gentler grade above the basin passes Trail 202 and ends as it joins Trails 132 and 158 (3,800 ft).

**Trail 132, Observation.** *7.2 miles/m (H,S).* One mile from the start of Trail 192 (1,300 ft) this route climbs 200 feet, then begins a steady diagonal ascent of the west flank of Howe Ridge. The path swings through the steep Lush Creek drainage, then heads up through old-growth forest to the crest (3,200 ft), passing spur Trail 195 en route. It crosses the ridge, at its junction with Trail 198, to continue the ascent across rocky slopes on the east flank of Observation Peak. At a saddle northwest of the summit, a spur heads to the top of the peak (4,207 ft), a former lookout site, and what a

*Trapper Creek streams through moss-covered rocks in the Trapper Creek Wilderness.*

sight indeed! The tops of St. Helens, Adams, Rainier, and Hood are seemingly a touch away, and on a clear day vistas stretch across a vast sea of forested ridges as far north as Mount Baker and as far south as Mount Jefferson.

Trail 132 continues northwest to a saddle junction with Trails 158 and 192 (3,800 ft). A gentle climb north leads to the shoulder of Sister Rocks where an 0.5-mile cross-country scramble southwest gains their summits (4,261 ft and 4,268 ft), a former look-out site. An easy descent north through huckleberry-laden meadows arrives at FR 58 (3,550 ft).

**Trail 194, Dry Creek.** *4 miles/m (H,S).* From the joint trailhead with Trail 192 on FR 5401 (1,150 ft), the route meanders along the west bank of Dry Creek, passing through intermittent old-growth groves. After crossing Bourbon Creek, the path ends on Trail 158 (1,550 ft).

**Trail 158, Big Hollow.** *3.2 miles/d (H,S).* The way leaves FR 64 (1,480 ft), crosses Big Hollow Creek, passes the north end of Trail 194, and climbs due west up an ever-steepening spur from Howe Ridge. A sometimes testy wade of a fork of Big Hollow Creek leads to huckleberry meadows and the junction with Trails 132 and 192 (3,800 ft) northwest of Observation Peak.

# 40 Silver Star Mountain Roadless Area

**Location:** In Clark and Skamania Counties, between the East Fork of the Lewis River and the Washougal River

**Size:** 12,545 acres

**Status:** Semiprimitive Nonmotorized; Washington State Department of Natural Resources (DNR) and private timber production

**Terrain:** Sharp ridges with rocky outcrops radiate in all directions from the top of Silver Star Mountain. Deep stream drainages cut steep-gradient slopes between ridge crests.

**Elevation:** 1,200 to 4,390 feet

**Management:** USFS, Gifford Pinchot National Forest, Mount St. Helens National Volcanic Monument; Washington State Department of Natural Resources (DNR); portions of one section privately owned

**Topographic maps:** Bobs Mountain, Dole, Gumboot Mtn., Larch Mtn.

This bald, rocky summit, more than 4,300 feet high, looms above the Columbia foothills northeast of the Portland–Vancouver area. It was heavily wooded prior to a 1902 forest fire; subsequently its burn-bald summit was made a fire lookout site. Although its forest cover has never regenerated to its former stature, the remaining rock and meadow slopes nurtured a variety of plant species that adapted to the new environmental conditions. Today these are diverse and unique enough that the area is a highly prized botanical reserve. In addition to its flora, the treeless ridge tops offer horizon-filling views of surrounding volcanic peaks and the urbanized lowlands along the Columbia River. Roads that invaded the western portion of the area in the 1940s were placed off-limits to motorized traffic in 1984, and have gradually degenerated to trails. The net is a wonderfully scenic semiwilderness within sight and easy hiking distance of Columbia River population centers.

## CLIMATE

The average annual precipitation ranges between 75 and 85 inches. Temperatures are mild; midwinter lows run in the mid- to upper 20s, and summer highs are usually a comfortable 80 degrees. The area is free of snow by May, and remains so until November. This area is one of the earliest to enjoy wildflowers, which generally begin blooming by the end of May.

## ECOSYSTEM

The bottoms of some creek drainages have pockets of old-growth Pacific fir, western hemlock, noble fir, and western red cedar, and some upper slopes have open stands of second-growth Douglas-fir. More than a third of the area has not recovered its forest cover since the 1902 Yacolt burn, and it remains meadows and rock outcrops. Common meadow species are beargrass, vine maple, salal, Oregon grape, big huckleberry, red huckleberry, and twinflower. The wide variety of bushes, herbs, and wildflowers found here, as well as several uncommon species such as the endangered *Clackamas corydalis*, has made Silver Star a candidate for a Biological Special Interest Area.

A large number of black-tailed deer live in the region's forests, as do black bear, cougar, Lewis woodpecker, blue grouse, and Larch Mountain salamander.

## GEOLOGY

The entire area lies atop a granitic pluton that intruded Eocene oceanic basalt, andesite, and rhyolite sometime in the mid-to-late Tertiary. Typical of such intrusions, the periphery became mineralized and has been the scene of intensive prospecting. More than a hundred unpatented mining claims were filed within the area's boundaries, and placer gold, some platinum, and low-grade copper have been found.

## HISTORY

The Silver Star region has attracted archaeological interest with the discovery of at least ten sites of prehistoric human activity. Among these are pits dug on a ridge near the top of the mountain. The purpose of these pits is unknown; speculation is that they were used either as spots for ritual isolation during a guardian spirit quest or possibly as blinds for hunting animals flushed upslope.

Placer gold was discovered in the East Fork of the Lewis River, the Washougal River, and their tributaries in the 1890s, and the Washougal Mining District was soon

*The summit of Silver Star has wide views, or surrounding peaks, including Mount Hood in Oregon.*

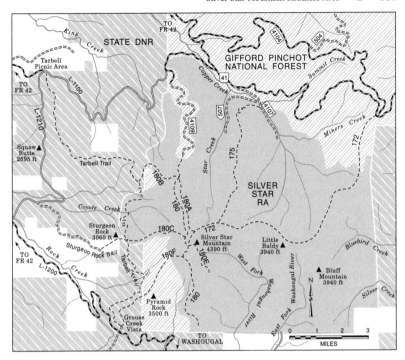

the site of heavy prospecting. No significant lode ores were found.

In 1902 the massive Yacolt burn consumed 283,000 acres of timber, including that in the Silver Star area; only isolated stands deep in creek drainages survived. Aged, silver snags from the burn are still found today in open meadows and second-growth patches of trees on the mountain. In the years following the fire, the Forest Service intensified its fire-control effort in the area. In the 1930s, CCC crews constructed a road to a lookout site atop Silver Star Mountain, and several ridge-top trails were put in to support fire suppression.

## HIKING

**Trail 180, Silver Star.** 2.5 miles/m (H,S). FR 4109 climbs south from Copper Creek to a gate (3,080 ft) where it is closed to motorized traffic and becomes Trail 180. The route continues up the old rocky roadbed through meadows bedecked with wildflowers, swaying stalks of beargrass, and huckleberries. It ends as it meets Trail 172 (4,130 ft); a short spur continues to the summit of Silver Star Mountain (4,390 ft) and wide views to Rainier, St. Helens, Adams, and Hood, as well as down to the Columbia River Gorge and segments of metropolitan Vancouver and Portland.

**Trail 180C, Sturgeon.** 1.6 miles/m (H,S,B). Another short connector links the upper end of Trail 180 (4,120 ft) to the Tarbell Trail at a saddle east of Sturgeon Rock (3,060 ft) and a primitive DNR road off Road L-1210.

**Trail 180E, Indian Pit.** *0.6 mile/m (H,S).* A short spur trail leaves the junction of Trail 180 and others, continues to the south, and descends through beargrass and huckleberries to a saddle. A short climb on the ridge to the south leads to the site of the Indian Pit, whose origin has variously been attributed to spirit quest sites, hunting blinds, or food caches—no one knows for sure.

**Trail 180F, Pyramid.** *2.5 miles/m (H,S,B)* A decommissioned road, converted to trail, heads south from the junction of Trails 180 and 180C (4,080 ft). It descends through old-burn meadows, thick with a carpet of beargrass and wildflowers, passes below Pyramid Rock, and drops to meet the Tarbell Trail and DNR Road L-1200 at Grouse Creek Vista (2,375 ft).

**Trail 175, Starway.** *3.3 miles/d (H,S).* The trail departs from rough, difficult FR 4107 (1,620 ft) in a switchback chain up the steep, rugged, wooded ridge on the east side of Star Creek. The never-ceasing grind continues up the narrowing ridge backbone to talus and brush, where the route becomes obscure and poorly marked in places. As the south-tending ridge merges with another from the east, the way ends on Trail 172 (3,800 ft).

**Trail 172, Bluff Mountain.** *6 miles/d (H,S).* At the junction of FR 41 and 4104 (3,550 ft), the path heads southward on an abandoned ridge-top roadbed, then drops to a saddle (3,100 ft). From here it contours through old burns above cliffs on the north side of Bluff Mountain. At a col west of the mountain the path shifts to the south side of the ridge and heads west below Little Baldy. West of this knob, the path traces the narrow, rocky crest past the upper end of Trail 175, then skirts the north flank of Silver Star Mountain to meet the spur to the top and Trail 180 (4,130 ft).

**Tarbell Trail.** *9 miles/m (H,S).* This DNR trail leaves a common trailhead with Trail 180F at Grouse Creek Vista (2,375 ft), contours through second-growth into the Rock Creek basin, and passes above a beautiful, 100-foot-high waterfall. The way switchbacks up to cross the Sturgeon Rock Trail at a narrow saddle (3,040 ft) east of the rock itself. Nine long switchbacks drop north to Coyote Creek (1,950 ft), then the route works its way uphill around the head of the basin, passing the lower end of Trail 180B. A traverse west along the side of Squaw Butte at 2,500 feet leads to a broad northwest-directed ridge. The way descends the gentle wooded rise to the Tarbell Picnic Area (1,700 ft).

## CLIMBING

Sturgeon Rock (3,060 ft), at the west side of the area north of Rock Creek, has a few leads of technical rock climbing on its north face.

## WINTER SPORTS

FR 4109 into Silver Star from the north is generally driveable in winter to within a mile or so of the start of Trail 180. A ski or snowshoe trip the remainder of the way to the top of Silver Star is easy and hazard-free, with the exception of large cornices that form on the edge of the ridge overlooking Star Creek. The trip offers excellent wintertime views of Portland, Vancouver, and the nearby volcanic summits of the Cascades.

# Big Lava Bed Region

## Big Lava Bed, Red Mountain, and Bear Creek Roadless Areas

**Location:** In Skamania County, between Indian Heaven Wilderness and the Columbia River

**Size:** Big Lava Bed, 19,030 acres; Red Mountain, 2,880 acres; Bear Creek, 8,060 acres

**Status:** Big Lava Bed is 39 percent Semiprimitive Nonmotorized; the remainder and all other roadless areas are Roaded Natural

**Terrain:** Big Lava Bed is a lightly forested jumble of huge basalt blocks of a fairly recent lava flow from a crater at its north end. Big Huckleberry Mountain/Grassy Knoll is a sharp, Y-shaped group of ridges that meet at the summit of Big Huckleberry Mountain. The Bear and Jimmy Creek areas are densely forested, extremely steep slopes rising to narrow crests flanking the two drainages.

**Elevation:** 2,400 to 4,202 feet

**Management:** USFS, Gifford Pinchot National Forest, Mount Adams Ranger District

**Topographic maps:** Big Huckleberry Mtn., Gifford Peak, Little Huckleberry Mtn., Willard

The unique feature of the Big Lava Bed Roadless Area is the 12,500-acre lava bed that covers a 9-mile-long by 1-to-4-mile-wide swath on its east side. The eruption that generated the lava flow occurred 3,000 years ago—a few moments ago, geologically speaking. As a result, it has not succumbed to inevitable erosion, but instead has a vast jumble of sharp rock towers, intriguing fractures in the lava surface, short caves, and a moonscape appearance. The crater that vented this eruption is at the north end of the area, rising about 600 feet above the surrounding landscape. A fairly uniform stubble of lodgepole pine combined with the scrambled landscape makes the lava bed an excellent place to get lost during cross-country explorations.

The western portion of the Big Lava Bed area consists of a trio of ridges radiating from Big Huckleberry Mountain. The crests are a combination of light forest and open subalpine meadows with fine views and an interesting diversity of botanical features. Unfortunately, logging activity has gnawed right up to the base of these ridges. The Bear Creek area has three southwest-trending drainages flanked by near-vertical walls that rise to narrow, jumbled, subalpine crests.

## CLIMATE

The mean annual precipitation for the area is 100 inches, with a substantial portion of that occurring as snow; average annual snowfall is about 8 feet. Winter low temperatures average in the mid-20s. Summers are dry and comfortably warm; average summer highs range in the lower 80s. Less than 5 percent of the precipitation falls between June and August, and the area is mostly snow-free between May and October.

## ECOSYSTEM

With only nominal soil, and no known source of underground water, the lava beds are still about 70 percent rock, although vegetation from the surrounding forests is slowly populating the area. Sparse stands of lodgepole pine have spread across most of the lava bed, and an occasional isolated Douglas-fir can also be found. The only shrub unique to the area is trailing juniper. In the surrounding forest, and making some inroads into the lava beds, are communities of Sitka willow, red alder, black cotton-wood, mountain wormwood, and subalpine fir. Understory members include hedge nettle, figwort, beargrass, vine maple, salal, Oregon grape, queen-cup beadlily, western prince's pine, bunchberry dogwood, deerfoot vanilla fern, various species of huckleberry, and a number of mosses and herbs. The ridge area between Big Huckleberry

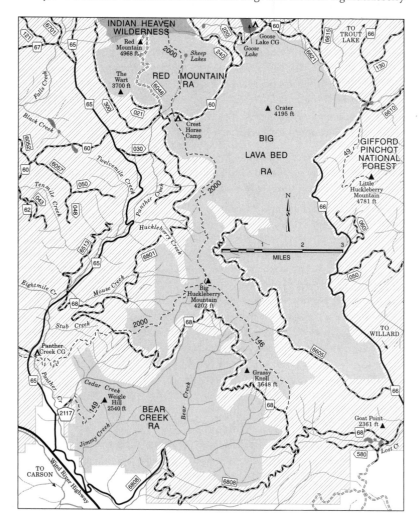

*Forest covers much of Big Lava Bed. In the center of the photo is the cinder cone that was the source of the flow.*

Mountain and Grassy Knoll has a typical forest of Pacific silver fir, western hemlock, noble fir, western white pine, western red cedar, and Douglas-fir. Grassy slopes along the crests have dense growths of huckleberries. Most of the Bear Creek area is covered with old-growth Douglas-fir, western hemlock, with a smattering of silver fir. Ridge tops sport the typical assortment of subalpine wildflowers.

Animals found in the region are black bear, black-tailed deer, a few elk, and marten. Larch Mountain salamanders hide in the lava, and the forests of the area are also habitat for blue grouse, Lewis woodpeckers, spotted owl, and pileated woodpeckers.

## GEOLOGY

The base rock beneath the area consists of several layers of mid-Tertiary pyroclastic volcanic flows. The unique surface formation of the Big Lava Bed is of far more recent origin; the cone at the north end of the area ejected one or more lava flows to create this bed less than 3,000 years ago. The lava is fractured by many cracks and folds, and has not suffered any significant smoothing erosion. Soil layers are sparse to nonexistent.

## HISTORY

The volcanic cone that created the Big Lava Bed erupted within historical times, but little is known about the area since then. Two primitive trails once crossed the area, possibly made by Indians, since they predated any Forest Service presence in the region. Big Huckleberry is thought to be a summer campsite used by the Klickitat tribe when gathering herbs, roots, and huckleberries. Peeled cedars have been reported near the trail to the mountain; the tree bark was used to make baskets in which to carry the harvest. Grassy Knoll was also once a fire lookout site. The meadows between Grassy Knoll and Big Huckleberry Mountain were used for sheep grazing between 1920 and 1940.

## HIKING

There are no maintained trails in the Big Lava Bed, and because of the jumble of lava blocks, the uniform thin cover of lodgepole pine, and the lack of unique identifiable features, it is very easy to get lost when exploring the area. The most interesting feature of the beds is the crater from which they erupted. The forested walls rise about 400 feet above the surrounding lava beds, and the 200-foot-deep depression in the crater's center holds a tiny meadow where a profusion of wildflowers grows in early summer. Also of interest is a deep, T-shaped trough with near-vertical sides, located a half-mile west of the crater. The nearest cross-country approach is from FR 60 south of the junction with FR 6000-240.

**Trail 146, Grassy Knoll.** *5.5 miles/m-d (H,S,B).* From the junction of FR 68 and FR 6800-511 (2,850 ft), the route heads uphill in swatches of forest between clearcuts to the top of a long northwest–southeast-trending ridge (3,600 ft). The way follows the crest northwest to Grassy Knoll, then continues along ridge-top meadows with brilliant spring wildflower displays, fall huckleberries, and fantastic views of Mounts Hood and Adams, the Big Lava Bed, Mount Defiance, and the Columbia Gorge. The trail then contours the forested west slopes just below the ridge top to intersect the PCT (4,000 ft) west of the summit of Big Huckleberry Mountain.

**Trail 149, Weigle Hill.** *3 miles/d (H).* A seldom-maintained trail leaves the end of County Road 2117 (960 ft) to switchback up a steep, wooded rib to the southeast. Reaching the ridge top (2,174 ft) southwest of Weigle Hill, the way traces the narrow, wildflower-clad meadows of the crest to the summit (2,540 ft). The trail once continued along the knife-edge ridge for another 3 miles to FR 68, but this segment has been abandoned.

## Trail 2000, Pacific Crest National Scenic Trail. *11.7 miles/m (H,S).*

After crossing FR 68 east of Panther Creek (2,786 ft), the PCT heads into the Big Lava Bed area atop the divide between Cedar and Mouse Creeks. It continues a gradual, winding ascent through forest and subalpine meadows to the west shoulder of Big Huckleberry Mountain, where it meets Trail 146 (4,000 ft). A spur pops up to the former lookout site atop the mountain (4,210 ft) for great views of the Columbia River Gorge and nearby volcanic summits in Washington and Oregon. The way now heads north through ridge-top meadows, then descends to the west edge of the Big Lava Bed (3,200 ft). The route traces the winding perimeter of the bed north for 3 miles before arriving at FR 60 and Crest Horse Camp (3,510 ft). It continues across the Red Mountain RA, passing close to the Sheep Lakes before entering the Indian Heaven Wilderness.

Opposite: *Hikers pause on the Chelan Lakeshore Trail in the Lake Chelan National Recreation Area.*

# Pasayten

## Pasayten Wilderness; Pasayten Rim Roadless Area

**Location:** In Whatcom and Okanogan Counties, along the Canadian border between Ross Lake and Toats Coulee Creek
**Size:** Wilderness, 530,000 acres; Pasayten Rim, 15,410 acres
**Status:** Designated Wilderness (1968, 1984); Roadless Area is Semiprimitive Nonmotorized
**Terrain:** High rugged ridges and peaks in the west and subalpine parkland plateaus in the east are both cut by deep, densely wooded drainages.
**Elevation:** 2,550 to 9,066 feet
**Management:** USFS, Okanogan National Forest, Methow Valley and Tonasket Ranger Districts
**Topographic maps:** Ashnola Mtn., Ashnola Pass, Bauerman Ridge, Billy Goat Mtn., Castle Peak, Coleman Peak, Crater Mountain, Frosty Creek, Horseshoe Basin, Hozomeen Mtn., Hurley Peak, Jack Mtn., Lost Peak, McLeod Mountain, Mount Lago, Mt. Barney, Pasayten Peak, Pumpkin Mtn., Remmel Mtn., Robinson Mtn., Shull Mtn., Slate Peak, Sweetgrass Butte, Tatoosh Buttes

"Immense" is the only adjective to appropriately describe the Pasayten Wilderness. It is 54 miles across, east to west, and from 10 to 23 miles deep, north to south. It contains more than 160 lakes, and at least as many creeks and rivers, a dozen of which flow through deep, steep-walled canyons. Nearly 150 of its summits exceed 7,500 feet in elevation. More than 600 miles of trails wander the wilderness; the longest runs 73 miles, from the eastern boundary to the Cascade crest.

## CLIMATE

The climate varies markedly across the vast expanse of the wilderness. Annual precipitation averages 106 inches on the west and 31 inches on the east. Average midwinter minimums swing from 15 degrees on the west to 8 degrees on the east; temperatures drop much lower with altitude and storms. Summer highs in the west are in the balmy 70s, while the east side sees average highs in the 80s and occasional days 10 to 15 degrees warmer. Eastern trails are generally snow-free by early July; high trails in the west often don't melt out until early August. Most snowfall occurs between October and May, but the entire area is susceptible to sudden storms.

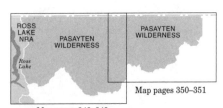

Map pages 348–349
Map pages 350–351
**MAP KEY**

*Remmel Mountain is one of the highest peaks in the Chewuch River area of the Pasayten Wilderness.*

## ECOSYSTEM

The forest communities in the wilderness are diverse, varying with both altitude and east–west location. At lower altitudes in the west the forest is mostly Pacific silver fir, Alaska cedar, and western hemlock, shifting with altitude to subalpine fir, Engelmann spruce, and subalpine larch. On the east slope of the Cascades the dominant species are grand fir, Douglas-fir, western white pine, and, at higher elevations, western larch and subalpine fir. Lodgepole pine is the first species to regenerate in burn areas, which are scattered throughout the wilderness. Subalpine parklands have growths of lupine, sedge, and cinquefoil.

The high steppes in the eastern portion of the wilderness have a varied cover of low sagebrush, fescue, Sandberg's bluegrass, tufted phlox, sedges, penstemon, cinquefoil, and alpine pussytoes. Lodgepole and ponderosa pine are the most common trees.

Wilderness inhabitants include white-tailed and mule deer, moose, marten, black bear, wolverine, gray wolf, grizzly bear, cougar, mountain goat, bighorn sheep, and the largest lynx population in the lower 48 states.

## GEOLOGY

According to plate tectonic theory, the western half of the wilderness was once part of a continental shelf on the east side of the North Cascades microcontinent originally located in the mid-Pacific. Thick layers of sandstone laced with marine fossils built up

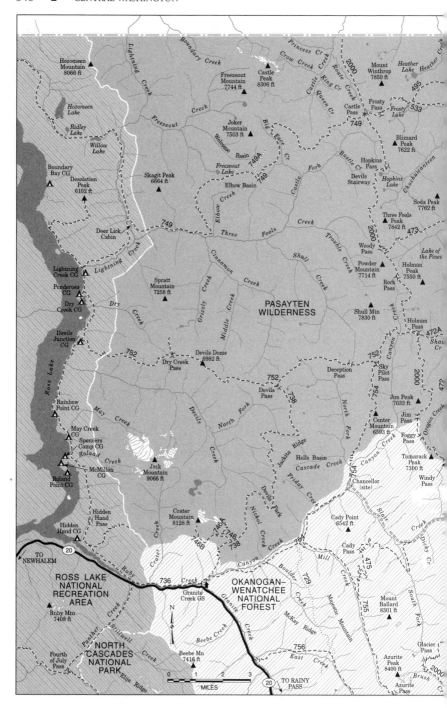

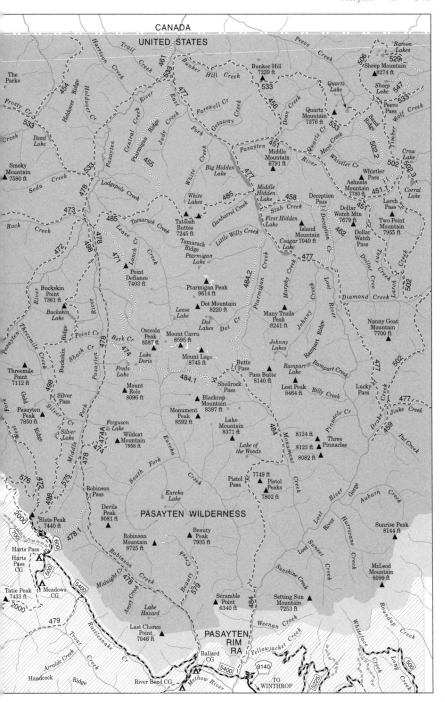

on this submerged shelf between 100 million and 140 million years ago. About 100 million years ago the shelf was raised above sea level, and plate movements brought this terrane and the North American continent closer together in the vicinity of southern California. Over the next 40 million years the new coastal plain was intruded by several granitic plutons along a north–south arc. The microcontinent slid north along the coast of North America to finally dock firmly in its present position about 50 million years ago. The crushing meeting of the two pieces of continental crust was followed by faulting and folding along the line of contact. The section between the Pasayten

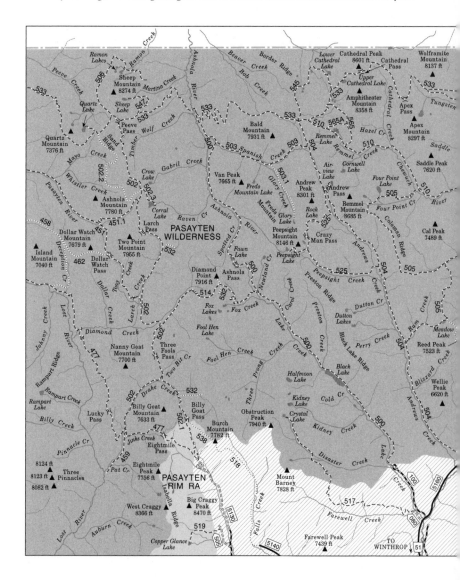

Fault (lying on a line trending northwest from Eightmile Creek to the Pasayten River) and the Ross Lake Fault (along the east side of that lake) dropped, forming the Methow graben.

The eastern half of the wilderness is underlaid by a vast granite batholith, which intruded somewhere between 80 million and 100 million years ago on the coast of another terrane that had merged earlier with the west coast of North America. The waves of ice sheets that moved south across the area up to 15 million years ago scraped and smoothed this granite to the large basins and broad saddles found in that area

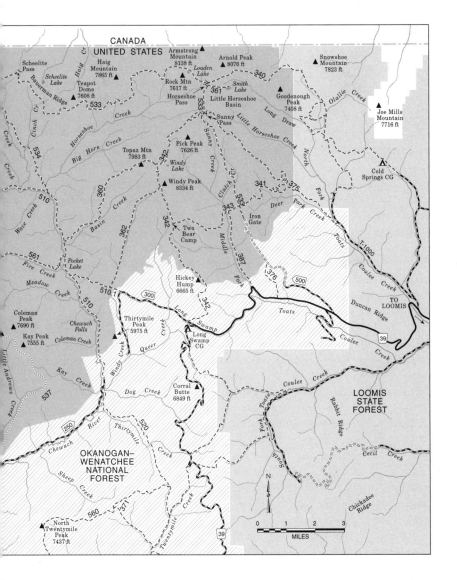

*The Pasayten Wilderness hosts the largest lynx population in the Lower 48 states.*

today. The glaciers also carved the deep channels throughout the wilderness, forming the characteristic U-shaped north–south valleys through which its major rivers and creeks flow. In post-glacial times the lower portions of several of these drainages have been incised by rapidly moving water to form deep, narrow gorges with near-vertical walls.

Local alpine glaciers that remained after the retreat of the continental ice sheet further molded the landscape to sharpen ridgelines and cut the cliff-walled cirques that contain many of the area's lakes. The largest glacier in the wilderness today is the Nohokomeen Glacier on the northwest side of Jack Mountain. Several other higher peaks also have small pocket glaciers clinging to their north faces.

## HISTORY

There is some evidence of prehistoric Indian travel in the upper Lost River area, and nomadic tribes are thought to have roamed the region as early as 6,500 B.C. The late 1800s saw the first contacts between natives and whites entering the region. By 1871 the question of Indian-versus-settler land ownership demanded resolution, and the U.S. government assigned the tribes to various reservations. In 1879 the Moses Reservation, encompassing most of the present-day Pasayten Wilderness, was established for the Columbia tribe under Chief Moses. The tribe, whose traditional lands were farther southeast near the Columbia, refused to move to the reserve. The few white miners and stockmen in the area were unhappy with the reservation designation and demanded that a 10-mile-wide strip along the Canadian border that held their mines and pastures be withdrawn from the reservation. In 1883 a 15-mile-wide strip here was restored to public domain. The remainder of the reservation was changed to public domain in 1884, and opened to settlement two years later.

Prospectors found promising placer deposits in the Canyon Creek and Slate Creek areas in the early 1890s. The search changed from placer to lode gold later in the 1890s, and camps with over 2,000 miners grew at Chancellor and Barron, on the southwest fringe of the wilderness, to exploit rich, gold-bearing quartz veins.

The first forest reserves in the state, established in 1897, were converted to national forests by the early 1900s. The Chelan National Forest, which encompassed most of the area between the Canadian border and the Entiat River, was divided in 1911; the portion in Okanogan County became the Okanogan National Forest. The forest lands were initially used for grazing, mostly by sheep. By 1912 the Forest Service had intensified its fire-suppression mission, and more than sixty-nine sites were identified as potential fire lookout locations. With the arrival of CCC labor in the 1930s, lookouts were built atop Windy Peak, Monument 83, Bunker Hill, Point Defiance, Dollar Watch Mountain, Diamond Point, Remmel Mountain, Crater Mountain, Slate Peak, and Mount Setting Sun, and miles of supporting trails were created.

Tungsten deposits were found near Scheelite Pass in 1904, and World War I demands triggered active mining here that peaked by 1916. The long, difficult trip to the mines, and the discovery of cheaper sources of the ore elsewhere, finally ended production by the 1930s.

The first logging in the area occurred in the 1920s, but many of the old-growth timber losses were due to large forest fires in 1929. More than 500,000 acres of the Pasayten were designated wilderness in 1968, and another 25,000 acres along the south and east borders were added to the wilderness in 1984.

## HIKING
### Ross Lake National Recreation Area Trails
**Trail 749, Elbow Basin.** *18.1 miles/m (H,S).* From the Lightning Creek Trail at Deer Lick Cabin (1,960 ft), the way swings into the Three Fools Creek drainage. A near-flat grade continues upstream to cliffs above the mouth of Elbow Creek. No fun now, as forty-seven switchbacks labor uphill northwest through second-growth timber, then meadows, to the divide (5,950 ft) between Elbow and Freezeout Creeks. The track, sketchy in places, heads east on or just below the open grassy crest. On the horizon are ragged peaks: Hozomeen, the Chilliwacks, the Pickets, and Jack and Crater Mountains.

After crossing a pass (6,350 ft) at the head of Elbow Basin, a spur follows the ridge north to a minor summit (6,898 ft) with knockout views to Castle Peak and Joker, Jack, and Crater Mountains. The main route drops steeply across avalanche tracks to Big Face Creek (4,830 ft), then switchbacks up to a long diagonal ascent of the opposite side of the basin to the ridge top (6,400 ft). The crest and trail bob up and down as they head east above Castle Fork and Two Buttes Creek. After a gradual descent of meadowed sidehills, switchbacks drop into the Castle Fork Basin. A brief ascent reaches Castle Pass (5,451 ft) and the PCT.

**Trail 752, Devils Ridge.** *17.6 miles/m (H,S).* From Devils Junction on Ross Lake (1,850 ft), the way climbs steadily through forest to enter the wilderness (3,400 ft).

The uphill grade continues to top the ridge at Dry Creek Pass (5,860 ft). The path crosses open parkland as it ascends to the top of Devils Dome (6,982 ft), a broad, bald knob and former lookout site, with an awesome view across the deep gulf of Devils Creek to the glacier-clad face of Jack Mountain (9,066 ft), the highest point in the wilderness. Switchbacks down a narrow rib east from the summit lead to a more gradual

*Copper Glance Lake, in the Pasayten Rim Roadless Area, is reached via a short trail.*

descent, first in meadows, then in forest, to Devils Pass (6,130 ft) and the north end of Trail 738.

The route contours the head of the North Fork of Canyon Creek to wooded, nondescript Deception Pass (5,300 ft). A brief ascent leads to Sky Pilot Pass (6,300 ft) to meet Trail 754. The way slowly descends the wooded Canyon Creek slopes, zigzags down to meet the rising creek (4,910 ft), then turns uphill to end on the PCT at Holman Pass (5,060 ft).

## Highway 20 Trails

**Trail 738, Jackita Ridge.** *15.2 miles/d (H,S).* From the Granite Creek Guard Station (1,904 ft), this route crosses Canyon Creek for a steep, switchback climb through big old-growth forest to the subalpine meadows of McMillan Park (5,500 ft). Here unmaintained Trail 746 climbs to two abandoned lookout sites on the summit of Crater Mountain. The gentle grade to the head of Nickol Creek steepens to gain a broad, wildflower-smothered ridge leading to Devils Park. A gradual ascent north across meadows offers great views of Jack and Crater Mountains. The way snakes around ribs and basins on the west side of Jackita Ridge, where tread slippage makes travel difficult. The route descends east, contours open grassy slopes at the head of the North Fork of Devils Creek (6,200 ft), then drops to Devils Pass (6,130 ft) to end on Trail 752.

## Trail 2000, Pacific Crest National Scenic Trail. *32 miles/m (H,S).*

This major north–south trail leaves FR 5400-600 (6,780 ft) at a switchback south of Slate Pass, then contours northwest above Barron, a mining town with a population of thousands in the late 1880s, but now just a few shacks fading into the forest. The way climbs to Windy Pass (6,280 ft), zigzags northwest to Foggy Pass (6,190 ft), then crosses Jim Pass (6,280 ft) to contour eastside slopes around Devils Backbone. A gradual ascent northwest rounds a wooded shoulder, then switchbacks drop to Holman Pass (5,060 ft) to meet Trail 752.

The way traverses slopes above Canyon Creek, then climbs the open southwest flank of Holman Peak to Rock Pass (6,550 ft). It crosses east of the crest to scree slopes below Powder Mountain, passes the west end of Trail 473, then climbs to Woody Pass (6,624 ft). The way contours the west side of the crest below Three Fools Peak, tops Lakeview Ridge (7,200 ft), then descends Devils Stairway. Switchbacks down an open sidehill to Hopkins Pass (6,122 ft) pass a way-trail dropping to Hopkins Lake (6,171 ft). A long gradual descent north through forest and across avalanche tracks reaches Castle Pass (5,451 ft) to meet Trails 749 and 533. Route Creek is followed north to the Canadian border (4,360 ft) and into British Columbia's Manning Park.

## Harts Pass Trails

**Trail 754, Chancellor.** *15.5 miles/m (H,S,B).* (The segment of the trail between Granite Creek and Chancellor is covered in the Liberty Bell section.) From the old Chancellor mining camp site (2,870 ft), the route heads north up Canyon Creek. Strenuous switchbacks climb 2,000 feet up a broad, wooded rib, then the way tapers to a steep uphill grade to a saddle (6,340 ft) north of Center Mountain. The crest, sometimes wooded, sometimes meadow, is followed north to Sky Pilot Pass (6,300 ft) and Trail 752.

**Trail 473, Rock Creek.** *7.1 miles/m (H,S).* From the PCT (6,400 ft), the path traverses steep, side slopes east of Woody Pass, with views of the abrupt north faces of Holman Peak and Powder Mountain. It then crosses numerous avalanche-track meadows as it descends into Rock Creek to meet Trail 478 (4,300 ft) above the Pasayten River.

**Trail 472, West Fork Pasayten.** *14 miles/m (H,S).* Just beyond the gate (7,200 ft) on FR 5400-600 near Slate Peak, the way heads northeast across meadows and open timber to the west side of Haystack Mountain. It swings down the West Fork of the Pasayten, traversing past old prospects before descending to the riverbank. The route follows the wooded drainage downstream, then wanders away from the river along the valley floor. It ends on Trail 478 (4,390 ft) at Rock Creek near the confluence of the West and Middle Forks of the Pasayten.

**Trail 498, Buckskin Ridge.** *11.5 miles/d (H,S).* From the second switchback on FR 5400-600 (6,860 ft), the route heads north and ascends meadows on the east side of Haystack Mountain. It weaves around several creek basins to Silver Lake (6,256 ft), drops to cross Silver Creek, then climbs to Silver Pass (6,500 ft). Switchbacks descend into the headwaters of Threemile Creek, then climb up east bank slopes. A traverse north rounds a sharp rib from Buckskin Ridge, then climbs east to cross Buckskin Ridge at a narrow, rocky col (7,300 ft). The way drops into the upper Point Creek basin, where a traverse north leads to Buckskin Lake (6,492 ft). After an ascent northwest below the rocky cliffs of Buckskin Point, the way makes a long drop down a broad wooded ridge to join Trail 478 at the Pasayten River (4,290 ft).

**Trail 478, Robinson Pass.** *27.4 miles/m (H,S).* From FR 5400 (2,520 ft), the way traces the banks of Robinson Creek through old-growth forest and across avalanche slopes to flower-covered meadows near Robinson Pass (6,220 ft). It descends to the Middle Fork of the Pasayten River, then wanders north through large, valley-bottom old growth. After leaving the river bottom to traverse side slopes for 4 miles, en route passing unmaintained Trail 474 and Trail 485, the track rejoins the river, crosses it, and meets Trail 498. Farther north it passes Trail 472, then Trail 473 near the south end of the abandoned Pasayten airstrip. The way ends at the north end of the strip, where it meets Trail 533 (4,279 ft).

**Trail 484, Monument Creek.** *25 miles/m (H; S, but not recommended beyond Eureka Creek bridge).* Near the mouth of the Lost River, the route leaves FR 5400 (2,400 ft) and heads north upstream through old-growth cedar and Douglas-fir along the base of cliffs framing the deep, U-shaped drainage. At the bridge across the mouth of Eureka Creek (2,640 ft), one can peer upstream into the impressive gorges of Eureka Creek and the Lost River. Vertical faces more than 2,000 feet high frame both of the narrow watercourses. Work begins at the bridge—more than eighty switchbacks gnaw up parched talus slopes to the 5,800-foot-high crest. The ascent continues along the crest for another mile, then traverses steep side slopes through vestiges of a large 1986 fire. Another switchback chain gains narrow Pistol Pass (7,100 ft) and dramatic views of the peaks flanking Monument Creek. The way drops to the creek (4,650 ft), then follows the drainage upstream to a headwater junction with Trail 484.1 near Butte Pass (6,560 ft). An abandoned, but followable continuation, Trail 484.2, heads north from the pass down the Ptarmigan Creek drainage to Trail 477.

**Trail 484.1, Shellrock Pass.** *8 miles/d (H,S).* An unmaintained trail with plenty of vigorous ups and downs heads west from Trail 484 (6,560 ft) just south of Butte Pass. It climbs talus slopes to Shellrock Pass (7,500 ft), then switchbacks west down a rocky face and the basin headwall of Eureka Creek. Here the path becomes Trail 474, the number of a long abandoned route up Eureka Creek. The trail climbs sidehills to a col (7,120 ft), then twists down into the small cirque enclosing Freds Lake (6,507 ft). A side-slope descent reaches a rib above Berk Creek, where switchbacks drop to Trail 478 (4,960 ft).

## Eightmile Creek Trails

**Trail 477, Hidden Lakes.** *26.7 miles/m (H,S).* The route leaves the end of FR 5130 (4,650 ft) for a gradual climb northwest across Eightmile Pass (5,440 ft). It descends Jinks Creek to meet Trail 502 (4,650 ft) at Drake Creek. One long switchback leads to Lucky Pass (5,780 ft); beyond, the route descends steep sidehills to Diamond Creek, then drifts down along the Lost River to Cougar Lake (4,270 ft). The way follows the glacier-cut valley northwest to First Hidden Lake (4,303 ft), then crosses a subtle divide, meets Trail 485, and slips down to Big Hidden Lake (4,316 ft). At the north end of the lake, Trail 451 heads east; Trail 477 continues down the East Fork of the Pasayten to end on Trail 533 (4,000 ft).

**Trail 485, Tatoosh Buttes.** *10.6 miles/d (H,S).* At the imperceptible divide between Middle and Big Hidden Lakes (4,318 ft) the track switchbacks up through big old-growth forest north of Gunbarrel Creek to break into the flowered meadows of Tatoosh Buttes (7,245 ft). Miles of bare ridges open to the south. The way descends through forest to Lease Creek, then continues west to the Pasayten River to meet Trail 478 (4,500 ft).

**Trail 502.1, Billy Goat.** *6 miles/m (H,S).* From the end of FR 5130 (5,000 ft), the route climbs north through old-growth forest to Billy Goat Pass (6,600 ft), where it passes Trail 538. North of the pass it drops past abandoned Trail 532, then joins Trail 502 near the mouth of Two Bit Creek (5,600 ft).

**Trail 502, Larch Creek.** *16.2 miles/m (H,S).* From Trail 477 (4,700 ft), this route follows Drake Creek upstream past Trail 502.1, then bends north through an old burn to cross Three Fools Pass (6,101 ft). It descends through woods past Trail 514 to Diamond Creek (5,500 ft), then swings into the Larch Creek drainage. The tread follows the creek upstream, passes Trail 451, then abandoned Trail 532, and crosses Larch Pass (7,150 ft). It passes Trail 451.1 as it climbs to a saddle (7,490 ft) at the head of McCall Gulch, where flower-splashed meadows offer broad views across the Ashnola River valley. Here Trail 502.3 drops east to Corral Lake, and unmaintained Trail 502.2 heads west for Whistler Basin. Rolling parkland continues north to Peeve Pass (6,880 ft), where the route ends on Trail 533.

**Trail 451, East Fork Pasayten.** *10.5 miles/e (H,S).* A long, valley-bottom path leaves Trail 477 at the north end of Big Hidden Lake (4,350 ft) and climbs east through lodgepole pine along the riverbank to a fork at McCall Gulch (5,950 ft). Trail 451.1 heads east to meet Trail 502 (7,180 ft) north of Larch Pass, while the main trail continues south to Dollar Watch Pass (6,950 ft) and expansive views of Dollar Watch and Two Point Mountains. The path descends steeply into the Tony Creek drainage, then switchbacks down a steep sidewall to cross Larch Creek and join Trail 502 (5,600 ft).

## Chewuch River Trails

**Trail 500, Lake Creek.** *18.9 miles/m (H,S).* From the end of FR 5160-100 (3,162 ft), the track follows the bottom of the broad, glacier-cut Lake Creek drainage northwest to Black Lake (3,982 ft). It continues up the narrowing valley, with wooded walls rising as much as 2,000 feet on either side of the stream course. The route becomes steeper by the mile as it climbs to Ashnola Pass. At the pass it skirts the shore of Fawn Lake (6,201 ft), then descends north into the Spotted Creek drainage. The way follows the creek downstream to meadows at the confluence with the Ashnola River (5,800 ft). The route then flows down to join Trail 533 on the banks of the Ashnola (5,081 ft).

**Trail 504, Andrews Creek.** *15.5 miles/e (H,S).* Another long, north–south thrust into the heart of the wilderness leaves the Chewuch River at Andrews Creek (3,050 ft). After a brief jump up the sidehill to cross Little Andrews Creek, the way settles to a gentle ascent through old-growth forest along Andrews Creek. Traces of a 1984 fire are evident between Little Andrews and Blizzard Creeks. At Ram Creek, Trail 505 leaves to the east, and Trail 525 heads west at Peepsight Creek. The way climbs steadily to Andrew Pass (6,690 ft), where glimpses open to the east face of Andrew Peak, and Trail 525 rejoins Trail 504. Meadows open to views of other peaks as the way descends from the pass along Spanish Creek. The path ends on Trail 533 (6,730 ft) at Spanish Camp.

**Trail 505, Coleman Ridge.** *10.7 miles/d (H; S, but sections impassable).* At the mouth of Ram Creek the route leaves Trail 504 (4,590 ft) and switchbacks up the lodgepole pine–covered slope to the head of the creek, where it threads through a wooded notch to Meadow Lake (6,361 ft). The way follows a gentle ridge north over a 6,827-foot knob, drops to a junction with Trail 561 at Fire Creek, then continues west across meadows and through open timber to the south end of Coleman Ridge. It rises steadily across the west side of the ridge, dips briefly into a wooded basin, then climbs to a saddle (7,200 ft) between Coleman Ridge and Remmel Mountain. The way worms over scree and boulders below a cliff to reach Four Point Creek (7,100 ft). Good backcountry sleuths can find the old route up the gully that once led to a lookout atop Remmel Mountain (8,685 ft). The rocky track contours the basin wall northeast past the way-trail to Four Point Lake (6,850 ft), then drops abruptly through switchbacks to the Chewuch River and Trail 510 (5,240 ft).

**Trail 525, Peepsight.** *8.1 miles/d (H; S, but sections impassable).* This loop trail on the west side of the Andrews Creek drainage initially leaves Trail 504 (5,310 ft) 0.5 mile north of the mouth of Peepsight Creek. It ascends through timber on the north side of the creek, then climbs steeply north to Crazy Man Pass (7,260 ft). Here are great views of rugged surrounding peaks—Peepsight Mountain, Andrew Peak, and

Remmel Mountain. The way slides down scree and boulders to the north to reach Rock Lake (7,170 ft). From here it meanders up, down, and around gullies and ribs before settling to a northward climb to Trail 504 at Andrew Pass (6,690 ft).

**Trail 510, Chewuch.** *18.1 miles/m (H,S).* Starting at the end of FR 5160-250 (3,440 ft), this route traces the banks of the Chewuch River to its headwaters deep in the heart of the wilderness. Two miles from the trailhead is the first attraction, Chewuch Falls. The way continues through river-bottom lodgepole pine to pass Trails 561 and 360. As the river makes a sharp bend west at 4,650 feet, Trail 534 heads off to the north. The way maintains its river-bottom slog, passes Trail 505, and reaches the junction of Remmel and Cathedral Creeks (5,600 ft). As it heads up Remmel Creek, trees slowly thin and the way breaks out to rumpled meadows painted in summer with the reds and blues of paintbrush and lupine. The trail skirts Remmel Lake (6,871 ft), with the ragged summits of Remmel and Amphitheater Mountains in view. The path wanders west across rolling parkland to end on Trail 533 (6,910 ft).

**Trail 360, Basin Creek.** *6 miles/m (H,S).* The way climbs steeply up the east wall of the Chewuch River drainage from Trail 510 (4,360 ft), then bends north away from Basin Creek. It climbs through lodgepole pine to larch and subalpine fir as it skirts the northwest edge of Topaz Mountain, then joins Trail 342 (7,340 ft) north of Windy Peak.

**Trail 534, Tungsten.** *6.2 miles/m (H,S).* At the westward bend of the Chewuch River (4,660 ft), this route climbs north through lodgepole forest, crosses Cinch Creek, then traces Tungsten Creek upstream to the Tungsten Mine (6,800 ft), where crumbling mining debris clutters the junction with Trail 533.

## Toats Coulee Creek Trails

**Trail 342, Windy Peak.** *11.5 miles/m (H,S).* Starting at Long Swamp Campground (5,500 ft) on FR 3900-300, the route heads north through lodgepole pine along the east side of Hickey Hump, then continues sharply uphill through Engelmann spruce and subalpine fir to Two Bear Camp (6,970 ft). The way plugs uphill across alpine meadows, where it meets the head of Trail 362 and a spur that continues uphill to the top of Windy Peak (8,334 ft), once the site of a fire lookout. Here are horizon-sweeping views of the entire east side of the Pasayten Wilderness. Trail 342 descends grassy slopes past the east end of Trail 360, then dips northeast through swampy meadowland before climbing to end on Trail 533 (6,910 ft) west of Sunny Pass.

**Trail 533, Boundary.** *64 miles/m (H,S).* The longest trail in the wilderness leaves its southeast corner, winds up and down west along the U.S.–Canada border, and ends on the PCT 15 miles from the west side of the wilderness. The east end starts at Iron Gate (6,120 ft) on the end of FR 3900-500, then climbs through a young lodgepole pine forest that opens to meadows at Sunny Pass (7,215 ft), where it meets Trails 342 and 375. The way continues north across broad parkland to Horseshoe Pass (7,000 ft).

The trail now bends west past shallow Louden Lake (7,070 ft) and below the north-face cliffs of Rock Mountain. The path then contours around the south sides of Haig Mountain, Teapot Dome, and Bauerman Ridge. Heading northwest along the lower slopes of that ridge, the trail crosses Scheelite Pass (6,713 ft), then worms west to the

*White-winged crossbills are commonly found in conifer forests such as those of the Pasayten Wilderness.*

remains of the Tungsten Mine, where it meets Trail 534. The path rounds parkland slopes at the head of Tungsten Creek, then bends west to broad Apex Pass (7,300 ft). A long sweep to the northwest turns at the head of Cathedral Creek, then climbs to Cathedral Pass (7,570 ft), where ghostly silver snags of trees burned in a 1920s fire haunt young growths of lodgepole pine. The path drops from the pass to the larch-lined shore of Upper Cathedral Lake (7,390 ft). The lake, below the imposing cliffs of Amphitheater Mountain, is one of the most photographed spots in the wilderness, especially when decorated by brilliant fall colors. The Boundary Trail ducks southwest through a flat meadowland pass and descends gradually to Spanish Camp (6,720 ft), passing the north end of Trail 510 en route.

From here to the Ashnola River, the original route high on the slopes of Bald Mountain has been replaced by a lower and gentler grade that includes long sweeping switchbacks down forested slopes to meet Trail 500 and cross the Ashnola River (5,020 ft). The way climbs the west side of the broad, U-shaped valley, then breaks into meadows. An easy grade reaches Peeve Pass (6,860 ft) where Trail 502 heads south.

At a narrow slot (6,750 ft) between Sand Ridge and Quartz Mountain, a short spur contours to the cirque enclosing Quartz Lake (6,741 ft). A swing across a long parkland slope on the southwest side of Quartz Mountain has continuous breathtaking views west to the peaks of the Cascade crest. The way twists around basins and wanders up and down in open timber to reach meadowland atop Bunker Hill (7,239 ft), an old lookout site, with even closer views of the crest peaks. The route now makes a long, tempered descent through forest to the Pasayten River.

Trail 477 is joined just before the Pasayten Bridge (3,910 ft), and the vague remains of Trail 461 head north just across the river. An easy grade follows the broad river valley southwest to reach the abandoned Pasayten airstrip (4,290 ft). Trail 478 continues south, but this route crosses the north end of the airstrip into densely wooded Soda Creek Canyon. At a stream fork the way bends northwest past Dead Lake (5,062 ft), then heads west up the wide, heavily forested Frosty Creek drainage past Frosty Lake (5,343 ft). The trail switchbacks up an avalanche slope, contours an open basin below Mount Winthrop, then climbs to Frosty Pass (6,500 ft). It then descends to Castle Pass (5,451 ft), where it ends on the PCT.

**Trail 375, Albert Camp.** *8.5 miles/m (H,S).* One of the most scenic trails on the eastern rim of the wilderness leaves FR T-1000 at the Fourteenmile trailhead and follows Deer Park Creek northwest through state forest land to the wilderness boundary. The first 3 miles of tread through Deer Park have been rebuilt into lazy, easy-grade switchbacks to the ridge top (6,890 ft). A traverse northwest through subalpine forest crosses a pair of saddles, then climbs to broad parkland (7,700 ft) with good views southwest of the high, rugged face of Windy Peak. The path then switchbacks down to end on Trail 533 north of Sunny Pass (7,220 ft).

## CLIMBING

Although more than fifty peaks in the wilderness are listed in climbing guides, and over one hundred have sheer, rocky north or west faces ranging between 200 and 1,000 vertical feet, simple scramble routes lead up south and east slopes or along north–south ridges. Only a handful of peaks demand any technical skill to reach their summits.

West of the Cascade crest is Jack Mountain (9,066 ft), the highest point in the wilderness, and one of the ten non-volcanic peaks in the state over 9,000 feet. Easy, although steep, routes work up a south-face gully to a single C-4 pitch. The north ridge and northeast glacier have C-4 routes, and the most challenging approach via the southeast ridge has one C-5.6 pitch.

One of the few north-face challenges that has been attacked is Castle Peak (8,306 ft) west of the Cascade crest near the Canadian border. Routes up the wall rate between C-5 and C-5.8. The route to the top of Shull Mountain (7,830 ft), northwest of Holman Pass, is not difficult, but several pinnacles on the long north–south ridge that makes up the summit are worthy of a lead or two of interesting climbing. Holman Peak (7,550 ft), just east of the crest, has a few hundred feet of pleasant rock on the summit block.

Two other summits in the north-central portion of the wilderness that have seen development of north-face routes are Amphitheater Mountain (8,358 ft) and Apex Mountain (8,297 ft). The former has routes that range from C-5.3 to C-5.9. The latter has multiple pitches between C-5.7 and C-5.9. Just north of Cathedral Pass, Cathedral Peak (8,601 ft) has solid C-5.6 to C-5.9 routes, and other pinnacles on the ridge northeast at the Canadian border appear to have equally challenging crags.

The only other peaks of climbing interest are in the south-central portion of the area along ragged Isabella Ridge. The long rocky ridge has precipitous north and northeast faces, but much gentler slopes on the south side. North along the ridge from Burgett Peak (7,365 ft) is Sherman Peak (8,138 ft). Although it has a vertical 1,600-foot north face, an easy southwest slope reaches the summit. Other possible routes along flanking ridges must bypass a number of ridge-top gendarmes. The arête northwest of Sherman has several crags just over 8,100 feet.

The north end of Isabella Ridge ends in the wishbone crest capped by the Craggy Peaks. Big Craggy (8,470 ft) has rock faces on either side of a northern buttress, but its south slope is a steep, nontechnical scree climb. West Craggy (8,366 ft) is gentle on its hard-to-reach southwest slope; its precipitous north ridge has one difficult C-5.8 route up the east face.

# Liberty Bell Region

## Liberty Bell and Sawtooth (North) Roadless Areas

**Location:** In Okanogan, Skagit, and Chelan Counties, between the Pasayten Wilderness and North Cascades National Park and the Lake Chelan–Sawtooth Wilderness

**Size:** Liberty Bell, 112,430 acres; Sawtooth (north), 36,038 acres

**Status:** Semiprimitive Nonmotorized, with the exception of the North Cascades Scenic Highway, which crosses the lower portion of the area

**Terrain:** This area's steep, rugged mountains are frequently capped by serrated knife-edge ridges. Streams and rivers drop abruptly from lakes in rock-rimmed cirques or headwall basins to broad, U-shaped, glacier-cut valleys. Some small pocket glaciers are found, mostly below sheer north faces of peaks.

**Elevation:** 1,904 to 8,444 feet

**Management:** USFS, Okanogan National Forest, Methow Valley Ranger District

**Topographic maps:** Azurite Peak, Crater Mountain, Gilbert, Mazama, McAlester Mtn., McLeod Mountain, Mt. Arriva, Robinson Mtn., Slate Peak, Silver Star Mtn., Washington Pass

It is said that the Liberty Bell Roadless Area is Washington's equivalent of Yosemite Valley. Although not directly comparable, the two regions have many similar features. The Liberty Bell area is nearly bisected by the long, deep, U-shaped valley of the upper Methow River, a beautiful and classic example of the cutting and shaping action of glacial ice. The dominant features of the southern half of the area are massive peaks and ridges formed by granitic intrusions through the metamorphic base rock. These peaks exhibit sheer, solid granite faces, several more than 1,000 feet high, a challenge to the best of climbers. Other ridges are crowned with a series of fins, spires, and towers of comparable difficulty, though with lesser vertical extent.

The area cannot truly be called roadless, as it is spanned by Highway 20, the North Cascades Scenic Highway. However, as its name implies, it was constructed and is maintained for minimal intrusion into the scenic beauty of the region. Aside from this road, the remainder of Liberty Bell deserves protection similar to that afforded the areas along its boundaries: the Pasayten Wilderness, North Cascades National Park, and the Lake Chelan–Sawtooth Wilderness. Its exclusion from wilderness status was possibly prompted by about 150 mining claims that still exist in the area.

An abundance of trails leads into the region; many originated as narrow-gauge wagon roads built to serve the area's mines and prospects. While several of these routes ply brushy creek bottoms and are poorly maintained, others, including a segment of the Pacific Crest National Scenic Trail, cross high passes and traverse alpine slopes that offer breathtaking scenic views. Lakes are sparse—there are just twenty-eight in the

*Golden Horn, seen here from Cutthroat Pass, displays a sheer, 17,000-foot north face.*

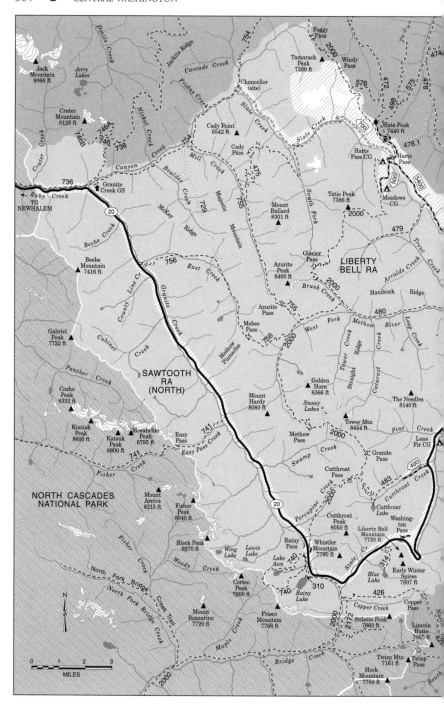

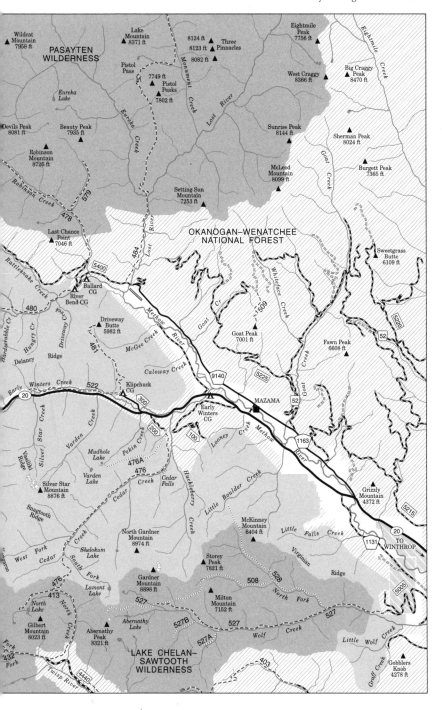

Wildcat
Mountain
7958 ft ▲

PASAYTEN
WILDERNESS

Lake
Mountain
8371 ft ▲

8124 ft ▲   Three
8123 ft ▲   Pinnacles
8082 ft ▲

Eightmile
Peak
7756 ft ▲

Eightmile Creek

Pistol
Pass
7749 ft
Pistol ▲
Peaks
7802 ft

Monument Creek

Lost River

West Craggy
8366 ft ▲

Big Craggy
Peak ▲
8470 ft

Eureka
Lake

Eureka Creek

Sunrise Peak
8144 ft ▲

Goat Creek

Sherman Peak
8024 ft ▲

Burgett Peak
7365 ft ▲

Devils Peak
8081 ft ▲

Beauty Peak
7935 ft ▲

Robinson
Mountain
8726 ft ▲

McLeod
Mountain
8099 ft ▲

Robinson Creek

579

478

Setting Sun
Mountain
7253 ft ▲

OKANOGAN–WENATCHEE
NATIONAL FOREST

Last Chance
Point
7046 ft ▲

Lost River

484

Rattlesnake Creek

5400

Sweetgrass
Butte
6109 ft ▲

Ballard
CG
River
Bend CG

480

481

Driveway
Butte
5982 ft ▲

McGee Creek

Methow River

Goat Cr

Whiteface Creek

1509

5220

52

Driveway Cr

Hardscrabble Cr

Hungry Cr

Delancy     Ridge

Caloway Creek

9140

5225

Goat Peak
7001 ft ▲

Fawn Peak
6608 ft ▲

Early Winters Creek

522

Klipchuck
CG

300

20

MAZAMA

52

1163

Silver Star Creek

Varden Creek

200

Pekin Creek

100

Early
Winters
CG

Looney Creek

Methow River

Vasiliki
Ridge

Mudhole
Lake

476A

476

Varden
Lake

Cedar
Falls

Cedar     Creek

Huckleberry Creek

Little Boulder Creek

Grizzly
Mountain
4372 ft ▲

5215

Silver Star
Mountain
8876 ft ▲

Snagtooth
Ridge

North Gardner
Mountain
8974 ft ▲

McKinney
Mountain
6404 ft ▲

Little     Falls     Creek

20

1131

TO
WINTHROP

West     Fork

Cedar

Shelokum
Lake

Storey
Peak
7821 ft ▲

Virginian

Ridge

5005

476

413

South Fork

Lamont
Lake

Gardner
Mountain
8898 ft ▲

527

Milton
Mountain
7152 ft ▲

508

528

North     Fork

527

North
Lake

Gilbert
Mountain
8023 ft ▲

Abernathy
Peak ▲
8321 ft

North Creek

Abernathy
Lake

527B

527A

527

Wolf     Creek

Little     Wolf     Creek

Graff Creek

432

Fork

Fork

4440

Twisp River

LAKE CHELAN–
SAWTOOTH
WILDERNESS

403

Gobblers
Knob
4278 ft ▲

entire area, and only ten are significant enough to bear a name. However, most are scenic gems, set in tight cirques surrounded by imposing cliffs with tiny shore-side meadows bordered by subalpine fir and larch. They are especially beautiful in the fall, when their turquoise surfaces reflect the golden larch and crimson bushes.

## CLIMATE

Because the Liberty Bell area straddles the Cascade crest, weather varies markedly over its 20-mile, east–west span. On the west side, average annual precipitation is about 100 inches; on the east, about 60 inches. Most of this precipitation occurs between November and April, with as much as 45 feet of snow falling on higher westside elevations over the winter period. Average winter minimums are 16 degrees on the west side of the range, and 9 degrees on the east side. Maximum summer temperatures average in the low 70s on both sides of the crest.

## ECOSYSTEM

The forest in the lower portion of the region west of the crest is dominated by lodgepole pine and Douglas-fir, with an understory of Oregon grape, spirea, willow, bracken fern, Oregon boxwood, oceanspray, twinflower, serviceberry, honeysuckle, prince's pine, and starflower. At higher elevations, Engelmann spruce, mountain hemlock, western red cedar, Pacific silver fir, and subalpine fir join the forest mix. East of the crest, the mid-elevation forest is a mix of ponderosa pine, lodgepole pine, and western larch, while at higher elevations grand fir, white fir, white pine, mountain hemlock, and subalpine fir replace the ponderosa. The understory here includes huckleberry, prickly currant, Oregon boxwood, baldhip rose, and beargrass.

Among the forest animals are mule deer, cougar, black bear, and, at high elevations, mountain goat. Rarer species, in need of special preservation efforts, are spotted owl, lynx, wolverine, water vole, western gray squirrel, and three-toed woodpecker.

## GEOLOGY

Approximately 50 million years ago the North Cascades microcontinent collided with the west coast of North America; the metamorphic rocks off the east coast of that terrane were twisted and uplifted to form this segment of the Cascade Range. South from Rainy and Washington Passes, the base had already been intruded by the granitic Black Peak batholith prior to the meeting of the two plates. About 40 million years ago, the Golden Horn batholith pushed up into the heart of the Liberty Bell area. The intrusive contact zones between this batholith and the base metamorphic suite are highly mineralized, thus the extensive mining in this region. The Gardiner Mountain fault, which marks the west side of the Methow graben, runs northwest to southeast through the area, roughly in the vicinity of the South Fork of Slate Creek. The fault line is not discernible; it is masked by the Golden Horn batholith. The sedimentary base of the sunken Methow graben has been overlaid by a thick layer of glacial debris.

About 15 million years ago the continental ice sheet covered all but a few of the high points of the Liberty Bell area, and its advance can be recognized in the deep, U-shaped valleys that were carved by the glacier, and in the scrape marks etched into exposed granite outcrops. The steep knife-edge crests, with their many towers and spires, are a result of flaking caused by the expansion of water that accumulated in fine cracks in rock structures and then froze.

## HISTORY

The early history of the Liberty Bell area is dominated by its mineral riches. Prospectors probed the area in the late 1880s, entering it from both the Skagit and Methow Valleys. In 1892, Alex Barron discovered a rich strike near Harts Pass. The mining camp of Barron blossomed quickly to a population of 1,000, and reached 2,500 at the peak of its activity. More than $300,000 in gold was extracted from this one claim.

Transportation of supplies in, and ore out, was a major obstacle to capitalizing on the area's riches. In 1893, Charles Ballard was hired to put a road in to Harts Pass. When completed, the road was so narrow it required specially built narrow-gauge wagons to negotiate it. One precarious section at Deadhorse Point consisted of planks laid over steel pins that had been driven into the face of a sheer cliff. A panicky runaway pack string gave the location its name. Despite this hazardous route, huge compressors with 9-foot-diameter flywheels, multi-ton rock crushers, and tons of ore were moved in and out via the primitive Harts Pass road.

In 1915, Ballard opened the Azurite Mine, one of the richest in the area. It produced nearly $1 million in gold and silver between 1929 and 1939. Lode mines were located around Barron, Tatie Peak, Hells Basin, Boulder Creek, Mill Creek, Majestic Mountain, and Granite Creek. Placer mines along the creeks of the region took out more

*A family outing at Cutthroat Pass, with Golden Horn in the distance.*

than $225,000 in gold. In total, more than 3,000 claims were staked in the area between 1894 and 1937. Today 140 unpatented claims and 10 patented claims still remain.

At peak production, some of the mines were operated year-round, but avalanches took a heavy toll in buildings and lives, and dog teams were the only source of supplies during winter months. Access was an ongoing nemesis, and the Harts Pass road wasn't improved to its present condition (still not for the faint hearted) until the 1930s. Methow Valley miners and merchants lobbied fruitlessly for a road across the Cascades to the Skagit Valley, but it wasn't until 1962 that the route over Washington Pass was selected. The road was finally completed in 1972, but this highway is still closed by heavy snow from late November to mid-May.

In the early 1900s sheep herders arrived on the scene and drove flocks from their winter pastures in the Columbia Basin to high alpine meadows in the Pasayten for summer grazing. As many as 300,000 sheep per year were taken to the high meadows via a "driveway" that went over Driveway Butte, then up Rattlesnake Creek. Grazing permits have since been drastically reduced; at present only one herd is permitted into the area in alternate years.

The primitive scenic beauty of the North Cascades was recognized in 1934, when the Whatcom Primitive Area was expanded to the 801,000-acre North Cascades Primitive Area. In 1968 most of this primitive area became North Cascades National Park. Unfortunately, Liberty Bell was excluded from both the park and the wilderness classification. Its striking topography certainly merits such protection.

## HIKING
### Ruby Creek to Rainy Pass Trails

**Trail 754, Chancellor/Canyon Creek.** *15.5 miles/d (H,S,B)*. From Granite Creek Guard Station on Highway 20 (1,930 ft), this path enters the dense old-growth forest along Canyon Creek. It follows the creek upstream, crossing several tributaries, passing moldering fragments of cabins and piles of rusting mining equipment. Just after the route crosses Mill Creek, Trail 755 heads off to the east. Trail 754 widens as it follows an old narrow-gauge wagon road for the remaining distance to Chancellor (2,844 ft) northwest of Harts Pass. Chancellor was once a booming mining camp. The trail continues into the Pasayten Wilderness.

**Trail 755, Mill Creek.** *10 miles/m (H; S, but not recommended)*. Branching off from the 5.9-mile point on Trail 475 (2,820 ft), this scenic, rarely used trail began as a route to the Azurite Mine. Its narrow track follows the steep, forested sidehill along Mill Creek. At 3.5 miles the path passes the west end of Trail 475 from Cady Pass, the main route to the mine, and at 4.7 miles the mine itself is reached (4,500 ft). Open spots at tailings give glimpses up to the rugged west face of Mount Ballard. The route continues south along Mill Creek through a 1987 burn, then switchbacks up to Azurite Pass (6,700 ft). Here are great views of Azurite Peak and the impressive north face of Golden Horn. The track descends a steep forested slope along Jet Creek to join the PCT (4,390 ft).

**Trail 756, Mebee Pass/East Creek.** *8 miles/m (H,S)*. From Highway 20 (2,580 ft), switchbacks up a forested nose lead to a rock outcrop with good views down Granite

Creek, and beyond to Crater Mountain. A long, timbered traverse crosses East Creek, then gradually climbs above its north bank to the Gold Hill Mine (4,700 ft). The route drops back to East Creek and follows it south, becoming more obscure as it crosses and recrosses the creek. A mile from the head of the basin the trail zigzags up steep wooded slopes to Mebee Pass (6,500 ft), once a lookout site. From the pass, the way descends gradually to the West Fork of the Methow, where it joins the PCT 0.3 mile south of Jet Creek (4,370 ft).

## Rainy Pass Trails

**Trail 740, Lake Ann/Maple Pass Loop.** *1 mile to Lake Ann/e (H); 6.5 miles for Maple Pass Loop/m (H).* A wide, gentle track leaves south from Rainy Pass (4,900 ft), switchbacks a few times up through dense forest, traverses an open avalanche track, then splits. The spur to the west soon arrives at the cliff-walled cirque containing Lake Ann (5,475 ft); a tiny island pokes through its turquoise surface. The northwest fork climbs above the north side of the lake, then makes a few steep switchbacks to Heather Pass (6,200 ft) and views west across Lewis and Wing Lakes to the imposing summit of Black Peak. The track continues along the top of the cliffs above Lake Ann to Maple Pass (6,300 ft). Imposing scenery includes nearby Corteo Peak and, in the distance, Dome Peak, Spire Point, and Glacier Peak. The route continues along the narrow, open crest above the Lake Ann cirque, then tiptoes down rock steps along the divide between Lake Ann and Rainy Lake. It descends this steep, forested rib to meet Trail 310 and follow it back to Rainy Pass.

## Rainy Pass to Washington Pass Trails

**Trail 426, Copper Pass.** *3.5 miles/m (H,S).* This brushy, seldom-used path leaves Bridge Creek Trail 2172 just north of Copper Creek (4,250 ft) and heads east up that creek's drainage. A few switchbacks take the route out of the creek bottom to wooded slopes above its north bank, where it continues a gentle, but obscure, ascent to bouldery meadows at the head of the drainage. Here it climbs to Copper Pass (6,700 ft), then descends into the Lake Chelan–Sawtooth Wilderness.

**Trail 314, Blue Lake.** *2.2 miles/m (H).* From a pullout on Highway 20 (5,200 ft), this National Recreation Trail enters the forest and parallels the road for a short distance. It then heads up ever-steepening slopes, surmounting them by switchbacks, to reach the north shore of Blue Lake (6,254 ft). The surface reflects a 1,000-foot rock wall above it. East of the lake the towers of Liberty Bell and Early Winter Spires jut into the sky, and ragged Cutthroat Peak decorates the northwest horizon.

## Washington Pass to Mazama Trails

**Trail 483, Cutthroat Pass.** *5.5 miles/e (H,S,B).* A gentle path leaves FR 2000-400 (4,500 ft) and follows the bank of Cutthroat Creek southwest for 1.7 miles to a junction. The spur south leads to Cutthroat Lake (4,935 ft), set in a wide basin surrounded by rugged peaks. The west fork switchbacks up through huge old-growth forest, then enjoys a respite at a bench meadow framed with immense larch. The climb resumes,

*The Liberty Bell massif, seen here from Washington Pass, is one of the most striking sights in the North Cascades. From left to right are Early Winter Spires (pair of tall peaks on the left), Lexington Tower (mid-level peak with small knob on top), Concord Tower, and Liberty Bell.*

swings around the head of a small rocky basin, and arrives at Cutthroat Pass (6,820 ft), where it joins the PCT. At the pass, a panorama of peaks—Silver Star, Liberty Bell, Cutthroat, Dome, Azurite, Ballard, Golden Horn, Tower, and The Needles—encircles the horizon.

**Trail 481, Driveway Butte.** *4 miles/m (H,S,B).* This segment of an old sheep drive leaves Klipchuck Campground (2,900 ft) and heads north alongside Indian Creek. The climb through forest to the head of the creek is steep, but from there the grade eases. It becomes brushy and obscure as it continues northwest, then turns northeast up open slopes to the top of Driveway Butte (5,982 ft). This old lookout site has expansive views down the Methow Valley and across Early Winters Creek to the crags and spires of Silver Star Mountain.

**Trail 476, Cedar Creek.** *9.6 miles/m (H,S,B).* From the gravel pit at the end of FR 5310-200 (3,030 ft), the route, a National Recreation Trail, starts gently up the Cedar Creek drainage, passing through old-growth fir, spruce, and cedar. At 2 miles (3,500 ft) the creek drops 50 to 60 feet over a beautiful falls. The path continues upstream along the bank, reaching meadows with views of Gardner and Silver Star Mountains and the long row of towers that caps the ridge at the head of the valley. The track leaves the meadow for forest as it continues uphill and crosses the west and main forks of the creek. It heads steeply uphill toward seemingly impenetrable Abernathy Ridge. Switchbacks gain the narrow defile of Abernathy Pass (6,420 ft), where the trail drops into North Creek and joins Trail 413 (5,450 ft). Knobs above either side of the pass offer views of Silver Star and the spires along Kangaroo and Snagtooth Ridges.

## Harts Pass Trails

**Trail 480, West Fork of the Methow.** *8 miles/e (H,S,B).* The route leaves River Bend Campground (2,710 ft) and wanders along the bottom of the deep West Fork of the Methow drainage, most of the way in lodgepole pine, except for a few brushy meadows cut by avalanche chutes. At 7 miles the track heads uphill along Brush Creek to join the PCT (4,280 ft).

**Trail 475, Cady Pass.** *10 miles/m (H,S,B).* The trail was once a narrow-gauge road over which supplies were hauled to, and ore from, the Azurite Mine. It heads south from FR 5400-700 (3,850 ft) into the South Fork of Slate Creek drainage. In 1.5 miles the route crosses the creek, then heads northwest in a long lateral climb through beautiful old-growth forest to meadows at 5,200 feet. Switchbacks up an open rib reach Cady Pass (5,980 ft) and a grand scenic display that includes Mount Ballard, Majestic Mountain, Jack Mountain, and Snowfield Peak. A scamper northwest along the ridge for 0.9 mile to an old lookout site at Cady Point has even better views. West of the pass the track swings back and forth as it gradually descends open hillside, then forest, to meet Trail 755 (4,240 ft) a mile north of the Azurite Mine.

## Trail 2000, Pacific Crest National Scenic Trail. *30.7 miles/m (H,S).*

**PCT: Rainy Pass to Methow Pass.** *10.5 miles/m (H,S).* From the north side of Rainy Pass, the trail enters dense fir forest as it gradually climbs into the Porcupine Creek drainage. After crossing the creek, switchbacks take the track high on the slopes above the west bank, where a gradual ascent swings around the head of the basin. A chain of easy-grade switchbacks climbs to Cutthroat Pass (6,830 ft) to meet Trail 483. Here grand views open to Silver Star, Liberty Bell, Cutthroat, and Kangaroo and Sawtooth Ridges. The route continues north from the pass, staying high as it swings across the rocky east side of the crest. It then switchbacks down a narrow rib to Granite Pass (6,300 ft), with views north to The Needles and Tower Mountain. Northwest of the pass, the path contours the steep headwall below Tower Mountain to meadows in a small alpine bowl. A boot-path heads a short distance uphill to Snowy Lakes. The PCT climbs west out of the basin, then traverses to Methow Pass (6,590 ft).

**PCT: Methow Pass to Glacier Pass.** *12 miles/m (H,S).* After leaving Methow Pass, the path switchbacks down the forested lower flank of Golden Horn to the headwaters of the West Fork of the Methow, then follows the dense river bottom north past Trails 756 and 755. As the river bends east, the trail climbs higher above its bank and swings into the Brush Creek drainage, where it meets Trail 480, then ascends along the narrow creek bottom. Near the head of the basin it zigzags uphill to Glacier Pass (5,580 ft), a low saddle between Brush Creek and the South Fork of Slate Creek. There are a few glimpses here of Azurite Peak and Mount Ballard.

**PCT: Glacier Pass to Harts Pass.** *8.2 miles/m (H,S).* From Glacier Pass, switch-backs climb the steep west end of Handcock Ridge, where more meadows overlook Azurite and Ballard. The crest is followed north to the wide meadow of Grasshopper Pass (6,750 ft), where the path crosses into the South Fork of Trout Creek drainage. A contour north near timberline leads to a col (6,890 ft) on the shoulder of Tatie Peak and more views of Mount Ballard. The track traverses around the head of the wide basin southeast of Tatie Peak, passes a col (6,950 ft) at the head of Ninetynine Basin, then swings around a buttress ridge to yet another saddle (6,660 ft) above the North Fork of Trout Creek. A descent north passes the Brown Bear Mine and reaches FR 5400-500 (6,420 ft) 0.5 mile south of Meadows Campground. The road is hiked north to Harts Pass (6,194 ft).

## CLIMBING

The Liberty Bell area has some of the most challenging rock climbing in the Washington Cascades. There are both Dolomite-like spires and Yosemite-like faces within easy hiking distance from Highway 20. Rising dramatically above the south side of Washington Pass is Liberty Bell Mountain (7,720 ft), a dome-shaped peak with near-vertical granite walls jutting more than 1,100 feet above the valley floor. Eleven routes have been put up the peak, all ranging between C-5 and C-5.9. The massif south from Liberty Bell is fractured into five more distinct granite towers: Minuteman, Concord, and Lexington Towers, and North and South Early Winter Spires. All range around 7,500 feet, and all offer vertical wall climbs in the C-5 to C-5.10 range.

Paralleling the Liberty Bell massif to the east is Kangaroo Ridge, a wild, 3-mile-long collection of fins, spires, and crags with vertical north and east sides; each has at least 200 to 500 feet of C-5 to C-5.10 climbing.

Northeast of Kangaroo Ridge is another mile-long group of towers atop Snagtooth Ridge, all with 100- to 300-foot final pitches ranging between C-4 and C-5.7.

North of Snagtooth Ridge is the massive bastion of Silver Star Mountain (8,876 ft), with a star-shaped glacier on its northeast flank and two distinct sets of towers on its northwest ridge. The easiest ascent is a C-3 glacier and rock route, but other climbs reach the summit from the south, southwest buttress, southeast face, and west face; the latter is a complex C-5.8 challenge.

The first group of towers (8,350 to 8,441 ft) north of Silver Star are the Wine Spires: Chablis, Pernod, Chianti, and Burgundy; the latter is the most difficult, C-5.6 to C-5.9. The next group of crags, with moderate faces on the west and sheer ones on the east, are collectively referred to as Vasiliki Ridge. The individual towers are Vasiliki Tower (7,920 ft) and the Acropolis (8,040 ft), C-4 to C-5.5 in difficulty. Farther north are Charon, Ares, Juno-Jupiter, Aphrodite, and Bacchus Towers, all with relatively easy C-3 routes.

On the north side of Highway 20, between Washington and Rainy Passes, is another massive ridge, anchored on the south by Whistler Mountain (7,790 ft), a small, pointed peak with C-4 to C-5.7 routes. The most prominent summit here is Cutthroat Peak (8,050 ft), whose summit block has no trivial routes; all are rated between C-4 and C-5.10. Near Cutthroat Pass is Molar Tooth (7,547 ft), a fang requiring six leads, one C-5.6.

At the east end of the granitic Golden Horn batholith are The Needles (8,140 ft), an isolated group of spires, each with a few leads of rock climbing. The highest has 200 feet of solid rock, with one C-5.5 lead. Tower Mountain (8,444 ft) has an impressive 1,400-foot north face, but can be topped by C-3 to C-4 routes from the south and west. Golden Horn (8,366 ft) is a distinctive-looking rock horn with a sheer 1,700-foot north face, an easy C-3 climb from the south.

A long ridge north of the Golden Horn–Tower massif is capped by Azurite Peak (8,400 ft) and Mount Ballard (8,301 ft). Both have impressive-looking faces, but neither is a technical challenge.

South of Mebee Pass are the Methow Pinnacles, a group of three pyramidal summits atop a long, 1,400-foot-high wall. The highest of these (7,564 ft) has some delicate slab climbing rated C-5; the others are less difficult.

## Winter Sports

Although the Methow Valley is renowned for its ski touring, most of this activity is associated with valley-bottom lodges and ski trails, and very little winter activity penetrates the backcountry of the Liberty Bell Roadless Area. The treeless scars that lace the steep slopes in the heart of the area testify to winter avalanche hazards that justify its avoidance. A few cross-country tours are safe either in early fall when the snow is light, or in late spring when the snowpack is mostly stabilized. These offer an opportunity to enjoy the scenic beauty of the area enhanced by a blanket of snow.

After the first fall snows, but before Highway 20 is closed for the winter, a ski tour to Lake Ann and continuing above it to Heather and Maple Passes offers a winterized sample of the stunning scenery found along this summer trail. Once snows close Highway 20, the road is a popular snowmobiling route, except in conditions of high avalanche danger.

A popular midwinter tour continues up the barricaded highway above Early Winters to the Cedar Creek Trail 476, then heads up that trail to Cedar Falls. The trail is narrow, however, so the downhill run can be dicey.

After Highway 20 reopens in late May, and with stable snow conditions, the PCT can be skied north from Rainy Pass into Porcupine Creek and up to Cutthroat Pass. Avalanche slopes in upper Porcupine Creek must be watched carefully, however. Cutthroat Pass can also be reached by skiing Cutthroat Lake Trail 483, a beautiful trip that is safe from any avalanche hazard until it reaches the final small bowl just below the pass.

When the Harts Pass road first opens, a great, relatively safe, tour heads south past Meadows Campground, then up the ridge above the Brown Bear Mine. After skiers feast on the views from a 7,200-foot knob at the head of the ridge, a downhill run through the forested basin to the east leads back to the campground.

## 44 Chewuch River Region

### Long Swamp, Long Draw, and Tiffany Roadless Areas

**Location:** In Okanogan County, along the southeast rim of the Pasayten Wilderness, west of Salmon and Toats Coulee Creeks

**Size:** Long Swamp, 70,180 acres; Long Draw, 4,652 acres; Tiffany, 24,027 acres

**Status:** Semiprimitive Roadless; motorized recreation permitted on some trails

**Terrain:** Creeks and rivers run through deep canyons with moderately steep side slopes, topped by benches and rounded ridge tops.

**Elevation:** 2,500 to 8,250 feet

**Management:** USFS, Okanogan–Wenatchee National Forest, Methow Valley and Tonasket Ranger Districts

**Topographic maps:** Billy Goat Mtn., Conconully West, Coleman Peak, Coxit Mountain, Doe Mountain, Mt. Barney, Old Baldy, Spur Peak, Sweetgrass Butte, Tiffany Mtn.

Long Swamp, a large wedge-shaped roadless area south of the Pasayten Wilderness, is bisected by the Chewuch River Road. Logging has encroached on the southern fringes of the area. The side-slopes of Long Swamp's high, rounded ridges are cut by deep peripheral stream drainages and are covered mostly by a terminal succession of lodgepole pine. Larger Douglas-fir, ponderosa pine, and Engelmann spruce grow in drainages and

*This early photo shows a ranger carrying water for the lookout on North Twentymile Peak. The lookout is no longer staffed, although the structure still stands.*

draws, but these have been rapidly reduced by selective logging. The extensive meadows that line ridge tops and wider valley floors have colorful wildflower displays in spring. The Long Draw Roadless Area is a long, rolling, lodgepole pine–covered ridge off the southeast tip of the Pasayten Wilderness.

The forested flanks and open parklands of the north–south backbone of the Tiffany Roadless Area are a utopia of leisurely hikes. The longest single trail is just over 6 miles, and almost all of the routes can be linked to form day-hike loops. Although logging has chewed around the borders of Tiffany, old-growth stands remain untouched in the lower portions of the area. Once above timberline, both dry and damp meadows are covered by multiple species of grasses, flowers, and shrubs. Although the area has only four lakes, two are in beautiful subalpine settings. The open ridges and two timber-free summits that once held fire lookouts provide sweeping views of both distant snow-clad peaks and dry rolling plateaus.

## CLIMATE

A relatively dry eastern Washington climate pervades the area, with mean annual precipitation between 19 and 26 inches, much falling as winter snows. The mean midwinter minimum temperatures are 8 to 12 degrees, and mean midsummer maximums range from 77 to 84. Extended periods in which temperatures exceed these averages are not uncommon.

## ECOSYSTEM

North slopes and creek drainages support stands of Douglas-fir and ponderosa pine, with Engelmann spruce in draws. Old-growth stands are found on Middle Tiffany Mountain and along Isabel, Clark, Pelican, and the North Fork of Salmon Creeks. Higher elevations are covered mostly by lodgepole pine, with some occurrences of western white pine, Engelmann spruce, subalpine fir, and some western larch. The ground cover on open ridge-top meadows includes sedges, bluegrass, fescue, Indian paintbrush, lupine, columbine, valerian, needlegrass, wheatgrass, buckwheat, gilia, penstemon, saxifrage, stonecrop, lupine, paintbrush, and pussytoes.

The upper Chewuch River drainage has been proposed as a 10,000-acre RNA because of its unique ecosystem, which includes riparian hardwoods, black cottonwood, and willow along the river; Engelmann spruce and subalpine fir on lower slopes; an upwelling spring; and lodgepole pine forest with subalpine meadows at higher altitudes. Tiffany has been proposed as a Research Natural Area by virtue of several unique ecosystems represented here. Specific ecological cells are an Engelmann spruce–subalpine forest; an alpine community mosaic; an oligothorpic lake; a permanent pond; a vernal pond; and subalpine sagebrush parkland.

The forest is home for mule deer, black bear, marten, fisher, blue grouse, and one of the largest lynx populations in the country. The Chewuch River corridor is a wintering ground and spring fawning habitat for the large Methow mule deer herd. Among threatened or sensitive species in the area are grizzly bear, golden eagle, northern bog lemming, water vole, wolverine, and three-toed woodpecker.

## GEOLOGY

The base rock of the region was created 60 million to 150 million years ago when the west side of the Okanogan microcontinent fractured and was subducted by oceanic crust, leaving its cover of sedimentary rock in a trench along the west side of the tiny plate. Hot basalt rising above the sinking slab and magma from newly emerging volcanoes along the continental rim transformed this trench rock into the granitic base of the area. Base rock is highly mineralized in the upper Bernhart Creek drainage, at the southwest corner of the Tiffany area, and near Rock Mountain, on its north border. Lode ore consists of veins of silver and lead; some low-grade surface uranium deposits also exist. This granite is covered in most places with a layer of glacial till and volcanic ash from the last series of eruptions of Glacier Peak. The principal drainages of the area display the characteristic U-shaped form of glacier-carved valleys, created when the last continental ice sheets overrode the area 15 million years ago.

## HISTORY

The Chewuch River and its main tributaries were identified on maps dated as early as 1873, so some exploration had been done prior to that time. In 1879 all of present-day Okanogan County was designated as a reservation for the Columbia tribe headed by Chief Moses. The reservation was opened to homesteading in 1886, but only a few settlers dribbled into the area. Prospectors soon thronged to the hills north and west of Conconully to engage in hard-rock mining of its silver deposits. Prosperity was short-lived, and most mines closed when the bottom dropped out of the silver market in 1893.

Tiffany Mountain, and its present surrounding roadless area, are thought to be

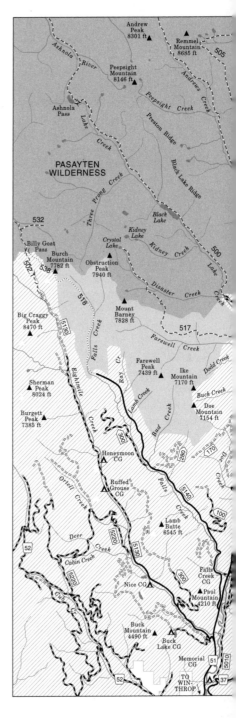

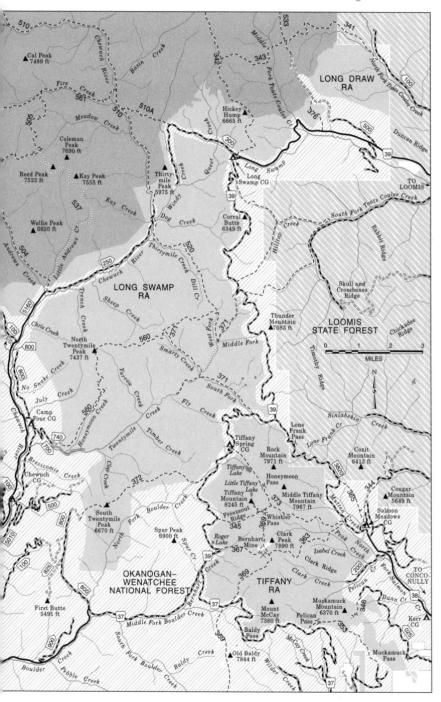

named for Perry and William Tiffany, brothers who came to the area at the height of the mining boom. Although the brothers were rumored to be members of the wealthy Tiffany Jewelry Company family, archive searches indicated that they were probably just distant relatives of the founder of that firm.

The first forest reserves in Washington were established in 1897, and they rapidly became grazing ranges for cattle and sheep as newly arriving settlers began claiming and fencing the fertile valley floors. In 1911 the huge Chelan National Forest was partitioned, and the portion in Okanogan County became the Okanogan National Forest. Throughout its early history the forest was used mostly for grazing, and several of today's trails are old stock driveways.

During the 1920s, the Forest Service put fire lookouts atop Burch and Doe Mountains and North Twentymile Peak, and built trails to serve them. The original lookout on North Twentymile Creek still stands, with its unique cupola atop a log-cabin ground house. It is believed to be one of the last lookouts of this style still in existence. As is obvious around the perimeters of the roadless areas, logging has been the dominant industry in the area over the past 50 years.

## HIKING

Trails originating in the roadless areas that continue into the Pasayten Wilderness are described under region 42, Pasayten.

### Eightmile Creek Trails

*Trail 518, Falls Creek.* 5.2 *miles/m* (H). An unmaintained trail, once used to support a lookout atop Burch Mountain, heads southeast from Trail 502.1 at Billy Goat Pass (6,600 ft). The tread may be washed out or it may disappear in places, but it is relatively easy to follow. The long traverse of an open southwest-facing sidehill has continuous views of the vertical rock faces of the Craggy group of peaks, and Isabella Ridge beyond. After a few switchbacks at the end of the traverse, the path rounds a small rib to a bench, reverses direction, and climbs to the former lookout site atop the mountain (7,782 ft). In addition to the Craggys, the Pasayten Wilderness now comes into view. The route continues down the ridge to the south, then dips into the Falls Creek headwater basin. The poorly maintained path follows the steeply dropping creek to the end of FR 5140 (4,900 ft).

### Chewuch River Trails

*Trail 517, Crystal Lake.* 9.2 *miles/m* (H,S). After leaving FR 5160-080 (2,800 ft) the trail makes long lazy switchbacks up the forested slopes north of Farewell Creek, then follows the valley west, keeping high above the creek. In 3.5 miles, the way bends north into a marshy basin and climbs across a 6,100-foot saddle into the Pasayten Wilderness. It drops to cross Disaster Creek, then follows it upstream to Crystal Lake (7,114 ft), a beautiful little alpine lake hidden in tall timber stands.

*Trail 560, North Fork Twentymile.* 5.7 *miles/d* (H,S,B). After starting on abandoned FR 5010-740 (3,200 ft), the track turns into the Honeymoon Creek drainage for a long, gradual ascent up the west bank of the creek. Near the steeper head of the basin switchbacks climb to the broad ridge crest (6,800 ft), where meadows escort the path to the top of North Twentymile Peak (7,437 ft). Here are a pair of fire lookouts, an ancient cupola-style one built in 1923 and a more modern one completed in 1948. A sea of timbered ridges rolls west to Silver Star Mountain, southeast to Tiffany Mountain, and north to the Pasayten Wilderness. A seldom-maintained section of trail continues east in ridge-top meadows, then slowly descends the broad crest to join Trail 371 at the head of the Smarty Creek basin (6,480 ft).

**Trail 371, Smarty Creek.** *11.7 miles/m (H,S,B).* From FR 39 at the point it crosses the South Fork of Twentymile Creek (5,840 ft), the route heads downstream to the northwest, along boggy South Twentymile Meadows. At 2.5 miles (5,450 ft) the path crosses Twentymile Creek to reach the mouth of Smarty Creek, then follows the latter creek upstream to a saddle (6,480 ft) where it meets Trail 560 from North Twentymile Peak. The route heads east, ascends a broad gentle ridge to 6,890 feet, then drops down a steep hillside to the West Fork of Twentymile Creek. It follows meadows northeast along the West Fork, then turns north to Thirtymile Meadows.

## Tiffany Area Trails

**Trail 373, Tiffany Lake.** *8.5 miles/m (H,S,B).* This route runs east–west across the north end of the Tiffany area. From Tiffany Spring Campground on FR 39 (6,750 ft), the trail descends a short distance east to Tiffany Lake (6,550 ft). From the lake, it climbs through forest and a succession of meadows to Honeymoon Pass (7,150 ft). A short scramble through the woods to the southwest reaches cliff-bound Little Tiffany Lake (7,370 ft). From Honeymoon Pass, the track drops briefly into the headwaters of the North Fork of Salmon Creek, then climbs diagonally up a cliff face to a ridge-crest meeting with Trail 345 (7,300 ft). The route follows the narrow rib east to meadows along the broadening crest above Peak Creek. A descent of the forested ridge nose leads to FR 3820 (4,920 ft).

**Trail 345, Freezeout Ridge.** *3.7 miles/m (H,S,B).* The trail leaves FR 39 at a saddle (6,580 ft) and heads up the forested ridge to the east to break into meadows at 1.5 miles. A steady ascent of the broad open shoulder of Tiffany Mountain passes spurs to the summit and works around its steeper south side to meet Trail 369 at Whistler Pass (7,600 ft). The track ends 0.5 mile farther east where it joins Trail 373 (7,300 ft).

**Trail 367, Bernhart Mine.** *3 miles/m (H,S,B).* From FR 39 (5,740 ft), this old miners' route heads east through woods along the bank of Bernhart Creek. It follows a fork of the creek to the southeast past boggy meadows, then swings north up the basin wall to the Bernhart Mine (6,640 ft). From the mine, the trail shoots up steep slopes, with nary a switchback, to a parkland junction with Trail 369 (7,360 ft).

**Trail 369, North Summit.** *6.5 miles/m (H,S,B).* This old stock driveway heads into the woods north of FR 37 (5,840 ft) and follows the ridge to the northeast, sometimes in forest, sometimes in meadow. After skirting several ridge-top knobs, the way reaches a narrow saddle with views north to the long, meadow-capped crest between Clark and Tiffany Mountains. The route heads east up a narrow ridge, traverses past two

*The Bernhart Mine trail follows an old miners' route; Tiffany Mountain is in the distance.*

knobs, and meets Trail 363 on the south rib of Clark Peak. A long sidehill contour of meadows on the east flank of Clark passes the head of Trail 367, then the way ascends to Whistler Pass (7,600 ft) where it meets Trail 345.

**Trail 363, Clark Ridge.** *4.5 miles/m (H,S,B).* A hundred yards beyond the east end of Trail 373 (5,030 ft), this route turns southwest into the Peak Creek drainage, descends to a creek crossing, then climbs to the divide between Peak and Isabel Creeks. The way follows this wooded crest west, then traverses south around the head of Isabel Creek to Clark Ridge. A gradual ascent on south slopes below the ridge top reaches the rocky headwall below the south face of Clark Peak. A few switchbacks gain a saddle at the head of the basin where Trail 369 is joined (7,320 ft).

## Winter Sports

The west flank of the Tiffany area is inaccessible in the winter except for long snow-mobile approaches over snowbound forest roads. FR 38, up the North Fork of Salmon Creek, is generally plowed as far as Salmon Meadows Campground, so eastside trails are within easy reach of cross-country skiers, and there are few avalanche hazards along the paths of summer trails.

# Sawtooth Ridge Region

### Lake Chelan–Sawtooth Wilderness; Sawtooth (South), Chelan (East), Hungry Ridge, and Black Canyon Roadless Areas

**Location:** In Chelan and Okanogan Counties, between the east side of Lake Chelan, the Lake Chelan National Recreation Area, and North Cascades National Park, and Highways 20 and 153.

**Size:** Wilderness, 145,667 acres; Sawtooth (South), 96,682 acres; Chelan (East), 23,780 acres; Hungry Ridge, 11,431 acres; Black Canyon, 11,935 acres

**Status:** Designated Wilderness (1984); Roadless areas are Semiprimitive, some Motorized, some Nonmotorized

**Terrain:** A high backbone ridge running northwest to southeast the length of the wilderness continues into the roadless areas to the south. Several creeks originate high on the central rib, then drain through steep-sided lateral valleys separated by subalpine ridges whose outer ends drop abruptly to Lake Chelan, and the Twisp and Methow Rivers.

**Elevation:** 1,098 to 8,974 feet

**Management:** USFS, Okanogan–Wenatchee National Forest, Chelan and Methow Valley Ranger Districts; and a few patented private mining claims

**Topographic maps:** Big Goat Mtn., Cooper Mtn., Gilbert, Hoodoo Peak, Hungry Mtn., Lucerne, Martin Peak, Mazama, McAlester Mtn., Midnight Mountain, Oss Peak, Oval Peak, Pateros, Prince Creek, Rendevous Mountain, Silver Star Mtn., South Navarre Peak, Sun Mountain, Thompson Ridge, Washington Pass

On the west the wilderness rises abruptly from Lake Chelan to the subalpine crest of the Sawtooth Range, which runs northwest–southeast through the wilderness and the roadless areas to its south. On the northeast side of the crest, the terrain drops to the wide, glacier-carved valley of the Twisp and Methow Rivers. Another steep subrange rises on both sides of Wolf Creek between the head of the Twisp and Winthrop Rivers, in the Methow Valley. Creeks cut deep, narrow lateral drainages northeast and southwest from the summit backbone. The range is capped by pyramid-shaped summits, most with gentle slopes to the southwest and vertical rock faces on the north.

High cirques hold 96 lakes, more than half so small that they don't even bear names. Most are in rugged alpine settings, and only eighteen or so

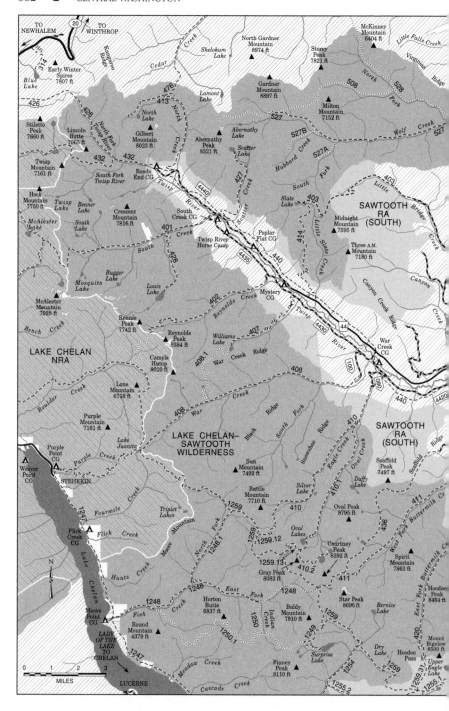

are reached by spur trails (mercifully, most closed to motorized traffic). In many cases the lack of trails is not a deterrent to visiting lakes, as cross-country travel is relatively easy in the open timber and parkland at upper elevations on the southeast side of the crest.

Unfortunately, acceding to multiple-use concepts, the Forest Service accepted the existing motorized use in the non-wilderness portions of Sawtooth Ridge, and has reconstructed 22 miles of trails, converting them to motorcycle highways. This use would have been precluded had the roadless areas been originally included in the wilderness. Thankfully, a few trails (mostly old sheep drives) are too delicate, steep, or rough for motorized travel. These tend to follow the tops of the area's highest ridges, and therefore offer outstanding scenery.

A diverse group of biological communities can be found in the wilderness, and the trails here climb through the spectrum of east Cascade timber, bushes, grasses, and flowers. The sunny drier climate of eastern Washington means that flowers bloom earlier and trails open sooner than in areas in the heart of the Cascades. These favorable climatic conditions bring with them certain negatives, including an increased likelihood of encountering such annoyances as rattlesnakes and ticks.

## CLIMATE

The Methow Valley is influenced more by continental weather patterns than by the Pacific Ocean weather systems that dominate the climate west of the Cascades. As a result, winters are colder and clearer, and summers drier and hotter, than the same seasons in regions 50 miles to the west. Midwinter temperatures average in the 20s, with lows from minus 30 to 10 degrees. Average summer temperatures are in the 70s, and the summer highs are over 90. Annual precipitation is a sparse 18 to 23 inches in the Methow Valley, and up to 75 inches at the crest, mostly falling as snow during winter months. Snow depths reach 4 to 5 feet at mid-level elevations, and as deep as 12 feet at the crest.

## ECOSYSTEM

Because of the wide elevation differential in the Lake Chelan–Sawtooth Wilderness and surrounding roadless areas, several east-slope ecological zones are represented within its boundaries. West of the crest its lower-level forests are mostly ponderosa pine, Pacific silver fir, Douglas-fir, and western larch, while the east side forests are mostly western larch and lodgepole pine. The understory varies with soil composition: the finer-textured soils support snowberry, oceanspray, sedges, arnica, and woods rose; the rockier areas grow fescue, wheatgrass, balsamroot, dwarf mountain fleabane, and needle and thread. Above 3,500 feet, pinegrass is added to this mix.

With another 500 to 1,000 feet of altitude, subalpine fir, Engelmann spruce, western white pine, and mountain hemlock may appear. Understory shrubs include huckleberry, baldhip rose, and prickly currant; herbs and flowers here are bigleaf sandwort, wild ginger, anemone, arnica, trillium, queencup beadlily, wood violet, and dwarf blackberry.

Above 4,800 feet the trees shade to subalpine fir, Engelmann spruce, whitebark pine, and lodgepole pine. Ground cover includes huckleberry, beargrass, and, on damper north slopes, Cascades azalea, rustyleaf, and Labrador tea.

Wildlife common to the area includes mule deer, mountain goat, cougar, and black bear. Part of the Methow Valley mule deer herd, the largest in the state, spends summer in the wilderness and migrates in fall; fawns are born in the vicinity of Gilbert Mountain. Bald and golden eagles are often seen in the winter along the Methow River, and peregrine falcons are occasionally spotted during their spring and fall migrations.

## GEOLOGY

The wilderness lies adjacent to the point of collision, some 60 million years ago, between the North Cascades microcontinent and the west coast of North America. Most of the rock in the area is metamorphic, formed from sedimentary and volcanic strata on the flanks of the two continents about 100 million to 140 million years ago. Their meeting resulted in tight folding and uplifting of this metamorphic base, forming the precursor to the Sawtooth Range of today.

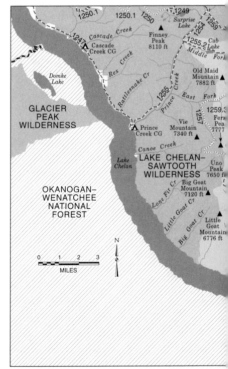

Continued northerly movement of the microcontinent resulted in the Gardner Fault, which runs roughly along the ridgeline northeast of the Twisp River. This fault marks the west edge of the Methow graben, a wide strip of rock between this fault line and the parallel Pasayten Fault to the east that dropped relative to surrounding rock and was later overlaid with sedimentary deposits. A large granitic intrusion in the vicinity of Gilbert, at the head of the Twisp Valley, created the extensive mineral deposits along its margins that later brought prospectors to the region.

The U-shaped valley of the Twisp typifies the sculpting of glaciers over the last two million years. Although most glaciers have disappeared from the area, small hanging ice fields on a few peaks have extensive moraines below, testifying to their once-larger expanse. Creeks have more recently eroded narrow and deep, V-shaped drainages that carve through many of the lateral ridges.

Soils are granitic glacial till covered with volcanic ash of varying thickness, laid down in the last eruptions of Glacier Peak.

## HISTORY

Alexander Ross, of the British North West Company, and three Indian guides explored the north end of the Twisp River in 1814. They probed northwest from South Creek, possibly through Rainy Pass, to the headwaters of the Skagit River. In 1853, Army survey crews under the command of Captain George B. McClellan, looking for possible railroad routes across the Cascades, tested the headwaters of the Twisp and found no practical route to breach the range. In 1882, another Army party, under Lieutenant Henry Pierce, searching for a military route across the Cascades, left the middle Twisp, crossed War Creek Pass, and continued on to Lake Chelan and beyond to the Skagit River.

The first mineral discoveries were made in 1884, and these brought hordes of prospectors to the area over the next six to ten years. The mining camp of Gilbert grew near the head of the Twisp River, and more than two hundred claims were soon plastered over most of Gilbert Mountain, Twisp Pass, Crescent Mountain, and Abernathy Peak. Other mines were developed on the forks of Gold Creek, five miles to the southeast. The ores were mostly silver-bearing, with some occurrences of copper and placer gold. Although the surface ores had a high assay value, few mines had significant production,

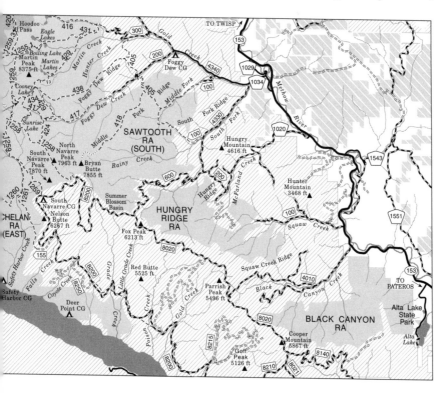

and by 1921 Gilbert lay deserted. Limited mining activity is still carried on at a few of the old claims.

The meadows along ridge tops and in high basins have been used since the 1920s for grazing sheep; short sections of a long sheep driveway from Chelan to the Pasayten still exist on the eastern slopes, and are still used for this purpose. A number of the area's trails were put in and maintained by sheepherders.

In the 1930s fire lookouts were constructed atop ten of the area peaks and ridge tops, and more trails were added for their support. All of these lookouts were destroyed in the 1950s. Lower portions of the ridges on the east and southeast sides of the region have been heavily logged in recent years.

## HIKING

Note: In the summer of 2001 the Rex Creek fire burned more than 50,000 acres of timber on the west slope of the Lake Chelan–Sawtooth Wilderness and adjoining roadless areas. Numerous trails suffered severe damage. Repairs are planned; however, when all will be completed is uncertain. When planning a hike in this area, first check with the Chelan Ranger District office for trail conditions.

### Lake Chelan Trails

All trailheads on Lake Chelan must be reached via either private boat or passenger ferry from Chelan. Passengers can board or disembark at Prince Creek, Moore Point, and Stehekin; stops must be prearranged with the Lake Chelan Boat Company.

*Trail 1247, Lakeshore Trail. 18 miles (14 miles in the wilderness)/e (H,S).* This path runs through the north half of the wilderness bordering Lake Chelan; there are no trails along the precipitous south half of the shoreline. The trail runs from Prince Creek Campground, on the south, to Flick Creek Campground, just inside the Lake Chelan NRA on the north, then continues to Stehekin. As the way leaves Prince Creek (1,128 ft) it passes the lower end of Trail 1255, then gradually works up to 400 feet above the lake. It stays at this level, with minor ups and downs, as it crosses cascades of several creeks and periodically breaks into viewpoints of the lake and surrounding peaks.

The way wanders up to 1,720 feet, then drops in a few lazy switchbacks to Fish Creek. Here a spur leads west to Moore Point, one of the ferry stops. En route it passes the site of an old hotel, built in 1889–92 to accommodate the rush of prospectors, visitors, and settlers into the upper lake region. Trail 1248 heads east up the Fish Creek drainage, and Trail 1247 continues north near the 1,600-foot level to the NRA boundary.

*Trail 1255, Prince Creek. 14 miles/m (H,S; B,M east of Cub Lake).* From Trail 1247 (1,128 ft), switchbacks climb above the northwest side of the narrow, deep, lower Prince Creek drainage. The path then ascends gradually through a ponderosa forest, crosses the creek (2,715 ft), and continues up its east side to the confluence of the Middle and North Forks (4,200 ft). Here, at a junction with Trail 1254, it swings east and follows the Middle Fork of Prince Creek east past Cub Lake (5,235 ft), crosses Trail 1259, then climbs to Boiling Lake (6,950 ft). From this pretty, meadow-rimmed lake, gentle switchbacks climb to Horsehead Pass (7,580 ft), where the path becomes Trail 431.

**Trail 1248, Fish Creek.** *10 miles/m (H,S).* From Trail 1247 (1,320 ft), this route ascends the steep sidehill above the north bank of Fish Creek to 2,400 feet, where Trail 1250.1 leaves to the southeast. The path continues its ascent above the creek, finally closing to it at the confluence of the North and East Forks, the junction (3,560 ft) with Trail 1248.1.

The only maintenance on Trail 1248 above this point is by a guide service, just prior to hunting season. The route follows the boggy East Fork another 3 miles, staying within a few hundred feet of its bank, then crosses the creek to the lower end of Trail 1250. The ascending track crosses the creek three more times before it reaches an alpine meadow and meets Trail 1259 (6,750 ft). The

*A boat brings hikers to several Lake Chelan trailheads.*

two trails share the tread for 0.2 mile, then Trail 1248 heads uphill, crosses the outlet from Star Lake (7,173 ft), and climbs to Fish Creek Pass (7,500 ft), where it becomes Trail 411.

**Trail 1248.1, North Fork of Fish Creek.** *3 miles/m (H,S).* A link to Trail 1259 leaves Trail 1248 at the confluence of the North and East Forks of Fish Creek. The grade through dense forest is steep, but eventually it levels at a meadow with the first of two creek crossings (both hazardous at high water). A more gradual ascent with a final steep scamper leads to Trail 1259 (5,640 ft).

**Trail 1250, Indianhead Basin.** *4 miles/m (H,S).* From Trail 1248 (5,030 ft), switchbacks out of the East Fork of Fish Creek lead up the west bank of a tributary. The route rounds a nose into the Indian Creek drainage, crosses the creek, and follows gentle slopes below cliffs to the rocky head of the basin. The way climbs talus to a deep narrow col (7,350 ft). Here are great views south to Finney Peak and the steep north face of the ridge between it and Surprise Lake. The route traverses east from the pass below a cliff band to join Trail 1249 (6,880 ft). The trail is only maintained by hunting party guides.

**Trail 1249, Surprise Lake.** *2.5 miles/m-d (H,S).* Leaving Trail 1259 (6,530 ft) east of Baldy Mountain, this path climbs through forest and across rocky slopes to a broad saddle on the ridge to the south (7,050 ft). It descends the rocky sidehill west of the saddle, meets the upper end of Trail 1250, then swings east and switchbacks down a rough path to the west shore of Surprise Lake (6,150 ft). The long lake is wedged in a deep basin at the base of the 800-foot-high cliffs of Finney Ridge.

## South Navarre Campground Trails

**Trail 1261, Safety Harbor.** *4.5 miles/m (H,S,B,M).* Starting at the end of FR 8200-155 (4,325 ft), the trail follows an old roadbed beside an abandoned aqueduct northwest for 2 miles, to where it meets Safety Harbor Creek and Trail 1260. Here the trail twists uphill along the creek to meet Trail 1259 (5,520 ft).

**Trail 1260, Uno Peak.** *6.5 miles/m (H,S,B,M).* From Trail 1261 at Safety Harbor Creek (4,500 ft), the route heads up across the broad, steep, timbered southeast face

*Hikers follow the Chelan Lakeshore Trail in the Sawtooth Wilderness.*

of Uno Peak. Switchbacks lead to a ridge-crest notch where the way swings onto the south face of the peak and makes a diagonal ascent to another saddle on the west edge of that face. The route climbs along the west side of the peak, then drops to a bench above Miners Basin. It follows this bench around the head of the basin to meet Trail 1259 (6,260 ft).

**Trail 1259, Summit Trail.** *27 miles (11.5 miles outside the wilderness boundary)/m (H,S; B,M from South Navarre Campground to junction with Trail 1255).* From South Navarre Campground (6,410 ft), the trail descends through forest and meadow to Safety Harbor Creek, where it meets the north end of Trail 1261 (6,100 ft). It follows the creek northwest into Miners Basin to meet Trail 1260, then climbs steeply to reach the west slopes of Horsethief Basin.

At the pass at the head of this basin (7,390 ft), the path meets Trail 1258. Switchbacks descend to the headwaters of the East Fork of Prince Creek, where a traverse of the basin meadows leads to Trail 1259.32. The route continues north to the headwaters of the Middle Fork of Prince Creek. At the creek the route crosses Trail 1255, turns sharply west, and ascends steep side slopes to Chipmunk Pass (7,040 ft) on the divide between the Middle and North Forks of Prince Creek, the wilderness boundary. En route it passes the lower end of Trail 1259.31 to Hoodoo Pass.

From Chipmunk Pass, the route drops steeply to a tributary of the North Fork of Prince Creek and follows it down to the head of Trail 1254. A diagonal ascent through the forested basin east of Baldy Mountain leads to Trail 1249. The way climbs north from the basin to reach ridge-top meadows at a divide (7,640 ft) above the East Fork of Fish Creek.

The route switchbacks down a wooded cliff to the basin at the head of the East Fork of Fish Creek, then makes a long traverse through timberline parkland to pass Trail 1248. The path swings around the southwest flank of Gray Peak, where Trail 1259.13 heads uphill for Horsethief Basin. After crossing a narrow saddle (7,390 ft), a short traverse to yet another pass (7,050 ft) leads to the headwaters of the North Fork of Fish Creek.

The route descends into forest as it heads north past Trail 1259.12, then continues down to meet the upper end of Trail 1248.1 (5,640 ft). It swings west to follow the North Fork of Fish Creek to its headwaters, then climbs above them to a 7,240-foot pass where it enters the Lake Chelan NRA.

**Trail 1258, Summer Blossom.** *6 miles/m-d (H).* Another old sheep driveway, improved in the 1930s by the CCC, leaves FR 8200 (6,430 ft) in the Summer Blossom Basin and heads northwest along Sawtooth Ridge. Much of the way is in meadows and rocky flower gardens along the crest, where the tread is faint. Views of the peaks of the Glacier Peak Wilderness and the Methow Valley are priceless. The path strays off the ridge to avoid North Navarre Peak, but sightseers can scramble to its top (7,963 ft) for expanded scenic views. After meeting the upper end of Trail 424, the route slips from the crest to its upper west slope and bends around a rocky rib into Horsethief Basin. It continues to a saddle at the head of the basin (7,390 ft), where it merges with Trail 1259.

**Trail 1259.31, Hoodoo Pass.** *1.3 miles/e (H,S).* The route leaves Trail 1259 (6,650 ft) and climbs gradually through a broad, open, timber-and-meadow basin to Hoodoo Pass (7,430 ft), where it crosses into the wilderness and becomes Trail 420.

## East Slope Trails, South of the Twisp River

**Trail 405, Pasayten Drive.** *5 miles/m (H,S,B,M).* This is one of the few remaining sections of an 80-mile-long sheep drive from the Chelan area north to the Pasayten highlands. Most of the route has been decimated by roads and logging, but this short piece is still used to access ridge-crest grazing trails. The north end of this trail segment starts at Crater Creek on FR 4340-300 (3,200 ft) and switchbacks south to the top of Foggy Dew Ridge (4,550 ft), where it meets the east end of Trail 438. From here, it drops steeply southeast to Foggy Dew Creek and FR 4340-200 (2,922 ft). Switchbacks regain lost elevation, and the way joins Trail 418 atop Middle Fork Ridge (4,685 ft). After sharing a tread for 1.3 miles, this path leaves Trail 418 and traverses south to the Middle Fork of Gold Creek (3,270 ft). A short climb reaches a saddle in South Fork Ridge (4,005 ft), then the route descends to FR 4330-100 (3,380 ft) in the South Fork of Gold Creek drainage.

**Trail 418, Bryan Butte.** *10 miles/m (H,S,B,M).* This unmaintained sheep drive starts from the end of a spur up the Middle Fork of Gold Creek off FR 4340 (2,200 ft). It continues up the creek to join Trail 405 and shares its tread to the top of Middle Fork Ridge (4,685 ft). The route heads southwest, keeping atop the broad ridge as it climbs through open forest and meadows with excellent views of the south end of the Sawtooth crest. At 7 miles the ridge top narrows, with steep drop-offs on both sides; the trail stays steadfastly along its top. The path swings sharply south on a ridge north from Bryan Butte and ascends arrow-straight to the top of the butte (7,855 ft).

**Trail 417, Foggy Dew.** *7.6 miles/m-d (H,S,B,M).* From the end of FR 4340-200 (3,440 ft), the track follows the north bank of Foggy Dew Creek, passing the flashing cascade of Foggy Dew Falls in 1.6 miles. The path continues upstream for 3.4 more miles to meet Trail 429, beyond which it is closed to motorbikes. Switchbacks leave forest for the meadows of Merchants Basin. Shortly Trail 417.2 heads south; Trail 417 continues up to Merchants Basin. An indistinct tread leads to switchbacks up talus slopes to a notch (7,970 ft) on the east rib of Switchback Peak, where Trail 434 is joined. The path now contours the south face of the peak to the Sawtooth crest (8,040 ft), where it continues west as Trail 1259.32.

**Trail 438, Foggy Dew Ridge.** *4.8 miles/d (H,S,B,M).* This sheep driveway runs along the crest of Foggy Dew Ridge. It leaves Trail 405 (4,550 ft) at a ridge-top saddle and climbs abruptly up a steep forested nose to a long gentle ascent atop the rounded crest. Breaks in the timber give views down into the Martin and Foggy Dew drainages, and occasional glimpses of the Sawtooth crest. The trail, unmaintained and indistinct in places, stays on the ridge top for 3 miles to where the crest swings north around upper Hunter Creek. The way contours the hillside, maintaining a constant elevation until it joins Trail 429 (6,800 ft) a short distance below Cooney Lake.

**Trail 429, Martin Creek.** *8.9 miles/e (H,S,B,M).* From the 2.5-mile point on Trail

431 (5,720 ft), this route weaves down to cross Eagle Creek (5,235 ft), then gradually ascends side slopes northwest of Martin Creek through old-growth forest. At 6.5 miles a side path, Trail 429.1, reaches the twin Martin Lakes (6,729 ft and 6,820 ft) lying in larch-rimmed meadows. The route wanders gradually uphill around the headwaters of Martin Creek to meet Trail 434 (7,240 ft). A short descent southeast passes the west end of Trail 438, then the way drops down slopes above a fork of Foggy Dew Creek to end on Trail 417 (6,645 ft).

**Trail 434, Cooney Lake.** *1.5 miles/m-d (H,S).* In a meadow just 0.2 mile from Trail 429 lies Cooney Lake (7,241 ft), with more than a half-dozen small ponds above its west shore. A primitive path continues southwest from the lake, where tight switchbacks up a steep talus slope reach a notch (7,970 ft) on the east rib of Switchback Peak and the junction with Trail 417 from Merchants Basin and Trail 1259.32 from the west.

**Trail 431, Eagle Lakes.** *7 miles/e (H,S,B,M).* From the end of FR 4340-300 (4,750 ft), the route follows Crater Creek upstream to a fork in 1 mile, then swings south as it climbs around the nose of the ridge between Crater and Martin Creeks. Long diagonal ascents linked by tailored-for-motorcycle switchbacks gradually work up the forested side slope past the junction with Trail 429. The ascent becomes steeper as it passes Trail 431.1 to Upper Eagle Lake (7,110 ft). Trail 431.2 descends from the first of the switchbacks below Horsehead Pass to Lower Eagle Lake (6,490 ft). The way climbs to Horsehead Pass (7,580 ft), where it continues west as Trail 1255.11.

**Trail 420, East Fork of Buttermilk Creek.** *6.5 miles/m (H,S).* The first 2 miles beyond FR 4300-400 (4,750 ft) are on an abandoned road along the East Fork of Buttermilk Creek. At the road's end the track crosses the creek and continues a gentle ascent of the wooded creek bottom. The way crosses the creek twice near the head of the basin, where it becomes steep and rocky as it breaks into the talus and boulder slope on the north side of Hoodoo Pass. The pass (7,630 ft) marks the wilderness boundary, where this trail becomes 1259.31 and drops down the south side of the pass to Trail 1259.

**Trail 411, West Fork of Buttermilk Creek.** *9.5 miles/m (H,S).* At the end of FR 4300-500 (3,800 ft), the way gradually ascends the wooded bottom of the West Fork of Buttermilk Creek drainage. After a potentially dangerous creek crossing at 0.1 mile, the path continues up the deep, wedge-shaped valley, through boggy sections where the path closes with the creek. Near the head of the drainage, the route crosses to the southeast side of the creek; switchbacks gain a tree-covered bench. After another creek crossing, a steep ascent breaks into rocky scrub with a glimpse of talus marking the terminal moraine of a onetime pocket glacier on the north side of Star Peak. At Fish Creek Pass (7,530 ft) this route becomes Trail 1248 as it descends the west side of the range.

**Trail 436, Oval Peak.** *9 miles/m (H,S).* This old stock drive high above the West Fork of Buttermilk Creek may be difficult to follow in places. From the end of FR 4300-560 (5,000 ft), the track heads southwest up a broad timbered ridge, then traverses the rim of Buttermilk Meadows, on the south slopes of Scaffold Ridge. The route contours a wooded bluff about 1,000 feet above the valley floor, then reaches a small, unnamed lake (6,936 ft). After a lateral descent of steep slopes, the path joins Trail 411 (6,850 ft) at the last series of switchbacks climbing to Fish Creek Pass.

## Twisp River Trails

**Trail 410, Eagle Creek.** *7.3 miles/m (H,S).* At the end of FR 4420-080 (3,010 ft) the path heads into the narrow Eagle Creek drainage to where the beak of Duckbill Mountain splits Eagle Creek from Oval Creek, its tributary to the south. This route continues up the densely forested bottom along Eagle Creek. At 5,700 feet the drainage widens to a wooded basin with a sprinkling of meadows. The track follows the creek west toward Battle Mountain, swings around the head of the basin, and with a few switchbacks reaches the parkland bench of Eagle Pass (7,280 ft). To the west the route becomes Trail 1259.12.

**Trail 410.1, Oval Creek.** *6.9 miles/m (H,S).* At the 2-mile point on Trail 410 (3,800 ft), this route crosses Eagle Creek and zigzags up a rib to get above a deep narrow cleft at the mouth of Oval Creek. The path then traverses to meet the rising creek as it heads up the narrow valley floor. The creek and trail continue in tandem as they ascend southwest for 5 miles. At the drainage-head basin, the trail climbs to the rock-rimmed cirque containing West Oval Lake (6,860 ft); it continues from here as Trail 410.2 to Middle and East Oval Lakes.

**Trail 408, War Creek.** *9.3 miles/e (H,S).* From the end of FR 4430-100, the route enters the mouth of the War Creek drainage (3,140 ft). Steep, forested valley walls sweep up 2,000 feet to enclosing ridge tops. The way follows the north side of the creek, climbing for 9 miles to War Creek Pass (6,780 ft). The ascent passes through the Douglas-fir, Pacific silver fir, and subalpine fir zones, presenting a botany lesson in the trees, shrubs, and grasses of each. At the pass the route enters the Lake Chelan NRA to meet the Boulder Creek, Purple Creek, and Summit Trails.

**Trail 414, Slate Lake.** *5 miles/d (H,S).* From FR 44 on the west side of Little Slate Creek (2,860 ft), the route heads uphill in dense forest, picking its way up narrow benches in the steep side-slope. When these wide spots run out, switchbacks attack the slope directly, gaining the nose of a ridge at the wilderness boundary (4,800 ft). The uphill slog continues to the ridge crest (6,200 ft), where the climb slackens a bit and alpine meadows offer views of Midnight Mountain, Abernathy Ridge, and the vertical north face of Reynolds Peak. The way swings across a poorly marked parkland bench high above Little Slate Creek, crosses between bands of cliffs, and turns in to the cirque enclosing Slate Lake (6,400 ft).

**Trail 402, Reynolds Creek.** *6.6 miles/d (H,S).* From the end of FR 4435-015 (3,160 ft), the route heads into the narrow maw of lower Reynolds Creek to traverse a steep side slope above the creek. The basin slowly widens, and meadows give glimpses of the 2,400-foot-high north face of Reynolds Peak. At a wooded bench below these cliffs, the path zigzags up to a tiny meadow flat, then struggles on, picking its way up a final rock cliff to Reynolds Pass (6,874 ft), the boundary with the Lake Chelan NRA.

**Trail 401, South Creek.** *7.3 miles/d (H,S).* From South Creek Campground

*Boiling Lake, an alpine tarn in the Sawtooth Ridge Roadless Area, drains to the Middle Fork of Prince Creek.*

(3,180 ft), the route heads into forest at the bottom of the deep, V-shaped slopes of the South Creek valley. The track follows the creek west through avalanche-cut meadows in the ever-widening valley floor. These openings provide peeks at Crescent Mountain to the north and the long imposing face of Rennie Peak to the south. The gentle grade continues up to the headwater basin, where a climb through flowered parkland reaches South Pass (6,300 ft), the Lake Chelan NRA border. Here an expansive view takes in nearby McAlester Mountain and the more distant icy summits of North Cascades National Park. Beyond, the path becomes the South Creek Pass Trail.

**Trail 413, North Creek.** *4.6 miles/e (H,S)*. The route starts amid prospect pockmarks alongside FR 4440 (3,662 ft), makes a couple of long swings uphill to pass a mine, then snakes along North Creek. Timber and meadows alternate as the valley bends from north to west and rounds the flank of Gilbert Mountain. At 3.6 miles the way passes the south end of Trail 476 (5,460 ft), a path that climbs steeply to a narrow notch (6,420 ft) through a long stretch of sawtooth pinnacles along the wilderness boundary, then enters the Liberty Bell Roadless Area. Trail 413 ascends to meadows; beyond a tiny tarn (5,700 ft) it splits, the south fork continuing to North Lake (5,780 ft), and the southwest fork climbing to mining operations in the cliffs above (6,600 ft).

**Trail 432, Twisp Pass.** *4.2 miles/e (H,S)*. The route leaves FR 4440 at Roads End Campground (3,690 ft) and heads up the glacier-cut Twisp River valley. In 1.5 miles the east rib of Lincoln Butte splits the Twisp into the North and South Forks; this trail follows the South Fork, while Trail 426 heads up the North Fork. The track climbs the nose of Lincoln Butte to a clearing with great views of the sheer north faces of Crescent Mountain and companion peaks to the west. A traverse reaches cliffs, where the tread has been chiseled from a rock wall, then the way enters flower meadows as it continues to Twisp Pass (6,064 ft). Here it enters North Cascades National Park as the Twisp Pass (Fireweed) Trail.

**Trail 426, Copper Pass.** *3.2 miles/m (H,S)*. At 1.5 miles up Trail 432 (4,500 ft), the route heads up the North Fork of the Twisp River. This old prospector track between Gilbert and Stehekin was once abandoned, but was partially restored in the early 1980s by volunteers from outdoor groups. The lower portion of the route follows the wooded bottom of the North Fork to a small basin where the river splits into two major tributaries. The trail continues along the northwest branch and heads straight uphill with scarcely a breath-catching pause. The forest breaks into meadows, which yield to heather by the time the trail reaches Copper Pass (6,700 ft). The panorama of rugged peaks includes nearby Kangaroo Ridge, Early Winter Spires, and Stiletto Peak; beyond are Corteo Peak and the glaciated face of Goode Mountain. The trail continuing west down Copper Creek to Bridge Creek is brushy, but can be followed.

## Wolf Creek Trails

**Trail 527, Wolf Creek.** *10.5 miles/e-m (H,S)*. At the end of FR 5005 (2,700 ft), a long valley-bottom path heads west along the bank of Wolf Creek. Most of the lower valley is heavily wooded, though occasional meadows have early-season splashes of wildflower color. The route continues its gradual ascent along Wolf Creek to reach the broad expanse of Gardner Meadows (5,780 ft), with views up the vertical north face of Abernathy Ridge. The trail ends at the meadows, but skilled cross-country hikers can continue another mile up either fork of the creek to small alpine lakes.

## CLIMBING

Although several peaks in the wilderness are in the 7,500- to 8,800-foot range, and many have massive, near-vertical north faces, all of the summits can be reached by relatively simple scramble routes. The higher and more impressive peaks are listed here.

Gilbert Mountain (8,023 ft) has a 600-foot north wall that encircles a small pocket of glacial ice. It can be climbed via the west ridge or south slope on mine trails to the upper slopes. Crescent Mountain (7,816 ft) has an abrupt north wall that continues west for almost 3 miles. Abernathy Peak (8,321 ft) is a rugged-looking pyramid at the west end of Abernathy Ridge.

Gardner Mountain (8,898 ft), the highest point in the Lake Chelan–Sawtooth Wilderness, has a massive, 1,800-foot northeast face. A cross-country hike up the south slopes to the southeast ridge offers an easy summit route. Oval Peak (8,795 ft) is a large rounded dome, easily accessible from any side except via northeast cliffs. Courtney

Peak (8,392 ft) is a triangular summit with a sheer, 1,000-foot north face that rises above Oval Lakes; it is an easy ridge walk from Fish Creek Pass. Star Peak (8,690 ft), one of the highest summits on the Sawtooth crest, also is an easy ascent from Fish Creek Pass.

## WINTER SPORTS

The main winter recreation in the area is snowmobiling on roads on the east side of the area. Check with local ranger districts regarding specific trails that are open to snowmobiling.

## 46  Granite Mountain Region

### Granite Mountain and South Ridge Roadless Areas

**Location:** In Okanogan County, north of Highway 20 between Winthrop and Conconully

**Size:** Granite Mountain, 28,860 acres; South Ridge, 5,510 acres

**Status:** Semiprimitive, Nonmotorized and Motorized, and Roaded Natural

**Terrain:** The region consists of broad low ridges, forested most densely on the northern slopes. Deep, stream-cut drainages fan out in all directions from the heart of the area. The summits of Old Baldy, and Granite and Starvation Mountains are the dominant landscape features.

**Elevation:** 2,600 to 7,850 feet

**Management:** USFS, Okanogan–Wenatchee National Forest, Methow Valley and Tonasket Ranger Districts

**Topographic maps:** Blue Buck Mountain, Buck Mountain, Conconully West, Loup Loup Summit, Old Baldy, Pearrygin Peak

Logging roads encircle the two segments of the Granite Creek area and the South Ridge area, and only the recent policy shift by the Forest Service to preserve such areas as roadless has prevented them from being choked out of existence. Roadless does not mean motorless, unfortunately, and all trails in these areas are open to motorized recreation. A long, high backbone ridge runs north–south from Old Baldy to Starvation Mountain, both former lookout sites on the eastern side of the northernmost section of the Granite Mountain roadless area. Several creeks drain laterally from these focal points, cutting V-shaped valleys framing high, wooded crests radiating from the backbone ridge.

The southern section of the Granite Mountain roadless area wraps around the steep, forested ridgeline connecting Little Granite, Granite, and McDaniel Mountains. The main features of South Ridge are two steep-walled, east–west crests, South and Coyote Ridges, north of Highway 20 and west of Loup Loup Summit.

## CLIMATE

The climate in the area is typical for Washington east of the Cascades. Precipitation is light, ranging from 20 to 25 inches annually, with much of this in the form of snow; summers are dry, sunny, and warm. Winter temperature lows average around a brisk 10 degrees. Midsummer highs are generally in the 80s, although 90-degree weather for extended periods is not uncommon.

## ECOSYSTEM

The lower marshy areas and northern slopes are primarily covered with Douglas-fir mixed with ponderosa pine, while south-facing slopes are more open with a bunch grass and bitterbrush cover and seasonal wildflowers such as Indian paintbrush, syringa, verbena, and goldenrod. Old burns and logged areas support a thick new growth of lodgepole pine. At higher elevations subalpine fir, Engelmann spruce, and western larch emerge. Stunted firs and heathers are found atop the highest point, Old Baldy.

Substantial herds of mule and white-tailed deer inhabit the area, and the many snags and broken trees harbor birds and small mammals common to this environment. Threatened or endangered species found in the area include lynx, great gray owl, and Freija's fritillary.

## GEOLOGY

The metamorphic base of the region was created during the late Cretaceous period from fractured and subducted sediments on the west side of the Okanogan microcontinent. The impinging oceanic crust from the west sank beneath this continental crust and melted, forming hot basalts that rose above the sinking slab. These magmas crystallized beneath the base rock in the northeast portion of this area forming large granitic plutons exposed by later erosion. Base rock on the periphery of these plutons was highly mineralized with lode ore consisting of veins of copper, molybdenum, gold, zinc, and uranium. Erosion filled the perimeter of these granite intrusions with a thick cover of sediments combined with volcanic ash from the last series of eruptions of Glacier Peak. The principal drainages of the area display the characteristic V-shaped form of stream-incised valleys.

## HISTORY

In 1888 Loup Loup became the first platted town in Okanogan County; it and its rivals to the east, Ruby and Conconully, attracted hundreds of miners to work the rich silver deposits found in the vicinity. The region's first crude roads were punched through to transport mining supplies in and ore out, and many of today's roads follow these original routes. The silver towns were boisterous, with drinking, gambling, and prostitution carried on round the clock, and quick trigger fingers the norm. At the height of the boom Loup Loup had thirty to forty homes, a boardinghouse, general store, meat market, post office, and a population of over 400. The bottom fell out of the silver market in the depression of 1893 and by 1895 the town had died. Only a few rotting logs, faint piles of rock foundations, and scattered chimney bricks remain today.

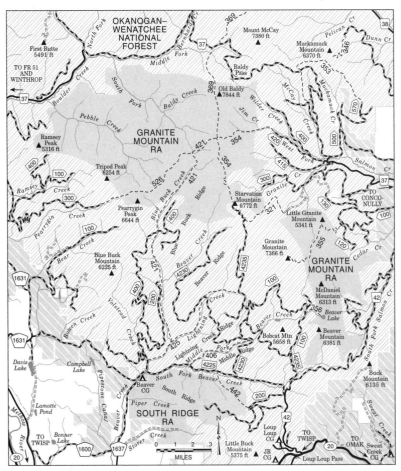

With the decline in mining, the primary interest in the region has been timber harvest, and to a lesser extent, cattle grazing. In the 1930s fire lookouts were built atop Pearrygin Peak, Old Baldy, Starvation Mountain, Granite Mountain, Little Buck Mountain, and Buck Mountain. Only the last remains; the rest have been removed or destroyed. Trails put in to support the lookouts form the backbone of today's trail system; however, most of the final paths to the lookout sites themselves have been abandoned.

## HIKING

*Trail 369, North Summit. 6.5 miles/m (H,S,B,M).* From FR 37 (5,780 ft) 2 miles west of Baldy Pass, the route descends to cross the Middle Fork of Boulder Creek, then starts a gradual climb through wooded slopes to the south to pick up a broad ridge crest. The narrowing ridge is followed south to Baldy Pass (7,400 ft), with outstanding views of the North Cascades. The route crosses the ridge, traverses the wooded west flank of Old Baldy, and then regains the broad ridge south from the peak where a spur once lead to the summit lookout site. The way follows the broad ridge southward, breaking into view meadows, then descends to a saddle junction with Trails 354 and 421 (6,390 ft).

**Trail 354, Golden Stairway.** *6.2 miles/m (H,S,B,M).* From the end of FR 3700-420 (4,150 ft) at the West Fork of Salmon Creek, the trail follows the wooded drainage westward to the streamhead basin. It then climbs the steep headwall, and breaks out of timber in a series of switchbacks to reach a ridge crest junction (6,402 ft) with Trails 369 and 421. Here are far-reaching views, both to the east and to the west. The route then heads south along the top of the ridge, dipping and climbing over intermediate humps to reach the top of Starvation Mountain (6,772 ft) and the end of FR 4235.

**Trail 421, Blue Buck.** *8.5 miles/e (H,S,B,M).* Leaving Trail 425 at the confluence of Beaver and Lightning Creeks (3,300 ft), the route follows the drainage northward,

*Western bluebirds nest in old woodpecker holes of the Granite Mountain region.*

parallel and not far from FR 4225-200. After crossing a roadend clearcut, the path enters an uncut side-slope above Blue Buck Creek as it continues upstream. As the valley floor widens the path again encounters logging roads and more "harvest units." The route reenters untouched forest, the valley walls narrow, and the trail is forced close to the creek bed. At 5,700 feet, just south of Beaver Meadows, the path heads eastward up a small wooded gully and reaches the backbone crest with wide views at a junction with Trail 369 (6,450 ft).

**Trail 355, Granite Mountain.** *5.5 miles/m (H,S,B,M).* A logging road maze leads to the trailhead on FR 3700-120 (3,840 ft). The route weaves swiftly up the steep timbered slope to a saddle (5,060 ft) in the ridge south from Little Granite Mountain. Traversing side-slopes to the south, the way reaches the forested east face of Granite Mountain, where relentless switchbacks grind up to the old lookout site atop the peak (7,366 ft) with broad views to the west and northwest to Starvation Mountain.

# 47 Mount Bonaparte Roadless Area

**Location:** In Okanogan County, north of Highway 20, between Tonasket and Wacounda Summit
**Size:** 10,790 acres
**Status:** Semiprimitive Motorized
**Terrain:** Mount Bonaparte sits atop a massive northeast–southwest trending ridge. With the exception of the summit and a little of the east edge, the massif is heavily forested.
**Elevation:** 4,200 to 7,257 feet
**Management:** USFS, Okanogan National Forest, Tonasket Ranger District
**Topographic maps:** Cayuse Mountain, Havillah, Mt. Bonaparte

Mount Bonaparte offers an unsurpassed view of the expanses of the Okanogan Highland. Its open, 7,257-foot summit, the highest point within a 50-mile radius and one of the highest peaks in Washington east of the Okanogan River, has panoramic views that stretch west to the far Cascades and the Pasayten Wilderness, north to the Canadian border, over the Kettle Range to Abercrombie–Hooknose, and south over forested ridges to the brown Columbia Plateau. Trails running from the top of the peak down the long ridge on which it sits eventually dissolve in logging incursions that whittle away at the area's borders.

## CLIMATE

The mean annual precipitation is between 13 and 14 inches. About a third of this falls between October and January, starting as rain and changing to snow by late November. Midwinter mean minimum temperatures run 14 to 16 degrees, and midsummer mean highs are in the high 80s to low 90s.

## ECOSYSTEM

Lodgepole pine is dominant on the heavily forested slopes of Mount Bonaparte. Other species include Douglas-fir, western larch, and Engelmann spruce, along with scatterings of ponderosa pine and subalpine fir. The south side of the mountain holds some good-sized stands of old-growth trees. Small meadows with subalpine vegetation coat the barren summit and a portion of the ridge top on which it sits.

The lower portions of the mountain are a winter range for mule and white-tailed deer, and lower ridges are winter habitat for blue grouse. Occasionally coyotes, martens, and raptors such as golden eagles, hawks, and the rare great gray owl may be seen. The preponderance of lodgepole pine means few snags for typical cavity dwellers such as woodpeckers or porcupines, which are seldom found here.

## GEOLOGY

Mount Bonaparte is at the northern edge of a massive granite dome that was intruded about 60 million years ago. As this dome rose, it dragged with it a fringe of older gneiss

*The summit of Mount Bonaparte has two fire lookouts: the old one, built on the ground in 1914, and a more recent conventional tower.*

that surrounds this granite core. Surface soils are mostly glacial till left after the melting of continental ice sheets, plus more recent alluvium.

## HISTORY

Mount Bonaparte is the primary fire lookout site for the Tonasket Ranger District; two generations of lookout structures are perched atop its summit. One, a hand-hewn log cabin built in 1914, is on the National Register of Historic Places. The more recent one is a conventional tower.

## HIKING

**Trail 304, Antoine Trail.** *4.2 miles/m (H,S,B).* The lower trailhead on FR 3230-150 (4,400 ft) has been obscured by several clearcuts on the west side of Antoine Creek, so it may be difficult to find. If in doubt, follow the southeast rim of the cuts to pick it up as it parallels the creek, about 350 yards above its west bank. A gentle grade continues upstream, rounds the upper drainage, and heads north in a gradual ascent to the nose of the ridge to the east. It turns southeast up this broad ridge, climbing first through older fir and larch, then lodgepole pine. About 0.5 mile from the top of Mount Bonaparte it joins Trail 306 from Myers Creek (6,920 ft).

**Trail 307, Fourth of July.** *7.3 miles/m (H,S,B,M).* From FR 3230 at the divide between Mill Creek and the North Fork of Siwash Creek (5,078 ft), the route heads east, then south along a bench, crosses the North Fork of Siwash Creek, then begins a long, gradual ascent of the wooded southeast side of the ridge running southwest from Mount Bonaparte. The way twists around minor ridges and basins at the head of Lightning and Pettijohn Creeks. After traversing the steeper south flank of Mount Bonaparte, it weaves north to meet Trail 308 on the east side of the mountain (5,820 ft).

**Trail 306, Bonaparte.** *4.5 miles/m (H,S,B,M).* The most direct route to the top of the mountain starts from FR 3300-300 (4,640 ft). After negotiating a path through clearcuts, the way enters virgin forest and climbs south to meet Trail 308 (5,680 ft). More uphill grind reaches the top of Trail 304 (6,120 ft). The route breaks into subalpine trees and meadows at the summit (7,257 ft).

**Trail 308, Southside.** *5.6 miles/m (H,S,B,M).* FR 3300-100 provides a new trailhead for this path, which once started 1,000 feet lower at Bonaparte Lake Campground (the lower trail section is still followable). The trail leaves the road (4,550 ft) and climbs

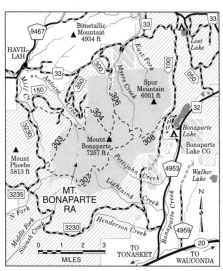

southwest up the steep sidehill past Duff Spring to a cliffy area, switchbacks north, rounds a broad ridge nose, then meets Trail 307. The route traverses northwest through timber to merge with Trail 306 (5,680 ft).

**Trail 303, Cabin.** *2.5 miles/m (H,S,B,M).* This near-flat, wooded connector trail between the east ends of Trails 307 (5,160 ft) and 304 (4,800 ft) opens the opportunity for a long loop trip all the way around the base of Mount Bonaparte.

## 48 Sherman Pass North Region

### Profanity, Twin Sisters, and Hoodoo Roadless Areas

**Location:** In Ferry County, along the Kettle Range, extending north from Highway 20 at Sherman Pass to FR 61 at Deer Creek Summit

**Size:** Profanity, 29,418 acres; Twin Sisters, 13,311 acres; Hoodoo, 7,103 acres

**Status:** Semiprimitive Nonmotorized and Motorized

**Terrain:** A series of broad, rounded summits surrounding a long north–south crest encompass east–west-trending, broad, glacier-sculpted ridges.

**Elevation:** 3,000 to 7,135 feet

**Management:** USFS, Colville National Forest, Republic and Kettle Falls Ranger Districts

**Topographic maps:** Bangs Mountain, Big Goat, Boyds, Bulldog Mtn., Cooke Mountain, Copper Butte, Edds Mountain, Jackknife Mtn., Malo, Mt. Leona, Orient, Sherman Peak, South Huckleberry Mtn.

Lateral streams from the hydrological divide of the northern Kettle Range flow west to the Sanpoil and Curlew Valleys, and east to the Columbia River. The Twin Sisters and Hoodoo areas lie on the east side of the Kettle Range divide. The long backbone of the Kettle Range is a distance hikers' nirvana, since its 30-mile-length is closed to motorbikes—a rarity for trails east of the Cascades. The entire distance is at ridge-top level, passing over a series of local high spots or near enough to them for view-seeking side trips. These summits have fascinating names—Jungle Hill, Wapaloosie Mountain, Scar Mountain, Midnight Mountain, Stickpin Hill, and Profanity Peak. For hikers who wish to break the long crest trail into more digestible sections, several lateral access trails, 3 miles or less, intersect it from both sides of the ridge. All three ridge-top trails in the Twin Sisters area, and the sole trail in Hoodoo are tailored to and heavily used for motorized recreation.

Early summer travelers are rewarded by a profusion of wildflowers in open alpine meadows, and in fall bird-watchers can spot raptors migrating through the region. Views from high spots are expansive but—as real estate agents put it—"territorial." Most open spots overlook a sea of rolling wooded hills on either side of the range that drop to unseen valley drainages and rise on the opposite side to distant ranges on the horizon.

## CLIMATE

Because the Kettle Range is a major obstacle to eastward-flowing weather systems, it tends to get more precipitation than areas of the Okanogan Highlands that border it on either side. Annual precipitation ranges between 28 and 35 inches, with more than half falling between October and March, a substantial portion of this in the form of snow. Periods of heavy rain also occur in May and June. Midwinter temperatures average in the 20s, with lows in the mid-teens. Summer temperatures average in the mid- to high 60s, with highs in the lower 90s.

## ECOSYSTEM

Where the climax forest has not been touched by fire, the dominant species of trees are Douglas-fir, western red cedar, and subalpine fir, with Engelmann spruce, quaking aspen, birch, and cottonwood in damper stream drainages. Understory vegetation for this segment of forest includes pinegrass, sedges, arnica, Oregon boxwood, huckleberry, trail plant, queencup beadlily, wood violet, and anemone. Dense stands of pole-sized western larch, lodgepole pine, and ponderosa pine have replaced large portions of the original forest consumed by large fires in 1929. Open slopes on drier southern exposures have a cover of fescues and sagebrush.

*Shootingstars grow in dry, sunny areas of the old burn.*

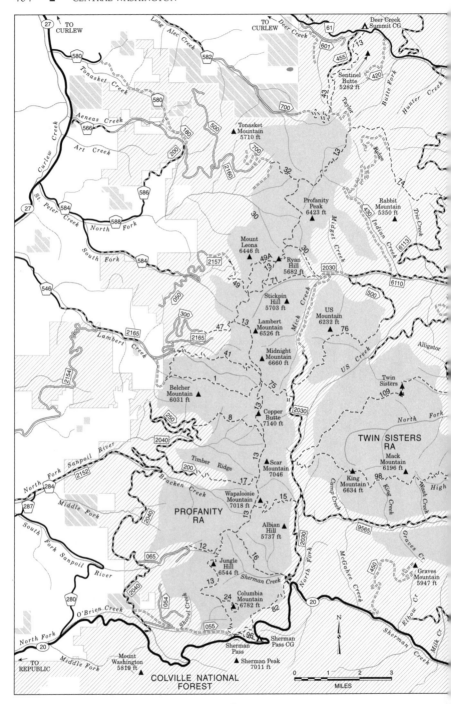

Wildlife includes mule and white-tailed deer, with the population shifting toward the latter in recent years. Other forest inhabitants are black bear, cougar, bobcat, marten, lynx, ruffed and blue grouse, and snowshoe hare. The range is on the migration route for raptors such as golden eagles and peregrine falcons.

## GEOLOGY

The northern portion of the range is composed mainly of older, pre-Jurassic metamorphic gneiss, schist, and quartzite. About 60 million years ago this base was intruded in the south, near Sherman Pass, by younger granite. Soils are composed of volcanic ash, loess, and glacial till, with the ash component more heavily eroded on steeper south and west slopes. The northern portion of Profanity, in the vicinity of Mount Leona, and the southeast corner of Twin Sisters have significant deposits of uranium, tungsten, silver, gold, and copper ores.

## HISTORY

In 1872, a large area that includes the Kettle Range was designated as the Colville Indian Reservation. Its reservation status was short-lived, as the north portion of the reservation was opened to homesteading and mining in 1892. An Army group under the command of Lieutenant Henry H. Pierce was one of the first to explore the area; they crossed Sherman Pass in 1882. A second Army contingent traversed the region a year later, and the pass was named for its leader, General William Tecumseh Sherman, later of Civil War fame. An old stage road later crossed the range some 7 miles north of Sherman Pass, and its route is followed today by Trails 1 and 75.

The Colville National Forest was created in 1907, and the Forest Service built fire lookouts on four area summits, Columbia Mountain, Copper Butte, Twin Sisters, and Graves Mountain. Only faint remains exist today, but hikes to three of those summits still reward visitors with outstanding views.

## HIKING

The Profanity area is a narrow, 30-mile-long strip of the Kettle Range between Sherman Pass on Highway 20, to the south, and Deer Creek Summit on FR 61, to the north. Trail 13 runs the length of this backbone ridge, and all other trails in the area are primarily access routes to Trail 13.

**Trail 13, Kettle Crest North.** *30.2 miles/m (H,S,B).* A long route atop the Kettle Crest switchbacks north out of Sherman Pass (5,513 ft) to a bench, then contours the west flank of Columbia Mountain. As the forest breaks to meadows, a spur climbs southeast across an open hillside to a former lookout site atop the mountain (6,782 ft). Here are excellent views north and south along the crest, west to the Sanpoil River valley and Republic, and east across the Columbia River drainage. The crest trail swings west around a ridge finger, then returns east to a saddle (6,186 ft). It traverses the west and north sides of Jungle Hill, then zigzags down to meet the upper end of Trail 12. Switchbacks regain lost altitude as the way passes Trail 16, and then heads northeast into alpine meadows to the junction with Trail 15, just south of Wapaloosie Mountain. After rounding the west side of the mountain, a drop north down a rocky face leads to the east end of Trail 17 (6,570 ft) from Bracken Creek.

The path contours the west side of Scar Mountain, drops to a col (6,430 ft) to meet Trail 8 from the west, then climbs the ridge to the top of Copper Butte, the highest summit in the North Kettle Range (7,140 ft). Here are the remains of a lookout cabin, and views west to Republic, east to Colville, and southeast to Mount Spokane. A few gentle switchbacks down through lodgepole pine reach a saddle (6,050 ft) once crossed by a stage road over the Kettle Range. Trails 1, to the west, and 75, to the east, follow its route.

After passing Trail 41 from the west, the track continues through meadows with wide westward views as it gradually ascends to the south slopes of Lambert Mountain. The trail swings west across open slopes to meet Trail 47, then drops north across a steep, thickly forested sidehill. At a junction with Trail 49 at a narrow saddle (5,648 ft) south of Mount Leona, the way bends sharply east.

The trail contours a creek-head basin, passes the upper end of Trail 71, then climbs to a narrow saddle (5,520 ft) on the west ridge of Ryan Hill. Switchbacks drop down the steep north shoulder of the hill to the head of a tributary of the South Fork of Boulder Creek, and the junction with Trail 30.

The route climbs a wooded knob to the north, descends to a pair of saddles west of Profanity Peak, and follows the west side of the ridge through a meadow, then Douglas-fir and lodgepole pine forest, to the east end of Trail 32. The way now swings east, drops to cross Indian Creek, then ascends to an old logging road atop Taylor Ridge (6,082 ft). After following the road a short distance, the trail shifts back to the crest, heads up and down over humps to the northeast, skirts the top of Sentinel Butte, and drops to the Deer Creek Summit Campground on FR 61 (4,630 ft).

## West Side of Kettle Crest Trails

**Trail 17, Timber Ridge.** *3.2 miles/d (H,S,B).* From a logging clearcut (5,520 ft) on FR 2040-200, the path swings uphill northwest to gain a ridge-top meadow. It follows the broad, forested crest of Timber Ridge east to a steeper, narrower rib, and ascends it to join Trail 13 atop a small knob (6,570 ft) between Wapaloosie and Scar Mountains.

**Trail 8, Marcus.** *3.5 miles/m (H,S,B).* The route leaves the north side of FR 2040-250 (4,750 ft) to wander up and cross the heads of three streams feeding the North Fork of the Sanpoil. An ascent, first in forest, then in dry side-slope meadows, reaches Trail 13 at a saddle (6,430 ft) on the ridge south of Copper Butte.

**Trail 1, Old Stage Road.** *5.8 miles/m (H,S,B; wagons are also allowed).* Follow a piece of history, the old stage road across the Kettle Range, as it leaves FR 2165 (3,914 ft), crosses a bridge over Lambert Creek, and takes a few easy-grade switchbacks to gain a broad, forested ridge crest. After following the ridge east a short way, the path makes a diagonal ascent across the north-facing slope of upper Lambert Creek basin. The trail swings northeast as it cuts up across the basin headwall to a saddle (6,050 ft) between Copper Butte and Midnight Mountain, where it meets with Trails 13 and 75.

*Steel plate Wagon Wheel Memorial markers on the Old Stage Road commemorate this historic route.*

**Trail 41, Midnight Ridge.** *4.4 miles/m (H,S,B).* From a common trailhead with Trail 1 (3,914 ft), the route switchbacks to gain the crest of Midnight Ridge. It follows the ridge eastward through pine-rimmed wildflower meadows to reach Trail 13 (6,050 ft) south of Midnight Mountain.

**Trail 49, Leona.** *1.6 miles/e (H,S,B).* At the end of the driveable portion of FR 2157 (5,150 ft), walk 0.75 mile on road and another 0.75 mile on trail to reach Trail 13 atop the Kettle crest (5,550 ft). Spur Trail 49A continues around the wooded base of Mount Leona to rejoin Trail 13 in 1.5 miles, offering an easy loop opportunity.

## East Side of Kettle Crest Trails

**Trail 16, Jungle Hill.** *2.5 miles/d (H,S).* This steep, sometimes obscure route leaves FR 2030 (4,300 ft) and starts a ceaseless climb up the steep, pine-covered ridge nose north of Sherman Creek. Near the Kettle Crest, breaks in the forest offer open views to the northeast as the way joins Trail 13 (6,560 ft).

**Trail 15, Wapaloosie.** *2.5 miles/e-m (H,S,B).* Just after leaving FR 2030 (4,980 ft), this trail crosses the North Fork of Sherman Creek and heads up the lodgepole pine–covered slope in long, gentle switchbacks. At 6,000 feet the path turns south, to a diagonal ascent across broad meadows on the east flank of Wapaloosie Mountain. Two more swings up through the meadows open views east of Graves and Mack Mountains. The way then works around the south side of the mountain to join Trail 13 (6,860 ft).

*The fire lookout on the summit of Columbia Mountain was built in 1914. No vestiges remain today.*

**Trail 75, Old Stage Road.** *1.7 miles/m (H,S,B; wagons are also allowed).* This is the eastern continuation of the old wagon road (reconstructed in 1992) that Trail 1 follows from the west. The gentle grade departs the west side of FR 2030 (5,478 ft), makes a pair of easy swings across the forested east slope, and gradually ascends to a saddle to meet Trails 1 and 13 (6,050 ft).

## Twin Sisters Roadless Area

**Trail 76, US Mountain.** *5.4 miles/m (H,S).* The first 2 miles of this trail are an ATV road that leaves FR 2030 at 5,380 feet and climbs northeast past a saddle (5,920 ft) on the south flank of US Mountain. Here the real trail begins as it contours the southeast side of the mountain, with occasional open views of logging cuts lower in US Creek. The route then swings steeply downhill, then contours the drainage side-slope to reach the end of FR 6110-500 (4,120 ft).

## Hoodoo Roadless Area

**Trail 17, Hoodoo Canyon.** *2.5 miles/e-m (H).* From FR 9565 (2,800 ft), the path drops to cross the South Fork of Deadman Creek, then heads up the ridge to the southeast, passing through old logging cuts. The route continues a steady climb through larch and cedar to an open saddle (3,760 ft) with great views west to the Kettle Range and down into cliff-framed Hoodoo Canyon. A path leads along a bench that diagonals down the steep canyon wall, where a spur switchbacks down to Emerald Lake (3,100 ft). The trail continues south, descending to the flat canyon bottom that leads to Trout Lake and its campground at the end of FR 2000-020 (3,060 ft).

## WINTER SPORTS

It only takes a couple of feet of snow to blanket the low ground cover of Kettle Ridge and open summer trails to cross-country skiing. Experienced skiers often head north from Sherman Pass, following the route of Trail 13 as far as skill and endurance can take them. The tour to the top of Columbia Mountain rewards the hardy with around-the-compass views of the Kettle Range and the drainages on either side, made even more beautiful by the crystal cover of snow.

At the north end of the Profanity area, at Deer Creek Summit, a conservation group from the town of Curlew has constructed and maintains a group of five Nordic trails. Two follow old logging and 4WD roads north from the pass for loops of 5 and 8 kilometers (3 and 5 miles). South from the summit, one track traces the summer route of Trail 13 to the head of West Deer Creek, then returns north via abandoned FR 6110-430. This loop is 10 kilometers (6 miles), but a spur closer to the summit cuts the loop by a third. For the adventuresome, another abandoned forest road at the south end of the longer loop continues west down Long Alec Creek, eventually coming out on County Road 582 east of Curlew. The length of this trip will vary, depending on how far the county has plowed the road, but it averages 16 kilometers and requires prearranged transportation at either end.

# Sherman Pass South Region

### Bald Snow, Thirteenmile, Cougar Mountain, South Huckleberry, and Bangs Roadless Areas

**Location:** In Ferry County, in the Kettle Range, south of Highway 20 and east of Highway 21

**Size:** Bald Snow, 24,383 acres; Thirteenmile, 12,714 acres; Cougar Mountain, 4,735 acres; South Huckleberry, 10,090 acres; Bangs, 3,733 acres

**Status:** Semiprimitive Nonmotorized

**Terrain:** The region holds rolling to moderately steep ridges with a few deep, cliff-rimmed drainages. Slopes are mostly wooded, except for the core area, which was burned by a major forest fire in 1988.

**Elevation:** 1,840 to 7,103 feet

**Management:** USFS, Colville National Forest, Republic and Kettle Falls Ranger Districts

**Topographic maps:** Bangs Mountain, Bear Mountain, Edds Mountain, La Fleur Lake, Seventeenmile Mountain, Sherman Peak, Sitdown Mountain, South Huckleberry Mtn., Thirteenmile Creek

This area provides visitors with an opportunity to witness the rebirth of a forest. In the summer of 1988, lightning strikes in the White Mountain and Bald Mountain areas set six small spot fires. The extremely dry weather preceding the lightning storm, and the winds of up to 35 miles per hour that followed it, caused these small fires to merge and overwhelm fire-suppression efforts. The resulting inferno raged for nearly three weeks, consuming 20,126 acres before it was finally controlled. Nearly all of the Bald Snow Roadless Area was turned into charred snags, with only small, isolated patches of trees surviving. Salvage logging removed dead but marketable timber, and reforestation began, attempting to match planted seedling species with those that had previously existed in each section of the forest. As of this writing, thirteen years later, vegetation has transformed the blackened rocky landscape to a new, green, regenerating ecosystem.

## CLIMATE

The Kettle Range is a major obstacle to the west–east storm systems that cross this section of the state, and as a result it receives more precipitation than the drier highland valleys on either side. The mountains in the southwest Thirteenmile area are lower, and therefore drier, than those on the crest of the range. The Bald Snow area, abreast of the range, has an average annual precipitation of 35 inches, while Thirteenmile, to the west, and South Huckleberry–Bangs to the east, average only 20 inches. About 50 percent of this occurs between October and March, much as snow. After a relatively dry early spring, May and June often see extended rainy periods. Midwinter temperatures

*The summit of Thirteenmile Mountain, reached by Trail 23, reveals rolling, forested hills.*

range between 10 and 20 degrees; summer highs are in the lower 90s, and sometimes warmer in the southwest part of the area.

## ECOSYSTEM

In sections outside of the 1988 burn, the climax forest consists of Douglas-fir, ponderosa pine, western red cedar, and subalpine fir. In areas that had been burned over in the past, these species were replaced by dense stands of western larch and lodgepole pine. Forest composition varies with the moisture content of the soil; streams and damper areas also support Engelmann spruce, quaking aspen, cottonwood, and birch. Drier south-facing slopes have larger open patches of grass. The understory, depending on specific location, includes sedges, arnica, spirea, huckleberries, sweetscented bedstraw, hawkweed, Oregon boxwood, various species of rose, wood violet, and ninebark. Rarer sensitive species found in the area are phacelia, twinflower, Umatilla gooseberry, Idaho gooseberry, Okanogan flameflower, and Robinson's onion.

Wildlife is plentiful in the forest; among the creatures that may be spotted on hikes here are mule deer, black bear, cougar, lynx, bobcat, coyote, wolverine, pine marten, snowshoe hare, blue grouse, and pika, along with a variety of songbirds.

## GEOLOGY

The Bald Snow–Thirteenmile area east of the line of summits between Mount Washington and Seventeenmile Mountain is underlaid with an intrusive granite dome that rose through the existing mantle about 50 million to 70 million years ago. Outcrops of this base granite are evident in many places along the Kettle crest. A north–south fault just west of this chain of summits marks an abrupt change from granitic rock to younger (50 million years old) andesite and rhyolite of volcanic origin. The soil cover of the area is composed of thick layers of glacial till left after several retreats of continental ice sheets, plus later additions of volcanic ash. Moderate amounts of tungsten and uranium ores are found in the western half of the region, and some zinc and silver composites occur south of Sherman Pass.

## HISTORY

The entire area was once part of the Colville Indian Reservation, set aside in 1872. In 1892 reservation boundaries were adjusted, and the northern half of this region, which includes Bald Snow–Thirteenmile, reverted to public domain. The southern half remained, as it is today, the Colville Reservation. Four years later the north portion was

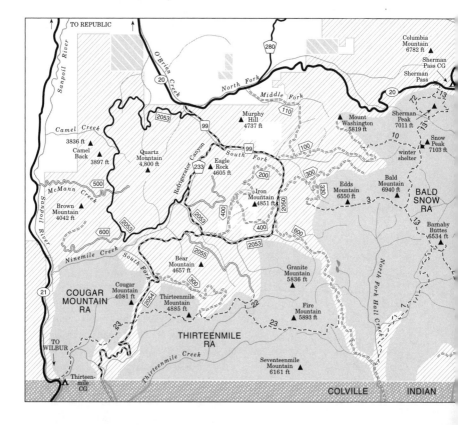

opened to homesteading, but few settlers arrived until the early 1900s. Despite having lost reservation status, the mountains just north of the reservation boundary were of great significance to the Colville Indians. As a portion of the rite of transition into adulthood, tribe members sought out the summits as a place to seek contact with guardian spirits.

The first forest reserves in the state were created in 1897, and in 1907 the Colville National Forest was established. Over the next 25 years the Forest Service built fire lookouts atop Barnaby Buttes and White, Thirteenmile, and South Huckleberry Mountains, and trails were put in to supply the lookouts and accommodate fire-crew access to the area. None of these lookouts remains today.

## HIKING

There are two long trails in the Bald Snow/Thirteenmile/Cougar Mountain areas: Trail 13, running north–south along the Kettle Crest, and Trail 23, running east–west along the southwest border of the region. All other trails in these areas are feeders for these two. South Huckleberry has a single ATV trail, and Bangs has no trails.

**Trail 13, Kettle Ridge South.** *13.3 miles/m (H,S,B).* This high ridge-top route offers

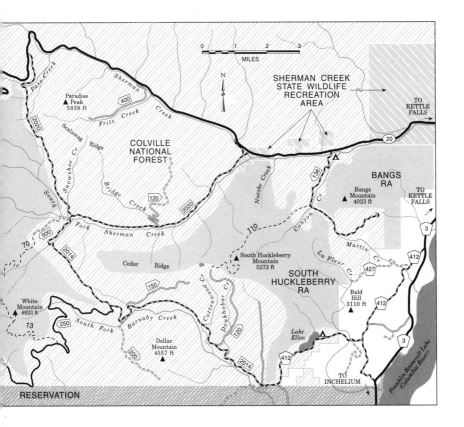

wide burn-cleared views east to Lake Roosevelt (the Columbia River), west to the Okanogan Highlands, and north and south to the Kettle Crest summits. At the southeast side of Sherman Pass (5,587 ft), switchbacks climb to the head of a fork of Pass Creek; then the route twists around flanking ridges northeast and east from Sherman Peak. At a saddle south of the peak (6,390 ft) the path switches to the west side of the crest and traverses the west slope of Snow Peak, passing the head of Trail 10 en route. The trail snakes over a ridge-top knob, returns to the east side of the crest, and traverses the east side of Bald Mountain. On the south flank of the mountain, it meets Trail 3 and returns to the ridge top that trends southeast to Barnaby Buttes. The path crosses a broad low saddle between the two buttes, then continues south to meet Trail 70. A climb south through talus and boulders reaches a short spur to the summit of White Mountain (6,923 ft). From here, the way is all downhill, first in tight switchbacks, then long ones, and finally a straight gradual descent to FR 2014-250 (5,200 ft).

## East Side of Kettle Crest Trail

**Trail 70, Barnaby Buttes.** *2.8 miles/m (H,S).* This trail was once a supply road to the lookout atop Barnaby Buttes; although it reverted to trail status when the lookout was abandoned, it retains the wide tread and gentle grade of the old road. The last 2 miles of FR 2014-500 to the trailhead (4,520 ft) are very rough, and impassable by low-clearance vehicles. The way starts in forest, passes through one steep stretch, then ascends gradually to meet Trail 13 at a saddle on the ridge south of Barnaby Buttes (6,050 ft).

## West Side of Kettle Crest Trails

**Trail 10, Snow Peak.** *2.7 miles/m (H,S,B).* After leaving FR 2050-100 (5,120 ft) the route climbs diagonally up south-facing slopes to a broad ridge top (6,100 ft), then follows the crest east to meet Trail 13 (6,300 ft) on the west side of Snow Peak. The entire way passes through the White Mountain burn; though new trees offer only nominal shade, grasses and wildflowers have recovered and add color to the hike.

**Trail 3, Edds Mountain.** *4.2 miles/d (H,S).* The track starts at the end of FR 2050-300 (4,884 ft) and heads steeply up slabs and boulder fields on the prominent ridge west from Edds Mountain. After crossing the south flank of the mountain (6,472 ft), the route drops to a broad saddle between Edds and Bald Mountains (6,076 ft). The path then ascends the open ridge toward Bald, with views to the south down the broad Hall Creek drainage to the Colville Indian Reservation. About 1,400 feet below the summit of Bald, the route starts a gradual descent east to join Trail 13 (5,920 ft). The tread may be hard to find in rocky or grassy areas, but cairns mark the way.

**Trail 7, Barnaby Buttes.** *7 miles/m (H,S,B).* The route leaves FR 2050-600 (3,420 ft) and follows a onetime road, now trail, northeast up a creek basin for 3 miles before it reaches the original trail. The way continues to the head of the drainage, then climbs along the side of a gentle ridge in broken forest and meadows. Switchbacks climb to reach Trail 13 (6,180 ft) just west of the top of Barnaby Buttes.

**Trail 23, Thirteenmile.** *16.5 miles/m (H,S,B).* This path is west of the White

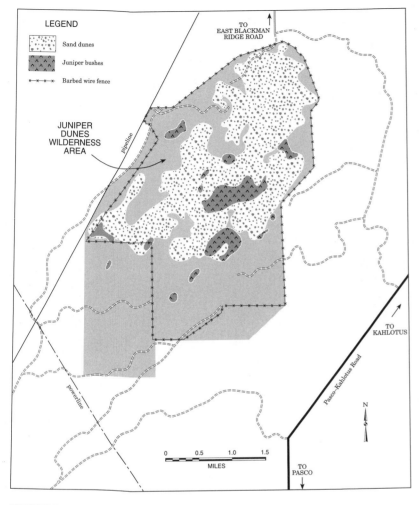

Mountain burn, so it is blessed by a variety of forest cover, including magnificent old-growth stands of ponderosa pine. The east end of the trail starts from FR 2050-600 at the head of a small Hall Creek tributary (4,327 ft). It climbs west through forest to a saddle on the ridge between Fire and Seventeenmile Mountains (5,130 ft). Side trips can be made to the top of either for panoramic views of the area.

The track gradually winds down to the upper end of Thirteenmile Creek, where a spur leads north to a marsh at the end of FR 2055 (4,200 ft). Trail 23 climbs above the steep-walled banks of the creek and meanders west toward Thirteenmile Mountain. Just east of the mountain it touches the end of FR 2054-300, then continues around the south side of the mountain through alternating patches of forest and meadow. A convoluted ridge is followed west to the canyon that contains FR 2054; the track drops and crosses the road (3,550 ft). The trail climbs out of the canyon, crosses a broad rib, and starts a twisting descent into the narrow canyon cut by Thirteenmile Creek. Soaring rock cliffs frame both sides of the creek as it drops to its confluence with the Sanpoil River at the Thirteenmile Campground (2,020 ft) on Highway 21.

## WINTER SPORTS

On the plus side for the White Mountain burn, in winter the bare slopes offer seemingly limitless acres of deep, untracked powder snow for the enjoyment of skilled cross-country skiers. Summer Trails 10 and 13 are frequently used as access routes to reach the snow-clad ridges and bowls for fantastic runs unencumbered by timber, and a winter shelter has been built near the junction of Trails 13 and 10.

## 50  Juniper Dunes Wilderness

**Location:** In Franklin County, 16 miles northeast of Pasco, northwest of Pasco–Kahlotus Road
**Size:** 7,100 acres
**Status:** Designated Wilderness (1984)
**Terrain:** The wilderness is a low, rolling landscape covered by sand dunes and groves of western juniper.
**Elevation:** 750 to 1,130 feet
**Management:** US Bureau of Land Management (BLM), Spokane District
**Topographic maps:** Levey NE, Levey SE, Levey SW, Rye Grass Coulee

Juniper Dunes is the last remaining vestige of the ecosystem that once covered nearly 250,000 acres between the Columbia and Snake Rivers. It encompasses the largest sand dunes and the largest remaining natural groves of western juniper in the state. Strong, persistent southwesterly winds build dunes up to 130 feet high and more than 1,000 feet wide. This is the northernmost limit for western juniper—the groves in the wilderness are between 80 and 150 years old. This distinctive ecosystem is habitat for a

## HIKING

There are no established trails within the wilderness, and only a half-dozen 4WD roads make short probes into the perimeter of the area. All of the peripheral land is privately held, so at present there is no legal access to it without permission from surrounding landholders. The BLM is attempting to negotiate public access to the south and west sides of the wilderness, but until that effort is successful, persons wishing to visit the dunes should contact the Spokane district office of the BLM (see Appendix A, Managing Agency Offices) to find out whom to contact to obtain access approval.

Opposite: *The Wenaha–Tucannon Wilderness Area boasts one of the largest elk populations in Eastern Washington.*

unique group of mammal, bird, and plant species that have adapted to its demanding features. A number of other species of birds also migrate through the area seasonally.

## CLIMATE

The climate is that of a northern-latitude desert, with an average annual rainfall of only 7 to 8 inches, more than 80 percent of which occurs between the months of September and May. Since the area is cold during the winter, much of that season's precipitation occurs in the form of snow, about 13 inches annually. Minimum midwinter temperatures average in the low 20s, and the midsummer maximums are in the 90s, with many days above 100. Obviously the best times to visit are in the spring and fall.

## ECOSYSTEM

The western juniper is the only significant tree species in the wilderness; however, there are more than sixty species of plants present. Among these are hoary aster, balsamroot, rabbitbrush, cryptantha, Russian thistle, milk vetch, psoralea, phacelia, yellow bells, blue flax, verbena, wheatgrass, wild rye, cordgrass, phlox, knotweed, larkspur, bitterbrush, prairie star, and blue-eyed Mary.

Larger mammals found in the area are mule deer, coyote, bobcat, badger, skunk, weasel, and porcupine. Smaller creatures include pocket gophers, kangaroo rats, pocket mice, harvest mice, deermice, and grasshopper mice. (Those coyotes and bobcats have to eat something!)

The resident bird species include raptors such as red-tailed hawks, ferruginous hawks, Swainson's hawks, sparrow hawks, merlins, great horned owls, long-eared owls, and short-eared owls (more trouble for the mice). Other residents are quail, partridge, pheasant, magpies, ravens, and horned larks. Among summer-only visitors are mourning doves, kingbirds, Say's phoebes, violet-green swallows, shrikes, Macgillivray's warblers, orioles, blackbirds, cowbirds, and a variety of sparrows. Migrant bird populations include bluebirds, kinglets, pipits, vireos, Townsend's warblers, buntings, song sparrows, Canada geese, pintails, goshawks, sharp-shinned hawks, hummingbirds, nighthawks, Lewis woodpeckers, sapsuckers, flycatchers, and pewees.

Reptiles here are not to be slighted; among these are skinks, four species of lizards, and six species of snakes (including rattlesnakes!).

## GEOLOGY

The base rock below the wilderness is Columbia Plateau basalt. In Miocene times, about 15 million years ago, stretching of the Earth's crust in southeastern Washington opened fissures from which enormous lava flows emerged and spread across the plateaus to the west. A succession—maybe hundreds—of such basalt floods occurred over the following 4 million years, building up a thick crust of layered basalt.

About 12,000 to 10,000 years ago, the continental ice sheets that had covered most of the northern part of the present-day United States began to retreat. The melting glaciers formed huge lakes behind ice dams in northern Idaho and western Montana. When these dams gave way, immense floods swept across eastern Washington. The magnitude

*A hiker surveys windswept sand near a trailhead in the Juniper Dunes Wilderness.*

of the larger floods is almost unimaginable—in one, more than 500 cubic miles of water was released and flowed across the Columbia Plateau in a 300-foot-high surge. The floods carried away surface soils and carved deep channels in the basalt plateau, then fanned out and temporarily formed large lakes in central Washington before draining through Wallula Gap and on down the Columbia River channel. These slack-water lakes, one of which formed above Juniper Dunes, deposited their finer sediments in the basins beneath them, providing the sand that is shaped by winds into today's dunes.

## HISTORY

The area has been used since the 1960s for recreational activities, some benign such as picnicking, sightseeing, and nature studies, others more ecologically damaging such as camping, Air Force survival training, horseback riding, and motorcycle and ATV travel. Studies by the Bureau of Land Management (BLM) in 1971 established the uniqueness of this ecosystem, and the bureau acquired and consolidated parcels of land from private owners. By 1975, 5,300 acres had been gathered and were designated an Outstanding Natural Area, which closed the area to grazing and ATV use. 1984 an additional 1,800 acres were added, and the entire 7,100 acres were designated the Juniper Dunes Wilderness.

# Abercrombie–Hooknose Roadless Area

**Location:** In Stevens and Pend Oreille Counties, on the west side of Highway 31, just south of the Canadian border
**Size:** 32,021 acres
**Status:** Semiprimitive Nonmotorized
**Terrain:** The Roadless Area spans a long, rounded, north–south ridge that is the hydrologic divide between the Columbia and Pend Oreille Rivers. The highest points have steep-walled, wooded cirques on their north or east sides. Creeks carve deep drainages east and west from the crest, defining lateral ridges that slope gradually to steep drop-offs into the valleys flanking either side of the area.
**Elevation:** 2,800 to 7,308 feet
**Management:** USFS, Colville National Forest, Colville and Sullivan Lake Ranger Districts; 1.5 sections under Washington State Department of Natural Resources (DNR) management; some private inholdings
**Topographic maps:** Abercrombie Mountain, Boundary Dam, Deep Lake, Leadpoint, Metaline

If you crave cross-country travel but don't warm to the possibility of bushwhacking or getting lost, then Abercrombie–Hooknose is the place for you. Short (albeit steep) lateral trails, none exceeding 4 miles in length, reach broad, open meadows and lightly forested saddles along the 7-mile-long, north–south backbone of the region. In early summer alpine meadows are ablaze with wildflowers, and in fall lower slopes provide ample patches of huckleberries on approach hikes.

## CLIMATE

The area is damper than most other portions of eastern Washington. It receives nearly 28 inches of precipitation annually, about half of which falls as snow, beginning in November and continuing until March. May and June also have periods of heavy rain. Temperatures are typical of the eastern part of the state, with midwinter minimums averaging in the teens, and summer maximums in the mid-80s, with some periods in the 90s.

## ECOSYSTEM

A large portion of the area was burned in 1926, thus most of the forest cover is second-growth western larch and lodgepole pine, with occasional Douglas-fir and ponderosa pine that survived the blaze. Some of the wetter draws and westside slopes have stands of old-growth Douglas-fir, western hemlock, and western red cedar. The understory here includes ninebark, snowberry, oceanspray, spirea, Oregon boxwood, and huckleberry. At higher elevations Engelmann spruce and subalpine fir stands are found, and damper locations on northern slopes and in ravines host vegetation such as Labrador tea and Cascades azalea. Drier south slopes have huckleberry, western juniper, arnica, serviceberry, huckleberry, and spirea. Meadow cover atop alpine ridges consists of bunchgrass, heather, moss, and lichen.

Found in the forest are mule deer, black bear, coyote, moose, elk, bobcat, cougar,

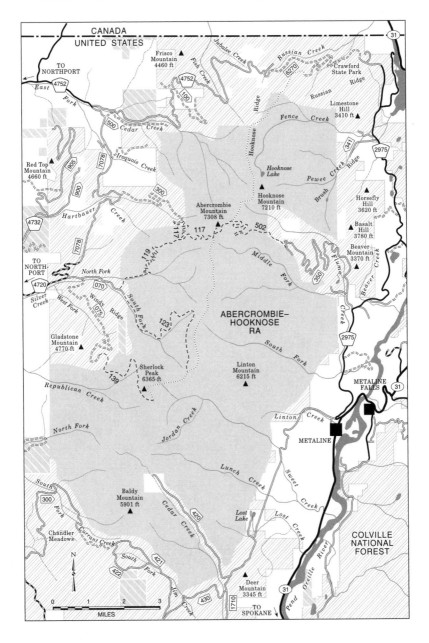

grouse, pine marten, wolverine, goshawk, barred owl, and pileated woodpecker. Grizzly bears and gray wolves have been sighted occasionally. A small herd of mountain goats is located near Linton Peak, west of Metaline.

## GEOLOGY

The high crest running through the Abercrombie–Hooknose region belies its origins, for it was once a broad coastal plain on the western flank of the North American continent. The plain built up over ancient continental crust, beginning more than 600 million years ago. Throughout the ensuing Paleozoic era, deposition continued on the plain; layers of limestones alternating with black muds were transformed into slates and argillites.

About 200 million years ago, the North American plate was pushed westward by a flow of new crust in the mid-Atlantic trench, and its western margins were forced against, and then over, the crust of the Pacific Ocean. This collision folded and tilted the coastal plain upward in a series of fractured blocks. Pressures metamorphosed portions of these ancient sedimentary rocks, and granitic magma, heated by the subducting Pacific crust, intruded into the fault zones of the older rock. Erosion and continental glaciation smoothed this newly formed range, forming today's broad rounded ridges. Only Abercrombie and Hooknose Mountains stood above the continental ice sheets. Alpine glaciers that formed on these two peaks carved the steep cirques that are now evident on their sides.

*Heavy underbrush of the Abercrombie–Hooknose Roadless Area provides habitat for ruffed grouse.*

The oldest limestones and dolomites harbored solutions of lead, silver, and zinc ores that were trapped beneath the subsequent impervious layer of slate. Extensive mining that occurred along the western flank of the region exploited these rich deposits. Later limestone deposits, concentrated closer to the top of the formation, were tapped for many years by a cement factory at Metaline.

## HISTORY

The history of the Abercrombie–Hooknose area focuses on the development of its mineral wealth. The arrival of the Idaho and Washington Northern Railroad in 1910 created Metaline, a company town with one purpose in mind—the production of cement. Starting in the early 1900s, extensive mining for lead and zinc caused shafts to be sunk all over the tops of Gladstone and Red Top Mountains. The demand for these ores peaked during World War I; today only a few mines remain active. In the Metaline vicinity, mining started in the 1930s. Small amounts of lead, zinc, and tungsten ores, and some placer gold, have been taken from that area.

The eastern boundary of the Abercrombie–Hooknose area is partially defined by large power transmission lines from Boundary Dam on the Pend Oreille River, just south of the Canadian border. The 340-foot-high dam is a Seattle City Light project that was completed in 1967.

## HIKING

**Trail 502, Flume Creek.** *4 miles/m (H,S).* From the end of FR 2975-350 (5,120 ft), the route heads west up a broad ridge, then across a steep sidehill to a scree slope where four long switchbacks gain the crest northeast of Abercrombie Mountain. The strenuous rocky route climbs southwest to the barren summit (7,308 ft), once the site of a fire lookout, with great views over northeast Washington. From Abercrombie, cross-country hikers can follow the open alpine crest northeast to Hooknose Mountain (7,210 ft), or chase cairns south along the open ridge to the upper end of Trail 117 and trek beyond, over several intermediate knobs, to Sherlock Peak (6,365 ft), nearly 5 miles to the south.

### Westside Trails

**Trail 139, Sherlock Peak.** *3.6 miles/m (H,S).* From the end of FR 7078-075 (4,620 ft), at the top of Gladstone Mountain, the track winds around a small knob, then climbs southeast across a steep wooded hillside heavy with huckleberries in the fall. A few slow zigzags up the final slope reach a ridge-top meadow south of Sherlock Peak. An easy scramble to the north up the open crest reaches the summit (6,365 ft), with around-the-compass views of nearby Abercrombie and Linton Mountains, the Columbia River, the Salmo-Priest Wilderness, and, in the distance, rugged North Cascades and Canadian peaks. The scenic cross-country ridge-top route north to Abercrombie is an easy hike.

**Trail 123, South Fork Silver Creek.** *3.6 miles/d (H,S).* From the Y-intersection on FR 7078-070, above the confluence of the forks of Silver Creek, take the branch to the southeast (3,160 ft) along an old jeep path into the woods. The gentle grade follows the

*A female white-headed woodpecker forages for insects on a dead branch.*

huckleberry-rich creek bottom for about 2 miles before it takes on trail attributes and heads sharply uphill. Broad switchbacks climb the ever-steepening slope around a creek-head basin to gain a narrow saddle (5,450 ft) on the crest between Sherlock Peak and Abercrombie Mountain. From here hike cross-country to either of these two destinations via the north–south backbone ridge.

**Trail 119, Silver Creek.** *3.5 miles/d (H,S).* From the Y- intersection described above, take the northeast fork (3,160 ft) up the North Fork of Silver Creek. After a very brief stroll along the creek, it's uphill time, and seemingly endless switchbacks plow up the steep, timbered slope. A traverse from the last corner finds Trail 117 at a saddle (5,800 ft) on the west side of Abercrombie Mountain.

**Trail 117, Abercrombie.** *3.2 miles/m (H,S).* From the end of FR 7078-300 (5,000 ft), the way heads into second-growth timber where switchbacks climb to a ridge-top saddle and the junction with Trail 119. More zigs and zags up through an old burn break out into meadows and reach the crest south of Abercrombie Mountain; a large cairn marks the end of the formal trail (6,840 ft). The way north to the top of the mountain (7,308 ft) is obvious, marked by a sequence of small cairns.

# 52 Salmo–Priest Region

## Salmo–Priest Wilderness; Salmo–Priest A, B, and C Roadless Areas

**Location:** In Pend Oreille County, south of the Canadian border, between the Pend Oreille River and the Idaho border

**Size:** Wilderness: 39,937 acres; Salmo–Priest A, 895 acres; Salmo–Priest B, 12,117 acres; Salmo–Priest C, 725 acres; 17,600 acres in northern Idaho have been proposed for addition to the wilderness

**Status:** Designated Wilderness (1984); Roadless areas are Semiprimitive Non-motorized

**Terrain:** Two long northeast-to-southwest ridges are connected at their north ends by an east–west divide, capped by Salmo Mountain. The westernmost ridge has very steep side-slopes below a narrow, rocky crest fringed with several glacial cirques. The easternmost ridge top is lower, more rounded, and wooded. Both ridges are cut by several deep lateral drainages.

**Elevation:** 2,600 to 7,309 feet

**Management:** USFS, Colville National Forest, Sullivan Lake Ranger District, Idaho Panhandle National Forest, Priest River Ranger District

**Topographic maps:** Boundary Dam, Gypsy Peak, Helmer Mtn., Metaline Falls, Pass Creek, Salmo Mtn.

The Salmo–Priest Wilderness is the largest section of virgin forest in eastern Washington. However, even now its peripheral roadless areas are being carved by logging, and beautiful ridge-top vistas often include a substantial number of foreground clearcuts that degrade their aesthetic appeal. Trails that run the length of Crowell Ridge, on the west, and Shedroof Divide, on the east, offer extensive hiking and backwoods camping opportunities and broad scenic views of the Sullivan Creek drainage and Selkirk and Purcell Mountains.

*Badgers are among the varied wildlife found in the Salmo–Priest Wilderness.*

## CLIMATE

The north portion of the wilderness is one of the wettest sections of eastern

Washington, averaging about 50 inches of precipitation annually, compared to 28.4 inches at Metaline Falls, at its southwest corner. Snow, which accounts for most of this precipitation, can reach depths of more than 9 feet and persist well into midsummer. Although average midwinter temperatures range from zero to the low teens, extremes of minus 40 degrees have been recorded. Summers are relatively mild, with highs in the 80s and occasional 90-degree days.

## ECOSYSTEM

Most of the lower-elevation forest in the Salmo–Priest Wilderness consists of western red cedar, western hemlock, Douglas-fir, grand fir, and larch. At higher elevations, Engelmann spruce and subalpine fir are introduced into this mix, and the highest crests are mostly meadows with a cover of fescue and beargrass.

One research natural area (RNA) has been designated in the wilderness, and two more are proposed in it and surrounding roadless areas. The Salmo RNA, established in 1973, consists of 1,390 acres between Salmo Divide and the South Salmo River. It typifies a timbered stream drainage, with old-growth stands of western red cedar, western hemlock, Douglas-fir, and Engelmann spruce, and some areas of second-growth in spots burned by 1920s fires.

Round Top Mountain, at the southeast corner of the wilderness, has been proposed as another RNA. It is a gently rounded mountain covered with meadows and a few trees near the summit. Beargrass dominates portions of the meadows, which gradually taper to subalpine fir and isolated stands of whitebark pine. The other proposed RNA, Halliday Fens, lies in a roadless area on the west flank of the wilderness. This marsh, filled by wetland grasses and other vegetation, is a habitat for seven state-listed sensitive plant species: yellow

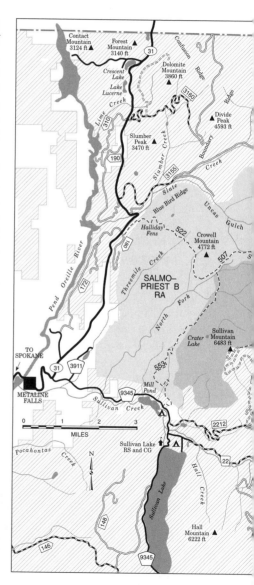

sedge, crested shield fern, green keeled cotton-grass, marsh muhly, hoary willow, McCall's willow, treelike clubmoss, and black snakeroot.

Among the wilderness wildlife are black bear, mule and white-tailed deer, elk, bighorn sheep, and a plethora of small rodents. Also found in the region are pine marten, badger, cougar, bobcat, lynx, moose, goshawk, and pileated woodpecker. This is the only part of the state where woodland caribou are found, and one of the few areas where grizzly bear and gray wolf are known to exist.

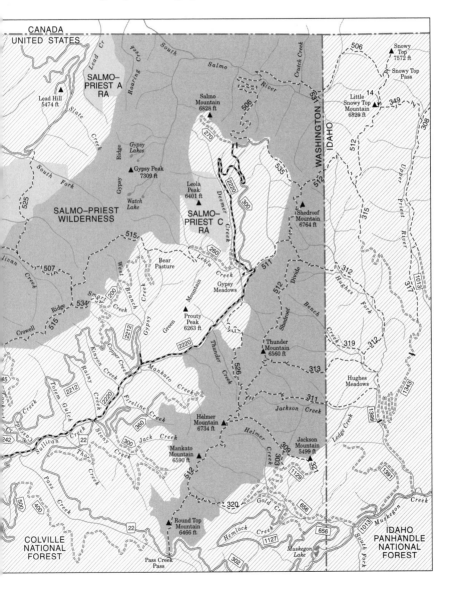

## GEOLOGY

This area is underlaid by some of the oldest rock in the state of Washington. This is the western fringe of the original North American continent; the base of Shedroof Divide, on the east side of the wilderness, is metamorphosed Precambrian sedimentary rock—phyllites and quartzites, more than 600 million years old. On the west side of the wilderness, the Crowell and Gypsy Ridge areas were once part of the younger western coastal plain of the North American continent. Westward drift of this continental plate caused it to ride over the Pacific Ocean crust, and the coastal lowlands were lifted and folded during early Paleozoic times to form this segment of the range. Continental

*Cool, clear water streams over rocks in the South Salmo River.*

ice sheets flowed across the area, grinding and rounding the mountains beneath them. Some of the higher portions of Crowell and Gypsy Ridges stood above the ice sheets and were later sculpted by local alpine glaciers that left a chain of cirques in vertical sides of these two ridges. Soil in the valleys is primarily glacial till and alluvium, with a thin layer of volcanic ash from the last-gasp eruptions of the North Cascades volcanoes.

## HISTORY

Aside from local Indian tribes, the first visitors were prospectors arriving in the late 1800s. Little is known of their efforts, and no productive mines are known to have existed in the wilderness.

Most of the trails throughout the area were cut in the early 1900s to support fire suppression and supply a chain of lookouts located along the higher summits. None of these lookouts is active today. As is obvious from the snarl of old logging roads and the clearcuts on the perimeter of the wilderness, logging has been the dominant industry in the region for the past fifty years.

## HIKING
### Highway 31 Trails

**Trail 522, Halliday.** *4.2 miles/m (H,S,B).* From FR 180 (2,580 ft), the path heads northeast along a low wooded bench, rounds a steep ridge nose, then starts up a deep, wooded drainage. After a brief ascent, the way arrives at the west end of Halliday Fens, a treasure of biological diversity that hopefully will be set aside as a research natural area. In ponds and marshes created by industrious beavers, this wetland boasts seven sensitive plant species. It is also a good spot for bird-watching. After a bench-top swing to the north, the track wanders along the northern perimeter of the fens, then makes a steady ascent to a broad wooded pass (4,080 ft) on the southwest side of Crowell Mountain. It then drops into the North Fork of Sullivan Creek drainage to meet Trail 507 (3,600 ft).

**Trail 525, Slate Creek Cutoff.** *4.2 miles/m (H,S).* From FR 3155 (3,780 ft), the trail descends to cross the South Fork of Slate Creek, heads south across another creek, then climbs a forested ridge to a broad saddle. It drops off the saddle, wanders past a shallow pond, then resumes a gradual ascent around the basin at the head of Uncas Gulch. The route swings into the North Fork of Sullivan Creek drainage, where it joins Trail 507 (4,550 ft).

### Sullivan Creek Trails

**Trail 507, North Fork.** *5.3 miles/m (H,S).* From Trail 522 (3,620 ft), the route proceeds northeast above the North Fork of Sullivan Creek. It gradually ascends to a broad, forested basin, then follows the creek as it twists uphill and southeast. After passing Trail 525, the track switchbacks up the basin headwall and breaks into meadows on Crowell Ridge, where it meets Trail 515 (6,530 ft).

**Trail 553, Red Bluff.** *5.2 miles/m (H,S,B).* From the north side of County Road

9345 (2,580 ft), the trail climbs gradually northwest to the forested nose of a broad ridge, passing a few open spots that look south over Sullivan Lake. The route continues an easy ascent north, rollercoastering over intermediate knobs (3,700 to 4,100 ft). It switchbacks down a steep bank to the North Fork of Sullivan Creek, then climbs the opposite side to meet Trails 507 and 522 (3,720 ft).

**Trail 515, Crowell Ridge.** *7.8 miles/m (H,S).* The premier scenic route on the west side of the wilderness starts on the sharp ridge (6,260 ft) east of the Sullivan Mountain lookout. The track runs first through open timber, then into beargrass-studded meadows. It stays atop the narrow rib except when skirting minor ridge-top knobs. Steep walls drop northwest to a chain of cirques. After meeting Trail 507 at a saddle above Smart Creek, the path continues northeast atop the bare crest to a col (6,540 ft) between two talus-laden humps, where it drops down the southeast side of the ridge to the Leola Creek drainage to meet FR 2212-200 (5,650 ft) just above Bear Pasture.

From the ridge top, the adventuresome can continue north cross-country along the bare rocky crest of Gypsy Ridge for about 4 miles. En route, hikers can cross the highest summit in the wilderness, Gypsy Peak (7,309 ft), or drop east off of the crest to either of two cliff-rimmed lakes, Watch Lake (6,471 ft) or Gypsy Lakes (6,426 ft).

**Trail 526, Thunder Creek.** *5 miles/m (H,S).* From Gypsy Meadows (4,170 ft) on FR 2220, walk a former road for 2.4 miles to the trail, which continues the gradual ascent south through huge old-growth timber. Sate yourself with trailside huckleberries in season as you head up the northeast side of Thunder Creek to meet Trail 512 (5,600 ft) between Thunder and Helmer Mountains.

**Trail 506, Salmo Basin.** *8.8 miles/m (H,S).* This is the first leg of a popular and scenic 2- to 3-day loop that includes Trail 535 and a section of Trail 512. Just beyond the junction with the road to the Salmo Mountain lookout, continue east on gated FR 2220 for 0.5 mile, where this trail heads north into the forest (5,920 ft). A pair of long, lazy switchbacks work down into a drainage, passing through old-growth cedar and hemlock and a carpet of ferns and mosses reminiscent of the damp western Cascade forests. A long diagonal descent leads to additional sweeping switchbacks that reach the South Salmo River (4,070 ft). Cross the river and turn east, making a gradual ascent to Crutch Creek. The path climbs away from the riverbank, passing spur Trail 531 to Salmo Cabin, then enters Idaho, bending north to stay high on the steep sideslope above the river. The river and trail once again twist east 0.5 mile south of the Canadian border, then turn southeast, where the track climbs the drainage headwall to meadows at Snowy Top Pass (6,300 ft). Trail 506 becomes Trail 512 at this point. A strenuous cross-country scramble to the top of Snowy Top (7,572 ft) rewards the effort with a panorama of some of the wildest mountain country in northern Idaho, southern British Columbia, and northeastern Washington.

**Trail 535, Salmo Divide.** *3 miles/m (H,S).* From the start of Trail 506 (5,290 ft), the route follows a closed road for a mile before becoming a true trail. It wanders along the forested top of Salmo Divide, between Salmo Mountain and Shedroof Divide, to link with Trail 512 (6,280 ft) at a saddle north of Shedroof Mountain.

## Priest River Trails

***Trail 512, Shedroof Divide.*** *21.8 miles/m (H,S).* The longest trail in the wilderness runs atop its eastern backbone ridge from the southeast tip of the area to just a mile short of the Canadian border. The entire distance is in semi-open to open timber, broken on occasion by alpine meadows. It offers wide views of the western portion of the wilderness, the Sullivan Creek drainage, and the upper Priest River country of Idaho. Starting on FR 22 just east of Pass Creek Pass (5,440 ft), the route heads north up the shoulder of Round Top Mountain. It skirts the east flank of the mountain, passes the upper end of Trail 320, and continues east of Mankato Mountain to reach a notch (6,491 ft) on the south ridge of Helmer Mountain.

*Sunset silhouettes a snag on Round Top Mountain.*

The way drops to a divide (5,600 ft) between Thunder and Jackson Creeks, passing Trail 526 from the west and Trail 311 from the east. The route climbs north, passes the upper end of Trail 313, then climbs over the top of Thunder Mountain (6,560 ft). The way follows the undulations of the divide as it continues north and passes the heads of Trails 312 and 511. A switchback ascent climbs toward Shedroof Mountain to 6,600 feet, where the route skirts the west flank of Shedroof and descends to a saddle to pass Trail 535.

Shedroof–Salmo Divide now bends northeast, rounds the head of Hughes Fork, and meets Trail 315. The crest is pursued north, to a spur to the lookout site atop Little Snowy Top (6,829 ft) with views encompassing the wilds of northern Idaho, northeastern Washington, and Canada. The way continues north past Trail 349, then joins Trail 506 at Snowy Top Pass.

### East Side of Shedroof Divide Trails

***Trail 320, North Gold.*** *3.3 miles/m (H,S).* From Trail 512 (6,010 ft) north of Round Top Mountain, switchbacks and a poor tread drop swiftly into the upper Gold Creek basin; the grade then eases, meeting and following an old logging road for an easy descent to the end of FR 656A (4,350 ft).

***Trail 311, Jackson Creek.*** *4.6 miles/m (H,S).* From Trail 512 (5,600 ft), 1.7 miles south of Thunder Mountain, the trail drops through brush to a gradual side-slope descent above upper Jackson Creek. In 1.5 miles switchbacks descend the steep sidehill to close with Jackson Creek. The stream bottom is followed west from there to a broad, widening slope and Hughes Meadows (2,920 ft).

**Trail 312, Hughes Fork.** *7.5 miles/m (H,S).* This seldom-maintained route departs Trail 512 (5,370 ft) 0.5 mile south of the junction with Trail 511. It drops quickly east down a brushy ridge crest, swings north into the Hughes Fork of the Priest River drainage, crosses the creek, and continues downstream above its north bank. It follows the stream as it bends south to end in Hughes Meadows on FR 662 (2,700 ft).

**Trail 315, Upper Hughes.** *5.3 miles/m (H,S).* A brushy obscure tread leaves Trail 512 (5,930 ft) as it drops off the ridge 2 miles south of Little Snowy Top. The path continues south along the crest for a mile, then switchbacks down to a saddle where it meets an abandoned alder-choked logging road. This road is followed south for a little over 4 miles to a gate on FR 1399 (4,240 ft) near Cabinet Pass.

**Trail 349, Little Snowy Top.** *4.7 miles/d (H).* From its intersection with Trail 512 (6,280 ft), this track makes a brutal teeth-jarring descent, losing nearly 4,000 feet of elevation in 1.5 miles via seventy-two switchbacks. After a no-bridge crossing of the Upper Priest River, the route ends on Trail 308 near the river's east bank (2,960 ft).

# 53  Sullivan Lake Region

## Grassy Top, Harvey Creek, and Dry Canyon Breaks Roadless Areas

**Location:** In Pend Oreille County, south of the Salmo–Priest Wilderness between the Pend Oreille River and the Idaho border

**Size:** Grassy Top, 10,709 acres; Harvey Creek, 7,082 acres; Dry Canyon Breaks, 5,098 acres

**Status:** Semiprimitive Nonmotorized

**Terrain:** An interconnected series of steep-walled forested ridges frame the headwaters and drainages of Noisy Creek, Tillicum Creek, Sema Creek, and the South Fork of Granite Creek.

**Elevation:** 2,600 to 6,784 feet

**Management:** USFS, Colville National Forest, Sullivan Lake Ranger District, and Idaho Panhandle National Forests, Priest Lake Ranger District; eight sections are owned by a private timber company

**Topographic maps:** Helmer Mtn., Metaline Falls, Monumental Mtn., Orwig Hump, Pass Creek, Scotchman Lake

On the west side of Grassy Top, slopes rise abruptly from Sullivan Lake to Hall Mountain, where a high ridge runs southeast for more than 6 miles to Grassy Top Mountain. East of Grassy Top, a rounded horseshoe-shaped chain of ridges joins High Rock Mountain, Tillicum Peak, and Orwig Hump in enclosing the Tillicum Creek drainage.

On the east these ridges drop sharply to the North Fork of Granite Creek, pausing briefly in a mid-level bench 200 to 400 feet above the creek. Although slopes on the north and south sides of the area have been heavily logged, a fringe of untouched timber left along ridge tops mercifully hides clearcuts from most of the trails. There is a fair chance of seeing Rocky Mountain bighorn sheep, which were introduced into the area, in the vicinity of Hall Mountain.

The Harvey Creek area encompasses an east–west ridge extending between Molybdenite Mountain and Monumental Mountain. Streams drain north from this crest into Harvey Creek, and south into Le Clerc Creek. Most of the forest cover is lodgepole pine covering areas denuded by 1926 fires. The main attractions of the area are berry picking in the Bunchgrass Meadow area, hunting, and fishing. The Dry Canyon Breaks is a narrow, steep, north/south roadless strip on the lower west slope of Molybdenite Mountain. The forest here is small Douglas-fir, western red cedar, and western hemlock. Neither of these areas has any developed trails. In recent years both areas have been used for survival training conducted by nearby Fairchild Air Force Base.

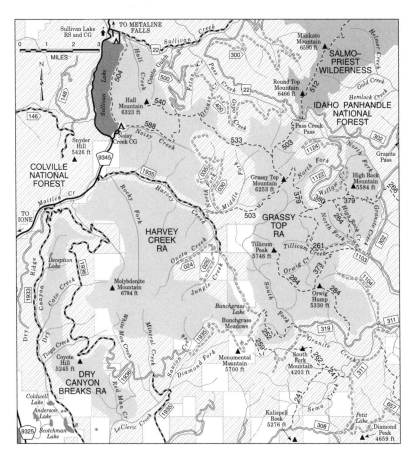

## CLIMATE

The average annual precipitation in the area is about 24 inches, most falling as snow, which can reach depths from 3 to 6 feet, depending on elevation. Midwinter temperatures average in the low- to mid-teens, with some below-zero stretches. Summer highs average in the mid-80s, with occasional periods over 90.

## ECOSYSTEM

The forest is a mixture of virgin old-growth and second-growth timber, the latter regenerating in areas burned by major fires in the 1920s. South-slope trees are mostly Douglas-fir and ponderosa pine, with an understory that includes ninebark, snowberry, spirea, woods rose, and oceanspray. Damper draws and north-slope forest stands hold western hemlock and cedar, with ground cover of Oregon boxwood, queencup beadlily, oak fern, and huckleberry. The higher elevations have a mix of subalpine fir and Engelmann spruce, with whitebark pine included near the top of Hall and Grassy Top Mountains. On the ground here are beargrass, rustyleaf, Labrador tea, and huckleberry, with mosses and lichen coating open rock outcrops. Hooker's bluegrass, poor sedge, meadow pussytoes, and saw-leaved sedge, all on the state sensitive species list, are found in the area.

Typical forest inhabitants include black bear, white-tailed deer, elk, cougar, bobcat, snowshoe hare, and a variety of small animals. The area is also habitat for rarer creatures: moose, grizzly bear, gray wolf, fisher, and wolverine. Bighorn sheep are sometimes seen in the vicinity of Hall Mountain, especially in early morning or late afternoon at salt blocks placed near the top of the mountain. The State Department of Wildlife, in cooperation with the Sullivan Lake Ranger District, maintains a winter feeding station for the sheep near the mouth of Noisy Creek. The South Fork of Granite Creek is a spawning and rearing stream for Priest Lake cutthroat. The bird population includes grouse, pine marten, pileated woodpeckers, and goshawks.

## GEOLOGY

The base under the area is ancient metamorphosed Precambrian sedimentary rock that formed on the original west coast of the North American continent. The south side of the area has been intruded by a granitic batholith that has forced the original crust north along an east–west thrust fault at Pass Creek. Sullivan Lake and the region to the west of it are underlaid by the lateral moraine of continental ice sheets that pushed down the Pend Oreille Valley some 15,000 years ago. The same glacial advance is responsible for the rounded ridge tops, occasionally broken by rock outcrops, on the east side of the area. Surface soil is primarily glacial till, colluvium, and alluvium covered by a thin layer of ash from Cascade volcano eruptions.

## HISTORY

Although the area is in territory traditionally used for hunting and gathering by the Kalispell Indians, no firm evidence of such activities has been found. Most of the trails were built in the 1930s to support fire lookouts that once existed on the six highest

*Hikers begin a trip to Grassy Top Mountain.*

summits, and to provide backcountry access to fire crews. Some of this construction was carried out by the CCC, and vestiges of their camps may be found in the vicinity. During the same period there was also some prospecting, and about 200 claims were filed in the area. Recent mineral exploration in the eastern half of the region has focused on gold, silver, tungsten, lead, zinc, molybdenum, and uranium. Since the 1950s the major industry in the area has been logging, attested to by miles of side-slope clearcuts on the periphery of the Grassy Top area and the south flank of the Harvey Creek area.

## HIKING
### Grassy Top Northside Trails
**Trail 504, Lakeshore.** *4.2 miles/e (H).* This level path (2,600 ft) follows the east shoreline of Sullivan Lake between the Sullivan Lake Campground, on the north, and Noisy Creek Campground, on the south. Most of the way is in dense forest broken by open scree slopes with views up to Hall Mountain. The southern portion of the trail has easy access to the lakeshore, and the entire route is especially beautiful when the rich yellows and golds of fall are reflected in the deep blue surface of the lake.

**Trail 540, Hall Mountain.** *2.5 miles/m (H,S,B).* FR 2200-500 is closed to motorized traffic in spring and fall; check with the local ranger district for specific dates. From the end of FR 2200-500 (5,300 ft), the track follows a short stretch of abandoned road up to a saddle (5,580 ft), the west end of Trail 533, and the north end of Trail 588. The route heads west along the south side of the grassy crest to the top of Hall Mountain (6,323 ft). The tread is rocky in places, but easy to follow. The mountaintop offers around-the-compass views of Sullivan Lake, the Salmo–Priest Wilderness, the remainder of the Grassy Top area, and the Pend Oreille Valley, as well as the possibility of close-up views of bighorn sheep.

**Trail 533, Hall Mountain–Grassy Top.** *5.1 miles/m (H,S,B).* From the junction of Trails 540 and 588 (5,560 ft) east of Hall Mountain, the route heads east, then southeast along the contorted crest, sometimes on top, sometimes weaving from one side to the other. It reaches a saddle (6,160 ft) northwest of Grassy Top Mountain where it meets Trail 503. Most of the way is heavily wooded (thankfully) with few views of nearby clearcuts until it breaks into a sidehill meadow near its east end.

**Trail 503, Pass Creek–Grassy Top.** *7.8 miles/m (H,S,B).* From FR 22 on the west side of Pass Creek Pass (5,360 ft), the trail drops to cross Pass Creek, switchbacks a few times up through dense forest, then swings south. A few more zigzags gain a ridge-top saddle (6,000 ft), where a wooded rib is followed southwest to join Trail 533. The path wanders across west-slope beargrass meadows before making the final ascent to the top of Grassy Top Mountain (6,253 ft) and broad views of the Salmo–Priest Wilderness and the Priest Lake area. The trail wanders through meadows southwest from Grassy Top for nearly a mile before it twists down a wooded nose to an abandoned logging road. The road is hiked west for about 3 miles to FR 1935-030 on the North Fork of Harvey Creek (4,120 ft).

**Trail 588, Noisy Creek.** *5.3 miles/m (H,S,B).* From the end of an old mine road (3,280 ft) at the southeast end of Sullivan Lake, this path takes long switchbacks up the ridge, then drops into the deep, narrow, wooded Noisy Creek drainage. It follows the creek bank upstream for about 2 miles, then turns uphill to the north, where the tread continues up a hogback to the backbone ridge top (5,580 ft) to meet Trails 540 and 533.

## Grassy Top Eastside Trails

**Trail 379, North Fork–Grassy Top.** *7.7 miles/m (H,S).* The route leaves the west side of FR 302 (3,250 ft), crosses the North Fork of Granite Creek, then attacks the steep face of a bluff in a series of switchbacks. A brief pause atop a midslope plateau gives way to an even steeper talus face, where more switchbacks gain the gentler, wooded east flank of High Rock Mountain. Here the path takes a straight shot west to the broad mountain crest (5,530 ft), south of the mountain's summit (5,584 ft).

The trail follows the flat, forested crest southwest for more than a mile, passing the upper ends of Trails 264 and 380 en route. At a junction with Trail 261, it bends northwest following a ridge toward Grassy Top. After wandering across two ridge-top knobs, the path gradually climbs to a rib running southwest. It turns up this narrow hogback, and breaks out into meadows studded with beargrass as it reaches the summit of Grassy Top and a junction with Trail 503 (6,253 ft).

**Trail 261, Tillicum Creek.** *4 miles/m (H,S).* The first stretch of trail is on an abandoned section of FR 1103 (3,521 ft). In 0.4 mile, Trail 373 leaves to the southwest, and in another 0.5 mile the road becomes a trail and follows Tillicum Creek into a narrow, forested draw. The way bends north up a tributary stream and climbs the tightening sidehill slope toward a broad saddle on a spur from the east–west backbone ridge.

A twist to the west and a diagonal ascent of a broad, wooded slope leads to the crest. Here the track swings northeast and meets Trail 379 (5,620 ft).

**Trail 284, Tillicum Peak.** *4 miles/m (H,S).* This route was once used to supply lookouts atop Orwig Hump and Tillicum Peak. It leaves FR 319 (3,520 ft) and works steadily uphill to the ridge running southeast from Orwig Hump. Once atop the ridge, a gentle grade goes arrow-straight to the old lookout site (5,330 ft). The path descends to the west, passes Trail 373, then follows the undulating crest west to the round, wooded summit of Tillicum Peak (5,740 ft). Here are views east down the wide Tillicum drainage and south down the deep canyon of the South Fork of Granite Creek.

# 54 Tucannon River Region

## Wenaha–Tucannon Wilderness; Mill Creek, Spangler, Meadow Creek, Willow Springs, Upper Tucannon, Asotin Creek, and Wenatchee Creek Roadless Areas

**Location:** In Columbia, Asotin, and Garfield Counties, in Washington, and in Wallowa County, Oregon; spans the Washington–Oregon border southeast of Dayton, Washington

**Size:** Wilderness total, 177,465 acres; in Washington, 111,048 acres; in Oregon, 66,417 acres. Mill Creek, 26,700; Spangler, 5,900 acres; Meadow Creek, 5,000; Willow Springs, 11,100; Upper Tucannon, 12,600 acres; Asotin Creek, 16,900 acres; Wenatchee Creek, 15,500 acres

**Status:** Designated Wilderness (1978); Roadless areas are mostly Semiprimitive Motorized

**Terrain:** This high basalt plateau is incised with deep canyons that have been cut by numerous creeks and rivers.

**Elevation:** 1,700 to 6,387 feet

**Management:** USFS, Umatilla National Forest, Pomeroy Ranger District; City of Walla Walla watershed (Mill Creek)

**Topographic maps:** (Washington) Deadman Peak, Diamond Peak, Eckler Mtn., Godman Spring, Hopkins Ridge, Kooskooskie, Mountain View, Panjab Creek, Pinkham Butte, Rose Springs Saddle Butte, Stentz Spring; (Oregon) Big Meadows, Bone Spring, Eden, Elbow Creek, Wenaha Forks

The Wenaha–Tucannon area was once a huge basalt plateau, formed by millions of years of passive eruptions and volcanic flows through underlying dikes. Over the past 10 million years, streams have cut through this volcanic layer cake, creating a labyrinth of deep, steep-walled canyons. The original tableland surface has been reduced to long, narrow ridge tops and broad, forested mesas dividing the various drainages. Trails through the area either stick to these crests, which often have clear, wide views of the surrounding ridges and the deep chasms between them, or closely follow the creeks and rivers at the base of steep-walled canyons. In most cases these ridges come to abrupt ends where creeks merge, and the gentle grades plunge precipitously down canyon walls for 2,000 feet or more to bordering streams. Some of the longer trails following streams and rivers through these narrow canyons offer a quick course in the region's geology, showcased in the multiple layers of basalt stacked in the walls above.

## CLIMATE

The mean annual precipitation varies with elevation, ranging from 24 inches in lower elevations to 32 inches at the highest points. Most of this falls between November and April as snow, which accumulates at depths up to 2 feet in the valley bottoms, and to 8 to 12 feet on ridge crests. Average midwinter lows are about 20 degrees; however, storms can easily drop temperatures to minus 20, and effectively much lower when the wind-chill factor is considered. Summer days are hot; highs average near 90, and days over 100 degrees are not uncommon, although evenings cool to the pleasant lower 70s.

## ECOSYSTEM

The biosystems in the wilderness vary with elevation and climate. Lower valleys and creek bottoms are wooded, mainly with ponderosa pine and some occurrences of western juniper. Ground cover is mostly bluebunch wheatgrass, Idaho fescue, and Sandberg's bluegrass, with lesser occurrences of such shrubs and plants as western yarrow, sagebrush buttercup, cheatgrass brome, littleflower collinsia, and smallflower forget-me-not.

Above 4,500 feet the forest changes to lodgepole pine, with occurrences of western larch, grand fir, white fir, Engelmann spruce,

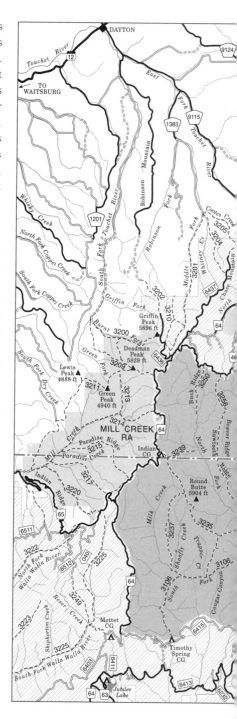

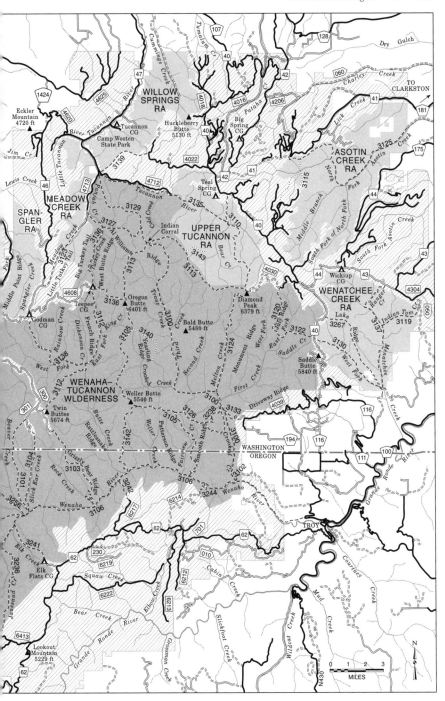

*Forested hillsides in the Wenaha–Tucannon Wilderness include ponderosa pine, western larch, and fir.*

western white pine, and Douglas-fir. Interspersed among the trees are bitterbrush, penstemon, lupine, heartleaf arnica, and white hawkweed.

At the highest elevations within the wilderness, the dominant tree species is subalpine fir, with associated growths of Oregon boxwood and queencup beadlily. Ridges and south-facing slopes are frequently bare of trees, with a cover ranging from sagebrush and Sandberg's bluegrass at lower elevations to Idaho fescue, scarlet paintbrush, and rosy pussytoes higher up the slopes.

The 576-acre Rainbow Creek Research Natural Area, northwest of the confluence of Preacher and Rainbow Creeks, was established in 1968. The RNA encloses a community of grand fir–white pine, grand fir–thinleaf huckleberry, and mixed conifers dominated by larch. Another proposed 1,665-acre RNA on the south side of the wilderness at Elk Flats–Wenaha Breaks holds grand fir–twinflower, grand fir–Pacific yew, and lodgepole pine–thinleaf huckleberry communities, and a low-elevation permanent pond.

Large herds of Rocky Mountain elk are found here, as are mule deer, white-tailed deer, black bear, cougar, bobcat, coyote, whistling marmot, and snowshoe hare. Avian inhabitants include bald and golden eagles, several species of hawks and owls, goshawks, quail, chukar, blue and ruffed grouse, and pileated, three-toed, and downy woodpeckers, as well as bluebirds and a variety of other songbirds. The warm, dry climate makes this ideal habitat for rattlesnakes.

## GEOLOGY

Between 17 million and 6 million years ago, an upwelling of basalts, thought to originate from a mantle plume associated with the Yellowstone Hot Spot, forced its way up through cracks in a north–south dike system near the Washington–Oregon–Idaho border, in a succession of massive basalt flows. Individual flows (50 to 150 feet thick) are interleaved with significant biological growth, indicating multiple eruptive events over an extended period; in places the total of the flows is nearly 5,000 feet thick.

A long northeast–southwest fault along the west side of the wilderness marks the boundary between the Columbia Basin, which was depressed beneath the weight of the volcanic flows, and a bulging anticline that forms the Blue Mountain region, which includes the wilderness along the Washington–Oregon border. After this high volcanic plateau was formed, creeks and rivers cut deep canyons through the layered basalt to expose the geological structures that created the original tableland.

## HISTORY

The Wenaha–Tucannon Wilderness was once the province of several Nez Perce Indian tribes, and many of today's trails throughout its expanse follow paths beaten by these native people. Trappers who entered the area in the 1880s used these paths, as did the sheep herders and cattlemen who followed them. In the 1930s this trail system was improved by the Forest Service to support grazing allotments and to assist in its fire-control mission.

During the late 1800s, the first settlers in the Blue Mountain region led a tenuous and hungry existence due to the scarcity of wild game in the area. In 1913, the Wenaha Game Protective Association was formed to introduce Rocky Mountain elk from Montana. The small new herds were protected by strict game laws and the creation of several game preserves; when hunting was first opened in 1927, the elk population had grown to one of the largest in the region, and it remains so today. In fact, hunters outnumber hikers as users of the wilderness.

## HIKING
### Westside Trails

**Trail 3256, Sawtooth.** *14 miles/d (H,S).* The way leaves Burnt Flat Corral (5,650 ft) on FR 46, heads along the broad ridge to the south, and after a few ups and downs arrives at Burnt Flat (5,900 ft), a 150-acre bench covered with a mixture of lodgepole pine and subalpine fir. The trail becomes more challenging as it picks its way along the rough, rocky crest of Sawtooth Ridge to cross the border into Oregon. It follows the ever-narrowing divide between the North Fork of the Wenaha River and Beaver Creek, then descends a rib to the Wenaha River and Trail 3106 (2,800 ft).

**Trail 3104, Slick Ear.** *5.2 miles/d (H,S).* From the end of FR 4600-301 (5,100 ft), the route traces the semi-open crest south to the Oregon border, where it switchbacks steeply down into the Slick Ear drainage, then follows the creek bank south to join Trail 3106 (2,800 ft), just above the Wenaha River.

**Trail 3103, Grizzly Bear.** *7.5 miles/m (H,S).* At the end of FR 4600-300 (5,380 ft), this route heads southeast across a plateau lightly covered with subalpine forest. Meadow openings permit glimpses east into the rugged, steep-walled canyons of Butte Creek and its tributaries. The way descends the broad, gently-sloping, top of Grizzly Bear Ridge for more than 2 miles before starting a series of switchbacks down a steep canyon wall into Rock Creek. It follows the creek downstream to the Wenaha River and Trail 3106 (2,600 ft).

**Trail 3112, East Butte.** *11 miles/m-d (H,S).* From Teepee Campground, at the end of FR 4608 (5,500 ft), steep, rocky switchbacks descend to the headwaters of the East Fork of Butte Creek. The way continues downstream to King Creek (3,580 f), where trail maintenance ends. A hikeable trail continues downstream to the confluence of the two forks of Butte Creek and the junction with Trail 3138. From here the route twists up a rocky ridge nose on the west side of Butte Creek and finally gains the ridge crest. The woods-and-meadow, ridge-top route to the southwest across Twin Buttes (5,674 ft) ends on FR 4600-300 (5,380 ft).

**Trail 3138, West Butte Creek.** *8 miles/m (H,S).* At Godman Campground (5,700 ft), the route leaves south from FR 46 and drops quickly down the ridge top to Happy Valley (4,100 ft). It climbs to a notch, then descends across the north end of the Rainbow Creek RNA to the banks of Rainbow Creek. The route parallels the creek as it bends east to the West Fork of Butte Creek. This fork is followed through ever-steepening canyon walls to the junction with Trail 3112 (3,110 ft).

**Trail 3136, Turkey Creek.** *4 miles/m (H,S).* Teepee Campground (5,500 ft) lies at the midpoint of Trail 3136. The route north is a wooded, valley-bottom trek that drops steeply to Turkey Creek, then follows the more gradual drainage floor north to join Panjab Creek and Trail 3127. The more popular segment winds through old-growth timber along the ridge east of the campground. After crossing West Butte Ridge, it descends to Oregon Butte Spring to meet Trails 3105 and 3113 (6,200 ft) on the north slopes of Oregon Butte. A short spur leads to the old lookout cabin atop the butte (6,401 ft), the highest point in the wilderness. Here are excellent views of the dozens of canyons that drop south to the Wenaha River and the forested ridges flowing north to the Tucannon River valley.

**Trail 3105, Smooth Ridge.** *16.7 miles/m (H,S).* From the junction with Trails 3136 and 3113, the route contours the east side of Oregon Butte to pick up the open ridge headed south. It follows a near-flat bench south for more than 3 miles to Lodgepole Spring. The way bends southeast across a divide, then makes a steep, wooded climb to top Weller Butte (5,540 ft). It then snakes east on the broad rim above the 2,000-foot-deep Crooked Creek drainage. After passing Trails 3142 and 3126, the route begins a long, gentle descent of Smooth Ridge. This ends in a sudden switchback drop to the confluence of Fairview Creek and the Wenaha River (2,070 ft), where it ends on Trail 3106.

**Trail 3126, Packer's.** *5.5 miles/m (H,S).* From Trail 3105 (4,780 ft), the route follows the south rim of the Crooked Creek drainage east, then gradually descends the broad ridge to the west rim of Crooked Creek canyon. It then makes a long, gentle, sidehill descent to the north to join Trail 3100 (2,150 ft) at Crooked Creek.

## Northside Trails

**Trail 3129, Rattlesnake.** *5 miles/m (H,S).* At the mouth of Panjab Creek (2,970 ft), the route leaves FR 4713 and heads for the sky. Switchbacks work up to a just plain steep climb of the forested ridge leading south to Alnus Spring (5,200 ft). As a reward for the agony of the first 2.5 miles of trail, the remainder is near flat as it weaves through woods and grassland to end on Trails 3127 and 3113 (5,720 ft).

**Trail 3100, Crooked Creek.** *17.4 miles/m (H,S).* Not for the claustrophobic, this long, rugged, creek-bottom route plumbs the deepest canyons in the wilderness. Starting on the north from Trail 3113 at Indian Corral (5,700 ft), the way drops immediately to the headwaters of Trout Creek, which it traces down through ever-deepening canyon walls to its confluence with Third Creek (3,250 ft). The snake-like path of this stream is followed down to its confluence with Crooked Creek (2,700 ft). To the south the canyon rim looms 2,000 feet above; to the north a mere 1,000 feet is needed to gain the ridge top. At this point Crooked Creek flows east, but 2.5 miles downstream, at the junction with Trail 3124, the stream bends sharply south and the valley floor widens briefly into meadows at the lower end of Trails 3133 and 3126 (2,350 ft). The route continues south along the creek and crosses the Oregon border. The creek is followed to its confluence with the Wenaha River and Trail 3106 (1,916 ft).

**Trail 3135, Tucannon.** *4.1 miles/e (H,S,B).* From the end of FR 4712 along the Tucannon River (3,520 ft), this easy-grade path in the Upper Tucannon Roadless Area continues along the wooded riverbank to Bear Creek (4,130 ft) and the junction with Trail 3110.

**Trail 3110, Bear Creek.** *7.3 miles/m (H,S,B; M to the wilderness boundary and trail's end).* From FR 4000 (5,670 ft), the way drops south swiftly in rocky switchbacks to Trail 3135 (4,130 ft) on the Tucannon River. From here the route switchbacks uphill with a vengeance to Jelly Spring (5,440 ft). The worst is now over, as the way meanders south along a broad ridge-top bench with periodic meadow breaks and views of the north half of the wilderness. The route ends as it meets Trail 3113 (6,250 ft) just north of the summit of Diamond Peak (6,379 ft).

## Eastside Trails

**Trail 3113, Mount Misery.** *16 miles/m (H,S).* This is a scenic route with good views of the wilderness, short side trips to regional high spots, and very few ups and downs to make life miserable. From the end of the Diamond Peak Road, FR 4030 (5,900 ft), a half-mile stroll west leads to the junction with Trail 3110 and the spur to the top of Diamond Peak (6,379 ft). Just east, at Diamond Spring, the route meets the upper end of Trail 3124, then continues west along the crest past Sheephead, Squaw, Bear Wallow, Clover, and Bullfrog Springs to meet Trails 3100 and 3129 at Indian Corral (5,700 ft). Soon after, the way bends south, then follows along an easy semi-open ridge top to meet Trails 3105 and 3136 on the north slope of Oregon Butte (6,170 ft).

**Trail 3124, Melton Creek.** *9.7 miles/m (H,S).* The north end of the route departs Trail 3113 at Diamond Spring (6,185 ft) and soon starts the first of several series of knee-jarring switchbacks in its rapid descent to Melton Creek at Chaparral Basin (3,470 ft). The wooded creek bottom is followed south across at least two dozen steep sidehill gullies to join Trail 3100 where Melton Creek meets Crooked Creek (2,420 ft).

## Oregon Trails

**Trail 3106, Wenaha River.** *31.3 miles/m (H,S).* This long, river-bottom trail runs east–west along the Wenaha River for the full width of the wilderness. The east end starts outside of the wilderness near Troy, Oregon, and in 9 miles reaches the wilderness at the junction with Trail 3100 at the mouth of Crooked Creek (1,916 ft). The way traces the twisting river course west, sometimes along the bank, and other times skirting a short distance up the canyon wall to avoid short riverside cliffs. After leaving Trail 3100, the way meets, in succession, east to west, Trails 3244, 3105, 3142, 3242, 3103, 3104, 3101, 3256, 3235, 3241, 3236, and 3237. At the confluence of the South Fork of the Wenaha and Milk Creek, the route swings south with the South Fork and climbs to join FR 6415 at Timothy Spring Campground (4,680 ft).

# APPENDIX A. MANAGING AGENCY OFFICES

## NATIONAL PARK SERVICE

Mount Rainier National Park, Tahoma Woods, Star Route, Ashford, WA 98304-9751; (360) 569-2211; www.nps.gov/mora

North Cascades National Park and Park Complex, 810 State Route 20, Sedro Wooley, WA 98284; (360) 856-5700; www.nps.gov/noca

- Purple Point Information Station, Stehekin, WA; (360) 856-5700, ext 340, then 14.
- North Cascades Visitor Center, Newhalem, WA; (206) 386-4495, ext 11.

Olympic National Park, 600 East Park Avenue, Port Angeles, WA 98362-6789; (360) 565-3100; www.nps.gov/olym

## U.S. FOREST SERVICE

U.S. Forest Service, Pacific Northwest Region, 333 SW First Avenue, Portland, OR 97204-3340; (503) 808-2200; www.fs.fed.us/R6

Colville National Forest, 765 South Main Street, Colville, WA 98114; (509) 684-7000

- Colville/Kettle Falls Ranger District, 255 West 11th, Kettle Falls, WA 99141; (509) 684-7001
- Republic Ranger District, 180 North Jefferson, Republic, WA 99166; (509) 775-7400
- Sullivan Lake Ranger District, 12461 Sullivan Lake Road, Metaline, WA 99153; (509) 446-7500

Gifford Pinchot National Forest, 10600 NE 51st Circle, Vancouver, WA 98682; (360) 891-5000; www.fs.fed.us/gpnf

- Cowlitz Valley Ranger District, 10024 Highway 12, PO Box 670, Randle, WA 98377-9105; (360) 497-1100
- Mount Adams Ranger District, 2455 Highway 141, Trout Lake, WA 98650-9724; (509) 395-3400
- Mount St. Helens National Volcanic Monument, 42218 NE Yale Bridge Road, Amboy, WA 98601-9715; (360) 247-3900

Idaho Panhandle National Forests, 3815 Schreiber Way, Coeur d'Alene, ID 83815-8363; (208) 765-7223; www.fs.fed.us/outernet/ipnf

- Priest River Ranger District, 32203 Highway 57, Priest River, ID 83856-9612; (208) 443-2512

Mount Baker–Snoqualmie National Forest, 21905 64th Avenue West, Mountlake Terrace, WA 98043; (425) 775-902; www.fs.fed.us/R6/mbs

- Darrington Ranger District, 1405 Emens Street, Darrington, WA 98241; (360) 436-1155
- Mount Baker Ranger District, 810 Highway 20, Sedro Wooley, WA 98284; (360) 856-5700

- Skykomish Ranger District, 74920 Northeast Stevens Pass Highway, PO Box 305, Skykomish, WA 98288; (360) 677-2414
- Snoqualmie Ranger District, 42404 SE North Bend Way, North Bend, WA 98045; (425) 888-1421

Okanogan–Wenatchee National Forest, 215 Melody Lake, Wenatchee, WA 98801-5933; (509) 662-4335; *www.fs.fed.us/R6/oka, www.fs.fed.us/R6/wenatchee*

- Chelan Ranger District, 428 West Woodin Avenue, Chelan, WA 98816; (509) 682-2576
- Cle Elum Ranger District, 803 West Second Street, Cle Elum, WA 98922; (509) 674-4411
- Entiat Ranger District, 2108 Entiat Way, Entiat, WA 98822; (509) 784-1511
- Lake Wenatchee Ranger District, 22976 Highway 207, Leavenworth, WA 98826; (509) 763-3103
- Leavenworth Ranger District, 600 Sherbourne Street, Leavenworth, WA 98826; (509) 548-6977
- Methow Valley Ranger District, 502 Glover, Twisp, WA 98856; (509) 997-2131
- Naches Ranger District, 10061 Highway 12, Naches, WA 98937; (509) 653-2205
- Tonasket Ranger District, 1 West Winesap, Tonasket, WA 98855; (509) 486-2186

Olympic National Forest, 1835 Black Lake Boulevard SW, Olympia, WA 98512-5623; (360) 956-2300; *www.fs.fed.us/R6/olympic*

- Hood Canal Ranger District, 150 North Lake Cushman Road, PO Box 68, Hoodsport, WA 98548; (360) 877-5254
- Pacific Ranger District, 353 South Shore Road, PO Box 9, Quinault, WA 98575; (360) 288-2525

Umatilla National Forest, 2517 SW Hailey Ave, Pendleton, OR 97801; (541) 278-3716

- Pomeroy Ranger District, Route 1, Box 53-F, Pomeroy, WA 99347; (509) 843-1891

## U.S. FISH AND WILDLIFE SERVICE

Nisqually National Wildlife Refuge Complex, 100 Brown Farm Road, Olympia, WA 98516-2302; (360) 753-9467

Washington Island National Wildlife Refuge, c/o Washington Maritime NWR Complex, 33 South Barr Road, Port Angeles, WA 98362-9202; (360) 457-8451

## BUREAU OF LAND MANAGEMENT

Bureau of Land Management, Spokane District Office, 1103 N. Fancher, Spokane, WA 99212-1275; (509) 536-1200; *www.blm.gov/orwa*

## WASHINGTON STATE

State Parks and Recreation Comission, PO Box 42650, Olympia, WA 98504-2669; (360) 902-8500, (800) 233-0321; *www.parks.wa.gov*

Department of Natural Resources, Olympia Headquarters, 1111 Washington Street SE, PO Box 47000, Olympia, WA 98504-7000; (360) 902-1000; *www.wa.gov/dnr/base/recreation.html*

# APPENDIX B. SUGGESTED READING

Arender, Barney. *Barney's Book on the Olympic Peninsula*. Olympia, Wash.: Nosado Press, 1990.

Beckey, Fred. *Cascade Alpine Guide, 1: Columbia River to Stevens Pass*, 3rd edition. Seattle: The Mountaineers Books, 2000.

————. *Cascade Alpine Guide, 2: Stevens Pass to Rainy Pass*, 2nd edition. Seattle: The Mountaineers Books, 1989.

————. *Cascade Alpine Guide, 3: Rainy Pass to the Fraser River,* 2nd edition. Seattle: The Mountaineers Books, 1995.

Beckey, Fred, and Van Steen, Alex. *Climbing Mount Rainier. The Essential Guide*. Mukilteo, Wash: AlpenBooks Press, 1999.

Gauthier, Mike. *Mount Rainier. A Climbing Guide*. Seattle: The Mountaineers Books, 1999.

Hooper, David. *Exploring Washington's Wild Olympic Coast*. Seattle: The Mountaineers Books, 1993.

Kirkendall, Tom, and Vicky Spring. *100 Best Cross-Country Ski Trails in Western Washington*, 3rd edition. Seattle: The Mountaineers Books, 2002.

Landers, Rich, Ida Rowe Dolphin, and the Spokane Mountaineers. *100 Hikes in the Inland Northwest*. Seattle: The Mountaineers Books, 1987.

Mueller, Marge, and Ted Mueller. *Fire, Faults, and Floods. A Road and Trail Guide Exploring the Origins of the Columbia River Basin*. Moscow, Ida.: University of Idaho Press, 1997.

————. *The San Juan Islands, Afoot and Afloat*, 3rd edition. Seattle: The Mountaineers Books, 1995.

————. *Washington's South Cascades' Volcanic Landscapes*. Seattle: The Mountaineers Books, 1995.

North, Douglas. *Washington Whitewater*. Seattle: The Mountaineers Books, 1992.

Olympic Mountain Rescue Group. *Climber's Guide to the Olympic Mountains*, 3rd edition. Seattle: The Mountaineers Books, 1988.

Seeholtz, David. *Mount St. Helens, Pathways to Discovery*. Vancouver, Wash.: A Plus Images, 1993.

Shane, Scott. *Discovering Mount St. Helens*. Seattle: University of Washington Press, 1985.

Spring, Ira, and Harvey Manning. *50 Hikes in Mount Rainier National Park*, 4th edition. Seattle: The Mountaineers Books, 1999.

————. *100 Hikes in the Glacier Peak Region: The North Cascades*, 3rd edition Seattle: The Mountaineers Books, 1996.

————. *100 Hikes in Washington's North Cascades National Park Region*, 3rd edition Seattle: The Mountaineers Books, 2000.

————. *100 Hikes in Washington's South Cascades and Olympics*, 3rd edition. Seattle: The Mountaineers Books, 1998.

Spring, Vicky, Ira Spring, and Harvey Manning. *100 Hikes in Washington's Alpine Lakes*, 3rd edition. Seattle: The Mountaineers Books, 2000.

Vielbig, Klindt. *A Complete Guide to Mount St. Helens National Volcanic Monument*. Seattle: The Mountaineers Books, 1997.

Wood, Robert L. *Olympic Mountains Trail Guide*, 3rd edition. Seattle: The Mountaineers Books, 2000.

# INDEX

# ABOUT THE AUTHORS

MARGE and TED MUELLER are avid outdoor enthusiasts and environmentalists who, along with their two children, have explored the Northwest's mountains, forests, deserts, and waterways for more than forty years. Ted taught classes on cruising in Northwest waters, and both Marge and Ted have instructed mountain climbing. They are members of several environmental advocacy groups, and are board members of Friends of Washington State Parks. They are the authors of over a dozen regional guidebooks, including the six volumes in the *Afoot and Afloat* series.

THE MOUNTAINEERS, founded in 1906, is a nonprofit outdoor activity and conservation club, whose mission is "to explore, study, preserve, and enjoy the natural beauty of the outdoors. . . ." Based in Seattle, Washington, the club is now the third-largest such organization in the United States, with 15,000 members and five branches throughout Washington State.

The Mountaineers sponsors both classes and year-round outdoor activities in the Pacific Northwest, which include hiking, mountain climbing, ski-touring, snowshoeing, bicycling, camping, kayaking and canoeing, nature study, sailing, and adventure travel. The club's conservation division supports environmental causes through educational activities, sponsoring legislation, and presenting informational programs. All club activities are led by skilled, experienced volunteers, who are dedicated to promoting safe and responsible enjoyment and preservation of the outdoors.

If you would like to participate in these organized outdoor activities or the club's programs, consider a membership in The Mountaineers. For information and an application, write or call The Mountaineers, Club Headquarters, 300 Third Avenue West, Seattle, WA 98119; 206-284-6310.

The Mountaineers Books, an active, nonprofit publishing program of the club, produces guidebooks, instructional texts, historical works, natural history guides, and works on environmental conservation. All books produced by The Mountaineers Books fulfill the club's mission.

*Send or call for our catalog of more than 500 outdoor titles:*

The Mountaineers Books
1001 SW Klickitat Way, Suite 201
Seattle, WA 98134
800-553-4453
*mbooks@mountaineersbooks.org*
*www.mountaineersbooks.org*

The Mountaineers Books is proud to be a corporate sponsor of Leave No Trace, whose mission is to promote and inspire responsible outdoor recreation through education, research, and partnerships. The Leave No Trace program is focused specifically on human-powered (nonmotorized) recreation.

Leave No Trace strives to educate visitors about the nature of their recreational impacts, as well as offer techniques to prevent and minimize such impacts. Leave No Trace is best understood as an educational and ethical program, not as a set of rules and regulations.

For more information, visit *www.LNT.org,* or call 800-332-4100.